CATHOLIC AUTHORS

Catholic Authors

CONTEMPORARY BIOGRAPHICAL SKETCHES

Edited by

MATTHEW HOEHN, O.S.B., B.L.S.

Librarian of St. Benedict's
Preparatory School, Newark, New Jersey

ST. MARY'S ABBEY

1952

IMPRIMI POTEST
† Patrick M. O'Brien, O.S.B.
Abbot

NIHIL OBSTAT
Joseph H. Brady, S.T.D.
Censor Librorum

IMPRIMATUR
† Thomas J. Walsh, S.T.D., J.C.D.

Newark, N. J., February 21, 1952

PREFACE

ABOUT four years have elapsed since the first volume of *Catholic Authors* was published. Its subtitle, *Contemporary Biographical Sketches, 1930–1947*, implies that the authors were either living at the time the book appeared or that they had died since 1930. The present volume also includes authors who have died since 1930 as well as those who are still living. Only authors of books are included. Authors whose works have been printed in a foreign language are included if at least one of their works has been translated into English.

This is not a revision of the previous work. All the 374 authors in this volume are new in the sense that they are not in the preceding volume. Some names that might have been expected in the first volume are also absent in this. Although the editor tried earnestly to make the list as complete as possible, some authors, for personal reasons, preferred to be omitted. The editor was unable to get in touch with a few others, whom he would have liked to include. And some who promised to send data failed to do so. The editor sincerely regrets their omission. Nor can he promise to include them in a future volume, because he has no plans to revise either of these books.

In compiling this volume the editor had in mind particularly librarians, who lose so much time in a frantic search for biographical material. Consequently, he included as many authors as possible in order to meet the needs and satisfy the varied clientele of libraries. The two volumes together give an intimate introduction to 994 contemporary Catholic authors. The term "Catholic author," as here used, means that the author is a practicing member of the Catholic Church. He need not write on Catholic themes, and his thought does not necessarily reflect the mind of the Church.

Searching out authors and gathering material is a most difficult task. Not every request for data meets with a response. Some authors broke down only after several years of pleading, while others thought they have revealed themselves in their books and saw no reason for a separate biography. In some cases it was only through the good offices of friends that a sketch could be obtained. All sorts of reference books were consulted. Thousands of letters were written by the editor to the authors themselves, their publishers and others, and every effort was made to get reliable data. The final draft of each sketch was sent to the author, if living, for corrections or approval. The sketches of deceased authors were checked by relatives or some reliable authority.

While he himself assembled most of the material and wrote 158 of the sketches, the editor engaged the services of several writers to help in composing 146 others. The initials of the writer are given at the end of each sketch, unless it is the result of multiple authorship,

or the work of a writer who does not want his name mentioned, or
unless it is principally autobiographical. There are 70 uninitialed
sketches. The editor is indebted to the following contributors: E.
Boyd Barrett (46); Rev. Kevin Mahoney, O.S.B. (10); Anne Fre-
mantle (7); Count Michael de la Bedoyere (England) (5); P. B. Ly-
saght (England) (5); Rev. Wilibald Berger, O.S.B. (Austria) (4);
Rev. Edmund Sutcliffe, S.J. (England) (4); Elise Lavelle (3); Helen
Landreth (3); Rev. Gerald Flynn, O.S.B. (3); Mildred B. Hughes (3);
Rev. Genadius Diez, O.S.B. (Spain) (2); Sister M. Serafina Mazza (2).
The following contributed one each: Theodore Maynard; Rev. Bona-
venture Schwinn, O.S.B.; Rev. Francis X. Murphy, C.SS.R.; Rev.
Gustave Bardy (France); Rev. Elred Olajos, O.S.B. (Hungary);
Franz Mueller; Canon Fernand Van Steenberghen (Belgium); Charles
Brady; Kathleen O'Flaherty (Ireland); Rev. J. C. Lehane; Francis
MacManus (Ireland); Rev. Henri Pouillon, O.S.B. (Belgium); Niall
O'Cuil (Ireland); Gertrude Helff; Rt. Rev. Hugo Lang, O.S.B. (Ger-
many); Rev. E. J. Coyne, S.J. (Ireland); Kurt Reinhardt; W. J.
White (Ireland); Rev. Paul Passelacq, O.S.B. (Belgium); Rev. Ludwig
Ott (Germany); Rev. Aloysius Kropp, O.S.B.; Mary Giesselmann;
Mother Mary Michael (England); Norbert Labsasz; Stanley Vish-
newski; Rev. Arthur McGratty, S.J.; Kevin MacGrath (Ireland);
Mary Ruth Bede; John E. Sparling; Rev. Sigmund Toenig, O.S.B.
(Austria); Ella M. Flick; Elizabeth Woods; G. Pran (Italy); Rev.
Henry E. G. Rope (English College, Rome); Rev. Patrick O'Connor,
S.S.C.; Rev. W. A. Kashmitter, M.M.; Rev. J. V. Ducattilon, O.P.
(France); Rev. Benedict Joseph, O.P. (Italy); Littleton C. Powys (Eng-
land); and those who prefer to be known merely as R. J. K.; J. C. L.;
Y. S.; Sr. M. P.; M. M. S., and Helpers of the Holy Souls.

It is impossible to mention the names of all who have helped in
one way or another with this book. The editor is particularly indebted
to His Excellency, Thomas Joseph Walsh, Archbishop of Newark; His
Excellency Archbishop Paul Yu-Pin; His Excellency Edwin V. Byrne,
Archbishop of Santa Fe; Rev. Joseph H. Brady; Patricia MacGill;
Professor Ludwig Ott (Germany); Eddie Doherty; Rev. Odilo Zurkin-
den, O.S.B. (Switzerland); Rev. Albert Nevins, M.M.; Julius Epstein;
Dorothy Day; D. Vincenzo Pugliese (Italy); Rev. Yves Congar, O.P.
(France); Rev. Bonaventure Schwinn, O.S.B.; Jan-Albert Goris,
Commissioner of Information for Belgium; Rev. Bede Ernsdorff,
O.S.B.; Rev. Andrew Kainzmaier (Germany); Rev. Rouzies (Librarian
of the Institut Catholique, Paris); Peter W. Hoguet; Rev. James B.
Clyne; Rev. René d'Ouince, S.J. (Editor of *Etudes*, Paris); Rev. Stephen
J. Brown, S.J. (Ireland); Rev. John J. Heenan, S.J.; Rev. Benignus
Benabarre, O.S.B. (Philippines); Rev. Leo Hudon, S.J. (Secretary
General of the Gregorian University, Rome); Mary Ellen Evans;
Virginia Patterson; Mary Bracken; Rev. Paul Passelacq, O.S.B. (Ed-
itor of Maredsous Publications, Maredsous Abbey, Belgium); Alma
Savage; Barbara Wescott; Very Rev. Leo Rudloff, O.S.B. (Israel); Rev.
William Heidt, O.S.B.; Valentine Tonone; Elizabeth Diller; Rev.
Alphonse O'Connell, O.S.B. (Scotland); Rev. F. Sheridan, C.S.Sp.
(Editor of *Missionary Annals*, Ireland); Rev. Edouard Neut, O.S.B.

(Belgium); Rev. Benoit Thoreau, O.S.B. (Belgium); Rev. D. Delteil; Rev. Bonaventure Kuo (China); James Shaw; Rt. Rev. Edward Hawks; Rev. Louis B. Blecharczyk; Rev. Hildebrand Yaiser, O.S.B. (Japan); Very Rev. Bernard O'Dea, O.S.B. (Ireland); Rev. Gregory Barry, O.S.B. (Ireland); Rev. Finbar O'Mahoney, O.S.B. (Ireland); Brian Doyle (Australia); Rt. Rev. Monsignor Sigismund Milalovics (Hungary); Sister Mary de Paul, O.P., and Alfred Vincent Kidder, and the publishers: The Macmillan Company; J. B. Lippincott Company; Viking Press; Sheed and Ward; Bruce Publishing Company; E. P. Dutton Company; Pellegrini and Cudahy; Pantheon Books; Beauchesne and Sons (France); Eason's Bulletin; B. Herder Book Company; Dodd, Mead and Company; Charles Scribner's Sons; British Information Services; William Morrow and Company; William Sloan Associates; Cosmopolitan; The Literary Guild of America; P. J. Kenedy and Sons; Doubleday and Company; Desclee de Brouwer (France); Coward-McCann, Inc.; Farrar and Strauss; Houghton, Mifflin Company; Little, Brown and Company; Longmans, Green and Company; Joseph Wagner, Inc.; Duell, Sloan and Pearce; Mercier Press (Ireland); Harvill Press (England); Harcourt, Brace and Company; G. P. Putnam's Sons; and Crown Publishing Company.

The translation of material from the German was made by Fathers Robert Baumgartner, O.S.B. and Wilibald Berger, O.S.B., and Norbert Labsasz; from the French by Fathers Kevin Mahoney, O.S.B., Elred Olajos, O.S.B., and Justin Csanyi, O.S.B.; from the Spanish and Italian by Father Genadius Diez, O.S.B.

For other help the editor wishes to thank Fathers Daniel Ready, O.S.B., and Christopher Lind, O.S.B. He would have been at a loss without the assistance of the typists who volunteered to work free of charge one night a week for the past two years. They are: Mrs. Marion (Hoehn) Dosch; Mrs. Rose Gallagher; Miss Rose Marie Gallagher; Mrs. Hilda (Riester) Heinrich; Mrs. Bette (Duncan) Hoehn; Mrs. Mary (Dwyer) Hughes; Miss Cecilia Koermaier; Miss Genevieve Lind; Mrs. Agnes (Koermaier) Oelkers; Mrs. Mildred (Hoehn) Ritter and Miss Rita Young. An expression of gratitude is also due to Fathers Bonaventure Schwinn, O.S.B., Kevin Mahoney, O.S.B., Gerald Flynn, O.S.B., and Miss Mary Flynn, for their help in correcting the proofs.

A very important item in the preparation of the book was a financial one. The Parent-Teacher Association of St. Benedict's Preparatory School, of which Father Thomas Long, O.S.B. is the moderator, contributed generously as it had done when Volume I was in preparation. The card party, of which Mrs. Teresa Fitzpatrick was the chairman, raised a further amount. To the members of these groups, to Rt. Rev. Patrick O'Brien, O.S.B., Abbot, and my confreres of St. Mary's Abbey for making the manufacture of this book possible, the editor wishes to express his heartfelt thanks.

CONTENTS

Page

Dorothy Adams (Mrs. Francis
McHugh).............. 1
Sister Mary Alfreda, O.S.B. *See*
Sister Mary Alfreda Elsen-
sohn, O.S.B............. 158
Robert Gordon Anderson...... 2
Valenti Angelo............ 4
Austin Joseph App.......... 6
Gladys Baker (Mrs. Roy Leon-
ard Patrick)............. 8
Rev. John Francis Bannon, S.J. 11
Vera Barclay.............. 12
Rev. Gustave Bardy.......... 14
Piero Bargellini............. 16
William Edmund Barrett..... 20
Rev. Bernard Basset, S.J...... 22
Margaret Bellasis (Francesca
Marton)................ 23
Joseph Bernhart............ 25
Princess Marthe Lucie
(Lahovary) Bibesco
(Lucile Decaux).......... 26
Claire Huchet Bishop........ 27
Rev. Celestine Bittle, O.F.M.
Cap.................... 29
Maurice Blondel............ 30
Thomas Bodkin............. 31
Hermann Borchardt......... 34
Rev. Eugene Boylan, O.C.S.O. 36
Charles Andrew Brady....... 39
Leo Brady................. 41
Theodor Brauer............. 43
Joseph Anthony Breig........ 45
Elizabeth Brennan........... 47
Rev. Gerald Thomas Brennan.. 49
Ann Bridge (Lady Mary
O'Malley).............. 50
Goetz Antony Briefs......... 53
Rev. Everett Francis
Briggs, M.M............. 54
Rev. Matthew Britt, O.S.B.... 56
Robert Carlton Broderick..... 57

Page

Colm Brogan............... 58
Beatrice Bradshaw Brown
(Michael Kent)......... 59
Rev. Raymond Leopold
Bruckberger, O.P........ 61
Dorothy M. Bryan........... 63
Louis Francis Budenz........ 65
Rev. Roger Buliard, O.M.I..... 67
David Burham.............. 69
Rev. Eric Norman Bromley
Burrows, S.J............ 71
Doris Burton............... 74
Charles Edward Butler....... 76
Rev. Joseph Cacella......... 77
William Edward Campbell..... 78
Mrs. Robert Capes
see Angela Verne........ 611
Mrs. Marcel Carbotte *see*
Gabrielle Roy............ 497
Rev. Maurus Carnot, O.S.B.... 80
Hans Carossa............... 81
Rev. John Carr, C.SS.R....... 82
Mary Jane Carr............. 83
Rev. Columba Cary-Elwes,
O.S.B.................. 85
Mother Cecily *see*
M. M. Merrick......... 350
Kadankavil C. Chacko....... 86
Rev. Pierre Charles, S.J...... 88
Jean Charlot............... 90
Bohdan Chudoba............ 92
Rev. André Combes.......... 93
Francis X. Connolly......... 95
Sister Mary Consolata
(Consolata Carroll)....... 96
Rev. Gustave Leon Constant... 99
Fred Copeman.............. 101
Rev. Frederick Charles
Copleston, S.J........... 104
Rev. John Coventry, S.J...... 105
Sister St. Michael Cowan
(Rosalia Cowan)........ 106

ix

Contents

Page

Rev. Francis Stanley Crocchiola
(Francis Stanley)......... 107
Rupert Croft-Cooke.......... 109
Rev. Patrick Cummins, O.S.B.. 110
Most Rev. John D'Alton...... 112
Sheila John Daly (Mrs. P. White) 113
Rev. Jean Daniélou, S.J....... 114
Daniel-Rops (Henry J. Petiot). 116
Rev. Henry Davis, S.J........ 118
Lucile Decaux see Princess
Marthe Lucie (Lahovary)
Bibesco................. 26
Rev. Maurice de la Taille, S.J... 120
Rev. Henri de Lubac see under
Lubac................. 313
Teresa Deevy................ 121
Rev. Martin Dempsey........ 122
(John) Michael Derrick....... 124
Paul Derrick................ 125
Sinead (O'Flanagan) de Valera
(Mrs. Eamon de Valera)... 126
Joseph Dever................ 128
Louis de Wohl............... 129
Maurice De Wulf............. 131
Alfred Döblin................ 133
Dorothy Dohen.............. 136
Mrs. Edward Doherty see
Catherine de Hueck....... 253
Mrs. Charles T. B. Donkin see
Dorothy Mackinder...... 329
Rev. John Donovan, S.J....... 137
Roger Burke Dooley.......... 138
Rev. William Lodewick Doty.. 141
(Edmund) Alan Downey...... 142
Rev. Francis Drinkwater..... 144
Rev. Jerome D'Souza........ 145
Douglas Valder Duff.......... 147
Rev. Avery Robert Dulles, S.J. 149
Pierre Lecomte Du Nöuy...... 150
Eleanor Early............... 152
Rev. Edward J. Edwards,
S.V.D.................. 154
Rev. John Tracy Ellis........ 156
Sister Mary Alfreda Elsen-
sohn, O.S.B.............. 158
Helen Margaret Mary af
Enehjelm (Mrs. Erik af
Enehjelm).............. 159
Rev. Omer Englebert........ 161

Page

Henry Outram Evennett...... 163
Rev. Denis Fahey, C.S.Sp..... 163
Eleanor Farjeon............. 166
James Aloysius Farley........ 168
Rev. Thomas Butler Feeney,
S.J..................... 170
Rev. William Noé Field....... 170
Kevin Fitzgerald............. 171
Robert Stuart Fitzgerald...... 172
Rev. Joseph David Flanagan
see Rev. M. Raymond,
O.C.S.O................. 461
Lawrence Francis Flick....... 174
Rev. (John Christian) Leopold
Fonck, S.J............... 176
Gene Fowler................. 178
Anne Fremantle............. 180
Rev. Louis Joseph Gallagher,
S.J..................... 182
Rev. David Gannon, S.A...... 185
Very Rev. Robert Gannon, S.J. 186
Rev. Noel Hamlyn Gascoigne.. 187
Rev. Jerome Gassner, O.S.B... 189
Laverne (Kels) Gay........... 191
Rev. (Edoardo) Agostino
Gemelli, O.F.M.......... 194
Theodate Geoffrey see
Dorothy G. Wayman..... 617
Most Rev. Martin Stanislaus
Gillet, O.P.............. 197
Henry Martin Gillett........ 199
Domenico Giuliotti.......... 201
George Glasgow............. 203
Sister M. Fides Glass........ 205
Liam Gogan................. 207
Guido Gonella.............. 208
Caroline Gordon (Mrs.
Allen Tate).............. 210
Maurice Anthony Gorham..... 211
Rt. Rev. Martin Grabmann.... 213
William Joseph Grace........ 216
Hilda Graef................. 218
Very Rev. Aelred Graham,
O.S.B................... 220
Rev. Andrew Green, O.S.B.... 221
Anne Green................. 223
Julian Green................. 224
Giovanni Guareschi.......... 226
Theodor Haecker............. 228

Contents

Page

Page

Robert Hamilton (John Robert Hamilton) 230
Mary Harris 231
Francis Burton Harrison 233
George Bagshawe Harrison 234
Lucile Hasley 235
Irene Haugh 238
Rev. Denis J. B. Hawkins 238
Rev. William Hayward 240
Jean Heavey 241
Most Rev. John Carmel Heenan 243
Rev. Paul Heinisch 244
Rt. Rev. Martin B. Hellriegel . . 245
Rev. Francis Herlihy 247
Ferdinand Aloysius Hermens . . . 249
James Hogan 251
Rev. Joseph Holzner 252
Catherine de Hueck (Mrs. Edward Doherty) 253
Rev. Robert Hull, S.J. 255
Marigold Hunt 257
Douglas Hyde 258
Leo Vincent Jacks 260
Carol Jackson (Peter Michaels) 261
Rev. Paul de Jaegher, S.J. 263
Pierre Janelle 264
Sister Mary Jeremy, O.P. 266
Kathleen M. Joyce-Prendergast 267
Constance Julian 268
Rev. Joseph Andrew Jungmann, S.J. 270
Mother Marie St. Justin *see* Marie René-Bazin 474
Harnett Thomas Kane 272
Rev. Otto Karrer 274
Oksana Stepanovna Kasenkina 276
Rev. Alan Keenan, O.F.M. 278
Daniel Lawrence Kelleher 279
Rev. James Gregory Keller 281
Rev. Bernard J. Kelly, C.S.Sp. 283
Michael Kent *see* Beatrice Bradshaw Brown 59
Rev. Neil Kevin 285
Robert Wendelin Keyserlingk . . 286
Benedict Kiely 288
Claude Francis Koch 289
Zofia Kossak (Mrs. Zygmunt Szatkowski) 290

Rev. Robert Kothen 292
Helen Landreth 294
Patrice de la Tour du Pin 296
Rev. William Lawson, S.J. 297
Robert Lax 298
Rev. Jules Marie Leon Lebreton, S.J. 300
Most Rev. James Leen, C.S.Sp. 302
Rev. Joseph Mary Lelen 304
Francis Joseph Henry Letters . . 305
Thomas Fanshawe Lindsay 306
Rev. Arthur Little, S.J. 307
George Aloysius Little 309
Rev. Riccardo Lombardi, S.J. . . 310
Rev. Joseph Adam Lortz 312
Rev. Henry de Lubac, S.J. 313
Barbara Lucas *see* Barbara Wall 613
Patricia Lynch 314
Stanislaus Lynch 316
Rt. Rev. Justin McCann, O.S.B. 318
John Bernard MacCarthy 320
Rev. Vincent Patrick McCorry, S.J. 320
William Henry McDougall, Jr. . 321
Maeve Cavanagh MacDowell . . 324
Sister Martha Mary McGaw, C.S.J. *see* under Martha . . 338
Rev. Fergal McGrath, S.J. 325
Rev. Arthur Raymond McGratty, S.J. 327
Mrs. Francis McHugh *see* Dorothy Adams 1
Dorothy Mackinder (Mrs. Charles T. B. Donkin) . . . 329
Bryan MacMahon 330
Francis MacManus 332
Neil MacNeil 334
Rev. Edward Mahoney 335
Clarence Emmet Manion 335
Eduardo Marquina 337
Sister Martha Mary McGaw, C.S.J. 338
Gregorio Martínez Sierra 340
Gustavo Martínez Zuviría (Hugo Wast) 341
Francesca Marton *see* Margaret Bellasis 23
Vera Laughton Mathews 344

Contents

Page

Rt. Rev. Olivier Maurault..... 346
Peter Maurin................ 347
Sister Maria Serafina Mazza ... 349
Rev. Denis Meehan........... 350
M.M. Merrick (Mother Cecily). 350
James J. Metcalfe........... 351
Peter Michaels *see* Carol
    Jackson................. 261
Ernest Milton................ 353
Mrs. Ernest Milton *see* Naomi
    Royde Smith............. 542
Joseph Cardinal Mindszenty ... 354
Margaret Theodora Monro..... 357
Rt. Rev. Edward Roberts Moore 359
Rev. Thomas Hendrick Moore. 362
Adolf Morath................ 364
Sylvanus Griswold Morley..... 365
Daphne D. C. Pochin Mould... 367
Rev. Jean Claude Mouroux.... 369
Rev. Senan Moynihan, O.F.M.
    Cap.................... 370
Rev. Hermann Muckermann... 371
Rev. Albert Muntsch, S.J..... 374
Gerard Murphy.............. 376
Rev. James George Murtagh... 377
Elizabeth Myers (Mrs. Littleton
    Powys) 378
Takashi Nagai.............. 380
Rev. Robert Nash, S.J......... 381
Thomas Patrick Neill........ 383
Jean Nesmy *see* Henry
    Surchamp.............. 566
May Nevin (Mrs. Canice
    Whyte)................ 384
Rev. Albert J. Nevins, M.M... 385
Mrs. Darcy Niland *see* Ruth
    Park................... 429
John Frederick Nims........ 388
Willis Dwight Nutting....... 390
Most Rev. Eris Michael
    O'Brien............... 392
Cathal O'Byrne............. 393
Rev. John O'Connell......... 394
Armel O'Connor............ 395
John O'Connor............. 396
Rt. Rev. John Joseph
    O'Connor.............. 397
Joseph O'Connor........... 399
Patrick O'Donovan......... 400

Page

Rev. John M. Oesterreicher.... 402
Kathleen O'Flaherty.......... 405
Terence O'Hanlon............ 406
Mary O'Hara (Mrs. Mary
    Alsop Parrot Sture-Vasa).. 408
Lady Mary O'Malley *see* Ann
    Bridge 50
James Milton O'Neill........ 411
Joseph O'Neill.............. 413
Alfred O'Rahilly............. 415
William Aylott Orton......... 417
Rev. Augustine J. Osgniach,
    O.S.B.................. 419
Rev. Denis O'Shea........... 421
Richard O'Sullivan.......... 424
Gretta Palmer.............. 425
Rev. Pascal P. Parente....... 428
Ruth Park (Mrs. Darcy
    Niland)................ 429
Rev. Pius Parsch, Can. Reg.
    Lat.................... 431
Howard Rollin Patch........ 433
Richard Pattee............. 435
José Maria Peman........... 437
Francesco Antonio Perri...... 439
Rev. Henri Perrin, S.J........ 440
Rev. Emery E. Petho........ 441
Henry J. Petiot *see* Daniel-Rops 116
Rev. Henry Petitot, O.P...... 442
Josef Pieper............... 444
Armand Pierhal............. 446
Catharine Plummer.......... 447
Count George Noble Plunkett... 450
Leo Politi.................. 451
Una Pope-Hennessy......... 453
Crawford Power............. 454
James Farl Powers........... 455
Mrs. Littleton Powys *see* Eliza-
    beth Myers............. 378
Rev. Ferdinand Prat, S.J..... 457
Mrs. Harry Rogers Pratt *see*
    Agnes Edwards Rothery... 493
Patrick Purcell............. 459
Rev. M. Raymond, O.C.S.O.
    (Rev. Joseph David
    Flanagan).............. 461
William Bernard Ready....... 463
Kenneth Reddin............. 465
Douglas Reed............... 466

Contents

Page

John Cowie Reid 468
Kurt Frank Reinhardt 470
Rev. Hans Anscar Reinhold 471
Marie René-Bazin (Mother
   Marie St. Justin) 474
Rt. Rev. Giuseppe Ricciotti 475
Rev. Joseph Rickaby, S.J. 477
Rt. Rev. (Andrew) Romanus
   Rios, O.S.B. 480
Rev. Francis J. Ripley, C.M.S. .. 481
Henry Morton Robinson 484
Rev. Aloysius Roche 485
Very Rev. Theodore Roemer,
   O.F.M.Cap. 486
Heinrich A. Rommen 488
Very Rev. Myles V. Ronan 489
Rev. Henry Edward George Rope 491
Agnes Edwards Rothery (Mrs.
   Harry Rogers Pratt) 493
Corinne Rocheleau Rouleau
   (Mrs. Wilfrid Rouleau) 495
Gabrielle Roy (Mrs. Marcel
   Carbotte) 497
Rev. Leslie Rumble 499
Mariadas Ruthnaswamy 501
John Julian Ryan 502
Very Rev. Dom Idesbald
   Ryelandt, O.S.B. 503
Edward Charles Sackville-West 505
Blanaid Salkeld 506
Nelle Margaret Scanlon 507
Most Rev. Joseph Henry
   Schlarman 509
Rev. Mark Schmid, O.S.B. 511
Rev. Philibert Schmitz, O.S.B. .. 512
Reinhold Schneider 513
William Greenough Schofield ... 517
Kurt von Schuschnigg 519
Ildephonse Cardinal Schuster,
   O.S.B. 521
Father Senan, O.F.M.Cap. *see*
   Rev. Senan Moynihan,
   O.F.M.Cap. 370
Elizabeth Sewell 523
Don Sharkey 525
Clare Consuelo Frewen Sheridan 527
John Desmond Sheridan 528
Walter Shewring (Hayward
   Francis) 530

Page

Gregorio Martínez Sierra *see*
   under Martínez 340
Paul Kwang Tsien Sih 532
Rev. M. Raphael Simon,
   O.C.S.O. (Kenneth Simon) 534
Liam C. Skinner 536
Henry Slesser 537
Most Rev. Jan Olav Smit 540
Helen Grace Smith 541
Naomi Royde Smith (Mrs.
   Ernest Milton) 542
Vincent Edward Smith 544
Anthony Joseph Stanley 547
Francis Stanley *see* Rev. Francis
   Stanley Crocchiola 107
Karl Stern 548
Richard Leroy Stokes 550
Rev. Anselm Stolz, O.S.B. 552
Rev. Benedict Stolz, O.S.B. 554
Geoffrey Stone 555
Rev. Francis Maria Stratmann,
   O.P. 556
Charles Stanley Strong 558
Mrs. Mary Alsop Parrot Sture-
   Vasa *see* Mary O'Hara 408
Emmanuel Celestin Cardinal
   Suhard 560
Mark Sullivan 561
Henry Surchamp (Jean Nesmy) 566
Rev. Edmund Felix Sutcliffe,
   S.J. 567
Rev. Francis Sweeney, S.J. 569
James Johnson Sweeney 571
Christopher Hugh Sykes 572
Mrs. Zygmunt Szatkowski *see*
   Zofia Kossak 290
Allen Tate 574
Mrs. Allen Tate *see* Caroline
   Gordon 210
Frank Sherwood Taylor 577
Rt. Rev. Patrick J. Temple 578
Rev. Dom Raymond Thibaut,
   O.S.B. 579
Rev. Newton Thompson 580
Rev. Francis Beauchesne
   Thornton 581
Felix Timmermans 585
Mari Tomasi 587
Maria Augusta Trapp 589

Contents

Page

Rev. Leo Trese.............. 591
Rt. Rev. Francis Trochu....... 592
Margaret Trouncer.......... 593
Rt. Rev. Pierre-Celestin Lou
   Tseng-Tsiang, O.S.B....... 595
Walter Ullman.............. 597
Rev. James (Herman Anthony)
   Van der Veldt, O.F.M..... 598
Rev. Ferdinand Valentine, O.P. 600
Rev. Dom Eugene Vandeur,
   O.S.B.................. 601
Kees Van Hoek............. 603
Rev. Dom Idesbald Van
   Houtryve, O.S.B.......... 605
Rev. Fernand Emmanuel
   Joseph van Steenberghen.. 607
Rev. Hubert van Zeller, O.S.B.
   (Hugh Venning)........ 609
Hugh Venning *see* Rev. Hubert
   van Zeller, O.S.B........ 609
Angela Verne (Mrs. Robert
   Capes)................ 611
David Esdaile Walker........ 612
Barbara Wall (Barbara Lucas). 613
Bernard Wall.............. 614

Page

Francis Wallace.............. 615
Hugo Wast *see* Gustavo
   Martínez Zuviría......... 341
Dorothy G. Wayman
   (Theodate Geoffrey)...... 617
Oliver John Grindon Welch.... 620
Antonia White.............. 621
Mrs. Peter White *see* Sheila
   John Daly.............. 113
Edmund Taylor Whittaker.... 623
Mrs. Canice Whyte *see* May
   Nevin.................. 384
Rev. Franz Michel Willam..... 624
Mother Mary Paula
   Williamson, R.C......... 626
Rev. Christopher John Wilmot,
   S.J.................... 628
Rt. Rev. Boniface Wohrmüller,
   O.S.B.................. 629
Hans Conrad Ernest Zacharias 630
Jacques Zeiller.............. 632
Gustavo Martínez Zuvería
   (Hugo Wast) *see* under
   Martínez............... 341

Dorothy Adams
(Mrs. Francis McHugh)

A literary spokesman for and an interpreter of the Polish people and their history is the earnest writer from Boston, Dorothy Adams.

Life offers few stranger paths than the one which led Miss Adams from her New England Unitarian home to Poland, there to become a Catholic, and back to America to wield her pen in bringing to the American public her conception of Poland as she found it.

Dorothy Adams was born in New York, the daughter of John D. Adams, member of an old Boston family. Her father, an assistant editor of *Harper's Magazine*, was a warm friend of Rudyard Kipling and knew Mark Twain and Du Maurier. His daughter Dorothy's childhood was spent in Boston, where she received her early education at the fashionable Miss Winsor's School. At Lincoln House Settlement, where her father was a director, she met, from an early age, people whose lives were far from privileged. Later she went to Baltimore to attend Goucher College, and on the day of her graduation was made the executive secretary of the Maryland League of Nations Association in 1924. For two years she traveled between America and Europe. She spent some time at Geneva, the League of Nations headquarters, and returning to America wrote and lectured on collective security in and about Baltimore. In 1926 the British Institute of Foreign Affairs assigned her to undertake a study of the Polish-German border question.

While in Europe she had met Jan Kostanecki, an economist, son of Professor Kasimir Kostanecki, rector of the University of Cracow. Later in London while at the London School of Economics she met Kostanecki again. "In a flash of self-recognition," she says, "I realized that I had identified John with Poland." They fell in love and were married. They built a house in Warsaw, had a son, traveled, and were happy. They went to Vienna where they saw the evidences of the growing threat of Nazism. Her husband, interested in forming a Danubian League, asked her to go back to Poland. Soon after their return to Poland they were separated again, and this time on his returning to her he was killed in an airplane accident.

Dorothy Adams returned to America and surveyed Poland and her happy family life there only as a memory. All this and much more she tells the world in her personal history, *We Stood Alone*, which was published in September, 1944.

She believes that Poland has a bad press in America, and through her book tries to counteract it. While traveling in the Balkans and in Italy, she became deeply interested in early Church History and archeology. Gradually she was led to the conclusion that history has but one answer for the seeker after truth, namely, that the Catholic Church is the true religion of Christ. So from the Unitarian background she had come all the way, and on September 10, 1938, she was received into the Church at Warsaw. She holds that the League of Nations failed for lack of spiritual guidance, and this guidance she deems necessary for any future conventicle of peace.

She is now living in Douglaston, Long Island, with her son and her husband, Mr. Francis Dodd McHugh, whom she married in 1940. She writes, speaks on the radio, and lectures, principally on Poland and is busy writing a novel with a Polish background. Before she could finish the novel, heartbreaking letters began pouring in from those she loves so dearly in Poland, as well as from the school for the blind at Laski, which she describes in her book. Since then she has spent all her energies in organizing an American committee to help the blind of Poland. She remarks: "With this daily tragedy before me I could not close my ears to concentrate in forgetfulness on my new book.

"I have also helped a Rosary Sewing Group for Mercy Hospital. We say the rosary as we sew every week, and in a few months we have earned $800.00 for the nuns." K. M.

Sister Mary Alfreda, O.S.B. See *Sister Mary Alfreda Elsensohn, O.S.B.*

Robert Gordon Anderson
1881–1950

Though almost the whole of Robert Gordon Anderson's life had been spent in connection with writing, it was not until the publication of his *Biography of a Cathedral* in 1944, followed by *The City and the Cathedral* in 1948, that he discovered his most eloquent line of work. And this work revealed an absorbing interest in Catholicism which led him at last, in the spring of 1950, to his reception into the Catholic Church.

He was born in Somerville, New Jersey, on April 18, 1881, the son of William Wallace and Mary (Davis) Anderson. His forebears, most of them early settlers, founded several townships in New England and elsewhere; and it was they who deeded to Bloomfield, New Jersey, the Village Green, which served as the training ground of the Minute Men during the Revolutionary War. The maternal homestead, which was built in 1667, was used by General Nathaniel Greene as a hospital; and Lafayette was entertained there. A great-great-grandfather furnished equipment for the local contingent; and was wounded while serving as a colonel on Washington's staff.

Alexander Gordon, paternal grandfather of Mr. Anderson, came to these shores from Scotland in the middle of the nineteenth century, adding the Anderson to his name, and fighting in the Mexican War. Mr. Anderson, in fact, had relatives in every war that the United States has fought. Other ancestors of his, shipbuilders in Maine, were related to Ralph Waldo Emerson.

Equally glorious has been the part played by his Gordon connections on the other side of the Atlantic; for one of them, the fourth Earl of Aberdeen, was at the head of a coalition cabinet from 1852–1854, and another Earl, the sixth, after serving briefly as Lord Lieutenant of Ireland in 1886, was afterwards appointed Governor General of Canada in 1893, and in 1905 once again resumed his old office in Ireland, being rewarded with a marquisate. Gordon is a very illustrious name in the British Isles.

Robert Gordon Anderson grew up to be a tall man, with a finely shaped head and clear, gray eyes, and an indefatigable worker until the last few years, when he developed serious heart trouble. His romantic interests early were stirred by the decorated well, made by a French emigré for the 1667 house, and by a tunnel it had, providing means for escape in the event of its being attacked. So also by the journey his grandmother made in a covered wagon in 1851 to find her husband, the Mexican War veteran, and by the stories related by others of his much travelled kin.

He himself taught for a while in his youth in a red schoolhouse, before studying at New York University. After this, he worked for an encyclopedia, wrote advertising copy, and was, in his day, the youngest reporter in New York City. After that, he spent two years on a Montana ranch, rubbing shoulders with bronco-busters, gamblers, desperadoes, and even murderers, in Custer County, until he settled down to the sedate management of a bookstore in downtown New York.

Then we find him, as a publisher's representative, visiting most of the great cities of the United States, going from this to positions as sales manager and literary advisor, finding time also for advertising campaigns and for "ghosting" some best sellers. But the goal he had set himself of becoming a serious writer on his own account had to be postponed until he was thirty-seven, after which he published twenty works as diversified as essays, biographies, novels, juveniles, verse, and travel books.

In 1911 he married Marion Blake. They had three children. Interested in French civilization since childhood, he spent a summer in France in 1920, which further drew him to that country. In two subsequent, and more extended, visits to Paris, accompanied by his wife and children, he felt that he came to know almost every stone of the city, every historic landmark, and every old church.

The fruit of this knowledge is apparent in his two major works. He also got to know something more important, for antiquarianism in his case was not something dead, but the key to the vivid and vigorous life of Catholicism. The Cathedral of Notre Dame with him was a passion, for he never tired of walking her aisles and aerial galleries, nor in meditating in the light of her rose windows, nor of attending her Masses and processions, thus unconsciously becoming saturated with Catholicism.

At first he wrote of the Cathedral as man's greatest artistic achievement, peopled throughout the ages with colorful characters. But gradually something more molded his first conception: the Cathedral was Christ, and the heart of the whole matter was the Host on the altar. In writing about the Cathedral, he found that he was writing himself into the Church. Probably it was some time before he was himself aware of what was happening, as it was some time before he brought himself to take what he saw later was for long an inevitable step.

One is reminded of Henry Adams' great book *Mont St. Michel and Chartres*. There is, however, this vast difference. All of Mr. Adams' learning and sympathy and literary charm were unable to penetrate the hard obstacle of his scepticism; his work therefore remains intellectual and abstract. But in the case of Robert Gordon Anderson there was a heart that generously responded to what he saw. These last two books by Mr. Anderson become therefore a tender and vibrant interpretation, not only of Paris and of its Cathedral, but of medieval culture and of Christian civilization. They constitute a remarkable crown to a very varied career.

Besides the books already mentioned, Mr. Anderson is also the author of *Not Taps but Reveille* (1918); *The Little Chap* (1919); *Leader of Men* (1920); *Seven O'Clock Stories* (juvenile) (1929); *Half-Past Seven Stories* (1922); *The Isle of Seven Moons* (1922); *Eight O'Clock Stories* (1923); *For Love of a Sinner* (1924); *Over the Hill Stories* (juvenile) (1925); *Those Quarrelsome Bonapartes* (1927); *An American Family Abroad* (1931); *The Tavern Rogue* (1934); *Villon* (grand opera libretto and poem) (1937).

Robert Gordon Anderson and his wife lived in Port Washington, Long Island, New York, in an English half-timbered cottage on one of the village's many hills. In a delightful garden adjoining deep woods, he and his friends, the birds, found mutual sanctuary.

On September twenty-fifth, 1950, he died of a heart attack.

                                                         T. M.

Valenti Angelo   1897–

Until he was eight years old, Valenti Angelo lived in Massarosa, Tuscany, Italy, "a little village nestled on a richly foliaged slope of the Tuscan Hills." Here he was born to his parents Augustino and Viclinda (Checchi) Angelo on June 23, 1897.

"My early school days," he writes, "were interesting. The solemn shaven-headed monk from the monastery taught the village children. In a corner of the whitewashed walls of the room there was always to be seen a row of switches standing neatly along the wall. It was seldom, however, that the kind, patient monk ever used one. At Christmas he would give all of them to an old woman of the village to make a fire with.

"I first became interested in drawing when Jacobo, the village wood-carver, found me making ducks of mud beside a puddle. From that time on I was allowed to go to his shop and might stay as long as I desired. 'Do it over again and again,' he would say. 'Do it until there is nothing more to do with it. And always do your best.'"

In 1905 Valenti came to America and lived for a while on New York's Bleecker Street. His brief stay in Little Italy made a vivid impression on him. When he returned thirty-eight years later to New York from California, where he had gone to live with his father, he was amazed to find how much he remembered.

He spent the first two years in California in school and then had to work in the fields. At fifteen he worked in a paper mill. Later he worked as a laborer in rubber, steel and glass works. And, while he worked he enjoyed drawing the things around him. "This," he says, "took up all my lunch hours and most of my time after work.

"At nineteen I left home and lived in the city of San Francisco, where I did ordinary labor. I haunted the library at night and the museums on Sundays and learned a great deal that my few school years had failed to provide. After much struggle I was hired by a photoengraving firm where I did any sort of art work that came into the shop. I worked there for three years." On July 23, 1923, he married Maxine Grimm. They have two children.

"In 1926," he writes, "I made my first illustrations for a book for the Grabhorn Press and since then I have devoted most of my time to decorating books. In the past twelve years I have decorated and illustrated some one hundred and thirty-five books and all have been a source of inspiration to do many more, and each one more fun than the last." Among these decorated works are the folio edition of *Leaves of Grass* and the *Song of Songs Which is Solomon's,* for which he hand-illuminated not less than 180,000 initials. In the American Institute of Graphic Arts "Fifty Books of the Year" exhibits, since 1927, thirty-seven books decorated by Angelo have been included. He has been a free lance artist in New York City since 1933.

Not until 1937 did he turn his hand to writing. In that year he published *Nino* "the offspring of my memories in the little village in the Tuscan Hills." This was followed up with *The Splendid Gift* (1938), and then *Golden Gate* (1939), "an account of Nino's early days in America. The horse and buggy days, and those of barefooted boys and dusty roads, peaceful rivers and graceful mountains, the rich golden fields of grain and the invasion of the four-wheeled carriages. All these went into it, and I felt again the long summer days, the green fields, the struggles and the long, long wait for manhood."

The other books to come from his pen were *Paradise Valley* (1940), *Hill of Little Miracles* (1942), *Look Out Yonder* (1943), *The Rooster Club* (1944) and *The Bells of Bleecker Street* (1949). What he had seen in 1905, when he had come to New York for the first time, he was eager to put down on paper: "the pushcarts, the children playing about the streets, the music, the roar of the elevated trains, the fluttering of pigeon wings amid the church bells," are vividly portrayed in *The Bells of Bleecker Street*.

L. S. Bechtel in her review (New York *Herald-Tribune Weekly Book Review*, p. 6, March 20, 1949) writes: "Here Mr. Angelo's many abilities combine in a complete success; his feeling for a place (this time Little Italy in New York), his remarkable insight into the hearts of small boys, his love of all people who do things well with their hands, his understanding of the Italian temperament, his keen artist's eye for detail, and his ability to write fluid, lively good English."

Valenti Angelo's latest book, *The Marble Fountain* (1951), is a story about a bombed Italian village in Tuscany. It treats of faith and reconstruction among the people there. M. A. H.

Austin Joseph App 1902–

The three basic theses of Austin J. App are: that, literally and really, the only hope for the world is Christianity; that the way to world peace is justice according to the Golden Rule, including particularly the weak and the vanquished; and that literature with the other arts is a divine instrument for harmonizing the emotions with right reason and the will of God.

Soon after his birth in Milwaukee, Wisconsin on May 24th, 1902, his parents August H. App and Katherine (Obermaier) App moved to a farm in Ozaukee County, near Lake Michigan, some ten miles north of Milwaukee. He was the first child of a large family, seven of whom are living.

At fourteen he entered the academy of St. Francis Seminary, where he got a thorough education in the classics and philosophy, and had one year of theology. He received his A.B. degree in 1924. He spent his summers working in mines and quarries, in the harvest fields of Kansas, Nebraska, and South Dakota and as a deck hand on an army transport between New York and Panama. After graduating, he won the four-year Knights of Columbus graduate scholarship to the Catholic University of America and received his master's degree in 1926. To further his knowledge of Spanish, he spent the summer of 1927 in Spain, and then vacationed in Lourdes and Paris.

Upon his return to the United States he was made assistant in English at Catholic University and continued his graduate work. He received his Ph.D. in June, 1929. His dissertation, *Lancelot in English Literature*, was his first published book. From 1929 to 1935 he was instructor of English at the Catholic University and at Catholic Sisters College. In the summer of 1931 he visited Central Europe and in the summers of 1932 and 1934, Great Britain and Ireland. Soon his articles began to appear in the American magazines.

In 1935 he became professor and head of the department of English at St. Thomas College, which became the University of Scranton. He was also moderator of debate, and in 1940–41 he was president of the Debating Association of the Pennsylvania colleges. In the spring of 1939 he conducted a series of radio programs on public affairs, entitled the Scranton Radio Forum. In June, 1939, he was awarded the University of Scranton Faculty Medal as "outstanding educator of men." In 1941 he became a co-founder with Mr. Eugene P. Willging and Dr. Leonard Wolf of the bi-monthly review magazine *Best Sellers*, for which until 1947 he wrote many unsigned reviews.

In 1942 he was drafted into the army, took his basic training at Fort Belvoir, Virginia, and served in headquarters at Camp Claiborne, Louisiana, from where in March, 1943, he was honorably discharged into war work as administrative assistant in personnel of the Jaeger Machine Co., Columbus, Ohio. When his sister, Martina, nursing arts graduate of Catholic University (now assistant professor there), also got a position in Columbus, he bought and furnished a house.

In September, 1944, he went to San Antonio, Texas, as associate professor of English at Incarnate Word College. Here for the first time in his life he was free from "extension" teaching, and more free to write. Shocked by the Morgenthauistic treatment of the German people and by the Potsdam Pact, he began pamphleteering and publishing on his own. His first pamphlet, "Ravishing the Women of Conquered Europe" (1946), sold 80,000 copies and has been translated into four foreign languages. The German edition, translated by Father E. J. Reichenberger, appeared in 1950 in Salzburg, Austria, *Der Erschreckendste Friede der Geschichte* (Hellbrunn Verlag). Then followed *History's Most Terrifying Peace* (1946); *Courtesy, Courtship and Marriage* (1947), and *The True Concept of Literature* (1948).

In the summer of 1948 he moved East again, to become associate professor of English at La Salle College, Philadelphia, where he is at present. He plans to stay in the East. In the summer of 1949 he visited Germany, Austria and Italy; two years later, he visited Luxemburg, Germany, Denmark, Holland and Austria. His chief interest was the welfare of the twelve million expellees from East Germany, the Sudetenland, and the Danube countries. He addressed them in Berlin, Regensburg, Kaernten, Vienna, and elsewhere.

His latest book is entitled *Making Good Talk: How to Improve Your Conversation* (Bruce Publishing Co., 1950). It was the November, 1950, selection of the Catholic Literary Foundation.

On November 16, 1951, he was elected a member of the Gallery of Living Catholic Authors. M. A. H.

Gladys Baker
(Mrs. Roy Leonard Patrick)

"My journalistic career started about twenty years ago at a wedding reception," writes Gladys Baker, author of *I Had to Know*. "It happened during my debutante year in my home town, Jacksonville, Florida.

"Everything contributed to the glamorous occasion. Flower-bedecked rooms of the bride's spacious home; strains of dance music drifting from the ballroom; guests in white-tie elegance.

"I had been asked 'to pour.' As I stood there ladling out the champagne punch, the scene dropped its mask of sensuous allure and I saw it as a wasteland. The guests, as in the old ballad, were 'dead men running.' Suddenly, I too wanted to run — not further into that world of artificiality but into the Real World, which I had sensed — since childhood — held eternal values. Taking French leave of hostess, escort and evening wrap, I fled the place.

"Next morning — seeking more solid ground on which to base my life — I asked for and got a job on *The Jacksonville Journal*."

A career of international journalism and "a compelling desire to find the other world of Reality which mystics, poets, and scientists of every age have found and affirmed with such clear conviction" have been the two drives that have dominated her life.

During the past twenty years she had interviewed practically every figure of our times as he attained celebrity.

Born in a well-to-do family, she received a classical education imparted by tutors and by private schools. At seventeen, as a "southern belle and beauty," she starred in a motion picture with a Southern locale. The stage, however, held no lure, so she turned down a Hollywood contract and took up journalism.

Every morning she climbed out of bed at six and reported for duty at seven. Like all beginners she had to do rewrites and "obits." But she felt she was Somebody when she received her first week's salary — $12.50.

One day the reporter who covered the hotel run complained of his inability to interview Anna Case, the noted concert singer, who had given a program the night before. Miss Baker told him she would try to get a story. She got it. This won for her the confidence of the city editor, who assigned her to interview Arthur Brisbane when he came to town. From then on she was given every interview assignment with famous people who stopped off in Jacksonville.

Her next job was with the *Birmingham News-Age-Herald*. Editor Charles A. Fell made her special New York correspondent. In New York she interviewed hundreds of celebrities. Later she became foreign correspondent for the North American Newspaper Alliance, interviewing dictators, crowned heads, statesmen, and world celebrities. She made journalistic history interviewing Kemal Ataturk and Mussolini, when these dictators had made themselves inaccessible to the press.

The following intimate pen portrait of Gladys Baker, at this time, is from the Protestant mystic, Adele Brooks Fort, author of *Splendor in the Night*.

"It was at the Opera that I first met Gladys Baker. She had recently come to the city in which I was living and the papers had given much space to her arrival. Her seat was next to mine that evening, and after our introduction I regarded her with interest. As I recall it she wore an evening gown of pale yellow which seemed to enhance the fairness of her hair and skin. I thought that she was beautiful, and as I had read about her success in writing, I determined to encourage her to talk, if possible, so that I could appraise independently her talent for expression.

"But here I met with a curious experience! It was I that did the talking, led on by a look of absorbed interest in Miss Baker's face. This flattering attention broke through my usual reserves, and it was only after I left her that I realized what a spell I must have been under to induce me, all unconsciously, to speak with ease and informality on topics I seldom discuss.

"This interest in people undoubtedly explains Miss Baker's success with many persons of various tastes with whom she has come in contact. It was inevitable, when later she was granted interviews with those in the limelight, that they should feel the tribute of her grave attention which must have invariably overcome their restraints. And in my own case (in thinking it over afterwards) I was astonished to realize that I had touched on subjects approaching the spiritual. And this with a stranger, at *Traviata*, between the acts!

"Either she had such charm that one forgot one's bearings or else, despite the shining quality of the opera and the glamour with which Gladys Baker herself was surrounded that night, she was searching for something deeper than appeared on the surface. We were, in fact, both seeking values beyond the material.

"I saw her again from time to time; later in New York after she had returned from Europe; in Washington; in Florida. And each time I found that she was still seeking, discarding tried and unrewarding paths for a trail that would lead her into truth she could accept. It was inevitable that she should find it! I, a Protestant, rejoice with her."

In 1941 — when war clouds broke over Europe — Gladys Baker was ordered home by her Southern editors. She commuted between New York and Washington. The lounge of the Mayflower Hotel was the listening post for her colleagues, especially those reporting international affairs. On one occasion she met there a New Englander, Roy Leonard Patrick, owner of Vermont granite and talc mines; director on boards of the Federal Reserve Bank, and the Boston and Maine Railroad, whom she later married. In February, 1942, she made her home in Vermont.

Four years later (1946) she became suddenly and mysteriously ill. The malady defied doctors. Treatment at Johns Hopkins Hospital, the Peter Bent Brigham Hospital in Boston, and the best experts availed nothing except to diagnose the malady as an incurable hypoproteinemia. She was given five years to live. Then in more earnest began her search for Truth.

In 1951 her autobiography, *I Had to Know*, was published by Appleton-Century-Crofts, Inc. The book combines the highlights of a fascinating journalistic career, a gallant battle for life and a life-long quest ending in a description of personal instruction in Catholicism by Monsignor (now Bishop) Fulton J. Sheen.

On Saturday before Palm Sunday, 1950, she was baptized and received into the Church by Monsignor Sheen, and from him the next day received her First Communion. On Memorial Day of the same year she was confirmed by Francis Cardinal Spellman. All the ceremonies, due to illness, took place at her bedside at the Ritz-Carlton Hotel in New York City. Since then her overwhelming desire has been to "breathe out the self and breathe in the Thou."

I Had to Know received a unanimously excellent press — both Protestant and Catholic. In a review of *I Had to Know* in the *New York Times Book Review*, Anne Fremantle compliments the author as well as her book. She writes . . . "for all her supernatural interests and experiences Miss Baker . . . a beautiful and charmingly feminine woman . . . is a very natural person, whose 'courage is cast about her like a cloak of handsome comeliness.'"

Frances Parkinson Keyes, author of *Dinner at Antoine's, Joy Street*, etc., said — "The flowing style makes very easy, as well as very delightful, reading. Moreover, many passages in the book either struck a responsive chord, or opened some new vista, the sight of which will greatly enrich my life."

Fulton Oursler, Editor of *Reader's Digest*, wrote: "Every man and woman in search of peace should read *I Had to Know*. Here is the history of a human soul that found its way from confusion to happiness — the kind of happiness that cannot fade and that surmounts even incurable illness, pain and loss. No one can read Miss Baker's book without being the better for it."

Gladys Baker says: "Journalists and especially reviewers must possess three faculties. The ability of swiftly summing-up a personality; an imagination which colors and enhances, but without distortion, the actual words which are spoken; and above all a sixth sense which penetrates the subjective sides of character and like the sensitive lens of a camera, catches the subtle lights and shadows."

In private life, she is Mrs. Roy Leonard Patrick. She makes her home at 275 South Willard Street, Burlington, Vermont, and the Carlton House, New York City. M. A. H.

Reverend John Francis Bannon, S.J. 1905–

The fascination which the medieval cathedral aroused led Father John Francis Bannon to a "desire to learn more about the people and the age which erected these splendid monuments." Thus he became immersed in the study of history, though he has strayed somewhat from his "first love," the Middle Ages.

John Bannon was born at St. Joseph, Missouri, on April 28, 1905, the son of William Joseph and Clara (Shortle) Bannon. He was educated at Rockhurst High School, Kansas City, Missouri, and at Saint Louis University, from which institution he received his A.B., A.M. and S.T.L. degrees in the years 1928, 1929 and 1936 respectively. He entered the Society of Jesus September 1, 1922. He took the course of philosophy with the French Jesuits at Collège Saint Louis, Jersey, Channel Islands. It was here the Jesuit Fathers of the Province of Paris had taken refuge in the 1880's when the first severe anti-clerical laws of the Third Republic were passed against the religious. During those years came an opportunity to travel in the British Isles and on the Continent for three summers.

When Father Bannon returned to the United States in the summer of 1929 he began the period of regency. For two years (1929–1931) he taught at St. Mary's College, Kansas, and when the superiors closed that venerable old institution to turn it into a Jesuit house of theology, he moved on to Regis College, Denver, Colorado, for the year 1931–1932. During these years he taught French and Spanish. From 1932 to 1936 he followed his theological studies at St. Mary's College, being ordained to the priesthood in June, 1935. In 1937 he went to the University of California at Berkeley, to complete his graduate studies in history under the direction of Herbert Eugene Bolton. The degree of Doctor of Philosophy was granted by the University of California in 1939. "The topic of the dissertation," he says, "turned on the advance of the mission frontier into the northern Mexican State of Sonora." At the University of California, he developed an interest in the history of the Americas, both Latin and Anglo, which has since absorbed most of his academic activity.

Father Bannon has been at Saint Louis University since 1939 where he holds the rank of Professor of History, and has been director of the Department of History since 1943. From that date to mid-year of 1950 he has also been editor of *The Historical Bulletin*, "a service quarterly for teachers and students of history" published by the Department of History, Saint Louis University.

Father Bannon has traveled in a number of the Latin Americas and has lectured widely on topics of Inter-American interest. He has also cooperated with foreign trade groups. He was director of the six

Institutes on Foreign Trade, sponsored by the Export Managers' Club of Saint Louis and is currently chairman of the Inter-American Division, Saint Louis Council on World Affairs.

In giving a reason for writing books, Father Bannon said: "I look upon myself as a teacher-historian first and foremost. I feel that the Catholic historian has very much to contribute to a better understanding of the past by drawing on his close connection with the truest roots of Western civilization, the elements which came through or from the Church during the formative centuries. Students should have a share of that fuller understanding, hence my books for the college-university student clientele.

"As an historian I am probably more of a synthesizer than a research scholar. Let others write profound studies for the members of the historical craft; I am much more interested in bringing their excellent historical scholarship into student focus. I would rather be known as a great teacher of history than a great research historian. History is too vital a subject to be locked up in the ponderous tomes for the delectation of the specialist. Youth's formation can be well served by history — it should be one of the most human, broadening and fascinating subjects in the academic curriculum."

Father Bannon is the author of *Epitome of Western Civilization* (1942); *Colonial North America, A Short History* (1946); and *Latin America, An Historical Survey* (1947) in collaboration with Peter Masten Dunne, S.J. Currently, he is working on a two-volume history of the Americas: *The Colonial Americas* and *The American Nations.* He is a not infrequent contributor to the historical journals, and is active in the important national and sectional historical associations, having served on the Executive Council of the American Catholic Historical Association, several times on the program committee of the Mississippi Valley Historical Association, and on the general committee of the Latin American Conference of the American Historical Association. He is a corresponding member of the Academy of American Franciscan History and past-president of the Jesuit Historical Association.   M. A. H.

Vera Barclay   1893–

Vera Barclay is an author who chooses to write for children, and a sentence of Francis Thompson, "who grasps the child, grasps the future," is her battle cry because she is embattled. Her feeling about children's literature is best described in her own words: "Serious novels have come to fill a very special role in modern life — they do something to fill the hiatus caused by the crowding out of religion, culture and leisurely talk and friendship from modern life. To many people, reading is a formative influence. To children, on the other hand, it is hardly more than distraction, recreation, superficial instruction or thrill. And yet children — who are beings too reserved, as well as too unconscious, to make their necessities known — need books *in the same way* as grown-ups do, and perhaps even to a greater degree."

This English author was born in 1893 at Hertford Heath, Herts, the daughter of Charles and Florence Barclay. Her mother was a novelist of the romantic period but it is to her great-great-aunt Maria that Vera Barclay traces her own literary gift. For this member of the Charlesworth family, to which her mother belonged, produced the Early Victorian classic for the young, *Ministering Children*, which foreshadows the work of Vera herself. A note of interest to American readers is that her father was a direct lineal descendant of the Scottish laird Robert Barclay (1648–1690) called "the Apologist," who was appointed Governor of East New Jersey by Charles II. This gentleman, although a strict Presbyterian himself, sent large numbers of Quakers, including his own brother David, to the colony. He owed much of his deep learning to the six years he spent in Paris at the Scots Theological College, a college for Catholic missionaries where his uncle, Father Robert Barclay, was rector.

All these diverse strands from her ancestry seem to have been woven into the fabric of Vera Barclay's life. She became a Catholic in 1916 through reading a book on education lent her by a nurse in the Red Cross hospital, Netley. Knowing nothing previously of Catholic people, worship, or doctrine, she learned during the first four years of her life in her newly adopted religion "to know the *Faith lived* as no grown-ups could have taught it," as she says, from the little Catholic ragamuffins in the vicinity of Westminster cathedral in which London quarter she was then living, occupied entirely with scout work.

She wrote, first, books on scouting at the direct request of Baden-Powell, the founder of scouting. Then followed books and articles on Catholic education. These were published anonymously in *The Sower*, a Catholic educational magazine. Some of these articles have been reissued in a volume called *The Way into the Kingdom* (1949). She was led to her main work, however, by being asked to judge the finals of a Children's Book Competition. Her interest was aroused by this experience and as a result she wrote the first of her *"Joe and Collette"* series, which was followed by her *Jane Will You Behave* series. Some of these tales have been broadcast by the B.B.C.

The war interrupted her writing, but since 1943 she has produced a number of children's books, of which *They Found an Elephant* is the most recent, and which she hopes to follow up with similar books, as she believes writing for children is work that is really worth while. She says "the present worrying developments in child behavior — ranging from tiresomeness at home to actual juvenile crime — is a reaction of the children (who are sound at heart) to the modern attitudes and environments that are in every way a misfit for children. To get absorbed in the right kind of a book or magazine should help, as a prophylactic and even as a cure."

Her writing for children has been, however, interrupted by work on two highly controversial books dealing with what she believes to be the harmful effect of popular evolutionary teaching. *Darwin is not for Children* (1950) was sufficiently well received, to be followed up by *Challenge to the Darwinians* (1951).

A small volume very different from any of her other writing is *Morning Star and Other Poems* (1951).   **M. B. H.**

Reverend Gustave Bardy   1881–

It can be said without prudent fear of contradiction that the man who knows most about the first six centuries of the Church, and has written most prolifically thereon, is a stately, bearded septuagenarian, Gustave (Léon Victor) Bardy, professor of positive theology and patristics at the Grand Séminaire of Dijon. Born on November 25, 1881, at Belfort, he has had a long, busy career as priest, professor, patriot and patrologist.

As a scholar, Father Bardy resembles most the seventeenth century historian, Le Nain de Tillemont, whose biography he has recently supplied for the *Dictionnaire de théologie catholique,* for the breadth, exactitude and concise expression of his knowledge of the early Church. There is hardly a modern, scholarly European publication dealing with the literature and theology of the first six centuries in which his articles, reviews, or notes do not frequently appear. Since the close of World War II he has produced on an average of two books a year, even taking over such a delicate task as the edition of De Labriolle's *Histoire de la littérature latine chrétienne* (2 vols., Paris, 1948), and furnishing several volumes of introduction and translation for the *Sources chrétiennes* (e.g. Athénagore: *Supplique au sujet des Chrétiens;* Hippolyte de Rome: *Commentaire sur Daniel;* Théophile d'Antioch: *Trois livres à Autolycus*), while independently producing an excellent two-volume study of the *Théologie de l'Église* (Vol. I: de saint Clément de Rome à saint Irénée, Paris, 1945; and Vol. II: de saint Irénée au concile de Nicée, Paris, 1947).

Having attended secondary school in his native Belfort, M. Bardy made his seminary studies at St. Sulpice in Paris, where he received his licentiate in philosophy and letters in 1904, and where he was advanced to the priesthood on June 30, 1906. He obtained his doctorate for superior studies in philosophy at the Institut Catholique of Paris, having turned his attention in particular to the history of the early Church and of the Fathers, producing in 1910 a well received, scholarly study on the life and writings of Didymus the Blind. He has recently brought this study up to date in a short article, "Du nouveau sur Didyme L'Aveugle," in *Science Religieuse Travaux et Recherches* (Paris, 1944, pp. 247–250).

Father Bardy's professorial career began at the College of Saint Jean de Besançon, where he taught philosophy from 1909 to 1914. In 1913 he contributed a volume on St. Athanasius to the *Collection des Saints;* then, with the outbreak of World War I, he hastened to join the medical corps of his regiment, being mobilized on August 2, 1914. He served in campaigns in Alsace and the Near East (Salonica), and was released from service in 1918 with a medal and citations for wounds and bravery in combat. After the war, he studied in Paris, then joined the faculty of theology at the University of Lille in 1919. In 1923 appeared a work of scholarly erudition that proved him a first class patrological student capable of the finest philological analysis, his *Recherches sur l'histoire du texte et des versions latines du De Principiis d'Origène.*

For the series *Les Moralistes chrétiens* Father Bardy wrote the volume on *Clement of Alexandria* (Paris, 1926), and on *Origen* (1931). Meanwhile he branched out on the dogmatic and spiritual plane, producing another book on Origen, his *De la prière: exhortation au martyre* (1932), an introductory volume on the Fathers, *En lisant les Pères* (2d ed., Paris, 1933); *La vie spirituelle, d'après les Pères des trois premiers siècles* (1935); *le Sauveur* (1937), and *le Rédempteur* (1933). He has contributed numerous studies on the Church in the fifth and sixth centuries for the monumental Fliche-Martin *Histoire de l'Église,* the first two volumes of which have been translated into English by E. H. Messenger. He edited *Les trophées de Damas* for the *Patrologia Orientalis* (t.XV, fasc. 2); did studies on Paul of Samosata and Lucien of Antioch, while contributing numerous articles to important reviews and dictionaries such as his appreciation of "Adolphe Harnack" in the *Vie Intellectuelle* (8, 1930, 193–203), "Saint Athanase, Saint Basile" for the *Dictionnaire d'Histoire et Géographie ecclésiastique,* "Montanism," "Origine," "Trinite" for the *Dictionnaire de Théologie Catholique;* "Ambrosiaster," "Hellenisme," for the *Dictionnaire de la Bible,* etc.

In the past decade, Father Bardy has turned out books and articles ranging over the whole field of general and special Church History including two studies on St. Augustine, a volume on *Conversion au christianisme durant les premiers siècles* (1949), *La Question des Langues dans l'Église ancienne* (1948), *l'Église et les derniers Romains* (1948), *Les religions non chrétiennes* (1950). Meanwhile he has served as editor of the *Vie Catholique* from 1924 to 1938, director of the *Vie Diocesaine of Dijon,* where he joined the Faculty of Theology in 1939, and where he exhibits his interest in contemporary problems by devoting himself to such exacting tasks as acting as spiritual director to a girls' academy. Indicative of his prominence as a civic figure is the fact that he was made a Chevalier of the Legion of Honor in 1948.

Two of Father Bardy's books translated into English by Mother Mary Reginald immediately upon their appearance are the very serviceable *Christian Latin Literature* and *Greek Literature of the Early Christian Church,* originally contributed to the series *Bibliothèque catholique des sciences religieuses* (1929) and (1930), and in 1938 appeared *The Church at the End of the First Century,* translated into

English by P. W. Singleton. A number of his articles have been translated into English, including his study on *"The Hellenistic Milieu"* in *Père Lagrange and the Scriptures* (1947) and "St. Jerome and Greek Thought" in a forthcoming *Monument to St. Jerome* (Sheed and Ward, New York).

Father Bardy is a man of universal theological interests who has spent his days and years serving his Maker by a scholarly and literary production that is easily the equivalent in volume, if not also in weight and importance, of many a Father of the Church.

F. X. M.

Piero Bargellini   1897–

Piero Bargellini, who with Igino Giordani and Giovanni Papini, enjoys the privilege of being among the three Italian writers in America's Gallery of Catholic Authors, has more than sixty published volumes to his credit. In 1951 he was elected to the Municipal Council of Florence, and given charge of the city's fine arts. He is called a genuine Florentine, not simply because he was born and reared in Florence, but because he seems to embody all the characteristics of the citizens of historic *Fiorenza* — which Dante calls "the most beauteous and most famous daughter of Rome," and which was originally dedicated to the god of war, and subsequently to the Precursor of the Prince of Peace.

This genuine Florentine was the son of Captain Carlo Bargellini, the founder of the Italian Naval League — who at the age of twelve had run away from his father's printing house in Siena to become a cabin boy — and Adele Cestoni, the charming young woman for whose sake the captain gave up life on board ship and settled down in Florence. Piero was born on August 5, 1897, in the Bargellini home on Via Pier Capponi, the favorite rendezvous of Captain Carlo's sailor friends, and the birthplace of their journal, *La Lega Navale*, published by them and the Captain. These shipmates welcomed Piero into the world with the cheer, "Viva l'ammiraglio," dubbing him "the Admiral," and predicting for him a career on the sea. Their prediction, however, has turned out to be entirely false, for "the Admiral" has never had any love for the sea, nor any desire to become a seaman.

When Piero was only a few years old, his family went to live in the Mugello, the countryside where Giotto and Fra Angelico had spent their early childhood. It was here that Piero first became interested in art. As a boy of seven he had been so fascinated with the work of an amateur whom he had watched painting a festoon on a wayside shrine near his home that then and there young Piero decided to become an artist. He undertook at once to teach himself to paint. Installing himself in his "private studio," a stationary washtub of stone in the courtyard below his window, he worked assiduously with improvised colors and canvas, dreaming of the glory that would be his when down through the ages posterity would honor him as an illustrious painter. Despite laborious work, the results did not measure up to the little lad's expectations, and so his dreams of glory vanished, leaving him utterly disconsolate. Fortunately, this unhappy experience, far from cooling the fervor of his artistic spirit, made him more eager than ever to learn about painting and about all the fine arts; so much so, that Bargellini's love of art has become an abiding inspiration, to which many of his books owe their being.

After a brief sojourn in the country, Bargellini's family moved back to the city, into a rented house, for Captain Bargellini could not afford to buy a home. Though the Bargellini family had but a scant supply of money and things that money can buy, it had an abundance of the joy and happiness a group of children can bring to one another and to devoted parents. Piero loves to recall the "sweetness of living together" in their humble, unspacious home on the top floor of one of those long and narrow buildings near the Convent of San Marco, in Florence. "What a tiny house," he writes, "but what a lovely home."

Mindful of the sacrifice his parents were making for their five children, Piero was anxious to give them a helping hand as soon as possible. Accordingly, instead of seeking to satisfy his desire for literature and art, he directed his efforts toward a remunerative position, matriculating at the *Istituto Tecnico* for the course in civil engineering. He was graduated from that school at the age of eighteen, the very year of Italy's intervention in World War I, and so Piero and the rest of his class were regimented right into the barracks.

This unfavorable turn of events, which frustrated Bargellini's plan for helping his family, might have likewise frustrated his hopes for a literary career; but, paradoxically, it provided the occasion for encouraging these hopes. His professor of Italian, Diego Garoglio, when conveying the good wishes of the faculty to the graduating class, happened to add, "We shall meet Bargellini in the field of literature." This remark, coming as it did from an aesthete of the literary group of the *Marzocco*, was a pleasant surprise for the youthful surveyor, and he accepted it as a challenge and as a prophecy.

This prophecy had actually captivated Bargellini, and he lost no time in working toward its fulfillment. Upon coming back from the war, Lieutenant Bargellini took advantage of the privilege granted by the Italian government to soldiers wishing to go to school, and went to Pisa to study. He abandoned the field of his specialization, and prepared himself for the teaching profession, concentrating on elementary education, in which he was still engaged on the eve of World War II, no longer as an instructor, however, but as an administrator.

At the same time, Bargellini continued the assiduous study he had begun in the army, making himself familiar with the classics of Italian and world literature, and with other subjects of cultural and spiritual value. He also ventured into journalism, writing articles that later appeared in his *Calendario*, founded by him in collaboration with Betocchi and Lisi. Speaking of this venture, Bargellini says, "I could never have had the courage of presenting myself with a fistful of my own writings to anyone, except to some intimate friend, poor like myself and unknown like myself — Carolo Betocchi, for example, or Nicola Lisi."

Despite this modesty and timidity, however, the first fruits of Bargellini's journalistic endeavors must not have been devoid of merit, for they attracted the attention of men like Giuliotti and Papini, who were among the first to recognize Bargellini as a promising young writer. In fact, it was Papini who recommended Bargellini for the post of editor-in-chief of the *Frontespizio*, a literary monthly which had just been founded, and through which — thanks to Piero Bargellini's encouragement and kindness — many of today's younger writers learned to climb the precarious rounds of the literary ladder.

Bargellini's first book, which was not published until several years after it was written, shows the author's transition from the columns of a periodical to the pages of a book, for it is merely a series of related articles, akin to those that appeared in the short-lived *Calendario*. Bargellini himself tells how this volume came into being: "Then came the month of May. I was in love with her to whom I have dedicated this book, and who was to be my wife. I would often pray to the Madonna for her and for myself. I even got into the habit of going to the first Mass every morning, in the church of the Santissima Annunziata nearby. Upon returning home, I would go to my desk and write. For thirty-one consecutive days I wrote about the Madonna, producing these pages entitled "Scritti a maggio" (Written in May) . . . More than six years have gone by, and I have been asked to publish a book. I have several books ready for publication, but I am doing like that father of several daughters, who would not give the youngest one in marriage unless the eldest was married first. This is my first book, and I want it published first."

Scritti a maggio (1931) came out exactly twenty years ago. During these twenty years, Piero Bargellini's books have been appearing at the rate of three or four a year. They are almost as varied as they are numerous, ranging from controversial discussions on architecture to graded readers for elementary schools — biography, hagiography, art appreciation, religion, literary criticism, history of literature. This diversity of subject matter, unusual as it may seem, is not surprising to those who recall that Piero Bargellini is a civil engineer who became a teacher, a painter who became a writer, and a well-informed militant Catholic who is also a fervent apostle.

Whether one considers Bargellini as a narrator, a biographer, a polemist, or a critic, he is ever the same literary artist. Notwithstanding the diversity of the subjects about which he writes, his works have unity by virtue of his art, which is one — like his personality. Keenness of comprehension and accuracy of expression are manifest in all his writings. He knows how to grasp the real meaning of the data found in documentary sources, and how to present his findings in lucid, accurate, vivid language. Thanks to this happy faculty, Bargellini can make even the most abstruse ideas stand out in tangible, palpable form. He can give new life to people that have long been buried in the lifeless pages of dead history books, make them live in the fervid world of their day, and take an active part in the current events that have since become history.

Even the stalest of old facts, when presented in Bargellini's animated style, take on a freshness that is invigorating and contagious.

In view of such talent, it is not surprising that, as one of the keenest literary critics in Italy says, some of the passages from Bargellini's pen are among the most beautiful that can be read in the Italian language. The excellence of his art is not unexpected, for Piero Bargellini was the leader of those outstanding Frontespizian artists, who insisted that Catholics should write artistically, or not write at all, because what they write should be worthy of the burden of their thought.

From the foregoing passages about Bargellini and his works, it is evident that he is a staunch Catholic who is endeavoring to live his faith according to the mind of the Church. In one of his earlier articles, he alludes to his "conversion," saying it was more like the return of the homesick son to his father's house than like the conversion of St. Paul on his way to Damascus. Bargellini does not say why or when he had left his "Father's House," or how long he had stayed away from it; but, before he began to write, evidently, he was already back Home to stay, for even his earliest writings manifest warmest love for the Church. Bargellini's entire career as a writer, consequently, reflects his life as a sturdy Catholic who takes interest in everything, because he believes that nothing human is alien to Catholicism.

Bargellini's Italian readers can be numbered by the tens of thousands, but to the English-reading public, he is, as yet, almost unknown. The first American study of his life and works was made during World War II, by the author of this article, and published in *Not for Art's Sake* (1948). Since then, Bargellini's *Pius XII: The Angelic Shepherd* (1951), a translation of the Italian *Pio XII, Il Pastor Angelico* (1948), has appeared in this country. In Florence, the English translations of some of his writings on art began to come out soon after the close of the war. The beautifully illustrated monographs, *The Medici Palace and the Frescoes of Benozzo Gozzoli* (1947), and *The Convent of San Marco and the Paintings of Fra Angelico* (1948), announced the forthcoming *Trilogy of Beauty*, a translation of "Trilogio della Bellezza," which consists of three volumes of more than two hundred pages each, with many reproductions of the works of the masters — Benozzo Gozzoli, Sandro Botticelli, and Domenico Ghirlandaio — in the same format as the Italian edition. These books are elegant. They are attractively printed, richly illustrated, and artistically bound. Even without reading the inviting text, lovers of art can derive much joy from these pages, simply by leafing through them, and looking at the exquisite pictures.

Today Piero and Lelia (Cartei) Bargellini live on Via Bolognese, in Florence. There they celebrated their silver jubilee in May of the Holy Year, and from there, shortly after this celebration, Piero set out for his Holy Year pilgrimage to Rome, going on foot all the way, like the pilgrims of Dante's time. The six Bargellini children (Silvestra, Monica, Simon, Bernardina, Mauro, and Antonina), with their diverse interests and talents, make home life delightfully normal for themselves and their parents, and unconsciously create the inspiration for Piero Bargellini to strive onward as a Catholic and as a writer in his work among the laborers in the Vineyard.   M. S. M.

William Edmund Barrett   1900–

The average sale of one thousand copies a week, and a total of more than fifty thousand copies of his latest book, *The Left Hand of God*, with its sale to RKO for production in a motion picture, has helped William Barrett, its author, to prove several things, writes Ed Miller in *The Denver Catholic Register*. "It proves," he says, "that a writer can make an adequate amount of money without resorting to a lusty, busty heroine, 'sexsational' scenes and the argot of the gutter; that a top 'slick' writer can graduate into the ranks of the top novelists; and that the man who gets his literary training writing for magazines is not necessarily handcuffed to the habit of using warmed-over plots every time out."

William Barrett was born in New York City on November 16, 1900, the son of John Joseph and Eleanor Margaret (Flannery) Barrett. He studied at Manhattan College. *Cosmopolitan* published a novel of his, which never appeared as a book, entitled *Before I Wake*. It is perhaps the first novel ever written against the background of the Christian Brothers schools, of which he is a product. Mr. Barrett is particulary pleased about this novel.

On February 15, 1925, he married Christine M. Rollman. They have two children — Marjorie Christine and William Edmund.

In 1929 he gave up his position as southwestern advertising manager for Westinghouse to devote his entire time to writing fiction. He started at the bottom by writing for the "pulps." In the thirties he wrote thrilling stories of war in the air for youths. Ten years later he contributed to such magazines as *Redbook*, *McCall's*, *Cosmopolitan* and *Reader's Digest*.

Mr. Barrett is grateful to the magazines. While he was still immature in a writing sense, they provided him with readers and encouragement and with the means of carrying on. "Some writers," he says, "seek fellowship and research grants, some have private means or family support or patrons; when a writer has none of these he can always support his own projects through extra writing. Only in the United States, with its large and prosperous magazines, is this possible."

Lamenting the fact that there are too few Catholics contributing regularly to the popular magazines he remarks: "Those of us who do work in that field compete, as Catholic authors, with all that the left-wingers and the unbelievers send against us from their very fine, if godless, schools of creative writing and we accept cheerfully a narrow field of plot and circumstance against their wide ones; solving no human problem by divorce, refusing to glamorize illicit love, weighing character motivation on Catholic scales. The readership of a single issue of a leading popular magazine, any of them, runs into millions and a Catholic author has a sense of responsibility (or should have). He knows that to touch millions of lives, however lightly, is no light thing — and the heavy reader mail tells him that he is touching those lives."

His first book, *Woman on Horseback*, was published in 1938. *The Saturday Review* said of it: "Mr. Barrett writes with the flair of a novelist for character and situation, but he writes also with the conscience of a historian and the archival patience of a specialist." The New York *Times* comments: "Luridly melodramatic, it is also true. It holds the attention and makes the hair stand on end. Imagination . . . a sense of character . . . and a style so good one forgets it exists." The New York *Herald-Tribune* states: "There is no story to parallel it. Terrifying, pathetic, engrossing. *Woman on Horseback* deserves wide reading." The Los Angeles *Times* remarked of this biography of the dictator Francisco Lopez and his mistress Eliza Lynch, "A narrative so lively, romantic and full of action that it might be taken for a novel." This book was translated into German, Swedish, Spanish and Portuguese.

When *The Left Hand of God* came out in 1951, Monsignor Matthew Smith, Editor of *The Register* said: "This story, presented in briefed form in four installments by the *Redbook Magazine*, drew more mail than had come to that magazine in ten years about any other story; and many persons who wrote in, including some fallen-away Catholics, told how it gripped them spiritually! They learned plenty about their faith in it. Few of the letters were disparaging. Barrett's book is a brilliant exhibition of what can be done with Catholic themes that are dramatically out of the ordinary."

His other works are: *Flight from Youth* (1939, bought by MGM); *The Last Man* (1946); *The Evil Heart* (1946); *The Number of My Days* (1946); *Man From Rome* (Motion Picture) (1949). He is also included in the following collections: *Best American Short Stories* (1944); *Son-of-a-Sun Stew* (1945); *Denver Murder* (1946).

Since 1939 Mr. Barrett has been a book reviewer for the Boston *Transcript* and the Boston *Post*.

His next novel has been tentatively scheduled by Doubleday for October, 1952, and he is hard at work on it. It is the story of spiritual conflict laid against the background of an American city in our own day. The priest who appears in it is a real priest and not, as in *The Left Hand of God*, an imposter. In 1953 he hopes to finish for publication a biography on which he has labored off and on for many years.

Since 1941 Mr. Barrett has been a consultant in aeronautics for the Denver Public Library. In 1942 he was a civilian lecturer for the Army Air Force. For the year 1943–44 he was president of the Colorado Authors League. His home is in Denver, Colorado.   M. A. H.

Reverend Bernard Basset, S.J.
1909–

Early in the thirties a series of short stories began to appear in *Stella Maris*, the English Catholic magazine. The author was quite unknown and the tales were unpretentious; simple little stories full of humor intended for plain ordinary folks in their homes. The heroine was Margery, a harassed housewife, and her husband told the tales. The readers of *Stella Maris* were enchanted with Margery and when at length they came to learn that the author was a very young Jesuit scholastic, they rubbed their eyes in astonishment at his knowledge of so many homely details of family life.

From this unusual Jesuit seminarist, immersed in prayer and study, came fifty-four Margery stories, and for each new story the host of readers increased. From England the stories spread to America and Canada and across the European Continent where they appeared in many languages. Too precious to remain in scattered form, they were, during the war, collected in two books, *Margery and Me* and *The Seven Deadly Virtues*. For each volume there was an immediate sell-out.

Catholic England had another brilliant, witty writer, capable, as a critic put it, of "atomic flashes of word and picture," who was soon to write of Jesuits and Hanoverians, and infidels and giants.

Bernard Basset was born in the city of Westminster in 1909. His father, a convert to Catholicism, came of an old English family; his mother was half-American, her mother being a first cousin to General Robert E. Lee. Bernard's first public school was the famous Jesuit College of Stonyhurst in Lancashire (England). There he remained until he was eighteen years old and of age to enter the noviceship of the Society of Jesus. During his studies in the Society he was sent for three years to Campion Hall, Oxford University, where he took a first-class honors degree in the school of Modern History. The M.A. (Oxon) came five years later. While at the University he competed for and won two University prizes: the Stanhope Historical Essay prize with a paper on George II; and the Lothian Prize with a monograph on the French Rationalists and their approach to history.

Father Bernard Basset was ordained in 1941 and was sent to teach at Beaumont College, which is situated near Windsor Castle. Soon he became immersed in Catholic Action, which took him traveling and lecturing, throughout England. Meanwhile he has edited for some years a column in the widely read *Catholic Herald*. He has been employed in giving retreats and lecturing to the boys of the Royal Air Force. Helping demobilized servicemen has been a first charge on his work.

Among Father Basset's published works, irrespective of his articles, and plays and pantomimes written for the young, are: *Margery and Me* (1945); *The Seven Deadly Virtues* (1947); *Farm Street* (1949), *The Blessed Edmund Campion* (verses) (1936).

To many who have visited and have known *Farm Street*, the famous Jesuit Church in Mayfair (London), Father Basset's brilliant little story about it will be delightful reading. "With a series of swift and shining strokes," says Douglas Newton, in a review, "Father Basset creates the picture of the Great Adventure . . . the courage and prescience of the Society in planning a church not in a back street style but in a grand manner that a hundred years have more than justified." Pugin built the sanctuary but Jesuits like Bernard Vaughan, Woodlock, Steuart, and Gavin made it part of the heart of Catholic England. Father Basset "flings an enchanting net" around the interesting events and personalities of Mayfair's hallowed mews.

E. B. B.

Margaret Bellasis
(Francesca Marton)

In 1948 a novel called *Attic and Area; or The Maidservant's Year* appeared in depressed, over-taxed, austerity England. In bookstore windows it lay among piles of fiction having to do with problems of war, sociology, the subconscious, and the spooks. There was nothing spookish about *Attic and Area*. It had to do with a maid-servant's life in the cheerful, plentiful, peaceful domesticity of 1840 London. A species of "gastric" nostalgia was awakened. It hit hungry men's fancy. "It proved welcome," wrote *The Tablet* reviewer, "as would be in our dehydrated days the solid meals it often describes — rich, unrationed, done to a turn." Critics became enthusiastic! "How tempting is that great kitchen!" to quote the *Woman's Journal*, "and how the mouth waters at the thought of such delectable food and menus. . . . An enjoyable affair."

It was the second novel of a gifted young writer and artist who had served five years in an Air Force uniform during the war — living among heroes about to die. "The inspiration of working beside some of the bravest men who ever died," she writes, "can never be forgotten. The comradeship, the adventure, and the broadening effect of meeting so many diverse people! Whenever I now require a model for any character, I can look back on a crowd of hundreds of once familiar faces from which to choose."

Margaret Bellasis was born in London, England. On her father's side the family had a long, North-country, Catholic tradition, though part of the family, the senior branch, had fallen away, grabbing a Yorkshire abbey during the Reformation. On her mother's side, the family was Anglo-Irish and non-Catholic, but through her mother, a convert, Margaret was baptized a Catholic and her father was converted to the faith. A hundred years before, Sergeant Bellasis, an eminent Victorian lawyer, and friend of Newman, who belonged to the elder branch of the family, had also been converted.

Margaret Bellasis' early education was at a convent school, and after, when she was fifteen years of age, at an art school. She had shown a talent for drawing, but never went very far as an artist, either with brush or pencil, and "after working hard, I concluded," she says, "that I wasn't good enough." Meanwhile she loved to read.

"I continued to devour books, and formed a devotion which has never since wavered for the quiet, deep perfection of Jane Austen, and the unquiet, imperfect, wild genius of Dickens. My strongest early influence perhaps was R. L. Stevenson, with his conscious delight in craftmanship; he taught me to try after a style, and by dint of scribbling through my 'teens I finally achieved a fairly serviceable one."

Margaret Bellasis tried her luck as an advertising copywriter but the war came along to stop the efforts. She had visited Canada and seen the States from across the Niagara bridge. Mindful of history she planned but never executed a novel about early settlers — preferring to write her first novel about the Kentish (English) coast, a novel she called *Over the Same Ground*. She wrote it while war went on overhead. Waiting to be called to serve in the Women's Auxiliary Air Force, she kept busy at her typewriter. "Such a time," she says, "of suspense and noise and danger seems hardly ideal for novel writing; but the book took shape rapidly, and was finally finished among all the distractions of that grimly-operational wasps' nest, a Bomber Station." Margaret was serving in the Air Force when her novel came out (June, 1944), just after D-Day. It was well received. One day, being relieved from duty for a few hours, she was thrilled to see her first-born on sale in bookshops.

The pen name "Francesca Marton" under which her novels are written, was chosen by Margaret Bellasis partly (the Marton part) from a place called Long Marton, in Westmorland, once the home of her family; and partly (the Francesca), in honor of St. Francis de Sales, patron of writers. When she writes non-fiction reviews for *The Tablet*, or magazine articles, she signs her work "M. Bellasis."

So far, Margaret Bellasis has only published two novels: *Over the Same Ground* (1944) and *Attic and Area* (1948), but she has plans for more, saying that "themes and characters of Catholic interest will always find their way naturally into my work . . . but I never wish them to look dragged in."

Margaret Bellasis admits mournfully that she has but two photographic expressions; "one is sullen defiance, the other rabbit-and-snake terror," but there is no sullenness or terror in her outlook on life. She rides, dressmakes, cooks, dances, and loves flying, . . . the sea, and the English countryside. She now lives at Shorelands, the Marina, Deal, Kent, England, a little old seafaring town near Dover, part of "Hellfire Corner" as it was called during World War II and noted for the "little ships" it sent to Dunkirk. "It's a town," she says, "I'm very fond of; and my room here opens on a balcony facing the sea. All day long, we can see ships from every part of the world passing the famous Goodwin Sands and at night the sound of the waves lulls me to sleep. It proves a good spot to work."   E. B. B.

Joseph Bernhart   1881–

Though a layman, Joseph Bernhart is one of the ablest Church historians of Germany.

He was born on August 8, 1881, in Ursberg, Bavaria, the son of an official, and was educated in the local schools as well as the Universities of Munich and Jena. During his philosophical and theological studies he was especially interested in esthetics. He was a lover of freedom. For many years he could not decide whether to devote himself to art, poetry or to scientific research.

Since the essay is almost unknown in Germany he longed to specialize in this field. His knowledge of history and philology, which he learned at Munich, Jena and Berlin, when studying for his degrees, enabled him to give full expression to his ideas. He contributed to leading periodicals, especially to *Hochland*, whose editor, Karl Muth, respected his scholarship and esteemed his friendship. Joseph Bernhart is known not only as an editor, anthologist and lecturer but also as an author. His book, *Hans Holbein der jungere*, published in 1922, was well received and so were his books *Der Engel des Deutschen Volkes* (*The Angelic Patron of the German People*); *Heilige und Tiere* (*Beasts and Saints*), and in 1931 appeared *Der Sinn der Geschichte*, an introductory volume of *Geschichte der führenden Völker* (*History of the Leading Nations*).

His first book to be translated into English is *Vatikan als Weltmacht: Geschichte gestalt des papsttums*. It was translated into English by George N. Shuster and was published in 1939 by Longmans, Green & Company under the title *The Vatican as a World Power*. W. T. Wells, in his review of the book (*The Spectator*, March 24, 1939, p. 494), writes: "Dr. Bernhart is a man of finished and profound scholarship, he is also quite clearly a man with a deep and religious faith. He is able to distinguish the sphere proper to scholarship from the sphere proper to belief, and he is sufficiently self-analytical to understand when he himself is actuated by the faith of a Catholic and when he is expressing the judgment of a historian." Up to 1949, 18,000 copies were sold.

In 1946 the Government nominated him a member of the newly founded Bavarian Academy of Fine Arts in recognition of his work.

                                                                M. A. H.

Princess Marthe Lucie (Lahovary) Bibesco (Lucile Decaux) 1887–

Although Princess Bibesco was born in Bucharest, Rumania, she has lived most of her life in Paris. When she was six years old, her father was named Minister of Rumania to France. "Looking back on those days," she says, "I recall the salon of our house in Paris, where I was sent every morning to practice on the piano on which were the photographs of the sovereigns my father represented — King Carol, with his gray beard, and Queen Elizabeth with her short hair, and below them on a small table, the portrait of the Crown Prince Ferdinand." Some years later her father was called back to Rumania to be Minister of Foreign Affairs. Her family arrived just at the time Prince Ferdinand fell ill with typhoid fever. During his illness the Prince had grown a beard. When Marthe heard of it, — she was eleven years old at the time — she told her doctor, one of the physicians of the court, who was taking care of her cold, "We children are going to sign a petition to ask Prince Ferdinand to shave his beard." The next day the physician said to her: "Prince Ferdinand has commissioned me to tell you that if he is letting his beard grow it is because he wants to resemble those ancient Rumanian princes who are shown with beards in the frescoes of the churches." "This explanation," Marthe said, "flattered my patriotism."

Princess Bibesco was born in Bucharest, Rumania in 1887, the daughter of John Lahovary, former Foreign Secretary and President of the Senate, and of Princess Smaranda (Emma) Mavrocordato. Her mother was a convert to the Catholic Church from the Greek Orthodox Church.

At the age of sixteen she (Marthe) married her cousin Prince George Bibesco, grandson of the Prince of Wallachia (now Rumania). Two years later she went to Persia with her husband, when the King of Rumania appointed him temporary ambassador on a special mission. Here Princess Bibesco wrote her first book, *The Eight Paradises*. It describes her journey and experiences. The book was crowned by the French Academy. Princess Bibesco believes she is the youngest French author to have had a book crowned by the French Academy. (Princess Bibesco writes in French.)

Under the pseudonym of "Lucile Decaux," she wrote six novels. One of these, *Katia*, was translated into English and later was made into a movie. Princess Bibesco thinks her book *Crusade for the Anemone: Letters from the Holy Land* is of the greatest interest from the Catholic point of view. The anemone is the flower that Christ called the "lily of the field." "The Crusade" is a plea to return to the fervor and faith which one must have to make the journey properly to the Holy Land. The book was chosen by the Catholic Book Club.

Her other books in English are: Novels — *Catherine Paris* (1928); *The Green Parrot* (1929); *Balloons* (1929); *Worlds Apart* (1935); *Katia* (1939); Non-Fiction — *The Eight Paradises* (1923); *Isvor: The Country of Willows* (1924); *Royal Portraits* (1928); *Egyptian Day* (1930); *Some Royalties and a Prime Minister* (1930); *Lord Thompson of Cardington* (1932); *Alexander of Asia* (1935); *A Daughter of Napoleon* (1937); *Flowers: Tulips, Hyacinths, Narcissi* (1940); *The Veiled Wanderer: Marcel Proust* (1950).

During World War I she was the head nurse of a hospital in Bucharest and was helped by French nuns of St. Vincent de Paul.

Since her husband's death in 1941, Princess Bibesco has devoted her time to writing and looking after her two grandsons. Her husband had been president of the International Aeronautical Foundation and was an air pilot since 1909. Both he and his wife traveled extensively. Princess Bibesco was a friend of the late Maurice Baring. When Lady Lovat published her book *Maurice Baring: A Postcript* (1948), she had as postscript to her book Princess Marthe Bibesco's answer to her request that she should "write a preface to the French translation of *Passing By*, Maurice's first novel, and the one on which his dying mind had concentrated in so remarkable a manner." Lady Lovat commenting on Marthe's preface adds: "Its beauty needs no comment."

When in 1945 her country lost its freedom and was seized by the Russian Communists, Princess Bibesco discontinued visiting her native country. She divides her time between France and England.

M. A. H.

Claire Huchet Bishop

Claire Huchet Bishop started telling stories in "L'Heure Joyeuse," the first French Children's Library which was founded in Paris, in 1924, as a gift from America and which she had opened on behalf of an American Committee. She told one story, "The Five Chinese Brothers," which was particularly popular and which many years after she re-told at the New York Public Library. "Then for fun," she writes, "I set it down." It was published by the Coward-McCann Company, and Claire Bishop's career as a writer began.

Storytelling had been an hereditary pastime in her Breton family. Her grandfather was the village storyteller with tales of Tristan and Yseult, King Arthur, Roland, and great episodes of French history. Her father and her mother were storytellers. "As a child," she says, "I used to feel chills running up and down my spine while she (my mother) was reciting, and then, when it was all over, she would look at my white face and give a robust, hearty laugh, shrug her shoulders and say to me, 'You are stupid!'"

One might think that a storyteller, such as Claire, would be, above all, interested in people — especially when the storyteller claims, as she does, "to be nothing else but a poet." Be that as it may, Claire Bishop protests: "I am more interested in ideas than in people . . . people make an impression on me only in relation to ideas . . . this may be partly the reason why I can write successfully for children. My world has not changed." To add to the enigma of our storytelling poet's mental make-up — and to be directed as to how and where to solve the riddle — Claire Bishop adds: "a writer is his work. To look for the writer anywhere else is bound, in most cases, to be misleading."

Looking for Claire Bishop in her recent writings about French "Communities of Work," and about the renewal of religious faith in France, in her first adult book, *France Alive*, we find an observant, logical, dispassionate mind, motivated by human and religious ideals. "I told some of my friends, Dominican friars in Paris," she says, "that this book, on the French Christian renewal, *France Alive*, should be written, if not by a saint, at least by someone very pious. Their answer was that it was precisely because I was so far away from sanctity that I could do the job. A person, more or less in it, would take much for granted. No question — Our Lord does make strange choice of His tools!"

Claire Huchet Bishop, completely French, and "more French than the 'French,'" hails from Brittany, from typical Breton stock. As a little girl she was bored by school. "It was far less interesting," she relates, "than listening to mother and father at home. I managed to prepare myself to go to the Sorbonne (Paris), but although I was fairly successful, I disliked intellectual life."

In Paris, apart from her occupations at the Children's Library, she wrote some poetry which was published in some of the avant-garde magazines. She also worked on the staff of the *Nouvelle Revue Française*.

In America, she married Frank Bishop, a concert pianist of genius. After the publication of *The Five Chinese Brothers*, other stories followed in quick succession. The Viking Press published four of her tales, among which was the popular *Pancakes-Paris*. Of this she says: "*Pancakes-Paris* just happened! A ten-year-old American boy who made pancakes for me; the hardships suffered by French children during the past seven years or more; an immense desire to try desperately to make the well-fed and warmly comfortable Americans realize what it was like in France, where I had just spent a bitter winter: all added up to this book, *Pancakes-Paris*, which was illustrated by George Schreiber." The juvenile book was honored by the New York *Herald-Tribune* Spring Books Award 1947.

Besides articles in *The Commonweal* and elsewhere, and poetry both in French and in English — one of the latter, to her great joy, appeared in *The Catholic Interracialist* — Claire Huchet Bishop has the following works to her credit: *The Five Chinese Brothers* (1938); *King's Day* (1940); *The Ferryman* (1941); *The Man Who Lost His Head* (1942); *Augustus* (1945); *Pancakes-Paris* (1947); *Blue Spring Farm* (1948); *France Alive* (1949); *Christopher the Giant* (1950); *All Things Common* (1950).

Claire Bishop's energy and enthusiasm can be seen from her itinerary through France, Switzerland, Italy, Belgium, and Holland . . . visiting over sixty "Communities of Work" in preparation for her writings on that subject. Through twenty years of American life, as a married American citizen, she still keeps in personal touch with her home-land and family. Like a good Gallic-American she loves to cook and to garden — she finds time, too, for music. Like an ardent Catholic she paints, in *France Alive*, a thrilling picture of "the apostolic zeal of priests who tour the countryside in trailers, or shed their clerical garb to become workers in mines and factories or on the docks" of the unsettled suffering land of her birth.   E. B. B.

Reverend Celestine Bittle, O.F.M. Cap. 1884–

When in 1927 the health of Father Celestine Bittle broke down, his superiors sent him to St. Joseph's Monastery and parish in Appleton, Wisconsin, to recuperate. "Doomed to inactivity because of ill-health," writes Father Bittle, "and not knowing what to do with my time, I wrote up the story of my service in the war (World War I), and the Bruce Publishing Company published the book as *Soldiering for Cross and Flag* in 1929."

Father Bittle was chaplain in World War I in 1918, and served with the 301st, 302nd, and 303rd Units of the Motor Transport Corps in France. Shortly after this first book was published his superiors gave him the assignment of writing the history of his province on the occasion of its 75th anniversary. *A Romance of Lady Poverty* (1933), his second book, was the result.

Born in Des Moines, Iowa, on September 22, 1884, of John and Mary (née Voegele) Bittle, he attended parochial schools in Ionia and Grand Rapids, Michigan, and in Milwaukee, Wisconsin, and studied humanities at St. Lawrence College, Mount Calvary, Wisconsin, from 1897 to 1902. After having spent one year in the novitiate of the Capuchin Order in Detroit, Michigan, he went to Milwaukee, Wisconsin, and studied philosophy and theology in the clericate, and was ordained to the priesthood on June 29, 1909. The next years (1909 to 1918) were spent as Professor of Philosophy, Religion and Literary Criticism at St. Lawrence College, Mount Calvary, Wisconsin. From 1918 to 1919 he was in the army serving as chaplain in France, after which he was assigned as curate to St. Michael's Church, Brooklyn, New York, where he spent five years. In 1924 he was appointed superior and pastor of St. Elizabeth's parish, Milwaukee, Wisconsin, remaining there until 1927.

After his ordination in 1909 the superiors of his province introduced a two-year course of philosophy in St. Lawrence College at Mount Calvary, Wisconsin. Father Bittle was appointed to teach the course. The only books available in English at that time were the books of the Stonyhurst Series, rather technical in style and content, and not suitable for undergraduates. He felt that it was desirable to have a series of texts, nontechnical in style, but with the breadth of a mono-graph. Other interests and activities, however, occupied most of his time until in 1935 there appeared the first in a series of philosophical texts, *The Science of Correct Thinking* (Logic). Then in quick succession appeared *Reality and The Mind* (Epistemology), 1936; *The Domain of Being* (Ontology), 1939; *From Aether to Cosmos* (Cosmology), 1941; *The Whole Man* (Psychology), 1945; *Man and Morals* (Ethics), 1950. The last of the series, a work on Theodicy, will complete the plan conceived over a quarter of a century ago.

These texts are used in more than a hundred colleges and universities. The book on logic has gone through fifteen printings, and the one on epistemology through ten printings. The success of these texts is proof that their fundamental idea is sound.   G. F.

Maurice Blondel   1861–1949

Maurice Blondel, a leader in the contemporary revival of Scholasticism in France, was born in Dijon, on November 2, 1861. He made his secondary studies in his native town, and earned a bachelor of science degree, a bachelor of law degree and a licentiate in literature. Then he entered the Ecole Normal Supérieure in 1881. His professors were Emile Boutroux and Leon Ollé-Laprune; the latter became his friend and exercised a profound influence upon him.

The great event in his life came on June 7, 1893, at the Sorbonne, when he defended his thesis, *L'Action, Essai d'une critique de la vie et d'une science de la pratique.*" This work was unfavorably received by the philosophers of the University who reproached him for having misunderstood the rights of pure reason. The book was also vehemently criticized by certain theologians who reproached him for not having accentuated enough the gratuity of the supernatural life. However, it was never condemned by the Church. Obliged to defend and to explain his teaching, Blondel, forced by circumstances, became an apologist.

After teaching in the Lycée of Chaumont and of Montauban, then at the College Stanislas in Paris he was appointed to the Faculté des Lettres of Lille in April 1895, which he left in 1897 for Aix-en-Provence. He held the latter position for over thirty years. He came to love this town so much that when he retired from teaching in 1927 he chose to spend the remaining days of his life there. Forced to retire because of eyestrain, which developed into almost complete blindness, Blondel took advantage of his rest from arduous teaching duties to complete his work *L'Action* which was awaited since 1893. Thus he published *La Pensée*, Paris 1934; *l'Etre et les Etres*, Paris 1935; and finally a completely revised edition of *L'Action* in 1935–1936. With this trilogy, his philosophical achievement ended. Since 1914 he was a corresponding member of the l'Academie des Sciences morales et politiques and in 1948 he was made an officer of the Legion of Honor.

Blondel wrote many articles and books. Some of the remarkable ones are: "Lettre sur les exigences de la pensée contemporaine en matiere d'apologetique et sur la méthode de la philosophie dans l'étude du problème religieux" in the *Annals de la philosophie chrétienne* '(1896); repeated partially in *Le problème de la philosophie catholique*; *Histoire et dogme* in *La Quinzaine* (Jan.–Feb., 1934); "La Semaine sociale de Bordeaux et la monophorisme" in the *Annales de philosophie chrétienne* (1909–1910), under the pseudonym of Testis; *Le procès de l'intelligence* (Paris, 1920); *Le problème de la mystique* (Paris, 1925); *Leon Ollé-Laprune et l'achèvement de son oeuvre* (Paris, 1923); *Une énigme historique, le vinculum substantiale d'après Leibnitz* (Paris, 1930) (this last book is a French translation and a repetition of the Latin thesis of the author's doctorate); *Le problème de la philosophie catholique* (Paris, 1932); *Patrie et humanité* (1938, Paris).

Blondel was working on the third volume of a second trilogy at the time of his death. This trilogy was entitled *La philosophie et l'esprit chrétien*. Only the first two volumes were published: *Antonomie essentielle et connexe indeclinable* (Paris, 1944); *Conditiones de la symbiose seule logique et salutaire* (Paris, 1946). The third volume, which remains unpublished, has the title *Crise de croissance et perspectives seules salutaires*. Blondel died before he could put on the finishing touches. On the eve of his death, June 3rd, 1949, he could, however, sign a publisher's contract for a book which, in a way, is his testament: *Les exigences philosophiques du christianisme*.

Blondel's influence was considerable during his life. It has not stopped growing as the great number of works published testify.

G. B. and E. O.

Thomas Bodkin   1887–

To look up Bodkin, Thomas in *Who's Who* is to be confronted with fifty-two and a half lines of such diverse honors and activities as recall the petulant Clerihew concerning Hilaire Belloc:

"He seems to think nobody minds
His (doings) being all of different kinds."

(*Biography for Beginners*, edited by E. Clerihew, B.A. Diagrams by Gilbert Keith Chesterton).

Twelve lines of academic titles and distinctions, most of them obviously acquired in the domain of art, are followed by three of family history.

Then come six lines listing his legal and oratorical achievements. The next entry records nineteen years as a civil servant. The following four and a half lines detail his advisory or honorary membership of many learned societies and administrative bodies in the art or educational world and the concluding lines list his books.

Born in Dublin July 21, 1887, Thomas Bodkin is the son of the late Mathias Bodkin, County Court Judge of Clare, M.P. for North Roscommon. He was educated at Clongowes Wood College and the Royal University of Ireland, graduating from the latter in 1908. At both institutions he won gold medals for oratory, legal debates, and essays. The National University of Ireland and the University of Dublin have each conferred on him the degree D.Litt. In 1911 he was called to the Bar, King's Inns, and practiced for five years. On February 2, 1917 he married Aileen Cox. They have five daughters.

From 1916 to 1935 he was Secretary to the Commissioners of Charitable Donations and Bequests in Ireland. His success as a civil servant may be judged from the fact that in 1925 the Government paid the Secretary the unprecedented tribute of appointing him to be a Commissioner himself, which office he still retains. In 1926 he was made a member of the Commission to advise the Minister of Finance on coinage. The following year (1927) he was a member of the Committees to advise the Minister of Education on National Museum organization and on Art Education. In the same year he was elected Director of the National Gallery of Ireland, which post he held till 1935.

Dr. Bodkin is probably most widely known for his innumerable lectures to academic bodies, learned societies and congresses in England, Ireland, Scotland. Wales, and many foreign universities. He has given many and varied broadcasts, ranging from Brain Trusts to poetry readings, and has given both through the microphone and television.

As Public Orator for the University of Birmingham on May 5, 1950, Professor Bodkin presented Mr. Lewis Douglas, the American Ambassador to Britain, for his honorary degree on the occasion of the University's fiftieth anniversary of the granting of its charter. Many requests poured in for his services as an after-dinner speaker and at school assemblies. The latter he particularly liked to take, for he valued the opportunity given him to remind the young of the fundamental basis of all true education for life — the relation in which man stands to his Creator, and the duties to God and to his fellow men arising therefrom.

In the spring of 1935, Dr. Bodkin left his native Ireland to become first Professor of Fine Arts and Director of the Barber Institute of the University of Birmingham. On his arrival not a brick of the building had been laid. Nor had there been bought a single work of art. A beautiful building built according to the plans of Mr. Robert Atkinson (after an investigatory tour of the most modern galleries of Europe, with the director) was completed in time to be opened by Her Majesty, Queen Mary in July, 1939, just before the outbreak of World War II put a stop to all construction. Today this building, which recently won for its architect an important medal, houses a magnificent collection of varied treasures in a series of carefully designed and well-lit galleries built round a central theatre in which the Barber professor of Music provides the University with first-rate concerts of chamber-music, a lecture theatre for the Professor of Fine Arts, art and music libraries, administrative offices, and ample storage.

Mr. Bodkin's first publication came out in 1917 under the title *May It Please Your Lordships*, reproductions of French poetry. The title suggests a nostalgic hark-back to the Law Courts he had lately left. For it and various researches on French pictorial art he was awarded the Legion d'Honneur, which is probably his most highly valued distinction. It is all the dearer to him since the family of the late Paul Jamot, formerly Director of the Louvre, perhaps the greatest of his many friends among art-historians, gave him Jamot's personal insignia of the order. Three years later (1920) he published *Four Irish Landscape Painters* and this was followed by *A Guide to Caper* (1924) in which he furnished the text to Denis Eden's illustrations of a fantastic burg of bears. In 1927 appeared the first edition of Dr. Bodkin's most important work to date *The Approach to Painting*, a steady seller, which, re-written and enlarged, was re-issued in 1945. *Hugh Lane and His Pictures* (1932), commissioned by Mr. Cosgrave's government to state Ireland's claim to these accidentally misbequeathed masterpieces, was brought out in a magnificent special edition for presentation to the heads of foreign governments. But before it was ready, Mr. de Valera had come into office, so it was with his commendatory message that each copy was sent out. Later it was made available to the ordinary book-buyer in a rather less gorgeous format. In 1940 appeared *Jan Vermeer* and *My Uncle Frank* in 1941; the latter was a piece of reminiscent escapism, dashed off by night in a month of distractingly noisy blitzes which made the normal nightly session of concentrated study an impossibility. His other books are: *Dismembered Masterpieces* (1945); *Virgin and Child, Flemish Painters* (1946); *The Wilton Diptych* (1947); *The Noble Science* (1948).

Dr. Bodkin contributes a series of notes on little known presentments of the Madonna to *Legio Mariae* (Legion of Mary).

M. A. H.

Hermann Borchardt   1888–1951

A foe of fascism and communism, in the latter part of his life, Hermann Borchardt found refuge in the United States in 1937.

Born in Berlin on June 14, 1888, the son of Jewish parents (Louis and Berta (Borchardt) Borchardt), Hermann, at the age of six, was sent to Wilhelm's Gymnasium in his native city and continued to attend there until 1903. From 1905 to 1907, he was a student apprentice in agriculture. Then followed a year of compulsory military training in Alsace-Lorraine. During the school year 1910–1911, he studied at the University of Berlin and from 1912 to 1913 at the University of Greifswald. With the outbreak of World War I, he was placed in the medical corps, where he served until 1916. Then he resumed his studies at the University of Greifswald and one year later received his Ph.D. degree *summa cum laude.*

In 1920 he began a thirteen-year teaching career in various Berlin universities. Borchardt in his youth had been a left-wing Socialist and after 1918 worked with the German communists. When Hitler came into power in 1933, Borchardt went to Beauchamps, near Paris, in France and not finding any work in France accepted a professorship at the University of Minsk in Russia. He arrived in February, 1934 and was installed as professor of "Methods of Teaching German." He was curious to see with his own eyes what was going on in "the workers' paradise." As time went on, he observed: "I found that Soviet conditions, the pall of fear, the constant police surveillance, the substitution of state propaganda for real learning, made the task of an honest professor an impossible one. True education and the totalitarian state simply can't be made to jibe."

Asked to write a new text book by the Culture Commissariat, and reminded that "at least fifty per cent of the reading matter, conversation pieces and the like, must carry a Marxist moral," Dr. Borchardt replied: "You have propaganda in all your other courses; in history, geography, biology, physics, and philosophy. You can have too much of a good thing." He refused to write the book.

"One day a woman in charge of the German Department in Minsk in a burst of candor, summed up for me the mentality of the Soviet teacher," writes Borchardt in his pamphlet, "I Was a Teacher in Soviet Russia." "You must understand, Dr. Borchardt," she explained, "that whatever Moscow says is *correct*. This applies even to a rule of grammar. If tomorrow the very reverse rule is prescribed, then that will become correct." "But isn't there such a thing as truth?" asked Borchardt. "No," she said. "That's a metaphysical abstraction."

For two years he remained in Soviet Russia as a foreign *spet* or specialist and was paid more than many of his colleagues, and he was "under none of the terrifying pressures which my colleagues suffered. In the final analysis I was a free man, entitled to my God-given human dignity; but they were slaves of the State."

When in 1936 he was asked to take out citizenship papers, he "hesitated." On January 22nd he was told to leave Russia within forty-eight hours. The confusion that followed in trying to pack and dispose of belongings he could not take with him is graphically told in his article "My Last Days in Soviet Russia," in *The Catholic World* (April, 1945, pp. 40–46). He returned to Berlin but was there only a few weeks when he was requested to leave Germany. He refused. Arrested by the Gestapo, he spent nearly a year in the concentration camps at Oranienburg, Sachsenhausen, and Dachau. While a prisoner of the Nazis, Dr. Borchardt lost his hearing, a finger and twelve teeth. He came to this country in 1937 with his wife Dorothy (Redmer) Borchardt and his two children. His third child, Franklin Lewis, was born in New York.

Franz Werfel, the novelist, encouraged him to write the novel, *The Conspiracy of Carpenters* (1943), and wrote the foreword. Werfel remarks: "One of the finest features of the present work is that it elevates the teacher's calling to be the supreme function of mankind. But by 'teacher's calling' Borchardt does not mean education in the ordinary sense, but the reception, keeping holy, and presenting undefiled of that which God has revealed and continued to reveal to the illustrious spirits of a nation, its priests, scholars, poets, and artists. If the teacher's calling among a people has been corrupted by lying, fear of truth, feebleness of spirit, and cowardly lip service then that people is close to destruction; then the bog is advancing."

The Conspiracy of the Carpenters is Dr. Borchardt's best work. Maxwell Geismar in his review (*New York Times Book Review*) remarks: "it is a novel of ideas — of provocative, elaborate and startling ideas. While we may disagree with its conclusions, we may still value — we must indeed cherish — the illumination at once comic, macabre and prophetic, that it throws on the more obvious blunders of modern progress." His friend Julius Epstein of the American Committee for the Investigation of the Katyn Massacre, says "this book is Borchardt's political testament." And Mr. Epstein adds: "I have never met in my life a man of Borchardt's love for truth and courage to express what he considered to be the truth. He expressed this truth in all circumstances, especially when this was dangerous and often very harmful to him. With not the slightest regard for personal consequences, he simply spoke the truth."

This desire for truth led him into the Catholic Church three years before his death. He died of a heart attack on January 23, 1951.

He is the author of *Philosophische Grundbegriffe* (1927), a book on philosophy; *The Bloody Deeds of Germersheim Before the Eternal Judge, Music of the Near Future, The Red Document* (1929); *The Conspiracy of Carpenters* (1943); *The Brethren of Halberstadt* (1938) and *The Wife of the Police-Commissionaire* (1946).   M. A. H.

Reverend Eugene Boylan, O.C.S.O.
1904–

"Anything I have written since I became a monk," writes Father Eugene Boylan "was written because I was asked to write it, and the request was framed in a mood that was categorically imperative. That is also the excuse for my writing now about myself, a necessary excuse since a contemplative monk is one whose business is to leave himself and cleave to God; so that any return to himself is a descent from the sublime to what may in kindness be called the ridiculous."

Born in Ireland at Bray, Co. Wicklow, in 1904, he was baptized Richard Kevin; Eugene being the name he received in religion. In 1912 his family moved to Derry. There, at the Brow-of-the-Hill Schools, the Irish Christian Brothers gave him his primary education. They were not allowed to teach Latin, so they gave a technical course instead. As a result he had studied science for two years before going to the O'Connell School in Dublin for his secondary education. "I had a great dislike, and even greater incompetence, for language as taught in our schools," he says, "but whatever tastes and talents I had were very definitely turned towards mathematics and science. Accordingly I got through school with a minimum of Latin and Gaelic, and a maximum of mathematics and science. English would have been more to my taste. Exhibitions and scholarships were important, if not essential, for my future education, since I was the eldest of five children born to a man with a limited income and it was then the time of the Great War; and accordingly I concentrated on my best subjects and after doing fairly well at school, I was fortunate enough to win a double university scholarship." In 1921, he entered University College, Dublin, and took an honors degree in experimental and mathematical physics in 1924. From 1921 until 1923 he was a student at the diocesan seminary with the intention of becoming a secular priest, but in 1923 he saw clearly that whatever his vocation might be, it was not for the secular priesthood in Ireland. He continued work in University College, Dublin, after leaving the seminary and in 1925 he got the M.Sc. degree for a thesis: *On the Large Ions of the Atmosphere*. Specializing in atmospherical electricity, he published another paper on *Large Ions and Condensation Nuclei*, and won the competition for a traveling studentship in physics.

During all this time his chief interests were music and swimming, and it was only lack of funds that prevented him from owning and sailing a boat. "I was intensely fond of good music and an enthusiastic, though very incompetent, pianist. During my school days, my chief reading outside scientific and engineering works consisted, I must confess, mostly of novels. At the university, a growing interest in the social question and the problems of democratic government, especially that of power without responsibility, led me to Chesterton and Belloc; and it was G. K. C. who first gave me a relish for style, though I was far more concerned with his policy of distributism." He was an active member of the university debating society, and won medals for oratory and for impromptu speaking. He became auditor of the society in 1925 and his inaugural address was his first effort at serious writing. The subject was democracy, and it was written in the hope of getting Mr. G. K. Chesterton to speak at the meeting, but the necessary arrangements could not be made. It represented the beginning of a line of thought that led him far from physics. All this period was one of the most active, and in some ways one of the most tragic, in Irish history, and it had no small influence on his future development. The Irish Free State was set up in 1921, and a civil war broke out immediately. Things had settled down by 1926 when he left Ireland for Vienna.

The next three years were spent in Austria, on a traveling studentship from the National University of Ireland, and later, with a Rockefeller Fellowship. In Vienna he was in close touch with research on radium, cosmic rays, and atomic disintegration, and he studied various techniques with a view to future research. "To read for the studentship, I had needed French, and life in Vienna made German necessary, so I had to teach myself these two languages. But even when I had acquired a certain facility in reading German, I never turned to literature for reading. In music I found all that I needed, and Vienna gave me a feast of music. In Vienna I tried my hand at journalism by acting as correspondent for an Irish Catholic weekly, for which I afterwards did some musical critiques. I soon became aware of the appalling misrepresentation which continental news and especially Catholic news suffered at the pens of English-speaking journalists. They made no secret that they had to write nothing but what their editors, proprietors, or advertisers wanted to publish, and most of them suffered from an absolute inability to see events and institutions other than in terms of their own provincialism. They were all prisoners of their time and of the temper of their readers. The fight made by Monsignor Seipel and Dollfuss to save Austria from Communism and Naziism got no sympathy or help from them."

In 1929 he came back to Dublin to act as assistant lecturer in physics at University College, Dublin, where he taught and did research for the next two years, publishing another paper on *Atmospheric Ionization and Condensation Nuclei*. "All this time," he says, "I was growing more and more conscious of the need of a firm foundation in scholastic philosophy and a training in the spiritual life. Neither was easy to find. I was also beginning to see the need for new methods and new organizations on the Catholic front. Had I known of the formation of the new secular institute in Madrid, I would have been its enthusiastic supporter. However the next two years brought a change in outlook. In various ways I discovered that persons were more important than things, and that the personal love of Our Lord matters far more than any service, however great. The question of a vocation, which was always in my mind, again came to the foreground. I thought for a moment of trying to become an active religious, but finally I decided to try to become a monk. My own idea was to try to be a Carthusian (and indeed my brother, then a secular priest, is now the only Irish Carthusian monk), but advice, which carried unmistakable marks of divine approval, indicated the Cistercian Order as God's will for me. In 1931, I entered Mt. St. Joseph at Roscrea, and I was ordained priest in 1937. Since then I have taught philosophy, dogma, and moral theology. I built a tower, taught in a school, and for the past few years I have been acting as confessor in our public church. In 1944 I published my first book, almost on my fortieth birthday.

"Any good that has been done through my pen is due to the sanctity of the community in which I live and to the Divine Office which we daily sing in public. As regards *Belles Lettres*, I am an absolute Philistine. I only read the English classics when, and as much as I had to, at school. The only writer whose style meant anything to me apart from its content was Chesterton, until I read Algernon Cecil's *Metternich*. I have never had any patience with the writer or the reader who is more concerned with how one says things than with what one says. And if one has something to say worth saying, why not say it directly, with clarity and conciseness, rather than drawing it out at length and wrapping it up in a wealth of verbiage that only obscures its meaning? I envy the man who can expand a statement into a paragraph or make a chapter out of an idea. My own whole tendency is very much in the opposite direction. In fact I might say that my ideal of literary expression and style is a differential equation!

"It was not until I commenced philosophy and theology that I began to enjoy serious reading. I can never forget the joy of reading Coffey's *Ontology* and *Epistemology*, where one was in contact with a mind thinking on paper and solving difficulties as they arose. I started theology with the *Summa* of Aquinas, which I read with avidity. Indeed the style of the theological textbook is the one I relish most, and the succinct clarity of scholastic Latin is a relief from the cultivated obscurity of English philosophical writing. Any urge I have is to condense and summarize. I like to start with a bird's-eye view of the subject and to end by seeing things as integrated wholes. So I am quite out of tune with humanistic letters. Beside Aristotle and Aquinas, Homer and Virgil fade into insignificance for me; and only clarity and completeness can make me appreciate any of the modern writers. Such an outlook does not help to produce an able writer.

"Nor does my life offer much opportunity for me to become one. As a Cistercian, writing is a spare time job, and a Cistercian has no spare time. The Divine Office takes six hours a day, and when the daily manual work has been added to that, there is still a day's work of prayer to be fitted in. Cistercian silence and use of signs take away one's facility in the use of words; reading Latin and French does not help the flow of English. I find my pen becoming more and more clumsy and labored, and the more I have to say, the fewer words there seem to be with which to say it. Besides, I can only write at night time, and the Cistercian day ends at seven in winter and eight in summer. Nor can I write to a schedule, and the whole monastic life is a schedule. I know nothing so repugnant as to have to reread what I have written, and nothing so impossible as to rewrite it; yet theological writing needs careful rereading and rewriting.

"The two topics in which I am most interested are Mariology and cosmology. Even were the latter subject my province, the physics with which it is connected is in such a state of flux that nothing much can be done until the physicists make up their own minds.

"Of two things I am quite convinced. The first is that the most urgent need of the moment is the extension and the intensification of the interior spiritual life among all Catholics, and the application of its influence to each and every phase of their activity. The second is that, after the spiritual life, nothing is so necessary as the restoration of metaphysics (in the Aristotelian sense) to its proper place and influence in the intellectual life of Europe and America. I feel no effort should be spared to provide suitable means of training Catholics, especially adult laymen, in the interior life, and of instructing them in philosophy, without unduly interfering with their normal career. There are, of course, many difficulties in the way of achieving this purpose, but we have to find a way of overcoming them.

"However all that is not my assignment — even by writing. Any writing I may yet do will only be done as a means and as a result of abiding in the Vine, for that is my real work and the only way of bringing forth fruit. In fact, all that I have said has almost nothing to do with my real life, for that is hid with Christ in God, and it cannot be told. It is summed up in silence — a silence that is the history of happiness unbroken and unbounded — a silence that is the fitting praise of Him Who has deigned to call me to a life of loving union with Himself for which there are no words save the one — the Word of God."

Father Eugene is the author of *Difficulties in Mental Prayer* (1943); *A Mystic under Arms* (1945); *This Tremendous Lover* (1947); *The Mystical Body* (1948); *The Spiritual Life of the Priest* (1950).

M. A. H.

Charles Andrew Brady   1912–

The literary critic, Charles A. Brady, was born in Buffalo, New York, on April 15, 1912, the son of Andrew J. Brady, born in County Cavan, Ireland, and Belinda Dowd Brady, whose parents were of Mayo-Connaught stock, via Yorkshire, England. He attended Canisius High School, Canisius College, and Harvard University. On August 16, 1937, he married Mary Eileen Larson. They have four daughters: Karen, Moira, Sheila, and Kristin More. Professor and Mrs. Brady live in Kenmore, a suburb of Buffalo.

In addition to his work as Chairman of the Department of English,

Canisius College, he is a weekly book columnist for the Buffalo *Evening News*, and on the review staff of the New York *Times, America, Renascence, Thought, Best Sellers,* and *The Catholic World.* He has contributed poetry to *The Saturday Review of Literature,* the *Harvard Advocate, America;* short stories to *The Catholic World;* numerous critical articles to *Thought, America, Renascence,* the *Catholic Library World.* His poem, *Is Acher In Gaith (Fierce is the Wind),* won the Archbishop Cushing Award for Poetry in 1949. One of his short stories won second place in the 1947 Catholic Press Association contest. He contributed the article on the *Volsungasaga* to volume three of Devin-Adair's *The Great Books,* and the John Marquand critique to a forthcoming Scribner evaluation of American fiction at mid-century. His critical specialities have been twentieth century French, English and Scandinavian fiction, most particularly the novelists of the Catholic Renaissance. His critiques include extensive estimates of Jules Romains, Upton Sinclair, Sigrid Undset, Graham Greene, Evelyn Waugh, Maurice Baring, Agnes Repplier, Scott Fitzgerald, Charles Williams, and Clive Staples Lewis.

Professor Brady's first book, *Cat Royal,* a Christmas fantasy for grown-ups as well as children, was written in Boston during 1938, but was not published until 1947. In that same year appeared the highly successful, *A Catholic Reader,* a personalized anthology for the Catholic common reader which he edited. Apropos *A Catholic Reader,* Father John S. Kennedy commented: "Mr. Brady, the editor, will one day, perhaps very soon, be a leading figure in Catholic letters. He is a young man steeped in literature, familiar with a surprising amount of it, a connoisseur of discriminating taste, a keen and scholarly critic, and a writer of parts."

It is not only Catholic literary figures who have complimented Professor Brady on his scholarly acumen and witty verve. Upton Sinclair, with whom he has broken more than one amicable lance in controversy, has paid tribute to his fairness and detachment. John Holmes, the New England poet, has remarked on his capacities as critic of contemporary poetry. The late William Rose Benét has congratulated him on certain of his poems. And, after the appearance of two articles on Oxford's C. S. Lewis in *America,* Dr. Lewis wrote: "You are the first of my critics so far who has really read and understood *all* my books and 'made up' the subject in a way that makes you an authority . . . let me congratulate you again on your very thorough and perceptive piece of work."

Declan McMullen is scheduled to publish Professor Brady's detailed critique of C. S. Lewis and Charles Williams, *Reclaim Imagination.* The Monastine Press will bring out *Valentine for Toby. Poems: 1937–1950.* He is currently (1951) working on a historical novel of the Henrician period, tentatively entitled *Stage of Fools,* and centered about the personality of St. Thomas More. It will be a kind of historical fugue of ideas and will probably appear sometime in 1952. Other work in progress includes, besides projected critical articles, three juveniles: one an adventure story for girls; another a version in verse of a traditional Polish tale; and a picture-book libretto about an elephant who visited a Renaissance Pope.

Leo Brady

Professor Brady is a familiar figure in the lecture forums of the East. He has appeared several times at the Hartford *Critics' Forum;* been Literary Awards Luncheon speaker for the Cleveland session of the Catholic Press Association; spoken at the Syracuse and Buffalo Catholic Book Fairs, and before the Children's Books section of the National Association of Teachers of English. In 1949 he gave the Candlemas Lectures at Boston College — a Jesuit Lecture Foundation which has featured such scholars as the critic, Allen Tate, and the medievalist, Father Denomy.

Leo Brady 1917–

Each year the Catholic Writers' Guild of America presents a Golden Book Award to the authors of the best books in fiction, non-fiction and in the religious classification. The 1949 Golden Book Award in fiction was given to Leo Brady on January 30, 1950 at the Waldorf-Astoria Hotel, New York City. In accepting the Award, Leo Brady said, "I hope I can write a novel as heavy as this plaque."

Born in Wheeling, West Virginia on January 23, 1917, the son of Joseph Thurman Brady and Nannie Beans Brady, he was educated at Central Catholic High, first grade through second year of high school. Here he wrote his first story in an English class under Brother Placidus, C.F.X. His final two years of high school were made at St. Paul's Academy, Washington, D. C., where his family moved in 1931.

Upon graduation he worked first as a clerk in a grocery store and then as a stenographer in a metal manufacturing company and later in a wholesale paper company.

In 1937 he matriculated at the Catholic University of America, Washington, D. C., and was graduated A.B. in 1941, having majored in English. He attended the university under the terms of a working scholarship as secretary to Father Gilbert V. Hartke, O.P., head of the then newly-established Speech and Drama Department. In 1942 he received his M.A. degree (Speech and Drama) under the terms of a Knights of Columbus fellowship. On October 16 of that year (1942), he joined the United States Army and served until January, 1946. He spent most of his time in Philadelphia in the recruiting service as a radio writer and producer.

From 1942 to 1945 he wrote a weekly show using guest stars who were appearing in local theaters. Helen Hayes was one of the guest stars. It was during this period that Mr. Brady, who was a master sergeant, met another sergeant named Eleanor Buchroeder. She is now Mrs. Brady. Five children were born of the marriage but one died in 1947.

After the war, Mr. Brady returned to Washington and became a member of the faculty of Catholic University. Since January, 1946, he is assistant professor in Speech and Drama and functions also as a director and an actor.

His first play was written in 1939 under the title *Brother Orchid*, adapted from the short story by Richard Connell. His verse play *Calidore* was produced at Catholic University in 1940. He collaborated with Walter Kerr in the writing of three musicals: *Count Me In*, produced at Catholic University in 1942 and later produced on Broadway in New York City, by the Schuberts, *Yankee Doodle Boy*, the story of George M. Cohan, and *Cook Book*, the life story of Joe Cook. Mr. Brady impersonated the celebrated comedian in the university production of *Cook Book* largely because he had absorbed so much of his style and had become acquainted with so many of his mannerisms while working on this project. On a later occasion he made joint appearances with Mr. Cook on the stage of the Earle Theatre, in Washington; the star would sit on a chair at the side of the stage while Mr. Brady performed his routines.

His other works besides numerous short stories and articles are: *One Punch Judy*, comedy for adolescents produced at Catholic University in 1941; *Likely Story*, a musical play with Sparty Donato, produced at Catholic University in 1945; *Grandstand Play*, a farce produced at Catholic University in 1949; *The Edge of Doom*, a novel, published by E. P. Dutton & Co. in 1949, and *A Trick of the Light* in 1947, an unproduced play.

Mr. Brady got the idea that started him working on *The Edge of Doom* shortly after his discharge from the army. Commenting on his book he says: "I had never written a novel before but I had a general idea of the possible techniques. Since I like novels with exciting plots and plenty of big scenes I tried to write that kind of novel. There is undoubtedly a hangover here from my training as a dramatist which may either be a good or bad thing. Historically, the novelist doesn't usually make out in the theater, although playwrights have often turned to the novel with successful results. Anyway, I tried to write the kind of novel which I like to read. I don't see how a writer can do anything else."

Leo Brady's novel was written with an eye to the Christopher Award. Its failure to win the award is ascribed by the *Tablet* as "presumably because by its nature it is likely to provoke the same type of controversy — only more so — as did Graham Greene's *Heart of the Matter.*" The manuscript was accepted by E. P. Dutton & Company and Samuel Goldwyn paid $125,000.00 for movie rights. On the night of the Catholic Writers' Guild of America Award, one of the speakers was Paul Stewart, the actor who plays the part of Craig in the movie *The Edge of Doom*. Paul Stewart remarked that while some of the scenes were being taken in Skid Row in Los Angeles a habitué came up to the actors to ask the name of the play. When told it was *The Edge of Doom*, he replied "Man, you came to the right place."

In addition to teaching, in 1947 Mr. Brady was assistant drama and movie critic on the Washington *Post*.

M. A. H.

Theodor Brauer 1880–1942

After the First World War, until the beginning of the Hitler regime, Dr. Brauer was unquestionably one of the top leaders of social Catholicism in Germany. He was generally regarded as the Catholic authority in Central Europe in the field of labor problems and unionism.

Theodor Brauer was born January 16, 1880 in Cleve on the Lower Rhine in the immediate neighborhood of the German-Dutch border. To his mother, a Dutchwoman, he owed his knowledge of the Dutch language; to the Fathers of the Sacred Heart in Belgium, he owed his education as a boy in high school and his knowledge of French. He left the high school shortly before reaching the senior class (*Prima*) in order to earn a livelihood in the grain business in his native town. He soon advanced to the position of assistant manager of the firm in which he was employed. Shortly afterwards he became active in the office workers' movement and in the local sick fund of Cleve. The German government, at that time, encouraged employees to send their representatives into the administrative boards of the semi-official health insurance agencies of their respective locality. The government even approved the sick funds established by the larger unions of salaried employees as subsidiaries or substitutes for the public sick insurance funds. Here was a field to do positive and constructive social reform work, and it was in this field and in this activity that Theodor Brauer found his way into the Catholic social movement, which was at that time very active and progressing in the Rhineland.

In 1907 he became assistant director of the Central Bureau of the world-famous Catholic *"Volksverein"* (People's Union) in M. Gladbach, not far from Cleve. In 1908 he was appointed staff member of the headquarters of the Christian Trade Unions in Cologne. In this capacity he had to attend especially to problems of international social policy and of the international cooperation of the Christian trade unions. He had, in the meantime, acquired knowledge of several other modern languages, and had frequently served as an interpreter and foreign representative of the Christian trade unions of Germany. Later the editorship of the *Deutsche Arbeit*, a monthly of the Christian trade unions, which was of rather scholarly standing, was added to his duties. Though he had by that time not yet acquired any college education, he began to publish books dealing in a scientific manner with social problems. These books soon won him high acclaim among sociologists and economists. He became personal assistant to such leading men in the union movement as Adam Stegerwald, later German Secretary of Labor and Prime Minister of Prussia, and of Heinrich Bruening, later chief of the Center Party and Chancellor of the German Reich and until recently professor at Harvard University.

Quickly familiarizing himself with the Catholic social tradition in Germany, Theodor Brauer soon found himself at odds with the dominant political and social movement of German Catholicism at the turn of the century. Tactfully he tried to convince his Catholic contemporaries in Germany that only a return to the sound social teachings of such thinkers of the past as Windthorst, Bishop von Ketteler, Carl von Vogelsang, and others would assure Catholic leadership in social reform and a real contribution of German Catholicism to the solution of the social question. Many years before the publication of the encyclical *Quadragesimo Anno*, he advocated the organization of national economy along vocational group lines or according to the industrial council plan.

He had already reached middle age when he took the college entrance examination, in order to make up for the classes (grades) he had missed when he had to leave the *gymnasium* (classical high school) prematurely, and to be admitted to the university. He passed the *Abiturium*, a very stiff examination in Latin, Greek, mathematics, etc., successfully, and enrolled as a student at the University of Bonn. Here he wrote his Ph.D. dissertation on the German legislation regarding work councils and shop committees under the direction of Professor Dietzel, then German authority on wage theory, receiving his degree in 1919, one year after the end of the First World War. Dr. Brauer then became a member of the executive staff of the Kolping Society (Catholic Journeymen's Guild) in Cologne, directing the educational activities of this world-wide organization, founded by the former shoemaker and later priest and social reformer, Adolf Kolping. As early as 1922 he handed over to the School of Philosophy of the University of Bonn his so-called "habilitation" thesis to be admitted as a Privatdozent (junior professor). But even before these "habilitation" (admission into the faculty) proceedings were brought to a conclusion, he was, in 1923, appointed full professor of economics at the Graduate School of Engineering in Karlsruhe, for the chair formerly held by such famous economists as Herkner, Buecher, etc.

In 1928 Professor Brauer was offered and accepted the chair of the renowned philosopher and sociologist, Max Scheler, in Cologne, and was at the same time appointed co-director of the Municipal Institute for Research in the Social Sciences at the University of Cologne. Here he dealt particularly with problems of industrial adult education, wage policy, and vocational organization. At the same time he directed the Christian Trade Union College in Königswinter, and acted as permanent advisor for the *Gesellenverein* (Kolping Society). After the dissolution of the Social Science Research Institute by the Nazis in 1933, he continued to teach at the University of Cologne as an honorary professor of social legislation and social work. The Nazis, however, jailed him and although he was soon released, it became obvious that he would never receive any position of influence under the new regime, and that he would some day be arrested anew and perhaps spend the rest of his life in a concentration camp.

Reverend Lambert Hoffmann, at that time professor at Nazareth Hall Preparatory Seminary of the Archdiocese of St. Paul, recommended Professor Brauer to His Excellency, the Most Reverend

Archbishop Murray, who offered Dr. Brauer a full professorship at the College of St. Thomas. Professor Brauer accepted the invitation, since he felt that because of the political conditions in Germany he would accomplish more as a teacher among his fellow-Catholics in the United States than he would living in his home country as a silenced man. His scholarly work and his experience as a long-time leader in the field of social reform were much appreciated in this country. His students liked the personal approach in his teaching and his kindness in and outside of the classroom. He died of a heart attack on the evening of March 19th, 1942, the Feast of St. Joseph, the patron of the dying. In the morning of that day he had attended Mass and received Holy Communion.

He is the author of *Gewerkschaft und Volkswirtschaft* (1912); (1922); *Bodenfrage und Arbeiterinteresse* (1916); *Das Recht auf Arbeit* (1919); *Das Betriebsrätegesetz und die Gewerkschaften* (1920); *Christentum und Sozialismus* (1920); *Die Gewerkschaft als Organ der Volkswirtschaft* (1921); *Lohnpolitik in der Nachkriegszeit* (1922); *Die moderne Gewerkschaftsbewegung* (1922); *Allgemeine Wirtschaftskunde* (1923); *Adolf Kolping* (1923); *Krisis der Gewerkschaften* (1924); *Produktionsfaktor Arbeit* (1925); *Christentum und öffentliches Leben* (1927); *Der moderne deutsche Sozialismus* (1929); *The Catholic Social Movement in Germany* (1932); *National Economy* (1939); and *Economy and Society* (1940). With others he published *Thomistic Principles in a Catholic School* (1943); (1947).   F. H. M.

Joseph Anthony Breig   1905–

Joseph A. Breig is a newspaperman. For twenty-odd years, he has worked in that field — covering the news, supporting his family, and learning to write. Of late, in his spare time, he has been turning out work for a great many of the American Catholic magazines; and he is beginning to be heard from in the literary world. He has written four books. Two he burned because he considered them junk. The third and fourth have been published. Other books are now coming from his typewriter.

Descended from Scotch, German, Irish and Swiss ancestors, some of whom arrived in this country before the Revolution and others much later, Joseph A. Breig was born in the "steel town" of Vandergrift, Pennsylvania, not far from Pittsburgh, February 28, 1905. He was the son of George and Clara (McKenzie) Breig. His father, an electrician, also operated a sort of general store. In addition, he set tile, installed mantels, carpentered, and was Fire Chief. "He could do almost anything," says his son, "except spell." Strangely enough, he read omnivorously. His wife never misspelled anything and never misused a word. From the two of them, their son drew a great desire to be a writer. His sister, now Sister Regina Clare of the Sisters of Charity, urged him on to do so, and got his first stories published in a high school magazine.

Joseph Anthony Breig

In Vandergrift there were no Catholic schools; and for six years the boy was sent to public school. Then he spent two years in the Benedictine scholasticate at St. Vincent Archabbey, Latrobe, Pennsylvania, where, as he says, "the Faith seeped into a lad through his very pores." Back in Vandergrift, he went to high school and then to the University of Notre Dame. He took a broad arts and letters course with journalism added. In his junior year, he became editor of the student publication, the *Scholastic*.

During vacations, he says, "I worked for a while in a steel mill, helped my father as an electrician's apprentice, clerked in his store, racked up balls in a pool room, and got a year's newspaper experience." After Notre Dame, he worked for ten years (1924–34) on his home town newspaper, the Vandergrift *News*, which was successively a weekly, semi-weekly and daily. He did every kind of reportorial and editorial work, and even had a year as acting publisher.

In July, 1930, Mr. Breig married Mary Agnes Hoffman, a home town girl, who was clerking in his father's store. Soon after, he went to the Pittsburgh *Sun-Telegraph*, a Hearst newspaper, where for another ten years he was rewrite man, reporter, columnist and political writer.

During this period, he became an apostolic Catholic. People on the *Sun-Telegraph* asked so many questions about the Catholic Faith that he decided to learn more himself in order to inform them correctly. With Father Howard J. Carroll, now executive secretary of NCWC in Washington, then an assistant in Sacred Heart Parish, he started a study club. One result was that he met Father Patrick Peyton when Father Peyton's Family Rosary Crusade was starting. He counselled Father Peyton to invite the movie stars of Hollywood to lend their talents and influence to the work of promoting family prayer.

Gradually, says Mr. Breig, "I developed a strong desire to devote myself to Catholic writing. The opening came when I was offered a job as assistant managing editor of the *Catholic Universe Bulletin*, Cleveland. I have been there since 1945."

Besides his full-time job with the *Universe Bulletin*, he writes a syndicated column published in eight Catholic newspapers in Ohio, California, Tennessee and Nova Scotia. He also writes a monthly column for *Information* magazine, published by the Paulists. For two years he wrote "The Word" column in *America*, the Jesuit national weekly, and believes he was the first layman to be invited to do so. Out of these articles grew his book, *God In Our House*, published by America Press in 1949.

Mr. Breig writes a monthly piece for *The Missionary Servant*, published by the Missionary Servants of the Most Holy Trinity. He turns out the Gospel column weekly for the *Young Catholic Messenger*. He is an associate editor of *The Family Digest*, published by Our Sunday Visitor Press. His work appears in *Sacred Heart Messenger*, *Marianist*, *Victorian*, *Extension*, *Columbia*, *Today*, *Catholic Boy*, *Cor*, *Catholic Digest*, *Crosier Missionary*, *Books on Trial* and other publications.

In 1950 the story of the Breig family ("Autobiography of a Christian Family") appeared serially in *The Missionary Servant*. In 1951, he published his latest book *The Devil You Say*.

Variety is the chief characteristic of Mr. Breig's writing. He comments on the news. He writes philosophical things. He writes for adults and for children. He turns out articles, short stories, and even an occasional prose poem. His newspaper work has taught him to turn his hand to whatever kind of writing an editor may need. Sometimes it is humorous, sometimes polemical, sometimes inspirational, informative or critical.

Mr. Breig's favorite author is Gilbert Keith Chesterton. "The greatest thing G.K.C. did for me," he says, "was to show me how to love everything God made, because God made it. Chesterton made me appreciate the marvel of existence."   M. A. H.

Elizabeth Brennan 1922–

At the age of twenty-four, Elizabeth Brennan published her first novel, *Out of the Darkness* (1945) and it exceeded all expectations by selling over seven thousand copies in Ireland and England.

Born in Clonmel, County Tipperary, Ireland, in the year 1922, she was educated at the Dominican Convent, Sion Hill, in Blackrock, County Dublin. Very early in her school career she showed promise of outstanding talent in the field of English and writing generally.

Speaking for herself Miss Brennan says —:

"When I was a mere beginner in the field of writing a wise old professor once said to me — 'If you wish to write good novels then make it your business to read three types of books: poetry in order to get a feeling for words; travel in order to broaden one's horizon, and works on philosophy in order to derive a knowledge of life and a love of faultless English.'

"I took his advice and found it to be sound. One cannot read poetry for long without developing a flair for putting the right word in the right place, and works on philosophy are certainly pure wells of English undefiled.

"It was the same professor who warned me — 'If you give yourself pleasure in the writing of your books then you are bound to transmit that pleasure to the reader. That is why it is so important never to write anything forced or wooden; never to express opinions that are false or hypocritical. Be true to yourself and you will succeed.'

"A wise old man indeed!

"I always feel that in writing books for children one holds a great trust. The childish mind is so malleable for good or evil that everything one sets before it must portray idealism. This can best be done through the medium of fantasy, for in fairy-tales knights and princesses are always high-minded and pure and good always triumphs over evil. In these later days one can only deplore that such a medium is now being discarded for the type of writing in which vice and violence predominate. In fantasy one may give children a glass mountain to climb, but at least it inspires them with the *desire* to climb it."

For many years she was employed as secretary to a Dublin company. She is now engaged in editing the *Fry-Cadbury C-Cubs Magazine*, and also runs a very successful children's club in a northern newspaper. Miss Brennan prefers to write for children but is also interested in people and is a student of psychology.

When her first novel, *Out of the Darkness*, appeared, the Edinburgh *Evening Dispatch* said of it: "She handles her characters and atmosphere in a masterly way." Two years later she brought out *Am I My Brother's Keeper?* Critic Philip Rooney in his review remarked: "Sheer downright competence and craftmanship are Miss Brennan's outstanding storytelling gifts . . . a fine novel!" This book was later translated into Danish by M/S Skandinavisk Bogforlag, of Odense. *Whispering Walls* came out in 1949 and prior to that Miss Brennan had written three children's books, entitled *The Wind Fairies*, *The Wind Fairies Again*, and *The Mystery of Hermit's Crest*, the last of which was translated into Danish. Two other stories have appeared in serial form in Irish newspapers entitled *The Mystery of the Goblin Pipes* and *The Island of Geese*.

In December, 1950, Miss Brennan published her first poetic effort — *Wind Over The Bogs*. The reviewer in the *Irish Independent* remarks the poems are "tuneful and well-wrought lyrics." One critic said of it that it is "a book of surprising quality. There is a nostalgic quality in her poetry that is very marked in poems such as 'The Dream.'

> Oh lovely dream upon a dreaming hill,
> Spiring aloft on rose flushed fires,
> Vague and silver swirled as thoughts that fill
> The human soul with conflict of desires.
> Oh, mystic torch of April afterglow,
> Burn slow . . . burn slow. . . .
> How can I bear to see you go?
> Burn till the dream itself is sinking low;
> Burn till its vestal fires are dimmed and gone,
> For even dreams should not be dreamed too long."

M. A. H.

Reverend Gerald Thomas Brennan
1898–

A friend dared Father Gerald T. Brennan, the popular author of children's books, to write a book, and he accepted the challenge. The readers of his first book, *Angel Food*, clamored for more books and the priest-author has tried to satisfy the demand.

Hanging above Father Brennan's desk are these two lines:

> . "He who gives a child a treat
> Makes Joy-bells ring in Heaven's street."

These lines have inspired the priest to write many books for children. Father Brennan loves children and children give him ideas for his stories. Father Brennan has a season box at the Rochester Red Wing Stadium and misses very few baseball games during the summer. Usually he takes some children with him to study their language, mode of expression, their likes and dislikes, etc.

Born in Rochester, New York on April 21, 1898, the son of Joseph Patrick and Mary (Fahy) Brennan, Gerald Thomas attended Cathedral Grammar School and Aquinas Institute (one year), and Saint Andrew's and Saint Bernard's Seminaries of that city. He was ordained a priest June 9, 1923. He has a licentiate in philosophy. From 1923 to 1932 he served as a curate in Our Lady of Mount Carmel Church, Rochester, New York and pastor from 1932 to 1937. In June 1937 he was appointed pastor of St. Bridget's Church where he is now stationed.

His sermons at the children's Mass usually consist in telling the children a story, and then drawing a moral or lesson from the story. "My children," he says, "have liked the stories and, in my books, I have passed on the stories to other children outside my parish." His books are now read by thousands of children. Each new book brings him new friends.

Father Brennan's first book *Angel Food* contains thirty-one stories. It was written principally for priests to help them in their instruction of the little ones.

When asked "Which one of your books do the children like best?" Father Brennan replied: "They seem to like them all. The younger children have a slight preference for *Angel City* and it is one of my favorites."

Father Brennan does not use any Thorndike list or any other vocabulary list to guide him in his writing. He relies on his twenty-seven years of close association with children to help him speak their language. He talks about things which the children know and understand.

In answer to the question "Do you enjoy writing for children?" Father Brennan replied: "I'm having more fun than the winner of the

Irish sweepstakes. The work is hard, but it fails to be work when you love doing it. If you want to have some fun for yourself, write a children's book! Then sit back and see what happens!"

Father Brennan is the author of *Angel City* (1938); *Angel Food* (1939); *The Ghost of Kingdom Come* (1940); *The Man Who Dared a King* (1941); *The Good Bad Boy* (1942); *For Heaven's Sake* (1942); *Toby's Shadow* (1944); *Going His Way* (1945); *The Man Who Never Died* (1946); *God Died at Three O'Clock* (1947); *Just for Juniors* (1948) and his latest *Angel Food for Jack and Jill* (1951).

He has also written stories and articles for *Young Catholic Messenger, The Cathedral Basic Reader, The Oratory Magazine*, and *Journal of Religious Instruction*.

Ann Bridge (Lady Mary O'Malley)

Ann Bridge is the pseudonym of a very gifted and successful novelist, who lives in Ireland. Since her first novel, *Peking Picnic*, which won the Atlantic Monthly Prize in 1932, she has published a decade of remarkable novels, four of which have been Book Society choices; and it is now generally known that her husband, Sir Owen O'Malley, was an official of the British Diplomatic Service (recently retired), who represented his country in China, Mexico, Hungary, and Portugal. She is known as an Alpine climber, an archaeologist of some distinction, an accomplished linguist (to whom even some Chinese is intelligible), an indefatigable war-relief worker, and one who took the American press into her confidence when on a visit to this country in 1941.

What is in particular remarkable about Ann Bridge's novels, many of which have to do with far-off countries, China, Italy, Albania, Yugoslavia, Spain, and the Scottish Hebrides, is the intimate and living knowledge which she displays of locale, and the social milieu about which she writes. Of course she insists upon residing in and studying a country before she writes about it. Then, when in a place she has the gift of absorbing swiftly and accurately all that observant eyes, quick ears, and intuitive understanding can absorb. After that, with her gift of character-portrayal, her story-telling where unexpected twists and exciting incidents figure, and while hidden meanings and sage reflections are scattered about, Ann Bridge entertains — and educates. Hers is an enquiring, cultured mind, mellowed by much travel, and hers the rare gift of kidnapping her reader to where she will. As Father Martindale, S.J., wrote of her in a review, "You simply find yourself in Dalmatia or wherever she chooses to put you."

Ann Bridge, of course, is offered opportunities that seldom befall other writers. Telling, for example, of the remote origin of her novel *Singing Waters* (1946) she says: "When I was in Albania in 1936 I was rather touched by the fact that both the then prime minister and foreign minister begged me to write a book about their country. It was poor, they said, and small; 'tourismo' would help their finances a lot; they had observed with envy that my book *Illyrian Spring* (1935) had, in the case of their next-door neighbor, Yugoslavia, doubled the number of American tourists, and multiplied the British four-fold, all in the space of twelve months. Could I not do the same for them? The Hotel Continental should be my home for as long as I wished to stay as the guest of the Government; guides and ponies and interpreters would be put at my disposal for any further expeditions I might wish to make, also at Government expense."

Ann Bridge was born at Porters Park, Shenley, Herts. She was called Mary Anne though the Anne is not a baptismal name. When seeking a pseudonym she took the Ann from Mary Anne and the Bridge from Bridge End to make Ann Bridge. She was seventh of nine children, her mother being from New Orleans, Louisiana, and an Episcopalian; her father, English, and extremely Low-Church. Her paternal grandmother was, in a sense, lowest of the low, a Plymouth Sister, and her religious spirit prevailed in Ann's home. There were no playing of cards; no going to theatres; no hot food on Sunday; and instead of games, one of Dr. Spurgeon's dour sermons was read aloud to the whole family after Sunday service. Each child had a "Sunday book" to read; one, chosen by Ann herself, when still very young, was Borrow's *The Bible in Spain*, which is hardly religious reading!

Education was through German governesses, and was in its way thorough. Ann began French at five, German at eight, Latin at twelve, Greek at thirteen, and Italian later. She would not or could not study mathematics. When the family moved to London, Ann took her diploma in Social Science at the London School of Economics in 1913. Of this diploma she made little use, as in the same year she married a young diplomat. Then began a life of varied and interesting foreign travel. In turn she lived in China, Hungary, Switzerland, Italy, France, Germany and Portugal and visited Yugoslavia and Spain. She also spent much time in Scotland.

Of young adventure, Ann Bridge had her fill. At the age of nineteen she became a member of the Ladies Alpine Club and was known as a climber of some skill in the Alps and the mountains of Central Europe. Among other adventures she spent seven weeks climbing at Courmayeur on the South side of Mont Blanc, then went on to Zermatt, where with her brother she made the fourth ascent of the northeast face of the Weisshorn by a new route, a climb which was recorded in the *Alpine Journal*.

The knowledge of archaeology that Ann Bridge displays in her novel *And Then You Came* (1949) is far from an affectation. She made excavations and quite important discoveries of vitrified forts in Scotland, and was invited to become a Fellow of the Society of Antiquaries of Scotland. In further preparation for this novel she records, "I spent six months of research in Edinburgh, London, Dublin, and Oxford. I corresponded with experts, made special journeys to Loch Etive and Barr-Nan-Gobhan to see again the sites and places I wanted to describe accurately, unvisited since childhood days when I had sailed to them with singing boatmen." She has a fascinating story to tell about the writing of each of her novels — in her case at least, publicity agents have had an easy task.

Most of her writing is done in the mornings from 7 A.M. until 9 A.M., before breakfast. Besides being an archaeologist, traveller, and mountain climber, Ann Bridge loves to ride, to ski, to swim, to sail a boat with "no paid hand aboard." She delights in gardening and in amateur botany. After her marriage she lived for nearly twenty years at Bridge End, Ockham, Surrey. She now lives in Ireland. "My main preoccupation," she writes, "is the garden. Our nearest greengrocer's shop . . . is 175 miles away, so in the matter of green vegetables what you do not grow you do not eat." She adds, "It is a perfect place to write in. A soothing climate, great tranquility, extreme beauty out of every window and just the right number of delightful neighbors, after a life overcrowded with people. The only drawback is that there are almost too many things to do . . . but it is nice to have too much to do." She has one grown son who served with the RAF during the war. While her son fought, Ann Bridge helped in Polish relief work; organized a factory in Chelsea (London) for reconditioning clothing for abroad; and (in 1945) handled relief work for civilian deportees in France.

Ann Bridge's approach to Catholicism was slow and highly fortuitous. As a little girl she had a Catholic cousin who, during visits to her home, was faithful in attending Mass; and for years she knew well the Reverend Dr. F. E. Hutchinson, the biographer of George Herbert, who, as a High Church Anglican, taught her to love St. Francis of Assisi and to read the "Fioretti" and Dante's poetry. Then there were visits to monasteries during her travels: a Trappist monastery in China in 1925, and a Franciscan monastery in Albania in 1936. While in Hungary in 1940 and 1941 she attended Mass as there was no Anglican church available. Finally there were friendships with the late Maurice Baring and with the late Archbishop MacDonald of Edinburgh and his relatives.

It was Father Charles Martindale, S.J., who received her into the Church in Farm Street, London, in 1948. She had travelled a long way from Spurgeon to Martindale.

Among Ann Bridge's published works are the following: *Peking Picnic* (1932); *The Ginger Griffin* (1934); *Illyrian Spring* (1935); *The Song in the House* (short stories, 1936); *Enchanter's Nightshade* (1937); *Four-Part Setting* (1939); *Frontier Passage* (1942); *Singing Waters* (1945); *And Then You Came* (1949); *The Selective Traveller in Portugal* (in conjunction with Susan Lowndes, 1949); *The House at Kilmartin* (a book for children, 1950); and *The Falcon in Flight* (1951). *The Dark Moment* is The Literary Guild of America selection for January 1952.

E. B. B.

Goetz Antony Briefs   1889–

Goetz Antony Briefs, fourth child of Francis and Anne (Vieten) Briefs, in a family of nine, was born near Aachen (Aix-la-Chapelle) in the Western Rhinelands which he calls "a blessed landscape, such as you do not find in the northern German plains, a baptized landscape." His family was Catholic. "The spirit of my family," writes Professor Briefs, "was profoundly religious without any narrowness. There was so much cultural 'touch' to the piety of our home that religion never became boring to us — thanks to the great and noble spirit of my parents, in particular of my mother."

Goetz Briefs' high school, a typical German gymnasium of those days, and of course not co-ed, lasted from 1899 to 1908 and embraced among other subjects Greek and Latin classics. "I shall remain thankful for the classical education I got," says Professor Briefs, "and I regret that this excellent intellectual training is not open to every gifted boy and girl. It gives its adept a background for which nothing else can make up." In his high school, religious training was obligatory on all, Catholics, Protestants and Jews alike. The standard of education was very high as is witnessed by the fact that of the 48 who entered with Briefs in 1899 only 6 graduated in 1908.

Gymnasium finished, Goetz Briefs entered Munich University aiming at a university career. He chose history and philosophy as his courses but soon transferred to economics which captured his interest. In 1909 he spent a term at Bonn, and then settled down in Freiburg University (Breisgau) which was at that time at the peak of its reputation in a variety of fields. "I picked my courses as I pleased," he says, "and dropped whatever was not promising or uninspiringly presented: I read profusely in addition to carefully attending seminars and seminar discussions."

In 1911 he won his doctorate *Rerum Politicarum*, with the highest honor, presenting a thesis on cartels. Shortly after, he went to England to write his habilitation thesis for a lectureship offered to him in the Freiburg Faculty of Law and Economics.

When war broke out in 1914, Goetz Briefs was not drafted owing to defective eyesight but entered, instead, the Prussian Ministry of Interior as an economic expert.

Having married Anna Stephanie Weltmann in 1919, Goetz Briefs returned to Freiburg where he taught as assistant professor. There his four children were born.

After a short interlude at Würzburg University, Goetz Briefs, in 1923, became full professor at Freiburg, occupying the chair originally established for and occupied by the famous sociologist Max Weber. In 1926 he transferred to the chair of economics at the Berlin (Charlottenburg) Institute of Technology. Soon after he was chosen Vice-president of the International Association for Research in Law and Economics. Of this period in Berlin, Professor Briefs writes: "Those were very fruitful and blessed years for an enterprising young professor. I lectured and published inside and outside my academic obligations, worked very hard, and enjoyed my life as never before or after. I was happy and blessed in my family life as few mortals may be. There did not seem to be any reason why things should not go on that way. . . . Then (having studied Donoso Cortez, Spanish philosopher and statesman), I began to grasp that there were, outside of all economic and political considerations, metaphysical reasons why, in all probability, things would not remain in their balance."

Several times he declined posts in the German cabinet and other high ranking positions in the government. He served as associate judge in the Reich's Cartel Court. Professor Briefs' happiness was upset by the depression which "kicked the props from under all illusions," then with the advent of Nazism, Briefs came to the United States because he did not want to live under a dictator. From 1934 to 1937 Professor Briefs taught economics at the Catholic University, Washington, D. C., and subsequently joined the faculty at Georgetown University. He has given summer courses at Columbia University since 1938.

Among his published works are the following: *The Proletariat: A Challenge to Western Civilization* (1937); *Sociology of Industrial Relations* (German, 1937); *Classical Economics; Theory of Trade-Unionism* (German, 1928). He is currently preparing articles on the theory and sociology of unionism for the *Encyclopaedia of Labor*.

Professor Briefs has always taken a lively interest in Catholic social thought, and has published quite a few articles along this line. One task he has set for himself is to determine how far post-New Deal Unionism fits into the pattern of American society.

E. B. B.

Reverend Everett Francis Briggs, M.M. 1908–

One of the eyewitnesses of the "Doolittle Bombing Raid" during World War II is Father Everett Briggs, a Maryknoll missioner. At the time he was interned in a Japanese prison camp.

Born in Fitchburg, Massachusetts on January 27, 1908, the son of Everett Thomas and Mary Lillian (Hughes) Briggs, he was educated at Maryknoll Preparatory School, Clarks Summit, Pennsylvania; Maryknoll College and Maryknoll Seminary, Ossining, New York, Pius X School of Liturgical Music (1931); Catholic University of America (S.T.B., 1932); School of Japanese Language and Culture (diploma 1935); Columbia University (1943); Rutgers University (1947), and

Fordham University (M.A., 1951). In 1950, Father Briggs was awarded the degree of Doctor of Humane Letters by Holy Cross College in recognition of his writings in English and Japanese.

Ordained to the priesthood in 1933 at Maryknoll Seminary in New York, he was sent to Japan in August of the same year. There he mastered the language, built a church in the Shiga Prefecture where he became pastor at Otsu from 1935 to 1942. From 1940 to 1942 he was Society superior of the Maryknoll Kyoto Mission. While in Japan he authored several doctrinal and apologetic works in the Japanese language. At the outbreak of the Second World War, he was interned in a prison camp. It was from there he saw one of General Doolittle's planes fly over Japan.

New Dawn in Japan, published by Father Briggs in 1948, gives an account of Christianity in Japan, the pre-war trials of the Christian Church and the wartime concentration camps.

When asked how he happened to go to Japan, Father Briggs replied: "How did I happen to go to Japan? That is a question which often occurs to my friends, one that occasionally occurred to me when, far from home, I found myself part of that strange Oriental civilization. The only answer I am able to suggest is the Providence of God.

"One of my earliest memories is the pageant of little people, men and women, dressed in their gay kimono, their gleaming raven hair arranged in strange coiffures, who decorated the cups and saucers of my mother's tea service. I never dreamed as I grew to young manhood, that the destinies of that distant race would be intertwined with my own some day. But truth is stranger far than fancy.

"As grammar school days drew to a close, my mother used to speak to me about the nobility of the priestly calling. But in my childish way, I esteemed no other vocation than devoting my life to the happiness of my mother. Never, I am convinced, would I have become a priest if my mother had lived to see me graduate from school. Nothing that could separate us two had the least attraction for me. Then, quite suddenly, God beckoned my dear mother to the 'pure land,' and the vocation which once I spurned, I came to prize.

"While I was struggling against God's call, relatives of mine had gone to Japan as missionaries representing various Protestant denominations. One of them, Francis Clayton Briggs, distant as a relative, but close in the bonds of the spirit, had labored for fifteen years in central Japan. When he died through overwork and exhaustion, the Japanese people acclaimed him for what he was: 'The Saint of Harima.' His funeral, in its impressiveness and solemnity, was an unprecedented event in the history of Himeji.

"Japan, however, had no particular interest for me. It was only one of many mission fields, where God's harvest was great, though the laborers were few. My eyes focused on China, then the foremost mission territory entrusted to the Catholic Foreign Mission Society of America. During my years in the major seminary at Maryknoll, my language was Chinese for, as far as one could judge, my future lay in far Cathay. Shortly before my ordination to the priesthood, however, Maryknoll was charged with a new territory: the mission field of Kyoto, in central

Japan. In the summer of 1933, I was one of three American Catholic pioneers assigned, simply in due course, to that templed land.

"A few hours distant from Kyoto by train, lay the district where another Briggs had endeared himself to the Japanese people by his radiant charity and his unexampled zeal. Only an hour's journey flowed the Inland Sea, where that other Briggs, with the prow of 'Ye Good Ship Gospel,' had furrowed the blue waters of Nippon's landlocked tides. There, in the vale of Kyoto, was I destined to labor, almost a decade until the whirlwind of war swept over the world, gathering me into prisons, and from prisons plucking me back to my own dear native land. Here, an exile at heart, I can never forget the people of my predilection, those humble millions essentially upright, for the most part soul-hungry, and for the nobler life eager with all the inherited yearning of their race. No quirk of fate could have woven those unrelated strands into the tapestry of my life. There is a God, Whose Providence disposed all things mightily and sweetly."

In September, 1942, Father Briggs was repatriated on the *Gripsholm*. Upon his return to the United States, he taught Naval V-12 cadets the Japanese language at Holy Cross College from 1942 to 1944. From 1944 to 1947 he was on the faculty of Maryknoll Preparatory College in Pennsylvania. In 1946, Father Briggs represented the National Catholic Welfare Conference War Relief Services on the executive committee of L.A.R.A. (Licensed Agency for Relief in Asia). For three years (1947–1950) he was vice-rector and dean of Maryknoll Junior College at Lakewood, N. J.

Father Briggs is the author of *Christ In Japan* (English, 1937); *Beginner's Grammar of Conversational and Written Japanese* (1944); *Catholic Manifesto of Human Rights* (Japanese, 1946); *Communism and Catholicism*, Vols. I and II (Japanese, 1947); *The Life of Christ* (Japanese, 1948); *New Dawn in Japan* (English, 1948); *This Is Social Justice* (Japanese, 1949); *My Catholic Faith* (Japanese, 1950); *The Pagan's Weak Point* (Japanese, 1951); *The Christian Program of Social Order* (Japanese, 1951). Father Briggs is also the author of poems in Japanese, several musical compositions, and various articles in magazines.

Reverend Matthew Britt, O.S.B.
1872–

For more than fifty years, Father Matthew Britt has taught Latin, English, literature, history and government. He has been interested in liturgical and medieval studies, especially in Latin hymnody.

Born on April 12, 1872, in Algona, Iowa, the son of James Britt and Katherine (Kearney) Britt, both of Thurles, Ireland, he was baptized William Britt. He received his primary education in local public schools and his secondary

and college education at St. John's University, Collegeville, Minnesota.
He was invested as a Benedictine novice on August 14, 1895, by Abbot
Peter Engel of St. John's Abbey and was professed on August 15, 1896.
On June 12, 1900, he was ordained deacon by Bishop James Trobec and
a few months later (August 12) he came to St. Martin's Abbey, Olympia,
Washington, and has been associated with that Abbey continuously
since that time. Ordained to the priesthood on June 14, 1901, he taught
in the school and engaged in missionary activities in surrounding com-
munities on week ends and for periods up to six months at various times.
He attended the Olympia parish for some time, traveling from the
Abbey to the church on his bicycle. He went to the Shelton church by
boat, and also served the churches at Pe Ell and Ballard.

Despite his many duties as instructor and guide to those following
the line of scholarly research in his Abbey, he has been Censor Librorum
in the Seattle Diocese for many years. Priest-authors often submit their
manuscripts to him before they send them to the Chancery Office. He
not only watches for doctrinal errors but also corrects grammatical mistakes and improves the style.

His own published works are: *Hymns of the Breviary and the Missal*
(1922, revised edition in 1949); *Dictionary of the Psalter* (1928); *How to
Serve in Simple, Solemn, and Pontifical Functions* (1933); *Gemma
Caelestis* (1926), and *Altar Linens* (1949).

Notwithstanding his poor eyes (he needs a magnifying glass to read)
he is an avid devotee of things scholarly in a wide variety of fields,
secular and religious.

He is a member of the Mediaevalists and The Catholic Biblical
Association.   M. A. H.

Robert Carlton Broderick   1913–

That Robert Broderick is a hard working person
is evident from his daily schedule. After early
Mass and breakfast he and his wife, Virginia,
who is an artist and who illustrates all of his
books, work for five hours straight; then after a
light lunch, they give five hours to reading,
sketching, note-taking, which with pleasant
weather they try to do out-of-doors. And often,
to meet a deadline, they work through the entire
day and night.

Mr. Broderick and his wife form a team in the arts, and manage to
work closely together in a small apartment with the least possible clash
of the so-called temperament one hears associated with artists and
writers. She, a college honor student in literature as well as art, serves
as his sounding board for the reading aloud of his writings; and he, in
turn, acts in a like capacity with her art work, with the added chore
that he must at times serve as a "living model." "Hence, between our-

selves," he says, "I am known as 'a man of parts' since portions of me have appeared in so many illustrations of one kind or another."

Born on June 4, 1913, at Fond du Lac, Wisconsin, Mr. Broderick attended grade school in his native city, and entered St. Francis Seminary, Milwaukee, Wisconsin, where he received the A.B. degree, and in 1936 the A.M. degree. He majored in philosophy and English.

From 1936 to 1945 he was employed as fiction editor by the Bruce Publishing Company. He married Virginia Joanne Gaertner in 1941. Since that year both he and his wife have been collaborating on Catholic literature and art.

Books from his pen are: *Concise Catholic Dictionary, Paul of St. Peter's,* and *Wreath of Song.* He has contributed articles to the following magazines: *Catholic School Journal, St. Anthony's Messenger, The Marianist, Sign, Catholic World, Ave Maria, The Salesianum, Books on Trial,* etc. He and his wife have often appeared together on the lecture platform.

Both of them are planning rather far-reaching projects in their respective fields. Mr. Broderick is writing a novel, the first of two planned works of fiction. He also is gathering data for two non-fiction books. His wife is working on a series of religious pictures.

G. F.

Colm Brogan   1902–

Colm Brogan, Scottish schoolmaster, journalist and publicist, was born in Glasgow in 1902. His father was a tailor, one of the pioneer Irish who fought for social justice for Catholics in Western Scotland. His mother was English, the sister of Bishop Toner of Galloway, who lived to over ninety and was the oldest bishop in Britain.

Educated by the Jesuits and at Glasgow University, where he obtained the M.A., Colm Brogan took up teaching, and to this profession he gave the first twenty years of his career. During that time, he became knowledgeable in more things than pedagogy. His own acute and incisive mind, expressing its dry, sharp, and witty judgments with a powerful Glasgow accent, got to know the people of his vast industrial native town and, what was more important, to learn from them. While teaching little boys, he himself was always learning in a greater school. And the great lesson he learnt was the good sense of the common people when they are not made the prey of the progressive intellectuals. In this school he learnt to detach himself from the illusions of contemporary liberalism and socialism, and thus came to associate himself with their political opposite, Toryism.

But his Toryism was highly individual, and it served him more as a conspicuous pedestal from which to denounce the Left than as a platform on which to build a different political structure. Fundamentally, the constructive side of his thought was Catholic and democratic in the serious sense of the word.

Thus his teaching career was punctuated with political activities, mainly anti-Communist and anti-Socialist speeches, together with lectures and expositions of Catholic social doctrine under the auspices of the Catholic Truth Society of Scotland. He also at the time engaged in many forms of journalism, from religious to sporting.

The full fruits of this varied and intense human experience came when Colm Brogan left Glasgow in 1946 to settle in London as a writer and speaker. This step was made possible by the publication of the brilliant book *Who are the People?*, a study of left wing intellectuals and their progressive propaganda. With this book, a new political pamphleteer harking back to the days when political pamphleteering was a power in the land, made his bow. The shock to the public was all the greater in that up till then the Left propagandists had enjoyed a monopoly of the clever popular style, which obtains the wide sales.

Who are the People? was followed by *The Democrat at the Supper Table*, a series of dialogues on various manifestations of contemporary ways of social and religious thinking, and the highly popular *Our New Masters*, a study of the personalities and purpose of the contemporary Labor Government.

These books enabled him to reach the highest ranks of the journalistic publicists in Fleet Street. His name became household property also, when he was delated to the Committee of Privileges of the House of Commons for accusing Socialist members of Communist leanings and loyalties. The case was dropped without his being called upon either to prove or withdraw the allegations.

In addition to large numbers of articles in papers and magazines, both Catholic and national, Colm Brogan edited for four years *Round the World*, a periodical chiefly devoted to the examination of socialist and secularist policies at home and Communism abroad.

M. DE LA B.

Beatrice Bradshaw Brown (Michael Kent)

Beatrice Bradshaw Brown was born in New York City. Her father, Harold Haven Brown, an artist, educator, lecturer, and writer, was at that time teaching drawing in the New York high schools. His father, O. B. Brown, was a church organist, composer, and music teacher in Boston, Massachusetts. Her mother, Florence Bradshaw, was born in Aiken, South Carolina. She is also an artist, specializing in the creation of character dolls and paintings of children. Harold Brown and Florence Bradshaw met as art students in Chartres and Paris. Following their marriage, they lived successively in New

York City, Yonkers, Chicago, Indianapolis, and Provincetown, where Harold Brown died in 1932, after serving as director of the John Herron Art Institute in Indianapolis, and, later, of the Provincetown Art Association.

Beatrice first attended public schools in New York City and Yonkers. Following a move to Chicago, where her father became instructor of art in the University High School, she was entered as a pupil in the University Elementary School. This she describes as "a truly idyllic institution of learning for children . . . we wrote plays and poetry, wrote and printed our own school magazine, and learned a foreign language" — French or German, as the pupil wished. Beatrice's choice of French was motivated by a devotion to St. Joan of Arc which had been roused in earliest childhood by Boutet de Monvel's illustrated life of the French saint and heroine — who, at that time, had not yet been canonized.

From Chicago, the family moved to Indianapolis, where Harold Brown was appointed director of the John Herron Art Institute and head of the art school. In this city, Beatrice received her secondary school education at Shortridge High School. After graduation, she returned to Chicago and attended the University. This formal education was supplemented by several years intensive study of music (among the arts, her first and deepest love), and by a stay of some months in Italy and France.

Her first professional writing assignment was a review for the *Indianapolis News* of an exhibition of drawings by Boutet de Monvel at the John Herron Art Institute. While in France, she collaborated with her sister Barbara in writing a book of verses and drawings for children, which was published by E. P. Dutton and Co. This was later followed by a second children's book, published by Little, Brown and Co. Thereafter she wrote steadily for various periodicals, including *The Youth's Companion*, *The Christian Science Monitor*, and *Pictorial Review*.

In 1933, on the advice of a friend, she submitted a story to *The Catholic World*. This story, *Debt of Honor*, was accepted by Father Gillis and published in January, 1934. It was subsequently listed in the O'Brien Best Short Stories Anthology for that year. This story pointedly illustrates the strong Catholic flavor that had always characterized her writings, long before she received any formal instruction in the faith. She does not like to be labeled a convert. "Conversion means a turning, but in my case there was no turning, but rather a discovery. Had I ever succeeded in being a Protestant, that would have been a conversion, or turning, from what I really was to something I could never be. . . . All the stories I wrote, even in school days, were essentially Catholic."

Yielding to this innate Catholicism, in 1933 she began to go regularly to Mass. In February 1934 she was received into the Church in New York City, having been instructed by Mother Hart of the Sacred Heart nuns, then on Madison Avenue at 54th Street. Of this instruction she says, "Mother Hart would seem surprised that I raised no objections. Sorry to disappoint her, I would go back to my room and try to think up something to object to. It was no use. I could not object to what, fundamentally, I had always believed." She was conditionally baptized by Father Blakely, S.J., of the staff of *America*, in the Church of the Ascension — where she would have been baptized had she received that rite in infancy, having been born nearby, in Ascension Parish.

The publication of *Debt of Honor* by Father Gillis marked her debut as a Catholic writer. From that time on her writings have appeared in *The Catholic World*, *The Sign*, *America*, *Good Housekeeping*, *The Catholic Choirmaster*, *Mount Carmel*, and other periodicals.

Besides the two juveniles already mentioned, her books include *The Mass of Brother Michel*, a novel, first published serially in a shorter version in *The Catholic World*, and *The Bond of Peace*, a plea for a crusade of sacrifice to repair the divisions caused in the modern world by the Protestant revolt.

During the summers of 1941 and 1942, she studied Gregorian Chant, Polyphony, and organ at the Pius X School of Liturgical Music in New York. She is at present (1951) organist and choir director at St. Peter's Church, Provincetown, Massachusetts, where she lives with her mother, who was received into the Church in 1940.

She has also studied painting, design, and lettering. She illustrated her book, *The Mass of Brother Michel*, and has lettered and illuminated altar cards for churches and chapels in this country and abroad.

E. B. B.

Reverend Raymond-Leopold Bruckberger, O.P.   1907–

Raymond-Leopold Bruckberger was born on April 10, 1907, in Murat, in central France, in the midst of mountains which were ancient volcanoes. His father was an Austrian; his mother, French. World War I in 1914 brought ruin to his family. "My childhood was very hard," he says, "but I would like to live again my youth; I was afraid of nothing."

Early in life he wanted to be a priest, a missionary above all. At seventeen years of age he entered the Grand Seminary of St. Flour, the superior of which later became Cardinal Salièges, Archbishop of Toulouse. It was he who advised Raymond-Leopold Bruckberger to become a Dominican.

At the age of twenty, he, like every Frenchman in good health, had to enter military service. He was stationed in the very pretty town of Montpellier, in the south of France. In his twenty-second year Raymond-Leopold Bruckberger applied for admission to the Dominican Order at their beautiful monastery, built in the thirteenth century, St. Maximin in Provence. This monastery resembles a fortress and guards the relics of St. Mary Magdalene.

After seven years of study, he was named secretary of the *Revue Thomiste*, a magazine devoted to philosophy and theology. He is still one of its directors.

When World War II started, he was again mustered into the army. He served as a petty officer in the Corps Francs (Commandos). He says, "We fought well but without hope. France was betrayed. Near Paris I refused to surrender to the Germans and received two bullets in the breast." Captured by the Germans, he was made a prisoner but escaped after a month and joined the "Resistance." In 1942 he was again taken prisoner by the Gestapo and describes his six months in prison as "horrible."

On leaving prison he made a film with Jean Giraudoux, "Les Anges Du Peche," which received the Grand Prix of the French cinema.

Then he became Chaplain-General of the "Resistance." "The life," he says, "was terribly hard." Finally liberation came. He was in Paris when it was freed, and De Gaulle entered. With the war over he returned to his monastery, St. Maximin. On his way back, he began to write the story of the Wolf of Gubbio. "My cruel war experience made me want to write this little book," he says. "In war, people become openly what they are at heart. Cowards are more cowardly; the brave are heroes. Liars lie to advantage and loose women are more so than ever. Misers take all and leave nothing to others. The generous leave nothing for themselves. I lashed politics and politicians who made use of victories which they did not deserve. The theme of *l'Imitation* which I am putting into book form shows the difficulty of keeping one's soul in peace amidst the tumult of the world. And what one can get from such an experience is peace of heart in conquering and not being conquered by war — namely the pardon of offences and the practice of charity.

"All I knew of the Wolf of Gubbio is what the Fioretti say. But what interested me was the life of the wolf after his conversion. I had then to invent it. The first miracle, that of the suspended child, was inspired by a miracle of St. Vincent Ferrer, who stopped the fall of a workman, who was falling into a furnace. For the second miracle of the torrent, I recalled the passage of the Red Sea. The stopping of an earthquake was brought about by a South American saint. The change of the ugly person of Formicella was brought to my mind by the universal fact that love makes people more beautiful. The overturn of the chair of Podestat called to my mind a game of my childhood and I have always loved tricks. The seventh miracle where the wolf escapes through the forest was inspired by St. Joseph of Cupertino, who has just been made the patron of aviation, of whom it is said he easily elevated himself above the sun. And the miracle of the throat of the wolf filled with honey, recalls the story of Samson, who, having killed a lion, found in his cadaver a throat filled with honey. This means that strong people are not really strong until they can contain their strength with kindness."

Father Bruckberger's other books are *Rejoindre Dieu*, theology of prayer; *La Valeur Humaine Du Saint Ligne De Faite*, a literary criticism; *Si Grande Peine*, a war story; *Nous N'Irons Plus Au Bois,* against the Purge; *Les Cosaques et le Saint-Ésprit* (against Communism); *One Sky to Share* (1952).

In the fall of 1951 Harper and Brothers published his book, *The Stork and the Jewels*. It deals with the legend of a boy who made a pet of a fledgling stork which flew away each winter to another land and returned on the boy's birthday bearing gifts. The same company also brought out a new edition of *The Seven Miracles of Gubbio*, as a school edition of the French text. Harper's also published his life of St. Mary Magdalen. Father Bruckberger is now preparing a commentary on the Nicene Creed.

In 1947 he founded a literary review which included some of the best French writers, Bernanos, Camus, Cendrars, Jouhandeau, Maritain, Marcel Aymé, Jules Roy, Gabriel Marcel, Patrice de la Tour du Pin and others. This review ceased publication when Father Bruckberger left France.

He also spent some time in Africa as Chaplain of the Foreign Legion.

Of his visit to America (1951) Father Bruckberger says, "I love it deeply. I believe that from now on my work will be to make America understood to those Europeans who do not understand it and likewise to make Europe understood here. If these two continents understand each other the peace of the world is assured. I am a writer but I always think that life and death are more precious than all the books one can write."

K. M.

Dorothy M. Bryan

The picture of a child, happy and gleeful as he (or she) reads a book, is the picture of Dorothy Bryan's achievement. Dorothy Bryan not only selects and edits good manuscripts for juveniles, but she selects writers capable of entertaining children and coaxes them into writing for her protégés. More than that, she writes stories herself. She is the "fairy Queen" of the children's library, filling its shelves with good taste and high art. Her background becomes her work. "Aside from my deep interest in my work as editor in charge of the books for younger readers . . . I like young people themselves, also horses and dogs and all other animals. I live on Long Island, and after being brought up in hotels for at least part of each year during my younger life, I now prefer living in the country to the city."

Out in her Long Island home she has hundreds and hundreds of books that she has published or reviewed and she shares them with the girls and boys who live nearby. She lets them have these books to read and then asks them for their comments. Such is her wonderful way of learning more and more about the likes and thoughts of little people!

Dorothy M. Bryan   64

Dorothy Bryan's early education was divided between the Sacred Heart Convent in New Orleans during the winter and the Visitation Academy in New York in the fall and spring, with interludes of travel in between. She graduated from Packer Collegiate Institute and then went on for two years at Barnard College with a mind made up to enter the publishing business. May Massee of Doubleday, Doran and Company gave her an opening as a volunteer reader of juvenile manuscripts and later took her on as assistant. The training was excellent: "whole-time occupation in every angle of publishing, from book-estimating, make-up and design, through to the planning of illustrations, and personal editorial cooperation with authors." The year 1931 found Dorothy Bryan, in collaboration with her sister Marguerite Bryan, writing *Johnny Penguin*. It was illustrated by Marguerite. The success of this charming story encouraged them to continue with their "Michael and Patsy" pictured dog stories, and from there on to "Tammie," "Bobby" and his pony, "Frisky," and "Jonathan."

In 1934 Dorothy Bryan was put in charge of the juvenile book department at Dodd, Mead and Company where her special gift as a publisher began at once to produce results. Apart from selecting the best stories offered, she set about "creative editing," namely selecting the best possibilities. "Who," she would ask herself, "can write me the best book for children?" And, having chosen her "possibility" she proceeded to coax the authors — Phil Stong, Ruth Bryan Owen, Lauren Ford, Frances Parkinson Keyes, Walter D. Edmonds, Agnes Rothery, Laura Benet, Frank Ernest Hill, May Lamberton Becker, and many others — to write the books for children she planned. "The thing I like to do best," she says, "is to make juvenile authors."

Then appeared Dorothy Bryan's great enterprise, "The Dodd, Mead Career Books." These books are written by people who have been successful in the careers they describe, and represent in live fiction form all the popular and possible careers for young people. Such distinguished authors as Helen Hayes, the beloved actress; Sara Pennoyer, now Vice-President of James McCreery's; Emma Bugbee of the New York *Herald-Tribune;* Mary Margaret McBride of ABC; Gladys Swarthout, Metropolitan Opera star; Caroline A. Chandler, M.D., of Johns Hopkins; Lieutenant Colonel John B. Stanley, West Point, and Arthur Kenney, Du Pont research chemist have written books for the series. There are over sixty of these Dodd, Mead Career Books which aim to "present in interesting story form the requirements, problems, pleasures and future possibilities of selected fields of work that are worth-while for young people today."

Dorothy Bryan's standards are high. As editor and publisher she demands that a book be well written, that it contain principles of good living, a fine family relationship, and the spirit of tolerance. The heroes she presents must be real, live heroes, even in such small but stalwart heroes as "Michael" and "Patsy," her own two Sealyham terriers whom she loved and studied before giving them to the young world.

In conjunction with her sister Marguerite Bryan she has written the following books: *Johnny Penguin* (1931); *Michael Who Missed His Train* (1932); *Michael and Patsy on the Golf Links* (1933); *Fun with Michael* (1934); *There Was Tammie* (1935); *Tammie and That Puppy* (1936); *Bobby Wanted a Pony* (1937); *Frisky Finding a Home* (1938); *Friendly Little Jonathan* (1939).

In an article published in *Poise*, Muriel Fuller states: "Dorothy Bryan chose a field of far wider influence than that of books for adults. Her originality and fine editing are turned to the publishing of books for boys and girls. She is helping to build men and women for the future."

For many years she has been an active member of the Personnel Division of the Girl Scouts of the United States of America.

Miss Bryan serves well the cause of Catholic literature. As editor of the recommended list of juvenile books for the Cardinal's Literature Committee, she is a wise and experienced guide for reading in Catholic schools. She is also chairman of the juvenile section of the Gallery of Living Catholic Authors.   E. B. B.

Louis Francis Budenz   1891–

Louis Francis Budenz's great-grandfather emigrated from western Germany, and his grandfather was one of the early Indiana settlers. His father, a convert, was for fifty-four years paying teller at the Capitol National Bank of Indianapolis. His mother, an orphan, was the daughter of Irish immigrants from Cork and Kerry. Louis Francis, one of five children, was born in Indianapolis, Indiana July 17, 1891. He had a pious and intellectual childhood, spent browsing in his father's library. He was especially devoted to Shakespeare, Guizot, and Jefferson. From Public School 34, he went to St. Xavier's College (now Xavier University) Cincinnati, and to St. Mary's College, Kansas. Admitted to the Indiana Bar in 1912, in the same year he became editor of *The Carpenter*, the official organ of the United Brotherhood of Carpenters and Joiners, at that time the largest organization in the American Federation of Labor. In 1913 he went to St. Louis to be associated with the Central Bureau of the Catholic Central Verein.

Of his first published work, *The Employers Tactics in the Industrial Struggle*, Mr. Budenz wrote in his autobiography, *This is My Story* (Whittlesey House, 1947) "it was an extensive résumé of what actually occurred on the industrial battlefield, and it aroused far-flung interest." In 1914 Mr. Budenz contracted a civil marriage with a divorced Catholic, and remained outside the Church for the next thirty-one years.

From 1915 to 1920, he was secretary of the Civic League, an organization for civic reform. At that time he wrote a series of articles for the *National Municipal Review*, summing up the attitude of civic reformers of the period. In 1920 he accepted an offer from Roger

Baldwin to go to New York as publicity director for the American Civil Liberties Union. As founder and editor of *Labor Age*, a magazine sponsored by officials of the leading union (which later became the CIO) Mr. Budenz helped direct the agitation for, and the legislation of, the social services throughout the United States. Although Mr. Budenz lived in New Jersey, he worked around Union Square for a quarter of a century. His first meeting with Earl Browder and William Z. Foster, later to be long associated with him in the Communist Party, took place in 1922, but at that time he found himself in strong opposition to the Communist Party line. But he spoke in New York for Sacco and Vanzetti, and was arrested, then acquitted. He was arrested and acquitted twenty-one times altogether, while representing American Federation of Labor Unions. He was in charge of the Allen-A strike in Kenosha, Wisconsin, and later, in Nazareth, Pennsylvania and Toledo, Ohio, he won outstanding labor victories.

On October 2, 1935, *The Daily Worker* publicly announced that Mr. Budenz had joined the Communist Party. He had taken this step because of the adoption of the People's Front policy by the Communist International. Earlier he had read and intellectually accepted Lenin and other Communist authorities, but had been wary of the Communist's un-American approach. It was George Dimitrov, speaking for Stalin, whose declaration that Communists in every country must have due regard for their respective national traditions, which converted Mr. Budenz to the Party. But he did make the required pledge of allegiance to Stalin, as he later testified.

For two years he worked as labor editor of *The Daily Worker* at 50 East Thirteenth Street in New York City; then in 1937 he became editor of the *Midwest Daily Record*, the Chicago Communist paper. In 1940 he returned to New York as managing editor of *The Daily Worker*, a position he held until his return to the Church in 1945.

In his best selling book *Men Without Faces* (Harper, 1950), Mr. Budenz has described how he managed his paper from "a guarded, locked, sound-proof room." He has given chapter and verse for Communist treason, even at the time when the Popular Front was the official Party policy. His revelations of the set-up on the "ninth-floor"; of his moving around New York, meeting undercover Moscow agents with false names in obviously innocuous restaurants; of the cold-blooded kidnapping of persons on Moscow's blacklist, and of the planning of Trotsky's murder, furnish startling information.

It was on October 10th, 1945, in St. Patrick's Cathedral that Mr. Budenz, with his wife Margaret, to whom he is now married, and his four daughters, were received back into the Church by Bishop Fulton Sheen. Immediately thereafter, Mr. Budenz spent a year on the faculty of Notre Dame. Later he was appointed assistant professor of economics at Fordham. He is responsible for the identification of Hans Berger with Gerhard Eisler, and many important criminal and deportation cases have been based on his testimony. In 1948, he testified before a Senate group that "perhaps thousands" of Communist party members held government jobs. In magazine articles and radio statements he has warned that Soviet Russia is waging war on the United

States through Asia and Europe, as he predicted would occur when he left the communist conspiracy. He has also stated that were open warfare to break out between the United States and the USSR, a "time of terrible decision" would follow S-Day (Soviet, or Stalin Day) on which American Communists would spring into instant action against their country. Mr. Budenz has been the government's principal witness in more cases and investigations than any other man. Conspicuous among these was his appearance as the first witness of the government in the famous trial of the eleven communist leaders under the Smith Act before Judge Medina. Then, Budenz was on the stand in examination and cross-examination for ten days. In addition to his other courses in Economics, he is now responsible for the new course in the "Techniques of Communism" in the Institute for Contemporary Russian Studies at Fordham University.   A. F.

Reverend Roger Buliard, O.M.I.
1909–

The first and only book of Father Roger Buliard, an Oblate, is *Inuk* (1949) (pronounced inook), and this came out of his experience living fifteen years among the Eskimos.

Born at Le Russey, France, on the Swiss border, January 18, 1909, he is the son of Louise Noroy and Louis Buliard. At the age of six he started school in Le Russey, under the tutelage of the Christian Brothers, "where I left sweet memories of my pranks," he says. In 1920 he entered the seminary of Our Lady of Consolation, with the firm conviction of becoming a missionary. While he never won anything but the sports awards, he was mentioned for prowess in literature and history. He hated mathematics. Even at the seminary he engaged in a few pranks and states: "I was kept on because of my unfaltering ideal of becoming a missionary." Six years later (1926) on September 29th he entered the novitiate of the Oblates of Mary Immaculate in Normandy, France, "specialists of difficult missions, 'an Order founded more than a century ago by a Bishop of Marseilles and commanded to evangelize the poor.'"

From 1929 to 1930 he did regular army service in the Blue Devils, the French mountain infantry, with the rank of sergeant. He soldiered at the mountain outpost in Savoie, on the Italian frontier and thus got his first foretaste of the Arctic.

After returning to the Scholasticate in Liége, Belgium, he continued his theological studies and was ordained priest July 26, 1933. In May, 1934 he was sent directly to the Eskimos, four months before the completion of his theological course. His assignment fulfilled a boyhood dream. As a boy, while in Besançon, his eye was caught by the title of a book displayed in a shop window, "a title that flashed before my eyes like a crusader's sword . . . *L'Epopée Blanche* . . . *The White Epic.* I fingered the few francs in my pocket, then entered the shop and bought the book, thus taking the first step on a road that was to lead to the Arctic and fifteen years as a missionary to the Eskimos."

Eight years after he bought a copy of *L'Epopée Blanche* he was on his way to Coppermine, his first assignment, and here he remained until 1937 working with Father Lucien Delalande, O.M.I., a loyal friend and "godfather" of his seminary days at Liége who saved him from expulsion while in the seminary. "Coppermine was the one place on earth I wanted most to go," says Father Buliard. "The first furrow of this mission was moistened by the blood of the first missionaries. One day, we hope, all the Eskimos will pray there, remembering with gratitude those who laid down their lives for them." Here his first task was to learn Eskimo and English. His second year at Coppermine was spent alone. Father Delalande had gone to Burnside to establish a mission. In his third year, a Father John Franche, O.M.I., a young priest, was sent to him. Then Father Buliard received his second assignment — the foundation of Christ the King Mission, which was farthest north — on top of the world. He made an exploration trip and sojourn alone to Uyaraktok, and lived in a snow-covered canvas shelter for one year. He spent another year alone at Minto Inlet, farther north and here had his first conversion. Then he settled at King's Bay, building up the mission, where he remained until 1946 when, after twelve years in the Arctic, he was given permission by Bishop Trocellier to return to France to see his family who had suffered so much during World War II. He flew all the way. "Of my ten brothers and sisters, I recognized two. One had been a prisoner in Germany for four years, another had been wounded with the Maquis, a third had been in Buchenwald and weighed only sixty pounds when the Americans liberated him. My fourth brother, then ten years old, dodged bayonets investigating the haystack in which he was hidden. Our home had been occupied and plundered by the invaders, and my sister had been struck by a Gestapo officer when she refused to answer his questions."

In 1947 he returned to King's Bay. "I felt lost," he writes, "so I wrote a book to help me think straight and occupy my solitude." The book, *Inuk,* was published in France and was crowned by the French Academy with the Prix Montyon. Three years later he accidentally shot himself in the hand. He was flown out to Edmonton, the gateway to the North and then began to translate *Inuk* into English. It is now being translated into five other languages.

It is a personal account of his battles, and eventual triumph, against the elements, the animals and the hostility of the people, stationed in the most northern settlement on the earth. For nine months of the year, land and water are a block of ice.

Written "to attract public and official interest for a people I have learned to admire for their courage and love despite their faults," he dedicates the book "to the many unknown, hidden missionaries, who, from their convents, hospitals and schools, by their ardent prayers and generous sacrifices, have really made possible the spiritual foundation of this mission (Christ the King Mission), who have made it possible for Christ to reign, here at the end of the world, according to the motto of our new apostolic vicar, His Excellency, Joseph M. Trocellier, O.M.I. — 'Thy Kingdom Come!'"

In 1951, Father Buliard visited the United States, where he was the guest of the Sisters of St. Peter's General Hospital, New Brunswick, New Jersey.

Early in July he went to Ottawa, Canada and is now (September, 1951) stationed at the Scholasticate of the Oblate Fathers. His new assignment is to write a book which will be a continuation of *Inuk* and will bear the title, *Falla (The Father)*. This book will endeavor to give the history of the Apostolate of the Oblate Fathers among the Eskimos, with stress on the psychology o the happenings in the Arctic and the difficulties of the missionaries.   M. A. H.

David Burnham   1907–

It is remarkable that David Burnham should be one of three brothers, all of whom are writers, one (Philip) being Corresponding Editor of *The Commonweal*, the other (James) a full professor in the Department of Philosophy at Washington Square College of New York University in New York and the author of four books.

David Burnham was born in Chicago, Illinois, the son of Claude George Burnham, the British-born executive vice-president of the Burlington Railroad at the time of his death in 1928, and of Mary (Gillis) Burnham. He was educated at the Joseph Sears School, Kenilworth, Illinois, New Trier Township High School, Kenilworth, and Canterbury School, New Milford, Connecticut from which he was graduated in 1925. He then entered Princeton University. His extra-curricular interests at Princeton were along literary lines. He was Editorial Chairman of the *Daily Princetonian*, Literary Editor of the *Princeton Tiger*, Managing Editor of the *Nassau Literary Magazine* and co-author of a Princeton Triangle Club musical comedy. In 1929 he was graduated *magna cum laude*.

Since graduation from Princeton University, David Burnham has devoted himself exclusively to writing except during his four years in the army. He was released in June, 1946 with the grade of major in the Military Intelligence Reserve. He lived two years in Europe and has travelled extensively in the Far East, Africa, West Indies, Mexico, Canada and forty-seven states in the Union. On September 27, 1947, he married Clare Napier-Martin of Great Bromley, Essex, England, in Africa, where he had been travelling for four or five months since World War II ended.

The Burnhams purchased Hollow Farm in New Milford, Connecticut. There they live all year round and there David does his work.

Burnham's first novel, *This Our Exile* was published in 1931. It is concerned with the lives of a prominent suburban Chicago family and its circle. The theme is that "more crimes are committed in the name of love and through the promptings of love than any other; that love is not the end but only the beginning, from which understanding must carry on." After writing this novel Burnham went to work on his next book *Wedding Song* of which he says: "I became increasingly impatient of the conventional form of the Georgian novel. So much must be included which in the final analysis is mere padding. My chief interest is not ideas but personal relationships and these, it seems to me, are most effectively presented directly, in dramatic form. Consequently, I tried to evolve a form that would present the characters directly, in action, as a movie presents them. The reader meets the characters in the midst of significant action. As would happen if the reader met these characters in real life, their actions are confusing at first, because the motives aren't understood. And neither are the motives clearly apprehended by the man who relates the story. He himself is caught within the action, which he can see only through the present stage of his personality. But the earlier stages of his personality, which condition his present, must somehow be supplied. I used the device of interspersing chapters written by his sister, who is another of the chief characters throughout the action. Her narrative begins many years earlier than his, when they were children together, and gradually approaches the present until their alternate chapters are contemporaneous. By this device, I could withhold the background events until their pertinence to the present situation could be apprehended; and I also wished to express that the present action necessarily contained all their mutual past, although he himself wilfully excluded and repudiated the past. Again, the double narration is meant to express the relativity of experience; a brother and his sister interpret the same events from divergent standpoints, conditioned by the personality and character and relationship of each. Neither is meant to be the 'true' interpretation; the reader is meant to make his own interpretation on the basis of what each reveals. This, evidently, put a strain upon the readers which many were unwilling to accept, having become accustomed to being informed by the author exactly how to respond." A reviewer in *Outlook* commented: "He writes good straightforward narrative that holds the interest. He should make a solid sober novelist."

Wedding Song, utilizing this device, was published in 1934 and is Burnham's favorite book. It is a story of worldly young Americans and Italian aristocrats living a life of presumed pleasure in Venice. Some reviewers dismissed it as obscure, but most of those who read it carefully considered it a definite advance over *This Our Exile*.

His next book *Winter in the Sun* represents, in a sense, a retrogression. "I wrote it at a time," writes Burnham, "when it was the fashion for the novelist to attempt in one volume to solve all the problems of humanity. Still in my 20's, it seemed a presumption to pretend to know enough about human character to tackle a 'major' work. And so I confined myself to a love affair between two contemporaries of myself, of my own class, in a purposely limited scene — an Arizona guest-ranch. The theme is simply the difficulty of complete surrender — indeed the impossibility for an educated, sophisticated adult of the sort of surrender each of us at the same time fears and hungers for." The critics praised this book more for its incidents than its plot.

To exercise himself in tight plot construction, Burnham next wrote a detective story, *Last Act in Bermuda,* 1940.

Burnham looks upon these three books as "to an extent, exercises, training myself for dealing with the larger canvas for which, with luck, maturing experience will fit me."

He uses first-person technique because it seems to him to allow an added dimension to fiction. "In place of the author dogmatically assuming divine prescience, he exhibits the action through the eyes of a by no means all-prescient narrator. That character's mistakes and insentiencies not only define the character's personality better than a mere description could do, but express what I referred to above as the relativity of experience. If, as has been lately proven to us, time and space are relative, how much more so are human perceptions, personality, etc. The acceptance of this viewpoint appears to me to distinguish the work of all of our progressive modern novelists — e.g. Proust, Virginia Woolf, Stephen Hudson, early Faulkner, etc."

In addition to his novels, Mr. Burnham has written short stories for *Scribner's, Saturday Evening Post, Liberty, This Week,* and various Canadian, Australian, English and South American magazines. Some articles appeared in *Reader's Digest, The Symposium* and syndicated newspapers. Previous to his military service he was dramatic critic for *The Commonweal.* He is still a director of that magazine and Vice President of the Commonweal Publishing Company and contributes book and art reviews.   M. A. H.

Reverend Eric Norman Bromley Burrows, S.J. 1882–1938

The eldest of an Anglican solicitor's family of five, Father Eric Burrows was born at Ramsgate, England on March 26, 1882. He was educated at a preparatory school at St. Leonards, from which he passed to Felsted School in 1897 and thence to Keble College, Oxford, in 1901. He took honors B.A. in Anglican theology in 1904. He was drawn to the Catholic Church almost as soon as he came in contact with it at Oxford, but at the suggestion of friends and parents he was persuaded to think it over again in a quieter atmosphere, which he did at an Anglican clergyman's house in the country, after taking his degree, and after a travelling tutorship to Switzerland and Germany. In December, 1904, he was received into the Church by Father Kelly, O.S.M., at Begbroke Priory, near Oxford; and with the full consent of his parents, he applied for admission in the Society of Jesus in March following, being received at Manresa House, Roehampton, on September 7, 1905.

In the Society he went through the usual curriculum of studies and tests of his vocation. After his noviceship he studied philosophy at St. Mary's Hall, Stonyhurst, from 1907 to 1910. He was sent to teach first at St. Ignatius' College, Stamford Hill, and then at Beaumont. In 1912 we find him at the Jesuit University, Beirut, in Syria, studying Oriental languages. At the end of two years he returned to England to study theology from 1914 to 1918, being ordained priest at St. Beuno's College, North Wales, on July 31st, 1917. At the end of his theology he had a year's valuable experience on the mission at St. Joseph's, Glasgow, after which he was sent to Tullabeg, in Ireland, for his third year of probation.

Having accomplished the prescribed tests, he was next sent to the Biblical Institute at Rome to do special research work in Holy Scripture, and in 1922 he was attached to Farm Street Residence, London, to enable him to study Assyriology at the British Museum. Two years later he took part in the conjoint expedition of the Oxford and Chicago Field Museums to Kish, "the little red mound" (Tellel-Uhaimir, sixty miles south and twenty miles east of Baghdad), where Professor Langdon had made extensive and valuable finds; and in 1925 Father Burrows was engaged as the official expert cuneiformist of Mr. (now Sir) Leonard Woolley's expedition on behalf of the British Museum and the University of Pennsylvania, at Uri, or "Ur of the Chaldees," Abraham's birthplace.

Full details of this expedition, which lasted till 1929, were given in *The Times*, 1928, 1929, with excellent illustrations, and an exhibition was held at the British Museum in August and September, 1929. An article by Father Burrows in *The Dublin Review*, January, 1930, on "The Discovery of the Deluge," gives the relevant finds in Iraq, and the handsome publication of the British Museum on the *The Ur Excavations* (Texts II: Archaic), is the first volume of the vast material collected by the expedition and deciphered by Father Burrows. This consists largely of the text as deciphered by him, and of a comparison with classics of similar material. Many articles of his and separate studies also appeared in *Orientalia* and *The Journal of the Royal Asiatic Society*.

Mr. C. J. Gadd, in charge of the Assyriological Department of the British Museum, comparing Father Burrows with Father N. Strassmeier (died 1920), looks upon the latter as the pioneer who laid the foundations of modern Assyriology, a more prolific writer, but grappling with elemental principles of the science; whilst Father Burrows, coming later in the field, is much more advanced and his work is "sound, very careful, a valuable contribution to Assyriological knowledge. In fact, his work is accepted, together with that of Falkenstein's *Archäische Texte aus Ur*, as one of the principal contributions to the most ancient Babylonian epigraphy." Sir Leonard Woolley wrote as follows in *The Times*, June 25, 1938: "The sad death of Father Burrows, S.J., means a loss to Assyriology the more serious in view of the scanty number of cuneiform scholars of which this country can boast. A pupil of the late Professor Langdon at Oxford, Burrows was led alike by his scientific training and by his clerical profession to concentrate rather on the religious legends and on the astronomical achievements of the Babylonians, but a new direction was given to his studies by his association with the Ur excavations. From 1926 to 1930 he was a member of the Ur Expedition Staff and spent each winter in the field dealing with the inscriptions. Much of his work there has yet to be published, but what has already appeared has established Burrows' position as a cuneiformist of the first rank. During his time at Ur the discovery of large numbers of ancient texts gave him an opportunity of original work which he was not slow to seize. To the second volume of the official publication, *The Royal Cemetery*, he contributed a profound study of the documents bearing on the date and character of the early dynastic period, and in *Archaic Texts* he followed this up with a work on archaic palaeography which is one of the two books whereon rests all our knowledge of the beginnings of cuneiform writing. On that basis his lasting reputation is assured. It is impossible to describe his worth as a scholar without adding a word of regret for one of the most charming personalities that ever triumphed over the difficulties of camp life, for the gaiety and whimsical humor that overlay his deeply-felt convictions. To a very great number at home the news of his death will have brought real sorrow."

These scholarly works did not absorb all Father Burrows' interests and activities, for he had a literary and philosophical bent of mind, and he exercised his priesthood during the summer sessions by supplying in various missions, giving retreats to religious and instructing converts. E. M., writing in *The Times*, June 29, 1938, says of Father Eric Burrows that he was "a very lovable character. We first met at Kish, in Iraq, where as Assyriologist he found much to fill his time. I shall think of the little chapel he created, with its simple altar of packing-cases surmounted by a very large Nebuchadnezzar brick, and of the respect held for him in consequence among the simple Arab laborers. It was a positive delight to the members of the expedition to sit with him after dinner and propound knotty problems to him, which he ably answered with his little red book on Canon Law. Clothed always in sober black — he would wear no other color — he daily returned to the camp after his hot and dusty labors looking like an old-time miller with the dust of the excavations thick upon him. When an Arab brought into the camp a number of clay tablets bearing archaic writing which he pronounced to be of very early date his excitement was infectious. His satisfaction when he located the site from which they had come, some thirteen miles from Kish, and picked up others there, was good to look upon. He will be remembered by his colleagues at both Kish and Ur as a very courtly gentleman and a noble example of his Faith."

Father Burrows' death was sudden. He died in 1938 in the Radcliffe Infirmary, Oxford, from injuries suffered in a car crash on the Oxford Northern by-pass, near Eynsham.

Two volumes of his Biblical studies were published posthumously. These are entitled *The Oracles of Jacob and Balaam* (1939), and *The Gospel of the Infancy and other Biblical Essays* (1941.)

Doris Burton

Doris Burton of Kensington, London, has become firmly established as a Catholic writer during the last few years. Her latest work, *Through a Convert's Window* (Duckett), described by Father Devas, S.J., in his preface as "a good and helpful book," is proving of great value to converts and would-be Catholics, and also to Catholics who wish to win their friends to the Church. Describing many of the difficulties and prejudices she herself had to overcome and using the steps which led to her own conversion, she leads the reader through this Business of Conversion, Confession, Patriotism, Work, Loneliness, Superstition, Justice, etc., to the Supernatural and to Sanctity.

As a child Doris Burton received a vague Church of England upbringing at home, while at the same time she was being taught at school by a Quaker and Unitarian, so it is not surprising that she got the impression that a certain code of behavior was right, but that it did not matter to what Christian sect one belonged. A finishing school in Switzerland and the reading of French atheistic literature convinced her that man is nothing more than an animal and death the end of everything.

To escape from her sense of futility, she embarked on a career of nursing just before the outbreak of the First World War, but appalled at the suffering she met she turned to Infant Welfare. Here, too, she was filled with dismay at the problems arising from poverty and overcrowding. What was the solution? Surely the limitation of the population through birth control, or some new political system such as socialism! During this time her values were becoming more confused and cynical through reading popular writers of the moment such as Shaw and Wells. There was marriage for example. What was the point of making vows if they could be broken through divorce?

After a brief return to Anglicanism which, being dependent on the personality of the popular Dick Shepherd, soon vanished, she went to South Africa and lived a social life of tennis, dances, bridge and tea parties. But she could not cast off her sense of futility. Returning to London, feeling no longer able to cope with the world's problems, she worked as a black and white illustrator, dabbling tentatively with theosophy and other strange beliefs including spiritualism which she decided to be both dangerous and completely unconvincing. Next she joined the Oxford Group led by Frank Buchman — now called Moral Rearmament — and gained her faith in God. Yet she sought much more than that. "I wanted a philosophy which would give me the true solution to the many spiritual and material problems of life. With this in mind I began to study Catholicism, finally reaching that happy occasion, my reception into the Catholic Church in 1936."

Doris Burton had at last reached her goal, a key to things both eternal and temporal; a religion which taught that suffering accepted as one's Christian cross has a redemptive value, which gave the solutions to poverty and social evils in its encyclicals, which expounded the Christian Moral Law, with Holy Matrimony as a sacramental life long union, its fundamental purpose the rearing of a family. Having discovered the answer to so much which had caused her bewilderment and unhappiness, her one desire was to help others who might be groping towards the Truth. Under the name of Lucis Amator, she began writing leaflets and pamphlets, one being *Spiritual Rearmament for Moral Rearmament*. Her first small book for study circles, *My Christian Stewardship* (Burns & Oates, 1942), received a personal recommendation from the late Cardinal Hinsley; her next work, written under her own name, was a collection of Catholic short stories, *A Penny for a Candle* (Organ, 1946). Since then she has been writing stories and articles for Catholic magazines in many countries, including America.

Doris Burton has a real love for children. Realizing through her own experience how essential for true happiness is the knowledge of Catholic doctrine, she concentrates also on stories for children, stories described by the reviewers as "enthralling and written with a delightful touch of humor, yet with a spiritual appeal which goes straight to the heart." Some have appeared as Irish C.T.S. (Catholic Truth Society) pamphlets, others in book form, *The Angel Who Guarded the Toys* (Sands, Illustrated. 1948), followed by *Saints and Heroes for Boys* (Sands, Illustrated. 1950), the keynote of the latter being adventure, the adventure which leads to heroic sanctity. Two more books of a different kind were published in the autumn of 1951, by Paternoster Publications, *Great Catholic Mothers of Yesterday and To-day*, and the life of *St. Emilie de Rodat*, founder of the Holy Family Congregation and the first saint to be canonized in the Holy Year, 1950.

Although Doris Burton lives in London she prefers country life, but in any case she finds her writing absorbs most of her time, her relaxation being reading and listening to good music. She also has a special interest in the foreign missions.

With the threat of communism and the atom bomb, she appreciates more than ever the inestimable blessing bestowed upon her through the gift of faith. Nevertheless, the price she paid was costly. For as the eldest and only unmarried daughter of a wealthy father, she found herself deprived at his death of her share in his estate, receiving instead but a small annual allowance. She admits it was a blow. "Nevertheless, even had I realized fully at the time of my reception into the Church what it would cost, I should have gone ahead," she declares, "for nothing is more precious than Truth, that Truth which brings with it a peace of mind and a unifying sense of purpose only to be found in its fulness as a member of the Mystical Body of Christ." Her greatest joy is the hope that through her pen she is serving in some small way Holy Mother Church — to the greater glory of God.

Charles Edward Butler   1909–

Charles Edward Butler was born in Denver, Colorado, on July 9, 1909, the second child and first son of Charles M. Butler and Gertrude Clunan Butler, natives of Ontario who moved to Denver in the early years of the century. After parochial schooling in Denver, Butler attended the University of Denver, receiving first an A.B. degree in 1931 and then, after a year in the University's School of Librarianship, a B.A. in Library Science. During his high school and college years, he worked as a page in the Denver Public Library.

While a student at the University, Butler began to write verse, some of which was published in *College Verse*. Five of his poems from this source were included in the anthology *Trial Balances* (Macmillan Co., 1936), accompanied by a commentary by Witter Bynner.

In 1933 he went to Chicago to work as assistant to the Secretary of the American Library Association until 1937. That year he resigned to study in the Graduate Library School of the University of Chicago on a fellowship awarded by the American Library Association, receiving passing grades in most of his courses but producing nothing of any merit in the way of a professional study. There followed a year in the Library of Western Washington College of Education at Bellingham; in the autumn of 1939 he was appointed Librarian of the Kanawha County Public Library in Charleston, West Virginia, where he remained until his induction into the army as a private in September, 1942.

Assigned to the Air Force, Butler was put into personnel work and sent to an air base in Texas. After a few weeks there, he was transferred to the New Orleans Army Air Base, where he remained until July, 1943, when he was shipped to England. In New Orleans, he entered some poems in a contest for service men sponsored by A. S. Barnes Company; his entries, five poems, won third prize, and were included in the anthology *Reveille: War Poems* (Barnes, 1943). They were reprinted in J. Donald Adams' *New York Times Book Review* column, and one was read on a March of Time radio broadcast.

For more than two years, Butler, by then a few grades higher than private, was occupied with personnel duties at an Air Force maintenance and repair base near Manchester. He continued to write poems, and some of these were published by the *New Yorker*, one of whose editorial staff had seen his *Reveille* poems and asked him to submit others. *Harper's*, too, accepted two poems, as did *Poetry*, and in 1944 Archibald MacLeish chose his collection *Cut Is The Branch* for the Yale University Press Series of Younger American Poets. The volume was issued in 1945.

Discharged in October, 1945, he was married to Eleanor Walters in November in the Lady Chapel of St. Patrick's Cathedral in New York, and returned to Charleston. For a year he was busy preparing for publication a manuscript called *Tangle of Shadows*, a journal of part of his life in the army. It failed to find a publisher, and he turned to the writing of *Follow Me Ever*. The theme of this novel had occurred to him sometime during the closing days of the war, but it was not until later that he began the actual writing in the form in which it was eventually published. Completed in 1948, the manuscript came to the attention of Mr. Hermann Broch, the distinguished Austrian writer, who recommended its publication to Kurt and Helen Wolff of Pantheon Books, Inc. Sharing Broch's enthusiasm, they issued the novel in 1951. Despite — or perhaps because of — the delicacy and difficulty of its theme — the most understanding reviews appeared in the Catholic press, although on the whole, in the contemporary sense, the book was neither a critical nor a popular success. Shortly after publication, however, Butler was awarded a Guggenheim Foundation Award in creative writing for the completion of a novel dealing with Red Hugh O'Donnell and his life and times in 16th century Ireland.

Since September, 1949, Butler has been Librarian of West Virginia University Library. During the summers of 1948, 1949, and 1950 he studied at the Graduate School of the University of Michigan, and in 1950 received the degree of Master of Arts in Library Science. In 1949 and 1950 he received Avery Hopwood Awards in poetry from the University of Michigan.

Reverend Joseph Cacella   1882–

Spreading devotion to Our Lady of Fatima is the motivating force behind the writing of Father Cacella. It is only natural that he should be imbued with that spirit because he was born near the now world famous and hallowed spot, Fatima, Portugal, the date of his birth being September 21, 1882. After his elementary and high school studies, he entered the seminary of Santarem in Lisbon, Portugal, the very same house of studies in which St. Anthony, the Wonder-Worker, had studied. Ordained to the priesthood in 1909, he was made pastor of Our Lady of Help parish in Vestiaria. A year later, he was forced into exile because he would not conform to the wishes and dictates of the radical government of the revolution of 1910. Father Cacella made his escape, aboard a freighter, bound for Manáos, Amazon, Brazil. There he presented his credentials to Don Frederico Costa, Bishop of Manáos, who appointed him a missionary to the Indians of Borba and Rio Madeira, Amazon Diocese, in the dark, disease-infested jungles of the Amazon. For five years, under primitive conditions, he brought the Gospel of Christ-crucified to the Indians. Tropical fevers and beri-beri brought him to death's door. Physicians at first despaired of his life. When he had sufficiently recuperated he was ordered to a cool climate.

In 1915 he came to the United States to live with his brothers and sisters in New Bedford, Massachusetts. When he felt stronger he went to the monastery of the Friars of the Atonement, in Graymoor, New York, and there his health improved. The Very Reverend Paul James Francis, of "treasured memory," founder of the Atonement Friars, placed Father Cacella on the faculty of St. John's College.

Then came the call from the late Patrick Cardinal Hayes, Archbishop of New York, who wanted a pastor for the Portuguese people of the Archdiocese. Father Cacella came to New York and founded St. Anthony's Welfare Centre. Here poor and homeless men and indigent families are cared for each day, irrespective of race, color or creed. Often he himself has dressed the sores of these poor unfortunates.

It was at St. Anthony's that the spread of the devotion to Our Lady of Fatima was started in the United States. Since 1931 over 18,-000,000 copies of Father Cacella's popular brochure, "Fatima and the Rosary," have been published and distributed by him. His books include *Our Lady of Fatima, The Wonders of Fatima, The White Doves of Peace* and *El Mensaje de Fatima.* All bear the Imprimatur of His Eminence Francis Cardinal Spellman, Archbishop of New York.

Among his brochures are "The Story of Fatima" and "The Message of Fatima."

He is the editor of *Our Lady of Fatima Magazine, St. Anthony's Visitor,* and *A Luta,* the only Portuguese Catholic weekly in America.

In addition, he has produced a thirty-five millimeter and sixteen millimeter slide film strip entitled "The Story of Fatima," and an album of records for the picture.

Currently (1952) he is working on a book that will tell of his experiences in the Amazon.

Now in his seventieth year, this great promoter of the cause of Our Lady of Fatima and Padre of the Poor, as he is called by those who know of his work, still spreads the message of Fatima — *repent or be destroyed.*   J. E. S.

William Edward Campbell   1875–

Born in 1875, at Torquay, William Edward Campbell was educated at Reading School, the school of the famous pre-Reformation Abbey. He was received into the Catholic Church on his twenty-first birthday by Father William Gordon of the London Oratory in 1896. In the autumn of the same year he went on a visit to Downside, then a Priory, and was an Assistant Master there from 1905 until his retirement in 1931. During this time (1907) he married Amy Elizabeth Catherine Marchant. In 1940 he returned to Downside to help out during the war and taught until 1945.

In the atmosphere of Downside Abbey and the School and in the company of Benedictines like Cardinal Gasquet, Abbots Ford, Butler and Ramsay, "it was natural," he says "that my literary tastes were cherished to the full." A sermon preached by Abbot Gasquet, on the occasion of the beatification of the English martyrs in 1896, made a lasting impression on him. Among other things, the Abbot said no better work could be done for the service of the Catholic faith than to edit pre-Reformation documents dealing therewith. Mr. Campbell accepted the service and began to read on that period of history selecting for his first book a small edition of Roper's *Life of Sir Thomas More*. From that time on he gradually prepared himself by reading through and annotating the *Letters and Papers of Henry VIII's Reign*, edited by H. W. Brewer and James Gairdner.

Mr. Campbell's first literary work was done for *The Catholic World*, at the invitation of the late Father John Joseph Burke, C.S.P. (1875–1936), then editor, who had visited Downside. Two articles on Gilbert Keith Chesterton were his first contributions. Then followed ten articles on Sir Thomas More, and the latter subject proved to be his major literary interest in life. Cardinal Gasquet urged him to publish the book *Last Letters of Sir Thomas More* (1924) and wrote the introduction.

In 1926 Mr. Campbell made the acquaintance of Dr. A. W. Reed, then Professor of English and Literature at King's College, in the University of London, and Professor R. W. Chambers. The three of them, with Mr. Campbell as editor, projected a new folio edition in seven volumes of the 1557 Black Letter Volume of *The English Works of Sir Thomas More*. The first volume appeared in 1927 under the title *The Dialogue of Sir Thomas More Concerning Tyndale*, with an introduction by Professor Reed and an essay on "The Spirit and Doctrine of the Dialogue," by W. E. Campbell, the editor, and a modern version of the same by him. In 1931, the second volume, though the first in the order of More's 1557 edition, came out under the title *Earlier English Works*. It contained More's *Early Poems*, his translation of the life of Pico della Mirandola, *The History of Richard III*, and the unfinished meditation on the *Four Last Things*. This volume also contained an essay "William Rastell and More's English Works" by Professor Reed, and an essay by the late Professor R. W. Chambers "On the Authorship of the History of Richard III," which established once and for all More's own authorship of that work. Professor Reed added some philological notes and Mr. W. A. G. Doyle-Davidson some *Collation with Notes* thereupon, of which Mr. Campbell contributed the *Modern Version*.

Before the third volume was ready, the Second World War broke out, and further publication seemed unlikely. During the years, Mr. Campbell had amassed a good deal of material for the remaining five volumes. Much of this he used in his book *Erasmus, Tyndale and More*, published in 1949.

With the cessation of the war, and because of the favorable reception of the last book, work on the publication of the folio edition was resumed. Volumes three and four are now (1951) ready for the press. The remaining three volumes of the projected set of seven will be published as soon as possible.

More's Utopia and His Social Teaching is Mr. Campbell's other book, first given as lectures to the Catholic Social Guild at Oxford in 1929, and published in 1930.

Mrs. Robert Capes. See Angela Verne

Mrs. Marcel Carbotte. See Gabrielle Roy

Reverend Maurus Carnot, O.S.B.
1865–1935

In his biography of Father Maurus Carnot, Dom Odilo Zurkinden, O.S.B. of the Abbey of Disentis, Switzerland, remarks: "Few Catholic authors during the first decades of our century were better known and more popular than the Benedictine monk of Disentis in Switzerland, Dom Maurus Carnot. By his numerous writings, and hardly less through his lectures in various literary circles, where the peculiar charm of his humble personality was clearly revealed, he had made many and devoted friends."

Father Maurus Carnot was born on January 26, 1865, at Sammann, Switzerland, a small village in the valley of the world-famous Engadine, which borders on Tyrol. At baptism he received the names of John Rudolph. After attending grammar school in his native village, he made his higher studies at Schwyz. From there he went to the University of Innsbruck, where he took up philosophy and theology for three years. Military training at Chur followed, and when he was graduated, he entered, as a novice in the fall of 1885, the ancient Benedictine abbey of Disentis, which gradually rose to a new life. There he took vows on December 22, 1886, and was ordained on July 8, 1888. All through his life he revered his mother as a saint. He was never more happy than when he was with her.

For nearly five decades he taught in the monastic school, having begun to teach even before his ordination. He taught the classics, chiefly, besides German and history. The two latter subjects he continued to teach until his death, having given up Latin and Greek to younger confreres. Kindness, the essential trait of his noble soul, pervaded his teaching. He hoped to achieve through it more lasting results than through strictness. A fellow monk says of him: "He was a splendid instructor, endowed with a marvelous gift of communication, which inspired the students with great enthusiasm."

Besides teaching, Father Maurus devoted much time to the care of souls. He was zealous in his attention to the sick and the poor. His confessional in the Abbey Church attracted crowds. One of his penitents was Emperor Charles of Austria. He was also much in demand as a preacher and a lecturer, for he enjoyed the gift of presenting eternal truths in a simple and popular manner. And when he mastered the "rätoromanische" language, the idiom of his forbears, he was able to talk to his "Oberländern" in their own dialect as though he were one of them. In many towns and villages of Graubunden, as well as in the German parts of Switzerland, he lectured on the character of the Romansch people and on the beauty and richness of its idiom and literature.

It is due to his untiring efforts that on the occasion of a federal vote on February 20, 1938, the "Raeto-romansch" language was recognized as the fourth official language of Switzerland.

In his younger days he slept little. Often he worked through the whole night, because as prior, he had so much official business to do and there were so many knocks at his door during the day that he had very little time to write.

Besides writing poetry, Father Maurus also wrote novels and about sixteen plays. He wrote in two languages — German and Romansch. His compendious volume of German poems appeared in two editions. The Romansch poems, which were published in various newspapers and periodicals, were collected and edited posthumously in a small volume. His children's book, *Sigisbert im rätischen Tale*, was translated into English by Mary E. Mannix, under the title *A Pilgrim from Ireland*. Another novel, *Steinbock und Adler*, was likewise translated into English by Mary E. Mannix.

Among his other prose works are: *General Demont* (1906); *Wo die Bündnertannen Rauschen* (1913); *Der Landrichter* (1914); *Roswitha; Die Geschichte der Jörg Jenatsch* (1930). Additional plays are: *Placidus von Hohenrhätien* (1891); *Der Friedensengel* (1899); *Venantius* (1903); and *Franz Pizarro* (1903).   S. T.

Hans Carossa   1878–

The German novelist and poet, Hans Carossa, was born at Bad Tölz in Bavaria, Germany, in 1878. He studied medicine in Munich and Leipzig and practiced in Passau, Nuremberg, and Munich. He served as a physician in the German army during the last two years of World War I (1916–1918) but when he was wounded he was sent home. After the war he continued his medical practice in Munich, then returned to his birthplace in the country.

Carossa's first prose work, *Doktor Bürgers Ende* (1913), tells of a young physician who is driven to despair by his intense sympathy with the suffering of his patients. The autobiographic features of this work reappear in stronger outline in the novel, *Der Arzt Gion* (1931; Engl. tr., *Doctor Gion*, 1933), dealing with the material and moral disintegration that followed the German defeat. *Geheimnisse des reifern Lebens* (1936) is another novelistic narrative, largely introspective and abounding with psychological reflection. The following of Carossa's works are strictly autobiographical: *Eine Kindheit* (1922; Engl. tr., *A Childhood*, 1930); *Rumänisches Tagebuch* (1924; Engl. tr., *A Roumanian Diary*, 1929); *Verwandlungen einer Jugend* (1928; Engl. tr., *Boyhood and Youth*, 1930); *Führung und Geleit* (1933); and *Das Jahr der schönen Täuschungen* (1941). They are documents of the modesty, inwardness, and moral and intellectual integrity of the author.

Carossa is not only an author of the highest ethical resolve but, artistically, a master stylist in his prose works and a poet of high rank in his lyrics. The simplicity and at times austere beauty of his literary expression place him in a category all by himself, beyond the narrow confines of any "ism."

Carossa's most recent work is again autobiographical: *Ungleiche Welten* (Wiesbaden, 1951) gives a personal accounting of the twelve years the author spent under the Nazi regime, the period "when the German fate fulfilled itself" and when the life of the spirit "was condemned to a catacomb-existence." The work strikingly demonstrates "the powerlessness of man in the clutches of the 'kingdom of this world.'" The subject matter allows the author to make use of his training in scientific observation, in viewing the history of the political crimes of that sinister era as a graphic picture of psychopathology.

K. R.

Reverend John Carr, C.SS.R.
1878–

Father Carr has been numbered with Father Martindale, Alice Curtayne and Henri Ghéon, as one of those all too rare writers who have the gift of making the life of a saint an interesting story. Saints and Blessed of the Redemptorist Order are his usual subjects, and when it is remembered that in many ways their lives were without any compelling dramatic content his achievement is all the more remarkable. While the popularity of his biographies is, no doubt, largely due to the fact that he writes well, with charm, Irish humor, and a good sense of proportion, it is also possible to see it as a natural reaction against those purely historical lives which buried the sanctity of the saint beneath a mass of minute historical detail.

Father Carr's biographies are more simple, more direct. Where miracles are concerned, Father Carr, like Ghéon, is well aware that miracles are not everyday occurrences, but he believes that, unless there are any solid reasons for not crediting a saint with a particular miracle, to reject it only because it may seem improbable is illogical. This is the principle he followed in *To Heaven Through A Window*, his life of Saint Gerard Majella, his best and most ambitious work, published in 1946.

Born in Limerick city, Ireland, November 9th, 1878, he received his early education at the Jesuit college there and at a preparatory school run by the Redemptorists. In 1897 he entered the Redemptorist novitiate in Paris, was recalled to open the new Irish novitiate in Dundalk in 1898, before studying for the priesthood in England, Ireland and Belgium. After his ordination in 1903 he spent the first five years of his priestly life teaching. Then followed many years giving missions and retreats throughout Ireland. Towards the end of 1922 he went to Australia and while there his writing career began with the publication in 1925 of *Teresa of Lisieux: Truly a Lover*. Returning home to Ireland in 1927 he has combined writing with giving retreats ever since.

The list of his publications follows: *Venerable Joseph Passerat, C.SS.R.*, a translation from the French (1928); *Venerable Peter Donders, C.SS.R., Apostle of the Lepers*, a translation from the French (1930); *Saint Clement, C.SS.R., Patron of Vienna* (1939); *Christ is All* (1928); Italian version (1932), French version (1934); Irish version (1936); *Saint Maria Goretti, Martyr for Purity* (1948), Dutch version (1950), Irish version (1950); *By the Way, Do You Ever?* (1949); *Saint Jeanne de Lestonnac* (1950).
P. B. L.

Mary Jane Carr   1899–

Mary Jane Carr, the author of four books for boys and girls, laid the foundation for her writing of historical fiction in her seventh or eighth grade of grammar school. Finding history her most difficult study she made stories of her history lessons to arouse her interest and to fasten the events in her memory.

Born in Portland, Oregon, on April 23, 1899, the fourth child in a family of nine she was educated in the Portland public schools and then spent two years (1917–19) at St. Mary's (now Marylhurst) College for girls. At the age of eight, Miss Carr attempted to write her first poem. Her ambition was to be a poet like her favorite poet, Longfellow. She had written only eight lines when she was overcome with emotion. While she was in this state, her father came into the room and seeing the tears dropping on her unfinished "poem" asked for the cause of them. "I've been writing a poem," said Mary, "and it's terrible sad." Her father, an attorney, who had been a teacher in his youth, paying his way through the University of Michigan by tutoring, and who had read much poetry and prose from the classics, could find no cause for tears in the eight lines his daughter had written. Mary explained there was lots more to the poem, but "it is in my head and it's the part in my head that is sad."

After her two years in St. Mary's College, Portland, Oregon, Miss Carr went to work as a journalist. Mr. John O'Hara, her college history teacher, gave her her first position on his newspaper, the *Catholic Sentinel*, where she worked in all the departments from proofreading to editorial writing. She remained there for several years, as assistant editor. Of those years Miss Carr says: "A wonderful training school for a writer, I believe." Later she joined the staff of the *Sunday Oregonian* of Portland where she contributed a half page of children's verse and story to that paper for several years. Her first book, *Children of the Covered Wagon*, was first published serially in that paper. This book, a narrative of the Old Oregon Trail for boys and girls, has gone into many printings. It was a Junior Literary Guild selection; it was transcribed into Braille; it was published in French by Librairie Hachette, under the title *Sur La Piste de L'Oregon*, and in 1949 Miss Carr signed a contract with Walt Disney for a motion picture version of it.

Her next book, *Peggy and Paul and Laddy* (1936) was printed also by Blackie and Son, Ltd., London and Glasgow in 1937, and was transcribed into Braille. Her third book, *Young Mac of Fort Vancouver* (1940), which deals with the fur trade history was the choice of two national book clubs, Pro Parvulis and the Junior Literary Guild. It was transcribed into Braille. It was also chosen by the National Broadcasting Company for the radio program "Carnival of Books." The New York *Herald Tribune* selected it for its list "Twenty-five Books to Grow On," as one of 25 books which should be in every home library.

In 1941 Crowell published her book of verse for young children, *Top of the Morning*. Poems from this book appear in several anthologies including Macmillan's *Bridled With Rainbows* (1949), and Scott Foresman & Company's anthology for teachers, *Time For Poetry* (1949), and in several anthologies for teachers of children with speech difficulties.

Miss Carr's short story, "Apple Ranch," represents the state of Oregon in "Stories From the West," one of three books in a regional series, "Children of the U.S.A.," published by Silver Burdett Company, New York, and compiled by Marion Belden Cook. The Braille edition of the series is in seven volumes. It is being offered to eighty-three classes and schools for the blind in the United States and its territories. Miss Carr's story is set on an apple ranch in the Hood River Valley. The action evolves around two children and a mysterious worker who appears at picking time. A unique feature of the story is the inclusion of a brief history about the origin of the first apples grown in the Oregon Country over a century ago.

One of her poems, "When a Ring's around the Moon," opens the 1951 Giant Golden Book, *Elves and Fairies*.

Miss Carr is a member of Theta Sigma Phi, national honorary professional fraternity for women in journalism. She was elected one of Oregon's five "Women of Achievement" for 1950 by the Portland Alumnae chapter of Theta Sigma Phi. Since 1942 she is a member of the Gallery of Living Catholic Authors.   M. A. H.

Reverend Columba Cary-Elwes, O.S.B. 1903–

Catholic writers in England have, especially since the Newman movement, devoted much effort to present the Church's case to the English-speaking world. In no small degree the scholarly labors of the English Benedictines have aided this cause. One of the latest names added to this Benedictine roster is that of Dom Columba Cary-Elwes.

Dom Cary-Elwes was born in London in 1903, the son of Charles and Edythe (Parkington) Cary-Elwes. It is an old English family whose roots are partly Anglican and partly very Catholic, in that Anglican bishops and the great martyr, Saint Thomas More, are among the ancestors. Two of Dom Columba's uncles were priests, one a Jesuit and another a Benedictine, a cousin was the Catholic Bishop of Northampton, and his great uncle, Father Augustus Law, S. J. was the apostle of the Zambezi area in Africa. On his mother's side he belongs to the city of London, and his grandfather Sir Roper Parkington was a well-known figure there in the early days of this century.

Dom Cary-Elwes attended school with the Jesuits at the École St. Michel in Brussels from 1913 to 1914, and for eight years thereafter he was enrolled at Ampleforth School, the Benedictine Abbey school in Yorkshire. He played on the school rugby team two years, and was head of the school in his last year. After his graduation from Ampleforth he spent two years in the business world in France and in London. Recognizing a vocation to the religious life, he returned to his alma mater, Ampleforth Abbey, this time as a novice for the Order. In due course his superiors sent him to Oxford to complete his secular education and he took an honors degree in French and Spanish. Three more years were spent at Oxford studying theology with the Dominicans at Blackfriars; his professors were Father Bede Jarrett, Father Hugh Pope, Father Luke Walker and others.

While at Oxford he became closely associated with Father Leo O'Hea of the Catholic Social Guild and he helped to found a society among the undergraduates for the study of the social encyclicals.

After ordination to the priesthood in 1933, Dom Cary-Elwes returned to his abbey at Ampleforth and joined the teaching staff of the school. He taught the History of Dogma to the younger monks, and in the school his subjects were French, Spanish and Political Philosophy. During this period he wrote many articles for magazines, among them the *Clergy Review*, *Blackfriars*, the *Ampleforth Journal* and the *Sower*. He is of the opinion that his most useful article was one on the Young Christian Workers Movement which helped to restart them in England.

In 1937 he was appointed House Master of St. Wilfrid's House and,

Kadankavil C. Chacko   **86**

soon after, his first little book appeared, *The Beginning of Goodness.*
This is a guide for young men going into the world and has been widely
read in England, Ireland and America and has been translated into
Polish. In 1949, *A Simple Way of Love,* a remarkable spiritual book by
two Poor Clare nuns, was edited by Dom Cary-Elwes. In 1950 his first
major work came out, *Law, Liberty and Love,* a study of the Christian
idea of obedience and a call to a healing of the breach caused by the
Reformation.

Dom Cary-Elwes has two other works nearly completed. One of
them has occupied his leisure time for fifteen years and it is a history of
the missionary efforts to bring China into the Church. He traces his inspiration for this book to his great-uncle Father Law, whose deep desire
was the conversion of China. In his other work, dealing with the religions
of the ancient world, he is attempting to show to what extent Christ, in
St. Paul's words, is the "heir of all things."

Dom Cary-Elwes is a great friend of the historian Arnold Toynbee.
His interest turning now as it does to history may yet be of great significance in the presentation of hitherto neglected fields of history to
the Catholic English-speaking world.   K. M.

Mother Cecily. See M. M. Merrick

Kadankavil C. Chacko   1915–

In India it is the custom for Catholics to be
known by their Christian names. Hence the
name of this author is Chacko, the Malayalam
equivalent of Jacob. The family name is Kadankavil. The father's Christian name gives the
second initial. That explains how Kadankavil
Chacko Chacko becomes K. C. Chacko. Another
interesting detail in the matter of names is that
the first son is always named after his grandfather
and that the second son will be named after the mother's father. Daughters also are similarly named after the mothers of the father and mother
successively. The author's mother is Mary of Kudakkachira, Palai.

Chacko, the first son among the fifteen children of his parents, was
born on May 19, 1915. After studies at the local elementary school
Chacko entered the St. Thomas English High School, Palai, in 1923,
walking a distance of eight miles every day. "It was a terrible ordeal for
me, a boy of eight, to walk along lanes and streams, all alone sometimes
reaching home late at night, crying and terrified," he writes.

In 1930, he went to St. Berchmans' College, Changanacherry, about
thirty-three miles from home. There he was faced with the problem of
earning a livelihood. While at college he used to serve at Mass. The
priests in charge learned of his need and offered to help him. He was

employed to check up the fee register of the college and prepare the de-
faulters' list. This work paid his hostel dues. The government scholarship which he received was sufficient to cover the cost of tuition and
books. He completed the intermediate in March 1932, coming out first
class and first not only at his college, but in the whole Travancore State.
He won the Dr. Kurialacherry Gold Medal. That year (1932) he was
also awarded a silver medal for proficiency in Christian Apologetics by
the Catholic Educational Council, Madras, on an intercollegiate basis.

After winning the Grigg Memorial Scholarship, he entered the
Maharaja's College of Science, Trivandrum, for the B.A. course in
mathematics. The scholarship, as before, covered the cost of tuition and
books. Several priests helped him financially at this time. Later he took
up work as tutor to the children of some prominent Catholic officers of
the state. On successfully passing the examination with first class honors, he was selected by the government for studies at the College of
Engineering, Madras. He had to meet his expenses, but had no funds.
Then Mr. K. C. Thomas, Personal Assistant to the Chief Engineer,
who knew Chacko personally, suggested that he should marry his niece
and that the father-in-law would meet the expenses of his engineering
education at Madras. He accepted the proposal. On July 1, 1935, he
married Mary Thomas of Karippaparampil, Kanjirapally. "The marriage," he says, "was a rather hasty affair, but one over which I never
had any occasion to repent." According to the dowry system prevalent
in India, the father of the girl offered him something more than sufficient
to meet the cost of his studies at Madras. In March, 1937, he passed the
first examination, and in March, 1939, the bachelor of engineering examination with honors, both times securing the second rank at the
university.

During his college career he frequently won the first prize in public
speaking in college competitions and served as the editor of several college magazines. He secured a trophy at an All India Inter-University
debate also.

Then he joined the government service as a lecturer in the College
of Engineering, Trivandrum, and later he became the principal of the
Maharaja's Technological Institute, Trichur, affiliated with the University of Travancore, until in August, 1951, he was awarded a fellowship at the University of Notre Dame. He was granted a Fulbright
Travel Grant by the United States authorities, to cover the cost of his
passage to the United States and back to India.

In November, 1946, he was deputed by the Travancore Government for advanced technical training abroad. He spent one year in
England working for the firms of Dorman Long & Co., steel manufacturers and constructional engineers at Middlesbrough, and the British
Reinforced Concrete Engineering Co. at Stafford. During this time he
was also teaching at the County Technical College, Stafford, England.
In 1947, he visited Lourdes, where he was introduced to His Eminence
Cardinal Griffin, of England. Before he returned to India in December
of the same year, Mr. Eamon de Valera granted him a private interview
in Dublin in the Premier's office. In 1951 (September) Mr. Chacko came
to the United States on the full expense fellowship offered him by the

University of Notre Dame. He has been engaged to lecture at the University while doing his own postgraduate studies.

Chacko is greatly interested in Catholic Action. He writes regularly for the Catholic press and gives lectures on the platform as well as over the radio, which in India is under state control. On his way to the United States he visited Rome and had a special audience with the Holy Father on August 28, 1951. On this occasion he presented the Holy Father with copies of some of his books, including *Sister Alphonsa*. "The Sacred Congregation for the Oriental Churches in Rome," he writes, "had officially asked me to give them two copies of my book *Sister Alphonsa*. The Congregation has directed the Bishop of Palai to begin the diocesan process of enquiry into her life." On the same day he broadcast a talk to India over the Vatican Radio, a privilege rarely extended to a layman, and the authorities presented him with a record of his speech.

The special theme for most of his talks is the Franciscan ideal of poverty, which his family is trying to practice. Chacko, his wife and eldest son are Franciscan tertiaries. His youngest daughter and sixth child is named Elizabeth Alphonsa after the Clarist Sister whose biography he has presented to the world. He recollects with great satisfaction memories of his visits to Assisi and Lisieux, and particularly his conversation with Mother Genevieve of the Holy Face, the sister of the Little Flower.

Among his books the most popular one is *Sister Alphonsa* (1948). It is the biography of a saintly nun who died in 1946 at the age of thirty-six. She lived and died in a convent close to his home in India. His books in Malayalam, the language of the country, include: *Collected Letters of the Little Flower; Three Minutes a Day; Jesus for Children; Practical Imitation of Christ; May Devotions to the Blessed Virgin; Latin Mass; St. Bernard; Democracy and Peace; Chesterton's Conversion; Christmas and Good Friday* (Radio Speeches); *Inspiration of Christianity; Christ Today,* and *Social Life in England* (3 vols.).

M. A. H.

Reverend Pierre Charles, S.J.
1883–

The Belgian missiologist, philosopher and theologian, Father Pierre Charles, was born at Brussels, Belgium, on July 3, 1883. His father was a judge and a member of the highest court of Justice in Belgium. Pierre Charles lost his mother when he was ten.

He was educated at the Jesuit Collège Saint Michel in Brussels, and on September 23, 1899, entered the novitiate of the Jesuits at Tronchiennes, near Ghent, Belgium. He took his first vows on September 24, 1901. After studying philosophy at the Jesuit Facultés Notre Dame de la Paix at Namur, Belgium, he began his study of theology with the Jesuits at Louvain and completed his studies with the French Jesuits, then refugees, at Hastings, England, where he had among his professors the well known Jesuit Father L. de Grandmaison. Two years after his ordination in 1910, he made special studies in theology at Louvain and Paris (1912–13) concentrating on Kantianism. He was then appointed professor of dogmatic theology for the Jesuits at Louvain (not the University), just before the First World War. When Belgium was invaded by the Germans in 1914, he volunteered as military chaplain. After the siege of Antwerp, he was recalled by his superiors to become professor of theology and remained at this post until Belgium was invaded a second time by the Germans on May 10, 1940. Father Charles then went to France with his students of theology. Later he spent a few weeks in Portugal and then sailed to South America, where he remained until December, 1945, save for a short stay in Mexico. Traveling through Argentina, Chile, Bolivia, Ecuador and Uruguay he gave lectures and preached numerous retreats.

He returned to Belgium in 1946 and resumed his professorship at the Jesuit House of Studies and since 1948 is Dean of the Faculty of Theology.

In 1924 he became interested in mission work and regularly attended Missiology Weeks of Louvain, for which he is the permanent secretary since 1925.

In 1924 he founded Aucam (Aide universitaire catholique aux missions — Help of Catholic University Students to the Missions). A year later he started to give courses in missiology to the students of the university on the history of the missions, and on Japan. When in 1929 the Belgian government founded the Royal Colonial Institute, Father Charles was appointed a titular member of the political and moral section At the same time he was made a member of the International Colonial Institute, and took an active part in the sessions at Paris (1931), Lisbon (1933), and London (1936). He is a member of the Conseil d'administration of the Colonial University of Antwerp, Belgium, and teaches there on the history of the missions. He is president of the Comité de surveillance of the Museum of the Belgian Congo at Tervueren near Brussels and a member of the Institut des civilisations différentes. He inspired the foundation of the F.O.M.U.L.A.C. (Fondation médicale de l'Université de Louvain au Congo). At the Jesuit House of Studies for theology at Louvain, he founded a museum of pre-history and is developing there a museum of Congolese ethnography, and an important library of missiology.

In 1932 he was called to Rome to help found a faculty of missiology at the Gregorian University and to teach dogmatic missiology and the history of the missions.

He did extensive traveling in North Africa and visited the Belgian Congo twice. In 1933 he traveled three months in India and Ceylon. In 1939 he visited the United States of America and he keeps in close contact with that country, especially with the Jesuit weekly *America*, for which he writes a series of short spiritual notes on the Credo.

In 1950 he celebrated his golden jubilee of religious life. Still in good health he is very active and greatly interested in mission work. He loves flowers, fishing, cross-word puzzles and traveling. He is very witty and optimistic.

Since 1921 he has been writing regularly for the *Nouvelle revue theologique*, the Jesuit periodical published at Louvain. In 1922 he helped found the collection Museum Lessianum, which he began by his book *Prière de toutes les heures* which was translated into eight modern languages, including Japanese. The French edition, in 1938, had sold more than one hundred and twenty thousand copies. This book has been his most successful thus far. Its new English edition contains a foreword by Father Martindale, S.J., and retains the same title, *Prayer For All Time*. His other works are: *La robe sans couture; un essai sur la haute Eglise allemande* (1923); *Dossiers de l'action missionaire* (1926–29, second edition in 1939); *La prière missionaire* (1935); *Le problème des centres extra-coutumiers et quelques-uns de ses Aspects* (1936); *Japon moderne* (1937); *Cuestiones eternas de la vida* (1943) in Spanish; *La prière de toutes les choses* (1947); *Tractatus dogmaticus de sacramento poenitentiae* is ready for publication.

He wrote numerous booklets for Xaveriana, which he founded. He contributed the extensive article on "Kant and Kantisme" to the *Dictionnaire de théologie Catholique*, and the long essay on "Europe and the Far East" in Eyre's *European Civilization*. His numerous articles appear in several periodicals.   H. P.

Jean Charlot   1898–

All the writings of Jean Charlot spring from his experience and love of the fine arts and the desire to contribute to the better understanding of them. He has been influenced by the three languages that he speaks and writes — French, English, and Spanish — rather than by writers.

Born in Paris, France, on February 8, 1898, he was educated in that city and studied art at the Beaux Arts. He boxed for recreation, and was once schoolboy lightweight champion of France. Before coming to the United States via Mexico, he served in the First World War, but since then most of his life has been spent in the Americas, where he became a naturalized American citizen. In May, 1939, he was married to Zohmah Day. They have four children. At present the family is living in Honolulu, where Charlot is doing murals on ancient Hawaiian themes. His particular interest is, of course, art, particularly mural painting in the technique of true fresco. He painted some of the frescoes in the Escuela Preparatoria and Secretary of Education Building in Mexico City; among others he painted murals for the Church of St. Bridget, Peapack, New Jersey, the post office of McDonough,

Georgia, the Fine Arts Building, and the Journalism Building in Athens, Georgia. His prints and paintings are represented in the Phillips Memorial Gallery, Washington, D. C.; the New York Museum of Modern Art; the Metropolitan Museum; the Uffizi Gallery, Florence, and many other museums.

The books he illustrated include: the *Book of Christopher Columbus* by Paul Claudel; *Picture Book* by Paul Claudel; *Carmen* by Prosper Merimée for the Limited Editions Club; *The Sun, The Moon,* and *The Rabbit* by Amelia del Rio; *Portraits of the Reformation* by Hilaire Belloc; *Pageant of the Popes* and others.

Mr. Charlot was first draftsman for the Chichen Itza project of the Carnegie Institute of Washington. From 1926 to 1929 he was with the Carnegie Institute archaeological expedition to Chichen-Itza in Yucatan. He taught and lectured at the Art Students League; Columbia University; University of Iowa; Disney Studios; Brooklyn Art Institute; University of Georgia, Smith College and several other institutions. He is now stationed at the University of Hawaii.

His first publication was the manuscript of a lecture he gave in 1917 at the Guilde Notre-Dame, a Catholic association of Parisian artists.

His first book, *The Temple of the Warriors,* was written in collaboration with Earl and Ann Morris and it was published in 1929 by the Carnegie Institute of Washington. It treats of Mayan archaeology. In 1939 *Art from the Mayans to Disney* was published by Sheed and Ward and is now out of print. A sequel to this volume, *Art-Making from Mexico to China,* was published by the same firm in 1950. The frescoes he painted in Georgia were published in book form by the University of Georgia Press in 1944, with a commentary by the artist himself. His latest book is the *Dance of Death* (1951). It is a collection of drawings and captions about death and the manner in which it visits various people. In preparation by the Stanford University Press is his book, *Mexican Mural Renaissance,* written with the help of a Guggenheim Fellowship in 1946–47.

For the September 15, 1951, issue of *The Saturday Review of Literature* he contributed the article "Painting and Revolution."

Jean Charlot does all the illustrating for *Sheed and Ward's Own Trumpet,* a publication which contains news and reviews of their books.

M. A. H.

Bohdan Chudoba   1909–

Bohdan Chudoba is the elder son of Francis Chudoba, one time lecturer in King's College, London, and Professor of English Literature in Masaryk University, Brno, Czechoslovakia. Bohdan Chudoba is one of the few Slavonic historians who have defied both the Nazi and the Communist doctrines and have stuck to the Christian and Catholic tradition of their people.

Born at Brno (then in Austria-Hungary, now in Czechoslovakia) in 1909, he was educated in Masaryk University in Brno and completed his graduate studies in the University of Vienna and in the Royal University of Madrid. He holds the Ph.D. degree of the Masaryk University and the Ph.D. and Litt.D. degrees of the Royal University of Madrid. The desire to get acquainted with the sources of European history led him to extensive research work in the Spanish General Archives in Simancas and in the Secret Archives of the Vatican as well as in the archives of Prague, Paris, Vienna and several other large cities.

At first, medieval history was his main field of interest. He has written several studies concerned with the great religious revival in Bohemia of the 14th and 15th centuries. To write a book on that subject is still his ambition. Soon, however, his research work in the archives of the ancient castle of Roudnice in Bohemia led him to studies devoted to the epoch of the "Spanish preponderance" in Europe in the 16th and 17th centuries.

"I did not have much luck," says the Czech historian. "Some of my shorter papers on Spanish imperialism appeared in various Czech reviews as well as in the *Bulletin of the Spanish Academy of History* and in the *Mitteilungen der Oesterreichischen Institute fuer Geschichtsforschung*, but the book in which I have reached my main conclusions, *The Spaniards on the White Mountain*, had been confiscated by the Nazis in 1939 before it left the printer's office. A new edition appeared in 1945 and sold very well, but in 1948, according to a decree of the Communist government, all public libraries in Czechoslovakia had to destroy their copies. During the spring of 1952, an English book on a similar subject, *Spain and the Empire*, will be published by the University of Chicago Press."

The general aspects of Slavonic history have been another of his fields of interest. As Professor of Modern History in the Franciscan "Studium Catholicum" in Prague he used to study it in special courses with his students. A book on Czech history, *The Past and the Present*, published in Prague in 1946 proved a best seller — until, as all his other works, it was confiscated by the Communist authorities.

As educator — he started teaching in 1937 — he had to face problems concerning the philosophy of history and philosophy in general. In this respect, the spirit of Central European education had been particularly pagan. Dr. Chudoba's first book in this field, *On History and Progress*, a collection of essays, had been written and published before the war. After having experienced the practical results of both the Nazi and the Marxist concepts of history, he developed his ideas into a major work, finished in 1950 and published in the autumn of 1951 in this country under the title of *The Meaning of Civilization*. The Christian concept of history as opposed to the positivist one, the heritage of the arrested civilizations, and the aspects of the Christian civilization are the subjects of the three parts of this concisely written, but erudite and stimulating book.

In the meantime he had to quit the secluded life of study which he always preferred. Having been ousted by the Nazis from his teaching occupation, he edited his late father's collected works, went into underground hiding, served in the Russian Army at the close of the war, helped to revive the Catholic intellectual life in Czechoslovakia after 1945, was jailed by the Communist police, but elected almost immediately afterwards to the Czechoslovak National Assembly, and, finally, had to leave his country on skis, in February, 1948, to escape deportation to Siberia. He is now Associate Professor at Iona College, New Rochelle, New York.

He was married in Paris in 1949 and has one daughter. His hobby is poetry and story writing. His plans for the future are focussed on a history of the world as seen from the Christian point of view of history as a drama and also on a return to medieval studies.

Reverend André Combes   1899–

Hesitant at first whether to make music his career (at the age of sixteen he was the organist of the cathedral), or science and literature, Abbé Combes finally chose the priesthood.

Born October 29, 1899, at Perigueux (Dordogne) France, the son of a director of the normal school, he studied at the Ferdinand Foch School (Rodez). Influenced by a zealous priest, Abbé Paul Carnus, to consider a higher vocation, he entered the Seminary of Saint Sulpice in 1917. Ordained a priest in 1924, this son of an intellectual father had no other wish than to become a country curé. He had no other ambition than to spend his life in convincing the most backward peasants that God deserves to be truly loved.

He did not refuse, however, an opportunity to study for the doctorate of theology. He matriculated at the Catholic Institute of Toulouse, which boasted such professors as Louis Saltet, Ferdinand Cavallera and Louis Desnoyers. His thesis was on "les Vies anciennes de saint Martial, et l'histoire de leur interpretation." Doubtless he entered upon a road from which he could never draw back. Then he was held up for some time by illness. With the recovery of his health he prepared for his licentiate at the Catholic Institute of Paris and at the Sorbonne. At the École des Hautes-Études religieuses, he devoted himself to the history of doctrines and dogma, a field so admirably cultivated by his master Étienne Gilson, whose ardent disciple he became. After graduating from this school with a thesis on "Un témoin du Socratisme chrétien au XV⁰ siècle: Robert Ciboule," he began to contribute to the progress of studies on Christian spirituality by doing research on the famous chancellor of the University of Paris, John Gerson, the period least-known of the Western Middle Ages; the end of the 14th and the beginning of the 15th centuries. Most of these studies on Gerson he published in the *Archives d'histoire doctrinale et littéraire du Moyen Âge*, of which he was soon to assume the co-directorship with Gilson and Father Thery, O.P., and later in the *Revue du Moyen Âge latin*. Then his principal books began to appear. In 1940 he brought out *Jean Gerson commentateur dionysien (Pour l'histoire des courants doctrinaux à l'Université de Paris à la fin du XIV⁰ siècle)* — a study of the relationship between theology and mysticism. In 1942 appeared *Jean de Montreuil et le chancelier Gerson (Pour l'histoire des rapports entre théologie et humanisme en France au début du XV⁰ siècle)*. In 1945 in the collection *Études de théologie et d'histoire de la spiritualité*, which he founded in 1943, the first volume was published and in 1948 the second, under the title: *Essai sur la critique de Ruysbroeck par Gerson*. In these enterprises having discovered, in the unedited commentary of John de Ripa on the *Sentences*, some fragments attributed to Saint Anselm, he published in 1943 what is, perhaps, the most unique of his works: *Un inédit de saint Anselme? Le "De unitate divinae essentiae et pluralitate creaturarum" d'après Jean de Ripa*.

In 1938 the fame of his researches opened for him the doors of the National Centre of Scientific Research. Soon, through the perfection of his method and the abundance of his publications he became "Master of Research." His method consisted in applying, to the problems relating to human science, principles drawn from microphysics and to seek reality by exhaustive exegesis and to reveal to himself his paths of intelligibility. An unforeseen event, obliging him to extend his method to a new field, led him to other discoveries, the finest of all. For in 1943 the Catholic Institute created for him a chair of history of Christian spirituality. Wanting to teach there comparative mysticism, he extended his research from the study of spirituality during the Middle Ages to the study of the spiritual teaching of Thérèse of Lisieux, whom Pope Pius X called the greatest saint of modern times. This was to embark on a great adventure. Submitted to the microanalytic and genetic method, texts universally known revealed unsuspected treasures. Working from the Carmel of Lisieux, the repository of unedited texts, he published his book, *Introduction à la spiritualité de sainte Thérèse de l'Enfant-Jésus;* and then the complete *Lettres* of the Saint, *l'Amour de Jesus chez sainte Thérèse; Sainte Thérèse et la souffrance; Le problème de l'Histoire d'une âme; Lisieux de Ste Thérèse capitale de l'Espérance; Ste*

Thérèse de l'Enfant-Jésus-Contemplation et apostolat and *Itineraire spirituel de Ste Thérèse*, which will make the study of this subject complete. Thus informed of the true Theresian doctrine, he was able "to safeguard Christian people against evident errors concealed in *La Petite sainte Thérèse* written by Maxence van der Meersch, and to point out in the Austrian magazine, *Der Grosse Entschluss*, the omissions in the monumental work of Ida Görres."

Representing the Carmel of Lisieux at the first International Congress of the Holy Winding Sheet of Turin in Rome in May, 1950, Father Combes had the honor of receiving a special blessing from the Holy Father for his works, especially for *Bibliothèque de Mystique comparée*.

He gave a number of conferences while in Rome on Saint Thérèse. The last conference in the presence of the Promotor of the Faith at the Gregorian University gained him the thanks of Monsignor Natucci: "You make us understand better why we canonized her. She is greater than we thought."

Upon his return to Paris, he began to prepare a critical edition of the *Determinations of John de Ripa* for the Corpus General des Philosophes français, and also a critical edition of the *De mystica Theologia of Gerson* for Thesaurus Mundi; for the collection, Grandes spirituels (Albin Michel), a *Gerson* and a *Thérèse of Lisieux*. He compiled, with the heliographer, Lescuyer, of Lyons, three albums, Lourdes, Bernadette, Lisieux, in which he condensed the real lessons of these spiritual entities. As a collaborator for the *Revue d'Histoire de l'Église de France*, *La Pensée catholique*, the *Dictionnaire de spiritualité*, the *Enciclopedia cattolica*, this chaplain of St. Anne's Retreat House in Neuilly does not hesitate to state that he owes all his technical rigor, and his fecundity to the fervor of his religious life and to the scientific loyalty which imposed on him the worship of the Incarnate Word.

P. J. Kenedy and Sons has published the English translation of his *Introduction (Spirituality of St. Thérèse)* and of *l'Amour de Jésus (The Heart of St. Thérèse)*. Sheed & Ward of London has published the English translation of the *Lettres de sainte Thérèse*.   K. M.

Francis X. Connolly   1909–

Francis X. Connolly was born on June 24, 1909, in New York City, the son of Thomas F. Connolly and Lillian Flynn Connolly. After graduating from Our Lady of Mercy Grammar School and Xavier High School he entered Fordham College, then called St. John's College. In 1930 he received his A.B., and his A.M. and Ph.D. degrees in 1933 and 1937 respectively. In 1940 he married Mary T. Kennedy.

Most of his teaching has been done at Fordham College, where he started as instructor in 1930, moving on to assistant professor in 1933.

From 1938 until his promotion in December, 1951, to the rank of full professor, he was associate professor and chairman of the English Department.

From 1943 to 1946 he was in the United States Naval Reserve. After his indoctrination (February to April 1943) at Quonset Point, Rhode Island, he joined the staff of the Commander of the Naval Air Intermediate Training Command, Corpus Christi, Texas, as officer-in charge of Enlisted Training and Classification Control Officer. From September, 1945, to January, 1946, he served in the executive office of the Secretary of the Navy, Washington, D. C., as educational adviser and acting project control officer in the Navy Photographic Service. The offices he holds are Associate Editor of *Spirit;* member of the editorial board of The Catholic Book Club; member of the Board of Directors of the Catholic Poetry Society and chairman of the board from 1936 to 1948. He has been elected to the Gallery of Living Catholic Authors and is a member of The Catholic Commission on Intellectual and Cultural Affairs.

His publications are: *From the Four Winds* (co-editor, 1939); *The Story of Fordham* (1941); *To an Unknown Country*, a Bibliography (co-author, 1942); *Drink from the Rock*, (co-editor, 1944); *Return to Poetry* (co-author, 1947); *Literature: The Channel of Culture* (1948); *Stories of Our Century by Catholic Authors* with John Gilland Brunini (1949); *Give Beauty Back* (1950).

He has contributed to *Spirit*, organ of the Catholic Poetry Society of America, *Thought, America, The Commonweal, The Catholic World, Best Sellers,* and other reviews. M. A. H.

Sister Mary Consolata, S.M. (Consolata Carroll)

Sister Mary Consolata (Alice Viola Carroll) was born in Rome, New York, the eldest of four children of Jeremiah H. and Alice Flanigan Carroll. She attended the Rome public schools and was graduated from the Rome Free Academy. She says, "I spent the formative years of my life close to the convent of the Sisters of the Holy Names. In the groves and on the waters that adjoined the convent grounds I shared the play of the young boarders under the supervision of these good nuns. The charm and the inevitable refining influences of that period left a lasting impression on my mind."

She completed her academy courses at a time when fathers believed a woman's place was in the home. It was a far-sighted mother's endeavor to make her daughter not only a good wife and mother, but also capable of coping with the world if thrown upon her own resources. Home Economics was a new field of education; many teachers were giving up their regular positions and turning to the specialized branches of this subject. So, due to the implied logic of better equipping her for the home and relieving the drain on father's pocketbook, since mother's relatives lived in Brooklyn, Viola was sent to Pratt Institute.

At the end of three years, she applied through the Institute for a position in a private school. She was recommended to Mount Saint Mary's College in North Plainfield, New Jersey. After four years of teaching in this institution, the Motherhouse of the Sisters of Mercy, she became a novice in the Order. The details of her early days in Rome, New York, and those of her experiences at Mount Saint Mary's College before and after becoming a nun form the subject matter of her two books: *Pray Love, Remember* and *I Hear in My Heart*, both of which were selections of the Catholic Literary Foundation for June, 1947, and June, 1949, respectively.

Her subsequent study was in the field of English. She was graduated from Fordham University with a Master of Arts degree. She spent a summer at Breadloaf School of English in Vermont and attended the Writers' Conference there. She studied several summers at Columbia University under the supervision of Professor Donald L. Clark and Miss Martha Foley, who conducted classes in various forms of writing for publication, particularly the short story. She says: "I became interested in creative writing because my pupils were; in order to help them, I took courses in writing. When I had finished a story that I thought would interest a student desiring to write, my friendly critic advised: 'You do not have to write about what your students know; they can do that. You must write about the things you know.' That remark was the beginning of my literary life. I wrote a series of stories based on my childhood experiences, having only one purpose in mind, to tell these with their original emotion of importance and for the sheer pleasure of releasing feelings that had been pent up for years awaiting this outlet."

Sister Consolata by this simplicity of purpose succeeded, as she readily admits, far beyond her own dreams and the reviews which commend her work are a testimony to her original purpose. The *Catholic News Letter* in referring to *Pray Love, Remember*, said: "Perhaps the greatest value of these simple reminiscences lies in the utter naturalness with which religion is depicted as a part of Catholic family life. A further interesting feature is the quietly natural way in which the young girl's vocation to a religious life develops. Younger readers will not have to fight shy of certain sentimentality or preciousness which too often throws an uncomfortable aura around those who are particularly devoted to our Lord in the life of the cloister." Ernestine Evans writing in the *Herald Tribune* said in part: "By the law of averages, the young teacher should have married and had a family. She was always a little aware of mystical experiences, and always a striver after perfection, sensitive to fears, eager with an almost unconscious and natural piety. She was always a good girl, devoted to her father even when she argued with him and chose her own course. Her final choice to take her vows as a nun comes to seem to the reader as normal as her wedding would have been; for had she married, she would have brought to the founding of her family the same dedication, the same vows in perpetuity. And the manner in which she writes of her decision, the way she remains in character, subject to a religious experience and a religious discipline without alienating, in the end, her family, is set down with real skill. We are so accustomed to psychological dramatics in accounts of religious crises, and such welters of political violence, that this story largely owes its appeal to its lack of them. This is a valid account of one woman's experience and her amiable appreciation of the boundaries of the world inhabited by adolescent girls."

"I always enjoyed being dramatic," Sister Consolata recalls. "I delighted to tell children I was born in Rome, and when they had barely recovered from that surprise, I added that I was baptized in St. Peter's. Rarely do listeners hear good of themselves and I was no exception. As a child I delighted to eavesdrop on my elders, and on one of those occasions I heard my mother complain to her dear friend: 'Phoene, you have no idea how Viola tantalizes me; and I get no satisfaction from punishing her. There is not a thing that I can deprive her of but that she finds something else to amuse her.' This inability to be chastised according to mother's formula, I believe, is the basis or inspiration for my having become a writer. The wit to find a substitute for a doll, toy, or game was exciting; to draw upon one's imagination to know what to play if forbidden the usual pastimes of dressing up in long clothes, playing with dolls, floating paper boats in the bathtub, blowing bubbles, or keeping store was equally challenging. I conceived an entire set of rooms by pasting together several folds of newspaper and covering these with new wrapping paper begged at the grocer's. They became stiff enough to stand against the chairs. I drew a floor and wall line and then set up my pictures and furniture. Other little girls never cut out paper dolls that were seated. Frequently, they wore the most beautiful dresses. I devised the idea of matching color sets. All the ladies standing or seated who wore suits or coats of the same color were arranged together. When, as hostess, I invited a paper doll to remove her coat or cape, I selected one in the same color dress to supplant her. As I continued the conversation and asked her to be seated, as I also would have to be, there was a scurry for two seated dolls wearing the proper colors. And this process of exchanging garments went on for hours if I had decided upon holding a large reception. This creative impulse, my fondness for books, and the aid of a photographic memory can be said to be the basis of any talent which I may have."

Sister Consolata spent the summer of 1950 abroad, six weeks of it at Oxford University enjoying a tutorial experience in the contemporary novel, and poetry. She also traveled in Switzerland, France, England, and Italy. There are several books waiting for that moment that will not longer allow them to remain mere dwellers of the mind. One is a collection of short stories; another is the sequel to *I Hear in My Heart;* and still another, a companion piece to *Pray Love, Remember* based on farm life in upstate New York. At present Sister Consolata is a member of the English department of Georgian Court College in Lakewood, New Jersey, where the routine of teaching Freshman composition and reading the weekly theme obviously claims first place. For it is the wheat among this chaff that is material out of which may come a writer.

Reverend Gustave Léon Marie Constant   1869–1940

For thirty-two years Abbé Gustave Constant taught at the Institut Catholique in Paris, France. Despite his poor eyes, especially in his declining years, he was an indefatigable worker. He told a fellow priest: "It is the only way I can work for the Church." His writings deal chiefly with the sixteenth and the first half of the nineteenth centuries.

Abbé Constant was born on January 28, 1869, in Saint-Laurent-sur-Sèvre (Vendée) France. He was ordained a priest in April, 1893. After obtaining a diploma in the higher studies of history and geography, he studied to become a doctor of literature. He pursued further studies at the École française de Rome. From Rome he was sent on a scientific mission to Austria and Spain by the Ministry of Public Education. Called to the University of Liverpool, he became a Fellow and Professor of Modern Ecclesiastical History. From November, 1908, on until his death, he taught Church History (modern times) at the Catholic Institute in Paris.

During World War I he was a titular chaplain of the navy, and was wounded. In June, 1917, he received the Cross of the Legion of Honor. He died at Cannes on April 19, 1940. In his will he bequeathed his books and papers to the Catholic Institute of Paris.

With the exception of *Histoire de L'Église de France sous le Consulat et l'Empire* (1928), the works of Abbé Constant deal principally with two great subjects — the relation of the Council of Trent to Germany and the Anglican Schism. On the first subject he produced in 1910, *Étude et catalogue critique de documents sur le Concile de Trent* (Archives des Missions scientifiques t.18°); in 1922, *La légation du Cardinal Morone près de l'empereur et le Concile de Trente,* published under the auspices of the Académie des Sciences morales et politiques, and in 1923 two large volumes, with footnotes and references: *Concession à L'Allemagne de la Communion sous les deux espèces,* a study on the beginnings of the Catholic reform in Germany, 1348–1621. He chose a personage (Morone) and an episode through which aspects the Catholic reform became a "little" Counter-Reformation. In 1930 appeared *La Reforme en Angleterre.* The English translation by Canon R. E. Scantlebury was published by Sheed & Ward in 1934 under the title, *The Reformation in England, I, The English Schism, Henry VIII (1509–1547).* Hilaire Belloc writes in the Preface: "A great interest attaches to this book. It is the history of that opening part of the English Reformation which can only be called with strict accuracy 'The Schism,' for its characteristic was not an effort at doctrinal heresy but rather an effort to set up a National Church identical or virtually identical in morals and doctrine with the universal Church and yet separated from the unity of the latter. That was the distinctive note of what happened in the latter part of the reign of King Henry VIII. It was not a Protestant movement such as was taking place everywhere throughout the rest of Europe. It was not a popular movement, such as was to take place a little later in Scotland. It was not an aristocratic movement such as took place in France; it was purely political, dynastic, and wholly due to the initiative of the king, and, urging the king, Anne Boleyn. . . . It did, indeed, deny the authority of the Pope, but it not only did not deny but fiercely affirmed Transubstantiation, the Mass, the whole of the sacramental system. . . . Let it be said in conclusion that this fine book is typically French in the multitude and accuracy of its evidence. The author has read everything, used everything and checked every date and name with the most industrious accuracy. It is in the best tradition of the oeuvre documentée which is the chief point, in historical study, of the University of France."

Volume Two of this work, *L'introduction de la Réforme en Angleterre, Edouard VI, 1547–1553* (1939), was translated into English by E. I. Watkin and published by Sheed and Ward in 1942 under the title: *The Reformation in England, II, Introduction of the Reformation into England, Edward VI (1547–1553)*. It discusses such points as "The Church of England at the Accession of Edward VI," "Protector Somerset and the Beginning of the Religious Revolution," "The Church of England Advances on the Road Towards Lutheranism," "The First Prayer Book," "Somerset's Fall," "Warwick and the Progress of the Religious Revolution," "The Church of England Turns Toward Calvinism," "The Second Prayer Book," "The Moderate Bishops and the Religious Revolution," "Cranmer and the Reformation," and "England Protestant."

Abbé Constant had in view two other volumes, *La restauration du catholicisme en Angleterre, Marie Tudor (The Catholic Restoration, Mary Tudor)* and *L'Établissement definitif de la Réforme en Angleterre, Elisabeth (The Establishment of the Reformation in England, Elizabeth)*.

He had promised a volume for *Histoire de l'Église* by A. Fliche and V. Martin, but death prevented him from fulfilling it. He collaborated on the *Dictionnaire d'histoire et de géographie ecclesiastique*, published by Louvain University. He contributed articles to *La Revue Historique, La Revue des Questions Historiques, Revue D'Histoire Diplomatique, La Revue D'Histoire Ecclésiastique, Revue De L'Histoire D'Église de France, Downside Review, Revue Hebdomadaire, Revue De Paris, Correspondent* and other periodicals.   M. A. H.

Fred Copeman 1907–

In appraising the hard, danger-filled life of Fred Copeman, author of *Reason in Revolt*, one has to keep well in mind that writers are of every genre, and that social philosophers, too, are of every genre. Also one is well advised to anticipate strange developments in lives in which juvenile grouches were profound. "Very early in life," Fred tells us, "I began to see and rebel against the inequalities and injustices in human society. I saw the difference between the life of the master (of Wangford Workhouse) and that of the inmates; to me, a lad of ten, the lavish meals served to him and his family in their private dining room, the ease and comfort of their surroundings, was a contrast to the poor food, scanty and badly cooked, the stone floors, drab bare walls and corridors and the plain hard furniture and tiny metal beds considered suitable for the inmates."

Twenty years of fighting, revolting, protesting was a sequel to this early grouch of Fred's. A violent quarrel after that with a fellow communist had momentous consequences. Fred describes the quarrel: "Words seemed out of place. I tore into him like a thunderbolt. He finished up unconscious. When he regained consciousness he rushed to the window, screaming, 'Murder! Help!' We dragged him back into the room and closed the window." This quarrel was but a little incident in the career of a hefty labor leader, prize fighting for social decency, and blundering his way into truth and honor.

Initiated into the art of leadership during the mutiny of British sailors at Invergordon (1931) in which he took part, he later led hunger marches and riots in England, and commanded 16th and 54th Battalions of the Brigada Internationale during the Spanish Civil War. Then, when Hitler's bombs fell on London, he led the citizens to safety in dugouts and shelters and organized protective measures for them. He was still an extreme leftist, but the day came when, enraged and disgusted at the technique of the Communists in England and elsewhere, he renounced his membership in the Party and led (and still leads) British Trades Unionists against them. Conquering his own personal doubts and pride, he has, with God's grace, led himself into the Catholic Church, and into a discipline that hitherto had been wanting in his life. "The beauty of the Church is that it gives the teaching of one God, whilst enabling and in fact demanding that individuals be masters of their own soul and responsible for the actions they take."

Still believing that "socialism is beautiful and practical" and still working towards social progress, Fred Copeman finds that "in my political work . . . my Christian experience has given me a fresh dynamic, to understand politics as morality enlarged and the Christian expression of the art of government." "I can imagine," he continues, "that many people will wonder why I, once a Communist, should become a Catholic, most of them assuming that Catholicism is politically reactionary. A study of the history of the Church will show that throughout the ages it has played its part in the struggle to build a system of universal education, and none will deny that this has been the foundation stone in the progress of democracy as we know it. . . . In my opinion no documents show a clearer understanding of the needs and aspirations of the working man than the two encylicals, *Rerum Novarum* and *Quadragesimo Anno.* . . . The Communist Manifesto of Karl Marx has nothing positive to give which cannot be found in one or other of them. Above all, they do not rely on inspiration through hate.''

Fred Copeman was born in Wangford Union, a workhouse near Beccles (Suffolk, England), in 1907. His mother was ''a little lady, thin and frail, and almost totally deaf. She seemed unhappy. She always seemed to be discussing what she would do when her ship came home.'' He had a younger brother, George, but had no knowledge whatever of his father. The workhouse was drab, a sad place for a youngster. ''Life was a continuous repetition of work, sleep and funerals. I could never make out why so many people had to die.''

When Fred was nine he was sent to work on the farm attached to the Union. He made friends among the animals, especially with a cow called Dixie. ''Dixie seemed to take a special liking to me. I expended much energy in keeping her clean. At one time I even got to the stage of polishing her horns.'' Then a tramp, Sam, an old sailor, gave him a mongrel dog, Bonny, for himself. ''He was as ugly as sin and full of fleas.'' ''But,'' says Fred, ''many a happy day I spent in the fields with Bonny . . . he was the truest friend of my early days.''

Fred's first big fight was at Watt's Naval Training School to which he went after leaving the Union. ''Watt's'' he says, ''was a wonderful place and I was proud to belong to it . . . nothing but good can be said of it or of any of the other branches of Dr. Barnardo's Homes.'' But at Watt's he fell out with another lad, Dingy Bell, who was umpiring a cricket match. ''A fight began which was stopped by one of the instructors. Dingy and I renewed our battle after the match, continued it after each meal, or whenever time could be found. This went on for some seven or eight days, the biggest part of the school attending most sessions. . . . The fight ended through Mr. Stokes getting me away and giving me a lecture on sportsmanship. I have always found it hard to lose, and always remember his final words, 'You've got plenty in you, but you'll never do anything until you learn to be humble.' Both Dingy and I were glad to call off the fight. We both had black eyes, split lips and crocked thumbs. We were so battered we couldn't eat or sleep for some time.''

In the Navy Fred had all the travel and experience of ''shore leave'' that is the lot of every British tar. He was a boxing champion and a well-known footballer. When, in 1931, at Invergordon a mutiny over pay-cuts broke out he was called on to lead the men on his ship. He made speeches and then organized the men. In the end the ''cuts'' were called off, but Fred found himself discharged.

Soon we find Fred Copeman joining the Communist party and leading the extremist labor wing in London. Next we find him fighting in Spain, as a member of the British Brigade. He fought at Jarama and Brumetti, and was seriously wounded. While in the Brigade he resented the political activities of the Communists who cared less for the interests of Spain than for the aggrandizement of their party. With them it was "All for the Party." Fred found them scheming and heartless. In particular Fred resented the Communist effort to introduce capital punishment for disciplinary offenses. To this he would never agree.

When the war was over he returned to London, still a member of the party but much disillusioned over its *aims*. His lack of loyalty was noticed and he was sent to Moscow, on a visit, to be reindoctrinated. This visit resulted in further disillusionment. At Moscow he had seen La Passionaria, the famous woman leader of the Spanish Reds, ignored and neglected. The Kremlin no longer found any use for her. "I expected to find her on the stage at the Bolshoi Theatre, holding the hand of Stalin, and being introduced as one of the greatest living Communists. I found her alone in a little room closely guarded by units of the Red Army. . . ."

Fred Copeman's work in London in connection with the air raids won him the respect and gratitude of important citizens and after the war he was decorated with the Order of the British Empire. Returning to Trade Union and Local Government work, he soon became President of Lewisham Trades Council, and later stood as Labor Candidate for Parliament for North Lewisham.

It was during the air raids that his thoughts turned towards the Catholic Church. He had never given up a certain faith in "a greater Being," nor had he ever been quite convinced that man is "complete unto himself." In his inner mind he believed in immortality and that once again, somehow, somewhere, he would meet his lost friends Wally Tapsall and Sandy Duncan. Then, on his staff controlling the deep shelters of bombed-out London, a Mrs. Margot Burridge, a devout Catholic, won his respect by her courage and tenacity. She began to talk religion to him, and with her husband took him to various Catholic churches. Next came his talks with Father Martindale, S. J. which continued for over a year and resulted in his reception into the Church and his First Communion at Farm Street, at Christmas Midnight Mass, 1946. With his wife Kitty and his three daughters, Diane, Barbara, and Mary, he lives in Lewisham, London S.E.

Of Fred Copeman's one and only published work, *Reason in Revolt* (1948) Father Martindale in a review says: "this rugged and red-blooded book is bound to create a deep impression whether or not each reader agrees with every one of its sentiments or opinions. And it has made one man at any rate — the reviewer — examine his conscience pretty seriously."   E. B. B.

Reverend Frederick Charles Copleston, S.J. 1907–

Popular interest in philosophy begins, and too often ends, in the lives that great philosophers lived. At most this interest gives an inkling to the significance of thinking as such. Those who dig a little deeper compare and contrast systems of thought, and here we have a healthy initiation into philosophy. To go further one pries into the development of philosophy and into its relations with other cultural elements.

This line of study, this 'Philosophy of the history of philosophy,' is the chosen field of Father Frederick Copleston. "Reflection on the historical development of philosophy," he writes, "and on its relations with other cultural elements opens up general philosophical problems of great interest and throws a light on the nature of philosophy and its cultural and spiritual functions."

Father Copleston's writings have covered much ground. First he wrote of Nietzsche, then of Schopenhauer, then of the ancient and medieval philosophers, and lastly of existentialism. He regards himself as an historian of philosophy rather than as a philosopher, though he recognizes that one can scarcely be the former without adopting a more or less definite position in regard to philosophy itself. He looks upon himself as a Thomist, in a broad sense; but he is convinced that it is foolish to suppose that philosophical thought reached the completion of its development in the thirteenth century. In particular, he says, "the Thomists are now faced with the task of examining anew the nature, function and method of metaphysics. This must be done with an open mind and with a full understanding and appreciation of the difficulties raised by modern anti-metaphysicians. From the philosophic standpoint a mere repetition of St. Thomas is useless."

Father Copleston was born in Taunton, Somerset (England) in 1907. His father, F. S. Copleston, was a former Chief Judge of Lower Burma. After elementary schooling at Naish House, Burnham-on-Sea, Frederick Copleston went to Marlborough College (1920–1925). Shortly before leaving he was, at the age of eighteen, received into the Catholic Church. There followed four years at St. John's College, Oxford, where he took the degrees of B.A. and M.A. in *Litterae Humaniores*. In his final year at Oxford his interest in philosophy began, awakened by the then still surviving Hegelian tradition.

After a year spent in studying Scholastic philosophy at Oscott College, Birmingham, Frederick Copleston entered the novitiate of the Society of Jesus (September, 1930). He did his ecclesiastical studies at Heythrop College, Chipping Norton, Oxford; philosophy from 1932 to 1934 and theology from 1934 to 1938. He was ordained priest in 1937. His tertianship finished, he was appointed professor of the history of philosophy at Heythrop College, Chipping Norton, Oxford, a post which he holds to date. In 1948 Father Copleston became a member of the Council and Executive Committee of the Royal Institute of Philosophy.

Father Copleston's publications include the following: *Friedrich Nietzsche, Philosopher of Culture* (1942); *Arthur Schopenhauer, Philosopher of Pessimism* (1946); *A History of Philosophy, vol. I, Greece and Rome* (1946); revised 1947; *vol. II, Augustine to Scotus* (1950); *St. Thomas and Nietzsche* (Aquinas Paper No. 2); *Existentialism and Modern Man* (Aquinas Paper No. 9). He has contributed to *Mind, Philosophy, Dublin Review, Month,* and other periodicals. For his book on Schopenhauer, the degree of D.Phil. was conferred on Father Copleston by the Gregorian University, Rome.

Since the war, Father Copleston has, at the invitation of the British Foreign Office, participated in University Vacation Courses at Bonn, Cologne, Aachen, Münster, lecturing on philosophy. In 1948 he lectured in the American Zone at the Bavarian Universities. In the spring of 1950 he lectured on philosophy in Barcelona and Madrid. Father Copleston frequently broadcasts over BBC. His two most important engagements have been his discussion on the existence of God with Bertrand Russell and on logical positivism with Professor A. J. Ayer.

Walking, the becoming exercise of great and simple minds, is, according to *Who's Who,* the recreation of Father Copleston.

E. B. B.

Reverend John Coventry, S.J.
1915–

When writing his slim volumes, Father Coventry always had in mind the Catholic of ordinary education. "It is what the French call 'vulgarization,' writes Father Coventry, "and when they are kind they prefix 'haute.'"

Born on January 21, 1915, he went to school at Stonyhurst College, Lancashire, and upon graduation in 1932, joined the Society of Jesus, at the age of seventeen. He spent four years studying at Campion Hall, Oxford, reading for *Litterae Humaniores* ("Greats") and there took his B.A. degree in 1942. His M.A. was obtained three years later. While at Oxford he was under Father Martin D'Arcy, S.J., and he considers this "one of the best things the Lord has sent me." Before beginning his theology, he taught as a scholastic at Beaumont College, Old Windsor, Berks, for three years. He was ordained at Farm Street Church, London, in 1947. Upon finishing his training, he became Prefect of Studies at Beaumont College.

His books thus far are: *Morals and Independence* (1949), an introduction to ethics; *The Breaking of Bread* (1950), a clear explanation of the Mass, and *Faith Seeks Understanding* (1951), an essay on faith and reason.   **M. A. H.**

Sister St. Michael Cowan (Rosalia Cowan) 1886–

Sister St. Michael Cowan (Rosalia Cowan) was born in Co. Armagh, Ireland in 1886. She received her primary education there at the National Schools. Before continuing her studies she spent a few years with aunts in Newry, Co. Down. These aunts were booksellers and stationers, and it is probably her contact with authors and books in Newry that enhanced her taste for them.

Wishing to enter religious life as a teacher, she went to England to study at St. Michael's Convent in Devonshire with the Sisters she was to join later — the Daughters of the Holy Ghost, whose mother house is in St. Brieuc, Brittany, France.

In 1904 she entered the novitiate taking the name of the convent in which she was a boarder in Devonshire. When she completed her canonical year in France she returned to England, to Bedford, to continue to study. When in 1906 she went back to France to take her vows she was assigned to the American mission, and arrived the same year in Hartford, Connecticut, where the Provincial House of the Congregation was then located. Her first mission was in Swanton, Vermont, where she taught in the grades, continuing her studies by summer school extension courses, etc.

In 1911 she returned to Connecticut to be principal of St. Mary's School, Jewett City, for eight years, after which she went back to the "north country"; this time to Holy Ghost Academy in the Adirondacks, to teach English and History under the Regents. This is a picturesque country in summer, but in winter it is bleak and isolated. It was here she wrote a great number of her poems, which were afterwards published at the instigation of a literary priest in Waterbury, Connecticut, who "in the goodness of his heart thought they deserved to be read." The collection was entitled *Between You and Me*, but it is long since off the market.

In 1925 she was sent to Swanton, Vermont, again; this time to teach in St. Anne's Academy, a high school for boys and girls. She was seven years in this mission and these years she considers the most prolific of her life, for the boys of the Fathers of St. Edmund's juniorate then made their high school studies at St. Anne's and they were an interesting and hard-working band who set the pace for the other pupils.

It was at St. Anne's one summer that *Rest Awhile* was written though it was not published there. *Rest Awhile* was called a compilation by the author, though in a strict sense it is not a compilation, but the fruit of many spiritual works read from French and Spanish writers — not translated but their thoughts consumed and expressed by the author in her own language. It was her idea of a book that would be a useful companion on closed or private retreats.

Rest Awhile was offered for publication and accepted by Benziger Brothers in 1936 while the author was on a year's retreat at St. Joseph's Convent in New Haven. It was during that year also that *To Heights Serene* was rather hurriedly written and also accepted in 1937 by the same publishers.

The following year another work, *Glimpses of Truth*, was privately published in Waterbury, Connecticut. Then, *When the World Was Hushed* was written in spare moments during the winter of 1945 at Stella Maris Rest House in Newport, Rhode Island, where the author is superior.

Reverend Francis Stanley Crocchiola (Francis Stanley) 1908–

Because of the difficulty people have had with his family name, Father Francis Stanley Crocchiola uses his first two names, Francis Stanley, as his pen name.

Born in New York of Italian parents on October 31, 1908, he began his schooling at Nanuet, where the influence of one of his teachers led him to desire the priesthood. He attended public schools in New York City, and then boarding schools at Catskill, Peekskill, and Garrison, all along the Hudson River.

At Catskill, when fourteen, he wrote his first story. It was for a private enterprise that went bankrupt before the magazine could be got out. Years later when he visited the shop, the half type-set story was still in the frame. It was the story of an East Side family that decided to go high-brow in an old mansion near Red Bank on the Hudson. After that he was active on all school publications until ordination. At Catholic University he took a course in journalism under Dr. App.

After his ordination to the priesthood at the National Shrine in Washington, he taught at St. John's College at Garrison, New York, from 1937 to 1939. Upon the advice of a doctor, he gave up teaching and went to the dry climate of the Southwest, working first as an assistant pastor in St. Anthony's Church, Hereford, Texas; then as administrator of Our Lady of Guadalupe Church in Lubbock (1939–1940). Feeling rested he again tried teaching at St. John's, "but the last state became worse than the first." The doctor gave him five years to live if he remained in the humid climate of the East. He was received into the Archdiocese of Santa Fe by the Most Reverend R. A. Gerken, D.D. His first assignment was to assist at Our Lady of Guadalupe Church, in Taos, the art and literary center of northern New Mexico. During that year (1940) he became acquainted with Sharp, Phillips, Berringhause, Spud Johnson, and others who encouraged his first literary attempt in New Mexico, a series of articles on the various postage stamps then in circulation. He was transferred to San Miguel's Church, Socorro, New Mexico, where he served as an assistant pastor for the year 1941–1942. Then he became pastor of Our Lady of Guadalupe, Sapello, New Mexico, in 1942; pastor of Our Lady of Guadalupe, Villanueva, New Mexico, in 1943; pastor of St. Joseph's Church, Raton, New Mexico, 1944–1949; pastor of San Miguel Church, Socorro, New Mexico, and at present (1952) he is pastor of St. Anthony's Church, Pecos, New Mexico.

All this time he kept on studying and writing. "New Mexico," he says, "is a mine of information as well as a museum for the historian. It was alive with activity long before the Pilgrim Fathers were aware that there was land on this side of the Atlantic. The Spaniards kept good records. In addition, there was the unbroken line of Franciscan missionaries working for centuries among the Pueblo Indians."

To make known to the world the work of the friars, conquistadors, Pueblos, Indians and scouts seems to be an obsession with Francis Stanley. Urged on by friends, he hopes to complete a set of thirty-five volumes on New Mexico. Encouraged in this work by the Most Reverend E. V. Byrne, D.D., Archbishop of Santa Fe, he brought out his first book, *Raton Chronicle*, which gives the history of a town from "railroad and six-shooter days" to a placid modern city.

"I never feel happier," he says, "than when I write for the Santa Fe *Register*." Among his other books are: *One Half Mile from Heaven; The Cimarron Story; Maxwell Land Grant Sketches and Documents; The Picuris Story; Socorro; The Oasis; Ghost Towns of New Mexico*. In preparation are: *New Mexico's Bad Men; Las Vegas, Frontier Town;* and *All about Albuquerque*.

Francis Stanley's hobbies are: oil painting of the old Pueblo Missions of New Mexico with a view of some day using them as plates in a six volume work on the Pueblo Missions of New Mexico, and searching through old Spanish documents, newspaper files and government documents.

His ambition is to do work on the generals of the Civil War who got their military training in the various military outposts in New Mexico.

Rupert Croft-Cooke   1904–

Since the age of eleven Rupert Croft-Cooke wanted to be a writer. When he finally plunged into this field, he spent ten years before reaching the point at which he could make a living at writing. Up to this time he followed at least a dozen callings, "all of which were a means to an essential end," he says, being in turn a schoolmaster, journalist, stablehand, circus hand, etc., etc. He now (1952) has thirty-nine books to his credit.

Born at Edenbridge, Kent, England, in 1904, of Protestant parents, he was educated at Tonbridge School and Wellington College, Shropshire. At the age of nineteen, when he was teaching in a preparatory school, he wrote a book of poems called *Songs of a Sussex Tramp*, and sent a copy to Kipling, who invited him to tea. Mr. Croft-Cooke remembers him saying: "As you go on writing you will get many criticisms, verbal and printed, but you, and only you, will know which of them are true."

When he lost his teaching job in England, he saw a similar one advertised for Buenos Aires. He applied for it and was accepted. He then went home to look up the place on his atlas. "Although I taught geography," he says, "I had an idea it was in Ceylon." Two years (1923–1925) he spent in Buenos Aires in Argentina teaching English, and editing a magazine called *La Estrella*. It was at Buenos Aires in San Isidro parish church that Mr. Croft-Cooke was baptized as a Catholic on his twenty-first birthday. He returned to London in 1925 as a free lance journalist and writer. In 1928 he opened a bookshop in Rochester, Kent, dealing in first editions. During this time, he wrote six unpublished novels, and many articles, poems, et cetera completing over one million words and covering ten thousand sheets of paper before his first novel *Troubadour* was accepted by Chapman and Hall and published in 1930.

In 1930 he went abroad again, this time to Germany in order to write. The following year (1931) he lectured in English at the Institut Montana, Switzerland. He spent several years travelling in thirty-six countries. He lived in Spain, Germany, Italy and France. His novel, *Picaro*, the life story of a Spanish waif, was so Latin in conception and sympathy that a Spanish critic refused to believe that it was the work of an Englishman. During part of the years 1937 and 1938 he made a tour of four months' duration through ten European countries to collect material for a book called *The Man in Europe Street* (1938). While Mr. Croft-Cooke describes this book as "an attempt to get the point of view of ordinary people in the cafes, streets, and homes of other countries," it is largely autobiographical. He describes his hobbies and recreations as "essentially those of the proletariat."

For two years he travelled with a family circus. From this experience resulted two books, *The Circus Has No Home* (1940) and *The Circus Book* (edited 1947).

His next interest was the English gypsies. Living in a horse-drawn caravan driven by a Romany friend, he learned their customs and their language and he wrote two books about them. He spends much of his time playing darts in public houses, motoring, walking, travelling — "in fact leading an essentially ordinary existence among people other than intellectuals." He served in World War II as a captain and received the decoration B.E.M. (Military) for his part in the Madagascar operation.

"The war was the best thing in my life," he says, "Just before the war I had got to the point of manufacturing adventures. The war was the thing itself. I went to Madagascar, Zululand, India."

Besides four early books of poems which he tries to forget now and consequently does not give their titles, he has published *Twenty Poems from the Spanish of Becquer* (1926); *How Psychology Can Help* (1928); *Some Poems* (1929); *Banquo's Chair* (1930); *Give Him the Earth* (novel) (1930); *Nights Out* (novel) (1932); *Cosmopolis* (novel) (1932); *Shoulder the Sky* (novel) (1934); *Blind Gunner* (novel) (1935); *Crusade* (novel) (1936); *Kingdom Come* (novel) (1937); *Rule, Britannia* (novel) (1938); *The World Is Young* (autobiography) (1937); *Darts* (1936); *How to Get More Out of Life* (1938); *Pharaoh With His Waggons* (short stories) (1937); *Same Way Home* (novel) (1939); *Glorious* (1940); *Ladies Gay* (1946); *Octopus* (1946), in the United States it was called *Miss Allick;* *The Moon in My Pocket* (1948); *Wilkie* (1948), his favorite book, called in the United States *Another Sun, Another Home; The White Mountain* (1950); *Brass Farthing* (novel) (1950); *A Football for the Brigadier* (short stories) (1950) and *Nine Days with Edward* (1952).

He has contributed to most of the English periodicals and reviews including the London *Mercury, Spectator, Time and Tide* and *Manchester Guardian.*

Among the Catholic papers for which he has written are *The Tablet, Blackfriars* in England and *The Sign* in the United States.

M. A. H.

Reverend Patrick Cummins, O.S.B.
1880–

John Thomas Benedict Cummins was born April 19, 1880, on a farm near Burlington Junction, Nodaway County, Missouri. His father, Patrick Cummins, was an immigrant from Callan, Kilkenny County, Ireland. His mother, Anna Ryan, born at Springfield, Massachusetts, was the daughter of an Irish immigrant who in 1859 moved on from Massachusetts to Missouri.

High Prairie, a country public school, and St. Mary's, a parochial school in Maryville, the county seat, gave Thomas his elementary training. In 1895 he entered Conception College, conducted by Conception Abbey, a daughter of the ancient Abbey of Engelberg in Switzerland. College completed, Thomas entered the novitiate in 1899, and a year later made profession under the name of Patrick.

The years 1902–1906 were given to study in Europe, chiefly in the Benedictine College of St. Anselm's in Rome, where in 1905, he received the doctorate in theology, and in the Maximilian University of Munich in Bavaria.

Returning to Conception in 1906, Father Patrick taught for fourteen years, chiefly languages and philosophy, acting also as chaplain of students and master of the clericate. Occasional articles appeared from his pen in the *Ecclesiastical Review*, in the *Catholic Educational Review*, and in the records of the National Catholic Education Association and of the National Benedictine Educational Association.

In 1920 Italy's uncertain political future, the aftermath of World War I, suggested the appointment of an American as rector of St. Anselm's in Rome. Father Patrick accordingly held that position for five years, simultaneously holding the professorship of dogmatic theology. On his return in 1925, he became for a year the pastor of Keuterville, Idaho. Since 1926 he was assigned to teach, in his home monastery, Sacred Scripture and Dante's *Divine Comedy* claiming his chief attention.

His first work on Scripture was *The Catholic School Bible* of Reverend James Ecker of Treves, Germany. This work was followed in recent years by a number of articles in the *Catholic Biblical Quarterly*. A new English version of Jeremias, the Prophet, is now in the hands of the editorial committee which has the final word on the text of the Old Testament which is soon to appear under the auspices of the Archconfraternity of Christian Doctrine. He has been president of the Catholic Biblical Association and is now one of its consultors.

Father Patrick's interest in Dante was first aroused by the encyclical which Pope Benedict XV wrote in 1921, to honor the sixth centenary of the poet's death. An intensive course of study and teaching followed, first in Roman centers of Dante learning, then in his own monastery. A first result of these labors was a paper entitled "The Keystone of the Arch," published by the Northwest Missouri State Teachers College in Maryville, Missouri. The *Divine Comedy's* central line, so runs the theme (i.e. line 125 of the Purgatorio), is likewise the only fully broken line in all of Dante's poetry. This line, the keystone of the great poem, enshrines a monogram of Christ, namely, the word "Amor," whose anagram is "Roma."

The work entitled *Dante, Theologian: The Divine Comedy* appeared in 1948. The translation offered is a close echo of the original, with triple alternate feminine rhyme, and each line a unit of eleven syllables. The version is accompanied by a twofold commentary, one literal, the other spiritual. Raphael's glorification of the Eucharistic Christ, the so-called "Disputa," is reproduced, as a perfect work of art, inspired by Dante and leading back to Dante.

Reality: A Synthesis of Thomistic Thought (1950) is a translation from the French of Reverend Reginald Garrigou-Lagrange's book. He also translated Reverend John Hofer's *St. John Capistran-Reformer* (1951).

In 1950 Father Patrick was lecturer in the Summer School of Liturgy at Notre Dame University, where, on July 11, he celebrated the Golden Jubilee of his profession. Fifty years ago his favorite sport was baseball, when, as catcher, so fame runs, he used to stop wild balls with his shins. He now prefers the Vergilian sport of barefoot gardening to baseball.

Most Reverend John D'Alton 1882–

His Grace, Most Reverend John D'Alton, Archbishop of Armagh and Primate of all Ireland, was born in Claremorris, County Mayo, on the 11th of October, 1882. His uncle was the late Monsignor E. D. D'Alton, M.R.I.A., Dean of Tuam, author of a *History of Tuam* and of the well-known *History of Ireland*.

His early studies were pursued at Blackrock College, Dublin. He was one of a brilliant class that included Eamon de Valera, Thomas O'Rahilly of University College, Dublin, and the late James A. Sweeney, who became a judge in India.

From 1900 to 1904 he studied at Clonliffe College, Dublin, and from 1904 to 1908 at the Irish College, Rome. On the 18th of April, 1908 he was ordained priest for the Archdiocese of Dublin. During the year after ordination he pursued a course of studies at Oxford and Cambridge, and in the following year he received the degree M.A. (Hons.) at University College, Dublin. In 1910 he was appointed Lecturer in Ancient Classics at St. Patrick's College, Maynooth, and in 1912 was appointed Professor of Classics, a position he held until 1936 when he was made President of Maynooth.

During the period of his professorship at Maynooth he published: *Horace and His Age; a Study in Historical Background* (1917), a volume that revealed not only a thorough acquaintance with the more important literature bearing on the interpretation of Horace, but a wide and careful study of the political and social history of Rome; *Roman Literary Theory and Criticism* (1930), an extensive study of the evolution of Roman literary criticism from its early leavening by Hellenic and Hellenistic influences.

A third volume, *Selections from St. John Chrysostom* (1940), consists of comprehensive extracts from the writings of St. John Chrysostom, prefaced by an introductory essay on the life and works of the saint.

On April 25th, 1942, he was elected Coadjutor Bishop of Meath, and on the death of Dr. Mulvany in 1943 he succeeded to the See. On the 13th of June 1946 he was translated to the See of Armagh.

                                                                    G. F.

Sheila John Daly (Mrs. Peter White) 1927–

Sheila John Daly of the Chicago *Tribune* is one of the teen-agers' columnists.

Born in Fond du Lac, Wisconsin, on November 7, 1927, Sheila is the youngest of the four daughters of Joseph Desmond and Margaret Mellon (Kelly) Daly, and the only one of the children to be born in the United States. The other three were born in Ireland. Sheila John (her middle name John is taken from her father, now dead) is one of three writers in the family. Maureen is the author of the best seller *Seventeenth Summer* and was associate editor of *Ladies' Home Journal* from 1945 to 1950, and Kathleen, former fashion and beauty editor of the Chicago *Herald-American*, is an account executive with the William Weintraub Advertising Agency. Marguerite, the oldest daughter, is a top Chicago model.

Sheila attended St. Mary's Springs Academy in Fond du Lac, Wisconsin, and while there was editor of the school paper and valedictorian of the senior class. On February 14, 1945, while she was still a senior in high school, Sheila took over her sister Maureen's job on the Chicago *Tribune* writing the column "On the Solid Side." In this column, Sheila handles many of the youthful problems in a helpful and understanding manner. She has been commended several times for her encouragement of Christian charity in the home and at school. Even while attending Rosary College, Sheila continued to write this column.

Her writing career began at the early age of eleven. One summer afternoon, she asked her two older sisters to take her swimming. They refused. They were too occupied "writing books." Sheila decided to do some writing herself. Her effort resulted in a story, "The Sisters," which later sold to *Woman's Day* magazine. Her next attempt was a series of three articles for children on "How to Spend Saturday." These were also sold to *Woman's Day*. Since then she has contributed short stories and articles to *Mademoiselle, Extension Magazine, Seventeen, Calling All Girls*, the Chicago *Daily News*, and a number of other magazines and newspapers.

In May 1945, an extra feature "Tops Among Teens," which every week spotlights an outstanding and talented teen-ager, was added to the weekly output. This, likewise, has been syndicated.

In August 1946, Sheila's first book, *Personality Plus!*, appeared. It gives informal advice in the current vernacular on behavior for high school boys and girls, covering such matters as "Shyness," "How to Make an Interesting Conversation," "How to Get a Date," "Telephone Technique" and so forth. Since then *Party Fun*, in which she describes forty-eight special kinds of parties with ideas for invitations, decorations, games and food was published.

This was followed by *Pretty, Please,* a book for girls who want to be looking lovely. Then in August, 1949, appeared an etiquette book for boys, *Blondes Prefer Gentlemen.* In March, 1949, Sheila began work on the *Ladies' Home Journal* Profile of Youth Series, travelling all over the United States gathering information on teen-agers.

Between her writing and lecturing she turns up as guest star on radio and television. In her spare time she spends hours in record shops and with her own record collection which ranges from Billy Eckstine and Skitch Henderson to Beethoven and ballet music. In 1949 she signed a contract for her column with the New York *Daily News.* Before her marriage to Peter White in November 1950, she lived with her widowed mother in a North Side Chicago apartment, but she now lives in New York.   M. A. H.

Reverend Jean Daniélou, S.J.
1905–

Widely known as a result of his influence in present-day theological trends, Father Jean Daniélou is professor of the history of Primitive Christianity at the Institut Catholique in Paris, editor of *Études* and one of the collaborators of *Dieu Vivant.*

He was born on May 14, 1905 in Paris, the son of Charles Daniélou, former Minister and friend of Aristide Briand, and of Madelin Daniélou, the foundress of the free university for young girls at Neuilly. After his higher studies at the Sorbonne, he received his degree in philology in 1927. Two years later he entered the Society of Jesus. Under Jesuit supervision he continued philosophical studies at the Maison St. Louis (Isle of Jersey) and his theology at Fourvière near Lyons. He was ordained a priest in 1938. The following year he served in World War II. In 1944 he received the doctorate in theology at the Institut Catholique of Paris for his thesis on the *Spiritualité de Saint Grégoire de Nysse.* The same year he was made a doctor of philosophy by the University of Paris. Also in the same year he was named professor of the history of primitive Christianity at the Catholic Institute of Paris where he succeeded Father Jules Lebreton, S.J.

In the intellectual world Father Daniélou is especially known for revitalizing the study of the Greek Fathers. His first book *Platonisme et théologie mystique* was dedicated to the relations between Platonism and Christian mysticism in Gregory of Nyssa. In 1948 he published *Origène,* a study of the Alexandrian theologian, the success of which has been considerable. In 1950 appeared *Sacramentum futuri* in which Father Daniélou studies the origins of typological interpretations of Scripture in the Fathers of the Church.

In 1942 Father Daniélou founded the collection *Sources chréti-enne*, a French translation of the Greek and Latin Fathers, twenty-five volumes of which have already appeared. For this collection, Father Daniélou published the French translation of *Vie de Moïse*, by Saint Grégoire de Nysse, and wrote many introductions. Since 1945 he has published regularly a bibliographical bulletin of patristic publications in the *Recherches de Science religieuse*. Father Daniélou, moreover, is editor of the magazine *Les Études* since 1944. He chronicles there the principal intellectual movements of the world of today. Among these articles might be mentioned "Les Courants intellectuels dans la France contemporaine" (1945) having to do principally with the relations between Christianity and Marxism and Existentialism. In 1947, "Christianisme et histoire" tackles the modern positions of Protestant theology, in particular the ideas of Oscar Cullman. In 1948, "le Saint et le Yogi," studies in *Neo-Hinduism*, the relations between natural mysticism and Christian mysticism.

Father Daniélou is also interested in various aspects of the spiritual and missionary revival in contemporary France. He gives frequent lectures on the Pastoral and Liturgical Movements. His cooperation in *La Messe et sa catéchèse* and in *Jour du Seigneur* and other books will show his practical interests in these movements. In this collection he has just published *Lex orandi, Bible et Liturgie*.

Father Daniélou is also one of the foremost workers in the revival of the missionary spirit. To this end he founded the Cercle St. Jean-Baptiste, a center of spirituality and missionary culture. The spiritual conferences which he has given to this group are published in two volumes: *Le mystère du salut des nations* and *Le mystère de l' Avent*, both translated into English. In 1950, Sheed and Ward brought out *The Salvation of the Nations*, his first book to be translated into English. Its theme is the conversion of the world to Christianity.

Father Daniélou has also taken part in the Ecumenical Movement. Many trips to Sweden, Denmark, Switzerland, Germany, England and the United States afforded him the opportunity to meet the principal personalities of this movement in non-Catholic countries.

During the summer of 1950 Father Daniélou taught in the University of Notre Dame liturgical summer school.   K. M.

Henry Daniel-Rops (Henry Jules Petiot) 1901–

One cannot but marvel at the output of France's brilliant Catholic novelist and historian, the winner of the Grand Prix of the French Academy (1946), Henry J. Petiot, known to readers by his pen-name, Daniel-Rops. Nominated by the French Government, Knight of the Legion of Honor (1948), and appointed by his Holiness, Pius XII, Commander of the Order of St. Gregory the Great (1949), he has written some fifty books, including twenty novels, outstanding historical studies, as well as works of art and science. Yet nothing he has written has been hastily or carelessly done.

Robert Barrat, who visited Daniel-Rops in his home, writes about him in *America*, April 9, 1949 and states that when he wrote *Jésus en son temps (Life of Christ)*: "For three years, surrounded by his library's 10,000 volumes, with his door shut, and the telephone disconnected, he worked calmly, perseveringly, lovingly, from seven in the morning to one in the afternoon. The fruit of this monk-like toil has won him a world-wide reputation . . . over 320,000 copies were sold and it was translated into a dozen languages. *Jésus en son temps*, combined with *Histoire Sainte, L'Église des Apôtres et des Martyrs, l'Église des temps barbares* and *Les Evangiles de la Vierge*, have made Daniel-Rops prominent and exceptionally distinguished among Catholic apologists."

"He has received the light that he may spread it," writes A. De Parvillez (in *Eaux Vives*), "and because he has been and will be faithful to this mission, the most noble mission with which a writer can be honored, his name will remain radiant in the eyes of his countless readers."

Like many another young Frenchman, Henry Petiot gave up the practice of his faith in college days, but it was not for long. His patient enquiring mind puzzled over the problems of man's destiny and nature. At twenty-five, while teaching history in the Lycée at Chambéry he published his first essay *Notre Inquiétude* (1926), a study of "le malaise d'une jeunesse désorientée." It was a promising essay in style and it indicated how seriously he was thinking about life. Four years later one could see Henry's spiritual progress in *Le Monde Sans Âme* (1932). With two years more of development of thought, and indeed of literary skill, the splendid novel *Mort, où est ta victoire?* (1934), the story of a woman who passed through sin and trial to find the faith, revealed Daniel-Rops' personal convictions. *L'Epée de Feu* (1939), a profound and moving picture of the world of the day, taught men to raise their eyes to God. Daniel-Rops had by this time become a great and enlightened apologist for Christ.

When asked by an interviewer what spiritual book he liked to read, he went to his desk and took from it a small worn book with a green cloth cover . . . a Brunschvig edition of Pascal's *Pensées*. Then he related, "at the age of sixteen I used to carry this with me often on my solitary tramps through the mountains of Dauphiny . . . later, a long time afterwards — after those years when Pascal's dogmatic conclusions came to appear unacceptable — one day at Port Royal, close to the old hedge which is all that remains of the abbey, I opened once more this little green book and chanced upon some phrases that touched me to the quick: 'The negligence of men in a matter that concerns themselves, their eternity, their all . . . etc.' What was that voice that spoke to me from those lines after years of solitude and silence? Should I not have recognized it? Pascal held the answer . . . a man wholly given to God who, at the end of his life, puts everything aside and devotes himself . . . to active charity . . . what a lesson!"

Henry J. Petiot was born at Epinal (Vosges), France in 1901. His father, whose family came from the Vendée region and from Meaux, was an artillery officer stationed at Grenoble. His mother's family came from the Jura Mountains. Henry attended school and then the University at Grenoble. At the university he studied, simultaneously, law, history and geography, the latter science under Raoul Blanchard, a friend of Péguy. Under Blanchard's direction he wrote his first work: *Briançon, étude de géographie urbaine.*

From Grenoble he went to the University of Lyons (1921), to take his degree l'agregation-en-arts, which he succeeded in doing. He received his "habilitation," being second of all the candidates, and "le plus jeune agrégé de France" (1922). . . . His first teaching position was at the Lycée at Chambéry (1923); then came Amiens (1928); and lastly Pasteur á Neuilly sur Seine (1930). Meanwhile, in 1923 he married Madelaine Bouvier and began his literary career as a novelist. For over twenty years Henry Petiot continued to teach. "He loved passionately his work as a pedagogue. His pupils were considered by him as his younger friends whom he sought to educate and lead as well." Many of his pupils had distinguished careers in later years.

Besides writing books Daniel-Rops contributed to several French and foreign magazines, such as *Revue des Deux Mondes* and the *Nouvelle Revue Française.* In the Plon editions, he directed the "Présences" collection, having for collaborators Claudel, Valéry, Mauriac, Maurois, Jules Romains, Cardinal Verdier, Raoul Dautry, Robert Lacoste, Maurice Schumann, and Charles de Gaulle, whose book, *La France et son armée*, appeared in the collection in 1937. Daniel-Rops writes for *La France Catholique, Témoignage Chretien*, and *La Bataille.* He has lectured in many foreign countries and has thrice won French Academy awards, namely: "Prix Paul Flat" (1927); "Prix Alfred Née" (1939); and "Grand Prix de la Littérature." Among his publications are the following: *Notre Inquiétude* (1926); *Sur le théâtre de Lenormand* (1926); *Carte d'Europe* (1927); *L'Ame obscure* (1929); *Deux hommes en moi* (1930); *Estaunié* (1931); *Le Monde sans Ame* (1932); *Les Années tournantees* (1933); *Pèguy* (1933); *Mort, où est ta victoire?* (1934); *Eléments de Notre Destin* (1934); *Le Coeur complice* (1935); *Rimbaud* (1935); *La Misère et nous* (1935); *Tournant de la France* (1937); *Ce qui meurt et ce qui naît* (1937); *La Maladie des Sentiments* (1938); *L'Epée de Feu* (1939); *L'Ombre de la Douleur* (1941); *Mystiques de France* (1941); *Vouloir* (1941); *Psichari* (1942); *L'Ouevre grandissante de Patrice de la Tour du Pin* (1942); *Par delà notre Nuit* (1943); *Saint Bernard et son message* (1943); *Comment connaissons-nous Jésus?* (1943); *Histoire Sainte* (1943); *Trois Images de Grandeur* (1944); *Jésus en son temps* (1945); *Quêtes de Dieu* (1946); *William Blake, le mariage du ciel et de l'enfer* (1946); *L'Église des Apôtres et des Martyrs* (1948); *Coeur Flambant* (1947); *Terre Fidele* (1948); *Marges de la Prière, La Colombe* (1945); *Sacred History* appeared in 1949.

All the finest gifts of Daniel-Rops' mind and heart went into the writing of *Histoire Sainte*, the story of the people of Israel in Old Testament times. For three years he labored at it, exhausting all the fruits of modern archaeological and literary research. His gifts of lucidity, penetration, and exposition of complex ideas and entangled facts, were all called into play. In a sense he was writing against time, to disabuse the world of the Nazi libels against the Jews. Hardly had his work been put in type and 14,000 copies printed, when the German Gestapo burst into the premises of Fayard, the publisher, and broke the plates. They failed, however, to find the copies already printed, and after the liberation of France, the book was reset and reissued.

Henry Petiot, still comparatively young, now finds some repose in his beautiful home called "Eau Vive" at Tresserve, in Savoy. From the house French gardens slope down to the wonderful Lake of Bourget. There with his youngest godchild, Christine, and with Francis, an adopted son to whom he dedicated the re-edition of *Où passent les Anges*, he is relieved of some of the stress of the busy Parisian life he lived for two decades.   E. B. B.

Reverend Henry Davis, S.J.
1866–1952

Students of moral theology are familiar with the four volume work on that subject by Father Henry Davis, who for over forty years taught moral and pastoral theology.

Born in Liverpool, England, on December 1, 1866, the eldest son of Edward and Mary Davis, he was educated at St. Francis Xavier's College in Liverpool. He entered the Society of Jesus on September 8, 1883. After his noviceship he studied classics for two years and passed London intermediate classical honors. Then he was sent to St. Mary's, Stonyhurst, to study classics and philosophy for four years. Later he earned a B.A. degree in classics at London University.

For six years (1891–1897) he taught poetry and rhetoric at Mount St. Mary's College, Derbyshire. From there he went to St. Beuno's

College, N. Wales, for his theological course of four years. Ordained priest in 1900, he served the Glasgow Mission for some months, and then proceeded to Tronchiennes, Belgium, for the customary year of probation, the tertianship.

In 1902 he was appointed prefect and professor of the junior members of the Society, preparing them for their London University degrees in classics. A year later he went to Stonyhurst as prefect of studies and remained there until 1911. From then on he began to teach moral and pastoral theology, first at St. Beuno's College and since 1926 at Heythrop College to which place the theologate was transferred.

In 1943 he celebrated his diamond jubilee of entrance into the Society of Jesus and in 1950 the golden jubilee of his ordination to the priesthood.

He is the author of the following books: *Birth Control Ethics; Birth Control, the Fallacies of Dr. Marie Stopes; Eugenics, Aims and Methods; State Sterilization of the Unfit; Moral and Pastoral Theology* (4 vols., six editions, 1935–1949); *Artificial Human Fecundation* (1951). Father Davis wrote *Moral and Pastoral Theology* to replace the *Moral Theology* of his own professor and predecessor, a work that had considerable vogue for many years but that had gotten out of date owing to the publication of the New Code of Canon Law. Its author, Father T. Slater, S.J., being threatened with blindness, could not do any work to bring his volumes up-to-date. Father Davis considered it easier to write a fresh treatment of this subject rather than to correct and improve an old work. Its reception proved that a popular treatise was wanted. This work contains discussions of many medico-moral problems and a treatment of ectopic gestation at some length.

He had also contributed articles to various Catholic periodicals and he revised the English translation of selections from Suarez's work, *De Legibus,* etc., in the Publications of the Carnegie Endowment for International Peace, Division of International Law, 1944.

He died in January, 1952.

Lucile Decaux. See *Princess Marthe Lucie (Lahovary) Bibesco*

Rev. Henri de Lubac, S.J. See under *Lubac*

Reverend Maurice de la Taille, S.J. 1872–1933

The distinguished theologian and famous Jesuit teacher Father Maurice de la Taille, was born on November 30, 1872 in the town of Semblancay, France, the son of Comte de la Taille. There were eleven boys in the family.

Since the religious laws interdicting Jesuit institutions were in force at the time and education in general was weakened as a result of these laws, he made his classical studies at St. Mary's College in Canterbury, England, and later on spent a year at Ramsgate College, on the east coast of England, under the supervision of the Benedictine Fathers, for whom throughout his life he had the greatest affection. He learned English and familiarized himself with British life for which he always had a strong liking.

In November 1890 he entered the Society of Jesus and made his novitiate in the province of Paris. The following three years were spent in the Isle of Jersey where he studied philosophy under La Bachelet, Antoine, and Bainvel. In 1898 he received the licentiate at the Sorbonne. In 1899 he went to Paris to study theology. Later he went to Lyons. In 1901 he was ordained to the priesthood at Tours and then completed his studies at Canterbury in 1902. A year later he did parish work at Preston, England and in 1904 made his tertianship at Mold.

From 1905 to 1916 he taught theology at the University of Angers. For two years he served as a chaplain in the Canadian Overseas Forces. In 1919 he was called to Rome and was named one of the three principal professors of Gregorian University, who lectured in the classes leading to the doctorate. Father de la Taille taught speculative theology. For some years he performed this duty so excellently that the students, whose minds he really formed, gave him most willingly the utmost attention. They found in him a man of keen ability with a lofty mind and the deepest erudition. By culling over in his own mind the doctrines handed down by others he was able to make them so plain and pleasing that they seemed, in truth, not to come from others but from himself.

In 1904 he published his first article in *Etudes*. It dealt with the principal errors of the modernists. At a solemn session of the faculty of theology of the University of Angers, attended by many bishops and learned men, he expounded the encyclical "Pascendi Dominici Gregis." Since Father de la Taille was then a young man it is an indication of the esteem his contemporaries had for him.

His best known work is *Mysterium Fidei*. It is known in Catholic circles all over the world. Although completed in 1915 it was not pub-

lished until 1921 because of World War I. Father Joyce says of it:
"We do not exaggerate in daring to affirm that there has been no work
edited since the Council of the Vatican which has drawn such universal
attention as the *Mysterium Fidei*. It is an immense treasure-store of
science, it diffuses a new light upon the old truths, and a first glance
will reveal to nearly everyone a profound skill in dialectics and a
suave piety, redolent, in the entire book." An English translation was
made of this book. His next work was to be a treatise on grace but after
a long and painful malady, Father de la Taille died in 1933 in Paris,
at the hospital of the nuns of Bon Secours, with the words "Dieu soit
béni!" upon his lips.   M. A. H.

Teresa Deevy   1894–

Teresa Deevy was born in Waterford, Ireland,
on January 21st, 1894, of Kilkenny-born parents. Her father had started a business in Waterford city, and the house in which she was born
overlooks the city and the river — which is perhaps the most beautiful of all Ireland's rivers —
the Suir.

She was educated at the Ursuline Convent
in Waterford, and later at the National Uni-
versity of Ireland. Before taking her degree, however, she became deaf,
and so gave up trying to hear lectures. She left the University and went
to London to study lip-reading.

While in London she went very often to the theatres there — reading the plays first, when possible, then following them on the stage. One
night returning from the theatre she felt very strongly the urge to put
"the sort of life we live in Ireland into a play. The piece we had just
seen, depicted English life, and I felt how very different these are from
the people I know. About this time one of the plays I read was *Heart-
break House*. Shaw had called it 'a fantasy in the Russian manner on
English themes,' and I said proudly to myself my play will be 'a fantasy
in the Russian manner on Irish themes.' But there was a long way to go.
I returned to Ireland — this was in 1919, and Ireland faced the Terror.
My play was pushed into the background: some few articles and stories
were published, a short novel was completed (but never published) but
it was not until 1925 that my first play went to the Abbey Theatre —
to be promptly rejected. Some people thrive on sympathy, others are
braced by set-backs. I tried again — and yet again — and the third
attempt won. At least it won approval from the Abbey Directors, and
production. When the great day came it seemed to me that I had been
working all my life for this one day — or rather night.

"The theatre was well filled, the play seemed to be liked: in a quiet,
unenthusiastic way the audience showed interest. *Reapers*, I had called
my piece, and the great players of the Abbey gave of their best — F. J.

McCormick, May Craig, Eileen Crowe, Arthur Shields, Denis O'Dea, Shelah Richards. I was happy. Without any illusions as to this being a huge success, I was unprepared for the very severe notice in *The Irish Times* next morning! Other notices which followed, in a more kindly vein, declared that the play showed 'promise' — Promise! No word could have seemed more deadly to me! Had I not put into this play all that I had felt and thought and believed! (No wonder *The Irish Times* had complained of 'a spate of words!') This had seemed to me the outcome of my life's work, and they talked of 'promise'!

"It took some time to realize that this was the start of a journey, not the road's end, as I had thought. But the journey is worth the making, with all its ups and downs. And now one thinks gratefully of those who helped in the beginning — Lennox Robinson, who, for me, opened the door leading to the life I wanted, always there, as producer, as adviser, with suggestions, never pressing, never dictating. A perfect producer seeks to reveal the author.

"But there are others to whose wise words, whether spoken to me, or written, I owe much. Words that have helped, stray gleanings to remember always. 'There is movement in a play when a character grows before our eyes' (grows, or unfolds, that is — reveals himself or herself more fully as the play proceeds, not necessarily changing). 'A play should have three things — suspense, surprise, inevitableness.'

"'The audience, as a collective whole, cannot move so swiftly as the author's mind; do not bewilder the audience.' And one more dictum — from the writing of J. J. Synge. 'The drama is made serious — not by the degree in which it is taken up with problems that are serious in themselves, but by the degree in which it gives that nourishment, not very easy to define, on which our imaginations live.' A great saying that — drama, to be worth the name, must nourish imagination."

Six of her plays have been done at the Abbey Theatre: *Reapers* in 1930; *A Disciple* (one act) in 1931; *Temporal Powers* in 1932; *The King of Spain's Daughter* in 1935; *Katie Roche* in 1936; and *The Wild Goose* in 1936. Six of her other plays have been broadcast — some by BBC and others by Radio Eireann.

Reverend Martin Dempsey   1903–

Upon his ordination to the priesthood in 1929, Father Martin Dempsey joined the Catholic Missionary Society. One of the regulations required members to specialize in some form of the written as well as the spoken word. Father Dempsey began with simple stories on the Blessed Sacrament, Our Lady, great priests and so forth.

Born in Dublin, Ireland in 1903, the son of Martin Dempsey, M.D., F.R.C.P.I. and Mary (Callaghan) Dempsey, he was educated at the Jesuit College of Clongowes Wood and the National University of Ireland. He pursued his theological studies at Clonliffe College, Dublin, and Beda College, Rome, Italy.

As a member of the Catholic Missionary Society he lived at Brondesbury Park, in North London. In winter the priests gave Evidence Missions in churches and halls. In summer they went out with the motor van and spoke from it to crowds in the open air. In public they stated the case for the Catholic Church, and answered all kinds of questions.

In October, 1939, he enlisted as a chaplain in World War II and nine days later felt "strange, awkward and self-conscious in uniform." On October, 18, a troopship carried him to Cherbourg, France. From there he was posted to No. 3, C.C.S. (Casualty Clearing Station) at a small town called Doullens. Within a week the Station moved to a village called Mondicourt. "A Casualty Clearing Station is a unit of about a dozen or fifteen doctors, eight or ten women nurses, medical orderlies and R.A.S.C. (Royal Army Service Corps) men for transport duties, numbering in full some one hundred personnel. It is intended to operate some few miles behind the front line of defense or battle. Casualties are first treated at the Field Dressing Stations, and then moved down to the C.C.S. In the absence of war casualties, No. 3 C.C.S. became a small general hospital."

He returned to London in 1940, and in May, 1941, he was appointed a Senior Chaplain to the London district and was honorably discharged in 1946.

At the invitation of Right Reverend Monsignor John P. Boland, of the Diocese of Buffalo, New York, Father Dempsey came to the United States in 1947 to go on a three-month lecture tour. He also gave retreats all over the Eastern States. In August, 1947, Cardinal Griffin reorganized the Mission Society leaving Father Dempsey free to rejoin the diocese of Hexham and Newcastle.

In 1948 he returned to the United States to teach apologetics and sociology in the Catholic Girls High School of Los Angeles, California, with the permission of his bishop. In 1950 he became administrator of the Church of Our Lady of the Snows.

Among his publications are: *Servants of the King*, a pageant of the priesthood (1933); *Way of the Queen* (1934); *From an Old Monk's Diary* (1939); *John Baptist de la Salle*, his life and his institute (1940); *Back in Civvy Street* (1947); *The Priest Among the Soldiers* (edited) (1947), *Our Lady of Fatima and Other Sermons*, and *People and the Blessed Sacrament*. In preparation is the *Life and Times of Blessed Julian Peter Eymard*, Founder of the Blessed Sacrament Fathers.   M. A. H.

(John) Michael Derrick   1915–

The affairs of the Church in the modern world, with particular reference to Eastern Europe, are the special interest of Michael Derrick. He was born January 3, 1915, at Congresbury, Somerset, England, the eldest son of Thomas Derrick, the artist. He is the grandson on his mother's side of another artist, the late Sir George Clausen, R.A.

Educated at Douai Abbey School from 1924 to 1933, he went on to read Modern History at Queen's College, Oxford, when Sir Oliver Franks, the present British Ambassador to Washington, was Dean of the College and when Monsignor Ronald A. Knox was chaplain to the Catholic students in the University. In 1938, on completing five years at Oxford, he became Assistant Editor of *The Tablet*, under Douglas Woodruff, a position which he occupies to this day.

Unfit for military service during World War II, in consequence of an illness contracted while travelling in Hungary in 1933, he wrote regular scripts for the Overseas Service of the BBC throughout the war period. He has been actively associated with the Sword of the Spirit Movement, the Council of Christians and Jews, and The Newman Association. He was Chairman of the Founding Committee of the Challoner Club, which is the only general residential club for Catholics in London. He remains Chairman and a Trustee of the Club. The membership numbers five thousand.

In 1948 he was one of the British delegation to the Conversaciones Catolicas at San Sebastian, Spain, and in 1949 he went on a lecture tour of German Catholic audiences in the British Zone of Germany. He is a member of the "Bureau Provisoire" of the "Federation Internationale des Journalistes Catholiques" which was set up in Rome in February, 1950. He is the only English speaking member of the bureau.

In 1950 he contested Reading North as a Liberal in the parliamentary general election but suffered the fate of many Liberals. His first book, *The Portugal of Salazar* (1938), dealt with the contemporary experiment in the application of Catholic social doctrine.

Mr. Derrick has published pamphlets on the persecution of the Uniates in the Western Ukraine (1946) and on the case of Cardinal Mindszenty. From the beginning of 1948 to the end of 1949 he was Managing Editor of *Soundings*, a short-lived political and economic monthly, in addition to his work on *The Tablet*.

He is editor of the *Catholic Yearbook* and contributes a special supplement each month to the *Clergy Review* on the relations of Church and State in different countries. He has also contributed for some years, on such topics, to the *Britannica Book of the Year* and the *Annual Register*. He contributes to a wide range of English and continental periodicals. Mr. Derrick was married in 1951.   M. A. H.

Paul Derrick   1916–

Born in June, 1916 at Congresbury, Somerset, England, Paul Derrick is the son of Thomas Derrick, the artist. He was educated at Douai School, Woolhampton (1928–1933), Reading, and at Reading University (1936–1938) where he took a diploma in horticulture.

Working on various nurseries and fruit farms he has at the same time contributed over three hundred articles to various journals in England, the United States, Italy, Denmark, India and New Zealand. Most of these have been concerned with the problem of distributing property in an age in which production is normally on a larger scale than that of the family enterprise. Mr. Derrick is Chairman of the Distributist Council, a body representing various Distributist groups in England and Secretary of the Political Section of the Personalist Group, an English group associated with the French Personalists and their journal *Esprit*, founded by the late Emmanuel Mounier. Paul Derrick's pamphlet "Production and the Person" was recently published by the Personalist Group.

Many of his articles have appeared in the *New English Weekly*, *Catholic Worker*, *People and Freedom*, *Catholic Herald*, *Blackfriars*, *Month*, *Tablet*, *New Review*, *Commonweal*, *Cronache Sociali*, and other periodicals.

His book *Lost Property* (1947) argues that the distribution of property necessarily involves the organization of production on a co-operative basis.

Mr. Derrick maintains that all the political parties in Britain are moving in a Distributist direction. "The Conservatives declare that their aim is to create a 'property owning democracy' while the Liberals talk about 'ownership for all.' The Labor Party, for its part, has recently abandoned the nationalization of insurance in favor of 'mutualization' and seems to be moving towards a cooperative interpretation of socialism."

Mr. Derrick is now working on another book and hopes some day to have his own co-operative fruit farm.   M. A. H.

Sinead (O' Flanagan) de Valera (Mrs. Eamon de Valera)

Sinead O'Flanagan was born in Balleriggan, a seaside town in north county Dublin. When nearly seven years old she came with her parents, brother and sisters to live in the city. After being trained as a teacher she took a position in a primary school. She liked teaching very much but her great interest outside of her work was centered in acting and the stage. Her father used to take her to see the Shakespearian plays, and the comedies of Sheridan and Goldsmith. "No visits to the theatre in after life," she says, "could ever give me the thrill and joy which these early ones did and half the pleasure of the evening was derived from the discussion on the plays with my father on the way home."

As a child she took part in school plays and later when she joined the Gaelic League (a society for the revival of the Irish language) she acted in several Irish plays. Some of these were written by Dr. Douglas Hyde, late President of Ireland. In some of these plays, e.g., "The Tinker and the Fairy," and "An Posadh" (The Marriage), Dr. Hyde and she took the leading parts.

After she joined the Gaelic League she devoted most of her spare time to the Irish Language Movement. "The work," she says, "was very interesting. Apart from the study of the language itself, we had Irish dancing, concerts, visits to historical places, debating societies and other enjoyable functions.

"Nearly all the members of the League were engaged at work during the day so that the classes were held in the evening. Such was the enthusiasm among the members that many of us while still possessing only a limited knowledge of the language, undertook to teach beginners." In the autumn of 1908 Eamon de Valera came to learn Irish in a class of which she was the teacher. Two years later (January, 1910) she married him.

"Our married life," she says, "was eventful and rather unsettled, for after the 1916 Rising my husband was condemned to death. His sentence was commuted but he was in prison on several occasions afterwards. We had many removings from house to house. After my husband was liberated in 1917 we went to live in Greystones, County Wicklow. He was again arrested in May 1918 and was absent from home for many months. In June 1919 he went to America and remained there a year and a half. I myself went to America while he was there. I arrived in New York in August, 1920, and returned home the following October.

"This, with a couple of visits to relatives in England, is all the travelling I have done. In November 1922 we returned from Greystones to Dublin with our family, five boys and two girls. This again was a disturbed and anxious period in our lives as my husband was absent from home for two years. In 1932 he was elected Taoiseach and for the sixteen years he was in office I had to attend many public functions.

"During the greater part of my married life my time and attention were devoted to my home and family, but when the children no longer needed all my care I began in a very limited way to work again for the Language Revival. My special interest was centered in the children. I have written many plays in Irish for the young folk and have sometimes gone to the schools to help in the production of these plays.

"As a child I loved to listen to the old stories that my mother told me and found in after life that other children liked them too. My own children were equally interested listeners, but it was only after my grandchildren came that I thought of publishing the stories.

"Fallon and Co., Dublin, published three of the stories I heard from my mother, together with four others which I found in an old book. The stories were very well received here, and last March, Dodd Mead and Co. brought out the same seven stories together with nine original ones which were founded on old Irish legends under the title *The Emerald Ring and Other Irish Fairy Tales* (1951). With the stories were published two plays which I had written in Irish and translated into English.

"Though so much of my time was devoted to the Language Movement, I read rather extensively in English. Most of my summer vacations were spent in Balleriggan and there by 'the sad sea waves' I had delightful leisure for reading.

"As a girl my favorite poets were Byron, Burns, and our own poet Mangan. Longfellow I have always regarded as a helpful friend. I like Dickens best of all the English novelists. My children used to enjoy his books when I read them aloud as we sat by the fireside. I have read with pleasure Thackeray, Lytton and George Eliot and other English authors.

"The Anglo-Irish poets, notably Kickham and Griffin, have a great interest for me as have also the poets John Boyle O'Reilly, Denis Florence MacCarthy and in our own time the sweet lyrist Ethna Carbery. I do not so much care for some of the more modern writers.

"At present, my time is fully occupied with home and grandchildren. All my family have homes of their own except my eldest son who lost his wife in June last. He and his two young children are living with us so that life is almost as busy as in the early days of my married life, but when the other grandchildren assemble here we have still time for stories and as the elder ones have heard many of them already invention is called into play to keep my audience entertained."

Joseph Dever   1919–

In 1945, a young Boston GI became famous. *Yank*, the official army weekly had sponsored a short story contest for GI's all over the world and Joseph Dever had captured first place with his remarkable story *Fifty Missions*. It told of a combat flyer in such a way that everyone could know a bit of the personal strife which a young man in war must undergo. The story, reprinted in *Omnibook*, *Liberty*, *The Best from Yank*, and *Our Father's House* received wide acclaim. "It had that truthful realism that makes people either *love* a story for the poignancy with which it touches the human emotion or *hate* it for the accuracy with which it strikes home." Joe Dever himself says that *Fifty Missions* is "my best piece of work."

Joe Dever had, of course, experience in writing before enlisting in the army. He had been editor-in-chief of the *Stylus*, the Boston College magazine, and had made it one of the best college magazines in the country. In the *Stylus* he had written freely and at times satirically, of all phases of college life. Often he incensed professors and students by his propensity *to make people feel* what he put on paper. However, there was "constructive freshness" rather than bitterness in what he wrote, and always there was his own brand of realism. On leaving college he began to contribute to *America, The Commonweal* and *The Sign*. Then came his enlistment in the Air Force and his transfer from gunnery to camp newspapers where copy rolled from his typewriter in reams at Lowry, Laredo, Luke and Kelly Fields.

Joe Dever says, jokingly, that "a natural aversion to the pick and shovel prompted me to choose writing as my means of livelihood." But there was more to his vocation than that. He had "an entertaining knack of discovering and dramatizing the humorous elements in situations." He has, more important still, a high ideal of a writer's art.

In his literary art, Joe Dever aims at realizing the teaching of François Mauriac: "It is the privilege of artists to describe their pain in its differences and its details, and it is this that gives to each his particular distinction." If a piece of fiction does not make the reader say, "That's just the way it is . . . ," Dever feels the author has failed.

Joe Dever finds delight in writing poetry and has for successive years contributed Christmas poems to *America* and other verse to *Today, Integrity* and *The Catholic Worker*. One of his pieces has been chosen for the Marian anthology, "I Sing of a Maiden" and he has been honored by being elected a member of the board of directors of the Milwaukee Chapter of the Catholic Poetry Society.

In 1947 Joe Dever's first novel, *No Lasting Home*, appeared. It sold extremely well and was received with enthusiasm in Boston. About it, the author wrote: "while it was no great shakes nationally, the Boston critics saw in it the first piece of book-length fiction which has given an authentic picture of the Boston Irish-Catholic majority. That was a great satisfaction to me simply because it was precisely what I set out to do."

Joseph Dever was born in 1919 in Somerville, Massachusetts, a suburb of Boston, the son of Bernard and Rosaleen (Feeney) Dever. He was educated at St. Joseph's parochial school, Somerville High School, and Boston College where he was graduated in 1942. He entered the Air Force in 1943, remaining in the army until 1946. He was, as noted above, transferred from gunnery to camp newspaper work, becoming editor of the "Lukomunique," an army tabloid weekly, while at Luke Field. In his spare time he free-lanced for *Yank*, the official army weekly. After the war Joseph Dever married Margaret Kermode of Monte Vista, Colorado, and settled down in Milwaukee. They have three children.

Then he became engaged in reviewing books, lecturing, and teaching creative writing at Marquette University. He has been an editor of the Bruce Publishing Company, and was until recently personal secretary to Most Reverend Bernard J. Sheil, Auxiliary Bishop of Chicago. At present (1951) he and his family are living on a small ranch in Monte Vista, Colorado, having moved there after finishing his second novel, *A Certain Widow*, published by Bruce in 1951.

Joseph Dever, still young, and a literary "dynamo," cherishes high ambitions as a novelist. Familiar with the life of Catholic Boston, he aims at painting authentic and realistic pictures of his native city.

E. B. B.

Louis de Wohl   1903–

This vast fellow of over 270 pounds was born at the modest weight of 10 pounds and some odd ounces on January 24th, 1903. His father was Lajos Wohl, Knight of Mucsiny, who had been in turn an officer in a crack Hungarian cavalry regiment, journalist, politician, doctor of law, judge and mine-owner; his mother was née Baroness Victoria von Dreifus, an Austrian. One uncle, Julius von Blaas, was the court painter of Emperor Francis Joseph of Austria-Hungary, another, Baron Novellis, an Italian admiral, a third was Felix von Weingartner, the conductor. Louis de Wohl was born in Berlin, Germany, and inherited his father's nationality. He was educated at the Prinz Heinrich's Gymnasium. But he taught himself how to read and write (in block letters, studying the names and inscriptions on shops) and wrote his first play at the age of a little over 6: it was called "Jesus of Nazareth." It was never performed, mainly because of the vacillation of the author who wanted to play a part in it but just could not decide whether it was going to be Caiphas or Mary Magdalene or some other character.

At the age of 17 he had to give up his original intention of study-ing music and art because his family had lost most of its possessions in World War I. He worked for a bank right through apprenticeship. Then he was fired because he did his work in three hours instead of eight and wrote short stories in the remaining hours. He made a short escapade into dress designing, then became a publicity man for "Ufa," the biggest German film company.

At the age of 21 he wrote, and one year later he published, his first novel, *Der grosse Kampf* (*The Big Fight*), the story of a heavy-weight boxer. He was rather keen on boxing in those days and once even stood in the training ring with Georges Carpentier. Fortunately, Carpentier did not deign to hit him. When the novel became a surpris-ing success, he left "Ufa" and did what he had really always wanted to do. He just wrote. From 1924 to 1935 he wrote thirty-three books — all light novels, sixteen of which were filmed. They were no literary masterpieces, just more or less good yarns with lots of action.

His vacations were spent travelling — right across Europe to Turkey, Egypt, Syria, Tripolitania, Algeria, Tunisia, to India and Ceylon. In 1933, when Hitler came to power and so many good writers had to flee the country, he was more busy than ever, but it did not give him any pleasure. When in 1935 he left for the opening night of one of his plays in Vienna, he never came back. Instead, he went to England. The first thing he did was not only to learn, but to master the English language. He decided that this could be done properly only by receiving an education similar to that of an Englishman and he began to read children's books — first those for children from six to eight, then from ten to twelve and so on, until he reached his new "maturity." After four years (1937) he wrote his first book in English: *I Follow My Stars* — his autobiography. Up to this time, only transla-tions of his German books had appeared in England and nothing in the United States. After five years in England he applied for naturaliza-tion in a country he had learnt to love. But war broke out and all naturalizations were stopped until the end of the war. He tried in vain to enlist with the British army, navy and air force. He was not even allowed to dig trenches in Hyde Park. But then — in June, 1940 — he suddenly realized what his task in that war was and im-mediately set out to achieve it. He knew that Hitler was astrologically advised and he knew by whom and according to what system. He knew that Hitler's famous "time-table" that had caused so much guess work all over the world was simply astrological timing. And it so happened that he had become curious about this strange art himself years ago and had studied it sufficiently to know, with St. Thomas Aquinas, the difference between true and false astrology, between the permissible and the forbidden. He suggested to the British authorities that he would make exactly the same calculations that Hitler's astrologer was bound to make and thus come to the same findings — and that it was an advantage for the British to know what Hitler was told by a man in whom he believed. The British were intelligent and wise enough to make use of this knowledge, alien to them, and in due course Louis de Wohl was made a captain in the British army and the head of a tiny hush hush department of his own, called the Psychological Research Bureau. He did a great deal of work on psychological lines and sent in regular reports about the findings of Hitler's astrologer.

After World War II, he went back to writing, but he found that both his style and his interests had changed very much. He now concentrated on historical novels. Ancient Rome had been one of the centres of his interest from childhood onward, but he had never written about it. His first novel, after the war, was *Julian*, published in the United States in 1950 under the title *Imperial Renegade*, the story of Julian the Apostate. The next was *The Living Wood* (1947), the story of St. Helen and of the discovery of the True Cross. Then followed *Throne of the World* (1949), the story of Attila and St. Leo.

In 1948 he set out for Rome and was received by His Holiness the Pope in a special audience on May 10th, 1948. In the course of that audience, the Holy Father suggested to him that the hero of his next novel should be St. Thomas Aquinas. He went to work on it at once. It was published under the title, *The Quiet Light*, in August, 1950 by J. B. Lippincott Company, Philadelphia, who had previously published *The Living Wood*, *Throne of the World* and *Imperial Renegade*.

He came to live in the United States — New York — in November, 1949. In March, 1950 he went on a pilgrimage to Rome and on that occasion delivered the first printed copy of the novel on St. Thomas to the Holy Father.

His historical novels have so far appeared in the United States, Great Britain, Belgium, France, Denmark, Sweden, Norway, Holland, Switzerland, Italy, Czechoslovakia, Finland and the Argentine. *The Living Wood*, *Throne of the World* and *The Quiet Light* have been Book Club choices — both of the Catholic Book Club and the Literary Foundation.

Besides the books already mentioned he is the author of *Plunge into Life* (1936); *Satan in Disguise* (1938); *Secret Service of the Sky* (1938); *Last Thug* (1940); *Introducing Doctor Zodiac* (1940), and *The Restless Flame* (1951).

Maurice De Wulf   1867–1947

Maurice De Wulf was born at Poperinghe, near Ypres, Belgium on the 6th of April, 1867. He began his humanities studies at the diocesan college of his native city and completed his studies at the Jesuit College of Alost, Belgium. He entered the University of Louvain in October, 1885, and became successively Doctor in Philosophy and Letters (1889), Doctor in Law (1891), Doctor in Philosophy according to St. Thomas, (1893).

During his studies, he had become a disciple and a friend of Msgr.

Désiré Mercier, who, since 1882, held the chair of "Philosophy according to St. Thomas," created at the University of Louvain at the request of Pope Leo XIII. Mercier wished to convert this chair into a complete school of philosophy and as he needed helpers in order to do it, as early as 1891 he asked Maurice De Wulf to specialize in the domain of Mediaeval Philosophy and he sent him to Berlin and to Paris. In 1893, De Wulf joined the group of Mercier's first four professors with whom he founded the "Institut Supérieur de Philosophie." De Wulf started teaching in October 1893; besides mediaeval philosophy, he taught, for many years, the general course of history of philosophy and the general course of Logic; for a few years, he taught also ontology and aesthetics.

In 1894, De Wulf founded, with Mercier, the *Revue Néo-Scolastique;* he was the secretary of the new periodical (1894–1901), then the director (1907–1947). In 1900, the first edition of the *Histoire de la Philosophie Medievale* was published; this work will remain the principal work of the eminent historian; it had six editions during the author's life and several translations (into English, 1909, 1926 and 1935–1938; German, 1913 and 1944–49; Italian, 1913, Spanish, 1945). It is a work of erudition and of historical synthesis. De Wulf's *Histoire* gives a very personal interpretation of the philosophical movement in the Middle Ages. Up to the end of his life, the author kept working on his *Histoire,* enriching it with the results of historical research and profiting by the criticisms which were made. In 1901, De Wulf founded the series *Les Philosophes Belges,* a collection of texts and studies which reached fifteen volumes at the founder's death. In 1904, he published a very characteristic work, *Introduction à la Philosophie néo-scolastique,* which has been translated into English by P. Coffey under the title *Scholasticism, Old and New* (1907).

In 1914, when the German Army invaded Belgium and burned a great deal of Louvain, De Wulf took refuge in France and taught at Poitiers from 1914 to 1918. In 1915 he came for the first time to America to give some lectures at Harvard and Cornell Universities. In 1918, he came back to America and lectured at Toronto (St. Michael's College), where he returned in 1919 and in 1923. In September, 1919, he accompanied Cardinal Mercier on his triumphal tour through the United States and Canada. In 1920, he undertook a new series of lectures in the States at Madison University, Chicago, Princeton and Harvard, where a special chair for Mediaeval Philosophy was created for him. He occupied it from 1920 until 1927. In Europe, he was successively invited to Madrid (1918), Poitiers (1926–1927), Switzerland (1917–1928), Grenoble (1930–1931) and Durham (1932–1933). Among the works published during the period 1914–1936, we have to mention: *Philosophy and Civilization in the Middle Ages* (Princeton, 1922), which was translated into Chinese in 1935 and into Flemish in 1947, and *Mediaeval Philosophy illustrated from the System of Thomas Aquinas* (Cambridge, Mass. 1922; new ed. 1929; French translation, 1932 and 1949).

On March 7th, 1934, a solemn session was held in Louvain in order to celebrate the forty years of teaching of Professor De Wulf. A magnificent *Miscellanea* volume was presented to him (*Hommage à*

Monsieur le Professeur Maurice De Wulf, being vol. 34 of the *Revue Néo-Scolastique*), and his friend Professor E. K. Rand (now deceased) made a speech on that occasion.

In July 1939, De Wulf was made Professor Emeritus. He used his remaining strength to complete the 6th edition of his *Histoire de la Philosophie Médiévale*, the third volume of which was published in 1947: he received the first copies from the printer on March 7th, the feast of St. Thomas. One month later, on Easter Sunday, April 6th, he celebrated his eightieth birthday. He died quietly in the same year, at Poperinghe (his native town), on December 23rd, 1947.

Maurice De Wulf had been the most active and the most faithful helper of Cardinal Mercier at Louvain. In the pages of history, he will remain one of the most deserving scholars of the Thomistic renaissance and of the development of mediaeval studies in Europe and especially in America.

He received innumerable scientific distinctions and he was a member of numerous learned societies, among which was the Medieval Academy of America. He was Professor Emeritus of Harvard University since 1927.   F. V. S.

Alfred Döblin   1878–

It is not uncommon these days to hear of a doctor who is also an author. Dr. Döblin, the German novelist and essayist, is one of these.

He was born on August 10, 1878, of Jewish parents in Stettin, the capital of the formerly Prussian (now Polish) Province of Pomerania. When his father left the family to go to Hamburg to live, Alfred Döblin's mother and her five children moved to Berlin to stay with her mother, when he was ten years of age. Alfred was sent to the "Gemeindeschule" and later to the humanistic gymnasium — the "Köllnisches Gymnasium" in Berlin where he was graduated in 1900. At this early time he wrote poetry and a lyrical novel, *a la Holderlin: Die jagenden Rosse*, not yet published.

During his college days he became deeply interested in the philosophy of Kant, Schopenauer and Nietzsche. "I was not particularly concerned with religion. We were born Jews, and all that mother cared about was that she observed the great feast days, otherwise religion did not bother her very much," he writes.

After graduating from college he decided to study medicine, which he says, "might be the best foundation of my interest in philosophy. This philosophical impulse urged me to know the world most thoroughly, its problems and backgrounds; feeling, too, the necessity of natural science, I took a two years' course when I started medicine." He obtained his M.D. in 1905. At the University of Freiburg in Berlin he had specialized in psychiatry and neurology and therefore wrote his thesis on "A Case of Korsakoff Psychosis."

During the time he was a medical student he wrote miscellaneous critical essays about Nietzsche as well as short novels, which were published later in the first collection of his short stories under the title *Die Ermordung einer Butterblume (The Assassination of a Marigold Flower)* (1913).

He began his practice, as a doctor, in insane asylums, the last of which was at Buch, near Berlin, and then he joined the staff of physicians at the City Hospital in Berlin.

He married in 1912 and had four sons. His eldest son, Peter, became an American citizen and is living in New York; three others of his sons became French citizens and one has a residence in Nice and the other in Paris; the second oldest son died in 1940 as a French soldier fighting against the Nazis.

After his marriage, he worked as an independent physician and neurologist, first at "Hallésches Tor" in Berlin, then in the East, in the "Frankfurter Allee." Early in his life Dr. Döblin got used to the earnestness of life, and later on when living among poor people he experienced more of it. He is a man of strong imagination, and seeing life as it is, he reflected upon it a great deal. It was in the East of Berlin where most of his early writings were produced. There he brought out a novel dealing with the religious uprising of poor people in China. "It is the story of a revolutionary whose struggle with the brute power of the absolute state pleads the cause of nonviolence." Dr. Döblin achieved his first great literary success with this "Chinese" novel, *Die drei Sprünge des Wanglun (The Three Leaps of Wanglun)* (1915), for which he received the Fontane Award.

During World War I, he was a surgeon in the army, "a man whose life was divided between medical and literary work, and after 1918 — political interests. My social consciousness, after the revolution of 1918, compelled me to participate in the activities of the German Social Democratic party, a member of which I had been up to 1927, when I left the party because I did not agree with the undue influence of party favorites, and their interference with freedom of thought." He then plunged into writing all kinds of literature; a turning point had come into his life. "I tried to get away from the mechanistic and realistic interpretation of the natural sciences. The very titles of two main works show that change in my mode of thinking; *Das Ich Über der Natur* and *Unser Dasein*." In addition to these writings he also produced political satires, some of which appeared in a book under the title, *Der deutsche Maskenball.*

In Berlin he also wrote the novel *Wadzecks Kampf mit der Dampfturbine (Wadzeck's Fight with the Steam Turbine)*, dealing with the problem of man versus the machine, which was followed by the completion of his two volumes on Wallenstein, an historical novel of the Thirty Years War, symbolically depicting the failure of political philosophy of sheer will to power.

In 1924 he published *Berge, Meere und Giganten (Mountains, Oceans and Giants)*, an expressionistic masterpiece, picturing in a sort of apocalyptic vision the doom of mere knowledge and science without wisdom and moral incentives.

Still another book to come from his pen, while he was in Berlin, was *Berlin Alexander Platz* (1928), a district of Berlin whose people he knew very well, a type of whom he described in a certain Mr. Franz Biberkopf of that book.

The rise of National Socialism and the persecution of the Jews in Germany forced Dr. Döblin to leave Germany in 1933. He, his wife Erma, ten years younger than himself, and his four children went to Zurich, Switzerland and then spent many years in Paris. After losing his German citizenship he became a French citizen. Now advanced in years, he is disinclined to practice medicine. He says: "In my old days I am given to thinking and writing, and writing and thinking, following the course of this world."

His other books are *Das Land ohne Tod* (*The Country Without Death*, 2 Vols.), which gives a description of the beautiful landscape of the Amazon River. Furthermore, religious and human problems are discussed; the chief subject, however is an appreciation of the interesting political experiment of the Jesuit Fathers who built up a truly Christian state by the Amazon River in times when the whole world was war-torn. "After two centuries, that Christian-social creation went down which I try to illustrate. In doing it I learned a lot about the Christian religion, which was to bear good fruit in the writing of another bigger work, *November 1918* (4 Vols). The third volume bore the title *Karl und Rosa* (1950).

Dr. Döblin's religious development is described in the booklet, *Schicksalsreise* (*Ways of My Fate*), "the religious dreams of my former life realized."

In 1941 Dr. Döblin, his wife and two sons (the eldest and the youngest) were baptized in the Catholic Church, at Hollywood, California.

Later on he wrote a book of self-reflection, a kind of religious monologue, *Der Unsterbliche Mensch* (*Immortal Man*) (1948).

It was also in Hollywood that he started a voluminous novel called *Hamlet*, which he finished after his return to Germany — in Baden-Baden, but it has not yet been published. Other publications during the years of exile include *Babylonische Wanderung* (1934); *Pardon wird nicht gegeben* (*Men Without Mercy*) (1935). In Germany he wrote *Die Pilgerin Ätheria* in which he says, "I wanted to prove that all the efforts men make in struggling against God's grace are futile."

William K. Pfeiler of the University of Nebraska writes in the *Columbia Dictionary of Modern European Literature:* "he (Döblin) had the greatest narrative talent of any of the members of the German expressionist movement. A writer of tremendous vitality, fertile imagery, and vision, he is thoroughly grounded in modern science and philosophy."

Dr. Döblin returned to Germany at the end of the Second World War and resides at present in the south German town of Mainz where he edits the monthly review *Das Goldene Tor* (*The Golden Gate*).

K. R., W. B. and M. A. H.

Dorothy Dohen   1923–

The young writer Dorothy Dohen began writing by accident — "one of those providential accidents with which God is always surprising us," she says. The first article she had published was in *Today*. Although she had been intimately acquainted with *Integrity* from its very inception, she did not do an article for it until May of 1948. Since then she has been a regular contributor, for awhile writing under the pen name of Elizabeth Williams. For two years (1949–1950) she has had a monthly feature — "Letters to Margaret" — appearing in the *Torch* magazine. In December 1949, *Cross and Crown* — the Thomistic review of spiritual theology — published her article "Sanctity in Lay Life."

Her first and only book thus far, *Vocation to Love* was published by Sheed and Ward on October 12, 1950. "This is a book," she says, "which tries to make lay people realize the glory of their vocation — the call of God to them to attain the fullness of love. I suppose it can be called a book on lay spirituality, but it is spirituality for people who realize that they cannot live their interior life in a vacuum but must bring Christ to all aspects of everyday living. It is intended especially for lay apostles and deals with some of the difficulties and problems of their life which sometimes seem to impede the way to sanctity. But because love is a universal vocation I do not feel presumptuous in saying that the material in this book is for religious as well."

Dorothy Dohen was born in New York City on April 15, 1923, the third of the five children born to her parents, Elizabeth (Gutscher) and William Jerome Dohen. She attended the parish elementary and high schools of Saint Barnabas and was graduated from high school in June 1941. Having been awarded a state scholarship and a full tuition scholarship to the College of Mount St. Vincent-on-Hudson she began her college career in the fall of that year. She majored in English and minored in mathematics. She received her A.B. degree from Mount St. Vincent in May, 1945, and was awarded membership in Kappa Gamma Pi, the national Catholic honor society.

During the time she was in college she became interested in the lay apostolate and the Catholic Action cells which were then starting in New York. "The fact that the Popes have called upon lay Catholics to restore all phases of our temporal order to Christ, and the realization that God calls lay people as well as religious to sanctity, have been the molding influences of my life and writing. I had a brief period of training at the *Grail* and have been vitally interested in the Young Christian Worker Movement started by Canon Cardijn twenty-five years ago." Miss Dohen has worked at various jobs. At present she helps her mother keep house and writes. She also does some lecturing.

"If God wills it," she says, "I should like to continue writing to awake lay people to their call to be apostles and saints."

M. A. H.

Mrs. Edward Doherty. See *Catherine De Hueck*

Mrs. Charles T. B. Donkin. See *Dorothy Mackinder*

Reverend John Donovan, S. J., 1861–1933

Father John Donovan, who was of Irish parentage, was born at Castleisland, County Kerry, on October 11, 1861. His father worked for the British Ordnance Survey, and was consequently engaged for much of his time on the other side of the channel. The boy showed early signs of his ability, and he was sent first to a private tutor and afterwards to the Jesuit School at Turnhout in Belgium. At the age of nearly eighteen he entered the English novitiate of the Society of Jesus at Manresa House, Roehampton. After completing his noviceship he spent the next two years in the same house. Father Donovan took his London B.A. degree in 1884 from St. Mary's Hall, Stonyhurst. This he took with honors in classics.

The next three years he remained at St. Mary's Hall for the course of philosophy usual in the Society of Jesus. After this he taught the B.A. class at Stonyhurst College, his pupils consisting partly of secular philosophers from the college and partly of younger religious from the seminary, as St. Mary's Hall was generally called. In the year 1888 he took his M.A. degree, and came out third on the list. Though a class of boys was given him at Mount St. Mary's College his real talent did not lie in teaching the young; and his better work was done with the B.A. class to which he returned more than once subsequently, and with the juniors whom he taught both before and after his ordination. In the juniorate at Manresa he taught Greek, Latin, and French. The first three years of his course of theology he passed at St. Beuno's College, N. Wales, and there he was raised to the priesthood on September 22, 1895. His fourth year of theology he spent in the French theologate, then at Mold. For his tertianship Father Donovan returned to Belgium where he spent the year 1897–1898 at Tronchiennes in the usual exercises of the third year of probation. His last vows as a professed Father he pronounced on February 2, 1907.

From 1896, apart from the year just mentioned, until 1907 Father John was engaged in teaching the classics. Four years of this period were passed at Wimbledon College in the newly initiated Army Class. For a while he was back at Stonyhurst, 1902–1907; and then took up work on the home mission. For four years he had charge of the parish at St. Asaph, and then in 1916 came a bad breakdown in health. This he attributed to cycling up the Welsh hills and the consequent strain on his heart. For the rest of his life he was an invalid, compelled to a severe moderation in his activities, as any even small exertion at once affected his heart. It was in this state of health amid chronic heart-trouble that he gave himself to the production of those works of erudition and Christian apologetics that made his name known.

For ten years, from 1918, he was stationed at St. Beuno's College, which till 1926 was the theologate of the English Jesuits, and consequently had access to a well-equipped theological library. From 1928 he was in retirement, most of the time in Ireland, where it was hoped that his native air would be beneficial, and it is remarkable how he was able to continue writing under conditions very unfavorable for a scholar's work.

The first fruits of the leisure forced on him by his precarious state of health were given to the public in the three volumes of his *Theory of Advanced Greek Prose Composition with Digest of Greek Idioms* (1921). One writer has spoken of the enormous erudition embodied in this work, and the *Classical Bulletin* says it is "a monument to his thorough acquaintance with Greek idioms."

Then in 1924 Father Donovan produced a work, the real importance of which might be obscured for some by the smallness of its bulk. This was entitled *The Logia in Ancient and Recent Literature.*

Father Donovan also brought out various translations. He translated from the German the *Christian Monism* of Father Wassmann, S.J., and *Bases of Belief* (1924), by Father F. X. Brors, S.J.

On June 23, 1933, he said Mass for the last time at Kerry. He insisted on attending the funeral of a relative, with the worst effects on his own health. On July 6 it was found necessary to send him to the hospital of the Bon Secours Nuns at Tralee, but he collapsed in the reception room on arrival. He was hurriedly absolved by a priest who was undergoing treatment in the hospital at the time; and as soon as the Holy Oils could be procured was anointed conditionally, as it was some minutes after apparent death.   E. F. S.

Roger Burke Dooley   1920–

The story of a story can be highly interesting. The story of *Less Than the Angels*, Roger Burke Dooley's first novel certainly is! Coming from Canisius College, as a very young and very bright graduate to the Catholic University, Washington, D. C., to write a thesis on Jane Austen, for his M.A. degree, Roger Dooley carried in his head the name and an outline of his future novel.

He was just twenty-one and artistically in love with Miss Austen, his eighteenth-century sweetheart. As he read more about her, he found that she had written her famous novel *Pride and Prejudice* when she was his age. Stirred by the co-incidence he felt that "it was high time for me to get under way." Jane "with exquisite touch" (according to Sir Walter Scott), "had described the involvements, feelings, and characters of ordinary life" which was what Roger Dooley aimed at. *Less Than the Angels* began to take shape on paper!

Like Jane Austen, Roger had had an agile pen from early days. "At grammar school I enjoyed writing compositions," he writes, "and presently I discovered that it was even more interesting to make up stories of my own — and biding my days at South Park High School, Buffalo, I was plotting, if not writing, elaborate novels — usually inspired, it must be admitted, by the movies I saw and the mysteries and costume romances I then enjoyed reading." His mental development, paralleling that of the Hampshire girl, found him, when halfway through high school, and only fourteen years of age, making what he calls, "fumbling attempts to interpret the familiar, prosaic life around me which has since become my main interest in writing."

At Canisius, when editing the college magazine, he had considered putting his future novel into short-story form, but rejected the idea, feeling that there was overmuch satire latent in it. He wanted to tell about a Catholic social-climber in his native city, Buffalo, against the background of Catholic life there. The "social-climber" was to be a girl, and he feared his "heroine" would cause offence on the campus. So, he kept his story in his head — and heart — and waited.

In Washington, while he worked for his degree and wrote his thesis he gave half his time to his novel. It was a good place for him to write about Buffalo. "Detachment from the Buffalo scene," he tells, "gave me a more objective view of the novel's background, so that I thought I might now write about it (as Edith Wharton was said to do about old New York), "as intimately as if I loved it and as lucidly as if I hated it."

Roger Dooley did not quite finish his novel at Washington, D. C. Having taken his degree, he taught in high school in Buffalo and, in the spare hours of exacting teaching, he revised and revised his manuscript. "My aim," he says, "was to achieve something new in American Catholic fiction — a novel about Catholic life as it is ordinarily lived with none of the miraculous conversions, sugar-coated sermons, or other pietistic clichés that so often cause sophisticated readers to turn with a shudder from anything labeled a 'Catholic novel'."

Roger Dooley was twenty-five when his manuscript was finished. On its publication in 1946 the reception, both popular and critical, was highly satisfactory to the author. It was selected by the Catholic Literary Foundation and acclaimed by the Catholic press. Obviously his realistic interpretation of Catholic life was approved . . . the *Forecast* reviewer hailed it as "a fresh and authentic portrayal of Catholic life."

Roger Dooley was born in Buffalo, New York in 1920, the only child of Roger J. and May E. (Riordan) Dooley. His family, of Irish descent on both sides, lived in Buffalo for four generations. Familiar with the city and its traditions, he chose in later years to write about it, deciding, Jane Austen-like, to write "of what I knew best." Roger attended grammar school and finished at twelve, having skipped two years. From 1932 to 1936 he attended high school (South Park), and entered Canisius College in 1936 at the age of sixteen, having won two scholarships. He graduated from Canisius in 1940, taking his A.B. degree, *magna cum laude*, having majored in English. "Among the few alternatives open to English majors," he says, "teaching seemed most likely to leave me time free for creative writing, so the next step was to attain a master's degree. A Knights of Columbus fellowship, won in a national competition, enabled me to do two years of graduate work at the Catholic University of America in Washington, D. C., where my writing ambitions took more definite form, in my first novel, *Less Than the Angels*." Leaving the Catholic University with his M.A. degree, Roger Dooley taught for four years in high schools in Buffalo, and then joined the English staff at his alma mater, Canisius College.

Back in his college days he had received much encouragement for his writing in the college newspaper and literary magazine from his Jesuit teachers. There he turned out short stories, light verse, reviews and essays and even planned a trilogy of novels on his native city. The first of this trilogy, *Days Beyond Recall*, appeared in 1949. In her review of this book in the New York *Times*, Barbara Bond wrote: "there is no mistaking the reality of his atmosphere — or the authenticity of the over-all picture he has presented." What indeed strikes every reader of Roger Dooley's novels is their *authenticity*.

Roger Dooley finds some disquietude in the insistence of many of his fellow-citizens of Buffalo in identifying his fictional characters and the places and situations depicted in his novels. "With the glee of a whodunit fan, they look for their friends or more commonly their worst enemies." But this preoccupation of his readers is unfair, for Roger Dooley has "objectified his experiences so that his novels (so far) are in no way autobiographical."

Apart from his short stories, reviews and articles, Roger Dooley has so far published: *Less Than the Angels* (1946); *Days Beyond Recall* (1949). His latest book is *The House of Shanahan* (1952).

Still in his youth, and full of literary ambitions, Roger Dooley is on the threshold of big achievements in a field where there is much to be done. Of that field he has a clear vision. "It seems to me," he says, "that vast areas of Catholic life in America have yet to be explored in any significant way; there must be dozens of potential novels in every diocese, if only the novelists appear to dig them out. It is my hope to mine the particular vein of material available to me and give it its proper place in the American scene."   E. B. B.

Reverend William Lodewick Doty
1919–

Three books thus far (1952) have been written by Father Doty, and a fourth is in preparation.

William Lodewick Doty was born in New York City on March 17, 1919. His father was the late Dr. George Espy Doty, for many years connected with the Postgraduate Hospital in New York, and a general-practitioner and surgeon. His mother, still living, is Lillian Gertrude Doty (née Bergen) and he has three living sisters, Josephine and Joan Doty, Mrs. Humburto B. Conesa, and one brother, George. Father Doty is a direct descendant of Edward Doty, one of the signers of the Mayflower Compact, and of David Doty, a lieutenant in the American forces during the Revolutionary War.

He attended the now defunct Blessed Sacrament Convent School on West 79th Street in Manhattan for a brief time and completed his primary and secondary education at Collegiate School, also in Manhattan, New York. In 1935, after he was graduated from Collegiate, he matriculated at Fordham College, from which he was graduated in 1939 with a bachelor of arts degree. While at Fordham, he wrote for the *Fordham Monthly*, the college literary magazine, of which he eventually became an associate editor. His writings at this time included literary essays, poems and short stories. At Fordham, Father Doty was also active in dramatics and debating. In his senior year he was elected president of the Council of Debate.

Upon graduating from Fordham College, Father Doty worked for a brief time as a life insurance salesman, and then as a law clerk for New York attorneys. He attended evening classes at Fordham Law School for a year. It was during this period that Father Doty's latent vocation to the priesthood came to full flower. Putting aside legal ambitions, he entered, in the fall of 1940, St. Joseph's Seminary, the major seminary for the Archdiocese of New York.

While in the seminary Father Doty devoted himself, in the writing field, to the production of sermons. One was required each week by the Professor of Homiletics, the well known Monsignor Edward M. Betowski. One of the extracurricular activities of the seminary was a Literary Society which Father Doty joined and of which he later became president. The Literary Society met each week to hear a lecture, on a prominent author, by one of the members. Contributing literary articles to parish bulletins was another function of the society. While a seminarian, he succeeded in having a short poem accepted by *The Messenger of the Sacred Heart*. This was his first piece of creative writing to be published in a popular magazine.

Ordained on January 27, 1945, he was assigned to St. Peter's Church, in Haverstraw, New York. His priestly duties allowed little or no time for writing, except sermons. During this period, however, he came to perceive the need of specially prepared story sermons for children at Sunday Mass and in catechism classes. In June 1946 he was transferred to St. Luke's Church in the Bronx, New York City. Here he began a book on a series of story-sermons which was published in April 1948 by Joseph F. Wagner, Inc., under the title, *Catechetical Stories for Children*. Meanwhile he had been assigned to Cardinal Hayes High School in the Bronx to teach religion and English. Prior to this period, and even while in Haverstraw, Father Doty had collaborated on scripts for the "Faith in Action" radio program, sponsored by the Confraternity of Christian Doctrine. Moreover, from the fall of 1947 until February 1949 he collaborated with Fathers Daniel Brady and Edward Kenrick and Mr. John Grace of the Hayes' Faculty, on a weekly current-events column for the *Bronx Home News*.

His first novel *Fire in the Rain* appeared in 1951. In telling how he came to write it, he said: "Too engaged in adjusting myself to the sublime work of the parish priesthood to have energy or time for writing anything but sermons, I nevertheless knew that some day I must pull my chair up to the writing table and get to work, to try to tell something of the wonder and the beauty and the loneliness, and the bitter-sweetness of a young priest's life in Christ's vineyard." This book tells that story of a young priest's struggle for renewed zeal which he feels he has lost in seven years of routine parish duties.

Father Doty's latest work, *Stories for Discussion* (1952), is a novel about a priest teaching in school.

In addition he contributes to *St. Anthony's Messenger*, *The Messenger of the Sacred Heart*, *The Torch* and *The Lamp*.

(Edmund) Alan Downey   1889–

Fidelity to Ireland is an outstanding characteristic of this writer, who lives (1952) in Tramore, County Waterford, Ireland, and edits two Waterford papers. Third son of the seven children of Edmund and Frances Margaret Allen Downey, both Waterford City people, (Edmund) Alan Downey, like all his brothers and sisters, was born in London and grew up in a house seven miles from the centre of the metropolis in sight of the Surrey hills, where his father had settled as a young married man. The elder Downey was a publisher and the author of thirty novels.

Mr. Downey began his formal education at Notre Dame Convent, Clapham, London, when he was seven years old. Later he attended

Clapham College, conducted by the Xaverian Brothers, London University and Waterpark College, Waterford. He is an Associate in Arts of Oxford University (A.A. Oxon).

His interest in the land of his ancestors was kept vivid by holiday visits to Irish relatives and return visits by them to the Downey household in London. When he was fifteen, he went to work as a Civil Service clerk. About the same time, he read a series of essays by G. K. Chesterton published in the London *Daily News*. He credits them with turning his thoughts toward literature and religion and inspiring him to creative essay writing.

Leaving the Civil Service, he worked on a London Catholic newspaper, now defunct, and also began writing verse. Some of his early work appeared in *T. P.'s Weekly*, a London literary periodical edited by T. P. O'Connor, who later became a Cabinet Minister. In 1906, Mr. Downey's father went back to the land of his birth and bought *The Waterford News*. His son went with him and now edits the same century-old weekly, also *The Waterford Evening News*, a daily. He was made a Freeman of the city of Waterford in 1938.

Mr. Downey's published works include two volumes of verse, *The Starry Threshold* and *Things Invisible* and a miracle play in blank verse, *One Thing Is Necessary*. His other books are: *The Green Path*, a collection of short stories inspired by Irish scenes and experiences; *Economic Interpretations; The Glamour of Waterford; Forty-One*, an historical novel now out of print, dealing with the 1641 uprising led by Hugh McMahon, a short life of Thomas Francis Meagher, the '48 leader; and *Jade House*. In this novel, Mr. Downey says he attempted to "interpret the spirit of the Irish countryside in an abstract way with no intrusion of politics." He is at present at work on a sequel to *Jade House* in which an outstanding character is Eamon de Valera and also on a verse-drama about Hugh O'Neill, "the Great Earl," who led the Irish people in the Elizabethan wars. In the press, shortly to be published, is a narrative poem, *The Prisoner of London*, on the tragic story of the youngest son of Hugh O'Neill, who should have succeeded to his principality in Ulster had he not been made captive under Elizabeth's successor to the British throne, James I, who inaugurated the Partition of Ulster. He has contributed verses to periodicals including the *Capuchin Annual*, and several stories to Irish newspapers, his first appearing in the Dublin weekly, *The Sunday Independent*.   E. L.

Reverend Francis Drinkwater
1886–

A desire to improve the teaching methods of imparting religious instruction has prompted Father Francis Drinkwater to write many of his books.

Born in 1886 at Wednesbury (Staffs), England he was educated at the Colleges of Cotton and Oscott. Ordained in 1910 he was assigned to St. Peter's, Leamington (Warwickshire) where he spent four pleasant years. His rector was Canon William Barry from whom he learned much, especially history.

In May, 1915, he became an army chaplain on the Western Front. That same year he was wounded at Loos and gassed in 1918. In the last month of the war (as may be gathered from one of his own books) he lay in a hospital with a considerable amount of time to think. He decided to start a monthly paper. He finished up army life in 1919 with a few months' light duty at Aldershot. Here he had much time to write articles for the future paper. He called it *The Sower*, the first number of which appeared in June, 1919. It was devoted to Catholic education. Some of Father Drinkwater's articles were reprinted later in a shilling booklet called *Religion in School* and still later this work was enlarged into a larger volume under the title, *The Givers*. As a result of *The Sower's* campaign for better methods of religious instruction, Father Drinkwater was made Diocesan Inspector of Schools. Archbishop McIntyre urged him to get rid of the parrot-system of learning the catechism, and a new Birmingham Diocesan syllabus (sometimes called the Sower Scheme) was introduced. Convinced that the important thing is the living teacher, Father Drinkwater prepared aid-books for teachers. Some of these are: *Doctrine for the Juniors; Stories in School; Teaching the Catechism; Catechism Stories*, and *Twelve and After*. Of these teaching aid-books, perhaps the one called *Twelve and After* has had the widest influence. First published in 1925, it amalgamated doctrine, devotion, history, scripture and liturgy into a single course in a way that was novel. He was now parish priest of a larger parish in Birmingham, and found the work of getting out a periodical burdensome. He relinquished *The Sower* in 1926 and it was edited by others until 1939 when he again took it over when its editor, Father S. J. Gosling, went into the army.

Some of the plays Father Drinkwater wrote for *The Sower* were collected in a book called *Gabriel's Ave*.

In 1940 Father Drinkwater's presbytery, school and church were bombed in an air raid. Till the end of the war he lived in the sacristy and gradually got some of the buildings into repair. When the war was over he moved (September, 1945) to a smaller parish at Lower Gornal, a mining village near the countryside, where he is now stationed, and where he still is editor of *The Sower.*

Besides the books already mentioned, he is the author of: *Short Instructions on the Mass* (1921); *Rough Sermon Notes on the Sunday Gospels* (1924); *Homily Notes on the Sunday Gospels* (1926); *Prayers Worth Learning by Heart* (1929); *Sermon Notes on the Sunday Propers* (1931); *Religion in School Again* (1933); *Readings and Addresses for the Holy Hour* (1934); *Two Hundred Evening Sermon Notes* (1934); *Why Not End Poverty?* (1935); *Money and Social Justice* (1934); *Seven Addresses on Social Justice* (1937); *My Church Book* (1942); *Catechism at Early Mass* (1946); *Another Two Hundred Sermon Notes* (1947); *Catholic Schools Assembly Book* (1948); *The Abbreviated Catechism with Explanations* (1950); *Catechism Plays* (1950), and *Educational Essays* (1951).

M. A. H.

Reverend Jerome D'Souza, S.J.
1897–

Into the 1949 sessions of the General Assembly of the United Nations at Lake Success there stepped a most commanding figure. Tall, bearded, distinguished, Father Jerome D'Souza looks, as one of his fellow-delegates remarked, like the father-image everyone subconsciously carries in their hearts. He is the first Catholic priest to be a regular member of the principal delegation of a non-Christian nation to the United Nations. He made a tremendous impression in debates. As a delegate from India, a member of the Indian Congress, and of the Society of Jesus, he spoke with a double authority. His articles in *The Commonweal* on the Communist policy in India and on Communist tactics in the Far East generally, and his analysis of the Indian political situation were masterly.

Born on August 6th — the Feast of the Transfiguration — 1897, of Brahmin Catholic parents in Mangalore, South Kanara, India, Father Jerome, in spite of his Portuguese name, is of Indian race. Converted in the seventeenth century, his family took a Portuguese name, given by the Portuguese missionaries, as was then the common practice among the Christian converts.

Father D'Souza has three brothers, all priests: Reverend Boniface D'Souza, S.J. is rector of St. Joseph's College, Bangalore; Reverend John D'Souza is Rector of the inter-diocesan major seminary at Mangalore; Father Leo D'Souza is a secular priest. And his only sister is Superior of a Community of Indian Sisters Apostolic Carmel, in Mangalore, India. Their mother, who gave all her family to God, received from the Holy Father the papal cross, "Pro Ecclesia et Pontifice."

Father Jerome was educated in St. Aloysius' College, Mangalore, and in Presidency College, Madras. He was graduated with a first class honors degree in English Literature in 1920. He joined the Society of Jesus in 1921, at Shembaganure, South India, and did his novitiate and philosophy there at the Sacred Heart College. Then he travelled to Europe, and did his theology in Enghein, Belgium, and in the theological faculties of the French Jesuit provinces of Champagne and Toulouse. His tertianship he completed under Father Louis Poullier at St. Acheul in Amiens. He was ordained a priest August 31, 1931. His knowledge of the French language and literature is as thorough as his knowledge of English.

He returned to India in 1933, and was appointed Professor of English in St. Joseph's University College, Trichinopoly. In 1934 he was appointed Principal, and in 1938 also Rector. In 1942 he was transferred to Loyola College as Rector and Principal. At the end of 1950 Father D'Souza finished his term of office as Rector of Loyola University, Madras. He was then appointed Director of the Indian Institute of Social Order, St. Vincent's Street, Poona, India.

Father D'Souza was a member of the academic and governing bodies of the State University of Madras, to which the Jesuit University College is affiliated. He was appointed a member of the Government of Madras Reconstruction Committee in 1943. In the same year he was elected by the Madras Legislature under instructions from the leaders of the Congress Party as member of the Constituent Assembly of India to represent the interest of the Christians in the new Republic of India. "Though the Catholic population of India is less than two percent of the total 420 millions in India and Pakistan, the spirit of India is such that religious minorities are considered an integral part of national life and have their proportional representation in national governing bodies. It is not strange, therefore, that in India Catholic leaders be appointed to such governing bodies. At the death of Mahatma Gandhi, Father D'Souza was chosen to represent the Christians in giving the public address in the Constituent Assembly." (Jesuit Seminary and Missions Bureau).

After serving as delegate to the General Assembly in 1949, Father D'Souza was invited to give a course of lectures at Fordham University during the spring term of 1950. And on January 29th he gave the commencement address and received the degree of Doctor of Laws at Loyola College in Baltimore, Maryland.

Father D'Souza is still a member of the Indian Parliament and is on its Advisory Council for Foreign Affairs. His was one of the five names sent by the Government of India to UNO for their Panel for International Arbitration. He was appointed to this office in 1949 and will serve three more years. He is also a member of the Governing Board of the Indian Council of Cultural Relations under the Indian Ministry of Education.

Father D'Souza had a volume of collected essays and papers published in the fall of 1950 in New York (J. M. Barret Corporation, publishers) and he has written extensively in both French and English for *Etudes, The Month, Thought, The Commonweal, America, The Catholic World, The Sign* and *Ave Maria.*   A. F.

Douglas Valder Duff 1901–

Son of an officer of the Royal Navy, Douglas Valder Duff was born in, Rosario De Sta. Fe, Argentina, in 1901 and was educated by the Sisters of the Visitation at Bridport (Dorset), England. As a little lad and as a grown man he loved the nuns and in particular, the saintly Superior, Mother Mary Elizabeth, with whom he corresponded all her life and to whom, in conjunction with his aunt Isabella Duff, he dedicated his autobiography, *May The Winds Blow*, published in 1948.

Leaving the convent school in July 1914 he entered the Royal Navy training ship "Conway" as a cadet. Before his training was completed he transferred to the Cunard Line as a merchant marine cadet and served on a "doddering old tramp," the "Thracia." In 1917 the "Thracia" was torpedoed in the Bay of Biscay. As Douglas drifted towards the mainland on half of a smashed and capsized lifeboat, the sole survivor of a crew of forty-eight, he first attempted to strangle himself and, when his attempt failed, made a vow to become a monk.

After rescue he rejoined the merchant marine only to be torpedoed again. There followed adventure with the White Russians and then, remembering his vow, Douglas Duff entered a monastery at Deeping St. James (England) where he remained for two years (1919–1921). Feeling he had no real vocation, he left the monastery on a Monday morning. The following Friday he was a "Black and Tan" fighting off attacks from Irish Republicans in the streets of Dublin. He bitterly regrets having helped to fight the gallant Irish patriots who were fighting such terrific odds for their just rights and liberties. He loves Ireland, and, incidentally, he was the godson of Sir Roger Casement.

Douglas Duff next joined the Palestine Gendarmerie which Winston Churchill organized to keep the peace in the Holy Land. In personnel it differed little from the "Black and Tans." Douglas eventually found himself at the head of two hundred Arab and Jewish police with the task of maintaining order in Jerusalem. In the five years he commanded the Holy City's police he had many strange experiences with brigands, fanatics, rioters and cranks. He lived unscathed through the terrible earthquake of July 11th, 1927, of which he gives a striking description in his autobiography.

Illness forced his return to England, where he married and settled down for a time, devoting himself to writing adventure stories for boys, and books and articles about the Near East. His period of repose, interrupted by visits to insurgent Palestine, Abyssinia, Iraq and Civil War Spain, was terminated by the outbreak of the Second World War. He joined the Naval Reserve (R.N.V.R.) and was eventually sent to join the staff of Admiral Sir Andrew Cunningham as a specialist in near Eastern Arab affairs and for other duties.

There followed three years of strenuous activity in Crete, the

Western Desert, Tobruk, Derna, Greece and the Suez region, during which his official title became Lieutenant Commander, R.N.V.R. (Royal Naval Volunteer Reserve). Strange experiences, hair-breadth escapes, incredible situations, dare-devil adventures followed. Douglas records fighting and capturing an Italian tank from the seat of an ordinary touring car; he describes engaging a submarine from the deck of a tiny cargo boat. He lists 1013 air raids and no end of land campaigns, including sieges, that he underwent. He tells of fist-fights and of verbal contests with his military or naval superiors conducted in lurid language. Meanwhile he kept up correspondence with his beloved saint-friend, Mother Mary Elizabeth, and, at times, displayed heroic devotion to his faith. On one occasion he came across a corpse in Italian uniform. To his amazement he saw a small pyx hanging by a thin chain around the rotting neck of a priest. Opening the pyx he found a dozen small Hosts in it. After making an Act of Contrition he consumed the Hosts.

Man of action and adventurer he did his best to keep to high ideals, but in such situations it is scarcely to be wondered at that he had what ordinary stay-at-home folk must consider to be lapses.

Douglas Duff lived lustily, doing his best when his administrative measures were harsh and violent, by reminding himself that he must live up to the vows he made one morning in the Church of the Holy Sepulchre in Jerusalem when His Beatitude, the Latin Patriarch, struck him on the shoulder with King Godfrey's sword and dubbed him a Knight of the Venerable Order of the Holy Sepulchre, the oldest order of chivalry in the world.

Among the published works of Lieutenant Commander Douglas Duff are the following: *Sword for Hire* (1934); *Hammer of Allah* (1936); *Horned Crescent* (1936); *Palestine Picture* (1936); *Half-Deck of the Bradstock* (1938); *Desert Knight* (1939); *Desert Peacemaker* (1939); *Galilee Galloper* (1939); *Harding and the Screaming Mantle* (1939); *Harding of the Palestine Police* (1938); *Harding's Mountain Treasure* (1938); *Poor Knight's Saddle* (1938); *Jack Harding's Quest* (1939); *Palestine Unveiled* (1940); *Passage at Arms* (1944); *Berenger to the Rescue* (1949); *Treasure of the Antarctic* (1940); *Danger Chasers* (1946); *Bill Berenger's First Case* (1948); *Smugglers on the Saltings* (1948); *On the World's Roof* (1949); *Sea Wren's Maiden Voyage* (1949); *Bill Berenger Wins Command* (1950), as well as some 41 other books, 163 broadcast radio stories and some 540 short stories and articles in British and United States periodicals. He writes also under three pseudonyms, "Peter Wickloe," mainly concerned with stories having an historical background; (2) "Douglas Stanhope," engaged in sea-stories and (3) "Leslie Savage."

Douglas Duff was given a Distinguished Service Cross and three citations for valor. He is also a Knight of the Order of the Crown of Rumania and holds the Italian Order of the Crown.   E. B. B.

Reverend Avery Robert Dulles, S.J.
1918–

The conversion of Avery Robert Dulles took place in November 1940. Each one of his years at Harvard University from 1936 to 1940 marked a definite stage in his progress toward Catholicism. He attributes his conversion, under God, to his undergraduate studies in philosophy and history during the four preceding years.

Born in 1918 in Auburn, New York the son of John Foster Dulles and Janet Pomeroy Avery Dulles, he was raised a Presbyterian. After completing grammar school in New York City he attended preparatory schools in Switzerland and New England. His family wanted him to go to Princeton for his college education but he insisted on going to Harvard, "partly because my best friends were going there, but principally because I felt I would have access to the most learned instruction of our day. Such names as Whitehead, Kittredge, Lowes and Conant cast a spell over my eagerness. I did not suspect that I would find light at Harvard, not from these gentlemen, but from quite another quarter." (O'Brien's, *Where I Found Christ*, p. 69.) He entered Harvard College in 1936 and received his A.B. degree in 1940. While in boarding school and college he had a summer home in Long Island, New York, but he spent large parts of his summers traveling in Europe or cruising on a sailboat in the Great Lakes and the Gulf of St. Lawrence. He was attracted by the beauty which he found in the churches and museums of Europe, and even more, perhaps, by the expansiveness of the silent sea. Each of these attractions, in its way, awakened within him a thirst for the uncreated Beauty of God.

In an *apologia* which he published in 1946 under the title of *A Testimonial to Grace*, he described how, as an undergraduate at Harvard, he found his way out of the doubt and confusion of modern materialism under the guidance of the ancient and medieval philosophers. After Plato and Aristotle had taught him the supremacy of reason and the objectivity of the moral law, he discovered the riches of the Faith in the medieval poets and theologians, supplemented by the writings of modern Catholic philosophers and apologists.

A few weeks after the bombing of Pearl Harbor, Mr. Dulles found himself abruptly transferred from the status of a law student to that of a junior officer in the United States Navy. After spending much of the war period on submarine chasers in the Caribbean Sea, he was later assigned to staff and liaison work in the Mediterranean theater. It was during a period of relative leisure at sea in the summer of 1944 that he penned his *Testimonial to Grace*.

Upon his release from the Navy at the end of the war, Mr. Dulles was faced with a new decision as to the career he should pursue. He seized the opportunity to follow what had been the deepest inclination of his·heart since the time of his conversion. With the purpose of fighting henceforth with the sword of the spirit for a Kingdom that is not of this world, he entered the Society of Jesus at St. Andrew-on-Hudson, Poughkeepsie, New York in August 1946. After a novitiate of two years, he pursued the usual three years' course in philosophy at the Jesuit seminary of Woodstock, Maryland. He has recently been made a member of the philosophy faculty at Fordham University, New York City. After a brief period of teaching, he expects to begin his theological studies in preparation for his ordination to the priesthood.

In addition to *A Testimonial to Grace*, Mr. Dulles has written a monograph on the Renaissance philosopher, Pico della Mirandola. It was published by the Harvard University Press under the auspices of the Phi Beta Kappa Society in 1941. He is a contributor to *Where I Found Christ*, a collection of autobiographical stories edited by Rev. John A. O'Brien (1950). He has published articles on religious topics in various periodicals including the *Journal of Religious Instruction*, *America*, and *The Catholic Mind*. To *Social Order* (October, 1951) he contributed an article on Brownson's political theory.   M. A. H.

Pierre Lecomte Du Noüy
1883–1947

The leading thought of all Pierre Lecomte Du Noüy's work is that science leads to God and that it is destined to demonstrate the scientific inconsistency of materialism and to prove the necessity of a Divine Creator.

In the introduction of one of Du Noüy's books, *The Road to Reason*, Dr. Ralph W. Wyckoff says of the author: "One of the very few men I have known of whom it can be said that every year he was greater, both intellectually and as a human being, than the year before." How true this is, Catholics can appreciate from the fact that in Roosevelt Hospital in New York, where he died, he returned to the Catholic Church shortly before his death on September 22, 1947. On his deathbed he explained that his greatest joy would have been to liberate the scientists from atheism and to lead them back to God, their Creator.

Had he lived longer, there is no doubt that he would have corrected some of the unorthodox ideas on religion which he expressed in his books.

Pierre Lecomte Du Noüy was born in Paris, France on December 20th, 1883. A descendant of writers and artists which included Corneille, he was brought up in free-thinking, intellectual circles. He obtained his degrees of LL.B., Ph.B., Sc.B., Ph.D., and Sc.D. at the Sorbonne in Paris and graduated from Law School, but never practiced.

He started life by writing short stories as well as several plays which were produced with success. His deep interest in philosophy and the belief that progress in it would have to be based on science led him to take up scientific studies under Pierre and Mme. Curie, Sir William Ramsay in England, Appell and others.

At the outbreak of the First World War, he was sent to the Front as a lieutenant in the famous "Chasseurs à Pied," but his knowledge of mechanics and driving soon put him in command of a motor section with headquarters at Compiègne, where he met Dr. Alexis Carrel with whom he worked in his spare hours on the problem of the cicatrization of wounds. At Dr. Carrel's request Du Noüy was attached, in 1915, to his unit where he remained until the end of the war, with the exception of a short mission to the United States. In 1920 he joined the Rockefeller Institute in New York as an associate member, leaving there in 1927 to go to the Pasteur Institute in Paris where he created the first laboratory of molecular bio-physics in Europe. Heisenberg's theory of indeterminism, as well as the laws of chance had convinced him that life and the steady progress of evolution cannot be accounted for by modern physical laws and that materialism can no longer be based on science. His articles and lectures on the subject aroused the enmity of the left wing and forced his resignation from the Pasteur Institute in 1936. The title of Director of the Ecole des Hautes Etudes at the Sorbonne did not provide the laboratories necessary to continue his scientific work so he left. After a trip around the world he wrote *L'Homme devant la Science* (1939), which shows that the laws of chance cannot account for life and evolution. Modern laboratories were being built for him by an industrialist outside of Paris when World War II broke out. Conditions under German occupation prevented experimental work and he devoted himself to writing *L'Avenir de l'Esprit*, published in 1941 and crowned in 1942 by the French Academy. In 1944 the University of Lausanne awarded him the Arnold Raymond prize for his most valuable contribution to the philosophy of science for the two books mentioned above and *Le Temps et la Vie* (Biological Time) which had come out in 1936 in London and in 1937 in America. This book gave his new concept of a biological time, different from sidereal time, deduced from his experiments on the cicatrization of wounds.

Together with Mrs. Mary Bishop Harriman, an American, whom he had taken for his second wife in 1923, he escaped from Paris at the end of 1942, reaching this country in January, 1943. *La Dignité Humaine*, which developed some of the ideas in his first two books and stressed the moral and spiritual conclusions, was published by Brentano in New York in 1944. That year he covered 35,000 miles in the United States, lecturing for the YMCA and the USO on his experiences in Paris under the Germans. *Human Destiny*, a synthesis of his three French books, was published in 1947, shortly before his death on September 22nd of the same year after a long and painful illness. The last rites were administered by Reverend John LaFarge, S.J. He was buried from St. Ignatius Loyola Church on September 25, 1947.

Lecomte Du Noüy's scientific work can be classed in four principal groups:

1. 1915–1920 — Cicatrization of wounds — He established the mathematical formula based on the surface of the wound and age of the patient and could thus calculate beforehand the exact date of cicatrization and scientifically check the treatments employed to deduce the physiological age.

2. 1920–1926 — Absorption phenomena of surface tension — The tensiometer which won a Franklin Institute award in 1923 enabled him to put in evidence the existence of monomolecular layers which in turn disclosed three minima in the surface tension of sodium oleate and enabled him to calculate the three dimensions of the molecule as well as the dimension of the ovalbumine molecule and give a determination of the Avogadro number in excellent accord with previous ones.

3. Physico-chemical characteristics of Immunity. The study of thin layers of serum on water led to the discovery of a physico-chemical phenomenon not due to immunization and showed that the serum is constituted of asymetric prismatic molecules capable of being polarized in monomolecular layers.

4. 1927–1933 — Experiments made by heating serum at a temperature above 55° C. showed an increase in surface tension, viscosity, rotatory power, rotatory dispersion, etc.; altogether twelve new phenomena were discovered proving that serum and plasma are true solutions molecularly dispersed and not colloids as had been thought heretofore. Most of these experiments were based on new instruments and new techniques which since have been used extensively in scientific and industrial laboratories. Amongst these figure the tensiometer, a microviscosimeter, an ionometer for the measurement of Ph up to the 4th and 5th decimal parts and an automatic spectrophotometer in the infra-red.

About two hundred of his original scientific papers were condensed in two books published both in French and in English.

M. A. H.

Eleanor Early

Described as "a spritely brunette with an enormous curiosity about people and places," Eleanor Early has specialized in travel books.

She was born in Newton, Massachusetts, the daughter of James A. and Sarah Dolan Early. After attending the public schools in Wellesley, she entered Miss Wheelock's school in Boston. Her diploma from there made her a kindergarten teacher, but she never worked at it. She got herself a job on the old Boston *Record*, where she did all things that cubs do. She re-wrote club notes, did obits, chased fires, and covered inconsequential things. Then she covered murders, breach of promise suits, the Federal Building and the Police Court. Pretty soon she was a feature writer. Later she went to Washington for International News Service and also went abroad.

Asked how she started to write travel books, she answered: "I was a newspaper reporter — very young. I had planned a vacation to Cuba with my cousin. We had made our reservations there, bought our tickets, and lots of pretty scenery (dresses). At the last minute the boss said I could not go. It was very unfair. Jobs were not scarce then, so I just went anyhow. When I came back I was fired. So I started freelancing. I had discovered I loved traveling and it seemed to me there were so many things one should learn, in order to get the most out of it. Anyhow, I wanted to know so many things — history, geography and background. I wanted to know where and what to eat, and where to shop. I try to write travel books that are instructive and readable. If one keeps only to the main roads, one misses the things that give a place its character and charm."

Her first book *And This is Boston!* was written at the instigation of some nostalgic Bostonians. At the time she was at the training camp of the Braves in St. Petersburg, Florida, covering them for the Boston *American*. The book was an immediate success, and she has been writing about travel ever since. When her second book *And This is Cape Cod!* was published, the reviewer in the New York *Times* stated: "Nobody writes better guide books than Eleanor Early — better, more interesting, more charming." The New York *Herald Tribune* said of her third book, *And This is Washington*, "As guide, companion, and friend, it is in the words of the old song, 'beyond compare.'" Clara E. Laughlin — a travel writer herself, said of Miss Early's fourth book, *Behold the White Mountains!* "A perfectly delightful little book. . . . You're simply not human if after reading it you can stay away from the mountains." *Ports of the Sun* and *Lands of Delight* are about Bermuda, the Virgin Islands, the French Islands, the British Islands, Haiti and Jamaica, Barranquilla and Cartagena, Panama, Nassau and Cuba. To write them Miss Early lived in Dominica for nearly a year, where she hired the "big house" of a $100,000 estate for $30.00 a month and the best cook on the island for $1.50 a week. She kept house in Haiti, Tortola and Tobago and spent many months on the other islands she describes. Other books of hers are: *A New England Sampler; She Knew What He Wanted; An Island Patchwork* (Nantucket); *Adirondack Tales; New Orleans Holiday; New York Holiday,* and *Washington Holiday.*

Before she writes about a place, Miss Early gets to know it intimately. She reads everything about its history and its people, visiting every nook and corner. "First I do all the things the tourists do," she explains, "then I explore on my own."

In gathering her material for *New York Holiday* she ate in most of the two hundred restaurants described in that book; she visited the Statue of Liberty half a dozen times. "It was on Bedloe's Island, incidentally, that she unearthed the story, since reprinted in magazines, of Mrs. Charles C. Marshall, who persuaded Congress to spend a million dollars cleaning up the Island for Miss Liberty. In *New York Holiday* she also tells why 'Miss Liberty is such a great big girl,' 'why McCreery's Fifth Avenue entrance is so modest,' 'why Lord & Taylor and the A & P are remembered in the prayers of the Little Sisters of the Poor,' 'where to get breakfast with twenty-six different kinds of fish,' and 'who has undisputed right to all dead whales that drift ashore in down-town Manhattan.'"

Miss Early believes she works harder than most travel writers. She admits to rewriting a single paragraph forty times.

Her hobbies are traveling and cooking. She picks up recipes everywhere, and tries them at home. M. A. H.

Reverend Edward J. Edwards, S.V.D. 1904–

For ten years Father Edward J. Edwards was a missioner in the Philippines and China. Frequent attacks of malaria necessitated his return to the United States in 1940, and since then he has turned to writing as a means of helping the missioners still in the field.

Born on November 4, 1904, in New York City, he attended the public and parochial schools there, and then studied for the missionary priesthood in the Society of the Divine Word at St. Mary's Mission Seminary, Techny, Illinois. He was ordained in April 1930. In the fall of the same year, he was on his way to the Philippines. For three years, he taught in the seminary for native clergy, which was located in the town of Vigan on the northwest tip of the island of Luzon. "Teaching in a seminary was not exactly the type of work that one visualizes for oneself when signing up with a missionary society," remarked Father Edwards, "but it was the work assigned me and I did my best to lead the students' minds into the mysteries of the English language, homiletics, dramatics and algebra. There were a public high school and junior college in the town and my leisure moments were taken up with forming the students into a Catholic club.

"Four hours journey from Vigan, on a directly eastern route, brought one into the province of Abra. The entire mission work in this province was in the hands of our Fathers and it was in the nature of a renovation and inspiration for me to get up there in the long vacation months and share, even if remotely, in the hardships which their pioneer work entailed. The experience had on these forays formed the basis for *Thy People, My People*, and *These Two Hands*.

"On a three day notice I was transferred to the Catholic University of Peking which had just been turned over to the Society of the Divine Word by the Holy See. At the University I taught rhetoric, managed the University Press, edited the *Fu Jen Magazine*, and was athletic director.

"After two years I was recalled to the Philippines where the Society had taken over a school in the Visayan Islands. Despite my interest in active pastoral work I was again sentenced to the professorial chair. The new college was located on the island of Cebu. Colegio de San Carlos was the name of the school and for five years I functioned as prefect of boarders, athletic director, moderator of the school magazine, *The Carolinian,* instructor in college composition and debate, teacher of religion, and head of the dramatic department.

"Outside the city of Cebu there was a leprosarium that housed about 1100 patients. The father in charge of the patients' spiritual care was a good friend of mine and I used to visit him quite regularly. Out of this relationship was gathered the material that formed the basis for the novel *White Fire.*

"I had had a great many malarial attacks over a period of years and the final one left me with a chest condition that necessitated my return to the United States.

"The devotion and self-sacrifice of the priests, brothers and sisters at work in the foreign missions are really an inspiration and I wanted to do something to relieve the financial handicaps under which most of them labor. That was what induced me to attempt the first novel. It did produce some results financially, and over and above that it produced the self-satisfying illusion that I was still functioning as a sort of second-hand missionary. All the financial returns from my writings have gone to assist the missionaries in the Philippines.

"Towards the close of the war a young man who had had some rather strange experiences came to me for advice. There were so many people at that time bewildered by the loss of dear ones through the war that I thought it opportune to bring to their minds the one great source of comfort left them. The young man had given me permission to use his experiences as a basis for composing a novel and the result was *This Night Called Day.*"

His book, *The Chosen* (1949), with a seminary as the locale, was an attempt to speak out against the selfishness that is so widespread today, and that is laying hold of youth from the very dawn of the age of reason.

In 1950 Father Edwards completed a biography of Arnold Janssen, the Founder of the Society of the Divine Word. His latest novel is *Three Days.*

"What started out as a sort of occupational therapy," remarks Father Edwards, "has grown into a full time job. It is no longer an avocation, but work, hard work. One never does get a story down on paper with the clarity and effectiveness with which it was visioned in one's mind, and I suppose that is and remains the great challenge for every writer: To hope and try and keep on striving to achieve that."

                                                                M. A. H.

Reverend John Tracy Ellis   1905–

John Tracy Ellis was born the son of Elmer L. and Ida C. (Murphy) Ellis in Seneca, Illinois, July 30, 1905. While a student at St. Viator College, Bourbonnais, Illinois, he came under the influence of a professor who awakened in him a love for history that has grown through the years. After receiving his bachelor's degree from St. Viator in 1927, he entered the Catholic University of America and began his graduate study under the late Monsignor Peter Guilday, whose enthusiasm and methodology greatly impressed him. He wrote his doctoral dissertation in the field of medieval history under Dr. Guilday, who at the time was teaching medieval as well as American Church history, and received his Ph.D. in 1930. He later did postgraduate work at the University of Chicago and at Harvard University. He was head of the department of history at St. Viator College 1930–32 and at the College of St. Teresa, Winona, Minnesota, 1932–34. In these colleges he taught "everything from the Hittites to F.D.R." He was co-author of a brochure entitled *The Catholic Church and Peace Efforts*, which was published by the Catholic Association for International Peace in 1934. He was director of the Southern Branch Summer Session of the Catholic University of America at Our Lady of the Lake College and Incarnate Word College, San Antonio, Texas, 1935–37.

Dr. Ellis returned to the Sulpician Seminary at the Catholic University of America in September, 1934, to take up his studies for the priesthood, and he was ordained in Winona, Minnesota, June 5, 1938. He taught part time in the University 1935–38 while studying theology, when his major interest was modern European history. He was named an instructor in history in 1938, promoted to the rank of assistant professor in 1941, associate professor in 1943, and full professor in 1947. In 1942 he published *Cardinal Consalvi and Anti-Papal Relations, 1814–1824*. Because of Dr. Guilday's failing health, the late Bishop Joseph M. Corrigan, Rector of the Catholic University of America, asked Dr. Ellis in July 1941, to prepare to take over Guilday's courses in American Church history in the Graduate School of Arts and Sciences. Dr. Ellis spent a year's leave of absence, 1941–42, at Harvard University auditing courses in American social history and reading intensively. In September, 1942, he began his present work of teaching and directing graduate students in the history of the Catholic Church in the United States at the University.

Studying the history of the American Church in the late nineteenth century, Father Ellis soon came to realize the important influence that Bishop John Lancaster Spalding, of Peoria, had wielded during that period, and he decided to write the biography of Spalding. In the course of his researches into Spalding's life the part played by

Spalding in the foundation of the Catholic University of America bulked larger and larger, and Dr. Ellis' work developed, not into a simple biography of the Bishop of Peoria, but into a book on the origin and early years of the University, which was entitled *The Formative Years of the Catholic University of America.* It appeared in June, 1946.

Dr. Ellis is convinced that James Cardinal Gibbons was "by all odds the greatest single figure in the history of the American Church," and in July, 1945, he began collecting material to write the definitive life of the Cardinal. He has searched all the important diocesan archives east of the Mississippi, the National Archives in Washington, the Division of Manuscripts of the Library of Congress, the archives of the Maryland Historical Society, the Duke University Library, the library of the University of North Carolina, and archives in Rome, Paris, London, and Dublin for manuscripts and documents containing information about Gibbons. The work will run to two large volumes of about 700 pages each, and it will be published in the late spring of 1952 by the Bruce Publishing Company of Milwaukee.

Father Ellis is a priest of the Archdiocese of Washington, and he is censor of books for that archdiocese. He is a member of the American Historical Association, the American Catholic Historical Association, the Catholic Historical Association, the Catholic Commission on Cultural and Intellectual Affairs, and the Mississippi Valley Historical Association. Since 1941 he has been secretary of the American Catholic Historical Association and managing editor of *The Catholic Historical Review.* In 1947 he published *A Select Bibliography of the History of the Catholic Church in the United States.*

The variety of history courses Dr. Ellis conducted as a young college teacher and his shifting from medieval to modern European to American Church history have prepared him well for his present position of professor of American Church history in the Catholic University of America and director of graduate students in that field. And his proximity to the archives of the Archdiocese of Baltimore is most advantageous, as those archives are the richest single treasury of unused manuscript sources on the American Church, sufficiently abundant to invite the investigation and study of research scholars for many years to come.   B. S.

Sister Mary Alfreda Elsensohn, O.S.B.   1897–

The long-time interest in the historical background of Idaho County in the State of Idaho, led Sister M. Alfreda to write *Pioneer Days in Idaho County.*

Sister Mary Alfreda, née Edith M. Elsensohn, was born in Grangeville, Idaho, February 7, 1897, the daughter of Lewis and Mary Elsensohn. Her father, to whom she dedicates *Pioneer Days in Idaho County*, was the first County Superintendent of Schools in Idaho County, Idaho. As a child, Edith would sit at his feet listening to him read poems of Longfellow, especially Hiawatha. Later he used to speak to her often of Lincoln's Gettysburg Address, and she was always a willing listener. Her father died in 1908.

Edith's early education was received in the public and private schools of Grangeville, and Pomeroy, Washington. In 1915 she entered the Order of Saint Benedict at Saint Gertrude's Convent, Cottonwood, Idaho, and was professed November 26, 1916, under the name Sister Mary Alfreda. She was graduated from Lewiston State Normal School, June 1924, and that same year attended Washington State College, at Pullman, Washington. Later she attended Gonzaga University and received her B.S. from that institution in 1927. In 1935 she took a course in the geography and geology of Idaho at the University of Idaho and in 1937 she enrolled in a graduate course in geographical research. Her master of science degree in education was obtained in 1939 from the University of Idaho.

Sister Mary Alfreda has taught in the parochial or public grade schools at Cottonwood, Ferdinand, and Keuterville, Idaho. In 1950 she completed thirty-four years of teaching, twenty-six of them in high school. Since she specialized in science she taught biology, chemistry, and sometimes physics, for many years. She has also taught many other subjects and at present (1952) she is teaching journalism, speech, typing, and Latin II.

In addition to her teaching schedule, she has served as librarian at Saint Scholastica's Academy, Colton, Washington, and at St. Gertrude's Academy.

Sister Mary Alfreda's writing career began in the high school at Pomeroy, Washington. It was during her senior year there that the seniors and juniors were asked to write the history of the public school of Pomeroy. Sister Alfreda won the prize of $10.00 and her story was published in the pioneer edition of the *East Washingtonian.*

She contributed many articles to the *Echo of St. Gertrude's*, during the lifetime of that magazine, 1923–1940. Occasionally she writes articles for the *Idaho County Free Press* or the *Cottonwood Chronicle.* She also has an article in the three editions of the regional publicity pamphlet, "Golden Road to Adventure." Since 1947 she has been a member of the Idaho Writers League.

In November, 1950, a pamphlet, *Sixty-Six Years of Service, 1884–1950*, dealing with the history of St. Gertrude's Convent and Community, and written by Sister Alfreda, was published.

The first volume of Sister Alfreda's *Pioneer Days in Idaho County*, appeared in 1947. Volume Two was published in December 1951. "My purpose," she writes in the Introduction "has been to record as far as possible the geographic and historic factors and associations which have entered into the naming of the towns of Idaho County, of her numerous mountain peaks, her creeks, her lakes, her rivers, and any other natural features of significance."   M. A. H.

Helen Margaret Mary af Enehjelm
(Mrs. Erik af Enehjelm) 1909–

Helen Margaret Mary af Enehjelm is one of Europe's many polyglots. She was born on April 9, 1909 in Bakersfield, Kern County, California, the daughter of Henry Moller and Ellen O'Doherty Moller, where her father was engaged in the oil business. Her Danish grandfather, a sea captain, fled as far as possible from the Germans in Schleswig-Holstein only "to marry one of the nicest Germans, half-Prussian and half-Bavarian Sophie Witte, whose uncle later became foreign minister of Russia, Russia at that time having been the other land of unlimited opportunity. The author's mother is pure Irish from Donegal, her father's uncle having been the first English-speaking settler in Mora, New Mexico. The first language she learned to speak was Spanish. The first languages heard by Helen Moller other than English were Danish and German, her father's home having been trilingual. Among the schools Helen Moller attended were St. Joseph's Academy in Trinidad, Colorado and Bakersfield High School, Kern County. She then took her B.A. degree in English and French literature at the University of California, Berkeley in 1930.

In January of the same year (1930) she married Hugo Erik Gustaf af Enehjelm, a mechanical engineer, of the ten per cent Swedish minority in Finland. After a year in Canada, with studies in sociology at McGill University, the Enehjelms moved to Finland, where they have lived ever since through wars and various crises. "We live," she writes, "in the ancient province of Tavastland (in Swedish, the people who inhabited this district 100 kilometers north of the capital, Helsingfors, having been called Tavasts by the Swedish conquerors of 1200: in Finish Häme) and from our house on rising ground we can see both a large lake and the river that flows out of it, although we are not situated in the lake district proper — Finland is called the land of 40,000 lakes, but in our province one can drive for 10 or 15 kilometers without seeing a lake. The first snow flurries usually occur in November but the heavy snow blanket does not conceal the earth until the end of December or early January. The snow has usually melted by the middle of April, but light snows occur as late as May if it is a cold spring. The first flowers appear around May 1st on sheltered hillsides and are pink daphne very close to the ground and blue anemones. Summers are warm, with very clear, bright light. Our parish contains very old farming lands and broad fields from which most of the stones were removed centuries ago, but it is also heavily forested. Our parish church, built of granite in 1431 by the Swedish missionary priests, Catholic, of course, at that time, is very beautiful and stands on a hill overlooking a picturesque landscape of cliffs, forests, a winding river with a hump-backed stone bridge (the favorite scene of medieval pitched battles between powerful landowners), fields and meadows, and last but not least, the well of St. Lawrence, which is a wishing well into which people throw coins. In pagan times (that is prior to the advent of the Swedish missionary fathers in 1200) this well, a sacrificial site because of its apparently magical properties — it never freezes in the coldest winters and it never dries up in the warmest summers — impressed people's minds. St. Lawrence became extremely popular among the Finns of the middle ages, perhaps because of his martyr death on the griddle appealed to their imaginations. There are many medieval churches in Tavastland, all of granite, and often called cathedrals of the wilderness because the devout but poverty-stricken Finns lived in log cabins themselves and their churches were such great contrasts. About 20 kilometers from where we live there is a famous church, Hattula, built at the beginning of the 14th century, and formerly dedicated to the Holy Cross, a place of pilgrimage all during Catholic times, and a tourist attraction today. It is made of brick-faced granite and is decorated inside with fresco paintings representing the chief episodes of the Old and New Testaments. These churches were the first architectural elements that attracted me in Finland's landscape and they give a definite style to the landscape. What I like best of all in it is the blue ridge of forested hillsides in the distance, an unusual horizon for this otherwise rather flat, green country with its winding threads of blue."

The Enehjelms now own the family estate, Monikkala, and have one daughter, Johanna Francisca Beata. She was born in 1933 and is at present (1951) studying agriculture at the University of Helsingfors. The Enehjelms live in a purely Finnish district and never speak less than three languages every day. During the Second World War, with Russian prisoners of war, taken by the Finns, helping with the farm work, the author's husband spoke five languages a day, as there were also German-speaking Baltic relatives present. Mrs. af Enehjelm says if one is equipped with Swedish, one can manage perfectly all over Scandinavia including Iceland.

Mrs. af Enehjelm began writing directly in Swedish in 1942, striving to identify herself with the brave and isolated Finnish people. She is now engaged in translating into English Dr. Osvald Sirén's authoritative work, *3000 Years of Chinese Art* from Swedish. Recently she completed the first volume of the trilogy. She says: "I thoroughly enjoy putting the beautiful history of Chinese art into my own language, for there is nothing like one's own mother tongue and I love mine."

Mrs. af Enehjelm has written seven books. They are: *Kajornas kyrka* — novel (Jackdaw Church) (1934), written in English, translated into Swedish, published by Holger Schildt in Helsingfors, Finland; *Cypresstunneln* — novel (The Cypress Tunnel) (1938), same as above; *Vor soliga vardag* (Our Sunny Days or Everyday Life) (sketches) (1942), written directly in Swedish and published by Holger Schildt in Finland and Medéns in Sweden; *I lä for östanvinden* (Sheltered from the East Wind) (1943), same as above (novel in diary form); *Promenad med favoriter* (A Walk with Favorites) (1945), essays on English, American and French writers, written in Swedish and published in Finland in both Swedish and Finnish (1948), and in Sweden. One of these essays was also translated into Danish and published in 1946 by Wivels Forlag with essays by four Swedes and one other Swedish-speaking Finlander, in a volume entitled *Essays fra Sverige og Finland* (Essays from Sweden and Finland). *Promenad med favoriter* won the Granberg-Sumelius literary prize. *Hemlangtan* (Homesickness) (1946), essays published by Schildt and Medéns; *Po stranden* (On the Shore) (1948), childhood memories in sketches, written in English, translated by the author into Swedish, published by Schildt in Helsingfors, and Medéns in Sweden, unplaced as yet in the United States; *Vor soliga vardag*, translated into Finnish (1943) with the title *Aurinkoista Arkea*, Werner Soderstrom O.Y., publisher; *I lä for östanvinden*, translated into German (1943) with the title *In Lee vor dem Ostwind*, Waldstatt Verlag, Einsiedeln, Switzerland, have been popular with her readers.

Mrs. af Enehjelm has made extensive lecture tours in Sweden for the popular education union subsidized by the state. She has also translated innumerable articles and speeches on every subject from psychosomatic disorders of military patients to modern art glass.

M. A. H.

Reverend Omer Englebert   1893–

Father Englebert was born in the Ardennes, at Ollomont-Nadrin, on March 31st, 1893. His father belonged to a local land-owning family, established in the Ardennes for many centuries. He taught his son to read, and also taught him music. His mother, also of local land-owning stock, had Rhenish and Spanish blood. She was very pious. Until the age of eleven, Omer lived in a little village hidden in the mountains, chiefly occupied with his two pet goats, his dog, and a tame crow. He studied at the Ecclesiastical College of Bastogne. He relates that he was a bad pupil, caring only for music and reading. He finished bottom of his class, and in five years brought home only two prizes: one for music, and one for history.

He spent an itinerant youth, devoted to study, but also to travel. He tried to become a Franciscan, but his health was not up to it. He continued his studies under very good masters, but was always poor at scholastic philosophy, and rather better at theology. Devoted both to literature and to history, he was influenced by St. Francis of Assisi, and by the historians Harnack and Pastor.

In 1919 he founded a monthly, *La Terre Wallonne*. In 1924 he received Holy Orders in the diocese of Malines, at the hands of Cardinal Mercier, who made him literary editor of the daily *Vingtieme Siècle*. His first book, *La Sagesse du Curé Pecquet*, appeared in 1927, and was an immediate and a lasting success. Henry Clouard, in his *Histoire de la Littérature Française*, devotes two pages to Father Englebert. Of *La Sagesse du Curé Pecquet* and the two later volumes, *Le Curé Pecquet Continue* (1934) and *Le Curé Pecquet Vit Encore* (1948), he writes: "Essentially true to type, this Father Pecquet is one of the few real priests in modern literature. He gives to orthodoxy the savor of paradox, and defends divine government with all the brilliance usually reserved to the opposition. Moreover, the remarks of this saintly individual reflect a wisdom which is marvellously, fully, and sweetly profane: a wonderful fusion of the Gospel and the Fables of La Fontaine." David McKay Company, Inc., published in one volume selections from the three Curé Pecquet books, in the fall of 1951, under the title *The Wisdom of Father Pecquet*.

Amongst Father Englebert's many books are the following: *The Apparitions of Beauraing* (1933); *Life and Conversion of Eve Lavalliere* (1936); *Life of Joan of Arc by herself* (1939); *Father Damian* (1940); *Life of St. Martin* (1941); *Life of St. Genevieve* (1943); *The Sayings of Brother Egidius* (1929); *Life of St. Pascal Baylon* (1944); *Life of St. Francis of Assisi* (1947). This last has been translated into English, Spanish, German, Dutch and Polish. Every one of the above-mentioned books has been translated into at least two languages. Father Englebert's *Les Saints*, for each month of the year, was published in France in 1949–50 in the Collection "Pages Catholiques" by Albin Michel, and they are also bringing them out later in one volume. David McKay Company, Inc., published the English translation of the *Lives of the Saints* in 1951. It gives the interesting facts of some 2,300 of the elect.

Since 1941 he has been in charge of publishing two series at Albin Michel, in Paris, one of which is *Pages Catholiques* (which numbers now some sixty titles, including Thomas Merton's *Seven Storey Mountain*) and *Les Grands Spirituels*. Father Englebert is a great traveller; he has visited all the countries of Europe, except Russia, and much of South America. He came to the United States in 1950, on a mission to raise funds for a new complete edition of Migne's *Patrologia*.

Henry Clouard summed up Father Englebert by saying "what distinguishes him is a robust and realistic spirit, exacting in substantial values, and therefore opposed to all that is confused and superficial, in psychology, morals and politics." A. F.

Henry Outram Evennett   1901–

Henry Outram Evennett, a fellow lecturer and tutor of Trinity College, was born in London, the son of a stockbroker, on May 15, 1901. He was educated by the English Benedictine Fathers of Ealing Priory School (1912–1917), and Downside School (1917–1920). He then went up to Trinity College, Cambridge, England, with an open exhibition in history in October 1920. He became a senior scholar of that college in 1921 and obtained First Class Honors in both parts of the Historical Tripos (1922 and 1923). Two years later (1925) he became a Fellow of Trinity College on the strength of a dissertation on the history of the Council of Trent. He was appointed a college lecturer in history in 1930 and shortly afterwards a university lecturer as well. Since 1945 he has held in addition the office of college tutor.

His main subject of historical interest is the history of the Council of Trent and of the Counter-Reformation period in general. In 1930 he published *The Cardinal of Lorraine and the Council of Trent* (Cambridge University Press). This book was recognized as an authentic work on the subject. He hopes in due course to publish further studies on the Counter-Reformation.

He has also a subsidiary historical interest in the history of Catholic educational institutions especially in Great Britain. As a result of this study he brought out in 1944, *The Catholic Schools of England and Wales* which was also published by the Cambridge University Press, in the Current Problems Series. He also contributed a study on "Catholics and the English Universities 1850–1950" to a volume of studies published in 1950 to mark the centenary of the restoration of the English hierarchy.

Professor Evennett is unmarried.   M. A. H.

Reverend Denis Fahey, C.S.Sp. 1883–

In Rome, where his studies culminated, in 1912, in the doctorate of theology at the Gregorian University, Father Denis Fahey made a promise to St. Peter that shaped his subsequent career. He had lived in Rome through the acute crisis of Modernism and had seen how "revolutions were bringing about the elimination of the rule of Christ the King by circumscribing and hampering the influence of the supernatural." In Rome, his studies under Billot and Mattiussi resulted in deep convictions. "I began," he writes, "to realize more fully the real significance of the history of the world as the account of the acceptance or rejection of our Lord's program for order. . . . I repeatedly promised St. Peter that if ever I got the chance, I would teach the truth about his Master in the way he and his successors, the Roman Pontiffs, wanted it done. This is what I have striven to do and am doing."

Twenty-five years after the young Irish priest made his promise to St. Peter in Rome, a distinguished Dominican Father was to write in Dublin, Ireland, "It is probable that only in another generation will the full import of all that Father Fahey has been doing for a quarter of a century now, be rightly appreciated. All through these years he has preached submission to the supernatural order established under the headship of Christ. Of the truth that: 'He must reign,' Dr. Fahey is passionately convinced."

Denis Fahey was born in 1883, at Kilmore, County Tipperary, Ireland. On his mother's side he inherited a long tradition of love of learning. She was an O'Cleary, a descendant of the famous O'Clearys of Donegal, the hereditary historians of the O'Donnell clan. After his primary education, in 1895, Denis Fahey entered Rockwell College, County Tipperary, where he spent five years and achieved distinction alike in scholarship and athletics. At seventeen he entered the Congregation of the Holy Ghost and was sent to Grignon-Orly, near Paris, to do his novitiate. Though he completed his novitiate, a serious illness prevented him from making his profession, and he returned to Ireland to recuperate his health and continue his studies. Five years later he took his degree of B.A. at the Royal University (Dublin) with the highest honors in civil and constitutional history, political economy, and general jurisprudence.

Of the literature he was constrained to read in preparation for his examinations in this non-sectarian institution, Father Fahey wrote later in life, "I loathed the anti-Catholic spirit and doctrine of a number of the books I had to study, especially in the history course. My reaction against the disgusting books of my B.A. course was strengthened by the fact that I lived in Rome during the struggle against Modernism with its naturalistic separation of the historian and the believer."

During the period 1906–1908, Denis Fahey studied philosophy in houses of his Congregation in England and France and made his religious profession on February 2, 1907. His theological studies (1908–1912) were, as we have mentioned, made at the Gregorian University, in Rome. There he was deeply influenced by the works of Kurth, Deschamps, and Cardinal Pie. "Kurth's book *Les origines de la Civilisation Moderne*," says Father Fahey, "one of the loveliest books ever written, showed the Mystical Body of Christ transforming the pagan society of the Roman Empire and preparing the upward movement of acknowledgment of the programme our Lord Jesus Christ, Priest and King. Deschamps' book, *Les Sociétés Secrètes et la Société*, showed that the revolutions of the modern world 'were but an episode in the development of a pre-arranged plan, which is being carried out over an ever-widening area to multiply the ruins of which we have previously spoken.' (Pope Leo XIII, Review of Our Pontificate, March 19, 1902.) Thus the young student understood 'that all the revolutions were bringing about the elimination of the rule of Christ the King in view of circumscribing and hampering the influence of the Mass and the Supernatural Life of Christ, the Supreme High Priest.' These two books furnished me with the guiding lines of the theological and historical studies which I have pursued ever since." He was ordained priest by Cardinal Respighi at St. John Lateran in September, 1910. In the following year he gained the doctorate in philosophy of the Academy of St. Thomas Aquinas and in 1912 he received the doctorate in theology from the Gregorian University.

On returning to Dublin in 1912 Father Fahey was appointed Professor of Philosophy at the Senior Scholasticate of the Irish Province of the Holy Ghost Fathers at Kimmage where he later also occupied the chair of Church history. During the First World War he acted as chaplain to prisoners of war in Berner-Oberland, Switzerland. After the armistice in 1918 he attended lectures for a year at Fribourg University — and then returned to Kimmage to teach philosophy.

The published works of Father Fahey are: *Mental Prayer* (1927); *The Kingship of Christ* (1931); *The Social Rights of Our Divine Lord, Jesus Christ, the King* (1932) (adapted from the French of Père Philippe, C.SS.R.); *The Mystical Body of Christ in the Modern World* (1935); *Oh Women! What You Could Be!* (1936) (adapted from French of Mlle. Joannès); *Mary, Mother of Divine Grace* (1937) (trans. from French of Père J. Le Rohellec, C.S.Sp.); *The Rulers of Russia* (1938); *The Workingmen's Guilds of the Middle Ages* (1943) (trans. with commentary, of a work by G. Kurth, Belgian historian); *The Kingship of Christ and Organized Naturalism* (1943); *Money Manipulation and Social Order* (1944); *The Mystical Body of Christ and the Reorganization of Society* (1945); *The Tragedy of James Connolly* (1947); *The Rulers of Russia and the Russian Farmers* (1948); *The Mystery of Christ, Our Head, Priest and King* (1950) (trans. from French of Père Héris, O.P.).

Father Fahey thus describes his program as a teacher: "I try to form the minds of the scholastics to judge historical epochs and movements, programmes of politicians as well as ideas of authors placed in their hands for the study of languages and of history, by reference to the Six Points of the Programme of Christ the King. Whatever is in harmony with the Divine Programme for order will make for real progress, and whatever is opposed to it spells naturalism, decay and death. Thus I try to train them to make of Our Lord the centre of their lives in every department."

A. K. Chesterton has summed up in pithy fashion the work and spirit of Father Denis Fahey. "Dr. Fahey," wrote Chesterton, "is capitally equipped for the task of examining and setting forth the evidence on the activities of supranational forces, for he has immense erudition, a quiet and judicial mind, complete fearlessness and no bees buzzing in his bonnet."   E. B. B.

Eleanor Farjeon   1881–

A member of a well-known literary family in England, Eleanor Farjeon was received into the Catholic Church on August 22, 1951.

She was born in the Strand, in London, in 1881, and was the third child of her parents: B. L. Farjeon, a popular English novelist of the Dickensian school, and Margaret Jane Jefferson, the eldest daughter of the American actor, Joseph Jefferson. Her elder brother, Harry, was a composer, who studied at the Royal Academy of Music in London, and after a brilliant career, became a famous professor of harmony and composition there for forty-five years. During his studentship, he and Eleanor wrote the first opera ever performed in public by the Royal Academy of Music students. Their work was called, "Floretta," and its theme was a love-adventure of Henry of Navarre, "which," she says, "I had turned into very naïve verse and Harry had set to very tuneful melodies; and I made my public bow (in pigtails) at the age of 16." Her brother Harry died in 1948. Joseph Jefferson, her younger brother, went first on the stage, and later became a novelist and dramatist. He is still living. Herbert, the youngest brother, was a writer, dramatist and critic. He and Eleanor began to collaborate during the 1920's; their most notable works being, "The Two Bouquets" (a Victorian operetta, produced in London in 1936, and in New York by Marc Connelly in 1938); "An Elephant in Arcady," a play in the Goldoni style, with 18th Century Italian music; and "The Glass Slipper," an unusual treatment of the Cinderella story, commissioned from the Farjeons by Robert Donat during the Second World War, and produced with great success for two Christmases, in 1944 and 1945. Herbert died before the second production. Another particular success was their book, *Kings and Queens*, a book of verses covering English history from William the Conqueror, with vivid pictures by Rosalind Thornycroft. This book is known to children in America and England, and has been frequently printed.

Eleanor Farjeon had no formal education. She was delicate, and beyond opening his bookcases of 8,000 books for her to browse in at will, her father would not allow her to be educated, except for a few French and German lessons in her teens. "But my parents," she says, "knew everybody in the Bohemian literary and dramatic world, and we grew up in an atmosphere rich with imaginative suggestion. From the age of four I, with my brothers, was taken to the theatre and opera freely."

She began to write tales and verses and fairy plays from the age of six and at seven was writing them on her father's typewriter. She had a fairy tale published before her father's death in 1903.

In 1904 Joseph Jefferson, her grandfather, sent for the children to spend the summer with him at Buzzards Bay in the United States. He had never seen them, or his daughter "Maggie" for twenty-five years.

This visit might have resulted in their settling in America, but for the appointment of Harry as professor at the Royal Academy of Music.

Returning to London, Miss Farjeon continued to develop, writing after her own fashion, till she had found her feet.

During the First World War, she lived in a cowman's cottage in Sussex, which the farmer allowed her to occupy at ten pounds a year till the cowman came back. From here she saw the publication of her *Nursery Rhymes of London Town*, her first success, and wrote *Martin Pippin in the Apple-Orchard*, the book that made her known in England and America. *Nursery Rhymes of London Town* were set later to simple tunes of her own and are now sung in most of the junior schools in London. After the war, having found her publishers and her public in both countries, she continued to write prolifically in a Hampstead cottage which replaced her Sussex one. She became the nonsense poet ("Tomfool") of the newly-established *Daily Herald*, and for thirteen years supplied an average of about four verses a week, which included much of the children's verse afterwards collected in book form. Almost every year she had produced a work of fiction, mostly fantastic; one of her serious novels, *Ladybrook*, was partly based on her Sussex experiences.

In the 1930's she developed a flair for cooking and a passion for cats — in fact for all animals — but her possession of cats led to the little book, *Golden Coney*, which brought letters and visitors to her cottage from all over England.

After her mother's death in 1933, she wrote what is perhaps her best-known work in England and America, the memoirs of her ancestors, parents, her brothers, and herself, called in America, *Portrait of a Family*, and in England, *A Nursery in the Nineties*. Just after this work, the dramatic collaboration with Herbert began to bear fruit. Then she bought another cottage in Sussex which she occupied till June, 1940. The fall of France in the Second World War sent her back to London to be near her brothers during the Battle of Britain. After the war, she sold her cottage, and confined herself to Hampstead. She wrote a fairy play, *The Silver Curlew*, based on the Rumpelstiltskin story, which was first produced in Liverpool, and then for two seasons at Christmas in London. In all, Miss Farjeon has published twenty-seven books in America and many more than that in England. These include ten for children, several collections of verse, and plays.

Miss Farjeon and her brothers had been brought up in a God-fearing manner by her parents, but without any particular religion. Her own belief in a supernatural life was profound, but it was not until 1950, when she was sixty-nine, that she began to consider seriously what this meant. All her life she had written poems, stories and other things which touched on the Christ-Child and His Mother with reverence and sincerity, and in 1936 at the request of the Oxford University Press in New York she wrote a book of saints' stories for children, *Ten Saints*. In January, 1951, she began to take instructions at Farm Street Church, London. She was baptized, on August 22 of that year, by Father Richard Mangan, S.J., and was confirmed on October 21 by Bernard Cardinal Griffin in Westminster Cathedral.   **M. A. H.**

James Aloysius Farley   1888–

Active in politics for over thirty-five years, James A. Farley is now (1952) Chairman of the Board, of the Coca-Cola Export Corporation.

Born on May 30, 1888 at Grassy Point on the shores of the Hudson River about thirty-five miles above New York City, James Farley is the son of James and Ellen (Goldrick) Farley. He received his early education at Grassy Point Grammar School and then moved on to the high school at near-by Stony Point, famous in American history as the scene of "Mad Anthony" Wayne's stirring victory over a superior British force during the crucial period of the Revolutionary War. He was graduated in 1905. In the fall of that year he enrolled in the Packard Commercial School of New York City to study bookkeeping. All in all he had thirteen years of schooling including high school and nine months of business training. "Most of my education," he says, "was received in the school of life." Upon completing the business course, Jim Farley procured a job with the Merlin Keilholtz Paper Company in New York. The salary was eight dollars a week. His next job was with the United States Gypsum Company, for whom he worked twenty years, serving successively as bookkeeper, company correspondent, and finally as salesman. He liked the latter assignment best of all because it provided an opportunity for him to travel about the state and meet people — "an invaluable asset to a young man who had his heart set on a political career," as Farley had.

In the spring of 1920 he married Elizabeth A. Finnegan who lived in Haverstraw. They have three children.

In his twenty-first year, even before he cast his first ballot, the neighboring Democrats elected him a member of the County Committee. Burning with ambition for political preferment, he thrust aside all forms of social activity, "devoting the daylight hours to business and the nights to studying whatever paths might be open to political success."

His first office — that of Town Clerk of Stony Point — was won at the early age of twenty-four in 1912. The voters re-elected him on three successive occasions. The Town Clerk was not a salaried official; he got his pay in the form of fees for services rendered. Farley being "more concerned about building a political future than he was about cash on hand" never accepted the ten-cent fee from hunters and fishermen due him when granting a license at $1.10 of which amount $1.00 was forwarded to the State Treasury at Albany and the other ten cents was for the Town Clerk. "And of course it would be unthinkable to take a dollar from a young man and his bride-to-be who were about to set up housekeeping. I learned also that young ladies about to enter the marriage state were as a rule bashful about coming to the Town

Hall to apply for a necessary license. In that case, it was a good idea to bring the license to the bride's home or the home of the bridegroom." All these kind services helped him tremendously in getting votes.

The years in the Town Clerkship also marked his beginning as a letter-writer, "a form of electioneering which came to occupy an extremely important place in my later career." On page 193 of his book *Behind the Ballots* he gives the reason. "The receiver knows that it was intended for him personally and no one else in the world and far more important he can keep the letter telling about the fine help he rendered in electing the President of the United States, or the Governor, or the Senator until his dying day." Green ink was used because it occurred to him that it would be wise to have some little distinguishing mark that would induce the receiver to remember him as an individual, something that would stick in his mind long after the contents of the letter were forgotten.

After serving as Town Clerk, he was also elected as Town Supervisor for a few terms. Then came the first really important political position he ever filled — the office of Democratic County Chairman for Rockland County to which he was elected in 1918. It was at this time that he paid a visit to Alfred E. Smith, then President of the Board of Aldermen of New York City, to urge him to run for Governor. The following year he was appointed Port Warden in New York City by Governor Alfred E. Smith. The other public offices that he held were: member of the New York State Assembly from Rockland County for the 1923 Session; appointed member of the New York State Athletic Commission by Governor Alfred E. Smith in 1924; reappointed in 1926, and 1928; reappointed by Secretary of State Edward J. Flynn in 1930 and 1932; made Chairman of Commission in 1925 and remained Chairman until he resigned, February 28, 1933.

He was appointed Postmaster General of the United States in President Franklin D. Roosevelt's Cabinet in March, 1933; reappointed in President Roosevelt's Cabinet on January 22, 1937. He resigned as Postmaster General on August 31, 1940. During his administration from seventy-five to one hundred special stamps had been issued to the delight of philatelists. From 1930 to 1944 he was Chairman of the New York Democratic State Committee, and Chairman of the Democratic National Committee from 1932 to 1940.

His business activities, as we noted above, began as bookkeeper in 1906. Then he worked for the United States Gypsum Company in New York City. In 1926 he founded the James A. Farley & Co., Inc., dealers in masons' materials, and in 1929 merged his firm with five other building material firms. On September 1, 1940 he was appointed Chairman of the Board of the Coca-Cola Export Corporation. Later he became President and Director of the Coca-Cola Bottling Company of Boston and Director of the Coca-Cola Bottling Company of Canada and still later Director of the Coca-Cola International.

He is the recipient of twelve honorary doctorate degrees from twelve colleges and universities.

Although not an alumnus of St. Bonaventure's College he was chosen as general chairman of the drive for four million dollars, necessary for the building program at St. Bonaventure.

His only two books published thus far are: *Behind the Ballots* (1938) and *Jim Farley's Story* (1948).   M. A. H.

Reverend Thomas Butler Feeney, S.J.

Father Thomas Butler Feeney, of the Society of Jesus, was born in Lynn, Massachusetts. After his graduation from Boston College High School, he entered the Jesuit Order and subsequently continued his education at various Jesuit Houses of Studies in Poughkeepsie, New York, Woodstock, Maryland, and Ghent, Belgium. He is at present Professor of English and French in Boston College.

Father Feeney's first book appeared in 1938 under the title, *Ave Maria*, verse for children based on the Hail Mary. His second book, *When the Wind Blows*, also a book of verses, was published in 1947. These poems cover a wide range and there are some for every mood. Sister M. Madeleva says of them: "These verses of Father Thomas Feeney are as quaintly buoyant with his humor as they are earnest with the reverence of his faith."

In addition to his poetry, Father Feeney has written sketches, short stories and one-act plays. His favorite pastime is writing amateur songs, words and music. The songs have been described as a "mixed melody and thought of an Irish ballad and Gregorian Chant." He has set to music some of the verses included in *When the Wind Blows*.

M. A. H.

Reverend William Noé Field   *1915–*

Born in Orange, New Jersey, on December 22, 1915, Father William Noé Field received his early elementary education in the public schools of East Orange and Newark. From 1928 to 1936 he attended Seton Hall Preparatory School and from 1932 to 1936 Seton Hall College. Then he entered Immaculate Conception Seminary in Darlington and was ordained to the priesthood four years later. Presently, he is a student for a degree at Columbia University, and an instructor in English in Seton Hall Preparatory School and in the University College of Seton Hall University.

He was the first editor of the Newark Junior Museum publication *Drums*, and was editor of the *Seton Quarterly* from 1934 to 1935. He is co-editor of the *Seton Review,* "a journal dedicated to the expression of contemporary thought" — the new graduate quarterly of Seton Hall University, and a contributor critic to *Best Sellers,* a semi-monthly review of books published by the University of Scranton.

His only book thus far is, *Hear My Heart,* a book of poetry published in 1951. In the Foreword, William York Tindall, Professor of English, Columbia University writes: "His poems belong to a great tradition, that of Alice Meynell, Sister Madeleva, T. S. Eliot, and Joyce Kilmer. Like his predecessors, Father Field finds in this world — in all the glories of the four seasons, in city and country alike — the evidence of another world. Natural beauty, whether of snow or flower, and the artifice of bridge and spire, shadow forth divine beauty and provide a way to apprehend it. . . . He has found an honest, forthright way to communicate his love of nature and his deep religious feeling."

Father John Davis in his review of the book (*Seton Review,* November, 1951) says: "The poems in this collection are refreshingly spiritual and for those of us who know some of Father Field's 'voices,' they are nostalgic and even whimsical."

During his undergraduate days, his poetry appeared in various periodicals. A monograph on the ancient Mayan and Aztec civilizations of Mexico was privately printed and *The Catholic World* (April, 1945), published his article, "Newman in Ireland."

Kevin Fitzgerald 1902–

The following autobiography of Kevin Fitzgerald was written for *Eason's Bulletin* (Dublin, Ireland), at the urgent request of Keith Eason, Fitzgerald's old personal friend. It appeared in the June, 1949 issue and is reprinted here with permission.

"I was born a long time ago (June 19, 1902), in London, of Irish parentage, and lived in England continuously until I was seventeen years of age when I came to Ireland for the first time on a holiday. My father returned to Ireland to live, after retirement from business and was resident in the county Tipperary until his death in 1949 in his ninetieth year. The holiday led directly to my spending a year on a big group of farms in Offaly, and thereafter to four years at Sealehayne Agricultural College and the West of Scotland Agricultural College. As a result of these activities I became reasonably qualified as a technical agriculturist, but not so well equipped for the practical farming in Tipperary in which I then indulged. After a year or two of this I went to Canada as a farm laborer and returning to England became an agricultural adviser in the North Midlands, my work principally being to comment on the use of nitrogen fertilizers. This post gradually expanded itself on the general industrial side and after service in association with the Ministry of Agriculture and Fisheries during the war I came back to Ireland to manage a business of some chemical and industrial importance.

"Throughout all these years I have never stopped writing, at first largely technical articles for trade and semi-scientific papers. Later on I began to submit stories and talks to the British Broadcasting Corporation which was kind enough to accept a considerable number of them.

"About 1941 I wrote my first novel which, as with so many other similar attempts, remains unpublished. The war years provided little further opportunity for serious writing and it was not until I came to Ireland in September, 1944, that I could begin again. This proved a moderately successful venture as the book, *Not So Quickly*, was accepted by Messrs. Heinemann, and was treated kindly by most reviewers. Since then I have written two more books; one, *It's Safe in England*, published in 1949, the other, a long serious novel, requires a great deal more work than I have at present time to give to it.

"At the moment of writing this short note I am about five chapters into another story because I find that in the turmoil of Irish business life, a week-end devoted to writing is the best possible means of relaxation.

"Most of my friends seem to want an answer to the question: 'How do you do it?' Everything I have ever written has been done by hand in an armchair. I write on my knee using as my invariable support a book called *The Crafty Farmer*, a translation from the Spanish, and bearing inside it an inscription from a very dear friend of mine: 'To Fitzgerald, the one O. Henry missed.'"

Mr. Fitzgerald added: "I write in an armchair because I have always done this and prefer it to sitting at a desk or hammering at a typewriter."

Robert Stuart Fitzgerald   1910–

Born at Geneva, New York, on October 12, 1910, Robert Stuart Fitzgerald is the son of Robert Emmet Fitzgerald and Anne (Montague Stuart) Fitzgerald. After his mother's death in 1913, Robert Fitzgerald grew up in the household of his paternal grandmother in Springfield, Illinois. There his younger brother died and there, soon afterward, his father became an invalid with tuberculosis of the bone. Robert went to a parochial school, St. Agnes, and to the city high school, where he began writing. After finishing high school he spent a year at the Choate School, Wallingford, Connecticut, and entered Harvard in 1929. During his year at Choate his father died of pneumonia after having begun a recovery from his bedridden condition of ten years.

In 1931 a group of Robert Fitzgerald's poems, submitted to *Poetry* on Vachel Lindsay's recommendation, won the Midland Authors Prize awarded by that magazine. In the same year he went to Trinity College, Cambridge, for a year's study, corresponding to his junior year at Harvard; Greek and Latin literature and philosophy were his chief interests. He had now given up the practice of Catholicism in favor of a private mysticism connected with the art of poetry. In this condition he was to spend the next fifteen years. In his last year at Harvard he became impressed with Greek literature, took the leading part in a production in Greek of Sophocles' *Philoctetes*, and read much philosophy. He had decided not to study law and, despite his lapse from Catholicism, formed the intention of going to Paris to study medieval philosophy under Gilson. After his graduation in 1933 he had, however, to earn his living, and in November he got a job as a reporter on the New York *Herald Tribune*.

Newspaper work interested him greatly but it was difficult for him to write as quickly and equably as necessary; he was not a success at it, though he persisted until March, 1935. He then left the newspaper and left New York, going later in the summer to the MacDowell Colony at Peterborough, New Hampshire, where he put together a book of his poems and completed, with his collaborator Dudley Fitts, a translation into English verse of Euripides' *Alcestis*. In the fall he returned to New York, where he found work with an advertising trade paper and, in December, married Eleanor Green, of Portage, Wisconsin. In February, 1936, he was employed by *Time* to write book notes and, later, financial news stories, a job he labored at until the autumn of 1937 when he was made editor of the Art Section of the magazine. For two years, thereafter, he was constantly occupied with news, and to a modest extent with criticism of painting, sculpture and architecture, and in this job he had some journalistic success. From the fall of 1939 to the summer of 1940 he was editor of the Books Section. He then left *Time*, having saved enough money to live on for a year.

He and his wife went to Sante Fe, New Mexico, and there he did an English translation of the play that he admired most among classic tragedies: the *Oedipus at Colonus* of Sophocles. He wrote much and discarded much, returning to New York and to *Time* in 1941 with the nucleus of a second book of poems, finally published as *A Wreath for the Sea* late in 1943. By that time he had entered the navy, getting a commission as lieutenant, junior grade, with two months of officer training at Fort Schuyler and assignment, in August, 1943, to a shore station in New York. His work there was absorbing and highly exacting, and he did scarcely any writing until he was sent to the Pacific early in 1945 to join Admiral Nimitz's staff, first at Pearl Harbor and later at Guam. During the rest of that year he reread Virgil, read the Vulgate for the first time, and kept a daily journal which was later destroyed. After his discharge from the navy early in 1946, he and his wife were separated and he returned, by the mercy of God, to the Catholic faith. He spent the late winter and spring on a retreat with the Benedictines at St. Mary's Monastery, Morristown, New Jersey. A civil divorce was granted to Eleanor Green in June, and later in the year the invalidity of that marriage was confirmed by the appropriate authority of the archdiocese of New York.

In June, 1946, he began writing a weekly book review for *Time;* in September he began teaching English literature at Sarah Lawrence College, Bronxville, New York. His first considerable work of criticism as a Catholic was a review of Robert Graves' *King Jesus* in *The Nation* in 1946; his first poem in four years, *Seaman's Luck,* also appeared in *The Nation* early in 1947. In April, 1947, he married Sarah Morgan at the church of St. Jean Baptiste, in New York. That summer he began a collaboration with Dudley Fitts on a translation of the *Oedipus Rex* of Sophocles, which was published in September, 1949. In February, 1948, his wife gave birth to their first child, a girl who was christened Hugh Linane. In June he wrote his first piece of Catholic apologetics in answer to a series of anti-Catholic articles by Paul Blanshard that had appeared in *The Nation;* his reply was published by that magazine under the title *My Own Pinch of Salt.* In September, 1948 with his wife and child he went to Europe and attended the celebration of the feast of Saint Teresa in Avila, Spain; in October, during November and December they stayed in Rome. Soon after their return to the United States their second child, a boy, was born in March, 1949, and christened Benedict Robert Campion.

When the *Oedipus Rex* was finished he began to devote himself to a long poem, a work that would occupy several years. In August, 1949, he resigned from *Time* and moved with his family from New York to a house near Ridgefield, Connecticut. In the academic year 1949–50 he again taught at Sarah Lawrence; in 1950–51 he spent half of each week as resident fellow in creative writing at Princeton where he also helped conduct the Princeton seminars in literary criticism. A third child, Maria Juliana, was born in May, 1950; a fourth, in April, 1951.

Reverend Joseph David Flanagan. See *Reverend M. Raymond, O.C.S.O.*

Lawrence Francis Flick   1856–1938

Some years before his death Dr. Flick was heard to remark concerning a fellow physician, "It is too bad a man has to die just when he is beginning to be of some use to his brother man." Always a hard student and a very humble one, he considered his deep knowledge and practice of medicine a mere prelude to the things he had hoped to do.

A writer along medical and historical lines, he was the author of three books and about two hundred papers and pamphlets. His life work was the study of tuberculosis.

His greatest Catholic undertaking was his attempt (and failure) to found a Catholic daily newspaper in Philadelphia, Pennsylvania. He had gathered the money, sold stock, and formed a company. But World War I came along; also his friend and co-worker, Archbishop Prendergast, died. His list of stockholders, with the written opinion of every Cardinal, Archbishop, Bishop, educator, layman, and laywoman of any importance in the United States, makes a unique historical collection to be put into print someday.

Lawrence Francis Flick, physician and historian, was born on the feast of St. Lawrence, August 10, 1856, in Carrolltown, Cambria County, Pennsylvania. His grandparents on both sides of his family lived in the days of Prince Gallitzin and were his parishioners. His grandfather Flick came from France; his grandfather Sharbaugh, from Bavaria. Both families were among the pioneer settlers in the Allegheny mountain district attracted to that locality by the facility to practice their religion. Elizabeth Sharbaugh, mother of Dr. Flick, and John Flick, her future husband, met as very young children on the long trek over the mountains to Sunday Mass.

He received his early education at subscription schools in his home town and at St. Vincent College, Latrobe, Pennsylvania. He studied law under Benjamin Brewster in Philadelphia, and medicine at Jefferson College in the same city. He made his internship at Old Blockley, Philadelphia and practiced medicine for over fifty years on Pine Street in Old St. Mary's parish.

In his chosen field, the study and cure of tuberculosis, he rose to great fame. As a young man he himself had the disease and was sent West to die. His successful self-treatment of milk, eggs, rest and fresh air became the basis of his famous cure.

In 1885 he married Ella J. Stone, daughter of Thomas Stone and Ella Jane (Jones) Stone. The Stones came to Philadelphia from Liverpool, England in 1830. Thomas Stone was a master craftsman and one of those chosen to help mend the famous Liberty Bell.

Mrs. Flick became a convert to the Catholic Church some years before her marriage. She and Dr. Flick were the parents of seven children.

Dr. Flick, nationally known as a consultant on tuberculosis, having started the crusade against it in 1886, helped to found the Society for Prevention of Tuberculosis in 1892. He also founded the Free Hospital for Poor Consumptives in 1895, the White Haven Sanatorium, serving at this latter institution as president from 1901 to 1935 inclusive and was co-founder and first medical director of Phipps Institute for the Study and Treatment of Tuberculosis.

Dr. Flick was the author of three books: *Consumption: a Curable and Preventable Disease* (1903); *The Development of Our Knowledge of Tuberculosis* (1925), and *Tuberculosis: a Book of Practical Knowledge to Guide the General Practitioner of Medicine* (1937). A prolific writer, he was also author of some two hundred pamphlets and magazine articles.

In Catholic circles Dr. Flick was known as a lecturer on historical and literary topics. He was one of the founders of the American Catholic Historical Society, Philadelphia in 1884, and one of the founders of the American Catholic Historical Association in Washington in 1919 and its first president. Dr. Flick achieved a place for himself in American historiography which, together with his greatest work, that of his successful fight on tuberculosis, won him imperishable honor. The best known of his historical articles were: *The Study of History from a Christian Point of View* (1897); *Biographical Sketch: Rev. Henry Lemke O.S.B.* (1898); *Biographical Sketch: Matthew O'Conway* (1899); *Faith as a Factor of Happiness* (1914); *A Catholic Daily Newspaper* (three pamphlets printed privately) (1914–1916), and *History as a Science* (1921).

Few educational, cultural or charity movements were started in Philadelphia during his lifetime without his active participation. He was known for his hospitality. Noted educators and lecturers, ecclesiastical and lay, when in Philadelphia, were entertained by Dr. Flick.

In 1920 he received the Laetare Medal of Notre Dame University, and in 1933 he was given the Strittmatter Medal, the highest award of the Philadelphia County Medical Society.

Dr. Flick died July 7, 1938. E. F.

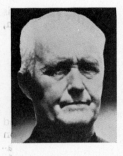

Reverend (John Christian) Leopold Fonck, S.J. 1865–1930

The outstanding German Jesuit Biblical scholar, the late Father Leopold Fonck was born on January 14, 1865, at Wissen near Düsseldorf in the Rhineland. From 1875 to 1883 he studied the humanities at the Thomas Gymnasium in Kempen and was graduated with honors. From 1883 to 1890 he studied philosophy and theology at the Gregorian University in Rome, and received the doctorate in each branch.

After returning to his home diocese of Münster in Westphalia, Father Fonck spent two years as spiritual director and teacher of religion at the "Knickenbergischen Erziehungs-anstalt" at Telgte. Up to then Father Fonck had been a secular priest. On September 20, 1892, Father Fonck entered the Jesuit novitiate at Blijenbeck in Holland. In the fall of 1893 his superiors sent him to Ditton Hall in Lancashire, England, to resume the Biblical and oriental studies he had started under Father Rudolph Cornely in Rome. In 1895 he went to Egypt and Palestine in order to better acquaint himself with the language, geography and the nature of the Holy Land. From there he went to the universities of Berlin and Munich, whose libraries helped him to give the finishing touch to his preparatory work for a Biblical professorship. Then followed his third year of probation, 1899–1900, in Wijnandsrade near Valkenburg in Holland, and at the College of Valkenburg he had collaborated in the compilation of the *Lexicon Biblicum* of the *Cursus Scripturae Sacrae*. In 1901 he was appointed professor of the New Testament at the University of Innsbruck. During the years he was stationed there (1901–1908), Father Fonck published an astonishing number of theological works, such as: *Streifzüge durch die biblische Flora* (Biblische Studien V/1) (1900); *Die Parabeln des Herrn im Evangelium* (1902); *Die Wunder des Herrn im Evangelium* (1903); *Der Kampf um die Wahrheit der Hl. Schrift* (1905); *Wissenschaftliches Arbeiten, Beiträge zur Methodik des akademischen Studiums* (1908).

One of Father Fonck's greatest and lasting achievements at Innsbruck was the foundation of a Biblical seminary with a library in the theological department of the university. Father Fonck also served as retreat master and wrote for his students the spiritual vademecum, *Thesaurus precum ad usum privatum theologorum* (1906) (3 ed. 1921).

In 1907 Father Fonck made a second educational trip to Palestine, for six months. Then he was called to Rome in 1908 and appointed professor of the New Testament of the newly founded "Cursus Superior S. Scripturae" of the Gregorian University.

On December 28, 1908 Pope Pius X appointed him Consultor of the Pontifical Biblical Commission. Shortly afterward he opened special schools. In February 1909, Pope Pius X entrusted Father Fonck with the duty of working out the program of a new institution of the Holy See. Father Fonck with his great experience in doing things, his great zeal working for the honor of the Apostolic See, and finally with his great alacrity in carrying out plans, within a few months, had so taken care of and managed everything that the Holy Father in the month of May, of the same year, was able to promulgate the solemn and public erection of the Pontifical Biblical Institute, with the publishing of the Apostolic letter "Vinea electa" (May 7, 1909). A little later, Father Fonck was named the first president of the Institute, but the Institute still lacked its own home. To obtain one, Father Fonck and Pope Pius X prayed continuously one novena after the other in honor of the Sacred Heart that benefactors would be found. After Father Fonck had prayed about ten novenas and the Pope himself more than thirty, a very rich French family gave the Pope sufficient money to purchase a Roman palace in the Piazza della Pilotta, opposite the North American College, and to reconstruct it to serve both as a library and as a house of studies. In the autumn of 1911 the Institute was transferred to its new home. Thus Father Fonck was able not only to establish the Biblical Institute and guide its destiny for nine years (1909–1918), but at the same time lay the foundation and personally direct one of the best and finest Biblical libraries in the world. With extraordinary zeal, he built up a valuable Biblical museum. He himself collected many objects for it when in the East in 1907. At that time even the liberals of Italy commended his work. The *Il Messaggero* said of him: "That which our government officials could not accomplish in fifty years, Father Fonck has done in one year."

In 1911 and again in 1913, Pope Pius X ordered Father Fonck to go to Palestine to erect a Biblical branch Institute. In 1913 he acquired a building site, but only after the war, on October 18, 1925 was the foundation stone laid. In October, 1927 the construction was finished.

Father Fonck had also a part in the reform of the *Breviary* and was appointed Consultor of the Congregation of Rites.

When war between Austria and Italy broke out, Father Fonck, because he was a German, had to leave Rome. At the request of the Pope, and the General of the Jesuits, he left Rome in May 1915 to go first to the Seminary of Chur, and then to the Maximilianeum in Zurich, where he remained until October 1919, doing all kinds of priestly work. In that year (1919) he returned to the Biblical Institute in Rome to teach Exegesis, and the History of the New Testament. For a time he also taught the History of Exegesis, Biblical Theology and Methodology, teaching the latter also at the Gregorian University.

On December 10, 1918 he relinquished his post as president of the Biblical Institute and was succeeded by Professor A. Fernandez, a Spanish Jesuit. From 1920 to 1925, Father Fonck was entrusted with the editorship of the periodical *Biblica*.

In 1929 Father Fonck was transferred from the Eternal City to Prague, Bohemia, to preach the Gospel he knew so well. A year later he was sent to Vienna in Austria to become spiritual adviser and chaplain to the students of the University there (Akademiker Seelsorger).

While giving a retreat to nuns in Vienna, Austria, Father Fonck was suddenly taken ill. Cancer had taken deep root in his system. As the end approached he raised himself from his bed and uttered the words: "Into Thy hands, O Lord, I commend my spirit." Thereupon he fell unconscious. He died on October 19, 1930.

He did a prodigious amount of writing. He wrote about two hundred and thirty-four essays and articles for different magazines; one hundred and ninety-seven articles for the *Lexicon Biblicum* and forty-two books and pamphlets.

Among his books in English are: *The Parables of the Gospel* (1914) and *The Light of the World* (1926).   W. B. and M. A. H.

Gene Fowler   1890–

Back in 1946 Gene Fowler published his autobiography *A Solo In Tom-Toms*. The title was prompted by the sudden death of Floyd Irwin, a young man and the best trick rider of the West, who had fallen from his horse while practicing his rides. The flying hooves fractured his skull. A medicine man came to the funeral parlor and played a solo with the leg bone of a wild turkey on the horsehide drumhead of a tom-tom. "In his song of mourning," writes Gene Fowler, "I heard good-by to the West, a good-by to youth and in this valedictory I began to find a meaning of my own young years. . . . The sudden close of youth's bright time. . . . Was not youth itself a solo in tom-toms?"

Born in Denver, Colorado on March 8, 1890, the son of Charles

Francis and Dora Grace Devlan, he received the name of Fowler from his stepfather who adopted him.

Gene's own father left the homestead because he believed his wife had divided her loyalty between himself and her mother. The test came when Mr. Devlan wanted a cup of coffee and Mrs. Wheeler insisted he say "please" — which he would not say. Kissing his wife good-by, he left.

It was not until thirty years later that Gene was to see his father for the first time. The meeting took place in New York, where Gene had gone to work for the Hearst newspaper. Of the event, Gene writes: "We were both wordless for a time. Then referring to his beard, I said, "So that's where you've been hiding all these years?""

Gene left grammar school when he was ten to work for a taxidermist. Since then he has had a disrelish for meat. In his thirteenth year his mother died. Later he attended West Denver High School and while there was described as "a lad of unbridled vitality." He took part in several activities of the school, winning a gold medal in an oratorical contest. He edited the school magazine, *The Heraldo*, for two years. When he was graduated, he worked for a printer and this experience enticed him to enter the field of journalism. The guidance came from Professor Ferd James Lockhart who said: "A fellow like you belongs to the newspaper business . . . you will see life firsthand in the newspaper business." As a reporter on the Denver *Republican* of the Rocky Mountain West he met a girl whose first name was Gloria. She took him for drives in her "splendid electric automobile, a black brougham model with a silvered steering bar. It was like trundling along the avenues in a show case." When Mr. MacLennan (the editor) chanced to see him riding with such elegance, he lifted his hat with an overdone flourish and the next day he made a point of saying in front of the other reporters, "We have the rare privilege of knowing a male Cinderella." Soon after the romance ended. Gene fittingly closes this chapter of his life and the twenty-fifth chapter of his book with the words "Sic transit Gloria."

Gene married Agnes Hubbard in July, 1916, whom he met while she worked for the Health Department in Denver. The Fowlers have three children; all married, and five grandchildren.

In 1950 Mr. Fowler joined the Catholic Church. Writing to the Editor of the Denver *Register*, he said: "I have long wanted to be received into the true Church. My decision was not a sudden, emotional event. Also, I did not wish to be a 'deathbed Catholic.' I am now sixty, and perhaps I can work in a small way to earn my right to be a son of that Church. Part of my reluctance to have myself publicized was due to my feeling that converts sometimes are overzealous in proclaiming their conversion. You who have been born, fortunately, as Catholics can only surmise the great joys that come to one who has found peace after a life of dark groping for salvation. It is this very ecstasy that sometimes causes the happy convert to proclaim his new found status to the world, and thus, unwittingly, he is apt to draw censure from worldlings who look upon him as a braggart and even a nuisance. This I desire to avoid, and would seek to be a devout Catholic, to strive for the achievement of good works but to be modest about it all." Father Duane Theobald who instructed Mr. Fowler for several months says: "Gene tells everybody, 'I've had such a good time here on earth, that now I want to make sure I have a good time in the next life.'"

To Mr. Jules Levine, Gene wrote: "I think it only fair that I perform at least a few years' work for the Church that, to my mind, offers so many spiritual privileges to an old man. I, who have lived in a whirlwind, wish to die in peace."

After several years on the papers of his native city of Denver, Gene went to New York, in 1924, as sports editor of the *Daily Mirror*. A year later he was transferred to the New York *American* as managing editor. In 1928 he became editor of the New York *Morning Telegraph* and secured reporters from other papers by increasing their salaries by $200.00 per week. When his publisher discovered that his payroll resembled the government's, Mr. Fowler lost his job.

He has worked as a writer for RKO, 20th Century Fox, Paramount, Universal, United Artists, Selznick International, Samuel Goldwyn and Metro-Goldwyn-Mayer. In February, 1952 he announced that he and Gene Towne, screenwriter, have formed the Fowler-Towne Enterprises to produce movies for the theatre and TV. He also has contributed to magazines, including *Cosmopolitan* and *Collier's*.

Mr. Fowler is the author of the following books: *Trumpet in the Dust* (1930); *Shoe the Wild Mare* (1931); *The Great Mouthpiece* (the life story of William J. Fallon, a New York City lawyer) (1931); *Timberline* (1933); *Father Goose* (1934); *Mighty Barnum* (with B. Meredith) (1935); *Salute to Yesterday* (1937); *The Great McGoo* (with Ben Hecht; play) (1931); *The Jervis Bay Goes Down* (poem) (1940); *Illusion in Java* (novel) (1939); *A Solo in Tom-Toms* (1933); *Good Night, Sweet Prince* (biography of John Barrymore) (1943); *Beau James* (a biography of James J. Walker, former New York Mayor) (1949), and *Schnozzola* (a biography of Jimmy Durante) (1951).

M. A. H.

Anne Fremantle 1910–

In Carlyle's famous *Heroes and Hero Worship* the old sage of Cheyne Row saw fit to devote one chapter to the man of letters as hero. Mrs. Anne Fremantle might fitly be described as the woman of letters as heroine. There is an eighteenth century sweep and an eighteenth century breadth to her work. She is novelist, biographer, critic, historian, journalist, editor, reviewer, broadcaster, and occasional civil servant. To paraphrase the great Johnson on Goldsmith, there is no literary form she has touched which she did not adorn. Nevertheless, it probably is fair to say that her prime specialty is literary criticism. On this particular plane she is the equal of any living writer in English. The peculiar pellucid quality of her criticism, so bright yet so profound, is probably best communicated by the suggestion that, in a deeply Catholic way, she is the feminine equivalent of the liberal critic, Lionel Trilling.

To the romantic American reader the background of Mrs. Fremantle's life reads like a memoir by Maurice Baring or a novel by Evelyn Waugh. Her father, the late Right Honorable Frederick Huth Jackson was, during his lifetime, Privy Councillor, Sheriff of London, and a Director of the Bank of England. Her maternal grandfather, the Right Honorable Mount Start Grant-Duff — a name straight out of *David Balfour;* Mrs. Fremantle comes by her romanticism as honestly as she does by her complementary classicism — had held such important offices as the Governorship of Madras, the Undersecretaryship for India, the Rectorship of Aberdeen University, and was Member of Parliament for the Elgin Boroughs for thirty years. In 1930 she married the Honorable Christopher Fremantle, son of Lord Cottesloe. They have three sons: Adam born in 1934; Richard born in 1936; and Hugh born in 1944.

Mrs. Fremantle's academic career is quite impressive, to start with. She is both an Oxford M.A. and a graduate of the London School of Economics. Her literary career began, as is, perhaps, more usual in England than in the States, with journalism. She was, by turns, Assistant Editor of Sir John Squire's *London Mercury,* occasional correspondent for the *Sunday Times,* the *Manchester Guardian,* the *Daily Herald,* the *Evening News,* the *Spectator, London Times* dramatic correspondent in Sicily and the United States, novel reviewer for the *New Statesman,* and contributor to periodicals such as the *News Chronicle, Time and Tide, Life and Letters,* and the *Field.*

In this same interval which stretched from 1931 to 1936 Mrs. Fremantle found time to publish a book of poems and a life of George Eliot, to rewrite a guidebook to Sicily, to edit two volumes of the *Wynne Diaries* for the Oxford University Press, to visit Moscow for the *London Times,* to write numerous scripts for the BBC, and to stand as Labor Candidate for St. George's, Westminster. Not daunted by her parliamentary defeat at the hands of Alfred Duff Cooper, then Minister for War, she occupied herself, in the interregnum between 1936 and the outbreak of war, by visiting America on a lecture tour for the English Speaking Union, doing a stint as drama critic, writing a long military-political biography of Marmaduke Pickthall, which Harold Nicolson has highly extolled, and continuing to turn out scripts for the BBC.

In the first year of the war she drove an ambulance for the London County Council, broadcast for the BBC in both French and German, and assisted Mr. Michael Huxley in New York in his organization of the United Nations Information Centre. The duration of the war was divided into tours of the U.S.A., sponsored by the British Ministry of Information, research work for India in Washington on the staff of Sir Girja Bajpai, and the task of seeing her first novel through the press.

Since January, 1946 Mrs. Fremantle has been living in New York. She is currently on the regular staffs of *The Commonweal*, the New York *Times*, *Tomorrow*, and *Town and Country*. Some of her best critical work is done in this usually ephemeral form. She has also, in this period, translated the *True Visage of the Saints* from the German, edited two anthologies, one of *Bible Stories by Great Authors* and one of *Mothers: A Catholic Treasury of Great Stories*, and published a highly successful novel, *James and Joan*. In 1950, she published the strong and sensitive biography, *Desert Calling*, a life of the French soldier-monk, Charles de Foucauld.

With David Marshall and Father Demetrius, she was one of the founders of *A.D.*, the new Catholic magazine, which hopes to specialize in the contemporary short story as well as in cultural subjects from art to the theater.

It is obvious that Mrs. Fremantle writes and works as naturally and easily as she breathes. What is most remarkable about her is the uniform excellence of her encyclopedic output. C. A. B.

Reverend Louis Joseph Gallagher, S.J. 1885–

At the present writing (1952), Father Louis J. Gallagher's latest book, *Episode on Beacon Hill* is being favorably received. It is a story of the fusion of the Yankee and Gaelic cultures in the city of Boston, resulting in the development of an ideal American citizen.

Born in Boston, Massachusetts on July 22, 1885, the son of James and Sarah (Dempsey) Gallagher, he made his early studies at a parochial school in Malden, and the Boston College High School. Then he went to Boston College. He entered the Jesuit Order in 1905 and after studies in classics and philosophy at Woodstock College, Maryland, and in Montreal, Canada he became professor of classical languages at Fordham University in New York, from 1912 to 1917. He returned to Woodstock College for his theological studies. Ordained in 1920 by Cardinal Gibbons, Father Gallagher, in the following year, was appointed headmaster at Xavier High School in New York City. For the year 1922–23 he was Assistant Director of the Vatican Relief Mission to Russia and was assigned as Vatican courier to transport the relics of Blessed Andrew Bobola. Asked to give a description of this assignment, Father Gallagher wrote: "Traveling as a diplomatic courier of the Vatican, and as a specially appointed courier of the State Department of the Soviet Government, we left Odessa for Constantinople aboard the packet-boat Tchicherin, at 5 P.M., October 15th, 1923. It was a still night and very dark. The ship was rolling leisurely and making good time. By midnight most of the several hundred passengers had retired to their staterooms. The weather was mild and we were seated on a bench on the upper foredeck; the captain of the ship, the ship's doctor, your courier and a formerly prominent Russian businessman, who was getting out of Russia with his wife, on falsified passports. The lady had been released from prison only a month before after serving a year and a half for a former attempt to escape, in the same manner.

"The captain had just told us of the capture of a Russian ship by Roumanian pirates, right about the middle of the Black Sea, and only a few weeks previous. We thought he was telling sea tales. He was, and was about to have another one to relate, on his way back to Odessa. Within half an hour the night was awakened by a cannon shot, which sounded to starboard. Five minutes later we heard another boom, somewhat closer, and something seemed to whiz over the bow of the boat. Then there was someone calling through a megaphone and ordering the Tchicherin to hold up, in the name of the G.P.U. The businessman turned to me and asked, 'Do you carry a gun?' I answered, 'No.' 'Well, I do,' he said, 'and so does my wife. We have decided not to go back to Russia, so please stand aside, if there is any shooting.'

"After a minute of play in all directions, our ship's searchlight showed a submarine chaser, now about two hundred feet away from the ship. The G.P.U. at that time was the Russian Government secret-service. What they were doing in neutral waters at midnight without a single light showing was a puzzle, even to the captain of the Tchicherin. At first he doubted the command, but carrying only small arms in the face of pointed guns, he slowed down his ship and finally came to a stop. The settling of the vessel into the water as she lost speed brought a host of passengers onto the decks, but they were ordered back to their staterooms and they immediately obeyed. The captain had a gun in his hand when he gave the order. The sea was calm, only gently rolling, and in five minutes the sub-chaser was made fast to the side of the Tchicherin. The first order to the captain was to light up the starboard deck and throw over rope-ladders. Five minutes more and four men climbed aboard the packet-boat, each flashing an automatic. The tension was increasing on the deck. It must have been breath-taking below decks, where the passengers were confined, with armed members of the crew stationed at the hatches. Our own chief concern was for our diplomatic baggage, meaning the box containing the casket with the body of Blessed Andrew Bobola, which was buried in a cargo of wheat in the hold of the ship. After a minute of whispered conversation between the captain and the leader of the four intruders, we felt more at ease. All five of them went below without calling us for questioning, and during their absence, our friend, the Russian businessman, was standing at the door through which they had disappeared, with an automatic in his hand, and waiting for them to return. A few long minutes of dead silence and of nerve tightening suspense had passed before they reappeared on the deck, escorting a man at gun point, with his hands tied behind his back. The businessman heaved a heavy sigh of relief. A few orders from below on the starboard side and the prisoner was taken down a rope-ladder with an armed guard preceding him, and hurried out of sight when he landed on the deck of the sub-chaser. The ships were unlashed and the chaser disappeared into the night, as mysteriously as she had come out of it.

"It was early dawn, with all quiet aboard the Tchicherin, as she was plowing a choppy sea toward Constantinople. The ship's doctor, the businessman and the courier were taking coffee in the captain's cabin and listening to his latest sea tale. The G.P.U. had chased the Tchicherin from Odessa to arrest a member of the ship's cheka, an ordinary plain clothes government spy, and one of their own organization, who had been assigned to that ship. There was something wrong with papers he had signed before leaving port and he was taken off to be returned to Odessa for explanations. 'What will happen to him?' the doctor asked. 'No telling,' said the captain, 'but may the Lord have mercy on his soul.'

"Two months later we met the Russian businessman on the Rue de Rivoli in Paris, and he said the man who was taken off the Tchicherin in the middle of the Black Sea was a former officer in the Czar's army, who had presumably gone over to the Bolsheviks after the First World War, and he went on to explain: as a member of the Bolshevik secret service, the G.P.U., he spent most of his time collecting information for future use and was getting out of Russia, once and for all, when the sub-chaser appeared. 'Maybe the captain knew something,' we commented, and as he went along, in somewhat of a hurry, he said, 'You never can tell.'"

After a year of tertianship in Ireland, Father Gallagher returned to the United States and was appointed Dean of the College of Arts and Sciences at Georgetown University. Back in New England in 1926, he served as Socius to the Provincial of the New England Province of the Jesuit Order until 1932. The following five and a half years (1932–1937) he was president of Boston College. At the present time (1952) he is the archivist of the New England Province of the Society of Jesus and is also devoting his time to writing and lecturing.

Father Gallagher is the author of: *The Test of Heritage*, a Russian class war novel (1938); *The Life of Saint Andrew Bobola* (1939) and *The China That Was* (1942). This latter work is being used as collateral reading matter in the Chinese Department of the Graduate Schools at Harvard, Yale, and Chicago Universities.   E. W.

Reverend David Gannon, S.A.
1904–

Father David Gannon, S.A., was born in New York City, September 16, 1904. Left an orphan at twelve years of age, the realization of the dreams of his early years — to study for the priesthood — had to be postponed for many years. All his education during this time was acquired by attending night schools. In the meantime, he entered the business world, and eventually became a member of the management staff of the Waldorf-Astoria Hotel, in New York City.

In 1931, after a conversation with the Very Reverend Paul James Francis, S.A., eminent convert from Anglicanism, and the founder of the Society of the Atonement, he entered St. John's Seminary at Graymoor, to begin his clerical studies. He was ordained to the priesthood at the age of thirty-five, at Catholic University of America, after completing his theological studies. Until the death of Father Paul in 1940, Father Gannon was closely associated with him in the administration affairs of Graymoor. Then followed eight fruitful missionary years among the Negroes of Kinston, North Carolina. Broken in health, he returned to Graymoor in 1948.

In the summer of that year, the Graymoor Friars acquired an abandoned Baptist college at Montour Falls, New York, in the Diocese of Rochester. Fully recovered in health, Father Gannon undertook the gigantic task of reconstruction. The abandoned college eventually became a fine senior seminary — Saint John's — rated among the best in the United States.

Returning to Graymoor in the winter of 1949–50 for a much needed rest, he was stricken again. In the spring of 1950, during a period of convalescence, he was given what he terms, "The most pleasant assignment of my life" — writing the biography of Graymoor's Founder — Father Paul. The book was published under the title of *Father Paul of Graymoor*, on May 29, 1950. The publisher is the Macmillan Company.

Father Paul was Anglican by birth and training. His convictions were strongly imbued with the urgency of corporate union with the Catholic Church. The story of that struggle and of the encouragement received from another Anglican, Sister Lurana, leads to a fuller understanding of the heart of Graymoor. The reader is given a clear-cut picture of those early days of hardship, with the strain of poverty and the pressure of Anglican skepticism about the world of Father Paul's ideal: "That all may be one." This ideal of corporate union was finally realized when by special dispensation Pope Pius X arranged for a corporate reception of the Friars and Sisters of the Atonement into the fold. From that point onward the Society prospered and grew into the organization now recognized as the Society of the Atonement.

Very Reverend Robert Gannon, S.J. 1893–

Father Gannon describes himself as a reluctant author: "I have always been handicapped as a writer by the obsession that there should be some sufficient reason for getting out another book. Lacking any inspiration that might drive me on, I have waited until late in life for the prompting of my public or at least of my superiors, only to find that they are less inclined than ever to prompt. The book on the *One Act Play* was done because there wasn't any and I needed one, and *After Black Coffee* was my lazy answer to a Fordham boy, who had gone into the publishing business and would not take 'no.' What possible crisis might produce a third, I can't imagine."

Born in St. George, Staten Island, New York on April 20, 1893, the son of Frank Stanislaus and Marietta (Burrows) Gannon, he was graduated from Loyola High School, New York and Georgetown University, Washington, D. C. He then entered the Society of Jesus and went to Woodstock College, Maryland. After receiving his M.A. degree in 1919 he became an instructor in English and philosophy at Fordham University. Ordained a priest in 1926, he earned an S.T.D. degree at the Gregorian University in Rome in 1927. Then he went to Christ's College, Cambridge University, and received an M.A. degree in 1930. He has honorary degrees from Alfred University, Boston College, Bowdoin, Colgate University, Columbia University, Detroit University, Georgetown University, Hobart, Hofstra, Holy Cross, Lafayette, Manhattan, Rutgers University, University of Toledo and New York University. He is a Fellow of the Royal Society of Arts in London.

In 1937 Father Gannon went to Venezuela on the invitation of Lopez Contreras, then President, as a consultant of educational problems and to Brazil to assist in the inauguration of the Brazilian Academy of Letters. The New York Academy of Public Education, of which he was president for two terms, bestowed on him the 1942 award for distinguished services in the field of education. He was three times president of the Association of Colleges and Universities of the State of New York, and was Dean of St. Peter's College from 1930 to 1936 when he became President of Fordham University. His was the longest term in office of any Fordham University president. During his term he liquidated a debt of half a million dollars, increased the endowment by a like amount, put one million dollars into new buildings and a half a million into reconstruction. Fordham's enrollment, which was 7,300 when Father Gannon took office, could boast of 13,200 when he retired. He had the honor of welcoming to the campus six presidents of various countries, President Roosevelt, President Truman and the present Pope Pius XII, as Eugenio Cardinal Pacelli.

The New York *Times* (Jan. 7, 1949) commenting on his retirement stated: "Few educators in this generation have so happily combined the virtues of intellectual brilliancy, urbanity and wit. Whether called upon for an after-dinner talk or delivering a series of scholarly lectures, or writing a book, Father Gannon was invariably broadgauged and good-humored. Upper and lower Manhattan will alike feel a pang at the severance of his highly constructive career at Fordham."

Father Gannon is now Director of the Jesuit Retreat House at Manresa, Staten Island. In his 1949 report he could state that the number of retreatants exceeded 4,000.

As we have seen above, Father Gannon has written only two books: *One Act Play* and *After Black Coffee.* The latter is a collection of twenty-one after-dinner addresses, which have genuine, polished literary quality. The speeches were delivered before alumni and professional groups, the New York Academy of Public Education, the New York Bar Association, the Conference of Christians and Jews, and the Society of the Friendly Sons of St. Patrick. Harry Hansen in the New York *World-Telegram* in his review comments: "His talks are direct, informal, often witty, but his convictions are clearly expressed. His eloquence has the rhythm and melody of the Irish orators of old — and they were no mean spellbinders."

It is hoped that his present position as director of the Mount Manresa House of Retreats will permit him to do more writing.

M. A. H.

Reverend Noel Hamlyn Gascoigne
1910–

Born in Palmerston North, New Zealand, Father Noel Gascoigne is the son of a lawyer, from whom he inherited a love of the legal profession, and of a mother whose most priceless legacy to him was the Faith which she taught him and nobly practiced herself. He spent his boyhood in a back-block (American back-woods) district wherein there was no Catholic school and thus his sole teacher in the Faith was his mother.

In 1929, he entered Auckland University College to study law, but the seeds of a vocation to the priesthood cultivated by his mother came to fruition, and the following year he entered the National Seminary, Holy Cross College. In 1934, as a deacon, he left his native country to continue his studies in Rome where he was ordained in 1935. The following year, he obtained his degree of doctorate of philosophy at the Angelicum University, Rome.

The three following years found him studying educational problems in England, Scotland and Ireland. He followed two main lines of research, catechetics under the direction of Father F. H. Drinkwater, the well known writer on that subject and the founder and editor of the Catholic Educational Quarterly, *The Sower*, and an examination of the question of State Aid for Church Schools with particular attention to the Scottish solution of this vexed question. In conducting the latter research, he was under the direction of the Most Reverend W. Brown, the Bishop of Pella, who as Apostolic Visitor to Scotland in 1917 did so much to secure the passage of the Act in the following year. Among the many to whom Bishop Brown introduced him was Lord Alness, the Secretary for Scotland in Lloyd George's Cabinet in 1918, and the statesman in whose charge was the famous Education (Scotland) Act, 1918. "I met Lord Alness on many occasions," says Father Gascoigne, "and I well recall his tribute to Bishop Brown: 'In all my long years of public life, I have met many negotiators with the government, but I can recall none more able than Bishop Brown. Always adamant when a question of principle was concerned, yet always knowing when to concede a point which did not involve principle.' To both Bishop Brown and Father Drinkwater, I owe a debt I can never repay."

In 1938 he entered Oxford University to study for the Diploma of Education. A rather interesting anecdote is connected with his seeking to enter this postgraduate course. A degree was required by the university authorities, and he submitted his Roman doctorate. He was informed that Oxford had not so far considered such a degree, but that if he would submit his doctorate thesis for scrutiny by someone on the professorial or lectureship board of the university, a decision would be given him. The examiner appointed by the university was Father Martin D'Arcy, S.J. The university ruled that the doctorate was acceptable in their eyes, a decision which established the precedent that Roman degrees would henceforth be recognized by the University of Oxford. The following year he gained the diploma with honors and left England for his native land via the United States.

In Washington he carried out further catechetical research under the guidance of the late Father Felix Kirsch, O.M.Cap., at the Catholic University of America. On his return to New Zealand he was appointed Director of Catholic Education, and later representative of the hierarchy in negotiations with the government on educational matters.

His first published work was *Christ and Youth* (1938). "I owe a great debt to Mr. Denis Gwynn," he says, "for the encouragement and advice he gave me on this initial work in the literary field." In 1940, he was commissioned to write the official account of New Zealand's First National Eucharistic Congress, a book which came out under the title, *The Story of the Congress*. In the meantime, he had interested himself in the Apostleship of the Sea activities, an interest first aroused when he listened to G. K. Chesterton speaking on the work of the Apostleship at the International Congress in London in 1936, one of Chesterton's last public appearances. His work as a Port Chaplain and later as a Naval Chaplain led him to write, during the war, *Manual for Catholic Soldiers and Airmen*. The men of the sea had a splendid manual in Father Martindale's *A Prayerbook for Catholic Seafarers*, and it was his desire to give the men of the other two services something along the same lines. His own manual drew upon Father Martindale's work, but was adapted to meet the special circumstances of the army and the air force and aligned to cover wartime conditions. That manual found its way to many battlefields and was very extensively used by the United States forces in the Pacific theatre. Perhaps the furthest place from New Zealand it reached was the Arctic Ocean, for "one of my most prized possessions," he says, "is a letter from one of the four survivors of H.M.S. Hood, which was sunk in those waters by the German battleship Bismarck. The sailor wrote informing me that the Chaplain of the Hood, who lost his life in the action, had framed his talks to the men on my prayerbook, and doubtless the copy of it now rested on the bed of the Arctic Ocean."

Father Gascoigne has written many articles for Catholic periodicals, one of which quite recently appeared in digest form in *The Catholic Digest* (America). He is engaged at the present time in writing two books, one on portrayals of characters he met during his work as Port and Naval Chaplain, and the other a catechetical work on a method of teaching the doctrine of the Mystical Body to children of both primary and high school levels.

Father Gascoigne visited the United States in 1951 as a Fulbright and Carnegie Scholar, conducting research in the Progressive Education of the school of John Dewey. This field took him to Columbia, Harvard, as well as to the University of Chicago. The survey was a critical one for in the last fifteen years, the public or state system of education in New Zealand has followed Dewey's philosophy with extremely adverse effects as regards discipline and the standards of scholarship. The New Zealand Government is interested in the report which he will prepare after conferring with many leading American educators. Father Gascoigne is also conducting research in catechetics and in the Liturgical Movement as well as the relationship between the State, and notably the Federal Government, and the private school systems of America. Father Gascoigne is the first priest to be awarded both a Fulbright and a Carnegie Scholarship.

Reverend Jerome Joseph Gassner, O.S.B.   1901–

Born in Ybbsitz, a medieval town in a valley of the Austrian Alps in the province of Lower Austria on August 12, 1901, Father Jerome Gassner received his education in the gymnasium of the Benedictines in Seitenstetten, Austria. He entered Seitenstetten Abbey as a novice in 1920. The following year he was sent by his abbot to the International Benedictine College, St. Anselm's, Rome, where he made his philosophical and theological studies and

received the laurea in scholastic philosophy in 1925. On July 19 of
the same year he was ordained priest. Returning to Austria he continued
the theological studies at the University of Innsbruck, took up studies
of history, particularly of classic archaeology and received on July 20,
1928 both the laurea of philosophy (history) and theology. The same
year he was called to St. Anselm's, Rome, as professor of philosophy.
From 1930 to 1938 he was professor of philosophy at the College in
Seitenstetten and lectured at the same time at the "Urania" in Vienna
about Thomistic philosophy. During those years he wrote (in Latin)
"Philosophia calculi infinitesimalis," a contribution to the philosophy
of mathematics; (in German) "St. Paul und die stoische Philosophie";
"Die Entwicklung der griechischen Architektur"; "Christliche Philosophie im christlichen Staate" (an open letter to the Austrian Government). In 1938 Hitler closed the gymnasium of Seitenstetten and
barred priests from the universities. In September 1938 Father Gassner
came to the United States and became an American citizen. Until 1941
he taught philosophy in the seminary of St. John's University, Minnesota; from 1942 until 1947 he taught philosophy and theology in the seminary of St. Gregory's Abbey, Oklahoma. In 1947 he returned to Rome as
professor of theology. That same year he was elected Procurator General
of the Austrian Benedictine Congregation to represent this branch of the
Benedictine Order at the Holy See. In 1948 he was appointed Postulator
General in causes of beatification. In 1949 the Holy Father appointed
him, for a period of ten years, ecclesiastical judge at the Roman
Curia.

From the beginning of his priestly and educational career he was
much interested in the care of souls; he gave many sermons and conferences and retreats to various groups of men, particularly to priests and
religious. From this experience he was incited to write on the liturgy.
Anxious to select the most inspiring subject for his retreats, which had
to be practical and at the same time afford the opportunity of theological, historical and aesthetical studies, he came to the liturgy, to the
Missal, to the Canon of the Mass, for the source of his material. Here he
found theology close to life, taught in a timeless method, presented in
artistic form. He started writing articles about the seasons and feasts of
the liturgical year. Since 1943 he is a regular contributor of studies on
liturgical subjects to the *Homiletic and Pastoral Review;* he wrote articles
for *Orate Fratres* and *The Liturgical Arts Magazine.*

In 1949 he published *The Canon of the Mass — Its History, Theology
and Art.* With his book on the Canon he did not wish to increase the
mass of devotional literature on the Holy Eucharist, nor did he intend
to give a formal dogmatic treatise for students and scholars. He does not
pretend to have done research work with new results for specialists in
the history of liturgy. "What I wished to do," he says, "was to select
from theological and historical literature what seemed to me necessary
and useful to get the substantial spiritual value of the Canon. I wrote
the book for priests and students of theology, as well as for the large and
increasing number of the faithful who pray the Mass. Since it is an interpretation of the Canon of the Mass, it may be said to be the primordial
theology of the Holy Eucharist in the beautiful language of the Church;

as the Church has taught it and continually is teaching it in liturgy: wherein she exercises her *magisterium ordinarium.*" Critics say that he is at his best in the chapters where he speaks about the scriptural background of the parts of the Canon. It is this method of exegetical-theology, characteristic of the time of the origin of the Canon, that he applied systematically. The interesting relations of the New Testament cult to the liturgy of the Old Testament — it is this scriptural background that is termed 'Theology of the Canon.'

"Of particular interest," he says, "is the approach to the better understanding of the Canon as a work of art. Those who look in the book for a history of liturgical arts, or for an analysis of works of art inspired by the Canon, are mistaken. It is the literary-artistic nature of the Canon, its artistic structure which is analyzed and serves to give a better understanding of it and of the intention of the Church. The Canon is a hymn, — a dramatic poem unfolding in successive events what is accomplished at the moment of consecration. It is a painting, a mosaic of a spiritual kind. It is an architectural edifice, a work of art proper to the Roman genius. Of particular interest may be the conception of the Canon as a mosaic: historically, inasmuch as apostles and martyrs, the Roman Pontiffs with the Fathers of the Church, have contributed colors, figures, ideas, prayers. The Canon is a mosaic of Scripture texts selected from the Old and the New Testament, which make it a comprehensive picture of God's revelation about the Eucharistic Sacrifice. But in particular the Canon is a mosaic of the classic period of this early Christian art: the same motives are found in the Canon as in the mosaics of Rome and Ravenna. It is a fact that Canon and mosaics have mutually inspired each other. Furthermore, their identical motives are presented in similar style, concept, and composition. The beautiful relationship between the perennial art of the colored stones and the art of the 'unchangeable rule' in the celebration of Holy Eucharist deserves particular attention as a key for the interpretation of the Canon, for its adequate understanding and appreciation."

Laverne (Kels) Gay   1914–

Born in Lodi, California, Laverne Gay is of Irish and Austro-German descent. From her Irish grandfather she inherited "an enthusiasm for historical personalities and the patterns of human progress." She writes of him that "history, especially the Napoleonic period, and the stormy politics of his own time were the deep and passionate interests of an existence otherwise divided between world travel and quiet country life in the California grape-lands. Hours of talk in those last years, under the family apple-tree, enkindled a spellbound granddaughter to spurts of childish poetry and essay-writing, and the grim, determined

conquest of several of those library lists of 'the hundred best books.'"
At school with the Dominican Sisters, first at Lodi (St. Anne's), and
later at Stockton (St. Mary's), her interest in poetry and journalism
was encouraged. In her graduating year, 1932, she was editor of the
convent newspaper and yearbook.

Entering the University of California, she majored in Latin and
history and was junior editor of the *Daily Californian*. She spent
time in dramatics and choral work and finally took a teacher's degree
which led to instructing in Oakland high schools for two years.

It was at the university that her interest in medieval history awakened, due to the lectures on the Middle Ages given by Professor James
Westfall Thompson, one of the great medievalists of his generation.
Professor Thompson was not a Catholic but, writes Laverne Gay, "in
mind and spiritual outlook he was always close to the Faith, and certain
of his inspiring lectures, like his famous one on the *City of God*, were
campus tradition and auditors of these were 'jammed to the halls' each
year. It was during his new graduate lectures on 'The Irish Element in
Medieval Culture' that I came upon St. Columban's royal friend
Theudelinda of the Lombards, whom he later characterized to me as
neglected by history and a 'natural' for me to do. So she became the
subject, first of the original research and later of a first novel, *The
Unspeakables*."

In 1939 Laverne Kels was married to Arthur Gay at the Newman
Hall campus chapel of the university. With the outbreak of war the
couple became "war-wanderers under Navy orders" but Laverne's
writing went on, first in Texas and then in the mountains of Idaho. In
1942 their first child, Stephen, was born; in 1947 Janis, their daughter,
arrived. In the meantime *The Unspeakables* was published.

Laverne Gay now decided to write about Bohemond, the leader of
the First Crusade. He was to be the hero of her second novel, *Wine of
Satan*. Of her purpose in this novel, she writes: "*Wine of Satan* was on
Bohemond, leader of the First Crusade, with a more serious attempt at
original creation, especially in character, with the same intention of
soundness in historical content and interpretation. My main interest
creatively in the novel (beside the basic one of sheer pleasure in the
'telling of all things made') is the delineation of the conflict in man's
nature in all its complexities, and how this dramatic struggle figures in
human responsibility and in the difficult and increasingly critical
achievement of individuals and civilizations in what du Noüy has called
'human progression in depth.' I realize that this idea is quite an assignment, and I am deeply aware of not having achieved with adequate
clarification in that direction as yet, but it is anyway the intention of
my work, as indeed it seems to be the growing consciousness of more
and more of modern creative effort."

Laverne Gay's work has been praised on many counts. Firstly, her
history is authentic. Next her story is well told and colorful. Wrote the
New York *Times* reviewer, Charles Lee, "Like a feudal tapestry, *Wine
of Satan* unfolds on one vivid scene after another. Here are square-sailed
Norman fleets, white-mantled squires with swords upheld in hush of
knighting rites, silken pavilions dotting Palestine dunes, the din of

Antioch in siege and sack, feastings around tables heavy with wine and roast heron, weepings at the slave marts amid the odor of branded flesh, the glow of moonlight on pink-walled Salerno, and the bizarre theatrics of medieval mimes in a miracle play." Apart from being capable of "a fine achievement in historical resurrection," Laverne Gay distinguishes herself in the difficult art of characterization. Her Bohemond and her Zoë are true persons in their ambitions and in their failings. "Bohemond," writes Father A. J. Brenner, S.J., in reviewing for the *New World*, "is shown not only as a courageous daring military leader of many varied experiences but as a human being with thoughts, desires and feelings similar to those of the majority of mankind." Mrs. Gay has shown herself richly endowed with creative imagination, good judgment, and insight into the patterns of human conduct.

So far, her published works are comprised of the two novels: *The Unspeakables* (1945); and *Wine of Satan* (1949). She confesses to be "freshly at work on what she hopes will be a contemporary novel."

Writing of her home in Sacramento where her husband Dr. Gay has his optometry practice she says: "Our hobbies are gardening and active sports when we find time for them, but most leisure now is directed to the increasing activities of the children. My professional affiliations are the Authors' League; Pen and Brush; California Writers' Club; and the American Association of University Women." Mrs. Gay does some reviewing for *Books on Trial* of the Thomas More Association.

Mrs. Gay is a warm admirer of Evelyn Waugh. She likes contemporary French literature, notably the work of the late Georges Bernanos, for style and "for his straightforward and realistic treatment of the inner life. He seems to have floated a whole modern school whose hallmarks are honesty, moral courage and a growing wholeness of vision." A book that is her "all-time favorite" is *Kristin Lavransdatter*, while Father Osgniach's work *Must It Be Communism?* on the world's need for Christian social reform turned her mind to the problems of international cooperation and to manifestations of the movement in this country. "There would seem to be," she says, "despite the thorny ambivalences of our present struggles, a general outcropping of true political creativeness in men of vision and uncynical good will (in the manifold trends toward cooperation of nations) in the same way that the great Gothic cathedrals appeared almost simultaneously in scattered places over Europe in the Middle Ages."   E. B. B.

Reverend (Edoardo) Agostino Gemelli, O.F.M. 1878–

Edoardo Gemelli was born in Milan, on January 18, 1878, of an old, well-to-do family of Lombard extraction. His father, a Freemason, and his mother gave their son an education founded merely on natural honesty, wholly exempt from any religious influences.

Having finished his elementary and secondary education in Milan, in 1896 he entered the Faculty of Medicine at the University of Pavia, where he absorbed the positivistic and anticlerical atmosphere which dominated the place. Feeling a strong inclination not only to study, but to a life of action, he very soon entered the social struggle, which was at the time particularly bitter, setting up and editing a number of "avant-garde" publications, and conducting heated controversies in newspapers, private and public meetings. His activities were chiefly addressed to the masses, in conformity with the Marxist theories in which he believed at the time. The greater part of his time, however, was given over to study.

Under the guidance of Professor Camillo Golgi, Gemelli specialized on the structure of the nervous system, and in 1902 he obtained a *cum laude* degree in medicine and surgery. He then became laboratory assistant to Professor Golgi, and conducted research in histology, embryology, and the physiology of the hypophysis.

After having received his degree, he returned to Milan to live, and was fortunate to serve his period of conscription in the Italian Army as a doctor in the S. Ambrogio Military Hospital in Milan itself, together with his friend and former schoolfellow, Dr. Ludovico Necchi. Dr. Necchi was a man of such Christian virtues as to induce his friends, after his death in 1930, to begin a movement for his beatification. Inspired by the example of Necchi's rectitude and charity, and by his discussions with him, Gemelli felt the strongest urge to a religious conversion. This feeling had been maturing for some time, owing, first to his dissatisfaction with positivist philosophy, which he felt more and more was clearly inadequate to scientific knowledge, and secondly, to the failure of Marxism, which showed, in the actions of its representative figures, its inmost incapacity to solve social problems.

In 1903, with sudden, unexpected finality, Gemelli entered the Franciscan monastery of Rezzato (Brescia) as a novice; and in 1908, under the name of Father Agostino, he was ordained, and celebrated his first Mass at the S. Antonio Monastery in Milan.

Determined to serve the cause of Christian truth, he soon began a vast program of practical action. In 1909 Gemelli set up a review, *Rivista di filosofia neoscolastica*, which soon collected the best minds of Italian neo-scholastic thought, then engaged in a campaign against the old positivists and the new idealists, who found expression in Croce's review, *La Critica*.

In 1914 Gemelli and his collaborators set up a new review, devoted to general culture interest, *Vita e Pensiero*, today one of the most important and best known in Italy, and which, even from its first number, showed its energetic, controversial attitude in an article written by Gemelli himself, under the title "Medievalismo." In this article the author maintained that the only solution to the serious problems created by the crisis of modern civilization can be found in an intelligent return to the organic, theocentric conception of the Christian Middle Ages.

In those same years, Father Gemelli also fought what was later called the "Lourdes Controversy," defending the Lourdes' miracles against the negations of certain medical circles, which inspired by Masonic principles, were trying to spread their agnosticism among the people and the cultured classes. A memorable episode of this controversy was a discussion held at the "Associazione Sanitaria Milanese" (Milan Medical Society) one night in 1909. The discussion ended with the expulsion of Father Gemelli from the Society, whose leaders had been clearly defeated by his trenchant arguments.

In two famous books, *La lotta contro Lourdes* (1911) and *Cio che rispondono gli avversari di Lourdes* (1912), Father Gemelli gave a detailed account of the discussion, which remains today a precious apologetic instrument.

In the meantime he continued his research work in laboratories in Italy and abroad, at Bonn, Frankfurt, Munich, Vienna, Amsterdam, Cologne, Paris, Louvain, and Mannheim.

In 1911 Father Gemelli obtained, at Louvain University, a special degree in histology, and later another degree in philosophy. He then devoted himself to research work on experimental psychology: first with Kiesow, at the laboratory of the Turin University, then with Kuelpe at Munich University, and at the Kraepelin Psychiatric Clinic, until 1914, when he became a lecturer on experimental psychology. Soon after, he refused an invitation to become a professor of psychology in the University of Tokyo, in Japan.

During the First World War, Father Gemelli was in the field, both as a doctor and a priest. He organized the "Opera di consacrazione dei soldati dell'esercito e della marina d'Italia," which brought nearly two million Italian soldiers to Holy Communion on the first Friday of 1917. He also founded and directed a psychophysiological laboratory at the Army Supreme Headquarters.

In 1921, after a memorable interview with Pope Benedict XV, Father Gemelli established the Catholic University of the Sacred Heart of Jesus, Milan, thus carrying into effect a desired, often expressed wish of all Italian Catholics, and fulfilling a promise which he himself had made in 1917 at the deathbed of the holy Catholic sociologist Giuseppe Toniolo. In the same year 1921 the Catholic University of Milan was canonically established and recognized by the Holy See; and in 1924 it was officially recognized by the Italian Government as a free university, with authority to grant degrees having the same rating as those granted by state universities.

Father Gemelli became, and still is, the first head of the University, while also being a regular professor in it, and the director of the laboratory of experimental psychology. To this science, Father Gemelli has given a place of honor, a fitting vindication against the neglect which it had suffered in other Italian universities.

Father Gemelli and his collaborators, in their scientific activities, touched on many branches of pure and applied psychology, while remaining faithful to a principle which can be called "organic" or "total." Thus, in the field of perception, Father Gemelli took a position against every atomistic conception, and upheld the principle that sensorial data are normally unified in perceptive activity. Differing from the tenets of the Gestaltist school, however, Gemelli proved that such unification is effected under the guidance of a presiding factor, operating as a selective process, so that, among the meaningless mass of sensorial data, only those which answer to a definite aim are chosen, brought forth, and organized. It is therefore sensorial organization which gives a meaning and a direction to the perceptive process, and makes it possible to reach a knowledge of "objects." This process of selection and synthesis, producing the "object," is also conducted according to a biological aim, which is to allow the subject to operate in the environment in which he is pleased.

Also with regard to personality Father Gemelli remained faithful to the "totalizing" principle, so that he always sought to study man as a whole, in his complete and organic state; having here ascertained the insufficiency of the introspective method, Gemelli accepted, from the different behavioristic methods, everything good they could offer in the study of personality. In particular he proved that the tasks assigned to subjects always surpass and reassume the physiological performance, thus unifying the action which must be done, and making the succession of phases "intelligible."

In the field of criminology Gemelli proved the advantage of a behavioristic study, taking into account the directing character of psychological activity.

He did some brilliant research work on language, which he examined from an electroacoustical viewpoint, with the help of delicate and elaborate apparatus; with the same apparatus and laboratory machinery he studied bioelectrical cortical rhythms.

Not to be forgotten are his studies on the psychology of soldiers, and particularly of pilots, and his research on professional and industrial psychotechnique, which round off the vast gamut of Father Gemelli's scientific interests.

Today Father Gemelli is also the Chairman of the Pontifical Academy of Sciences, which numbers among its members famous scientists and scholars of all nations; he is the Secretary of the Catholic Universities Federation, a member of the High Council of the Italian Ministry of Education, and an adviser to the Sacred Congregation of Seminaries and Universities.

Owing to his exceptional merits, he has been made an honorary member of several academies and societies, and has been given honorary degrees by many Italian and foreign universities.

The chief publications by Father Gemelli are: *Nuovi metodi ed orizzonti della psicologia sperimentale* (1924); *Il mio contributo alla filosofia neoscolastica* (1932); *The Franciscan Message to the World* (1934); *L'analisi elettroacustica del linguaggio* (with Pastori) (1935); *Idee e battaglie per la cultura cattolica* (1940); *Proposta sul riordinamento delle Università italiane* (1942); *La psicofisiologia del pilota del velivolo* (1942); *La psicotennica applicata all'industria* (1944); *La psicologia dell'eta evolutiva* (with Sidlauskaité) (1945); *L'operaio nell'industria moderna* (1946); *La personalità del delinquente nei suoi fondamenti biologici e psicologici* (1946); *Metodo per l'analisi statistica dell'intensità sonora del linguaggio* (1947); *Punti di vista psicologici e nuovi metodi per la determinazione dell'acuità stereoscopica* (1944); *L'orientamento professionale dei giovani nelle scuole* (1947); *Introduzione alla psicologia* (with Zunini) (1947).

G. P.

Theodate Geoffrey. See *Dorothy G. Wayman*

The Most Reverend Martin Stanislaus Gillet, O.P.   1875–1951

Stanislaus Gillet — he received the name of Martin when he joined the Dominican Order — was born in Louppy-sur-Loison, the department of Meuse in the diocese of Verdun, France, on December 14, 1875. Heeding a call to the priesthood he entered the diocesan seminary of Verdun, but, finding that the religious life, especially that of the Dominicans, appealed to him more, he left the seminary after a year to become a Dominican friar. At the age of twenty-two (1897) he was received as a novice at Amiens and clothed in the white habit of St. Dominic.

After his religious profession on November 7, 1908, Frater Martin was transferred to Flavigny to pursue his philosophical and theological studies. When France enacted its suppression laws in 1901 young Gillet went to Ghent, Belgium and there took his examination for the lectorship in sacred theology. Ordained a priest on September 28, 1902 he was sent to the renowned University of Fribourg to prepare for the doctorate. There he became a doctor of philosophy after having defended his thesis on Aristotle: "Du fondement intellectuel de la morale d'après Aristote."

In 1905 he was appointed professor of moral theology at Louvain, preaching there every Sunday at the university Mass. These sermons were the source of a series of works which were published under the title *l'Education du caractère*. Then he taught dogma at the monastery of Saulchoir at Kain from 1910 to 1914. During World War I he was a hospital attendant. From 1921 to 1927 he was professor of moral philosophy and social philosophy at the Catholic Institute of Paris. While there he increased his activities. He gave spiritual conferences to various groups; he was in demand as a preacher; he took part in all the Social Weeks of the French Catholics, bringing to them the teaching of St. Thomas. He has made one of the best French translations of the *Summa* of St. Thomas. For all these achievements he was, in 1923, given the title of master of sacred theology, and in 1926 he was made director of the Dominican magazine *Revue des jeunes*.

On July 22, 1927, he was elected provincial of his province. In 1928 he founded the Catholic Union of the Theater of which he was the spiritual director. A year later, he was elected Master General of the Dominican Order by the General Chapter when it met on September 21st, 1929. He remained Master General until September 21st, 1946, five years longer than the period prescribed by the constitutions of the Dominican Order, his term having been prolonged by the Holy See because of the difficulties created by World War II, which made it impossible to hold the regular General Chapter.

During his seventeen years of office he ruled with firmness but always for the good of the Order. His desire was to make the Order remain faithful to the principles which had animated the great Patriarch of Calaroga in the foundation of the Order seven centuries ago. One of his first projects was the recovery of the entire magnificent edifice of the old monastery of Saints Dominic and Sixtus to make it the seat of the Angelicum (1932). "The construction of the 'Aula Magna,'" writes Antonio Silli in the *L'Osservatore Romano* (October 3, 1951, p. 2), "with all the modern comforts and improvements, gave to the Pontifical University of the Dominican Order a seat worthy of the Order and of Rome, equal to the other Institutes of ecclesiastical learning in Rome." After the transfer of the Angelicum it became necessary to think of a location for the General's Curia, and Father Gillet thought it opportune to bring it back to its primitive seat, that is, to Saint Sabina, on the Aventine, donated by Pope Honorius III to St. Dominic himself who lived there. Through negotiations with the government of Italy he was able to gain possession of the entire monastery and there at the cost of much labor and expense he prepared a most worthy seat for the General's Curia (1936). The classical and beautiful basilica of Saint Sabina, dating from the fifth century, acquired through the munificence of the Most Reverend General, has been restored to its primitive splendor. There, at Saint Sabina, Father Gillet established not only his Curia and the Commission for the Leonine Edition of the works of St. Thomas but also the Historical Institute of the Order, the Dominican Liturgical Institute and the Normal School for the Masters of Novices and students.

On September 21, 1946, the General Chapter elected the Most Reverend Manuel Suárez as Master General of the Order to succeed the Most Reverend Martin Gillet. Father Gillet was named a Consultor of the Sacred Congregations of the Holy Office and of Studies. On the thirtieth of September, 1946, Father Gillet was made titular Archbishop of Nicea. On November 17th, he was consecrated by His Eminence Cardinal Carlo Raffaele Rossi. From then on Archbishop Gillet lived at the convent of the Most Holy Trinity in Rome and devoted his time principally to writing, until his death on September 4, 1951.

He wrote about thirty volumes, principally on education, moral philosophy and sociology.

His principal works are: *L'Education du caractère* (1908); *L'Education de la conscience* (1910); *L'Education du coeur* (1911); *Valeur éducative de la morale catholique* (1911); *Religion et pedagogie* (1914); *Conscience chrétienne et justice sociale* (1922); *La morale et les morales* (1925); *Paul Valery et la métaphysique* (1928); *Appel au bon sens* ((1936); *La Sainteté française* (1938); *Guide moral du chretien* (1940); *Réveil de l'âme française* (1942); *Saint-Dominique* (1942); *La Mission de Sainte Catherine de Sienne* (1945); *Thomas d'Aquin* ("Les Constructeurs") (1949).

His works in English are: *Education of Character*, translated by Benjamin Green; *Innocence and Ignorance*, translated with foreword by J. Elliot Ross, and *St. Thomas Aquinas.*

He was made an Officer of the Legion of Honor and was a Doctor "Honoris Causa" of many universities in France and in other lands.

B. J., G. D. and K. M.

Henry Martin Gillett   1902–

H. M. Gillett was born in Andover, Hants, England in 1902, the son of a Hampshire physician, and nephew of Admiral O. F. Gillett. He comes of a well-known Norfolk family with Tractarian associations. He was educated at Blundell's School and at Saint Chad's College, Durham. Always adventurous, as a boy he had a ride in the airship "Beta," and tea in the "Titanic" before she sailed from Southampton. At the early age of twelve he started to write books which he admits were never published! His first articles appeared when he was 15, and a series on Old Churches, in a Hampshire newspaper, attracted attention while he was yet 17. At this period, his study of mediaeval architecture led to a particular interest in Lady Chapels, and to the subject of devotion to Our Blessed Lady. He has visited about 400 shrines all over the world. This interest, which he never forsook, led him ultimately into the Catholic Church.

Still too young to take Anglican Orders, he accepted a post in Havana, and shortly afterwards in an Episcopalian Mission School in the Oriente Province of Cuba, where he organized the first scouts seen there, and attended the 1923 West Indian Scout Camp in Jamaica as deputy chief. From Cuba, by oil and banana boats, he worked his way to and through as many of the Central American Republics as possible, always visiting Shrines of Our Lady when he found them.

On being invited to take up important organizational work in the West Indies, he went to the University of the South from which he was graduated to the Protestant Episcopal Divinity School in Philadelphia. Here he found himself increasingly opposed to the prevailing modernist school, though during these years he found time to organize the American branch of the Anglo-Catholic Literature Association, which enabled him to visit and lecture in many places in Eastern and Mid-Western States.

Unable to find *terra firma* in the modernistic quagmire of the Protestant Episcopal Church, he abandoned ideas of permanent work there, and returned to take Orders from the Protestant Bishop of Durham. A serious illness obliged him to convalesce in Italy, where he made many important Catholic contacts. More and more he found his interest in Marian devotion to be utterly incompatible with the doctrine and discipline of the Church of England. Studying the facts of the various apparitions of Our Lady, including those at Fatima and La Salette, he became conscious, he says, that the urgent messages addressed by Our Lady to "her people" contained singularly little reference to the Church of England, wherein appeals to say the Rosary could hardly be obeyed without fundamental dishonesty. Finally, in 1933, he abandoned Anglicanism and was received into the Church in the Brompton Oratory, London.

The following month, Cardinal Bourne invited the author to undertake to write the history of Walsingham in Norfolk, which he had known since childhood, in connection with the restoration of the historic devotion and the opening of the Shrine of Our Lady of Walsingham in the ancient Slipper Chapel. This book was well received in the secular as well as the religious press, and ultimately led to the author's presentation of a copy to Pope Pius XI. From 1934 to 1940 he was largely absorbed in the task of promoting devotion to Our Lady of Walsingham, lecturing to more than 100,000 people. He organized many of the "first" pilgrimages "back to Walsingham," being the first to lead a party on foot back along the old Pilgrim's Way, 117 miles long, from London to Walsingham. In 1938 he was chief organizer of the 19,000 strong National Pilgrimage of Catholic Youth, led by Cardinal Hinsley and many bishops.

During these years, however, he found time for much writing and, in addition to numerous articles, wrote *St. Bede the Venerable* (1935) with a Foreword by his very close friend, the late Abbot Vonier of Buckfast; and the *Story of the Relics of the Passion* (1935), which was very widely reviewed.

His literary activities were seriously interrupted by the war years, when he was much engaged in civilian relief in many of the bigger air raids. In 1946, his new book *Walsingham* was published, with a Foreword by His Grace, Archbishop Godfrey, Apostolic Delegate to Great Britain. This book was received in September, 1946, by His Holiness, Pope Pius XII, who kept the author in private audience for nearly an hour. Arising from this came the work of collating the history and descriptions of many of the more famous shrines of Our Lady in preparation for his newest work.

In May, 1949, the author was again received by His Holiness, who graciously accepted the first copy of *Famous Shrines of Our Lady* and gave his personal permission for the work to be dedicated to himself. The book was published in the autumn of 1949.

H. M. Gillett has already given a number of broadcast talks on his favorite subject. He was invited to give the monthly series of talks on Our Lady's National Shrines on Radio Vatican, in honor of the Holy Year.

He served as history and English master at the recently opened St. Raphael's College, Market Harborough, conducted by the Missionaries of St. Francis of Sales. He is a member of the Royal British Institute of Archaeology and Fellow of the Society of Antiquaries of Scotland. Besides innumerable articles, usually illustrated, he has also written: *Folklore and Legends of Andover; The Story of the London Oratory Church* (1946); *Walsingham: The History of a Famous Shrine* (1946), and *Pluscarden Priory* (1950).

Domenico Giuliotti   1877–

Domenico Giuliotti, like his friend Papini, is a native of Tuscany. He was born in San Casciano, Val di Pesa, on February 18, 1877, on a farm only a few miles from the city of Florence. When he was barely old enough to go to school — in the days when his flaming red hair graced the shoulders of his little velvet suit — his parents sent him to live with an uncle, in a little hamlet near his birthplace. This uncle, Signor Virgilio, was a notary public who had become the *vice pretore* of the district. As a magistrate he took pride in his judicial duties, and he and his wife, having no children of their own, hoped that some day their young nephew would follow in the footsteps of his jurist uncle. Consequently, Giuliotti, much against his inclinations, eventually went to Siena "to study jurisprudence," as Signor Virgilio used to say when boasting about him.

Giuliotti's sojourn in Siena afforded him many exciting adventures — utterly "extra curricular," for his studies in "jurisprudence" did not worry him in the least. His head was as devoid of *juris* as it was of *prudence:* in it the banner of anarchy fluttered in the breeze of dithyrambs that whirled through his mind at that time. When this wayward schoolfellow had enjoyed all that Siena could offer in the way of distractions and diversions, he took himself to Rome, explaining to Signor Virgilio that he wanted to study under the renowned professors of law "in the city of the she-wolf." Speaking of this bluff, Giuliotti says that during his stay in Rome, not only did he never see the renowned professors of law, but that he did not even know them by name. Fortunately, his uncle finally realized that "that crazy poet" was not meant to be a jurist, and so his vagabond nephew was free to poetize to his heart's content.

As the years went by, however, Giuliotti began to acquire sense, and his outlook changed. He was no longer the lawless, anarchical ruffian who loved to wear a crimson tie to annoy the police. He had become serious-minded. He was terrified at the sight of the havoc wrought by the godless principles of a godless society with its worship of wealth and of everything that wealth can buy. The situation seemed hopeless, and Giuliotti was depressed almost to the point of despair, for it seemed to him that these diabolical principles were "preparing a generation capable of making hell turn pale."

In his endeavor to find something to counteract these evils, Giuliotti wandered from 'ism to 'ism. Finally, thanks to his reading the works of those fiery Catholic Frenchmen of the past century — De Maistre, De Bonald, Hello, Veuillot, Bloy, and the rest — he went back to the faith of his childhood, "to the Eternal Church that commands and teaches from Rome," as Papini puts it.

Upon coming back to the Church, Giuliotti was overwhelmed with joy to see how much the Church has to offer to those who hunger and thirst for Truth, and for the "peace that the world cannot give." At the same time he was appalled to see the indifference of those Catholics who make no effort to avail themselves of the inestimable treasures of Catholicism. This two-fold discovery directed his zeal toward a two-fold program: to improve his own spiritual well-being, and to promote the well-being of his neighbor. These aims are very evident in his writings, even as far back as the early days of *La Torre*, the periodical founded by Giuliotti and Tozzi with the express purpose of combatting socialism, anarchism, and everything opposed to the principles of the "Throne and the Altar."

Besides the well-known *Dizionario dell'omo salvatico*, written in collaboration with Papini, Giuliotti has published a score of books — books of sublime poetry, books of simple twice-told-tales, books about saints and books about sinners. Most of these are of a fragmentary nature, consisting of essays, sketches, book reviews, and journalistic articles such as an editor or a columnist might write. As one would expect, the spirit and the tone of these writings vary with the purpose and the content of the work. So much so, that as a certain French critic says of Giuliotti, "in him one finds the sweetness of Jacopone da Todi, the severe and serious naturalism of Giotto's frescoes, the winged flight of Dante's terzine, and often enough, a violence of reproach and satire that reminds one of Savonarola."

Despite these varied qualities, readers usually think of Giuliotti only as the author of his harsh *L'Ora di Barabba* (The Hour of Barabbas) and *Tizzi e fiamme* (Flames and Firebrands), which make one think of Leon Bloy, of Ernest Hello, of Louis Veuillot, and the other "bellowing writers" of this ardent group of Catholics, whom Giuliotti admires and emulates in their unconditional and uncompromising condemnation of the society of their day. Not all of Giuliotti's writings come under this category, however. His *San Francesco d'Assisi* and his *Ponte sul mondo* (The Bridge over the World), for example, are of an entirely different tone, for they sing the praises of God and His Church, and of those who lived and died for the glory of God and the salvation of souls. When thinking of Giuliotti's writings, therefore, it is well to remember that whether his words are as harsh as the lictor's axe, or as gentle as the breath of an angel, they all flow out of the same pen, the pen of a contrite penitent, a zealous Catholic layman who is spending himself in his endeavor to follow his Master ever more closely, and to induce others to do likewise.

Domenico Giuliotti is not too well known in America, and as yet, only one of his books is available in English: *The Bridge over the World* (1935), which is a commentary on the Holy Sacrifice of the Mass. In this country, very little has been written about Giuliotti. There is a brief article on his literary career in *The Columbia Dictionary of Modern European Literature* (1947), and a detailed study of him and his writings in *Not for Art's Sake* (1948), by Sister M. Serafina Mazza. Prior to these publications, Papini's chapter on him in *Laborers in the Vineyard* (1930) was perhaps the first work on Giuliotti known to the English-reading public.

Papini says that Giuliotti is one of those men whom the world fails to appreciate until they are dead. Papini himself, however, and the younger writers who had the privilege of associating with Giuliotti in the militant days of his literary career are not unaware of what Giuliotti meant to them. "Giuliotti taught us," says Piero Bargellini, "to be undaunted by human respect, and to write the truth, even at a time when falsehood is in vogue."

Giuliotti is still living in his native region, in the vicinity of Greve in Chianti, not far from the farm where he was born almost seventy-five years ago. He lives alone, close to the soil, a voluntary exile from the world of today, whose ungodly principles he abhors. He is proud to call himself a peasant, and happy to live the glorious faith of his Catholic ancestry. Since Giuliotti spurns the material progress of our day, "with its ghastly inventions and discoveries," his country home is genuinely rustic, and so is the country gentleman living there — a country gentleman in the noblest sense of the term.   M. S. M.

George Glasgow   1891–

"The son of an illiterate and *therefore* a charming and intelligent father — the argument being that the intellect often obstructs the flow of God's graces — my literary work has centred on the miracle of God's help to the helpless, the blessed state of the poor in spirit, and the beauty of simplicity." So George Glasgow has written about himself.

Born in 1891 in Bolton, Lancashire, George Glasgow became a journalist and an authority on finance, two callings at first sight somewhat out of keeping with the ideal described above. But these explain subsequent developments.

As a journalist, George Glasgow rose to the front rank, becoming the diplomatic correspondent of Britain's chief Sunday paper, the *Observer*, and special correspondent in foreign affairs of the *Manchester Guardian*, the English provincial daily of the highest reputation in the country. With these positions he became a journalist of international fame, attending the numerous international conferences between the world wars, and contributing regularly to American, Canadian, Belgian, French, German, Czechoslovak and Greek newspapers, as well as writing various books. During this period he constantly met and knew, often intimately, the leading world statesmen.

At the same time he pursued his financial researches and wrote three massive volumes on Investment Trust Companies, on which subject he is a leading expert.

Such occupations, however successful and rewarding, grew less and less to the taste of the son of illiterate Thomas Glasgow who, though not a Catholic, had had the grace of God in him. The grace of God called to George Glasgow also, and in the specific form which soon convinced a person of his intellectual ability. Walking in London one day, he noticed the entrance to a little pre-Reformation church in Ely Place. It was St. Ethelreda's, which Catholics had bought back from its Protestant owners. Within the church a light burned before the altar, the light that was to guide the footsteps of George Glasgow with the help of Father Martindale, just as it was to guide his wife, a daughter of an Anglican bishop. Just on the eve of the Second World War, Mr. and Mrs. George Glasgow were received into the Church.

Many others have done the same, and yet without feeling that the Truth necessarily called for the radical alterations of their daily work. But George Glasgow found himself unable to reconcile the light of Truth with a great deal of the higher journalism which earned him his bread and butter. So gradually he dropped one position after another in order to write for Catholic papers and to concentrate on his summing up of the whole matter in his book *Diplomacy and God* (1941). He retains only one regular outside post, that of the writer of the foreign affairs section of the monthly *Contemporary Review*. This Nonconformist review of great prestige, despite an editorial policy which is very different from Glasgow's mind, has for three decades been broad-minded enough to allow George Glasgow to have his monthly say — a fine record on both sides.

George Glasgow's other books include: *The Minoans* (1923); *Ronald Burrows* (1924); *MacDonald as Diplomatist* (1924); *From Dawes to Locarno* (1925); *General Strikes and Road Transport* (1926); *Continental Statesmen* (1930); *Peace with Gangsters?* (1939); *The Dupe as Hero* (under pen name Logistes) (1930).   M. de la B.

Sister M. Fides Glass   1889–

On January 11, 1945 President Franklin D. Roosevelt took time off amid his crowded hours to write to a Sister of Charity about a ballad she had written on Mother Seton, whose nephew was his second cousin. To his greetings and expression of appreciation he added: "You see the ballad has struck a responsive chord." The Sister of Charity was Sister M. Fides Glass, artist, teacher and writer: the ballad, "The Seton Ballad," represented work accomplished in the cause of the beatification of Elizabeth A. (Bayley) Seton.

"I am by training an artist. . . . I am a sort of accidental author," Sister Fides tells us. In each sphere her success has been achieved. But neither brush nor pen exhaust all Sister's energies. Her work for the canonization cause of Mother Seton, foundress of the American Sisters of Charity, has been immense. She painted an original life-size portrait of Mother Seton, after diligent research, as this view is rare. The picture was approved by Reverend Salvator Burgio, Vice-Postulator in America and Rome for the cause. The portrait now hangs in the nurses' home of the Pittsburgh Hospital. She wrote the pamphlets "A Valiant Woman" and "Mother Seton's Zeal"; she made a broadcasting record of the foundress's life for St. John's Mission in South Carolina, which was also heard over Greensburg and Pittsburgh radio stations; she designed 60 colored slides of Mother Seton's life with an accompanying lecture and she folded and pasted 50,000 pieces of literature and relics of the foundress. The literature has a reproduction of the new portrait. In Pittsburgh, Pennsylvania, in February, 1935, she wrote and produced the play "In God's Design," dramatizing episodes in the life of Elizabeth Bayley Seton. "It was the first drama of Mother Seton's life ever opened to the general public and drew huge crowds."

To date her most popular book has been *The Prince Who Gave His Gold Away.* "I wish," wrote Bishop R. Guilfoyle about this book, "we could make it a must book for every school child in the Diocese!" This book made hosts of friends for Sister Fides among young people in whose eyes she is "a great author." It was written in bed, at a time when physicians warned Sister Fides that, on account of her heart condition, she would have to give up painting.

Encouragement to write came to Sister Fides from her faithful friend Father Will Whalen, whose tragic death by fire occurred in 1949. Back in 1930 she showed Father Whalen a little ballad she had written called *Ballad of the Golden Squaw.* Father Whalen liked the ballad so well that he took it away with him and had it published. Thereafter he encouraged her "to write for young people" for whom he himself worked until his death.

Charity makes various demands on Sister Fides. "I am a semi-invalid and slow," she says in a letter of July, 1948, "however, I managed about a week ago to spend a few days at Carmel in Loretto teaching an enclosed nun some *tricks* in liturgical art. She is Sister Cecilia (Schwab), sister of the former steel-king, Charles M. Schwab. She was once a great musician . . . now her artistic talent has found another outlet. She was an apt pupil."

Then, there was dear, very old (ninety years!) Sister M. Xavier Farrell whose memories went back to the earliest days of the Sisterhood, and whose humor delighted the community. Her life had to be written. The book, *Happy Memories of a Sister of Charity,* "by" Sister M. Xavier, was the felicitous result. Whispers Sister Fides to a friend: "Sister Mary Xavier told me her story and I did all the composing, typing, galley work, and illustrations — but I knew it would take better under her name to which she objected at first." In reviewing the book Father J. T. Lanigan, S.J., said: "There is not a dull page."

Sister M. Fides was born at Summit Cresson, Pennsylvania. Her father was Thomas William Glass; her mother, Margaret Anne (McDermott) Glass. She was professed as a Sister of Charity at Seton Hill on July 19, 1910. In 1913 she took her teacher's diploma and taught art at St. Joseph's Academy, Seton Hill, from 1914 to 1920. She was assistant art teacher at Seton Hill College from 1921 to 1927. Meanwhile she attended art classes at Cape Cod School of Art; Christian Walter Summer Art School, and the University of Pittsburgh Art School. In 1927 she took an Art Teachers' Certificate and in 1930 she took the B.A. degree in fine arts in Carnegie College. From 1930 to 1936, when she retired, due to illness, she was engaged as art supervisor in parish grade and high schools in Pittsburgh and Altoona dioceses. Sister M. Fides' published works are: *Ballad of the Golden Squaw* (1930); *The Prince Who Gave His Gold Away* (1938); *Jesus, The Divine Physician* (1942); *Happy Memories of a Sister of Charity* (1941 — in conjunction with Sister M. Xavier); *Seton Ballad* (1945); *America's Indian Queen* (1948); *Prince Dimitri's Mountaineers* (1950).

Sister M. Fides has painted many portraits and other pictures. Her portrait of Mother Seton has already been referred to. Others of her paintings are St. Apollonia, patron saint of dentists, for Dr. John F. Blanch of Philadelphia, portraits of Archbishop Canevin and Bishop Hugh C. Boyle for the parlors at Seton Hill College. "Maybe," writes Sister Fides, "I'll turn back to painting completely, even though I'm all 'pepped up' to write again after my success in publishing. I hardly know which beckoning way to go as I have just acquired a wonderful belfry studio. It has a back door where I can walk right into the organ loft in the chapel gallery and pray in unison with the novices when I get tired of my palette and canvas."

Sister M. Fides is ready to admit being busy, but she disclaims achieving anything great. She says: "I'm gathering no moss — but I doubt if I am gathering anything else of worth — but I *do* say: 'All for Thee, my God!'"

E. B. B.

Liam Gogan   1891–

Liam Gogan, Keeper of the Art Division of the National Museum, and one of his country's leading authorities on Celtic art and archaeology, was born in Dublin, October 24, 1891 of English-speaking parents, successful business people. Like many others who grew up with the revival of Irish culture and language he feels that his effective education began when he immersed himself in Celtic studies — Old, Middle and Modern Irish, Welsh, Archaeology and Old Irish History at University College, Dublin, one of the National University Colleges.

After graduation with honors in 1913 he became a member of the National Museum of Ireland in the Irish Antiquities Department (1914).

Politically, like his father, a member of the Irish Republican Brotherhood, he was a Republican and for a time was assistant-secretary to the Irish Volunteers, the revolutionary body which was responsible, with the Irish Citizen Army, for the Easter Rising of 1916. His political attitude and activities brought about his internment and dismissal from the museum. Soon after, the first of his five volumes of poetry was published (1919) through the influence of Stephen McKenna, the internationally known Graecist. Some of his poems have been translated into English. He translated Gougaud's *Pioneers of Gaelic Christianity* into Irish. For four years he worked on the final revision of Dinneen's *Irish-English Dictionary*, being responsible for about three-quarters of the existing text. He is also preparing a supplement to this work. He has prepared a technical dictionary of art and architectural terms in Irish which has been published serially in various journals.

He rejoined the staff of the museum after the establishment of the then Irish Free State in 1921 and transferred from the antiquities to the art department in 1936. In 1932 Browne and Nolan, Ltd., Dublin, published his monograph (in English) on the *Ardagh Chalice, Ireland's Holy Grail*. It is inscribed to the Academy of Christian Art of which he was honorary secretary for several years and is now a vice-president.

He writes frequent articles and papers on art and archaeology and gave, some years ago, a series of radio-talks on the *Sacred Places of Ireland* (pagan and Christian). He recently gave a course of twenty lectures in Irish at Dublin University, the first of their kind. He has been much in demand as a public lecturer. In a recent paper (Ir. Eccles, Rec., Mar. 1951) he produced a definitive solution to the long debated problem of St. Patrick's place of origin.

As a young poet his main thought was the restoration of the broken link between the present and the last of the native poets who survived into the 19th century, later adapting himself to general modern trends, helped out by borrowings from French, German, Italian, Spanish and Latin and even English poetry.

He is an active participant in the Celtic Congress which he hopes may eventually have the success of the famous Indian Congress, and has been Irish delegate to its meetings of 1944 (Dublin), 1949 (Bangor, Wales), 1950 (Truro, Cornwall), 1951 (Quimper, Brittany).

After that he thinks the prime concern of the poet is the liberty of "the folk" and the preservation and the creation of tradition in all planes of the national life. He himself must never be the victim of anything whether wine, women or words. He thinks Rilke exaggerates sentimentally the poet's function as being "to praise": not uncommonly he has also "to blast." For politicians and politics, therefore, his esteem is somewhat measured and his *Ceannairc na nAinmhidhthe* (Animals in Revolt) illustrates this theme. He fully believes in Pearse's formula for the Irish Republic, "not free but Gaelic also," and considers that the politicals who also control the universities have wandered far from this objective. (Poem: *Na Teipeamhnaigh:* The Failures.) Like Rilke he believes in the duty of poets to translate themselves. Translations of long poems include Goethe's *Zueignung* and Francis Thompson's *Hound of Heaven.* The appearance of a new brood of poets, some quite modernistic, bears out his early belief in the possibility of a complete restoration of the Irish mentality and the creation of a new poetic tradition fully continuous with the past when poets numbered about a third of the Irish population!

He has visited most parts of Ireland; also the United States, Wales, Cornwall, France, Brittany, Germany, Belgium, Holland and claims to understand them all pretty well. Unlike Americans he admires American architecture and one of his young poems (Poésies Modernes) acclaims the skyscraper (Scríoboir Spéire).

He has contributed the article, Ireland: Art and Architecture to the *Encyclopedia Americana.*   H. L.

Guido Gonella   1905–

Philosophy is the domain of Guido Gonella but not his sole interest.

Born on September 18, 1905 in Verona, Italy, he pursued his higher studies in Paris, London and Berlin. Having earned his Ph.D. degree, he returned to Rome to become assistant professor of philosophy of law at the University of Rome. Despite his youth he distinguished himself by his clear and profound thinking as well as by a keen sense of justice. In time he became secretary of the Italian Society of the Philosophy of Law, secretary of the Juridical Section of the Italian Society for the Progress of the Sciences, and titular member of the Institut International de Philosophie du Droit et de Sociologie Juridique.

Owing to his active propaganda against Fascism and war, he was denounced as an anti-Nazi by the German press and expelled from the University. Then he continued his political activities through the press until 1939 when he was jailed for his anti-Fascist writings. He was released by papal protest and housed inside the Vatican. Clandestinely, he worked with De Gasperi on the foundation of a Christian Democracy.

From 1933 to 1944 he was on the staff of *Osservatore Romano,* which President Roosevelt referred to, during the hysterical last hours before World War II, as "the one newspaper in Europe that was telling the truth." In 1944 Signor Guido Gonella founded the paper *Il Popolo* which later became a daily and of which he was editor till his election as Education Minister.

He was elected to the first Italian Democratic Parliament. Because of his solid moral and intellectual training he was elected in 1946 Minister of Education, the position he still holds.

Guido Gonella is married and has five children.

He began his literary career when appointed editor of the *Studium* review. His works number about thirty volumes, of which the most important are his studies on the juridical philosophy of Rosmini and Hegel and those philosophers devoting themselves to the problem of personality and contractualism. His two books, *Presupposti ad un Ordine Internazionale* (1943) and *Principi di un Ordine Sociale* (1943), have been translated into eight languages.

A sample of his work was presented to the American public by Father T. Lincoln Bouscaren, S. J., with the publication of *A World to Reconstruct.* This volume contains a series of articles by Guido Gonella which were published in the *Osservatore Romano* from January to May, 1942. As the Introduction of this book states: "the author proposed to furnish matter for study to any who might wish to meditate on the enlightened teachings of His Holiness Pope Pius XII on the fundamental problems of international life. In England the book was published under the title *The Papacy and World Peace.*

"The plan of the work comprises a comparative study of the five points of each of the Christmas messages of 1939, 1940 and 1941 in which are defined those 'essential prerequisites of an international order' which cannot be disregarded by those, who, after the storm has subsided, will labor to rebuild a new international order founded on moral principles." It was through the Bishops' Committee on Publicizing the Pope's Plan that a translation of the series of articles appearing in book form in Rome was undertaken.

Among the principal works of this born statesman and accomplished scholar are: *la valutazione del machiavellismonell' etica di Benedetto Croce* (1930); *Il contributo del P. Cathrein agli' studi di diritto naturale* (1932); *Mente e Spirito* (1932); *Al di qua del bene e del male* (1932); *L' essenza dello spinozismo* (1933); *Classificazione dei concetti di "natura" nella filosofia del diritto* (1933); *La filosofia del diritto secondo Antonio Rosmini* (1934); *La dottrina della personalità ed alcuni suoi riflessi sociali* (1934); *Etudes critiques* (1936); *Schopenhauer Studien in Rom* (1937); *La filosofia come logica della scienza giuridica* (1938); *Aspetti teologici del proglema della guistizia* (1938); *Cartesio giurista* (1938); *La crisi del contrattualismo* (1938).   M. A. H.

Caroline Gordon (Mrs. Allen Tate)
1895–

The tobacco country around Clarksville, Tennessee, commonly called "The Black Patch" because "dark-fired" tobacco is grown there, was the birthplace of Caroline Gordon and she says it is the scene of her six (1951) novels.

The novelist, critic and short story writer was born October 6, 1895 on "Merry Mont," a farm in Todd County on the state line between Kentucky and Tennessee. Her parents were James M. Gordon and Nancy Minor (Meriwether) Gordon. On both paternal and distaff sides she stems from Virginia stock. Her mother's people, tobacco planters since the weed was first cultivated here by white men, came to Tennessee from Virginia early in the nineteenth century. Her father, a Virginian, came nearly a century later as tutor in her mother's family.

A classical scholar, he later conducted a school for boys in Clarksville. It was from him Miss Gordon received her early education. In 1916, she was graduated from Bethany College, West Virginia, with the degree of bachelor of arts. Thirty years later, her alma mater honored her with the degree of doctor of literature.

For some time after her graduation Miss Gordon taught school. Then she entered newspaper work. She was a reporter on the Chattanooga *News* from 1920 to 1924 and also worked for a New York feature service.

On November 2, 1924, she married Allen Tate, poet and critic and a member of a group of Southern writers who called themselves "The Agrarians." After her marriage, she turned to creative writing. The 1930 edition of Edward J. O'Brien's "Best Short Stories" was dedicated to her and her story was chosen as the best of the year.

Penhally, Miss Gordon's first novel, was published in 1931. A tale of the South in Civil War days, it won wide critical approval. The late Ford Madox Ford, the English novelist, called it "the best novel that modern America has produced."

In 1932, Miss Gordon won a Guggenheim Fellowship. Two years later, her second novel, *Aleck Maury, Sportsman* was published.

Asked to evaluate her own work, Miss Gordon said recently, "Many people consider *Aleck Maury* my most representative work. It purports to be the biography of my father and presents a man who believed that sport was an art rather than a relaxation, in conflict with his age, and, in a way, victorious over it. I am really not capable of judging which of my books is most representative. They all have the same theme or aspects of the same theme. Like most novelists I regard my novels, which, it seems to me, are chiefly concerned with man in an order of natural grace, as a preparation for work which I hope to accomplish."

Miss Gordon joined the faculty of Woman's College of the University of North Carolina in 1938 and for a year gave a course in short story writing. She lectured on creative writing at Columbia University from 1946 to 1951.

A contributor to leading English magazines, to the *Yale Review, New Republic, Southern Review, Criterion, Harper's, Madamoiselle* and *Sewanee Review,* Miss Gordon is represented in many anthologies. She has reviewed important books for the New York *Times* and the New York *Herald Tribune.*

For a few years after their marriage Miss Gordon and her husband lived in New York City and traveled in Europe. In 1930 they returned to Tennessee where they lived for years on a farm overlooking the Cumberland River near Clarksville. Recently they returned to the East to live in Princeton. They have one child, Mrs. Percy Wood, the former Nancy Tate. Both Miss Gordon and her husband are converts to the Catholic Church.

Miss Gordon's books include: *None Shall Look Back* (1937) a Civil War novel; *The Garden of Adonis,* published the same year, a study of class conflict in the contemporary South; *Green Centuries* (1941); *The Women on the Porch* (1944); and the *Forest of the South* (1945), a collection of short stories. *The House of Fiction,* an anthology of the short story, which she edited with her husband, was published in 1950. Her latest novel, *The Strange Children,* appeared in 1951.

E. L.

Maurice Anthony Gorham   1902–

For twenty-one years (1926–1947) Maurice Gorham was employed by the BBC. He had gone into the BBC as a journalist and had no desire to get into actual broadcasting until the war. His experiences in a fairly wide variety of jobs are told in his autobiography *Sound and Fury.* He had a distinguished career as editor of *Radio Times* and a broadcaster.

During the war he was Director of the Allied Expeditionary Forces' Programme but spent more time during the war running the BBC's broadcasts to the United States and Canada and in postwar days he reformed and launched the television service, which it was claimed was the best in the world. Then he resigned because he disagreed with the BBC and so found himself free to write.

"I always wanted to write," he tells us, "and enjoyed writing more than anything. I wrote stories as soon as I learned to write, mostly adventure stories based on current events like the Balkan War and the Yellow Peril (this was before 1914). . . . Since leaving the BBC I have done practically nothing but write, mostly on subjects of which I have special knowledge, but I hope that in time I may branch out and even possibly rediscover the vein of fiction that I possessed when I was ten."

The subjects, there are two such, of which Maurice Gorham has special knowledge, are wide apart. The first is radio-television; the other is the London "pub" or "local." On the first subject he has written three books (listed below) which are distinguished by the clarity and charm of his way of writing. One of them, *Sound and Fury* (1948), is autobiographical and abounds in pen-pictures of interesting characters and events belonging to his days with BBC.

He admits in *Sound and Fury* that when he first went there he pre-ferred to spend his lunch-hour alone, trying out the pubs not too far from Savoy Hill. Sometimes he went to "Mooney's" in the Strand; other days to "Gow's," or the "Tivoli Bar," or the "Old Bell"; but he avoided the "Coal Hole" where others of the staff used to go. He loved London, and says: "I am very fond of London and spend all the time I can walking around enjoying its streets, rivers, markets, music-halls, and pubs. These last are great social resorts of the English and despite increasing modern uniformity still present you with fascinating varia-tions all the time; also I am very fond of beer." Once he brought A. J. Alan, "the unexampled storyteller," to "Gow's." Alan said to him: "What will you drink, stout-and-bitter?" Maurice asked: "How do you know I drink stout-and-bitter?" Alan shot back: "I thought you looked as if you would." Maurice Gorham classifies himself, psycholog-ically, by the tale.

He had an early enthusiasm for the American scene, and has mem-ories of visits to many American cities, from Boston to San Francisco and New Orleans. His first trip to New York was made as a steerage passenger in 1929 and his last in 1947, when he made a flying visit to see for himself how American television compared with British. He then found, as he expected, that "their studios were no better than ours but they were building where we were not; their standard television sets were no bigger but they were making far more of them; new stations were opening almost every day . . . their studio programmes were not nearly so expertly produced nor so varied as ours but their outside broadcasts were amazingly slick . . . to sum it up, if we had had their equipment our staff could have produced a really terrific service."

Apart from television, he did not altogether welcome the changes he saw in America since the war. "I was rather alarmed," he writes (*Sound and Fury*, p. 230), "by the rampant nationalism that was evi-dent in the newspapers and on the radio and even at the football games. The United States seemed to me to be fast growing as self-confident and self-righteous as Victorian England, but more dangerous because it really thought foreigners should adopt the American way of life as soon as they heard of it, whereas the English always knew that foreigners are queer. The American point of view really seemed to be that any foreign country that is not morally corrupt need only be shown a refrigerator and a personal radio and a shiny automobile and it must at once decide to have a federal constitution, an electoral college, a two-party system, and forty-eight states." It should be mentioned, in fairness, that Maurice Gorham, in his Foreword to *Sound and Fury*, admits that "it is all too easy to make people who disagree with one's own opinions sound a little more stupid than they really are."

Maurice Anthony Coneys Gorham was born in London in 1902. His father J. J. Gorham, M.D., came from Clifden, County Galway; his mother, Mary Smith, from Lancaster, England. His early education was at the hands of the Xaverian Brothers at Clapham College, London. Afterwards he went to Stonyhurst and from there to Balliol College, Oxford where he graduated with Honors in Modern History in 1923. His first employment was to the editorial staff of the *Weekly Westminster* where he remained for three years (1923–1926). After a few months work with the *Westminster Gazette*, he joined BBC as assistant-editor of the *Radio Times*, a weekly journal. In 1928 he became art editor of *Radio Times*, a job he found most enjoyable, especially in a period of new ideas in commercial illustration and type display. Later he became its editor (1933–41). During his editorship the circulation rose to three million before World War II.

In 1941, owing to wartime needs, he shifted from journalism to broadcasting, taking over the direction of BBC's North American Service. In 1944 he was appointed Director of the Allied Expeditionary Forces' Programmes.

After the war, Maurice Gorham created the popular BBC "Light Programme" and then moved on to reform and launch BBC Television Service (1945–47). Since resigning from BBC he occupies himself writing. He lives in London in the "flat" he has always occupied in Ashley Gardens, S. W., opposite Westminster Cathedral. He is unmarried. He has been described as "tall, vigorous, open-air looking, and a fast talker." Besides walking in London, and visiting his favorite "locals," where he picks up material for his books, he visits Ireland, as often as he can and never missing a year, seeing his sister.

The following books have been published by Maurice Gorham: *The Local* (1939); *Sound and Fury* (1948); *Back to the Local* (1949); *Television, Medium of the Future* (1949); *Inside the Pub* (with H. M. Dunnet) (1950); *Professional Training for Radio; Showmen and Suckers* (1951), and *Londoners: Studies of London Scenes and Types*.

E. B. B.

Right Reverend Martin Grabmann
1875–1949

Acclaimed as the "foremost Thomistic student and research scholar of modern times," Monsignor Martin Grabmann was wholeheartedly devoted to Christ and His Church as St. Thomas was. He covered the realm of philosophy and theology and its patristic foundations from Saint Augustine up to the neo-scholasticism of our day. Over three hundred of his writings were printed.

Born on January 5, 1875 in Winterzhofen in Bavaria, he was the child of deeply religious parents. He received his grammar school education at Eichstätt (1884–1893) and pursued his philosophical and theological training in the same city from 1893 to 1898. For a short while he tried out the novitiate of the Dominicans but decided it was not his vocation. As a young seminarian, Martin Grabmann became an enthusiastic follower of St. Thomas and an avid reader of the *Summa*. He was ordained to the priesthood in 1898.

After two years (1898–1900) of parish work, Bishop Baron Leopold Von Leonrod, of Eichstätt, sent Father Grabmann, then stationed at Neumarkt (Oberpfalz), to Rome to continue his studies at the Anima (1900–1902). In Rome, he came under the influence of two most learned priests, Reverend Henry Denifle, O.P., the archivist of the Holy See, and Reverend Franz Ehrle, S.J., prefect of the Vatican Library, both of whom he remembered in grateful appreciation. Father Grabmann's studies in Rome gave him the determination to devote his life to historical research in scholastic philosophy and theology. No other scholar's name appears more often than Grabmann's in *Ueberweg* — Geyer's compendium about research work in the history of patristic and scholastic philosophy.

On his return to Eichstätt, he worked again in the ministerial office there, and at the same time continued his historical studies at the State Library in Munich, Bavaria. In 1906 Bishop Leo von Mergel appointed him professor of dogma at the seminary of Eichstätt. He remained there for seven years. Then followed a professorship of Christian philosophy at the University of Vienna in Austria (1913). From 1918 on, he was professor of dogma at the University of Munich which years may be considered the most fruitful of his divinity career. His happiness in teaching, however, received a harsh blow when the Hitler regime suppressed the theological school at the University in 1939. During World War II, in 1943, when the air force of the Allies bombed Munich more frequently, Father Grabmann accepted the kind invitation of his dear friend and former pupil, Dr. Michael Rackl, Bishop of Eichstätt, to leave Munich and return to his old home at Eichstätt. He brought with him his valuable library. At the end of the war, Father Grabmann resumed teaching for one year at the University of Munich.

One of the first topics he became interested in was the relation between faith and science. His first printed publication was a treatise about speculative theology according to St. Thomas Aquinas. In 1909 he published the first volume of *Geschichte der scholastichen Methode* (*A History of Scholastic Methods*). Two years later the second volume appeared, dealing with early scholasticism (12th century), many works of which, up to that time, had not yet been printed. His research in the State Library of Bavaria in Munich, and in many other libraries, brought to light numerous unknown, scholastic writings.

Much of Monsignor Grabmann's writing was done to panegyrize Thomas Aquinas. In 1928, Father Virgil Michel, O.S.B., brought out an English translation of Grabmann's *Thomas Aquinas: His Personality and Thought*. This *vade mecum* was translated into the main languages of Europe and even into Japanese. In 1949 the original appeared in its eighth edition. *The Introduction to the Theological Summa of St. Thomas* was translated into English by Reverend John S. Zybura and was published by B. Herder Book Company. This book was first published in 1919 and had been out of print for several years; a second edition appeared in 1928. Father Zybura in the Translator's Preface remarks: "In the present work Dr. Grabmann accomplishes four things:

"He sets forth the historical origin of the *Summa Theologica*, its place among the works of the prince of Scholastics, and the influence it has exerted down to our day.

"In a historical commentary on the Prologue to the *Summa* he initiates us into the spirit and form of this monumental work; with the intellectual life of Scholasticism and Thomas' way of thinking and working as a background, he outlines and estimates the originality of method and content as well as the power and value of this greatest literary creation of Aquinas.

"He then shows its significance for today by stimulating reflections on the proper manner of interpreting and utilizing it.

"In a final chapter he unfolds the structure of the entire work, gives a summary of its contents, and adds illuminating comments on the outstanding excellences of its several parts."

The most important work, which Father Grabmann had done on the study of St. Thomas, is a historical and critical research on the writings of St. Thomas. It appeared under the title: *Die Werke des Hl. Thomas von Aquin (The Works of St. Thomas Aquinas)*, third edition, 1949.

Numerous learned treatises on the history of scholastic philosophy and theology by Father Grabmann are collected in the two volumes: *Mittelalterliches Geistesleben* (1926 and 1936). Twenty studies on the history of medieval thought appeared in the series: *Sitzungsberichte der Bayerischen Akademie der Wissenschaften* (Jahrgang 1921–1943, Munich 1922–1944).

About fifty of Grabmann's writings concern Aristotelianism. He took great pains in explaining the medieval translations of Aristotle and stressed the importance of the so-called *Logica Nova*, that is, the second part of Aristotle's *Organum*, for the development of Scholasticism in the twelfth and thirteenth centuries.

In 1951 Bruce Publishing Co. brought out Grabmann's *The Interior Life of St. Thomas Aquinas*, which was translated into English by Nicholas Ashenbnener, O.P.

Father Grabmann received an honorary doctorate from the Universities of Innsbruck, Louvain, Milan, and Budapest. He was a member of the Bavarian Academy of Science; a member of the Medieval Academy of America, a member of the *zentraldirektion* of the *Monumenta Germaniae*, and a member of many other scientific academies and institutes. The Holy Father conferred on him the title of Prothonotary Apostolic.

Soon after he celebrated his golden jubilee in the priesthood (1948) his heart ailment became worse. After a ten-day illness, he died January 9, 1949 at Eichstätt, mourned by a host of friends in the scientific world.

L. O.

William Joseph Grace   1910–

William J. Grace was born the son of William Joseph and Catherine (Hickey) Grace, in New York City in 1910. When he was about five years old his family left the United States to live in Leghorn, Italy, where his father had been appointed American Consul. It was here that he lived during World War I, "for the most part preoccupied with a child's world of swimming and fishing in the Mediterranean, marred only by desultory subjection to education at the hands of private tutors. Occasionally, intermittent echoes of the adult world of war threatened, and I can still recall the hysterical joy of Armistice Day, but I am afraid that I and my contemporaries were chiefly interested in competing for the finest collection of propaganda postals."

After World War I his family moved to Sheffield, England, an industrial center in the British Midlands. It was there that he first settled down to the routine of regular attendance at a secondary school. Then he went to Balliol College, Oxford and received a M.A. degree.

In 1935 he returned to the United States where he has remained ever since. He was assistant professor of English at St. Bonaventure College (1936–37) and then joined the faculty of Fordham University where he is at present Assistant Professor of English at the School of Education. He also teaches at Notre Dame College of Staten Island, New York.

"During World War II," he says, "I had almost as quiet a time as in World War I, but as a classification specialist in the United States Navy, my understanding of war was at least increased."

Mr. Grace has contributed to *America, The Commonweal, Journal of the History of Ideas, English Journal, Thomist, Renascence, American Journal of Economics and Sociology, Thought, Sewanee Review, Comparative Literature, Journal of Higher Education, College English* and *The Catholic Worker.*

He also contributed to volumes one and three of Father Harold Gardiner's *A Guide to the Great Books.*

Triple City, a book of poems, some of which have appeared in *The Commonweal* and other magazines, is his first book. Mr. Grace sings of Man, who in our day is a citizen of a triple city — the city of God, the city of Man and the city of Satan.

"Elements of experience that have borne upon the content of *Triple City* include a first hand observation of the effect of an unenlightened industrialism upon the human culture and otherwise beautiful country of Derbyshire and Yorkshire, a destructive effect that has made me sympathetic to Eric Gill (see previous volume, *Catholic Authors: Biographical Sketches, 1930–1947*) and appreciative of his social doctrine," writes William Grace.

He continues: "My attitude toward war is partly explained by the fact that I have been subjected to propaganda of many kinds and variety so that I can take a disinterested and non-nationalistic view of this prevailing occupation of our times, which seems to have an important analogy with the ruthless competition and cupidity of the nineteenth century attack upon human dignity. Wars of themselves cannot, in my opinion, settle the validity or invalidity of ideas; they can only settle questions of power, self-confidence, survival.

"What I am attempting essentially to stress is the social meaning of the Incarnation. Unless this central truth is clear to us, we are apt to go wrong, even as Catholics. In a recent article I have said "The human being is of immeasurably more worth than the national state considered as a material entity, a 'power,' which with its great extent, wealth, and productivity, cannot even be compared with the value of a single person. . . . Even the stellar systems and their multitudes of worlds are not as important as one glimpse of truth in his head. Humility, as we know, is simply the realization of truth, the capacity to see being as it is, to see with reverence and wonder the Creator in His creation including man.

"*Triple City* is a succinct summary of the values I have presented in my prose writings. It is also an attempt to dramatize the age of crisis objectively and impersonally." Padraic Colum says, "*Triple City* is a poem, which, while recognizing the tensions of the world of today, ends with affirmation and reconciliation." A. M. Sullivan, president of the Poetry Society of America, states "William J. Grace is a metaphysical poet who maintains a high level of spiritual and intellectual integrity." Jacques Maritain wrote to the author: "I read your poems with great emotion. What is said about them in the preliminary pages seems quite true to me. I find in them a striking sense of the tragedy of life, winding up in supernatural peace." *America*, (Oct. 13, 1951) states, "This is the poetry of a mind that has pondered with rare understanding the phenomenon of the modern world's flight from God. It is a profound philosophical statement which has enlisted the resources of an exact eye for natural beauty and a wide-ranging facility of metaphor."

Mr. Grace's other serious interest besides teaching and writing consists in trout fishing. In fact the composition that gives him the greatest pleasure is "Fisherman's Song," which was recently set to music. He intends to bring the record along next time and see whether it is not as good a lure as the new-fangled spinning outfits.

Hilda C. Graef

Hilda C. Graef was born in Berlin into a family of artists and scholars. At the remarkably early age of six she had already made up her mind to study Latin and Greek — subjects which were taught at the first school to which she was sent. She studied English and German literature as well as Scripture at Berlin University. Although early attracted to journalism, she trained as a teacher after completing her studies at the University on the advice of her mother who felt that teaching was a far safer career. For eighteen months she taught at a Berlin Protestant school, but was finally dismissed — to her great relief, as she never liked teaching — "because there was Jewish blood in her family." Her next eighteen months were spent as lady housekeeper in the house of a professor at Marburg University, where she finally made up her mind to leave Germany.

She settled in England in 1936. At first she was a kind of mothers' help, then accepted a job at a private school where her principal duties were teaching the three R's to the little ones, washing them, seeing them safely across the road, and giving them a few German lessons. After four terms of this work a friend offered her a bursary for studying theology at King's College, London, for the Lambeth Diploma issued by the Archbishop of Canterbury. In January, 1940, after a two years' course, she received the diploma with First Class Honors, having won the Trench prize for New Testament Greek in between. But, in the meantime, the war had begun, and as she was of German nationality, she could not find a suitable post; she had to live precariously on assistance given by a British-German association, and a little money earned by some theology coachings.

Although brought up a "Liberal" Protestant, she was early attracted to Catholic forms of worship — attracted only, because for many years she lived practically without any religion. In the second year of her theological course, when she studied doctrine, she discovered that Christianity, which her Protestant teachers had always presented as some emotional experience divorced from reason, was a perfectly reasonable and consistent whole. She then began to practice the Anglican religion. In her spare time she read St. Thomas and St. John of the Cross, with the result that in January, 1941, she presented herself at the Jesuit Church in Farm Street, London, accompanied by the thunder of anti-aircraft guns, and was received into the Church two months later.

Already as an Anglican she had contributed articles on prayer to some religious periodicals, and when after her reception into the Church, her financial circumstances became even worse than they had been before, she made contact with the Dominican periodical,

Blackfriars, for which she wrote several articles on Dominican and other mystics. A few months after her reception she was offered a job as assistant to the Anglican editor of the *Lexicon of Patristic Greek* at Oxford. This work was being carried on at Pusey House, Oxford, the library of which had till then been barred to women. Thus she was the first woman to cross its threshold. She continued to write for *Blackfriars,* and occasionally, *The Tablet.* One day in 1945 she had a letter from a publisher, then unknown to her, who had seen her articles in *Blackfriars,* asking her whether she had a manuscript which she might want published. She had none, never having thought of writing a book, but she was advised to collect her previous articles on the mystics, which were then enlarged to form her first book, *The Way of the Mystics,* a readable and reverent introduction to the ways of holiness followed by some of God's most faithful children.

The same enterprising firm commissioned her to write her next book on Therese Neumann. This involved visiting the stigmatic of Konnersreuth and consulting all the accepted authorities who have written on the subject. The resulting book, *The Case of Therese Neumann,* the first critical examination to appear in the English language, had a mixed reception, but the general consensus of opinion seems to have been that it is well that such a book has been written.

When asked whether she would like to reply to the criticisms hurled at her, Miss Graef jotted down a "few observations" which were published in *The Commonweal* (November 2, 1951).

Also in November, 1951, her book, *God In Our Daily Life,* was published by the Newman Bookshop. "Covering our everyday life — from joy to pain, from duties of state to recreation — she demonstrates why all these must belong to God, then points to several pitfalls for the devout and suggests how we may reasonably make time for God."

Collaborating on the work of the *Greek Lexicon* and writing leaves very little time for hobbies — unless saying the Divine Office be taken as such. By way of relaxation she likes walking, which she finds most restful if done aimlessly and without timetable. She has an interest in politics, and also confesses to a trait common to most women, a glance at the fashion page of her morning paper.

She is the author of: *The Way of the Mystics* (Mercier Press, Cork) (1948); *The Case of Therese Neumann* (Mercier Press) (1950), and *God in Our Daily Life* (1951).   P. B. L.

Very Reverend Aelred Graham, O.S.B. 1907–

Aelred Graham, second son of Peter and Mary Graham, was born in Liverpool (England) in 1907. He was educated at St. Edward's College (Liverpool) and at the age of twenty-three entered Ampleforth Abbey, where he was professed as a member of the Benedictine Order in the following year. Ordained in 1938, he was appointed professor of dogmatic theology at Ampleforth (1939), publishing his first remarkable work, *The Love of God*, an epitome of spiritual theology, the same year. He had already, while a young monk, contributed learned articles to the *Ampleforth Journal; Blackfriars;* and *The Clergy Review.* In the latter journal, in December, 1938, his article on "Faith and the Motives of Credibility" attracted attention both in England and America.

Though by profession a theologian and metaphysician, Dom Graham must not be thought of as a dry-as-dust thinker living in an ivory tower. He had charge of Ampleforth Parish from 1940 to 1945; he was the Abbey guestmaster for two years; he teaches boys, of 14 to 18 years, English and Christian Doctrine, finding in that occupation practice in the art of explaining matters (however abstruse) in simple and intelligible terms. Dom Graham read learned papers to groups at Oxford and Cambridge; he has preached on the radio for BBC: he gives retreats to seminarians and to nuns; and all the time his able pen is ready to engage, with charm and courtesy, in controversy. "Intellectually," he writes, "the chief influence in my formation has been St. Thomas; but this has been combined with a characteristically Benedictine interest in humane letters."

Dom Graham has published many articles which have appeared in *The Tablet, The Clergy Review, Blackfriars, The Dublin Review, Eastern Churches Quarterly, Life of the Spirit, Dominican Studies,* and *The Ampleforth Journal.* In Reverend Canon G. D. Smith's recent work, *The Teaching of the Catholic Church,* Dom Graham contributed the chapter entitled "The Church on Earth." His published books are the following: *The Love of God* (1939); *The Final Victory* (1943); *The Christ of Catholicism* (1947). His second book, *The Final Victory,* was published at the height of World War II and was acclaimed in an editorial in *The Catholic World* as "the best little treatise I have seen on the causes and cure of war and on what we must do to prevent a third world catastrophe." But *The Christ of Catholicism* is, in the author's opinion, his most important work and it has been amazingly well received by the press. *The Catholic Worker* voiced a common opinion in declaring it: "easily the most significant work published on the life and message of Our Lord in years." As a "meditative study," intended chiefly for laymen, it is erudite without being pedantic, clear, succinct, and well-reasoned, expounding

Catholic Christology devoutly and convincingly. His book *Catholicism and the World Today*, published in February, 1952, was chosen as the selection of The Catholic Book of the Month Club.

In November, 1949, Dom Graham made his contribution to the important controversy initiated in *The Times* (London) on the subject *Catholicism Today*. His letter appeared in *The Tablet* commenting on salient aspects of the discussion. There was a word of mild reproof for convert laymen who wrote letters that insisted overmuch on "intransigence" without perhaps being sufficiently aware of the extreme complexity of the underlying theological questions. Dom Graham endorsed "the need for closer co-operation among Christians in the undertaking of practical good works." He said: "For Catholics to show even the appearance of being reluctant to work together with our fellow Christians in supporting 'all that rings true, all that commands reverence, and all that makes for right; all that is pure, all that is lovely, all that is gracious in the telling; virtue and merit wherever virtue and merit are found . . . (Philippians iv.8) would today be a major calamity.'" Liberally and graciously, Dom Graham admits agreement with the Protestant Bishop of Winchester that "if 'those who acknowledge Christ as Lord' cannot say the Our Father together then 'co-operation in other directions feels in experience to be frozen at the start.'" "On what principle, based on Scripture and Tradition," Dom Graham asks, "is the saying of the Our Father in unison with non-Catholics at a gathering to be disallowed?"

Father Aelred's contribution to this rather "exciting" and momentous controversy in England's great public forum, the letters to *The Times*, was so able, honest, urbane and sympathetic that it places him high in the ranks of spokesmen of the Faith.

In 1951 he was appointed Prior of Portsmouth Priory in Rhode Island.   E. B. B.

Reverend Andrew Green, O.S.B.
1865–1950

The most versatile monk in the almost one-hundred year history of St. Benedict's Abbey in Atchison, Kansas, was Father Andrew Green. As a monk, priest, pastor, retreat master, hospital chaplain, musician, composer, poet, author, translator, speaker, professor, administrator and alumni secretary, he lived a very active life. Born at Marak (near Everest), Kansas on October 5, 1865, he received the name of Francis. He attended the district school and then at the age of thirteen enrolled at St. Benedict's College in Atchison, Kansas. Scholastically he was a brilliant student, having won many prizes. His extra-curricular activities included playing the violin in the orchestra and the clarinet in the band. He was an excellent ball player.

In 1884–1885 he made his novitiate at St. Vincent's Archabbey in Latrobe, Pennsylvania, and took the name of Andrew. He was the last Atchison Benedictine to make his profession to Archabbot Boniface Wimmer, the first Benedictine abbot in America. On May 26, 1890, he was ordained to the priesthood by the Most Reverend Louis Mary Fink, the first man from St. Benedict's to become a bishop. Through forty-eight years he had been uninterruptedly engaged at the college before entering upon parochial work.

For sixteen years he was faculty adviser of the former students' publication, *The Abbey Student*, which he helped found in 1891. As moderator and also as professor of rhetoric, poetry, and literature he encouraged many students to write and to read good literature. He taught religion, Latin, drawing, mathematics, geography, German, logic, painting, history and oratory.

On April 24, 1898, he was the prime mover in founding the Alumni Association and was elected its first temporary president. For many years he was secretary to the organization and personally maintained the alumni files until 1928.

In the fourth year of his priesthood (1894) Abbot Innocent Wolf chose him as his prior, a position he held for three years. For twenty years he was secretary of the faculty and for one year each he was students' chaplain, registrar and manager of the printing press.

In January, 1935, he left St. Benedict's Abbey to become pastor of Sacred Heart Church, Baileyville, Kansas and remained there until June, 1936. Then he became an assistant pastor at the Old Cathedral, Leavenworth, Kansas from 1937 to 1938. The following three years he served as pastor of St. Mary's Church, Purcell, Kansas, and then for two years was an assistant at St. John the Evangelist Church, Lawrence, Kansas. He was chaplain of Mercy Hospital, Fort Scott, Kansas, from 1943 to 1948 and active to the last. At the time of his death he was assistant pastor to his own nephew, Father Maurus Kennedy, O.S.B., of St. Benedict's Church, Kansas City, Kansas.

His first literary work was a collection of poems, *The Bells of Atchison*, published in 1908. He wrote *Retreat for Religious* in 1944 and *The Love of God*, conferences to religious, in 1946. Although of Irish extraction, he compiled a German grammar and translated from the German *The Pastoral Care of Souls*, in 1944 and *The Messias*, in 1946.

Father Green was better known as a composer of music. A secret tryout of the violin, used by his father, a Brown County, Kansas blacksmith who "fiddled" for country dances, started him off to a successful career in the field of music. His greatest musical work is his symphony "Peregrinus" (The Pilgrim), completed and presented in 1932, after thirty years of painstaking creative work and revision. He helped compile the first edition of the diocesan hymnal, *Laudate*, and collaborated in its revision in 1942. He published "The Proper of the Mass" set to Gregorian themes in 1946 and composed his own "Mass."

His other musical pieces include a patriotic song, the music of which was composed by Father Andrew. In 1918 he published *The Chancellor Prize*, a popular school operetta and in 1920 he published his "Maur Hill Song," which he dedicated to the additional institution that St.

Benedict's Abbey acquired. For twenty years he headed the music department, and he directed the students' orchestra and band for at least eighteen years. He was in charge of the students' choir and vocal quartette for seven years. He played and taught practically every musical instrument.

In his sixty-fifth year as a monk and in his sixtieth year as a priest, Father Andrew Green died on January 2, 1950.   A. K.

Anne Green   1899–

The best seller, *The Selbys*, came as it were by accident. Anne Green, its author, daughter of Edward Moon and Mary (Hartridge) Green, had lived in Paris since she was six months old. As a girl in her teens she served as a nurse in World War I. After the war she toured Europe and then settled down with her family in Paris. A little desultory writing came from her pen, but the years were slipping by and she was now thirty.

One day a letter came from her cousin, John Macrae, president of E. P. Dutton & Co. urging her to "go ahead and write a novel." On impulse she obeyed. "The book, to my publisher's amazement, was a best seller chiefly because it was true, I suppose, in feeling."

Anne Green began *The Selbys* "without any idea of how it would work out." She told, in a gay and frolicsome vein, about an American girl in Paris. "With my own family background in mind," she says, "I started out, and I suppose all the subconscious observations of my life came to my help. I spun a tale around the only family that I knew intimately, my own.

"When," as she confesses, "my imagination 'ran dry,' I had the idea of writing two historical novels," and thus she wrote *The Silent Duchess*, a study of the eighteenth century in France, and *The Lady in the Mask*, a similar historical story about sixteenth century Milan. Anne's father, Edward Green, a Presbyterian, and her brother Julian, had joined the Catholic Church in 1915. Her conversion to the faith came in July, 1947.

Anne Green is critical of her own work, "hyper-critical" indeed, to use her own word. Only one of all her books pleases her. "The only book I like," she says, "is the last, *With Much Love*, because it is the story of my parents, as I saw it. The memory of them is so tender that anything connected with them is a joy to remember. The book had a certain success largely because of my affection for them.

"My novels," Anne Green says, "are not written with any plan. They are begun with one main character in mind and this personage usually provides the plot and adds extraneous characters without the conscious knowledge of the author."

Among Miss Green's writings are the following: *The Selbys* (1930);

Reader, I Married Him (1931); *Marietta* (1933); *A Marriage of Convenience* (1933), (also with title *Painter's Despair*, 1933); *Fools Rush In* (1934); *That Fellow Percival* (1935); *Winchester House* (1936); *16 rue Cortambert* (1937); *Paris* (1938); *Silent Duchess* (1939); *Delamer Curse* (1940); *The Lady in the Mask* (1942); *Just Before Dawn* (1943); *With Much Love* (1948); and *The Old Lady* (1947). She translated into English Georges Bernanos' book *Crime* in 1947. She and her brother Julian rendered into English Charles Péguy's *Basic Verities*, prose and poetry (1943) and his *Men and Saints*, in 1944.

Anne Green has lived, save for five years spent in America during the Second World War, in France and all her associations, apart from her immediate family, are French. Her education was at the Lycée Molière in Paris. It was not until late in life that she revisited Savannah, Georgia where she had been born on November 11, 1899. In her literary career, subsequent to her first great success, she has had some disappointments, which she expresses in her own personal way.

"The reason why I am not fond of my books is probably because having written one, *The Selbys*, that was light and gay and ended well, I have been expected to continue eternally in the same vein. I consider *Marietta*, my third novel, where I tried to escape from the beaten track, a better book than the others but it ended sadly and no one seemed to be able to stand that from me. Nevertheless the book remains truer to life, as I understand it, than any of the others."

E. B. B.

Julian Green   1900–

Julian Green's early career was unusually romantic and colorful. Born in 1900, in Paris, the son of Edward and Mary (Hartridge) Green, Americans, he attended the Lycée Janson, passing his baccalaureate in 1917, and at once joining the American Field Service in the First World War. From Field Service he passed to Red Cross and finally into the French Army. In order to secure entry into the regular French Army he had to join the French Foreign Legion because he was an American. For *one hour* he was a legionnaire.

In 1919 he was demobilized after 'distinguished war service' and faced the problem of his early life — the choice between painting and writing. Possessed with the idea that the ABC of painting is to look at pictures, for five months he went to the Louvre every day. Examining a dozen pictures a day, he became familiar with most of the pictures on the second floor of the Louvre. "My debt," he writes, "to the Louvre is immense. I feel as though it has fed me and brought me up."

From Paris he went for three years to the University of Virginia in America, where he studied English, German, Latin and Greek literature, while he shunned mathematics which he hated. At the University of Virginia he published a long story called "The Apprentice Psychiatrist." On his return to Paris he wrote "Le Voyageur sur La Terre." It appeared as a serial in the *Nouvelle Revue Française*. This strange tale caught the fancy of the famous André Gide.

Julian's basic problem, whether to paint or to continue writing, was still unsolved. With the mind to become an artist he entered the atelier of the Grande-Chaumière — but only for a brief spell. One day while watching the water from the Pont-Royal a revulsion seized him. "Damn the Grande-Chaumière," he thought. "I am a writer." At last he had decided on his vocation. Meanwhile Julian had followed his father into the Catholic Church (1915) and began to experience the ups and downs of piety. For a time he would be full of zeal, attending daily Mass — then for a spell he would be overcome with lukewarmness, even indifference. In the end the faith of a practicing Catholic became his.

Julian Green acknowledges the influence of Jacques Maritain, and his study of St. Catherine of Genoa, as factors in bringing him closer to his religion. For the great, if erratic, Catholic writer and leader in France before 1914, Charles Péguy, Julian Green expresses profound admiration. "I doubt," he says, "if any poet has ever spoken for France as Péguy did." In conjunction with his sister Anne Green, Julian has served well the Catholic world in America by his translations of Péguy. In 1950 he brought out a translation of one of his works under the title *The Mystery of the Charity of Joan of Arc*.

As a boy, Julian read largely but mostly in French, which was in a sense his "native" language. Even when speaking English, traces of his French accent were noticeable — and alarming to his American mother. Of English authors, he liked best Jane Austen and Charles Dickens. Of French poets, in those early days, he preferred Baudelaire.

Julian Green's first full-length novel, which appeared in 1926, was called *Mont-Cinère*. He laid the scene of his story in his aunt's house back in Virginia. His father ruefully reproached him with filling the family with misers. *Mont-Cinère* appeared in an English translation the following year under the title *Avarice House*. *Avarice House* was the first of the 'grim psychological novels' that Julian wrote. Of his method in writing, Mr. Green says: "I need some object to look at (when writing), some picture to place in front of me and to which I can apply for information. Thus for *Mont-Cinère*, I had a photograph of an interior, taken in an unknown house at about the year 1880. . . . While writing *Adrienne Mesurat*, I had in front of me a photograph of a painting by Utrillo.

Among Julian Green's publications are the following: *Mont-Cinère* (1926); (in English, *Avarice House*, 1930); *Adrienne Mesurat* (in English, *The Closed Garden*, 1928); *Leviathan* (in English, *The Dark Journey*, 1929); *Christine and Other Stories* (1930); *Strange River* (1932); *The Dreamer* (1934); *Midnight* (1936); *Personal Record, 1928–1939; Then Shall the Dust Return* (1941); *Memories of Happy Days* (1942); *If I Were You* (1949); *Basic Verities* (1943) (a translation in partnership with Anne Green); *Men and Saints* (1944) (also a translation in partnership with his sister).

His latest book is *Moira;* a study of sexual obsession. A reviewer for *The Times Literary Supplement* (June 22, 1951, p. 382) remarks: "It was only with *Moira,* published in the summer of 1950 and now available in an English translation by Miss Denise Folliot, that Mr. Green re-established himself as one of the most important novelists in France. *Moira,* in fact, takes rank beside the best of M. Mauriac and Bernanos and Gide. For the first time, perhaps, since *Adrienne Mesurat* the writer is in full possession of his powers; his hold on dialogue is firmer; and since he now knows more, both about literature and about life, the book has a maturity, an ease, which give it already the stamp of permanence."

The same writer on the front page of the same *Literary Supplement* mentioned above — it is a very long article — states: "Mr. Green himself seems unable to explain why he chose to write in French: 'I learned English when I was a child and I have always spoken it, but whenever I attempt to write it, I feel as if I am trying on a coat that has not been made for me. It worries me and I know that I am not wearing it as well as I ought to. It is a uniform which fits too tight. My dressing-gown, my everyday suit of clothes, in which I feel happy and at ease is French.'"

Julian Green was fortunate in winning the Harper Prize in 1929 for *The Dark Journey* and a half share in Harper's "Anniversary Prize" in 1942, for *Memories of Happy Days.* Julian Green was awarded the one million franc Literary Grand Prize of Monaco by a nine-man jury of French, Belgian, and Swiss academicians. The prize was presented in Monte Carlo in 1951.

Julian Green has achieved high success in "the study of violent emotion against the background of French provincial life." In this field his artistic craftsmanship wins unequivocal praise.

                                                                    E. B. B.

Giovanni Guareschi   1908–

When *The Little World of Don Camillo* was published in 1950, a new Italian author was brought to the attention of the American reader. His name is Giovanni Guareschi. His success surprised no one more than himself. "You really believe all that, about my success?" he inquired in astonishment when Mrs. Hedy Maria Clark interviewed him for the New York *Times* (Dec. 17, 1950, p. 13). "Believe it! Surely you know *Don Camillo* was a selection of the Book-of-the-Month Club, and that it is a consistent best seller."

"I've heard of that club — is it important?"

When Mrs. Clark told him it made quite a big difference, he replied: "Funny, very funny! I find it hard to believe that people really like my work. First there was the editor of *Bertoldo.* Then there was my wife. I once wrote a novel, *Destiny is Called Clotilde,* which I thought was pretty good stuff. I gave my wife a copy, inscribed with my most tender sentiments. Then one day when I was rummaging through some books in a second-hand dealer's cart, and what did I find? You guessed it! My masterpiece which my wife had turned in to get a thriller."

Guareschi was working one day at his hobby of carpentry when his secretary brought him a long letter from Pellegrini & Cudahy, his publishers, and told him it appeared to contain some important news. "Just tell me what it's about quickly because I don't have much time," Guareschi ordered. His secretary began to read. The publisher had set the publication date for August 15, and explained all the details for the launching of the book. Guareschi continued to struggle with the 2 x 4. The publisher was pleased to announce that *The Little World of Don Camillo* had been chosen by the Book-of-the-Month Club and this involved an edition of at least 150,000 copies. The publisher had set aside $10,000 for promoting the book, and would be happy if Guareschi would accept an invitation to come to New York. "What are you going to say?" asked his secretary. "Oh say that everything is fine but I can't come," said Guareschi, and began to plane down a board destined for the left wall of the little house for a pair of pigeons, the gift of an aunt. "But why can't you go? The international situation?" Guareschi began to nail the boards together. "Certainly not. Don't you see that I still have to make the roof, and the doorway, and the gables of the little house for my pigeons?"

Out of ten new talents, his book was judged "the most exquisitely wrought and the most moving. It has a quality of which today only the Italian writers seem capable, a quality that must come from the soil and some changeless and harmonious human relationship with nature, with God and the people whom the earth nourishes." (Harrison Smith, in the *Saturday Review of Literature,* Feb. 17, 1951, p. 9.)

Guareschi was born in Parma near the Po River in Italy, where he says, "people have heads as hard as pig iron and thus I succeeded in becoming editor-in-chief of *Bertoldo,*" a humor magazine. This is the magazine in which Saul Steinberg, who at that time was studying architecture in Milan, published his first drawings and for which he worked until he left for America. The people from Guareschi's part of Parma "are noted for their shrewdness masked by an air of naïveté, their sly humor which often tends to erupt in barbaric practical jokes. Guareschi himself explains it thus: 'It must be the sun, a terrible sun which beats on their brains during the summer, or perhaps it is the fog, a heavy fog, which oppresses them in winter.'"

During World War II, Guareschi spent most of the time in German concentration camps. He refers to this period as the most active time of his life — the activity being to stay alive which he barely succeeded in doing. When he was released he had lost much weight. To quote his own words: "I was reduced to a sack of bones of which the total weight was one hundred pounds and this included lice, bedbugs, fleas, hunger, and melancholy."

Guareschi now lives in Milan with his wife and two children. He is editor-in-chief of *Candido*, a political magazine, though he maintains his standing as an independent. During the electoral campaign of 1948 Guareschi ridiculed the Communists in his cartoons. He drew them as "earnest-looking little men with three nostrils . . . doing something ineffably stupid, following the party line to the letter, including typographical errors." (Hedy Maria Clark.) He thus shared in the victory over the Communists.

Douglas Newton reviewing the book, *The Little World of Don Camillo* for *Duckett's Register* (Feb. 1951) writes: "One of the things the Middle Ages disliked was *tristitia*, that is sadness, which was regarded as something of a sin against the promise of Redemption. Giovanni Guareschi is surely infected by that spirit in his puckish gathering of tales telling of the rivalry between a priest in a primitive little Italian parish, and its Communist mayor, Peppone. . . . It has the homely and simple naïveté of the Middle Ages, but is nonetheless reverent for that."   M. A. H.

Theodor Haecker   1879–1945

One of the genuine anti-Nazis who lived in the Third Reich during World War II, was Theodor Haecker. In fact "he was among the first" writes Alick Dru, "to discern the real character of the Nazi Movement, and his first article attacking its philosophy was published at the time Hitler came to power. He was arrested a few weeks later and was released only through the help of Karl Muth and Cardinal Faulhaber."

Born on June 4, 1879 in Eberbach in Würtemberg, Germany, he spent the greater part of his life in Munich. He was educated at a school in Esslingen but had to leave to go to work because of the poverty of his parents. After about two years of work, a generous friend sent him to the University in Berlin. Upon completing his studies in ancient and modern literature at the University, he worked for an export company in Antwerp, Belgium. A year later he transferred to the small publishing firm in Munich of F. S. Schreiver and he worked for him until his death.

Theodor Haecker married late in life and for the last twenty years of his life lived with his wife and three children in a flat above his office. His wife died in 1935. Apart from his family, his was a solitary existence. He rarely travelled and took no part in the social activities of the time. Strange to relate, however, as a young man his ambition was to become an actor and he abandoned this calling only after a long illness, due to an infection of the sinus which left a small disfigurement on his nose.

Haecker became a Catholic in 1921 and attributed his conversion to the influence of Newman, whose works as well as Francis Thompson's, he translated into German. In his critical essay in Kierkegaard's *Cognizance of Truth* he wrote: "I am still too strongly under the impression which Kierkegaard made upon me as a young man to speak of him without gratitude and admiration." Haecker saw in the Church a fulfillment of his *fidélité*. For a man such as Haecker, a conflict with the Nazis was inevitable. In a letter written in 1939 from Switzerland he says: "I was able to lecture in St. Gallen (in Switzerland) yesterday. The permission was given as a result of a blunder. And in my own country I am not allowed to say one word in public, because my books are a success and are beginning to have some influence. I have been declared an enemy of the State, a *Staatsfeind*. My name is starred three times in the books of the police, our tscheka, and my safety is always threatened more and more. I have the feeling and the belief that I am in the hands of God, but I am not on that account freed from anxiety and worry about my children. In a couple of hours I shall be back in Germany, and cannot tell what may happen. At any rate, once there I shall no longer be able to write the truth." Haecker was refused permission to lecture and to speak over the radio.

All of Haecker's writing was done at night. His first pamphlet *Kierkegaard und die Philosophie der Innerlichkeit (Kierkegaard and the Philosophy of Inwardness)* was published by F. S. Schreiber in 1913; *Satire and Polemik* (1914–1920); *Christentum und Kultur* in 1927; *Der Christ und die Geschichte (The Christian and History)* in 1935, and *Der Buckel Kierkegaard* posthumously in 1946. The English translation appeared in 1950 under the title *Kierkegaard the Cripple*.

His book, *Journal in the Night, 1939–1945,* consists of brief aphorisms, maxims, and meditations, such as number 103, page 24: "Ultimately, after all, we are made for happiness which is, so to say, the normal and the certain. The Church declares that certain men whom she named by name — her saints — are, with unquestionable certainty, in heaven. She does not say of any man, that he is quite certainly in hell — not even Judas, the betrayer of the Lord. She says it only of the devil, over whom she has no jurisdiction."

The *Journal* was kept hidden in Karl Muth's house outside Munich lest it be seized by the Gestapo. One day the Gestapo did enter his flat. "The current pages of the *Journal* lay in a music portfolio on the sofa in his room. Only the presence of mind of his daughter, who caught her father's whispered word '*mappe*' (portfolio) saved it from discovery. She ran into the room shouting that she was late for her music lesson, and ran off with the portfolio."

On one occasion when Haecker was arrested he was asked what he meant by his words "above all things the Germans lacked humility." Haecker replied: "Literally, what I said." He was dismissed with the remark: "Ach so, das ist in Ordnung."

In 1944 Haecker's house in Munich was bombed out. He went to the little village of Ustersbach near Augsburg to live. At the time his eldest son was a prisoner in England. His youngest son was sent in 1945 to the Russian front and was shortly afterwards reported missing. His sight began to fail and not long afterward, on the 9th of April, 1945 he died. He is buried at Ustersbach.   **M. A. H.**

Robert Hamilton
(John Robert Hamilton)   1908–

Robert Hamilton was born July 8, 1908, at Parson's Green, London, England, the second son of Edward Hamilton, who was the eldest son of Edward Wallace Hamilton, President of the Royal College of Surgeons, Dublin; and of Agatha Marion Triebner, who was descended on her mother's side from the ancient family, Annesley of Annesley, Nottinghamshire. Her mother was a convert from nonconformity.

Robert was educated at various private schools, and at Westminster Cathedral: "I did as little work as possible," he says "but achieved one solitary distinction by writing an essay on a scientific experiment. Most of the time I made up blood curdling stories for the entertainment of the students." At his mother's wish, he studied music, and went to the Royal Academy of Music. He earned a living playing in orchestras, but his real interests lay elsewhere. During this period he became interested in theology, in which he was encouraged by a priest friend.

His earliest reading was Dickens to whom he is still devoted; then Milton, whose *Paradise Lost* made a deep impression. He later discovered Chesterton, who opened new worlds of thought, and W. H. Hudson, who intensified a lifelong devotion to the English countryside. "My first sight of that countryside," he says, "was when I was seven, and was taken, to escape the air raids of the First World War, to Haslemere on the borders of Surrey, Sussex, and Hampshire — one of the loveliest corners of England. I fell in love with this place, and though I do not yet live there it has always been my second home." He wrote some articles on nature and the countryside, gradually introducing theological and philosophical elements. Some of these were illustrated by Margaret Sheridan (daughter of Dr. Patrick Sheridan), Arts, Mistress at Notre Dame, Liverpool, and book reviewer, whom he married in 1937. They have two sons: Gervase, aged 13, and Adrian, aged 9 (1952).

After his marriage, he began a system of encyclopaedic reading, centered in philosophy but covering a wide range of subjects including psychology, science, politics, history, and English literature.

Stimulated by the reaction of this reading on certain problems that he had been thinking over for many years, he began to write articles for *The Quarterly Review*, *Nineteenth Century*, *Horizon* and others, and to review books on ideological subjects. He brought together under a broad scheme a number of short essays embodying his reflections at the time, and later produced a short study of the mind in history, which set him thinking on biographical lines. He decided to develop his ideas mainly in studies of persons who had lived and thought the subjects relevant to these ideas. His first book was *Hilaire Belloc. An Introduction to His Spirit and Work*, (first edition 1945, second edition 1947). This was fol-

lowed by *W. H. Hudson: The Vision of Earth* (1946). He is building up
material for a Schematic Notebook which will attempt to survey all
his ideas worked out in his biographies.

Mary Harris   1905–

Mary Harris was born at Harrow on September
22, 1905, the middle one of a family of three.
Her mother was the daughter of a High Church
parson, and the children were brought up in an
atmosphere of Anglican piety. "I can remember
being given her rosary", writes Miss Harris, "to
play with as I lay on my cot, and her book of
devotions, bulging with pictures and held together by an elastic band."

As soon as Mary went to school she realized that, by the accepted
standards of the time, they were an odd family. Their clothes were
different from other children's, their house was furnished in a different
way, and their religion, with its markedly "popish air", was different
too. She was not old enough then to appreciate her mother's unconcern
for suburban conventions or admire her artistic tastes; her mother went
straight for the essentials in everything, and sacrificed nothing to appearances — still, in those days, a major concern of the middle classes.
"I have never known anyone less afraid of human respect than she was
— whereas I was haunted by it," says Mary Harris.

She continues: "On my mother's maternal side we came of a line
of artists, and we all took naturally to painting. I was happiest messing
about with my box of paints, but I liked writing verse too. Like most
small children I found rhymes more of a help than a hindrance to composition. The metre arranged my clumsy thoughts for me, the non-
sensical rhyme supplied me with further thought.

"I disliked school very much. I lived in terror of something or
somebody, knew myself to be odd, and was inclined to stand about
looking dazed and owlish. Story-book children, with their characters
all revealed and explained, had become so intimate to me that real
children seemed less real in contrast, inimical and unpredictable.

"When I was about thirteen a change came over me. I now began
to take pride in my oddness and to cultivate it. When I was told that
I was like Waring out of Browning's poem of that name, I was very
pleased. I felt that it showed something elevated in my nature that,
whereas I was good at essays and painting, I was extremely bad at
mathematics. And now, after having been ashamed of the 'oddness'
of our religious upbringing, I advertised it on all occasions. I had reached
that stage of adolescence when I and those around me were unstable,
creative, egotistical, when ideas are exciting for their own sake. Moments of grand intellectual rebellion when I incited my friends to
agnosticism, alternated with an equally sweeping enthusiasm for ortho-

dox belief. I set myself up as an authority on 'English' Catholicism and extolled the sacrament of confession.

"In the meantime my mother suffered a complete breakdown in health, and when I left school she was very ill. It had been intended that I should go to an art school, but the idea had to be abandoned as I was needed at home. Gradually, in my spare time, I tended to do less painting and more writing. It was, I suppose, a gesture of independence. My writing self was a more remote one from the family than my painting self. It belonged to me exclusively, because it was less open to criticism. I was lucky enough to hear of a club for the training of writers, called The Scribbler. Sheila Kaye-Smith had not long left it when I joined. The initial effort of coming face to face with what one intends to say has always been a torment to me, and the fact of now having to write, month after month for The Scribbler, gave me the necessary impetus which otherwise I should have lacked. I turned out during those first years of writing quantities of short stories which have never found a market. I did, however, receive a lot of encouragement which gave me the confidence to go on.

"About this time my mother, who had always, even as a child, felt a strong attraction to the Catholic Church, became converted. Unlike most converts she did not seem to go through any transitional stage of doubt or mental conflict — it was not her nature. She rose out of bed one morning, an Anglican, and went to bed that night, so to speak, a Catholic. It was a mystery to her why everybody did not follow her example; although she did, in fact, make many converts.

"My own conversion came some years later. It was a difficult and tortuous one, unlike my mother's, with its utter simplicity. I had the great privilege of being instructed by Monsignor Canon Jackman, and was received by him into the Church in 1941. He had an extraordinary mind, subtle, restless, intuitive; mercifully, it understood mine. Before long I was making my anonymous debut in his *Holy Roodlets.*"

In 1947 her mother died. Most of the family were already dispersed. Her brother was killed on the aircraft carrier Illustrious, during the Second World War; her father is in a hospital; her sister teaches in a high school. She now lives alone and writes in an attic.

Religion and childhood have usually been the inspiration behind her writing. It is not surprising, then, that she has developed into what is called a "Catholic writer," and that she either writes for, or about, children. Some of her critics look upon the religious trend in her writing as a limitation which should be got rid of. "All I can say is that I can only write as I *must* write," Miss Harris retorts.

A novel of hers, *Salokina and the Pastor*, was lost by an American agent. "It was while I was at work at this novel that a good many of my difficulties about becoming a Catholic were clarified," she says. "Through the character of the Lutheran pastor I was able to see things in a more detached and objective light than I would have done had I faced them as personal problems only."

She is the author of *Grettel at St. Brides* (1940); *The Wolf* (1946); *The Niche Over the Door* (1948), and *Fear at My Heart* (1951).

She is a contributor to *Collin's Magazine* for children.

Francis Burton Harrison   1873–

The outstanding events in the life of Francis Burton Harrison have been the passage of the anti-narcotics bill, known today as the Harrison Narcotic Law, and his fight for the independence of the Philippines.

Francis Harrison was born in New York on December 18, 1873. His father, Burton Harrison, a lawyer, served as private secretary to Jefferson Davis, President of the Confederate States of America, from 1861 to 1865. His mother, Constance Cary Harrison, was a playwright, novelist and historian.

He attended Miss Parker's School from 1880 to 1883; the Gramercy Park Tool-House Association, 1883–1885; Cutlers School, 1885–1891; Yale University, 1891–1895 and New York School, 1895–1897. From 1897 to 1899 he was an instructor at the New York Law School, and was admitted to the bar in 1898. The following year he joined Troop A of the New York Volunteer Cavalry and served with the United States Volunteers in the Spanish-American War, June 20, 1898 — January 31, 1899, as captain and adjutant general.

In 1903 he was elected a member of the House of Representatives (58th Congress) where he represented the thirteenth district in New York for two years. He was again elected in 1907 and remained until 1913. While serving on the House Ways and Means Committee, Harrison was instrumental in gaining passage of the Harrison Narcotics Act. It was not until December 17, 1914, however, that Congress enacted the internal revenue measure effective April 1, 1915, commonly known as the Harrison Narcotic Law. This law, as amended, "requires all persons who import, manufacture, sell or dispense narcotics to register and pay an occupational tax, to render returns, and, with certain exceptions, to make all sales, exchanges, etc. of narcotics in pursuance of government order forms. All narcotics entering into domestic trade must be tax-stamped." (Dictionary of American History, Vol. 4, p. 52.)

In 1913 President Woodrow Wilson appointed Mr. Harrison to the post of Governor General of the Philippines. He arrived in Manila on September 2, 1913 and within an hour delivered Wilson's historic message: "We regard ourselves as trustees acting not for the advantage of the United States but for the benefit of the people of the Philippine Islands. Every step we take will be taken with a view to the ultimate independence of the islands and as a preparation for that independence." From that day on Mr. Harrison lived up to that pledge. He appointed Filipinos to government positions; he developed foreign trade and agriculture. His administration from 1913 to 1921 is known as the era of good feeling because he very largely delegated his powers to the Filipinos. When Warren Harding was elected President of the United States, Mr. Harrison resigned his post and retired to Alness in the north of Scotland.

Since the independence of the Philippines, Mr. Harrison has been an adviser to all the presidents. During his tenure of office, Mr. Harrison had worked very hard on a bill for land reform in the Philippine Islands, which was turned down by Congress. Observers now believe that if the bill had been passed there would be less agrarian trouble today.

When his very close friend, President Manuel Quezon, became very sick and went to Saranac Lake, New York, Mr. Harrison visited him often. Mr. Harrison will publish a book very shortly on President Quezon's administration. In 1946 the General Assembly of the Philippines conferred upon Mr. Harrison honorary citizenship of the Philippine Republic, without any solicitation on his part. He was appointed a major general in the Philippine National Guard.

On May 3, 1950, after several months of instruction, Mr. Harrison was received into the Catholic Church by the Reverend Louis Blecharczyk, then chaplain of the Villa Maria retreat house in Stamford, Connecticut.

Early in 1951 Mr. and Mrs. Harrison flew to the Philippines bent upon spending the rest of their lives there. Finding the islands too hot, however, he returned to the States, and then in December of the same year, the Harrisons went to Spain to make their home there.

Although in his 79th year he still possesses a brilliant mind with great charm and a pleasing personality.

His first book appeared in 1922 under the title, *The Corner Stone of Philippine Independence*. His other published writings are: *Burton Chronicles of Colonial Virginia* (1933) (privately printed); *Archibald Cary of Carysbrook, Virginia* (1942) (privately printed); *A Selection of the Letters of Fairfax Harrison* (1944) (privately printed), and *Origins of the Philippine Republic* (privately printed in Tangier, Morocco, but it will be published after he revises some of the chapters).

He contributed to the *Virginia Magazine of History*.   M. A. H.

George Bagshawe Harrison   1894–

Scholar and critic, Professor Harrison has specialized in Shakespeare and the Elizabethan period, his best known work being the four volumes of *Elizabethan* and *Jacobean Journals*.

He was born in Hove, Sussex, England on July 14, 1894, being the second son of the late Walter Harrison. He was educated at Brighton College, one of the smaller English Public Schools; and in 1913 went up to Queens' College, Cambridge, as a classical exhibitioner, but his studies were interrupted by the outbreak of the First World War. He received a commission in the infantry, and in October 1914 was sent out to India; a year later he accompanied his regiment to Mesopotamia, where he remained until the end of the war, having by this time become staff captain in an Indian infantry brigade; he was mentioned in despatches.

On returning to England in 1919 he married Dorothy Agnes, daughter of the late Reverend Thomas Barker; of their five children, two survive, both of whom have been received into the Catholic Church. Having completed his studies at Cambridge, in which he was placed in the first class of the English Tripos, Dr. Harrison taught for two years at Felsted School; thence he went to St. Paul's Training College, Cheltenham, an evangelical college for elementary teachers. He was appointed assistant-lecturer at King's College in the University of London in 1924, promoted lecturer in 1927, and reader in 1928. He remained in the University of London for fifteen years. During the Second World War, Dr. Harrison again served in the army, as supply officer in the Royal Army Service Corps, and later in Intelligence and at the War Office. In 1943 he was released from military service to take up the appointment of head of the Department of English at Queen's College, Kingston, Canada. In 1947, together with his wife, Dr. Harrison was received into the Church after a series of events related in his contribution to Father John O'Brien's *Road to Damascus*. In 1949, Dr. Harrison accepted an invitation to join the English faculty at the University of Michigan.

Dr. Harrison's best known works, in addition to the *Elizabethan* and *Jacobean Journals*, are: the *Bodley Head Quartos* (which he edited between 1922 and 1926); *The Life and Death of Robert Devereux, Earl of Essex, Elizabethan Plays and Players*, and *A Companion to Shakespeare Studies* (which he co-edited with Harley Granville-Barker). His edition of *Shakespeare: Major Plays and the Sonnets* was published by Harcourt, Brace in 1948.

Lucile Hasley   1909–

The Church has had, in her long history, apostles of penance, of love, of humility, of mercy. Now, in the person of Lucile Hasley, appears the apostolate of laughter: wise, engaging, "running laughter," to draw one tumbling helter-skelter towards truth and virtue. Some Catholics have not known how to take this surprising apostolate. "I get threats, boos, jeers from those who would like to excommunicate me," writes Mrs. Hasley, but, she adds slyly, "I get lavish bouquets from the clergy." Torquemada-minded Catholics have, perhaps, some little thing to say on their side, for Lucile Hasley can be unconventionally impish. Father James J. Quinn, S.J. hints at this in reviewing her book *Reproachfully Yours* when he remarks: "She kicks the solemn with the ridiculous, more to get an extra point on the laugh-board than to appear irreverent as some seem to think." However, most Catholics agree that seeming indiscretions are swallowed up and obliterated in the flood of her genuine charity. What a thing it is to find a way to laugh oneself into fervor and faith!

Asked for a story about her life, Lucile Hasley answered: "I am at a loss what to say. I mean, my biography doesn't amount to a hill of beans. I was born at 631 Diamond Avenue (South Bend, Indiana) and now live at 1253 Diamond Avenue. Very cosmopolitan, eh? The most interesting feature to my life these days is the mailman, who staggers up to 1253 with a fantastic amount of fan mail from all over the world. To be perfectly blunt, all I possess is a *public*. Like canasta I became popular overnight with my silly essays and, really, I am hardly the one to write this up."

Born of Presbyterian stock, in South Bend, Lucile attended Milwaukee-Downer College and later entered Wisconsin University where she majored in art. Not liking her Presbyterian religion at all, and rebelling against it at every turn, she finally managed to free herself from any sort of religious belief or observance. "Life, for me, came to mean only clothes, dancing, men, and the number of prom bids and fraternity pins one could collect in a season. As far as anything spiritual went, I was just waltzing along . . . not searching, not interested, not even aware that anything was missing. Certainly, a *most* unlikeable candidate for the gift of faith." Yet certain events during her senior year at college, which she describes very wittily and touchingly in the story of her conversion — it appeared first in *The Sign* and later in Father John A. O'Brien's book, *Where I Found Christ* — brought Lucile into the Church at the age of twenty-one. Four years later she met and married Louis Hasley, Professor of English at Notre Dame University, and is now (1951) the mother of three children: Susan, Janet and Danny.

As a busy housewife and mother, she never intended nor even desired to become a writer but it came about quite accidentally. Some six years ago, the threat of grave illness put her to bed for four months and during that time she began to read ascetical writers. This brought on what she terms a "regular one-man Catholic Revival" and she started to write her own essays, all of which were accepted as soon as offered. She continued to write — under difficulties. "If my readers knew the noisy conditions under which I write," she says, "they would forgive me almost anything." The judges of the Short Story Contest of the Catholic Press Association in 1948 did not know anything about the "noisy conditions" under which Lucile wrote "The Little Girls" but they awarded it first prize of $600 from among the 3100 entries. In 1949, Lucile Hasley's first and only book, destined to be a best-seller, was published by Sheed and Ward, under the title *Reproachfully Yours*. It was a collection of nineteen personal (very personal!) essays. Its success was immediate, and "the apostolate of laughter" was launched.

The author set herself to avoid triteness or stuffiness. "If I have any literary standard at all," she writes, "it is this. I consider it a mortal sin to bore people." But, of course, the avoidance of "sin" was not her only purpose. Her power and art in reaching through to people, while she keeps them merrily entertained, also bears weightier fruit. As she expresses it, "I sneak up on my readers."

She found little abuses in the way new converts were initiated into life in the Church and treated therein, and she set herself in a fighting yet beguiling way to correct the abuses. "She discusses," writes critic

Father John S. Kennedy, "the lay apostolate, confession, reading, priests, nuns, married life, the letters she gets from readers. Each subject is lightly handled, with a radiant humor and pin-point wit, and when I say 'lightly handled' I mean it in two senses; with the lightness of fun and the lightness of sun. This is prose that reveals as it revels. While she performs she informs. She has a place all her own in the galaxy of Catholic authors and it is to be hoped that she will long twinkle there."

As a "red-hot convert," Lucile Hasley has thrown herself wholeheartedly into the lay apostolate. "Catholics," she wrote (*The Sign*, March, 1950), "are called to spread Christ's fire upon the earth, not just hug their wonderful gift of faith to themselves." Her special interest is that of racial justice and understanding for the Negro. Five years ago she originated a unique experiment in South Bend: a Catholic study group, composed equally of white and Negro women, who hold their fortnightly meetings in each other's homes. This has proven very successful in breaking down — in a truly Catholic way and on a grass-roots level — the formidable problem of prejudice and segregation. In 1950 the group was nominated as an entry for the national $1000 Lane Bryant award for the "group contributing most to the welfare and happiness of the community."

Lucile frankly admits her non-intellectual approach to the Church. In the story of her conversion she writes: "I am outside the pale of that intellectually respectable league of converts who can say, 'It was Augustine who led the way'; or 'Aristotle left me strangely dissatisfied'; or 'The shackles fell from my eyes when I first read the *Summa* in the original'; or 'After twenty years as a Communist I one day chanced to read the Pope's Encyclical on Labor,' et cetera, et cetera. *My* sole intellectual approach to the Church consisted in lifting a finger and pushing the buzzer at a Catholic rectory."

Naturally, as all but the brightest wits do, she exaggerates her own lack of thinking. At the time of her conversion, she may not have dug deep into metaphysics or theology, but she used her keen faculty of observation and shrewd good sense. Grace and "Divine Providence crowding in on her" did the rest. Since then, however, she has piled up a good deal of spiritual reading behind her and her present writing, as someone has put it, reveals both "bounce and base." She can make theology as exciting as a detective story for she knows how to put big truths into little words.

For Lucile, baptism means only the beginning. "Only in a very limited sense can one say at the baptismal font: 'Here's the finale! Peace, it's wonderful!' The Church offers peace, yes, but if it's just a rocking-chair sort of peace you're after, I would recommend some nice, quiet sanitarium in the hills of New Hampshire rather than the Roman Catholic Church. In fact, *peace* is perhaps the last word to come to my mind. I can think only in terms of the adventure, the challenge, the diversity, and — *yes!* — the joyousness of the Catholic way of life."

To date, Lucile has but one slim book to her credit, *Reproachfully Yours*, but the public response has been considerable. There are many who are urging another offering from our "apostle of laughter."

Irene Haugh   1906–

Miss Irene Haugh was born in Dublin on November 30th, 1906. She was graduated from the National University in 1927. Her father, the late Professor John Joseph Haugh, was a well-known mathematician and one of the founders of the Gaelic League Movement in Ireland. He was the author of a popular arithmetic entitled *Haugh's Higher Arithmetic.*

During the year 1929–1930 Miss Haugh worked for George Russell (A.E.), when the latter was editor of *The Irish Statesman.* She was his secretary during that last year of the journal's existence and also wrote regular weekly reviews for it. "That year," she says "was the most interesting in my life. He was a delightful companion, a great help, and a good friend to me. All the interesting people who came to Dublin drifted into his office at one time or another. Then I, too, would be absorbed listening to the poet speaking." She wrote a long article on the subject for the *Ireland-America Review,* under the title "The Golden Heresy of Truth."

She was also a student of the Royal Irish Academy of Music — music being one of her chief interests in life — and wrote music criticisms for a Dublin paper and for *The Irish Statesman;* also contributing many poems, some of them inspired by music, to well known literary journals in Dublin, England and America: *The Spectator; The Sunday Times; The Saturday Review; Poetry; The Commonweal,* etc. Some of these poems were reprinted in anthologies such as: *The Best Poems of 1929; The Best Poems of 1932; The Best Poems of 1933* (all edited by Thomas Moult); *The Bedside Book; The European Scrapbook* (1930), and *Poems From Ireland,* edited by Donagh MacDonagh (1944).

In 1933 she published a book of poems, *The Valley of the Bells,* with a preface written by A.E.   W. J. W.

Reverend Denis J. B. Hawkins
1906–

Born at Croydon, Surrey, England, 1906, Denis Hawkins is directly descended from John Loudon McAdam, the inventor of macadamized roads, and collaterally connected with James Harris, the eighteenth-century philosophical writer. He was educated at Whitgift School and at the Venerable English College and Gregorian University, Rome (Ph.D. 1927 and D.D. 1931). Ordained a priest in 1930, he has been rector of the Catholic Church, Esber, Surrey since 1940.

His philosophical writings, apart from numerous articles and reviews, consist of five books: *Causality and Implication* (1937); *Approach to Philosophy* (1938); *The Criticism of Experience* (1945); *A Sketch of Mediaeval Philosophy* (1946), and *The Essentials of Theism* (1949).

Early in his studies he came to the conclusion that there was a great deal more to be done than most Thomists realized in presenting Thomistic philosophy in a language which could be understood by the average contemporary philosopher and in facing problems which had arisen since the Middle Ages. In *Causality and Implication* he tried to bring the traditional notion of causality into relation with the logical concept of implication or entailment. Many modern logicians "evacuate" the meaning of implication by treating it purely in terms of extension, but it acquired its proper meaning as an intentional relation, a connection between concepts or isolates of thought which we are able to recognize in abstraction and, therefore, to apprehend as universally valid. If that is so, the Kantian problem of the *a priori* synthesis is seen to be a pseudo-problem. We do not have to ask how we manage by some mental mechanism to bring distinct concepts into relation; in favorable cases, as in logic, metaphysics, mathematics and psychology, we simply perceive their connection. With the material world we are in a less happy position and have to use the logically roundabout methods of the experimental and hypothetical sciences, but these presuppose logical and metaphysical principles. Causal laws have validity because in favorable cases we are able directly to recognize that one state of affairs must lead, or tends to lead, to another. There is much in this first book which Father Hawkins would now want to express with greater accuracy, but he is still convinced that its main thesis is true and important.

In *The Criticism of Experience* he tackled the puzzles about our knowledge of the material world and of our other selves which have been especially prominent in English philosophy since Locke. He completely accepted the subjectivity of sensations and tried to show that this was the genuine view of Aristotle himself, if not of his followers. Nevertheless he argued that we could not have the confidence in the existence of the material world and of our other selves which we in fact possess, unless we had some direct and not merely inferential and problematic knowledge of these. His theory of direct perception depended upon a sharp distinction between our consciousness of permanent mass and our consciousness of transitory sensation; the consciousness of the permanent mass of our own organisms could be, when in dynamic contact with other bodies, the psychological means of a logically direct awareness of these other bodies. While most of our knowledge of the external world is inferential and merely probable, these inferences and probabilities are intelligible only in relation to a nucleus of immediate awareness of bodies with which we are in contact.

The Essentials of Theism is a presentation in contemporary philosophical language of the road to God by natural reason as St. Thomas Aquinas described it. For the sake of modern man, enmeshed in historical relativism or materialism, chapters on the contingency of history and the inadequacy of materialism precede the direct exposition of the

Thomistic proofs. Attention is given especially to the transition from the bare notion of a first cause to the identification of this with Infinite Being, and to the way in which the Augustinian argument to a subsistent External Truth fits in with the Thomistic process of thought towards God as supreme mind. The most original among the later chapters rejects both the Bannesian theory of physical premotion and the Molinist doctrine of *scientia media*, and suggests a different type of reconciliation between divine omnipotence and human free will.

Approach to Philosophy was an attempt at a synoptic view of the subject, both contemporary and Thomistic. *A Sketch of Mediaeval Philosophy* was the summary of a short course of lectures given twice verbally before being written down; it is less an historical handbook than an introduction to the climate of mediaeval thought, although it is presented in historical sequence and gives some account of each important mediaeval philosopher. Father Hawkins is extremely dissatisfied with all his writings as soon as he sees them in print, although he has some lingering tenderness for at least *The Criticism of Experience*, but he hopes to live long enough to do something which will satisfy himself more. At any rate he believes that it is the job of a philosopher to go on thinking and to present the results of his thinking with brevity and clearness, relapsing neither into a popularization which conceals the difficulties nor into that kind of academic research which veils the absence of individual reflection by an imposing abundance of historical footnotes. He would like to be understood by anyone who is willing to think really hard, whether a philosopher in the professional sense or not.

Reverend William Hayward
1870–1945

Near the close of the nineteenth century, a group of Episcopal clergymen, who honestly believed that they were true priests, banded themselves together in a religious organization in the city of Philadelphia under the name "The Companions of the Holy Savior."

One of the first and most consistent of these members was Father William Hayward. He was born at Morley, St. Lawrence County, New York on March 15, 1870 and was the son of an Episcopal clergyman. He attended elementary school in Wisconsin, where his father was rector of a little country parish, and then went to the Howe School, a military academy at Lima, Indiana, and was about to enter Hobart College for his third year when he was advised by his bishop to enter the Anglican seminary of Nashotah House near Milwaukee, which was at that time under the spiritual influence of the Companions. In the spring of 1893 he was ordained "deacon" and not being of canonical age to receive the order of "priest" he taught at Racine College for a year. When the Right Reverend William Mc-Garvey, the founder of the C.S.S.S. (the Companions of the Holy Savior), visited there, Father Hayward joined the community on October 19, 1893.

Ordained a "priest" in the Episcopal Cathedral in Milwaukee on May 13, 1894, he accepted a position as assistant under Reverend Maurice L. Cowl in St. Elizabeth Episcopal Church, Philadelphia which, under the succeeding rectorship of the late Monsignor William Mc-Garvey, became the motherhouse of the community and the center of all its activities. He arrived there on June 15, 1894, and remained until 1908, when together with other Episcopal clergymen he entered the Catholic Church.

After his ordination to the priesthood on May 27, 1911 he was sent as assistant to Our Lady of Lourdes Church, Overbrook, Pennsylvania for eighteen months and then to St. Michael's in Philadelphia where he remained for nine years as an assistant. In June 1922 he was appointed pastor of the new parish of St. Alice in Stonyhurst.

Besides writing a short life of St. Alice and an *Exequiale*, a set of prayers for the dead, Father Hayward also wrote, *The C.S.S.S.: The Quest and Goal of the Founder, the Right Rev. William McGarvey* (1940). The latter work was written at the request of His Eminence D. Cardinal Dougherty, Archbishop of Philadelphia (now deceased).

Father Hayward died on April 14, 1945 at the age of seventy-five.

M. A. H.

Jean Heavey

A native of Philadelphia, Jean Heavey attended Hallahan Catholic High School for Girls, and then entered the Philadelphia Normal School. Two years later, she found herself at the front of an elementary classroom, confronted by "children's faces looking up, holding wonder like a cup." Although Miss Heavey admits she has often encountered many things besides wonder in her pupils' faces, she still finds the challenge exciting and enjoys meeting it.

Her elementary teaching experience was a brief encounter. Having acquired a B.S. in education and later an M.A. in English, both from the University of Pennsylvania, she taught English in junior high school and then in senior high school. At one time or another, she has done all the things expected of the English teacher — made marionettes; edited the school newspaper and magazine; produced plays; devised and revised courses of study; written and directed assemblies; conducted classes in creative writing; written speeches, including the principal's; and led a life of her own.

At present Jean Heavey is a reading counsellor in one of the public high schools. Her work includes in-service training as well as instruction of students. A member of the faculty of the Annual Reading Institute at Temple University, Philadelphia, she participates as lecturer and demonstration teacher. Miss Heavey has also conducted an in-service course in reading techniques for the Sisters of St. Joseph at the College of Chestnut Hill. In the field of remedial reading, she has contributed militant articles to the following educational magazines: *The Philadelphia News Letter, School and Society, The School Review, The English Journal* and *The Educational Digest.*

Miss Heavey's interests are varied and many. They include people, young or old; dogs; old china; ceramics; interior decoration; art galleries; parades; travel; Ireland and the Irish; literature, past and present; the theatre; conversation and writing. Her summers and spare time are spent in enjoying as many of these as possible. She has studied stagecraft and playwriting at Cornell University, where her one-act play, "Sort of Like Capek," was produced. Having traveled by automobile, bus, train and foot in the United States, Canada, Mexico and Europe, she has attended the theatre wherever a curtain went up whether she could understand the language or not.

Ireland still remains for Jean Heavey, however, the country that she likes best to visit. Some of her experiences in the homeland of her four grandparents have been unique. They include attending a funeral and a ceilde on the Aran Islands, taking a walking trip in Connemara, and nearly losing her life in a squall off Galway Bay. Out of her familiarity with the Irish scene she wrote "The Spirit of Ballybaugh," the story of a poltergeist in a commercial hotel in Ulster, published in the English *Good Housekeeping.*

Jean Heavey remembers one red-letter day when her teacher of composition in normal school read the preface of Joseph Conrad's, *The Nigger of the Narcissus* to the class. For years, Conrad's inspiring words both awed and haunted her. One sonorous phrase in particular echoed in her memory: "To snatch in a moment of courage, from the remorseless rush of time, a passing phase of life, is only the beginning of the task." It was not until Jean Heavey realized how "remorseless the rush of time" had become and that, if she were to snatch anything, it had better be by the forelock, that she began to write.

Her first published story, "The Vanity of Father Coyle," appeared in *The Saturday Evening Post* in February, 1950. At the request of Alice Dalgliesh, Charles Scribner's Sons' Editor of Books for Younger Readers, she expanded the story into a juvenile, published October, 1951, under the title *The Pastor's Dog.*

It is a "tender story about a priest and a boy who loved the same dog. . . . Her thesis has that universality which personalizes it for everybody; her imaginative crisis could in real life befall any two menfolk who had to go separate ways and a dog torn between devotion to both of them." ("Keeping Posted," *The Saturday Evening Post.*)

Most Reverend John Carmel Heenan 1905–

At one time known as Britain's radio priest, Bishop John Carmel Heenan is an outstanding writer, preacher and lecturer who, as the former superior of the Catholic Missionary Society, and since February, 1951, as Bishop of Leeds, England, holds a position of exceptional responsibility in Catholic England.

Born in Ilford, an eastern district of London, in 1905, he was educated by the Jesuits in the North London College of St. Ignatius, and did his clerical studies in the historical seminary of Ushaw and the Venerabile in Rome where he obtained the degrees of Ph.D. and D.D. He was ordained in 1930.

Exceptionally early in his priestly career he was appointed parish priest at Manor Park, near where he was born, and very soon after the appointment, he was made the National Director of the Legion of Mary. From the first he showed signs of his peculiar gift, as a priest, of showing himself equally at home with the working class, the bourgeoisie, the intellectuals and the high officials of the Church who recognized him as a man of mark.

His rector at the Venerabile, Monsignor Hinsley, was appointed Archbishop of Westminster and made Cardinal, coincidentally with the development of Bishop Heenan's career, and it was known what high trust the Cardinal Archbishop put in his old pupil.

During the war years, Father Heenan became known as a broadcaster with a special gift for teaching and preaching in the language which the ordinary listener and the soldier could appreciate, and thus earned the title referred to above. He was less widely known for the courage and endurance he showed in ministering nightly to the casualties of a district which suffered heavily from the early waves of bombing and the V1's and V2's of the later phases of the war. But it was the same courage which brought his radio career to an end, since Father Heenan was never able to trim his talks to the pattern of a "safe" national broadcasting system. These talks, however, were published under the titles of "Were You Listening?" and "Untruisms."

Though already widely known as a lecturer, especially on subjects where the Catholic Faith impinged on national and international questions — Father Heenan was one of the few English Catholics who had visited Russia and had seen for himself, — his real and full work seemed to have begun in 1947 when Cardinal Griffin and the English hierarchy chose him to be the superior of a revived Catholic Missionary Society. To Father Heenan and his band of carefully selected colleagues the hierarchy looked for the organization and leadership of a great national campaign to revive religious fervor and to preach the Gospel to the whole people, as a preparation for the Holy Year and the Centenary of the Restoration of the Hierarchy.

Father Heenan was thus responsible for the organization of numberless missions, for special motor-chapel campaigns in the countryside, and for special lectures to non-Catholic audiences. He took his own full part in every phase of the work and himself trained his fellow members of the Missionary Society as key missioners.

Despite these activities, his pen was kept busy. He was chosen to write a Memoir of Cardinal Hinsley, and a flow of books included: *Priest and Penitent; Letters from Rush Green; They Made Me Sign,* and *The People's Priest* (1951). Special lecture tours to Ireland, where his candid criticism of some aspects of the social situation there earned him some unpopularity, and to America were fitted into his overburdened programme.

An exceptionally retentive memory, wide reading, clarity of mind, the gift of the telling phrase, and, above all, perhaps, his courage in saying what ought to be said, however unpopular, have been the chief elements in his success as a speaker.

As a priest Father Heenan was ever ready to serve God and his superiors without thought for himself, his personal tastes or his reputation. In February, 1951, he was named by Pope Pius XII to be Bishop of Leeds, England.   M. de la B.

Reverend Paul Heinisch   1878–

Generally regarded as one of the foremost living Catholic authors in the Old Testament field, Father Paul Heinisch has averaged a book every two years, a total of twenty-three, since 1908.

Father Heinisch was born on March 25, 1878, in Leobschütz, Upper Silesia, Austria. After attending the public gymnasium, he entered the University of Breslau. From the very beginning of his theological studies he became interested in the Old and New Testaments, which subjects were taught by Professors Paul Scholz (d.1900), John Nickel and Aloysius Schäfer. The latter became Bishop of Saxony. After Father Heinisch's ordination to the priesthood in Breslau on June 23, 1902, he was engaged in parish work for five years. During this period, he took courses in theology at the university to earn an S.T.D. degree in 1907, which was awarded *magna cum laude.* To better fit himself for a professorship in the Old Testament he returned to the University in 1908. Three years later (1911) he was appointed professor of this subject at the University of Strassburg, where he succeeded Professor Faulhaber, who left to become bishop of Speyer (now Cardinal Archbishop of Munich). In 1923, Father Heinisch was called to the newly founded Catholic University of Nijmegen, of which he has been professor emeritus since October 1st, 1945.

245   **Right Reverend Monsignor Martin B. Hellriegel**

After occupying the chair of Sacred Theology there for twenty-two years he was sent to Salzburg.

Perhaps the best known of his twenty-three books are his eight volumes in the celebrated "Bonn Bible" series. An English translation of his *Theologie des alten Testamentes* was made by Father William Heidt, O.S.B., under the title *Theology of the Old Testament,* which was published by The Liturgical Press, Collegeville, Minnesota in 1950.

Some of his works in German are: *Der Einfluss Philos von Alexandrien auf die Älteste Christliche Exegese (Barnabas, Justin, Clemens von Alexandrien)* (1908); *Die griechische Philosophie im Buche der Weisheit* (1908); *Griechentum und Judentum im letzten Jahrhundert vor Christus* (1908); *Griechische Philosophie und Altes Testament* (1913–1914); *Die Weissagungen des Alten Testaments von dem kommenden Erlöser*(1919); *Die Gottesmutter im Alten Testament* (1925); *Das "Wort" im AT und im Alten Orient* (1922); *Die persönliche Weisheit im AT in religionsgeschichtlicher Beleuchtung* (1923); *Das Buch Ezechiel übersetzt und erklärt* (1923); *Das Buch Genesis, Exodus übersetzt und erklärt* (1934); *Das Buch Leviticus, übersetzt und erklärt* (1935); *Das Buch Numeri übersetzt und erklärt* (1936); *Theologie des Alten Testamentes* (1940); *Probleme der biblischen Urgeschichte* (1948); and *Geschichte des Alten Testamentes* (1950).

Two of his books, *Theologie des Alten Testamentes* and *Probleme der biblischen Urgeschichte* were translated into Italian.

W. B.

Right Reverend Monsignor Martin B. Hellriegel 1890–

To anyone familiar with the Liturgical Movement, Monsignor Hellriegel needs no introduction; he is one of its outstanding leaders and well qualified to be, by both his background, steeped in liturgical living, and by his education.

Born November 9, 1890, in Heppenheim, in the diocese of Mainz, Germany, he was baptized a week later in St. Peter's Church in Heppenheim. This parish was given by Charlemagne as a benefice to the Benedictine Abbey of the nearby horsch. With roots that go back through eleven centuries of untainted Catholicism, it is not surprising that Monsignor Hellriegel should be such a leader in the return of the liturgy of the Church. The beginning of his interest in the revival of the Liturgy began quite accidentally: "simply with the problem of raising flowers, in his garden, suitable for the various feasts of the year. But since each part — even such a humble part as altar flowers — in the liturgy is linked up with every other part, one study led to another, till the whole plan was worked out." (America vol. 45, p. 570.)

His parents had three other children besides Martin and adopted seven orphan boys. The Hellriegel home was the ideal Catholic one in which a family, that can be described by no other name but Christ-like, lived a rich Catholic life that carried out the age old customs of Catholic Germany and Austria. For years he paid no attention to requests for biographical data. He says "No doubt I inherited that from my good mother. Her motto was: *Die Person ist unbedeutend, Gottes Sache ist hochbedeutend.*" Martin attended high school and college in Heppenheim and, in 1906 Father George W. Hoehn, born in Heppenheim and pastor at Starkenburg, Missouri, brought him to the United States. He studied his philosophy at St. Meinrad's Seminary, Indiana, and his theology at Kenrick Seminary in St. Louis, Missouri. Advanced studies were later carried on in various liturgical centers, such as Maria Laach, the Benedictine Abbey in Germany, Klosterneuburg, with Dr. Pius Parsch, and at the Rome stational Churches, under Monsignor Kirsch.

In 1914, Monsignor Hellriegel served as assistant at St. Peter's Church in St. Charles, Missouri. He remained there until he became chaplain in 1918 at the motherhouse of the Sisters of the Precious Blood at O'Fallon, Missouri. In 1940, he was made pastor of Holy Cross Church, St. Louis, Missouri, a parish which he has made famous by the vital liturgical life that goes on there throughout the year. When Abbot Wilfrid Upson, O.S.B., of Prinknash Abbey, England visited this country in 1947 he was a guest of the Monsignor for a week. What impressed the abbot was the interest of the people in the liturgy. In the winter issue of the *American Benedictine Review*, Vol. 1, No. 4, the abbot relates: "On every Sunday evening during Lent an instruction is given by Monsignor Hellriegel on a part of the Mass, while at a temporary altar, erected in the sanctuary, the pastor's assistant vested in chasuble and with servers goes through the appropriate ceremonies facing the congregation. The significance of each detail of the Mass, the prayers and their accompanying ceremonial and the importance of the congregation's part in assisting at the Sacrifice is thus brought home in a very vivid manner. The parish is one large family." On June 6, 1940, he was made Papal Chamberlain and on May 16, 1949, he was made Domestic Prelate.

In connection with Monsignor Hellriegel's zeal for the return to the Sacred Liturgy of the Church by "an intelligent, active participation" by the laity "in the life of the Church", he wrote *The Holy Sacrifice of the Mass* in 1944. *Orate Fratres* (now *Worship*) (Vol. 19, p. 88) says of it: "Although it (*The Holy Sacrifice of the Mass*) follows the usual approach, by treating the successive parts of the Mass in order, it is distinguished above most of its predecessors by the devotional warmth of its language, the directness of its personal applications, and its simplest manner of stating profound spiritual truths. In a word, it makes the Mass live in mind and heart." In 1948, he completed the first volume of homilies and meditations on the Church Year entitled *The Vine and the Branches*. He is writing the second volume which will deal with the sanctoral cycle. These books are published by the Pio Decimo Press for which Monsignor Hellriegel has done much to advance and which prints *The Living Parish*, a magazine whose title best describes his own Holy Cross Parish.

Monsignor Hellriegel is an Oblate of St. Benedict (Conception Abbey, Missouri) and has the name of Stephen. He is an associate editor of *Orate Fratres* (now *Worship*) since its beginning in 1926 and a frequent contributor to it.

For many years he has been active in the National Catholic Liturgical Conference. Since 1949 he is president of the Liturgical Conference of America. Commenting on his election, the *Bulletin of the Liturgical Conference* (November 1949) states: "Monsignor Hellriegel has become the incarnation of liturgical life; he is also the one who has perhaps been singularly successful in 'incarnating' the liturgy in the lives of others in the lives of his parishioners. In his presence in his parish, one feels and knows that the liturgy is not a passing superficial, and ephemeral nicety, but the deep, abiding, even eternal life, of Christ in His Church, with its many outward expressions."

M. T. G. and M. A. H.

Reverend Francis Herlihy   1912–

In reading Father Herlihy's book *Now Welcome Summer* one has a rare, many would think impossible, experience. The experience is that of finding that feelings of awe, I mean religious awe, and amusement can combine in harmony. One finds oneself smiling genially over incidents of Irish-Korean friendship, the while one's soul is raised to God in sincere rapture over apostolic charity. In Father Herlihy's story we see young Irish priests, emboldened by Christian zeal, playfully living the Korean life, and liking it, in spite of its hardships, while they skillfully and patiently teach their Korean friends the doctrine and imitation of Christ.

The Koreans found Irish names too complicated, so Herlihy had to be changed to Hu. Hu Sinbu (Sinbu, meaning Father) was therefore the name the young Irishman (from New Zealand) went by. He had little worldly experience, for neither in his Australian seminary, nor in Dalgan Park (Ireland) where he was ordained at the age of twenty-three, nor in the Gregorian University at Rome (1936–39) where he graduated in Canon Law, had he much opportunity of studying mundane affairs. His life began, at the age of twenty-eight, at Hongtcheng, in South-central Korea. There, with a fresh mind, and a bright intelligent eye, he observed, philosophized, and narrated.

Telling of one of the occasional get-togethers of the Irish priests scattered round the Syunsen region he writes, "I felt a flicker of amusement in recalling that missioners are said to be men cut off from, and forgotten by, the world. Indeed, it might be partly true; but to these men, shut off in the valleys of this remote peninsula, it would seem to be a fact of very little consequence. For their world was here. Their problems and ambitions and plans centered around these humble friendly people, of novel ways, and broad guttural speech, whose Faith was in their keeping. Preoccupations were such things as the land for a kang-dong (chapel); the need for a catechist at this other place; Tjyeng Marcu who wanted to find a Christian husband for his daughter; the hostility of the (Japanese) policeman Watanabe; young I Pauro, who seemed as though he might have a vocation."

Hu Sinbu and the others were continually spied upon by Japanese police. "Does the Japanese official think we are any different from the rest? Not at all! We don't go down. He doesn't believe our story about saving souls — because the only thing he knows foreigners to be good at is saving dollars. To him the Faith is a foreign commodity, and it is one he doesn't want." When a missioner referred in a letter to another to Thomas Aquinas, the letter was opened and the Japanese became suspicious of this "Thomas Aquinas." They wanted to know what he was doing in Korea and where he was hiding. Their suspicions were likewise aroused about Saint Patrick (Sung Pa-triku) when they came across some reference to him. The anti-foreign bogey scared away many potential converts. The prewar years, during which Hu Sinbu was in Korea, were especially trying.

There is no appeal for sympathy in Father Herlihy's story of the Korean mission, nor does he dwell upon the sufferings and privations of the missioners. He is content to give a vivid picture of the scene, letting the facts, as he recounts them, drive home the moral. He tells, of course, of the heroism of the early French missioners, and of the native Korean martyr-priest Blessed Andrew Kim. Also, when World War II broke out and he and his companions were herded into jail, he describes the features of the cruel imprisonment they underwent. He does not, however, bear any enmity against the Japanese, but tries to explain away their violence in terms of the hatred of foreigners to which they were educated. On the whole his story, as a reviewer declared, "abounds in delicate touches of tenderness and fun."

Francis Herlihy was born in Southland, New Zealand in 1912, of Irish parents. He was educated, first by the Sisters of Notre Dame des Missions at Dannevirke, and afterwards at the Dannevirke High School. In 1929 he entered the Seminary at Holy Cross College, Mosgiel, New Zealand, and after two years there entered St. Columban's Mission Society at Essendon, Melbourne. From Melbourne he went to Dalgan Park (Ireland) where he was ordained in 1935. After three years study at the Gregorian University (Rome) he was appointed to the Mission Staff of Korea (1939), arriving in Hongtchen in 1940. In 1942 he was repatriated to New Zealand by the Japanese, and at present is Superior of St. Columban's Society House in that country. His book, *Now Welcome Summer*, was published in Australia in 1946, and in Ireland in 1948. The title is derived from the Chaucerian verse:

> Now welcome Summer, with thy sunne soft
> That hath this winter's weather over-shake
> And driven away the long nightes black.

Father Herlihy (with a modesty that readers of his interesting and original book will recognize) disclaims the right to be regarded as an author — and that in spite of many favorable reviews. He says: "My feeling is that the word 'author' applied to me, has to be, as I have written it, in quotes. I am an author because St. Columban's Mission Society had my book published. I am not suffering from false modesty — I think it was quite good for an amateur — but I can describe its writing only as a sort of parenthesis; I hoped it would be useful as a less obvious form of mission propaganda, but I have neither the material nor the opportunity nor, perhaps, the justification for trying again. If you were home on holidays and you built quite a fair little barn, of which you and the family were reasonably proud, you would still hesitate about appearing among the listed national architects — wouldn't you?"   E. B. B.

Ferdinand Aloysius Hermens
1906–

The work of Ferdinand A. Hermens is in the field of political science and economics.

Born on December 20, 1906 in Nieheim, Germany, he studied economics and related subjects at the Universities of Münster, Freiburg, Berlin, and Bonn from 1925 to 1930. He did postgraduate studies at the Faculté de Droit in Paris from 1930 to 1931 and was favored with research fellowships from 1930 to 1934. Ever since his student days at Bonn, Professor Hermens was an active member of the Catholic Center Party, which vigorously opposed the Nazis. In his home town, Nieheim, his opposition to the Nazis, conducted with a group of young Catholic friends, was so effective that the Nazis did not succeed in establishing a branch of their party, or even holding one single meeting, before Hitler was appointed Chancellor. Besides, Mr. Hermens' first book, *Democracy and Capitalism*, contained a vigorous defense of democratic government, and among his articles there was one contributed to the monthly, *Hochland*, at the conclusion of which he subjected the political qualifications of the leading Nazis, beginning with Hitler himself, to scorching satire. Naturally, this made the following months rather uncomfortable for him, in particular since he had not yet been formally admitted as a university lecturer which, in the case of the Institute of Technology in Berlin where he had been invited to join the staff, presupposed three years of research after the Ph.D. The winter of 1933–34 and the first two-thirds of 1934 were filled with the battle of wits with Nazis in Berlin, who incessantly caused Mr. Hermens difficulties but who, like a great many Nazis, were sufficiently illiterate to be unable to locate the particular articles and the reports of his speeches, the discovery of which would have guaranteed a one-way ticket to the concentration camp desired by these opponents and rivals. Finally, the Nazi Commissar to the Institute of Technology simply forbade Mr. Hermens' admission as a lecturer, and the efforts of Professor Goetz Briefs made it possible for him to leave Germany in September, 1934. He went to England to write a book dealing with the anti-depression policies of the major countries, which was published in Vienna in 1936. Mr. Hermens also did some work at the London School of Economics and Political Science. At the end of the school year, he came to the United States to become assistant professor of economics at the Catholic University of America and taught there for three years (1935–1938).

In 1937 he was given a grant-in-aid of Social Science Research Council for the study of elections and anti-democratic movements in Northern Ireland, Ireland, Holland, Belgium, France, Switzerland and Austria.

From 1938 to 1945 he was associate professor of politics at the University of Notre Dame and since 1945 he is professor of political science at the same institution.

In the summer of 1948 he was visiting professor at the universities of Münster and Bonn, with a grant from the Rockefeller Foundation. Meanwhile, the University of Notre Dame had established, with the support of the Rockefeller Foundation, the Committee on International Relations, which Mr. Hermens joined as a research associate. With the aid of the committee he returned to Europe in the summer of 1950 in order to study recent political developments in France, Italy, Austria, Germany, The Netherlands, Belgium and England.

Professor Hermens' books in English are: *Democracy or Anarchy? A Study of Proportional Representation* (1941); *The Tyrants' War and the Peoples' Peace* (1944); *Europe Between Democracy and Anarchy* (1951).

Sidney B. Fay, Professor of History, Harvard University in his review (Current History, vol. 7, p. 209, Sept. 1944) of the work, *The Tyrants' War and the Peoples' Peace,* writes: "Here is a wise, well-informed and very readable book. It deserves the widest circulation because it deals with the most important task facing the American people — the terms to be imposed on the defeated Axis powers and their satellites. . . . He recognizes that stern measures must be taken to prevent German militarists, Junkers and industrialists from ever again throwing Europe into war. But he believes, as does the present reviewer, that there are still 'decent' Germans, and that a distinction is to be made between the Nazis and the German people."

Arnold Brecht of the Graduate Faculty of the New School for Social Research in his review of the previous work *Democracy or Anarchy? A Study of Proportional Representation* (*Social Research,* Sept. 1944, pp. 411–414) writes: "This book has long been due. European emigrants were under a particular obligation to bring it into existence. Excellently done, thorough and comprehensive, it delivers from a heavy burden those of us who otherwise would have to give years to fulfilling this moral duty . . . Hermens' book is sure to become the great classical manual of the influence exercised by electoral systems of modern history."

Besides his works in German: *Demokratie und Kapitalismus (De-*

mocracy and Capitalism) (1931); *Demokratie und Wahlrecht* (*Democracy and the Franchise*) (1933); *Unternehmer und Konjunktur* (*The Employer and the Business Cycle*) (1936); and *Der Staat und die Weltwirtschaftskrise* (*The State and the World Economic Crisis*) (1936), Professor Hermens has written three pamphlets in English: *Democracy and Proportional Representation* (1940); *Proportional Representation, Democracy and Good Government* (1943), and *Potsdam or Peace, The Choice Before Us* (1946).

He contributes to *Hochland* (German), *La Revue Politique et Parlementaire, La Republique Française* (French), *Social Research, Social Science, Forum, Current History, The Commonweal, The Catholic World, Centralblatt and Social Justice, Columbia, The Sign, The Review of Politics, America, Thought, Parliamentary Affairs* (the publication of the Hansard Society in London) and *World Politics* (published by the Institute for World Politics of the University of London).

M. A. H.

James Hogan 1898-

James Hogan was born at Kilrickle, Co. Galway, in October, 1898, the son of Michael and Brigid Hogan, and a grand-nephew of the Sulpician Father John Baptiste Hogan, widely influential in ecclesiastical circles in Paris, Washington, and Boston during the eighties and nineties. Educated at the Jesuit College of Clongowes Wood, University College, Dublin, and Paris, he holds a D. Litt. degree from the National University of Ireland, and has been for many years a member of the Senate of the National University and a member of the Royal Irish Academy. The publication of *Ireland in the European System* and a number of historical articles led to his appointment in 1920 to the chair of history in University College, Cork, which he still occupies.

It was Mommsen who said that "the Celts have shaken all states and have founded none." This view of the ineffectual Celt has been proved wrong often enough by Irishmen outside Ireland. It was important to disprove it in the Ireland of 1921–1923 when at long last a native Irish State was struggling into existence. Associated from his student days with the struggle for Irish independence and with the founders of the new State, including his brother Patrick Hogan, Kevin O'Higgins and Michael Collins, during these years he served in the Army. The institutional side of early and medieval Irish history claimed most of his attention from his return to his chair in 1923 until 1932. His studies, which threw new light on Indo-European survivals, were published principally in the *Proceedings* of the Royal Irish Academy. In 1928 he became a foundation member of the Irish Manuscripts Commission, and, with the late Professor Eoin MacNeill, joint editor of the Commission's periodical *Analecta Hibernica*, seventeen numbers of which have appeared. He also edited several of the series of sixty volumes of unpublished historical documents issued under the auspices of the Commission.

Since 1933 his dominating interest has been political theory and the philosophy of history. In 1935 he wrote a best selling booklet *Could Ireland Become Communist?* and in 1943 *Election and Representation.* The first three of a series of studies on the philosophical as distinct from the economic origins of Marxism appeared in the *Irish Ecclesiastical Record* of 1948–49. There is no stranger episode in the history of ideas, Dr. Hogan maintains, than the Marxist travesty of the Hegelian dialectic, surely nothing stranger than that Aristotle and Hegel should be made responsible for the pseudo-philosophy calling itself the Marxist dialectic.

He does not believe in the university man confining himself to one specialty. He has written on current literary as well as political questions, including tendencies in Soviet literature up to 1930, on the new Irish novelists, 1920–30, and on the antipathies of the famous Irish novelist George Moore to things Christian and to things Irish. The question of literary censorship has engaged him. For a while he acted on the Irish Censorship Appeal Board and joined in a symposium with George Bernard Shaw and Sean O'Casey and others on this subject. Together with Eric Gill he has written on the question of workers' ownership. Recently he has made himself the chief Irish advocate of Ireland's adherence *sans phrase* to the Atlantic Pact.   K. O.

Reverend Joseph Holzner
1875–1947

Descendant of a small middle class family in the village of Dorfen-Markt in Upper Bavaria, Germany, Joseph Holzner was born there on December 12, 1875, the son of Joseph and Ann Holzner. After graduating from the humanistic gymnasium in Freising, he entered the German-Hungarian College in Rome, under the tutelage of the Jesuit Fathers, and pursued his philosophical and theological studies at the Gregorian University, Rome, Italy and Munich University, Germany. He received the doctorate in both philosophy and theology. On October 28, 1901 he was ordained a priest, at the Germanicum, in Rome. He began his priestly duties in 1902 as a curate in St. Benno's Church in Munich, then in Markt Schwaben and later he was a curate at the cathedral in Upper Bavaria. He was a chaplain in the Bavarian Army during the First World War, and later became pastor in Lengries. At the same time he was a teacher of religion at the Wittelsbacher Gymnasium in Munich. His extensive travels through all the countries of Europe, as well as in the Far and Near East, broadened his international contacts. In Greece, Asia Minor, Syria and Palestine he followed the path of St. Paul and collected impressions and manuscripts for his book, *Paulus.* In 1934 he retired from active duty and spent his last years at Lengries. In 1940 he was made a papal chamberlain. In 1937 the Herder Book Co. in Freiburg published his masterpiece, *Paulus, sein Leben und seine Briefe,* which by 1949 had been published in 22 editions. This work has been translated into Italian, French, Spanish, Portuguese, Czech, English and Greek. While it was being translated into French, the work was interrupted by the Second World War. In 1946 under the pseudonym of Franz Josef Hylander he wrote *Universalismus and Foederalismus* (Universalism and Federalism), as a contribution to the analysis of the occidental crisis. The little book of seventy-five pages was published by Schnell & Steiner of Munich.

His last work, *Rings um Paulus,* appeared in 1947. After his death on August 8, 1947, this book was placed on his coffin on August 11, 1947. His townspeople of Dorfen-Markt buried him with full honors.

W. B.

Catherine de Hueck
(Mrs. Edward Doherty) 1900–

In his book, *Tumbleweed,* Eddie Doherty tells the exciting, picturesque tale of a Russian girl, Catherine de Kolyschkine, a Red Cross nurse in the First World War, who married a wealthy Russian, Baron de Hueck, at a very early age. The girl, flying to Canada, after the Bolshevik Revolution, was destined to achieve fame as the Foundress of Friendship House. Her marriage with Baron de Hueck was annulled in the early thirties; Baron de Hueck died soon after. In 1943 she was married to "the great Eddie Doherty" (as she called him), by Bishop Sheil in Chicago.

Catherine Doherty, commonly known as "Baroness de Hueck," known also among the poor of Chicago as "Katie the Polack," had a full life of adventure and travel. She had many harrowing experiences of war and revolution in the Old World, and of poverty and hardship in the New World. Finally she found her true vocation in Catholic Social Action, and succeeded in launching the fine charitable enterprise known as Friendship House, with foundations at Toronto, Hamilton, Ottawa, Harlem (New York City), Chicago, Illinois, Marathon City, Wisconsin, Newburg, New York, Washington, D. C., and Combermere, Ontario, Canada. She is still actively engaged in supervising this work, while she writes books and articles.

Catherine de Kolyschkine was born in Nijni-Novgorod, in 1900. Her father, Theodore de Kolyschkine, a retired colonel of hussars, was an unofficial diplomat under the Czar. Her mother, Emma (née Thompson), was of English descent. Her early education was at Our Lady of Sion Academy, at Alexandria (Egypt). Later she attended the Lycée Mme. Milliard at Paris, and Princess Obolensky College in Petrograd. At the age of fifteen she served as Red Cross nurse in the Russian Army. With her first husband she fled to Finland after the Revolution. They finally succeeded in reaching Canada in 1921, where their son, George de Hueck, was born. Faced with the duty of supporting Baron de Hueck, who was in ill health, and her son George, as well as other relations, Catherine went to work in a department store in Toronto. Subsequently, going to New York City, she secured a place as lecturer on the Chautauqua Circuit at $100 per week. She won popularity by her lectures on Communism and within a short time was invited to tour for the Leigh-Emmerich Lecture Bureau at $300 a week. After a few years of lecture tours she wished to quit but Mr. Emmerich said to her: "You can't go on forever talking about Communists. I know you have to quit but don't quit me. How would you like to go abroad and buy talent for the Bureau?" This meant big money and luxurious travel in Europe. Catherine accepted. "I said 'Gosh,' and hurried to St. Patrick's to thank God."

The year 1930 found Catherine back in Canada and intent on re-signing her career and her considerable wealth in the cause of Catholic charity. At the request of the late Archbishop Neil MacNeil of Toronto, Catherine undertook the work of investigating Communist activities. For a year she lived with the Communists of Toronto, participating in their activities as an observer. At the end of that period she presented the Archbishop with her report. In 1931 she opened the first Friendship House (in Toronto). Seven years later, in 1938, she opened the second Friendship House in Harlem. A Friendship House is a center for helping the poor. It is supported by charity; its staff give their services free. "It isn't a monastery, nor is it a convent. But it's something between the two and something of both of them. It's a *conastery*." It is Catholic Action as contrasted with Catholic apologetics. "Apologetics," Catherine says, "helps to break down barriers against conversions, and has a certain negative value, but for every person who is helped by reading a book, there must be a hundred who have been converted by the corporal works of mercy." "It is so easy to write about the Faith, so difficult to live it, as Catherine has done," comments Arnold Lunn.

Catherine Doherty, despite her Russian up-bringing, writes clear, vigorous English. Her pen is busy with articles and reports. So far she has published four books: *Dear Bishop* (1947); *Friendship House* (1948); *Dear Seminarian* (1950); *Russian Yesterdays* (1951).

In 1947, Eddie and Catherine accepted the invitation extended to Friendship House by Bishop William J. Smith of Pembroke, Ontario, Canada, to open a branch of Friendship House in his diocese, the goal of which would be the Rural Lay Apostolate. For this purpose Madonna House was bought. It has grown much. There are three cottages on its five acres, and there is a fifteen-room house named St. Joseph a little way down the road. There are five staff workers, besides Catherine and Eddie. They publish a little paper devoted to the vision of the whole Lay Apostolate under the title *Restoration*. They have the only Catholic

Lending Library in the whole of Canada that serves anyone at a rural address from coast to coast. A second branch of this new Friendship House Rural Apostolate is expected to open soon. Invitations have been received from Brazil and Chile. Only the Holy Ghost knows where Catherine, His tumbleweed, will end her exciting life.

E. B. B.

Reverend Robert Hull, S.J.
1886–1932

Father Robert Hull was the eldest son of the late Mr. Robert Hull, J.P. of Preston, and was born at Holly House, Fulwood, Preston, on September 30, 1886. After two years at the Catholic College, Preston, he entered the class of Figures at Stonyhurst in September, 1899, and remained there for five years. His career at the College was a successful one, and he won many prizes, being often awarded the Gold Medal for his class. In addition he won the Junior Scholarship in 1900. It was only as his school course drew to a close that he decided on his future career. This was not done without much deliberation and prayer, as is evident from the fact that he took the unusual step of making a private retreat in order that his decision should be based only on the highest motives. The decision he arrived at was to offer himself to the Society of Jesus, and he accordingly entered the novitiate at Roehampton on March 30, 1905.

From this time on his progress followed the customary lines. After a short period in the juniorate, 1907–8, during which he prosecuted his classical studies, he spent the years from 1908 to 1911 in the study of philosophy at St. Mary's Hall. There followed four years at Campion Hall, Oxford, during which he followed the "Greats'" course. In 1918 he took his M.A. degree. His theological studies in immediate preparation for the priesthood were preceded by three years spent in teaching at his old school. During these years at Stonyhurst, 1915–1918, he threw himself with characteristic zeal into his work, both as a master and as an officer in the Officers Training Corps. His ordination to the priesthood took place at St. Beuno's College on July 25, 1920.

There yet remained the year of his tertianship, which was passed in the usual spiritual exercises at Tullabeg in Ireland, 1922–23. As Father Robert's abilities had marked him out for the post of professor of fundamental theology, or of apologetics, as it is variously named, he now proceeded to the Gregorian University, Rome, in order to prepare himself for the work. During these two years in Rome, he took his last solemn vows as a Professed Father of the Society of Jesus on February 2, 1924.

His health had not been good in Italy, and on his return to England to take up his professorial work it soon met with a serious breakdown, which necessitated a prolonged rest in 1925. When Father Hull was ready to take up his lecturing again, the theologate had removed from St. Beuno's to Heythrop College, and in these new surroundings he carried on his work of writing and teaching with energy and success until Easter-time 1932. He had then been suffering for some time, and it was found necessary for him to go into a hospital. Father Robert was strong and had appeared to be in the possession of good health, and no one imagined how near the end was. But in the hospital it soon became apparent that he had not long to live, as his disease was beyond the possibility of cure by doctor or surgeon. On April 10, he received the Last Sacraments, and passed away eight days later. The funeral took place in the private cemetery of Heythrop College on April 21, 1932.

Such, in very brief outline, was Father Robert's career. It may be said of him that in a short space he fulfilled a long time. There was little of incident in his life for the chronicler to record, but all he put his hand to he did well. A man who is earnest at his prayers, assiduous at his work, devoted to duty, and charming to all has not lived in vain. Such was Father Robert. His frankness and cheeriness made him a delightful companion, popular with all with whom he came in contact. As a friend truly wrote after his death, he was "lovable and charming."

A Jesuit Father, who knew him well, wrote of him as being "of great promise, so well fitted for his work . . . I used to admire his untiring industry, even the ardor with which he approached the task of preparation. He had an inquisitive mind that would never be satisfied with anything superficial. I used to look up to him as a man with a great career before him . . . I entertained the very highest opinion of the late Father Hull."

As a lecturer his work was deeply appreciated by his hearers. One records that in the lecture-room he was always painstaking, patient and kind. "In his lectures he strove to give full consideration to objections which might be brought against his own opinions. The arguments pro and con were examined with the greatest care and impartiality. One felt his whole aim to be that the truth may appear. By reason of his sincerity he increased, unconsciously yet very powerfully, the force of all he said."

His only book, *Medieval Theories of the Papacy and other Essays,* was published posthumously in 1934.   E. F. S.

Marigold Hunt   1905–

Marigold Hunt is the author of two children's books and advertising manager of Sheed & Ward, publishers.

She was born on November 10, 1905 in London, and is the daughter of Rowland Hunt, who was for 15 years Member of Parliament for Ludlow, and of Veronica (Davidson) Hunt. She attended a number of schools for short periods, and in between times shared a governess with any other children who happened to be handy. The reason for this odd education was that most of it took place during the First World War, when her father was an officer in a regiment which was everlastingly being shifted around England, and where he went the family went, too.

In 1925 she came to London to study art with an idea that she might make a living illustrating books, but in 1928 she joined the Catholic Evidence Guild and rapidly lost her enthusiasm for art, though she did illustrate three books later — Henri Ghéon's *St. Germaine of the Wolf Country* and Joan Windham's *Six O'Clock Saints* and *More Saints for Six O'Clock*.

In 1929 she joined the staff of Sheed & Ward, publishers, to work as biller and to do various other things, the firm being then only three years or so old and very small.

When Sheed & Ward opened their New York office she went there, and was with them till June 1940 when she returned to England to visit her family, and to see if she could help with the war. She remained there till 1946, working in St. Vincent's Orthopaedic Hospital part of the time, and also in various Catholic hostels and canteens. Since then she has been back at Sheed & Ward in New York.

Her first book was *A Life of Our Lord for Children* (1939) and her second, *St. Patrick's Summer* (1950). This second one is a story for 10 to 14 year olds, designed to make them see that God is more interesting than anyone else, and the saints the best friends one could have.

Miss Hunt's favorite animals are cats and (she is sorry to say) she reads far too many detective stories.

Douglas Hyde   1911–

It was an astounded world that heard the news in March 1948 that Douglas Hyde, the news editor of the London *Daily Worker* resigned from the Communist Party after being one of Great Britain's most famous communists.

Douglas Hyde was born April 8, 1911, in Worthing, Sussex, England of Methodist parents. At the early age of seventeen he had "what in nonconformist circles is known as 'the call to preach,'" and, as a theological student, soon became known as the "Boy Preacher." As time went on he began to have doubts about nonconformist theology and came under Communist influence. He had a troubled conscience, too, about social injustices and other evils of society. Before his eighteenth birthday he joined the Communist Party.

Though never unemployed, he was active in unemployed agitations during the years of economic depression. While the Spanish Civil War was waging, he organized campaigns for raising funds to buy ambulances, machine guns and other equipment to help the anti-Franco cause. "I would sometimes hurry into the porch of a Catholic Church and make for the Catholic Truth Society's literature rack, where pamphlets were exhibited for sale. I would take out any which appeared to be anti-Communist and put others on Spain in their place." He combined free lance writing for the Left Wing press with running a small holding in the Welsh hills, where his work in dentistry had taken him.

Later he edited a Left Wing monthly and then a local weekly in the London area. He held positions at every level of the Communist Party, served on the Party's London Secretariat, organized strikes, demonstrations, and spoke at Communist meetings for which he was arrested several times. He even functioned as a crypto-Communist Party member inside the British Labor Party.

In December 1939, he was told by the party that he should wind up the weekly paper of which he was editor and prepare himself to work on the *Daily Worker* instead. The change was effective in January. The *Daily Worker* embodied all his hopes. He served on it as chief subeditor, chief reporter and news editor in that order. He was news editor, roughly comparable to the city editor of an American newspaper, for the last five years before his resignation. When the *Daily Worker* was suppressed in 1941, he organized the party's illegal press.

At a May Day celebration he met his wife, Carol Johnson, for the first time. She was the chairman, and Hyde the principal speaker. "Within a few months," Hyde says, "we had set up a partnership which has remained a source of strength to us both throughout the years."

Regarded as the foremost anti-Fascist writer in the party, Hyde made a specialty of unearthing allegedly Fascist organizations. His hatred of Catholics and Fascists led to an attempt to prove that *The Weekly Review* (with which Chesterton and Belloc were associated) was Fascist. For these articles he was brought to court for libel by Catholic writers.

"In preparing for the High Court cases," writes Hyde, "I set about trying to understand my opponents and came to understand them too well. Catholic thought, gaining entry through a love for medieval literature and art, slowly destroyed my Communism — with me resisting every inch of the way."

The reading of Chesterton, Belloc and *The Weekly Review* had convinced him that they were right on fundamentals and the Communists were wrong. St. Thomas Aquinas' five proofs for the existence of God seemed to him unanswerable and "while they carried with them intellectual conviction they had not made God come alive for me. Then I could accept His existence intellectually but that was all."

His wife Carol then revealed that she had for some time had a secret wish that Rowena, their daughter, should not grow up in a Communist home, with "the party's morals being what they were." With all their hearts they yearned for the belief in God but it did not come. They had even discovered with some surprise that the great thinkers and philosophers of the Church had made out a better case for God's existence than Marx and Engels had done for His non-existence.

Then he was asked to review Avro Manhattan's book, *The Catholic Church against the Twentieth Century*, along with a pamphlet by the Anglican, Reverend Stanley Evans. "The first was a large book which set out to prove, by means of telling the story of Vatican policies since World War I, that the Catholic Church was Fascist. The other had much the same intention, attempting to show that the Church was against all progress. Once, I would have had grand fun with them, using them to smear Catholics and Fascists at one and the same time. I tried to do the same now, failed, and hated myself for even attempting it. It was a last desperate attempt to salvage the way of life I had loved. It failed completely.

"Instead I found myself saying: The Catholic Church against the twentieth century? So what? So am I, if the twentieth century means the crazy world I see about me, which has endured two world wars and goodness knows how many revolutions already, and in which the war clouds gather so soon after the last war."

Later Hyde attended a "Brains Trust" meeting of the Sword of the Spirit. Up till then he "had never been to anything Catholic, had never known any Catholic personally, never seen Catholics together in the mass. . . . I soon warmed up to the speakers . . . and walked to the station with the question master, Father Francis Devas, S.J." After telling Father Devas who he was, he asked him "Could such a man become a Catholic?" The priest replied that the Church existed for sinners.

On January 16, 1948, Hyde telephoned the local Jesuit College and said: "I want to have my two children baptized." "Half-past three on Sunday," said a voice at the other end of the line. "Won't some godparents be needed?" Hyde questioned. "Bring them along too, at half-past three on Sunday," said the voice. "But we just don't know a Catholic in the world," Hyde said. "Aren't you Catholics yourselves either?" the voice asked. "No," Hyde answered, "and we want to have a chat with someone about that too." "That telephone conversation meant the end of twenty years of Communism," writes Hyde in his book, *I Believed* (p. 274). On the fourteenth of March he resigned from the *Daily Worker* and on the following day from the party.

His house telephone rang almost unceasingly when the story broke. — "Journalists and photographers were in and around the house . . . The tables had been turned on the news editor with a vengeance, for I had to hold a press conference then and there. . . . For the next few days, life was hectic, with broadcasts, newspaper articles, endless interviews. On the Sunday, Palm Sunday, British Movietone News came and filmed us in our home."

Then Hyde wanted a period of peace and quiet. He would enjoy his "new-found freedom to think, to live my life as a Catholic." He says, however, "I could not pick up a copy of the *Daily Worker*, still cannot, without seeing the name of someone I brought into the Party still working for the cause. . . . I took a vow to try to make more converts to the Faith in the next ten years than I had made for Communism in the past twenty."

Hyde is now on the staff of *The Catholic Herald* and comments: "With my Communist background, I almost expected directives to come from the Cardinal as once they had come from Party headquarters. None came. Soon I was enjoying to the full the freedom that comes from the self-imposed discipline of the mind that springs from a belief in that absolute truth which so many of our generation have rejected or forgotten. . . . I believe Catholicism has the answer to man's social and political needs."   M. A. H.

Leo Vincent Jacks   1896–

Author of five books and about thirty stories and sketches, Leo Vincent Jacks is a teacher by profession. He explains his writing career as an avocation. "I write because I like it."

Born in Grand Island, Nebraska, March 14, 1896, Leo Jacks is the son of Porter and Margaret Genevieve (McMullen) Jacks. He received his A.B. from St. Mary's College, St. Marys, Kansas, and his A.M. from the Catholic University of America in 1920. He took a degree of Doctor of Philosophy, in Greek, Latin and Sanskrit, from the same institution in 1922.

He has lived on farms and ranches, worked for railroads and hardware companies. From 1917 to 1919 he served in the 34th and 32nd combat divisions of the United States Army, as an artilleryman and machine gunner. He always liked firearms. Rifle marksmanship is still one of his hobbies.

On August 2, 1930 he married Maxine Frances White. They have two children.

Since 1930 he has been director of the departments of Greek and Latin languages at Creighton University, and has served continuously as professor in the same departments.

His first short story appeared in *Scribner's Magazine*. Other stories appeared in *Munsey's* and *Collier's*. He has contributed articles to the *Catholic Educational Review* and *The Catholic World*.

Mr. Jacks is director of the annual Writers' Conference, sponsored by the Omaha Writers' Club, since 1946, and is likewise director of the annual Writers' Workshop held at the Catholic University of America. He is at present (1951) engaged in making some translations from Saint John Chrysostom for the new series of the Fathers of the Church, edited by Dean Deferrari.

His books are: *Service Record by an Artilleryman* (1928); *Xenophon, Soldier of Fortune* (1930); *La Salle* (1931); *Mother Marianne of Molokai* (1935); and *Claude Dubuis* (1946).   **M. A. H.**

Carol Jackson (Peter Michaels)
1911–

The first two books of Carol Jackson were published under her pseudonym, Peter Michaels. Her reasons for choosing that name are three: (1) "I like it," (2) "It seemed at the time more useful to have a man's name," (3) "To prevent people from confusing my good ideas with my (then) belligerent personality."

Born in Oshkosh, Wisconsin, in 1911, of a mixed marriage, Carol Jackson was baptized a Catholic but not reared one. Her father was a corporation lawyer. When she was three years old, the family moved to Madison, Wisconsin, and to Pelham Manor, New York, when she was ten. When she was fifteen, she joined the local liberal Presbyterian Church. She was fervently religious for a year or more "among nice people who were innocent of any doctrinal knowledge."

"When I went to Wellesley, I became an atheist," she says, "in less than a year, owing largely to the Bible department which was piously rationalistic. When I was a sophomore, I took journalism. We had to compose a sample magazine. Mine was called *The Atheist*. By this time I had become rather neurotic and my slight ability to write disappeared (except for writing letters), and did not show itself again until I became a Catholic."

Her parents, hoping that coeducation would have a stimulating effect on her, sent her to the University of Wisconsin. When that failed, she returned to Wellesley for another year but lacked credits to graduate.

The following five years ("miserable" she calls them) were spent in New York City, working in department stores, "a menial in the advertising department." Then she returned to Wellesley, majored in philosophy "everything except Christian philosophy."

After she was graduated, she used a small inheritance, from her grandmother, to take a trip around the world in freighters.

"More unhappy, frustrating years in the business world" followed, where she revolted again and again against the "nasty commercialism, but found no encouragement whatever for my critical ideas (which were mostly exactly right and which I mostly still hold). During those years I lived in Greenwich Village (New York) with a lot of other college graduates seeking refuge from the bourgeois world. We were idealists going sour, and sickening even of ourselves. All this experience has been invaluable to me lately, God having a way of making even our sins and sorrows fruitful.

"When I was twenty-nine I had figured everything out — wrong — and I was in despair so completely, that I did not even realize it. Then for the first time, Catholicism was presented to me, in the person of Paul McGuire, who was here lecturing on Catholic Action, and whose very incompetent secretary I was for several months. When he left for Australia, I spent a few months devouring *The Question Box*, and before long started taking instructions from Father Wendell, O.P. It was in 1941 that I made my First Communion. Father Wendell started me off on the practice of daily Holy Communion and helped me with the doctrine which I literally devoured for the first three or four years. He also employed me as his secretary for a few years and also introduced me to Ed Willock, with whom I started *Integrity*. So gradually my neurosis unwound itself (courtesy of grace, and without benefit of psychoanalysis), and my ideas straightened out and I started writing. It was Father Wendell again who 'dared' publish my stuff — which was considered radical — in the *Torch*." The *Torch* articles were later published in book form by Sheed and Ward. The first series was called *Designs for Christian Living*. The second series had the title *This Perverse Generation*. Both were published under her pseudonym, Peter Michaels. A reviewer of her book, *This Perverse Generation* (*Tablet*, London, England, December 31, 1949, p. 47), calls it, "An American rocket," adding "this is an American rocket, and rockets, quite apart from the shower of sparks that follow in their trail, can be life-savers. At least they shed a little sudden light. Mr. Michaels is angry; with the Western world for its insane pride and muddle-mindedness; with his fellow Catholics, for their complacent reduction of their faith to a nerveless pietism."

To find a synthesis for our times between religion and daily life, Miss Jackson, Ed Willock and two others began *Integrity* in October, 1946. Miss Jackson writes for it about half or one third of the time — again under the name of Peter Michaels.

Humble and apostolic, Miss Jackson says: "I am a good example of the truth that God can use any old material as an instrument because

His grace is all-powerful. Please God someday I may be a good instrument. There is always in the back of my mind those people, who must be millions, wandering around New York, and literally from one end of the year to the next not hearing one single good idea or true principle. So far we are remote from reaching them. But maybe, someday."

Reverend Paul de Jaegher, S.J.
1880–

The fact that the sublime doctrine of sanctifying grace, of which Father Paul de Jaegher, the Jesuit, is very fond, had been somewhat neglected, prompted him to write his first book, *La vie d'identification au Christ-Jésus* in 1927. Since then other solid spiritual books have come from his pen on other subjects dear to his heart.

Paul de Jaegher was born in Courtrai, a town of Flanders, Belgium, on the 14th day of January, 1880. After having worked with his father for five years, at the head of an important weaving factory, he entered, in 1903, the novitiate of the Jesuits at Tronchiennes. His first studies were made at Courtrai. He studied philosophy in the college of the Jesuit Fathers at Louvain, and theology at Kurseong in the Himalayas.

Ordained a priest in 1909, he was sent to work as a missionary among the primitive tribes of Chota Nagpur. This meant first learning the numerous and very difficult languages spoken by these tribes, a study which he relished. "Being soon in charge of some thirteen thousand Christian Ouraons," he writes, "I had to visit regularly a hundred villages or hamlets and more than forty village schools scattered all over the country, some perched like an eagle's nest on the top of the mountains, others nestling among dales and valleys or lost in dense forests infested by tigers, leopards, bears and even bisons and wild elephants. When at home I had to be a bit of an architect to build schools, chapels, bungalows, etc.; to act as a physician giving medicines to patients every day; to direct our central school; to instruct the catechumens for First Communion or marriage. At times there would be more than sixty marriages in a day. I also had to busy myself with gardening and other duties.

"Amidst this medley of occupations there was little chance for me ever to write any spiritual books. And yet I felt prompted to write something on sanctifying grace and union with God, present in our soul, so as to join the few writers like Father Raoul Plus, S.J., and Dom Marmion, O.S.B., who had just started popularizing the beautiful doctrine of sanctifying grace.

"So it was not without great difficulties that I managed to write my spiritual books. What encouraged me in this difficult work was my opinion that there was a real need of more Catholic literature on some subjects. I would never have written anything on matters which have been abundantly treated as spiritual life in general, prayer, mortification and kindred topics."

Father de Jaegher's first book, *La vie d'identification au Christ-Jésus*, which appeared in French in 1927, was translated into English under the title *One with Jesus*. It has been translated into nearly all European languages as well as Malayalam (an Indian language), and Japanese.

"I next noticed," writes Father de Jaegher, "that little had been written on the virtue of trust — and nuns, especially, badly needed a book which might comfort and encourage them in the various trials of the spiritual life and would in some way compensate for the lack of spiritual direction of which they often suffer badly. So I felt impelled to write my book, *Confiance* (1930), which was translated into English as *The Virtue of Trust*." It has also been translated into Flemish, Spanish, Italian and other languages. This book was followed by an anthology of mystical authors under the title *Anthologie Mystique* (1930), translated into English under the title *An Anthology of Mysticism*.

There is one more subject dear to him. It is the joys of the life of union, the joys of unitive love. These joys are, especially, those of a soul, which has become "one with Jesus." The book which describes them is therefore like a complement to his little book, *One with Jesus*, and bears the title *The Lord Is My Joy*.

It is hoped Father de Jaegher will continue to write his comforting books to stimulate souls on the path to pure, selfless love and sanctity.

M. A. H.

Pierre Janelle   1891–

Through his book, *The Catholic Reformation*, published by Bruce in 1949, the French author, Pierre Janelle, became known to readers in the United States.

Born on September 17, 1891, at Mouy, Oise, France, he is the son of the late Ernest Janelle (1861–1940), headmaster of the Lycées Charlemagne and Pasteur in Paris, and of Maria Pommart. He made his secondary studies at the Lycée of Vendôme and at the Lycée Lakanal in Paris. His higher studies were pursued at the Sorbonne in Paris, where he was graduated in 1911, and succeeded at the "agrégation" competition in 1914. In 1935 he was awarded the D.Litt. degree by the Sorbonne.

From 1910 to 1911 he was Provincial Committee Assistant at Glasgow University (Scotland) and the following year (1912–1913) was a temporary master at the Lycée Henri IV in Paris. On July 5, 1917, he married Edith Fournioux. She died on November 27, 1948. On February 4, 1950 he married Madame Donneaud, the widow of a Lyons doctor.

From 1919 to 1925 he was an English master at the Lycée Fustel de Coulanges, Strasbourg, France. For the following two and a half years (1925–1928), he was the holder of the Ernest Lavisse research scholarship, awarded by the Sorbonne. In the meantime, in 1923, he lectured in Scotland on French education in Alsace and was congratulated by President Poincaré personally. Then, in 1928, he taught for two years at the Lycée Kleber before coming as lecturer to Clermont-Ferrand. Since 1935 Dr. Janelle has been professor of English language and literature at that university.

During World War I he was at the front on September 9th, 1914, as a private in the Fifty-first French Infantry Regiment. On October 21st, 1914 he was severely wounded and mentioned in dispatches. In July, 1915, he was sent to the British Expeditionary Force as an interpreter, and was attached to the 124th Brigade, Royal Field Artillery, then to the 110th Infantry Brigade, and later to the First Army H.Q. For his work he received a letter of congratulations from General Count Gleichen, O.C. of the 37th Division. After taking part in the battle of the Somme and the battle of Vimy Ridge with the Canadian Corps, he was sent back to the French artillery in July 1917. He ended the campaign with the rank of second lieutenant in the 290th Regiment of the French Artillery.

In World War II he was called up on September 4, 1939 and given the rank of captain in the French artillery. Assigned to the French First Army, he did liaison work with the British army and took part in the battle on the Belgian frontier until taken down with illness. He was a convalescent until December 1940. During the years 1940–43 he kept in close touch with the group of American officers resident at Sayat near Clermont, providing them with information and help until their arrest by the Germans. For his military work he was awarded the French war cross with palm, the Legion of Honor and the British military medal.

His main interest in literary work is religious history, especially in connection with the British Isles. His attention was first drawn to that subject, "owing to the influence of an English Catholic, a convert, Professor John Swinnerton Phillimore of Glasgow University." He also largely benefited from the advice of his father.

His first work of importance was a publication of three Latin political tracts by Bishop Stephen Gardiner, entitled *Obedience in Church and State* (Cambridge University Press, 1930), in which he tried to show how there was an underlying continuity in Gardiner's ideas of the relations of the Church with the civil power. Then he published in 1935 a volume, in French, on *Catholic England on the Eve of the Schism*, in which, taking Gardiner as a central figure, he attempted to show for what reasons England had let herself unconsciously lapse into schism. Dr. Janelle next turned to the Catholic Reformation with a further book on *Robert Southwell: A Study in Religious Inspiration*, which was meant to prove that the Catholic apostolate in England under Elizabeth had had deep and lasting results on devotional practices, education and culture, even within the Church of England. This thesis was amplified and made to cover the whole of Christendom in a volume, *The Catholic Reformation* (1949), in which this movement is described as beginning before Luther and a continuation of the movement known as Christian Humanism. His latest work is a history, in French, *The Reformation in the British Isles*, which is part of volume XVI of the *History of the Church*, published under the direction of Professor Fliche and Monsignor Amann.

Among the many articles he contributed to reviews, he prefers "Was England predestined to be Protestant?" which appeared in the review of Clermont Academy. Dr. Janelle has spoken over the BBC on modern education.   M. A. H.

Sister Mary Jeremy, O.P.

Music and dance interest Sister Mary Jeremy as being organically associated with religion and therefore with poetry. The new form which is tentatively called "symphonic drama" seems to her remarkably fluid and challenging to American writers.

Born in Chicago, Illinois, Sister Mary Jeremy was educated at parochial schools, the Chicago Teachers College and the University of Chicago. At the University she belonged to the Poetry Club and while there won the John Billings Fiske Prize for Poetry, Thornton Wilder being one of the judges. She also won honors in English and was elected to Phi Beta Kappa.

After traveling in Ireland, Scotland, Iona, Aran Islands, England and France she returned to the University of Chicago to obtain her master's degree in English and submitted for her master's dissertation: "The Witty Lady in Shakespeare."

Then she entered the Dominican novitiate of St. Clara Convent, at Sinsinawa, Wisconsin, remaining at the academy there. Later she was sent to Yale University to work for her doctorate under the direction of the late Karl Young. Her dissertation this time was on the *Legenda Aurea* by James of Voragine. Since 1942 Sister Mary Jeremy is a member of the English department of Rosary College in River Forest, Illinois.

Her literary preferences are medieval and seventeenth-century poetry; among modern poets she especially likes Léonie Adams, Elinor Wylie, Jessica Powers, John Crowe Ransom, Hilaire Belloc, and Gerald Manly Hopkins (the latter as a person as well as a poet).

In music she is fond of sixteenth-century composers, especially Thomas Campion, and medieval hymns.

Sister Mary Jeremy began her literary career at Chicago Teachers College where she edited *The Normalite*. Her poems have appeared in the *Saturday Review of Literature, Poetry, Catholic World, America, Horn Book Magazine, The Sign, Ave Maria, College English, Spirit, University of Chicago Magazine* and the Chicago *Daily News*. Because of her admiration for Emily Brontë, Sister Mary Jeremy's poems in the Chicago *Daily News* were signed "Emily's Niece."

She has also published articles on medieval literature in *Speculum, Traditio, Modern Language Notes, Medieval Studies* and *Orate Fratres.*

In the Preface to her first book, *Dialogue with an Angel,* Raymond E. Larsson writes: "The talent of Sister Mary Jeremy is a fastidious talent, which eschews over-generosity of detail, superfluous emphasis, choosing reserve, exactitude, balance, symbol, image and development, detail inherent and indispensable."

Thomas Merton's criticism of *Dialogue with an Angel* is: "This volume of verse is, I think, one of the best that has come from the pen of any Catholic poet in America. The poems show a most respectable craftsmanship, and are a welcome relief from the sentimentality of so much religious verse. Familiar experiences are expressed with a new and individual intensity and with the objectivity of true art. Sister Jeremy's poems are the product of a very definite literary personality: sensitive, individual and strong. May God bless her and prosper all that she does for His glory!"

Other excerpts from reviews are: *The Saturday Review of Literature:* "rigor, candor, and grace" . . . New York *Times:* "spare but rich." Los Angeles *Tidings:* "The key metaphor of the understanding of her poems: a tree — strong, graceful, tall, shaken by every wind, but rooted secure." And William Rose Benét comments: "Sister Jeremy is a remarkable poet."   M. A. H.

Kathleen M. Joyce-Prendergast

When Kathleen Joyce was young she used to love to listen to her father talk about his father and his uncles, and their achievements in the literary world. It made her think how fine it must be to have one's name in print as an author. It gave her the ambition to write. She did not do anything about it, however, for several years.

Very soon after her school days, spent with Ursuline, Passionist, and Dominican nuns in County Tipperary where she was born, Kathleen Joyce married Mr. Prendergast. Three years later, she, her husband and a fourteen months old daughter went to New Jersey in America and remained there five years. Three years after her return to Ireland she did some writing, mostly on spiritual topics. Then one day a priest, her confessor, told her she could write a book and insisted that she should do so. "I laughed at him at first and told him it was an impossible project, but he kept insisting, with the result I wrote my first 'big' work of about one hundred and eighty thousand words, and after several rejections as a book, it eventually appeared in *The Irish Catholic* as a serial entitled *The Triumphant Lover.* Its popularity amazed me. Letters poured in from just everywhere. I had dedicated it, in my heart, to Jesus to Whom I owed, at that particular time, more than I could ever express in words — so, the laurels went to Him," writes Mrs. Joyce-Prendergast.

This was followed by another serial, *The Sheltered Rose*, of some sixty-five or seventy thousand words, which was accepted immediately by *St. Anthony's Annals*. Then appeared *Red Gables* for the *Irish Catholic*, followed up with *Swallows Rest*, also for that paper. Soon after, her serials were published in other magazines. She has had over two hundred poems published in various papers and magazines.

Her first book, "dressed in pale grey with a green spine and a gay little dust-jacket of white with my heroine watching a golden sunset on the hills, beside a big shady tree and in big letters the title: *This — My Land*, a novel by K. M. Joyce-Prendergast" gave her breathless joy and utter bewilderment. After going into a third edition, her publishers, Messrs. Gill & Son, asked her to write another book. She complied with *Vintage*, which was also a best seller. Their popularity seems to rest on the fact that they were so utterly Irish and composed of real life characters and genuine Irish background and scenic descriptions.

In 1946 she published, *Windyhill*, a novel centred around a beautiful old-world country mansion, and in 1951, *The Opening Way*, the concluding chapters of which were written at the famous Cistercian abbey of Mount Melleray in County Waterford. The silent beauty of that remote "City of God" is the subject for several chapters. Also, in 1951, appeared *Timmiekins*, a storybook for children.

Coming from a literary family, Mrs. Joyce-Prendergast intends to continue writing and to do it in praise of God, "in homage, and gratitude and love."   **M. A. H.**

Constance Julian 1863–

"My people were of pioneer stock and set out from England in the fifties when my grandparents sought to find in the new world a better outlook for their sons. They came as landtakers and had no interest in the gold discoveries that brought thousands of 'diggers' from the Old Land and America, for, as earnest followers of the revivals of Whitfield and Wesley they were imbued with the ideal of righteousness — the putting of first things first. In those days much of the Old Faith lingered amongst the would-be 'Reformers,'" writes Constance Julian.

Constance Julian was born on the 29th of November, 1863, at Merri Creek, a suburb of Melbourne, Australia, at her grandmother's home — her mother came from her ranch on the Loddon for that event. Her father and mother were both English, having come to Australia in their early days in the 1850's. The home in which Constance spent the first twelve years of her life was two hundred and fifty miles from the city and fifty miles from the nearest town — Bendigo, of gold-finding fame.

Her childhood was passed on distant "stations" (ranches the Americans would call them) on the wild plains. "They were the days when the aboriginals who still remained made their miamias on the near-by creeks and would bring rugs made of possum skins and dilly bags woven of grass in exchange for grapes and meat; days when kangaroo and emu raced on the treeless plains and the dingoes' howl was heard at night. Days, too, of the bullock dray and weekly coaches, when the telegraph and steam engine were the latest discoveries of science. A life that might have been lived on another planet, when it seemed that civilization had come to stay, that war and barbarism were of the past and that Queen Victoria was an institution." Well-nigh thirty years were spent at various distant homes where she was taught by governesses. "There were long and lonely days in those distant homes, relieved by the coming of the weekly coach with letters and newspapers keeping the far-off ranches in touch with the outer world. The newspapers of those days were of literary interest — for men of fine intelligence were the contributors and the days had not come when the commercialized descendants of the gold-diggers had swung people's minds to sport and pleasure at the sacrifice of higher things. Such was the background of my early days — one that influenced my life in later days when I lived in cities and learnt their ways — an atmosphere that was to keep me from seeking success in social circles, or from aiming at wealth or power. I have longed for the approbation of my fellow-beings — the finding among them of the imaginative understanding I found in Browning and Emerson — my bible for many years." A year or two was spent at a private school in Melbourne where she studied for the university entrance examination.

Later she took a position as a governess in Tasmania, but this work did not appeal to her. She returned to Victoria to open a little private school in a near-by township. "It was a pleasant experience," she says, "but not a successful one, for all my life I have neither had the concentration nor the commercial ability necessary for success. An idealist and dreamer, I never met with sympathy nor understanding from my good little Puritan mother and my unfulfilled longing for both wrought in me an inferiority complex from which I have suffered all my life. It was only in books I found the companionship I sought."

For years Miss Julian threw religion overboard and sought satisfaction in Zola and Haeckel and the Wilhelm Meister of Goethe, "till the innate need for belief drew me to Christian Science and Theosophy, and later to the Liberal Catholic Church which introduced me for the first time to the depth and beauty of the liturgy and the ritual. From these earnest seekers after truth, I was led to the Church by devious ways and reached the goal of my long pilgrimage, and to the certitude that it — and it alone — was the custodian of the full and Holy Catholic Faith. The others — good and earnest though they be —have fed their flocks with fragments of the Perfect Thing which they have 'picked and chosen' for themselves — all have chosen the shifting sand rather than the Rock foundation. I think that this realization comes more vividly to converts who have wandered for so long outside. They realize, more than some Catholics do, the tragedy of the 'Reformation.'" Constance Julian became a Catholic in 1927 when she was sixty-four years of age. She refers to her conversion as "the one great achievement of my life."

She has contributed to most of the Catholic papers in Australia and has had a book published by Bruce and Co., in America. She called it *Shadows Over English Literature* because "having found the Light," she says "I realized how tragic has been the effect of its loss on the writers of the English classics, and how the England they might have led back to the Truth has been disorientated by their adoption of an emasculated Christianity. Though late, I hope to publish a spiritual autobiography to tell others what that life has meant to me."   M. A. H.

Reverend Joseph Andrew Jungmann, S.J. 1889–

Father Joseph Jungmann was born on November 16, 1889 at Sand in Taufers, South Tyrol. He studied the humanities and theology in Brixen. After his ordination to the priesthood in 1913 he served for four years in his native diocese of Brixen as an assistant pastor. Then in 1917 he joined the Society of Jesus. Later he was sent to Innsbruck for further studies in philosophy and theology. Awarded a degree in 1923, he made additional studies in pedagogy, liturgics and history in Munich, Vienna and Breslau. Since 1925 he is a member of the theological faculty of the University of Innsbruck, first as a private lecturer, later as a professor of pastoral theology. He remained in this office up to the present time (1952) save for the period 1939–1945, at which time the theological faculty was dissolved — it being a part of the State University and discontinued by the National-Socialist rulers. Since 1926 Father Jungmann has been editor of the periodical *Zeitschrift für Katholische Theologie*.

The starting point for his studies and for his literary activities has always been pastoral theology, or, as he puts it, "the interest in the theological foundations of the care of souls." He is especially concerned with the questions: Why is the Christendom of our time, on the average, lacking in that ardor, that enthusiasm, that has been peculiar to it in the first centuries? Why do most of the Catholic Christians no longer consider it as joyful tidings rather than a sum of doctrines one has to believe, and duties one has to fulfill, in order to save one's soul?

The answer that thrust itself upon the mind of Father Jungmann, as a consequence of his many years of study of pastoral theology, is "obviously we are no longer conscious of the positive contents or, should

I say, the supernatural character of Christianity; and this is so because in religious instruction the dogma of Grace is taught in a much too abstract manner and which is also much too detached from the personal bestower of Grace, Jesus Christ."

This was the reason why his *"Dissertation ad Lauream"* in 1923 dealt with *"Die Lehre von der Gnade in der Katechese der ersten drei Jahrhunderte"* (The Dogma of Grace in the Catechism of the First Three Centuries). Father Jungmann's first published work tried then to handle the problem from the opposite side, namely, by a historical survey of the forms in which Christ's intercession remained in the conscience of religious people, and by showing facts which caused the gradual decrease of this consciousness; it was his work "Die Stellung Christi im Liturgischen Gebet" (The Place of Christ in Liturgical Prayers), which had been accepted for the *Liturgiegeschichtliche Forschungen* (Investigations into the History of Liturgy) by the Society for the Development of Liturgical Science at Maria Laach in 1925.

Then followed an attempt at a more systematic presentation of the aforesaid group of questions relative to pastoral theology. The book, published as a consequence of this study, *Die Frohbotschaft und Unsere Glaubensverkündigung (The Joyful Tidings and the Spread of Our Faith,* (1936), had to be withdrawn from the book market three weeks after publication, by order of Rome, upon the complaint of an auxiliary bishop, but it has never been condemned publicly. One of the principal phases of that book was later handled in an article printed separately: *Christus als Mittelpunkt religiöser Erziehung (Christ as the Center of Religious Education).*

From then on Father Jungmann's work was devoted to the history of liturgy. In 1932 he published *"Die lateinischen Bussriten in ihrer geschichtlichen Entwicklung"* (The Latin Rites of Penance in Their Historical Development). Then followed in 1941: *Gewordene Liturgie,* a collection of single essays dealing mainly with the history of the Mass and the ecclesiastical year, most of which had appeared in the *Zeitschrift für Katholische Theologie.* A series of lectures, *Die Liturgische Feier* (1939), was devoted to questions connected with the idea of liturgy and the essential laws of its forms. This book was translated into English and published by Pustet in 1941 under the title *Liturgical Worship.*

The book that won the highest approval of all was written during the National Socialist rule, when he was expelled from the university and forbidden to exercise any influence whatsoever upon the public as a writer. He was at that time chaplain of a community of nuns in a country place near Vienna. The book was a comprehensive historical picture of the liturgy of the Mass and was published in 1948 under the title *Missarum Sollemnia,* an explanation of the development of the Roman Mass. An English translation by Reverend Father Francis Brunner, C.SS.R., was published by Benziger Brothers in New York under the title *The Mass of the Roman Rite: Its Origins and Development.*

In the summer school of the University of Notre Dame in Indiana in 1949, Father Jungmann gave twenty-eight lectures under the heading, "Primitive Liturgy up to Gregory the Great."   N. L.

Mother Marie St. Justin. See Marie René-Bazin

Harnett Thomas Kane   1910–

Harnett T. Kane, the author of eleven books largely about his native South — all of them best sellers — was born in New Orleans, Louisiana, on November 8, 1910, the son of William J. and Anna (Hirt) Kane. After graduating A.B. from Tulane University in New Orleans in 1931, he did graduate work in sociology and history for the following year (1932–1933) at the same university.

He began newspaper work at the age of eighteen, while he was a sophomore in college, as a part time reporter on the New Orleans *Item*, working on the rewrite desk of the *Item* from 3:00 P.M. until midnight. Mr. Kane covered politics during the Long regime and knew Huey well. He says he was on "good enough" terms with him, although Huey tried to get him fired for breaking the fact that the late dictator wore silk pajamas, while he told people he slept in cotton nightshirts. He received two Rosenwald fund fellowships for the study of Louisiana history, 1942–43 and 1943–44. During the year 1943–44 he taught journalism at Loyola University, New Orleans, Louisiana.

During World War II he made hundreds of talks over the radio at army camps, hospitals and USO centers.

After seventeen years as a star reporter and correspondent, he decided to devote his full time to his own writing.

Each of Mr. Kane's books — his first was *Louisiana Hayride* (1941) — has been a greater success than the one before it. They have sold in the millions, in original editions, in reprints, foreign editions, etc., and have been serialized and condensed. He has been called "one of the important new writers of the South." According to the *Saturday Review of Literature*, his first book "catapulted him to recognition." Jonathan Daniels said: "Hardly any American writer has done so fine a job in the portraiture of his state as Harnett T. Kane of Louisiana." Bennett Cerf declared: "Mr. Kane is one of the few writers of today whose appearances bring people into the bookstores in crowds."

After *Louisiana Hayride*, which had the subtitle *The American Rehearsal for Dictatorship*, since it was the story of the Huey Long regime, came *Bayous of Louisiana*, in 1943. *Deep Delta Country* was published in 1944, and *Plantation Parade* in 1945. The latter is the story of the sugar and cotton mansions along the Mississippi and of the Creole planters who built them. A companion volume is *Natchez on the Mississippi* (1947), a lively, richly colored study of Natchez, Mississippi.

Other books are *New Orleans Woman* (1946) and *Bride of Fortune*

(1948), a biographical novel of Mrs. Jefferson Davis. For ten years he had worked on this latter book. He was in the middle of a dull afternoon of research when he came accidentally upon an exchange of love letters. "A man and a woman had written what they thought might be their last messages. They were written in anguish, with bullets flying about them and children crying on the floor. They were written after twenty-five years of marriage and they were love letters of the most tender and beautiful relationship." (Fanny Butcher in the *Literary Spotlight*.)

Mr. Kane began seeking out old people who had known Varina Howell Davis, and digging in archives for material about Jefferson Davis. The actual writing of the book, he said, took thirteen months, from what in Louisiana they call "kin see to kain't see" — from dawn until dusk.

Queen New Orleans: City by the River (1949) gives all phases of New Orleans life through Mr. Kane's own observations and experiences.

Pathway to the Stars (1950) is a novel based upon the life of John McDonough "who amassed a huge fortune in and around New Orleans, where he arrived from Baltimore in 1800. He never married, although he is supposed to have had two romances. When he died he left his enormous Louisiana estate to the schools of his native Baltimore." He asked "as a favor" that children sometimes drop flowers on his grave. "Now," Mr. Kane said, "every year more than 125,000 children do him that favor."

The Scandalous Mrs. Blackford (1951), written in collaboration with Victor Leclerc, is the fabulous story of Harriet Blackford's love affair with the Grand Duke Nicholas of Russia. Like all of Harnett Kane's best selling historical novels this story is authentic, based upon facts uncovered by the Russian historian, Victor Leclerc. It reached the national best seller lists within a week, and has been sold to moving pictures.

In October, 1951, Mr. Kane published his latest book, *Gentlemen, Swords and Pistols*, based on the duels and fabulous duellists of the South, and covering all parts of his native region. Mr. Kane is now at work on a novel based on the life of Mrs. Robert E. Lee, due in 1952 — *The General's Wife*.

The secret formula behind Kane's literary success is a simple one — talent plus hard work. He describes his own philosophy by saying, "I believe in the application of the seat of the pants to the seat of the chair and not in 'the contemplation of his novel,' a literary paraphrase of the more anatomically described idleness of the Buddha."

In spite of his dedication to hard work, Mr. Kane possesses natural gayety and is a born raconteur.

Leonard Lyons in the New York *Post* declared that Harnett Kane told Father Edward Murphy, author of *Scarlet Lily*, about his television appearance on George Putnam's program, when he appeared with a St. Bernard dog in a Travelers' Aid Society appeal: "The dog was a ham," Kane complained. "He kept pushing me aside and jockeying for the center of the stage." "I'll bet," said Father Murphy, "that that dog is saying the same thing about you to his dog friends."

M. A. H.

Reverend Otto Karrer   1888–

Father Karrer's first important publication was a study of St. Francis Borgia. It was so excellent that Cardinal Ehrle, on reading it, successfully urged the author to go to Rome to study Church History in the Vatican archives.

In Rome, Father Karrer discovered that he "was not so much interested in pure science." His true vocation as a writer and scholar was hagiography. He wrote on Newman, on mysticism, on the *Religions of Mankind*, on various topics, and "always found more educating power in living and dead personalities than in abstract studies." Newman had appealed to him and influenced him because of his art in relating science to life. As pastor in Lucerne, Switzerland, where he returned in 1925 and lived with his mother (died 1947), Father Karrer "employed theology, history, and psychology (in terms of the experiences of everyday life) as a means to teach the common people." He found that "doctrines can be of help only if they are closely in touch with life itself."

Pastoral experience deepened his conviction about the good that results from studying the lives of the Church's great heroes. He set himself to write of St. Augustine, St. Francis of Assisi, Thomas a'Kempis, St. Ignatius Loyola, and St. Francis de Sales. Referring to the time spent at other work and writing, he says: "During all these years I still kept my great predilection for biographical religious writing, psychological studies of the lives of the saints. Whatever the great personalities of Christianity were thinking of, were fighting for, or were realizing in their lives, seems to me of greater value in forming Catholic opinion than any abstract learning and research." Father Karrer's *St. Francis of Assisi: The Legends and Lauds* was published in this country (1948), and was well received as "a unique and valuable work."

As a Catholic philosopher of religious trends, Father Karrer watches with interest and sympathy the various attempts at oecumenical assemblies of non-Catholic Christians. In these Protestant efforts after unity of Christendom he finds a challenge for ourselves. "The world today," he says, "needs a spiritual preparation and we Catholics can only give our treasures to our fellow-Christians if we have the knowledge and conviction derived from the Bible. This means the propagation of the Bible. And we can do it only with new and amply explained translations. That is what I have been working on now for years, hoping to bring the peoples of the world nearer to our aims." His *New Testament* (German translation with comments) was published in September, 1950, in Munich.

The son of peasant parents, Otto Karrer was born in Ballrechten (Baden) in 1888. He spent his childhood in his home-village in the Schwarzwald, in the upper regions of the Rhine, between Basel and

Freiburg. On the advice of his village pastor he went to study in Freiburg University. He decided to take theology. Going to the Canisianum, theological college of the Jesuits at Innsbruck (Austria), he met students from all over the world and among them Americans. On the outbreak of World War I, he went to Feldkirch, and taught there in a Jesuit College until 1918. Next he continued his theological studies at Valkenburg, Bonn, and Munich, being ordained in 1920.

After the publication of his study of St. Francis Borgia he went to Rome to study history. In 1925 he returned to Lucerne, Switzerland where he carried on his pastorate and wrote several articles and books which were published by *Ars Sacra*, in Munich, and by Herder (Freiburg). Father Karrer's researches into the history of mysticism resulted in his book: *Textgeschichte der Mystik* in three volumes, and was followed by studies on Eckhart, the great medieval mystic. "This work of mine," he claims, "played an important role in the defense of the Church against the attacks of A. Rosenberg's nationalistic 'Mythos.' "

From mysticism, Father Karrer turned to the history of religions, *Das Religiöse in der Menschheit* which was translated by E. I. Watkin and published in London and New York in 1936 under the title, *Religions of Mankind*. "In this work," the author says, "I tried to show the way to the Catholic Church to all those who are lost in the chaos of various religious teachings. The book was favorably received and assisted a great number of wavering people."

Among the published works of Father Karrer are the following: *Franz von Borja* (1921); *Textgeschichte der Mystick* (3 vols.); *Meister Eckhart; Das Religiöse in der Menschheit und das Christentum; Seele der Frau; Schicksal und Würde des Menschen; Unsterblichkeitsglaube; St. Matthew's Gospel; Geheime Offenbarung; Briefen des hl. Ignatius; Augustinus das religiöse Leben; Studien über Franz von Assisi* (1948); as well as text-books on Francis de Sales, Cardinal Newman, Thomas a'Kempis, Juliana of Norwich etc. and the newest work, *The New Testament* (text and explanation).

Father Karrer's literary activities were strictly curtailed from 1936 until the end of the war by a Nazi prohibition against the publication of his books in Germany. The book that he regards as his most personal achievement, based on his own research and discovery, helped by the road signs of the Christian past, is his work on the *Religions of Mankind, Das Religiöse in der Menschheit und das Christentum.*

E. B. B.

Oksana Stepanovna Kasenkina
1896–

The world was startled one summer day in 1948 when a Russian schoolteacher jumped from a third-story window of the Soviet Consulate in New York City. Her name is Mrs. Oksana Stepanovna Kasenkina and she tells her reason in her autobiography, *Leap to Freedom*, 1949.

Born of pious parents on June 24, 1896 in Kamenskaya of the Donets region in Russia, Oksana Stepanovna Kasenkina was baptized in the Russian Orthodox Church. Upon completing her high school studies in Kamenskaya in 1914, she received her "certificate of maturity" which qualified her to teach. Her first assignment as a teacher was in a school in the Chuhynsicy Khutor which was part of the Lugansk group of Khutors. From 1914 to 1917 she taught in the elementary schools in the Donets region. The year following, she spent in the Ukraine in the Kharkov region. Then came three years (1918–1921) of study at the Lomonosov University in Moscow, where she specialized in the natural sciences. In order to earn some money to meet her expenses and also to avoid a break in her teaching career, lest she lose out in her pension, she taught on Sundays and in the evenings. While she was at the university she met and married Dementy Kasenkina. The marriage took place after vespers in a little village church to the west of Moscow. From 1921 to 1937 she taught general science in a high school in Slavyansk. Her next assignment was in the Donets region, in the high school of Tuchkovo, a village seventy-five kilometers west of Moscow. Here she taught agricultural biology. Then she was evacuated to the city of Gorki to work in a hospital as a nurse for two years (1941–1943) and became director of an evening high school for evacuated children. The following year she was appointed director of the experimental agricultural high school of Podol, a suburb of Moscow. From 1944 to 1946 she taught in high school 218 in Moscow and also served as a method inspector for the teachers in the Timiriazev section of Moscow. She said "deplorable conditions obtained in all." Then on June 14, 1946 she arrived in New York City to teach the natural sciences in the high school of the General Soviet Consulate.

Her two years as a teacher of the children of the consulate members is graphically told in her autobiography *Leap to Freedom*. When the film, *The Iron Curtain*, was shown in New York she decided to see it and it helped her make up her mind to escape. Some talks with an elderly lady she met in a park, as well as her conversation with an elderly Russian gentleman who spoke to her on the street and a young man who spoke Russian to her in a park, strengthened her in her resolve to escape. Through Mr. Weinbaum and Mr. Zensinof, plans were made to take her to the Tolstoy Foundation near Nyack, New York, where she met

Alexandra Lvovna Tolstoy, the daughter of the author. She was received kindly and was assured she was among friends. Little difficulties arose, however, and fear gripped Mrs. Kasenkina. In this state, she wrote a hasty note to Consul Lomakin, "Would he come to take me back?" The Consul came and she and his companions left quickly. As they left, the car was stoned by some of the one hundred inmates. Soon after she arrived at the consulate she learned she "had done a monstrously wrong and futile thing in returning." Her departure from the Tolstoy Foundation attracted the attention of the American people and the interest spread to other lands. From her window she could see many people milling about on the Sixty-first Street side of the Consulate. Her incarceration became more and more unbearable. The moment of decision came. She ran to the window, climbed out, and jumped, aiming for a telephone cable to break her fall. She was taken to Roosevelt Hospital and spent ninety-nine days receiving treatment for a stomach hemorrhage, a fractured vertebra, dislocated and fractured bones in the right leg, a fractured pelvis and compound fracture of the right kneecap.

It was only after she had fully recovered that she realized what efforts Americans made in her behalf. "The three people who acted to liberate me," she writes, "were the two lawyers, Peter Hoguet and C. Dickerman Williams, who conceived the plan of appealing for a writ of habeas corpus to liberate me from the Consulate, and Christopher Emmet, Chairman of the Board of Common Cause who asked for and obtained that writ. Mr. Hoguet took charge of the difficult task of serving the writ on Consul Lomakin in person."

While in the hospital she requested Father Marianus Horishny of St. George's Ukrainian Catholic Church in New York to visit her, which he did several times. She decided to return to the original faith of her ancestors, the Catholic Church. Mrs. Kasenkina, before her conversion, belonged to the Russian Orthodox Church.

"We displaced persons," she writes, "believe we were saved by the hand of Providence so that the world could learn from us the truths of the horrors in the godless Soviet Union. We pray for our suffering homeland and believe in the near future in acquiring freedom from Communist despotism, and its adjuring priesthood (Russian Orthodox Church) who have forgotten their vows and duties."

Mrs. Kasenkina has made her home in Long Island, New York, where she lives alone in her four room apartment. Besides learning English, she is writing a novel under the title *The Red Devil.* Asked who the Red Devil is, she replied: "Stalin, of course, who else?" "The novel," she said, "will be mostly about life in Russia." She added, "I only write when I feel like writing; that is the way with novelists."

M. A. H.

Reverend Alan Keenan, O.F.M.
1920–

For five years, Father Alan Keenan has been working among neurotics. His experience with them prompted him to write his one book, *Neuroses and Sacraments*. This he wrote during the summer holidays of 1949.

Alan Keenan was born in the Irish slum quarter of Liverpool on the twenty-first of February, 1920. He is the son of Patrick Keenan and Esther (Coughlan) Keenan, and was educated by the Irish Christian Brothers of St. Edward's College, Liverpool and at St. Bernardine's College, Buckingham, a Franciscan preparatory college. In 1936 he entered the novitiate of the Franciscan Order and was professed the following year. Upon completing his studies in philosophy and theology, he was ordained a priest in 1944. That same year Father Keenan's superiors sent him to Cambridge University to take a degree in science and while there he spent most of his spare time playing a large number of games. Once he represented the university at soccer and played a number of games for the town football team. The town supporters used to call him "The sporting parson." For twelve months he was the unofficial chaplain for the U.S.A.A.F. Wing Headquarters at Sawiston, near Cambridge, during World War II.

At the University his subject was biology. "With no scientific background, I found it hard going," writes Father Keenan, "and kept at it only because my superiors wished me to do so. My happiest recollection there was degree day — not because I obtained my degree but because on that day I burned all my notes out at Grantchester where Rupert Brooke wrote his poems. I burned them with a co-worker, a Jew. I should have known better than to burn these notes, for I was sent in 1947 to teach boys science in a Franciscan school, St. Bonaventure's, in the East End of London. Here I am at the moment (1951)." He teaches from nine to four daily.

His other occupations are giving sermons, lectures and ministerial work. Occasionally, he speaks for the Catholic Evidence Guild in Hyde Park and in 1950 he gave the Sunday morning Lenten course of sermons in Westminster Cathedral.   M. A. H.

Daniel Lawrence Kelleher   1883–

D. L. Kelleher was born in Cork City, Ireland, in 1883, and is an alumnus of the Irish Christian Brothers' College there. Entering University College, Cork (then called Queen's College) he graduated B.A. in 1905. His university career revealed his interest in letters, for he not only founded Q.C.C., the first undergraduates' magazine to be published there, but he was also its first editor. While catering for the cultural interests of his fellow students (he also founded the College Philosophical Society) he did not neglect their more material interests for, through his efforts, a Students' Dining Club which extended the corporate life of the students was established.

After graduation he taught for some years in London and Liverpool but he threw up his position and joined a tourist agency. In 1912 he went abroad to work, mostly in Switzerland. After the outbreak of the First World War he returned to Ireland in 1915 and became modern languages master in the high school, Dublin. Three years later he joined the editorial staff of the New Catholic Press at Manchester. In 1922 he again resumed his travels and from then until 1928 he journeyed extensively through Italy, France, Switzerland and Spain. At the same time he acted as special representative for the *Herald* chain of Catholic newspapers, covering notable Catholic celebrations and ceremonies on the Continent. In 1930 he married Hilda Margaret Lacy of Wallasey.

His combined literary and tourist experience made him an ideal choice for the newly-founded Irish Tourist Association. In 1929 he was commissioned to undertake publicity work on behalf of his native country. By writing and lecturing he made the beauties of Ireland widely known in Britain. A year later he joined the staff and was subsequently appointed London manager of the association.

Despite the demands of a busy life, he soon became prominent in Irish literary circles in London and took a special interest in the National University of Ireland Club.

For the past forty years Mr. Kelleher has been prominent in the world of letters in Ireland. Best known for his poetry and prose, perhaps, he is also a playwright of distinction. All his literary work, written in a highly picturesque style, is informed by strong national sentiment and deep religious conviction, for he is a Catholic Irishman in the full sense of the term. Much of his finest work has appeared in the pages of *The Father Mathew Record* and *The Capuchin Annual*, to which he is a regular contributor.

His first volume of poetry, *Poems Twelve a Penny*, appeared in 1911. Two years later he published another collection under the same title and in 1920 there appeared the third and last book in this series. In the latter year the Talbot Press in Dublin issued his *Cork's Own Town*, a long romance in verse written in the rich vernacular of his native Cork in which the author's sense of humor is apparent in almost every line. This poem under the title of "Padua" was printed privately at Leeds, England, in 1924 and, exactly ten years later rewritten and enlarged, it appeared in the pages of *The Capuchin Annual*, the leading Irish literary magazine.

His religious poetry is worthy of special mention. Characterized by fervent religious feeling, it is marked by extreme simplicity of diction and a fine restraint of style. In their charming imagery, profundity of thought and sincerity of expression, his sacred poems are evocative of the wonderful hymns of the medieval Franciscan poets which have been absorbed by the Church into her liturgy. In 1928, having been invited by Ernest Benn, the London publisher, to compile a collection of Christmas carols, he inserted one of his own poems anonymously in the anthology. This poem, *The Five Lesser Joys of Mary*, achieved almost instantaneous success. It was set to music by Peter Warlock, the renowned British composer, and has since achieved widespread popularity.

Benn also published Mr. Kelleher's *A Poet Passes* in 1928 and his *Christian Anthology* was published by the Cresset Press of London.

He is also an accomplished prose-writer. In his *Paris; Lake Geneva; Lucerne and Lugano; Biarritz, Lourdes and the Basque Country; Italy* — five books written for George Lunn's Travel Guide series — he has managed to convey by the charm of his writing something of the beauty of these renowned places. His *The Glamor of Manchester* appeared in 1920. His works on Irish life and history include *The Glamor of Dublin, The Glamor of Cork, The Glamor of the West, Ireland of the Welcomes* (1930), *It's Ireland* (1932), *Lovelights of Ireland,* and *Great Days with O'Connell* (1929).

Mr. Kelleher first came into prominence as a playwright when his *Stephen Grey* was produced at the famous Abbey Theatre in Dublin in 1910 during the heyday of the Irish Literary Revival. In the same year the Irish Society of the University of Liverpool put on his *A Contrary Election* (for production by their dramatic group). *The Last Hostel* (written in collaboration with T. C. Murray) was staged in his native city of Cork in 1918. *Her Dowry* was published in *The Dublin Magazine*. Amongst his radio plays, *Prince of the North, The Normans Have Landed,* and *Great Days with Daniel O'Connell* — all broadcast over Radio Eireann, the Irish national broadcasting network, won considerable favor.

K. Mac G.

Reverend James Gregory Keller, M.M. 1900–

The old Chinese proverb, "Better to light one candle than to curse the darkness," is the guiding motto of the Christophers, and their founder, Father James G. Keller, M.M.

Born at Oakland, California, on June 27, 1900, he was educated at St. Patrick's Seminary, Menlo Park, California, before entering the Catholic Foreign Mission Society of America, popularly known as Maryknoll, in 1921. Upon the completion of his studies at Maryknoll Seminary and the Catholic University of America, he was ordained to the priesthood in 1925.

After several years as associate editor of *The Field Afar* magazine, Father Keller founded the Christophers as "an aid in restoring fundamental Christian principles to American public and private life." His purpose is "to change the world for the better by showing average individuals how they can make their influence for good be felt in vital fields, particularly those of government, education, labor, management, writing (newspapers, magazines, books, radio, motion pictures, television), social service and library work.

"Less than one per cent of humanity has been causing the major troubles which have wracked the globe for the past thirty years," says Father Keller. "This handful — no matter what their labels — shares a militant hatred for the basic truths upon which this nation and all Christian civilization are founded (and without which they cannot endure), that each and every human being shares the common Fatherhood of God, deriving his rights from God, not from the State. The aim of the Christophers is to get another one per cent to go as apostolic workers — as Christophers, or Christ-bearers — into the same six fields," explains Father Keller, "and strive with missionary zeal to restore the fundamental truth which the other one per cent are working furiously to eliminate. It is far more important to get workers of good *in* than it is to get workers of evil *out*, essential as the latter is. Positive, constructive action is needed." Although under Catholic auspices, many Protestants and Jews are among the supporters of the movement.

On March 1, 1947, Father Keller started a book contest to stimulate writing in accord with Christian principles. Theatrical producers and drama critics encouraged the Christophers to launch a drama contest along the same lines. The two contests attracted a total of 2,432 manuscripts — 1,784 books and 648 plays. It was estimated that if all the manuscripts were placed on top of one another it would make a pile six hundred and twelve feet high. Among the writers were twenty-three Protestant clergymen. All entrants maintained full publishing and movie rights to their manuscripts. The First Book Prize of $15,000 went to George Locke Howe, an architect and a Protestant, for his Nazi spy novel. The First Drama Prize ($50,000) was won by Miss Rosemary Casey of Pittsburgh. Six prizes totalling $40,000 were awarded.

Nine years ago (1943) Father Keller had an experience he will never forget. He wrote about Maryknoll's missionary men. Someone suggested that his literary effort would make a good book. A man from Scribner's said he could get Meyer Berger of the New York *Times* to help. Meyer Berger on reading the manuscript remarked: "This is a gold mine." He agreed to collaborate with Father Keller. The book appeared in 1943 under the title *Men of Maryknoll*. Father Keller in an interview with Harvey Breit (New York *Times*, September 25, 1949) declared: "When I wrote my first book, *Men of Maryknoll*, I was wanting to do some good and much of the credit for those stories goes to your paper's Meyer Berger. I was like a man who wants to make a wonderful dinner but couldn't cook well enough. Well, Meyer Berger supplied what I lacked. As I worked along with him, I learned a lot about writing."

Then came *The Priest and a World Vision* (1946), a plea to priests to broaden their zeal. This was followed by *You Can Change the World*, in 1948. This book gives a positive approach to the problems of the day. Its sales have passed the 100,000 mark. A Baptist businessman bought 10,000 copies to distribute. The New York *Daily News* told its 2,000,000 readers in an editorial: "The just published Keller book, *You Can Change the World*, strikes us as a gold mine of practical tips on how to move in on this battle (for the world) and make your punches register." On this book Father Keller had as his collaborator Charles Oxton, free lance writer and member of the Catholic Institute of the Press.

In 1949 Father Keller compiled a book of brief modern parables under the title *Three Minutes a Day*, one for each day of the year. When Father Keller had shown the galleys of this book to Bob Hope, then in a hospital — Bob Hope read a bit of it — he was in great pain at the time — then looked up and said, "Gee, Father, this is great stuff. After all, three minutes a day is little enough to *ad lib* with your conscience." Each page of these simple moral lessons can be read in three minutes or less.

Father Keller's other books, *One Moment Please* (1950), *Careers That Change Your World* (1950), *Government Is Your Business* (1951), also concern the Christopher Movement. His booklet, "You can be a Christopher," was translated by a Chinese non-Christian member of a strict Buddhist sect.

In addition to his writing, Father Keller is devoting his energy to motion picture work and lectures. Through a series of thirty films explaining all phases of the Christopher Movement, in March of Time style, to cost about one million dollars, he plans to spur people to more active citizenship and bring his message into every community in the nation. Leo McCarey, who suggested the series directed the first film, "You Can Change the World." Among the Hollywood stars who offered their services free for the first movie are: Bob Hope, Spencer Tracy, Loretta Young, Rosalind Russell, Jack Benny, Irene Dunne, Jeanne Crain and Jimmy Durante.

Father Keller is also planning to open fifty Christopher Career

Guidance Schools throughout the country. Among the subjects are: "You Can Change the World," which will serve as an introduction to the series; "What You Should Know About Parliamentary Law"; "Playing a Vital Role as a Government Worker"; "Library Work"; Introduction to Short Story Writing"; "Industrial Relations and Labor-Management"; "Radio and Television Script Writing." The series will be based on Father Keller's books which expand the Christopher philosophy.

Now in his fifty-second year, this dynamic personality looks and acts like a much younger man. Courageously and with good humor he labors tirelessly to spread good here on earth.   M. A. H.

Reverend Bernard J. Kelly, C.S.Sp. 1910–

Father Bernard Kelly's spiritual books, which have averaged one a year, and which have won for him the degree of D.Litt. of Duquesne University, Pittsburgh, are written according to an enlightened plan of which he tells, in referring to his first work *The Seven Gifts of the Holy Ghost.* "My method in writing it (a method I have followed more or less closely ever since)," Father Kelly says, "was to read all that St. Thomas wrote on it and allied subjects, as well as some of the principal commentators and any important works or articles I could lay hands on. I followed this up by reading the New Testament from beginning to end to see what light it threw on the problem or how it could be used to illustrate it. This preliminary work done, I thought out the matter afresh in my own way, and tried to present it in a simple and reasonably modern dress." Father Kelly adds, by way of comment, "one of the disadvantages of rethinking a subject and presenting it in a new form is that an occasional reader takes for granted that the writer has spun the whole thing out of his own head and is ignorant of the accepted elements of the questions he is writing about."

Born in Dublin, Ireland, in 1910, Bernard Kelly received his early education from the Christian Brothers. He completed his secondary schooling at Rockwell College, Tipperary, winning a scholarship there. In 1920 he entered the novitiate of the Holy Ghost Fathers, and after his profession he was sent to University College, Dublin. He won scholarships at the end of each of his three years at the university and he took his bachelor's degree in mental science with first class honors in 1933, capturing the Pierce Malone Prize in mental and moral science.

After a year's teaching at Blackrock College, Dublin, he was sent to Fribourg University, Switzerland, where he took a doctor's degree in theology. The theological faculty at Fribourg, being in the hands of the Dominican Fathers, their courses centered around the *Summa* of St. Thomas. Father Kelly's admiration for the Angelic Doctor grew apace. "I have made it my aim," he writes, "both in what I have written and what I have spoken to give voice to the mind of St. Thomas to the best of my ability. In tackling new problems I have always endeavored to approach them from what would have been St. Thomas' angle."

From Fribourg, Father Kelly returned to Kimmage College, Dublin in 1939 to teach philosophy and later theology. For four years he taught patrology and homiletics, then, in 1949 he was appointed to the Missionary Vicariate of Onitsha, Southern Nigeria.

During his teaching years at Kimmage College, Father Kelly directed the famous Kimmage Choir which broadcast liturgical music over Radio Eireann. Under his baton, the choir, in addition to plain chant, did classical polyphony and modern music. The recordings of liturgical music, made by Father Kelly, are used by Radio Eireann as a regular feature.

As a side line, among his many occupations, Father Kelly wrote theological articles in Irish for the *Irish Ecclesiastical Record*. "In this connection," he writes, "I published a glossary of theological terms, gathered from old Irish printed sources." An ardent Gael, Father Kelly believes that "the Irish language, if fostered in the spirit of our forefathers, would strengthen the faith in Ireland. As English would never cease to be at least the second official language, there is no danger that the revival of Irish would prevent us from contributing our quota to the work of converting the English-speaking world."

Among the books published by Father Bernard Kelly are: *The Seven Gifts of the Holy Ghost* (1941); *The Sacraments in Daily Life* (1942); *Thy Kingdom Come* (1943); *The Armor of Christ* (1948); *First Steps in the Religious Life* (1948); *Catholic Morality* (1948); *The Mother of the Saviour* (1949) (translated from the French of P. Garrigou-Lagrange O.P.); *Progress in the Religious Life* (1950), and *God, Man, and Satan* (1950).

"In the books I have written," Father Kelly writes, "I have aimed at being of some practical assistance to souls, with the help of God's grace. For that reason I have always kept theory and polemics in the background and when adopting one side in the argument I have tried not to delay over pros and cons. I have endeavored, too, to be traditional — even old-fashioned — in the substance of what I had to say, while being up-to-date in its expression. In the spiritual life as in everything else, there is such a thing as unbalanced enthusiasm. A forgotten point, or a neglected one, is sometimes proposed as if it were the only one of any importance, and the bulk of beliefs and practices which people hold dear are passed over as secondary. While saying the new thing, whenever I thought it needed saying, I have always tried to deepen my reader's appreciation of the things with which he was or was likely to be familiar. I have never been able to fall in line with the writers who speak as if the ages immediately preceding our own were off the right track of spirituality. I believe that, more than they think, they are missing the spirit of those ages simply because it expressed itself in a way which is not that of our time."

In 1949, Father Kelly was elected to the Gallery of Living Catholic Authors.   E. B. B.

Michael Kent. See *Beatrice Bradshaw Brown*

Reverend Neil Kevin   1903–

Father Neil Kevin was born in Templemore, Co. Tipperary, Ireland, in 1903. He was educated at the Cistercian College, Roscrea, at Saint Patrick's College, Thurles and at Maynooth College where he was ordained and took a postgraduate degree in English Language and Literature and received an M.A. degree. In 1932 he was appointed Professor of English Language and Literature at Maynooth College, a position which he still fills. His first book, *I Remember Maynooth*, was published in 1937. It came out under the pen-name of Don Boyne, the anonymity as well as the engaging combination of light and serious writing making it first quite a sensation amongst clerical readers, and later a book in which lay readers began to take considerable interest. Two editions with additional chapters appeared subsequently. A recent writer on Maynooth College has said of Father Kevin's book: "The book which has claims to being rated the Maynooth classic is *I Remember Maynooth* by Neil Kevin, of which the third edition appeared in 1944. For Maynooth men this has become and will remain a sort of second breviary, and for anyone who wishes to understand the Maynooth atmosphere and ethos it is absolutely indispensable."

For his second book Neil Kevin turned to such a small inland Irish town as he himself had grown up in. The book, *I Remember Karrigeen*, brings into focus a bit of that more usual, everyday Ireland which is generally rated not "typically" Irish enough for export and does not appear in the prevailing fiction and the tourist guides. *Karrigeen* is the remains of a garrison town since the days of the English occupation. There are no shillelaghs or red petticoats in this little town but there is diversity of interesting character and the author borrows space quite a bit for reflections of his own upon that scene. Neil Kevin's third book appeared in 1948. This was *No Applause in Church*. Lightly-penned but serious and semi-religious, the book adds up to a series of reflections that are in no way "churchy" on Christian and natural virtues, a sort of bright treatise on everyday profundities. Excerpts have been republished in journals of all persuasions. The shrewdness and the humorous reflection that distinguished the other two books has here its best field for operating, and while it has not overtaken the Maynooth book in popularity, the reviewers have considered it Father Kevin's best.

Robert Wendelin Keyserlingk
1905–

"Somebody once teased us that in our family the blue blood ran out in ink" writes Count Robert Keyserlingk, the journalist, in his book, *Unfinished History* (p. 248).

He was born in St. Petersburg, Russia, on November 2, 1905 "to the sound of revolutionary gunfire in the city's streets." "As my father told me," he says "the doctor arrived late because of mob disturbances; so my mother had to cope with the situation alone."

In 1916 his father, who had been a naval officer of the Imperial Russian navy, came out of retirement to serve in the First World War when it broke out. The family fled to Japan. There Robert Keyserlingk attended St. Joseph's College in Yokohama from 1917 to 1918 and came into contact with Catholics for the first time. "Lest the good Fathers (Marianists) might unduly influence me, my younger brother who was with me, and my sister studying at the Sacred Heart School in Tokyo, we were sent next year to the Canadian Academy in Kobe, a school run by the Methodist Mission of Ontario." Three years later he was in China to finish up at the Shanghai Public School, a Masonic foundation, with senior matriculation in 1922. On completing his schooling, he entered a leading Shanghai commercial house as shipping clerk in a very junior position.

In 1925 he went to Canada to work as a logger and then as a fisherman on the coast of British Columbia. With the money he earned, he took courses in economics at the University of British Columbia and was graduated with honors in 1929. That same year he started his career as a full-time journalist, working as a correspondent for the United Press, first in Berlin, then as bureau manager in Zurich. He remained with that organization for nearly twenty years. In 1936 he was made general manager of the British United Press, an affiliate of the United Press, and in 1942 became managing director. He resigned in 1948 to found Campion Press.

On December 1, 1931 he married Baroness Sigrid von der Recke, another Balt, whose parents had been murdered by the Bolsheviks. They have six children.

Asked why he became a Catholic he answered: "I think the most accurate answer would be: I could not help it. But grace did not descend with sudden enlightenment as in the case of St. Paul. Far from it. The voyage was long and sometimes imperceptible. Much of it I ascribe to my devout Lutheran parents, who had given me the simplicity of their God-loving and God-fearing example. My greatest surprise was the extent to which an average interested Protestant like myself was armed with a 'protective prejudice' against Catholicism which had no basis in fact.

"I could write pages on these misconceptions. I firmly believed, for example, as vast numbers of Protestants believe, that Catholics are convinced that a priest can give a fully effective absolution, irrespective of the state of mind, penitence, and contrition on the part of the sinner.

"As I came to rid myself of a number of erroneous and derogatory notions on Catholicism, numberless questions which I had been asking myself found, for the first time, their reasonable and natural answer. . . . One day my oldest boy came back from school. He gave us a poser. In church the boy had been told one thing. His teacher, also an Anglican, had contradicted the minister with another view held by Anglicans of the more 'Protestant' trend. Whose authority were we to undermine — the teacher's or the preacher's? I said to my wife as casually as I could: 'You know, these problems would not arise if we were Catholics. I am not surprised at religion disappearing out of the lives of children when they are unable to get clear answers.'

"Imagine my surprise when my wife shot back: 'Yes, I have also been thinking about that. Four hundred years away from the Catholic Church has certainly not helped us any.'

"That same week we all began taking instructions, and two months later (Holy Saturday, 1946) the family, united as never before, was received into the Church." (*The Sign*, March 1951, pp. 17–19.)

Fourteen months later he resigned his high salaried position as managing director of the British United Press to found with Murray Ballantyne, Canada's national news weekly, the *Ensign*, "on whose masthead we proudly carry the words of Pope Pius XII: 'Can there be anything nobler than to unfurl the Ensign of the King before those who have abandoned it?' Today I can definitely answer — no!"

The first issue rolled off the presses on October 30, 1948. It is printed in tabloid form with a national edition running to twenty-four pages. It covers foreign news, domestic news, religious news, women's news, sports, books, editorials, comics and syndicated columns. It adheres rigorously to Catholic principles.

In 1948 Robert Keyserlingk published *Unfinished History* which he says in the Introduction "is an attempt to show in concrete terms of one family and one man the sweep of social, political and economic change that has surged over the world in the last forty years and to analyze the cause of these changes, not in terms of the rise of a Lenin or a Hitler, but in more fundamental terms of the nature of man as a creature of God, formed of memories and traditions and group ties more than he is modified by the accidental circumstances in which he lives." The problems of World War I are still held over as *unfinished business*.   M. A. H.

Benedict Kiely 1919–

In appraising the character and work of Benedict Kiely, who is prominent among present-day Ireland's young writers, one has to take note of his belonging to a very glorious and beautiful Northern county, Tyrone. An Irishman very often belongs to the county of his birth first, and only after that to his country as a whole. The honor of his county is a vital consideration with him, and the sufferings of his county are personal griefs. Benedict Kiely certainly has deeply at heart Tyrone's honor and Tyrone's great woe. To glorify his county, he wrote a brilliant book about a great but forgotten Tyrone writer, William Carleton; to help undo his county's misfortune he wrote against "partition" which leaves Tyrone in exile from the rest of Ireland. And in between these books he told in a novel, *Land Without Stars*, about life in an Ulster town with an interlude in West Donegal. "What I was trying to get," he says, "was the atmosphere of the town at the beginning of the war."

His critical study of William Carleton, under the title *Poor Scholar*, was a brilliant and romantic achievement. *Eason's Bulletin* states: "The writing of the book was," the author tells us, "the fulfillment of the only ambition that he ever allowed himself to possess. A boy at school in his native Tyrone, already wanting to write something, and reading in serialized form in a local newspaper Carleton's novel *Fardorougha, the Miser*, he decided that some day a Tyrone man would write a book about the greatest novelist that Tyrone ever produced, and one of the greatest novelists that Ireland has given to the English language." It was not the first time that a boyish impulse fructified, in later life, in a great creation.

Benedict Kiely was born in 1919 in the pretty town of Dromore, Co. Tyrone. His father was Thomas Kiely; his mother's maiden name was Sarah A. Gormley. His early schooling was at the Christian Brothers' at Omagh (Co. Tyrone). Subsequently he took a degree at the National University, Dublin, and soon began to work on *The Standard*, a Dublin weekly, as feature writer and film critic. From *The Standard* he went to the very important Dublin daily, the *Irish Independent*, as a member of the editorial staff. Meanwhile he began to contribute to various Irish and English reviews, including *The Irish Bookman*, and Capuchin periodicals.

In 1944, Benedict married Maureen O'Connell. They have four children. In 1945 his first important book, *Counties of Contention*, which gave an account of the historical background of partition, appeared. While he concentrated mostly on the period 1911–1912, he allowed for everything back to the Stuart Plantation. His own comment on his book is self-revealing. "I flattered myself that it was non-partisan. I began by stating my prejudices so that the reader could allow for them.

I then tried by an objective account of the whole business to show that it was easier for Irishmen to agree than to disagree. Maybe I was expecting too much both from Orangemen and Nationalists." At heart, Benedict, as a patriotic Catholic, suffered much over what he called the "spiritual partition" of his country. As a professional journalist who travelled through the country and saw things at first hand this "spiritual partition" was very real.

Benedict Kiely calls himself "a very busy man" and adduces reasons. "Short of walking, drinking beer, collecting books and going to football matches, I have no definable recreations," he says. Talking, he does too, abundantly, but that exercise he, as a citizen of Dublin, looks upon as an art rather than a recreation. To talk is rather "an essential of civilized life," than a recreation, in the Irish capital. When he walks, his preference is the beautiful valley of the Boyne, or the Clogher Valley in his beloved native county.

Kiely's style has been praised by critics for its clarity and high poetic flavor. His character-drawing in his novels is "sure and human." His discernment as a critic is such that his analysis of Liam O'Flaherty has been described as the best appreciation of O'Flaherty yet written. In reading, among moderns, his favorites are Joyce, Graham Greene and Saroyan.

Benedict Kiely's published works are: *Counties of Contention* (1945); *Land Without Stars* (1946); *Poor Scholar* (1947); *In a Harbour Green* (1949); *Call For a Miracle* (1951).

One may sum up Benedict Kiely's standing, in a reviewer's words, as "a (very young) Irishman with a mounting literary reputation for outstanding excellence in many fields."   E. B. B.

Claude Francis Koch   1918–

Claude Francis Koch was born in Philadelphia on November 28, 1918, the only child of Claude and Madeline Koch. His grammar school education was under the guidance of the Sisters of Mercy at the Academy of Mercy in that city; his high school, under the Oblates of St. Francis de Sales at Philadelphia's Northeast Catholic High; his undergraduate college years were spent at La Salle, under the Christian Brothers. Graduating with a B.S. in accounting and a minor in English (in 1940), he was awarded a fellowship in English by the Vincentians of Niagara University. Before he completed his work for the A.M. he was called up to active duty by the Marine Corps in September 1941 — one week after his marriage to Mary P. Kane of Philadelphia (September 7, 1941). He served overseas for two and a half years, in the lower Solomons, Noumea, and New Zealand, and was returned to inactive duty in 1946, with the rank of captain; his appointment to major came in 1949.

Immediately after the war he and his wife bought a three acre plot and a 150-year-old home half-way between Adamant and Calais, in Vermont; there he worked as a clerk in a cooperative store, and saw his first published verse in *Vermont Life*. In the fall of 1946 he joined the faculty of La Salle College in English, as an instructor; his promotion to assistant professor came in 1951. While teaching at La Salle (composition, Shakespeare, contemporary poetry) he has continued his graduate work at the University of Pennsylvania — and at La Salle he has done his writing.

In 1949, he began to publish verse in *Spirit*. In the same year he was awarded the Dodd, Mead Intercollegiate Fellowship for a projected novel, which was published as *Island Interlude* in March of 1951. In May of 1951 his first short story was awarded the Catholic Press Association $600 first prize. The story is entitled "The Rest Camp," and, like the novel, has the Second World War as its background.

There are four boys in the Koch family at this writing (June, 1951): Michael, Christopher, Stephen, and Gerard Paul — and already the three story house at 113 West Gorgas Street, Philadelphia, threatens to grow smaller. Perhaps they will some day be able to satisfy their desire to return to the old place in Vermont.

Zofia Kossak
(Mrs. Zygmunt Szatkowski)

Zofia Kossak comes from a family that was well known in Poland (before the Russians seized that country), for its artistic talents. Her grandfather, Julius Kossak, was a famous painter; her cousin, Wojciech Kossak, painted not only portraits but also battle scenes; her two sisters, Maria Pawlikowska and Magdalena Samozwaniec, were writers of outstanding merit. Her mother, Anna Kisielnicka, and her father Thaddeus Kossak were descended from the old rural nobility. Zofia was born in 1890 in Central Poland, where her parents owned an estate, and there she spent her happy childhood in the midst of horses, dogs and other animals. There were no schools then (1890–1905) save Russian schools, abhorred by the whole Polish nation. The schools were set up to denationalize the conquered people. To spare her this humiliation, Zofia's parents kept her at home and engaged private tutors. These were individuals who had to flee the capital for political reasons and found the estate in the country an ideal refuge. "From them," Madame Kossak says, "I learned much. I learned only what interested me. God spared me the torture common to scholars of learning all sorts of useless things and contrary to innate dispositions. I studied history with zest — literature, the arts and philosophy helping me in my writing."

In the "little" Russian Revolution from 1904 to 1905 her father was arrested. Soon after, the family estate was sold. Her family moved to East Poland now under the domination of the Russian Soviet and called Volynien. There she lived during the First World War (1914–1918) and there she was married in 1915. She had two children from this marriage.

When her husband died in 1921, as a result of a shock suffered during the revolution, Madame Kossak went to Silesia to spend some time with her parents who had gone there to live. Three years later she entered into a second marriage with a childhood friend, Mr. Zygmunt Szatkowski.

Madame Kossak started to write at an early age. Her first book, *The Blaze*, published in 1923, was a great success. It was written in the form of a diary, dealing with the "great" Russian revolution and life in Poland during the years 1917 to 1920. It was not only popular in Poland but was also translated and published in English, French and Japanese. A year later, her second book, a novel about the story of a famous picture of the Mother of God appeared. This is translated into German and Italian.

Then Madame Kossak went to live in Polish Silesia near Teschen where she became interested in the people there. Here she wrote three books: *The Great and the Small*, *The Battlefield of Liegnitz* (translated into German) and *The Unknown Land*. This latter book enraged the Nazis and in his pamphlet "Poland at Work" Oertzen declared Kossak an enemy of Germany. Then followed *This Day* (contemporary) and *Golden Freedom*, a historical novel which has for its theme Dimitri, the usurper's fight for the Russian throne and the occupation of Moscow by the Poles in the seventeenth century. This latter story was translated into Swedish. During this time she also wrote several books for children, one of these, *Troubles of a Gnome*, was translated into English.

About the same time Madame Kossak wrote also a religious book called *God's Fools*, dealing with the life of various saints and also a romantic biography of St. Stanislas Kostka entitled *For Love*, and translated into Italian.

To gather material for her next three novels, Madame Kossak visited Egypt and Palestine in 1933, and wrote a book, *The Pilgrim Way*, describing her travels. After seven years she published her trilogy, *Angels in the Dust*, *The Leper King* and *Blessed are the Meek*. *Angels in the Dust* is a story of the first crusade and was published in Italian, Jugoslavian, Czechoslovakian, Dutch and English. *The Leper King* is the story of the last king of Jerusalem and has been translated in English, Danish and Czechoslovakian. *Blessed are the Meek* is written against the background of the fifth crusade, the tragic children's crusade and the part played by St. Francis of Assisi in the turbulent thirteenth century. In the United States it was chosen as "The Book of the Month." It was also published in England, Sweden, Denmark, Norway, Finland, Czechoslovakia, France, Germany, Switzerland, Spain, Portugal and Italy.

In 1939 Poland was occupied by Germany. Madame Kossak had become an active worker for the Underground Resistance Movement and wrote for the illegal press under assumed names. However, her well-known style betrayed her identity. The Gestapo finally arrested her in 1943 as Madame Sliwinska, one of her assumed names, and she was deported to the notorious Aufschwitz concentration camp. After ten months she was taken to Warsaw for further questioning. She was sentenced to death but was rescued by the Resistance Movement two days before the outbreak of the Warsaw Rising in which she and her children took an active part.

Now living with her husband in England and having access to the incomparable treasures of the British Museum, their richness and antiquity, Madame Kossak has decided to use this wealth of material in consecrating the remainder of her life, as a writer, to bringing Sacred Scripture (especially the Old Testament) to the modern reader. The first book of the projected series, *The Covenant* (1951), has for its subject Abraham, and is published in Polish and English. At present (1952) she is preparing a book on Moses. Others will follow. She would like to finish her series with *The Isle of Patmos* and the Assumption of the Blessed Virgin Mary.   M. A. H.

Reverend Robert Kothen   *1900–*

The horrors of World War I prompted Father Robert Kothen to devote his life to Catholic Social Action. While living in Antwerp, Belgium, in October 1914, the city was besieged. The British Commission of Refugees sent him and his parents to Birmingham, England. They were not able to take anything with them. There, he and his parents had to go to work in a factory to eke out a living. Face to face with hard social conditions, he decided to dedicate his life to the social apostolate.

Born at Brussels, Belgium in October 1900, of parents of the middle class he was educated at St. Philip's Grammar School (conducted by the Oratorians of Edgbaston), and later at St. Aloysius of Gonzaga School in Paris.

Immediately after the First World War (1914–1918), he entered Louvain University, where he received a degree in pharmacy in 1924, after a five-year course of studies.

After one year of military service, he passed the examination to qualify as a reserve officer and was appointed an assistant at the École de Pharmacie of Louvain. Here he was in charge of the laboratory work of the students. In that same year (1924), he had several conversations with Cardinal Mercier, Archbishop of Malines, who helped him in his decision to enter the Leo XIII Seminary in Louvain. A year later (1925) he got his licentiate in Thomistic philosophy. After four years of theology at the major seminary of Malines, he was ordained a priest by Cardinal van Roey, and was appointed auxiliary chaplain of the Jeunesse Ouvrière Chrétienne (J.O.C.) where he remained for twelve years as the assistant of Canon Joseph Cardijn, founder and general chaplain of that organization. At this time he founded a group of laymen, the "Société des Saints Cosme et Damien," or "Association des Pharmaciens Catholiques," of which he is still general chaplain. Since its foundation, he is the director of the *Bulletin de la Société des Saints Cosme et Damien,* to which he contributed many articles on deontology. In 1931 for his numerous publications on the "Problème des stupéfiants," he received at Louvain the Bruylants Prize.

As a lay student, since 1920, Father Kothen had worked with that institution, which was then called "Jeunesse Syndicaliste," and was groping its way. Father Kothen was also active in Catholic Action in one of the parishes of Brussels and attended all the congresses of that period (1920–1925).

During Father Kothen's twelve years as auxiliary chaplain of the J.O.C., he had to organize the intellectual and spiritual life of the young workers. This included preaching retreats to the Jocists, working with the chaplains of the parishes and publishing the periodical, *Notes de pastorale Jociste.*

In 1935 the J.O.C. became an international organization. Father Kothen became a liaison officer for all national organizations and the secretary of the Brussels secretariate. This office necessitated frequent trips through Europe, serving as host to many visitors and corresponding with persons in nearly all countries of the world. In this way he acquired an international outlook on things.

On May 10, 1940, he was mobilized as an officer in the medical corps, on the day the German Army invaded Belgium. He retreated, with the army, to the south of France. He returned to his country, in August of the same year. Since his health was impaired, in 1941 he was appointed chaplain of a convent of contemplative nuns of the Order of the Visitation, at Lennick Saint-Quentin, near Brussels. There he busied himself with writing. In 1946 he published a book on the spiritual life under the title *L'homme sera-t-il pulvérisé.* He found time then to take an active part in the meetings that took place each year in Paris, when specialists discussed religious life. For the volume, *Directoire des Supérieures,* he contributed the article *La Supérieure, servante du bien commun.* This book was translated into English under the title *Religious Sisters.* At this time he continued and expanded the courses he was giving at the social schools of Brussels and Louvain, and later at those of Charleroi and Namur. One part of these courses has been published in a collection that has already reached five volumes: "Histoire des théories sociales." I *Les écoles sociologiques* (1944); II *Les théories economiques contemporaines* (1944); III *La pensée et l'action sociales des Catholiques;* IV *Le socialisme* (1946); V *L'Enseignement social de l'Eglise* (1949). This last volume has been translated into Japanese and Vietnamese. In 1946 he published *Les prêtres ouvriers,* which was translated into English under the title *The Priest and the Proletariat* and published by Sheed and Ward in 1948. It tells of the work of the priests who have gone to work as dock-workers, factory workers or in other trades to win back the working classes to the Church.

Among his other works are: *Le triple demisme de Sun Yat Sen* (1930); *L'Ame russe en détresse* (1931); *L'Athéisme militant* (1932); *La direction spirituelle des jeunes ouvriers* (1933); *Christianisme et Société* (1948); *Documents pontificaux* (1948 and 1949); *Principes d'Education Populaire* (1945); and *Vers une Mystique familiale.*

This latter work was translated into English by E. J. Ross and published by the Newman Press under the title, *Marriage, the Great Mystery* (1945).

In 1939, he published an essay on Peter Maurin and Dorothy Day under the title *"La revolution verte."*

Father Kothen is now retired and lives in the country — at Sosoye — Maredret, Belgium, where he devotes his time to writing.

E. O.

Helen Landreth 1892–

One day in 1925 Helen Landreth stood on the deck of an Atlantic liner as it rode at anchor off Cobh. She knew nothing of Ireland or its history. But from that time on she was aware of an increasing attraction to the country, which eventually changed her whole life.

Helen Landreth was born on the campus of Vanderbilt University, Nashville, Tennessee, where her father, the late Olin H. Landreth, was Dean of the Engineering Faculty. When she was two years old her father went to Union College, Schenectady, New York to head the Engineering Department, and it was in Schenectady that she received her primary and secondary education, graduating from Schenectady High School in 1913. Her first published work was a description of the college garden written for the high school paper.

She matriculated at Teachers College, Columbia University, in 1914, at first majoring in fine arts, and then changing to science. For personal reasons she left college in February of 1918, and though she later took courses in philosophy she did not complete the requirements for a degree.

In 1922 she joined the staff of *Collier's* in New York, and still belonged to it when she accompanied her father to Europe in 1925 and saw Ireland for the first time. Back in America she began to read Irish history. Her reading had the effect of building up a great respect and affection for the ancient Irish civilization and the spirituality and fortitude of the Irish people. When she left *Collier's* in 1927 she devoted more and more time to it, interrupted by more editorial work on *McClure's Magazine,* of which she was assistant editor for a short while in 1928.

Her growing love of Ireland had made her decide to write a book about Ireland which would combine history, social history and the history of literature, the basis of choice being the development of the

Irish spirit of nationalism. That book was eventually published in 1936 under the title *Dear Dark Head: An Intimate Story of Ireland.* The research necessary for the chapters on St. Patrick and the saints and scholars who followed him, particularly the chapter on the so-called Reformation, pierced the almost invincible ignorance regarding the Catholic Church which was the result of her Protestant upbringing. After the publication of *Dear Dark Head* the prayers of its Catholic readers for the author helped prepare her to receive the grace of faith. When she went back to Dublin in 1938 to do research for another book she asked the Jesuit Fathers for instruction in the Catholic Faith, and on the Feast of the Immaculate Conception she was received into the Catholic Church by the Reverend Edward Dillon, S.J.

Plans for her second book were changed by the war and by the finding of some important material relating to Robert Emmet in the State Paper Office of Dublin Castle. She realized that the true story of his rising in 1803 had been suppressed and an entirely false one circulated for political purposes. As the intention of Emmet's enemies had been to destroy his influence as an idealistic democratic leader as well as execute his body she decided to call the new book *The Pursuit of Robert Emmet.* After years of work the book was published in New York by Whittlesey House in 1948 and in Dublin by Browne and Nolan, Ltd. in 1949.

"The research for the book," she says, "was a tremendous job of literary detective work, which eventually extended to all the archive sources in Dublin, then to Belfast and London." During the eight years she was abroad she collected more than a million words of notes, chiefly from the State Paper Office of Dublin Castle, the National Library, and the Library of the Royal Irish Academy, and the Public Record Office of Dublin, Belfast and London. The book has been called the most important contribution to Irish history in a generation.

In June 1948, Miss Landreth went to the Boston College Library, where she is in charge of the increasingly important Irish Collection. She gives many lectures on Irish topics and on her conversion, and writes an occasional book review or short article. She still hopes to be able to go on with historical writing, but admits that books such as hers requiring years of preparation are not economically profitable. Meanwhile she is glad to be in a position to spread knowledge of Ireland's importance, spiritual and otherwise.   E. B. B.

Patrice de la Tour du Pin   1911–

Stephen Spender, in his introduction to Patrice de la Tour du Pin's *The Dedicated Life in Poetry*, divides poets into two kinds: those whose experience is translated into verse, and essential to it, and those for whom verse is experience. Shelley, Stefan, George, D. H. Lawrence, are obviously of the first kind; Byron, Rilke and T. S. Eliot, of the second. Also Patrice de la Tour du Pin.

Born on March 16, 1911, in Paris, he studied at Ste. Croix de Neuilly and the École des Sciences Politiques. In World War II he was badly wounded and taken prisoner on October 17, 1939 on the Blier, and spent three years as a prisoner in Germany. On October 21, 1943, he married his cousin Anne de Bernis and has three daughters. His published six books of verse make up part of Volume I of his *Somme de Poésie*. Besides, he wrote many articles. "He has," Stephen Spender says, "much in common with the early Yeats, above all the same curious combination of romantic, legendary qualities, with a certain consciousness of purpose which the mistiness never quite obscures; the same anticipation of wider, more public responsibilities to come at a later stage of his development. He is a young French poet who represents a reintegration of the separate functions of poetry."

He lives in a nineteenth century castle, not far from Paris, in rather nondescript country. He has made of his castle a centre to which poets and writers and thinkers come for refreshment and peace. "Since the age of eighteen," he says, "I have tried to do but one immense work in my whole life and am remaining faithful to this task now that I have arrived almost in the middle of Volume II. This desire of unity is not merely an artistic or architectural literary motive but a more profound desire to find as far as possible on this earth, the unity of myself before God and in God." The first volume of his gigantic *Somme de Poésie* has appeared in France, and has been variously received: for some, the mysticism obscures the verse; for others, the verse obscures the meaning. No one, however, can read it without feeling that here is the living word of a poet who has something tremendously important to say, and knows how to say it. Of Volume II he writes, "I am working at this time at my second volume: I think I must wait until I have finished it, and must not let it appear in fragments. It is a long work which will take at least ten years more, and I need much patience; I hope the Lord will give it to me. The work moves slowly, in spite of the times in which we live, but happily I live far from the literary world in order to find time and silence."   A. F.

Reverend William Lawson, S.J.
1904–

Father Lawson is mainly of English stock; but his name is from a Scottish great-grandfather, and he has more than a tinge of the Irish from a Kerry grandmother. He was born in 1904 just beyond the industrialized part of Lancashire, in the hills. He began his education as the elder brother of a large and happy family, and he con-tinued it with the Jesuits in their school at Preston. On leaving school he joined the Society of Jesus. As a Jesuit he did the usual studies in England and special studies in Holland, France and Germany. He took the degree of M.A. in modern history at Oxford University. He has also the degree of S.T.L. of the Gregorian University. His last year of studies was spent in Austria where he was during the Nazi Anschluss. He was ordained in 1936. On the completion of his studies he went to the Gregorian University in Rome as a member of the history faculty and lectured there for two years. He played football with the Scots, disregarded the custom of siesta and exemplified the saying that "Mad dogs and Englishmen go out in the noonday sun;" and he enjoyed more and more the wide horizons which Rome gives to the mind. His hopes of finding his life's work in Rome were dashed when Italy entered the war and it was judged wiser that he should return to England, which he did by one of the last trains out of Rome to Paris. Back in England he lectured in the Jesuit house of theology at Heythrop near Oxford and at St. Mary's Hall, Stonyhurst, in the fells and what Gerard Manley Hopkins in his "Epithalamion" calls the "Lancashire cloughs," where the English College from Rome had established itself. He also helped in various parishes while there was a grave shortage of priests. His more serious publications began at this time with a pam-phlet called *Why Worry!* written to soothe his parishioners (and him-self!) during the heavy raids on Bristol.

After the war Father Lawson, being unable to return to Rome, settled in his present work as lecturer in the Institute of Education of the University of London. He is principal of the Jesuit College of St. Peter Canisius, at Roehampton on the outskirts of London, where Jesuit students are trained for the work of teaching in the many schools of the English Province in England and Scotland, and in the African and British Guiana missions. Besides lecturing in college, he lectures in many of the colleges of the University of London and the Institute of Education, at the Newman Society's headquarters, and at the central college of the Institute.

Father Lawson's writings, apart from regular contributions of arti-cles and reviews to the Catholic press, include a series of pamphlets written for the Catholic Truth Society; a short *Life*, written for the

Catholic Social Guild, of Léon Harmel, the great Catholic industrialist in France who planned his textile factory (and his own life) on completely Christian doctrines and whose cause for beatification is being prepared; a short *Life* of Mother Raphaela Porras, the foundress of the Handmaids of the Sacred Heart; *Red Letter Days*, written in collaboration with Father Joseph Christie S.J.; and *For Goodness' Sake*. He has recently finished a *Life* of Blessed Marie Thérèse de Soubiran, the remarkable foundress of the Society of Marie Auxiliatrice (Our Lady Help of Christians) who had the rare distinction of being expelled from her own congregation and of dying a member of another.

At present he is engaged in the remote preparation of three books, one on history, another on the spiritual life and a third to follow *Red Letter Days*. He suffers from the not unusual difficulty of shortage of time. He has to depend for his writing on uncertain, and at the best brief spells of leisure; and the writing has to be done in uneasy conditions. He finds that he gets his best work done in trains, scribbling away on any journey that lasts more than half an hour, and typing from the scribble when he returns to his room. This, for him, is the ideal way of working. What stimulates him to write is meeting people of all kinds, with problems, frustrations, difficulties and darknesses of mind, yet with patience, goodwill, and a hunger for truth. If then there is time over in which to write something in the hope of helping them, and to express in language they can understand their hopes of greater goodness, then he tries to write it. But if there is no time left, it does not matter. What does matter is to meet people in love of Christ.

M. M.

Robert Lax 1915–

Thomas Merton in his autobiography, *The Seven Storey Mountain* describes Robert Lax as "taller than all of them (the students in Mark Van Doren's class on Shakespeare at Columbia College in 1936) and more serious, with a long face, like a horse, and a great mane of black hair on top of it."

In 1943 Lax went to the Abbey Gethsemani to visit Merton — a surprise visit. Merton was one of the minor ministers at the Pontifical Mass. At the Agnus Dei, Frater Louis (Merton) came to the Epistle side of the altar to receive the kiss of peace. In order to get there he had to come near the benches placed close to the sanctuary. There he saw Lax.

After dinner Merton went to the Abbot's room to get permission to speak to Lax — stating that he was an old friend and that he might be ready to be baptized.

"Isn't he a Catholic?" asked Father Abbot.

"No, Reverend Father, not yet," replied Merton.

"Well, in that case, why did he receive Communion last night at the Midnight Mass?" asked the Abbot.

Up in the guest house, Lax told Merton how baptism came about. The ceremony had taken place on December 19, 1943, in the Church of St. Ignatius Loyola on Park Avenue, New York.

Born in Olean, New York on November 30, 1915, of Jewish parents, Robert Lax attended the elementary schools of Olean and then Newton High School, Jackson Heights, Long Island. He took his bachelor of arts degree at Columbia College, and while there he was editor of *The Jester*, the college magazine. For a while, after school, he tutored the children of the manager of the Hotel Taft.

He taught English at the University of North Carolina for one year (1943–44) and then (1944–45) took a fellowship in the philosophy department to work towards a doctor's degree, which he did not finish. During this time he was on the staff of the *Carolina Magazine*, a student literary publication, producing not only stories but also some very striking sketches and illustrations. During his first year at the University of North Carolina, and before his conversion he took an intense interest in St. Thomas and St. Augustine, under the tutelage of Helmut Kuhn, a refugee professor, who has since returned to Germany.

When Arthur Ripley, the movie director, came to Chapel Hill to take background pictures for a movie version of Thomas Wolfe's *Look Homeward Angel*, Lax appeared in many of the scenes with the Carolina Playmakers. Ripley took an interest in Lax and "Mike" Beam (a friend of Lax), because of their writing ability and offered them a job whenever they came to Hollywood.

Lax worked for *Time* as movie reviewer from October, 1945, to February, 1946, after he left Chapel Hill. He gave up this job because watching three or four movies a day strained his eyes too much. He wrote stories for *Parade*, a national Sunday magazine, and did free lance work, until about February. Then he went to Bermuda for a vacation. Here he took some fine color photos, which he sold to *Vogue* magazine as illustrations for a story of the Bermudas.

In August, 1946, he and Beam drove to Hollywood, where Ripley gave them employment as scenario writers. He stayed there two years collaborating on screen stories with another Columbia friend, Patrick Laughlin and got one screen credit. Then he sat around waiting for work to begin on *Look Homeward Angel*. When that work failed to materialize he returned home.

In October, 1948, while visiting his cousin, who was teaching at the Connecticut College for Women, a member of the English department who was ill asked Lax to take over his classes for the remainder of the year. He taught a course in pre-Shakespearean drama and several writing courses.

Immediately after school (June 1949), he travelled with the Cristiani family and their circus in Western Canada, then went to the Virgin Islands to work on his circus book and visit his friends, Mr. and Mrs. Robert Gibney, on an eleven-acre island in the Virgin Islands away from everyone (no other inhabitants on the island) to write. Here Lax wrote some poetry, attempting a psalmodic style.

For a year (1940–41) he worked on the editorial staff of *The New*

Yorker and had poetry and fables published in its pages. Some of his poems have been published in *The New Yorker, The Commonweal, The American Scholar, Spirit, St. Anthony's Messenger, Ave Maria, Queen of All Hearts, Restoration, Seconds Sanctified, Tomorrow* and *Furioso*.

On the forty-fifth anniversary of Mark van Doren's teaching days at Columbia most of his friends wrote poems to honor the occasion. Of all the poems written, just two were read at the banquet — one by Thomas Merton and the other by Robert Lax.

In the summer of 1951, he spent two months in Rome, a month of which he says was spent "hanging around the Alfred Court Zoo Circus which came over from France to play at the Circus Maximus. When, after three weeks in the city, they left for a run of towns along the Adriatic, I travelled with them, riding on a trailer with the tent, sleeping under the wagons and the stars, one of the happiest experiences of my life. And so I have written a lot more about the circus: some for the book (which I think will be called *The Circus of the Sun*) and some other pieces to be published separately." The first inspiration for the circus book came while travelling through Italy; he visited members of the Cristiani family and also the family of the famous juggler, Rastelli, who is also a central figure in the book.

In Marseille, France (1951) he wrote a poem "A Song for Our Lady: Notre Dame de la Garde." It is about ten pages long but he has not sent it to a publisher as yet.

"To me," he says, "art is a way of profoundly reflecting and communicating the concept and reality of peace; the harmony of order. Peace is the work of the artist as well as the statesman, and any work of art at best: poem, picture, or concerto, provides a pattern for, and is an instrument of peace. The artist is above all a peacemaker and prophet of peace: it is with this understanding and by this authority that he functions in the world."

He adds: "Some of us are planning a magazine consciously devoted to the work of peace through art." M. A. H.

Reverend Jules Marie Léon Lebreton, S.J.   1873–

Formerly a professor in the School of Theology at the Catholic Institute in Paris, and Dean of the School from 1935 until his retirement in 1943, Father Jules Lebreton still retains his mental powers and lives an exemplary religious life despite his old age.

Jules Marie Léon Lebreton was born in Tours (Indre-et-Loire) on March 20, 1873. After completing his secondary education at the Collège St. Grègoire in that city he entered the Society of Jesus at the age of seventeen. While very young, he was a professor in the scholasticate of his order, preparing at the same time his thesis on Cicero "Le Latin de Ciceron," which earned for him the degree of Doctor of Letters (with high praise) from the University of Paris. Later he was awarded the degree of Doctor of Theology. In the meantime he was ordained a priest on August 24, 1903.

In 1905 he was appointed professor of dogma at the Institut Catholique of Paris. He lectured principally on the Most Holy Trinity and the Holy Eucharist. Although he did not neglect the scholastic writers on these subjects he delved more and more into the study of the Fathers of the Church. He found his real interest in the study of the first Christian centuries. This is why, in 1907, he exchanged his professorship of theology for the then newly established professorship of the History of Christian Origins. He held this position until his retirement in 1943. In recognition of his long faithful service, he was made honorary dean of the Faculty of Theology of Paris. In spite of his ill health, Father Lebreton was an indefatigable worker.

In the periodical *Chronique d'Histoire des Origines Chrétiennes,* Father Lebreton published a number of articles on the origin of apologetics. He also played an important part in the controversy evoked by modernism. His polemics with Tyrrell had deep repercussions in France and abroad. A contributor to *Etudes,* he helped Father Grandmaison transform this periodical from one of general interest to the public into a more specific scientific organ for the study of Christian doctrine. When Father Grandmaison died, Father Lebreton took over the editing of *Recherches de Science Religieuse.* This publication had for its motto a quotation from St. Paul, "Prove all things; hold fast that which is good." 1. Thess. 5:21. To this principle he remained most faithful in examining scientific problems in their relations with Catholic doctrine. He held the directorship of this publication until 1948. In addition to this work, he published in 1910, the first volume of his *Histoire du Dogme de la Trinité des Origines a Saint Augustine.* The English translation by Algar Thorold was published in London by Burns and Oates in 1939 under the title *History of the Dogma of the Trinity.* In this volume he studies the dogma of the Trinity in the first centuries of Christianity. It comprises the study of the Old and New Testament and the Jewish-Greek era. After the publication of this work Father Lebreton's health broke down which forced him to inactivity for a long time. It was not until 1928 that he could publish the second book, which studied the same subject up to the Council of Nicea.

From 1917 to 1927 Father Lebreton had lectured at the Catholic Institute on the teachings of Our Lord. When these lectures were published in 1931, he was accused by some of having been too strongly influenced by Grandmaison's *Jesus Christ* but this accusation is without any foundation, as Grandmaison's book had an apologetical character while Lebreton studied the spiritual doctrines in the Gospels. The English translation, *Life and Teachings of Jesus Christ, Our Lord,* translated by Francis Day in two volumes, appeared in 1935.

In 1949, The Macmillan Company published the first two volumes of an American edition of a twenty-four volume history of the Roman

Catholic Church. The complete set is designed to cover the annals of the Catholic Church from its beginning to the present day. Originally published in France in 1942, it is under the general editorship of Augustin Fliche, dean of the Faculty of Letters at Montpellier, and Monsignor Victor Martin, dean of the Faculty of Catholic Theology at Strasbourg. The first two volumes by Father Jules Lebreton, S.J., and Jacques Zeiller cover the beginning of Christianity to the end of the persecutions with the so-called Edict of Milan in 312 and were translated into English by Father Ernest C. Messenger. Dr. Edward R. Hardy Jr., Professor of Church History at Berkeley Divinity School in his review of the work (New York *Times Book Review* Jan. 29, 1950) states: "Lebreton and Zeiller write as Roman Catholic scholars, but with complete honesty in presenting both their own convictions and the evidence which others read differently. Non-Catholic writers like Harnack and his successors figure conspicuously in their references, and those to whom the position of the Papacy and the Episcopate seem less clear and the formulation of the ¡Orthodox ¡Creed less inevitable are not ignored."

After this historical study, Father Lebreton was mainly interested in problems of spirituality. His books, especially *Lumen Christi; La Doctrine Spirituelle Du Nouveau Testament*, and *Tu Solus Sanctus, Jesus Christ Vivent Dans Les Saints*, prove him a master in this field.

He is also the author of *Dieu vivant la revelation de la Ste. Trinite dans le Nouveau Testament* (1919); *La Vie et L'Enseignement de Notre-Seigneur* (2 vols.), and a biography of Pere Léonce de Grandmaison with whom Father Lebreton had collaborated for a long time, notably in editing the magazine *Etudes* and whom he succeeded as Director of *Recherches de Science Religieuse.* M. A. H.

Most Reverend James Leen C.S.Sp. 1888–1949

The little island of Mauritius, "Pearl of the Indian Ocean," was the scene of twenty-three years of strenuous missionary work, of the great Bishop, and later Archbishop, James Leen. Famous for his probity, gentleness, wit and wisdom, he was at the time of his consecration in 1925, the world's youngest bishop. In 1933, before the completion of his first decade as bishop, Pope Pius XI named him Titular Archbishop of Phasis, an honor given in recognition of personal merit.

The island, originally a French, and now a British possession, comprises Hindus, Mohammedans, Buddhists (both Chinese and Indian), in all some 400,000 souls, of whom over 140,000 are Catholic. For Archbishop Leen the task of spiritualizing his own flock and converting those outside the fold was immense. "He devoted his energy," writes Reverend Michael Carroll, C.S.Sp. (*Missionary Annals*, February 1950), "to the fostering of priestly vocations; to the expansion of Christian education; to spreading among the masses the great riches of the Church's doctrine — his pastoral letters were remarkable documents and were frequently reproduced in French spiritual reviews; to the execution of a generous building programme which included a cathedral that would be worthy of Port Louis; and especially, following the call of Pius XI, to the recruitment, organization and active guidance of the lay apostolate."

Born in Abbeyfeale, County Limerick (Ireland), in 1888, James Leen was one of many children, two of whom, Daniel and Edward, were also destined for the altar. At fifteen years of age he went to Rockwell College where he won many distinctions in scholarship and sports. Joining the Congregation of the Holy Ghost, he took first class honors in the National University, Ireland; and having been sent to Rome to the Gregorian University, he took his doctorate in philosophy and theology in 1917. Ordained in 1920, he was retained in Rome to teach as *Repetiteur* in the French seminary. Returning to Dublin he was appointed professor of moral theology in the house of studies at Kimmage. There his remarkable gifts as a teacher and theologian attracted attention, and in 1925 he was named by the Holy See, Titular Bishop of Hippo-Zareth and Coadjutor of Port Louis with the right of succession. This right was exercised the following year on the death of Bishop John T. Murphy.

Archbishop Leen's busy apostolic life did not permit much time for literary pursuits, and indeed he attempted none. He wrote, besides his pastorals, a number of short essays on devotional subjects, but only one book came from his able and learned pen. *By Jacob's Well* was composed in French to provide retreat matter for the priests and religious who in his own diocese sought his enlightening and inspiring aid. It is, in its way, a complete work of solid doctrine, a spiritual guide in the true sense of the word.

By Jacob's Well was translated into English by the Archbishop's brother, Reverend Dr. Edward Leen, and had a wide circulation in America, England and Ireland. Few distinctively religious books in recent years have had a wider circulation. Writes a brother priest: "All the windows of Archbishop Leen's soul were thrown open to knowledge from every branch of science and the result was the presentation of truth characterized by simplicity, clarity, completeness and harmony. No better example of this can be cited than his book called *By Jacob's Well*, dealing with the spiritual life."

To the gravity and gentle firmness of Archbishop Leen's character there was added a kindly, lighter side, which made him all the more lovable. That lighter side was displayed on the occasion of the banquet given in honor of his consecration as bishop. Amongst those attending the banquet was the Reverend Dr. Crehan, former Dean of Discipline at Rockwell College, where as a lively youngster, the then James Leen had been caught at some pranks. In his speech Dr. Crehan referred, jestingly, to the time when he had to use his hands in punishment on the bishop consecrated that day. When his time to speak came, Archbishop Leen took occasion to thank Dr. Crehan for the good services he had rendered in the Rockwell College days: "without that first laying on of hands," he said, "this second would never have taken place."

Archbishop Leen died on December 19, 1949.

In memory of his work, by an unanimous vote, the Municipal Council of Port Louis, composed of Catholics and non-Catholics, has decided to name a street of the capital after Archbishop Leen. It will be known as "Avenue Monseigneur Leen." The street chosen is the most elevated in the city. It was the archbishop's favorite walk.

E. B. B.

Reverend Joseph Mary Lelen
1873–

A zealous country pastor, Father Lelen uses his spare time reviewing and writing spiritual books.

Born at Sailly, which he describes as a "very small hamlet in Northern France," on December 24, 1873, Father Lelen was baptized in the parish church of Sailly, on Christmas Day of the same year. He is the son of Joseph Victor and Irma (Hu) Lelen, both deceased. He was educated at the Petit Seminaire of Cambrai, at the Sorbonne and at the Seminary of St. Sulpice (a preparatory house of studies for members of St. Sulpice or auxiliary members). One year (1894) he served in the French Army. One of his co-soldiers was Hilaire Belloc.

After his ordination to the priesthood by Cardinal Richard, in Notre Dame Cathedral, Paris, in 1898, he labored for a short time as an auxiliary Sulpician priest in France and then came to the United States to teach at Dunwoodie Seminary in New York. From there he went to the seminary in Montreal but left to accept an invitation from Bishop Blenk to come to New Orleans. Since the sultry and humid climate of Louisiana was injurious to his health, he asked Bishop Camillus Paul Maes, Bishop of Covington, for permission to work in his diocese. The bishop accepted him at once and appointed him chaplain of the Good Shepherd Convent. He held this position from 1907 to 1915, when he became pastor of St. Paul's Church, Florence, Kentucky. Three years later he was made pastor of St. Francis Xavier Church in Falmouth and has held this pastorate ever since.

Besides being a regular contributor to the *Messenger, Emmanuel, The Priest,* and the founder and editor of *The Christian Year,* the official paper of the Diocese of Covington for the years 1912 to 1915, Father Lelen has written the following books: *Towards the Altar* (1908); *Towards the Tabernacle* (1908); *Towards the Sanctuary* (1908); *The Agony of Our Lord* (1920); *The Gospel of a Country Pastor* (1922); *Mysterium Amoris* (1935); *Toward the Eternal Priesthood* (1939), and *The Wisdom of Holiness* (1949).

M. A. H.

Francis Joseph Henry Letters
1897–

The classics have interested Francis Letters from the day he caught sight of a Latin primer. "The astonishing difference between a modern and an inflected language," he says, "kindled my imagination at once. Only later did I come to be absorbed in modern languages also. But I have always had what I may call a romantic interest in the classics. I think it was the romantic aspect of Virgil's genius that first drew me to him."

Francis Letters was born in Gympie, Queensland, Australia in December 1897, the son of Francis Lawrence Letters, a Scot, and Sophie (Bastian) Letters, an Australian. He was educated at Christian Brothers' College, Waverley, Sydney, Australia from 1911 to 1914. He received his B.A. degree in 1918, having graduated from Sydney University with first class honors in Latin and English and the winner of the Frederick Lloyd Memorial Prize for a Latin essay. He also won the Nicholson Gold Medal for Latin verse. From the same institution he was awarded an M.A. degree with first class honors in the Classics (Greek and Latin), and also an LL.B.

In 1926 he went to England and then travelled on the continent to perfect his French and German. A year later he was called to the bar of New South Wales, and practiced as a barrister until 1937. In 1938 he became senior lecturer in classics and English at the New England University College (University of Sydney), in Armidale, New South Wales, the position he still holds.

In addition to the languages already mentioned, Mr. Letters is an assiduous student of Hebrew, Italian and Spanish. For many years he made a special study of Dante and has recently become interested in scholastic philosophy. He came to study Sophocles because he seemed to him the most representative of the Greek tragedians. Mr. Letters remarks: "he fascinates me now because I find him the most remote from modern experience."

In 1933 Mr. Letters married Kathleen Mary Logue, an accomplished violinist. They have four children — all girls.

His publications include: *Virgil; J. K. Huysmans: A Study; Introduction to Thomas Mann, The Great Attainder* (a volume of verse); *In a Shaft of Sunlight* (volume of essays).

A portion of the monograph on Thomas Mann was included by Charles Neider, in his book, *The Stature of Thomas Mann.* In 1950 Mr. Letters completed a study of Sophocles.

His favorite authors are Dante and Thomas De Quincey. His hobbies are music, walking and conversation.   M. A. H.

Thomas Fanshawe Lindsay   1910–

Thomas Fanshawe Lindsay was born at Bhagal-
pur, India, on February 1, 1910. His father, Sir
Harry Lindsay, K.C.I.E., C.B.E., was a distinguished official of the British Government of
India, and has since combined the functions of
Director of the Imperial Institute, Chairman of
the Royal Society of Arts, and President of the
Royal Geographical Society in London. His
mother was born an American citizen, the
younger daughter of the late Thomas Huntington, of Norwich, Connecticut.

Mr. Lindsay was brought up as a member of the Church of England. He was educated at Charterhouse, one of the most ancient of the
famous British public schools, and at Corpus Christi College, Oxford. At both school and university he won classical scholarships. While
at Oxford he edited the *Isis*, the students' magazine, and coxed his
college crew in the "Eights' Week" bumping races. At this time, too,
he made the acquaintance of two well-known Catholic authors, Monsignor Ronald Knox and Father Martin D'Arcy, but it was not until
later that he was received into the Church.

After leaving the university, Mr. Lindsay joined the staff of the
London *News Chronicle* as a news reporter, with a side line in book reviewing. In 1935, after a visit to Prinknash Abbey, which awakened his
first real interest in Catholicism and in the Benedictine life, he put himself under the instruction of Father Francis Devas, S.J., and was received into the Catholic Church in Farm Street Church, London.

In 1936, when the *Tablet* passed into the hands of a new syndicate,
Mr. Douglas Woodruff appointed Mr. Lindsay assistant editor. Here
his principal duties, besides the supervision of make-up and lay-out,
included comment on home and foreign affairs. In 1938 Mr. Woodruff
sent him to Rome as special correspondent to cover Hitler's state visit
to Mussolini.

Shortly after his return to England, he accepted a position as Assistant Director of the Press and Receptions Department in the British
Council, a semi-official agency founded by the British Foreign Office for
the cultural projection of Britain abroad. Here he worked under the
late Lord Lloyd, a statesman of singular vision and energy who, although he was never received into the Church, always showed a sympathetic appreciation of the Catholic point of view.

During the war, Mr. Lindsay's Department was for a time responsible for the entertainment of groups of foreign journalists invited by
the British Government to view the British war effort. Many of these
visitors expressed a desire to meet the late Cardinal Hinsley, with
whom Mr. Lindsay established close personal contact.

After the war, Mr. Lindsay was promoted to the post of Assistant

Director of the Council's Production Division, in charge of a staff of three departments then working in "evacuation" at Blenheim Palace, Woodstock, the seat of the Dukes of Marlborough. In 1947, however, he resigned from the British Council in order to take up a post as Assistant Director of Information Services at the Conservative Central Office, London, the headquarters of the Conservative party. His new chief was Lord Woolton, Chairman of the Party and former Food Minister in Mr. Churchill's wartime Administration.

Mr. Lindsay's first book was published in 1942 by Messrs. Longmans, Green & Co. It was a translation from the French of a critique of Freud by Roland Dalbiez, professor, psychiatrist, and Thomist philosopher. This work, which is in two volumes and entitled *Psychoanalytical Method and the Doctrine of Freud*, is now in a second edition.

In 1947 Mr. Lindsay, who is an oblate of Prinknash Abbey, published *The Holy Rule for Laymen*, a study of St. Benedict's *Sancta Regula* for the use of Benedictine oblates and other laymen. This book has been well received in the United States, and applications for translation rights have reached the publishers (Messrs. Burns & Oates) from Germany, Switzerland and Austria.

Lately Mr. Lindsay has followed up this interest in the Benedictine way of life by writing a new Life of Saint Benedict, which was published in Britain (January, 1950) by Burns & Oates. He is a regular contributor to *Pax*, the periodical issued by the Benedictines of Prinknash Abbey, and to other Catholic journals in Britain and the United States.

When the Prinknash community took over Farnborough Abbey, the monastery founded by the late Empress Eugénie, Mr. Lindsay was invited to become a trustee of the property.

In 1943 Mr. Lindsay was created Chevalier of the Order of the Sun of Peru, for services rendered to a Peruvian envoy and guest of the British Government. He is widely travelled in Europe and speaks French and Italian fluently.

His favorite recreation is riding, and he is a keen fox-hunter.

Reverend Arthur Little, S.J.
1897–1949

The son of a lawyer and playwright, Father Arthur Little was born in Dublin on the 31st of March, 1897. He attended the Jesuit colleges of Belvedere from 1906 to 1911 and Clongowes Wood from 1911 to 1913, where he won several distinctions in State examinations.

In 1913 he matriculated at Trinity College, Dublin, to begin his course of law studies. While there he joined the Irish Volunteers, who in 1916 were to fight such a heroic struggle, resulting eventually in freedom for Ireland. In 1914 he entered the Jesuit noviceship at St. Stanislaus College, Tullabeg, Ireland, where he remained for two years. After another year at Tullabeg, in the juniorate, he went to University College, Dublin, and secured his B.A. first class honors degree in ancient classics. From 1920 to 1923 he studied scholastic philosophy in the Collegium Maximum of the Irish Jesuits at Milltown Park, Dublin. For the three following years he was in Sydney, Australia, teaching in the Jesuit College there. He returned to Milltown Park, Dublin, in 1926 to begin his course in theology. When these studies were completed in 1930 he was ordained to the priesthood by Most Rev. Dr. Alban Goodier, S.J. Then in 1932 he was sent to Tullabeg as professor of philosophy in the infant scholasticate of the Jesuits. His first subject was psychology, but he soon changed to theodicy which was his favorite treatise. A Scotist at first, he was suddenly converted to Thomism and gave himself entirely and untiringly to his work here until 1946.

From 1946 to his death, he was in Leeson St., as "Scriptor." The mortal disease which brought about his death at the height of his powers prevented him from taking up a professorship of theology at Milltown Park, to which the 1949 Status had assigned him.

The official Jesuit obituary states: "In the premature death of Father Arthur Little, after months of severe suffering, the Province has lost its most brilliant member. He possessed a remarkably wide range of gifts and some of them in a high degree. He was a classical scholar, a philosopher, a poet, a musician, a critic of art, a writer, a wit."

Among his published works are a small life of Isaac Jogues, numerous lyric poems in various periodicals as well as numerous articles in *Studies* and *Irish Monthly*. His major works are: *Christ Unconquered* (1945), an ambitious epic poem on the Passion; *Philosophy Without Tears*, a short introduction to some of the fundamental philosophical problems broadcast in the form of dialogues. The American edition published in 1947 received two Book Society awards. Also in 1947 appeared *The Nature of Art; or the Shield or Pallas*, a philosophical treatise on aesthetics, especially the relation of art to morality. Up to the last he was engaged on a study of the Platonic element in St. Thomas, an advanced copy of which was put into his hands on his death bed. The title is *The Platonic Heritage of Thomism* (1950).

An exemplary religious, he was highly esteemed as a retreat master. His patient and joyous resignation in his sufferings the last months of his life edified all who came near him. He died December 5, 1949.

E. J. C.

George Aloysius Little 1899–

George Aloysius Little was born in Dublin in 1899. His father is Francis J. Little, lawyer and playwright. His grandfather was Surgeon P. Little of Dublin. He is the grand-nephew of the Hon. Peter Little, Judge of the Supreme Court of Newfoundland who was for some years Premier of that country. Another grand-uncle of his was Sir Joseph Little, also of Newfoundland.

George Little was educated by the Jesuit Fathers at Belvedere College, Dublin from 1907 to 1911 and at Clongowes Wood College, Co. Kildare. Subsequently he read an Honors Degree at the Royal College of Surgeons and Physicians in Dublin and graduated in 1923 from this college which he had entered in 1918. In 1925 he was elected a fellow of the Academy of Medicine. Having spent some time serving in various capacities here and in England, he commenced practice in Dublin, where he is still working.

He served as medical officer towards the end of Ireland's war of independence and later in the civil war. He joined the national forces in Dublin at the outbreak of the Second World War and became Second in Command of the 2nd Field Ambulance, Dublin Brigade, of the Eastern Command.

For many years he has been a spare-time writer and lecturer, chiefly on literary and historical matters. His first public lecture was delivered to the National Literary Society under the presidency of the late Dr. Sigerson. Besides articles and short stories in various magazines, he has written three books: *The Ouzel Galley* (1940), *Malachi Horan Remembers* (1943), and *Brendan the Navigator* (1945). He has been president of the Old Dublin Society for almost ten years. (This society deals with the history of Dublin in its widest sense.) He has lectured at least once a year to this society for some twelve years. He is also a member of the Royal Society of Antiquaries. In 1923 he married Alice Mulhern, whose family originated in Donegal, and has four children living. His outdoor interests are archaeological research, fishing, shooting and riding. "The thing that I am most proud of," he says, "is the fact that I am a brother of the Jesuit philosopher, poet, writer and musician, Reverend Arthur Little, S.J., who died December 5th, 1949."

Reverend Riccardo Lombardi, S.J.
1908–

The bespectacled, white-haired Italian Jesuit, Father Riccardo Lombardi, toured many countries preaching his "Crusade of Love," which he says is "an appeal to all sane forces of the world for union in war against the city of Satan and in edification of the city of God. It tries to propagandize the Gospel as the only true ideology of the present and future."

Riccardo Lombardi was born in Naples, Italy on March 29, 1908 of Piedmont parents. His father, Luigi Lombardi, was a university professor and senator in the Italian Parliament; his mother is a sister of the celebrated Admiral Vallauri. One of his sisters, Pia Collini, is a member of the Italian Congress.

Father Lombardi first studied law at the University of Rome, but in 1926 he joined the Jesuits. After completing ten years in further studies, he was ordained a priest in 1936. He holds degrees from both the University of Rome and the Gregorian University.

Father Lombardi traces his crusade back to 1938 at the completion of his studies and at a time when "the philosophy of desolation" was prevailing in Italy. He was sent by his superiors to give conferences and lectures to point out the dangers of false philosophies. The keynote of his talks is: "We are living in the midst of the evolution of a plan, conceived by God, which is going to work out for the good of souls. The result will be a grandiose triumph of Christ, after which the coming era will be called the 'Age of Jesus.' World-wide communism is doomed to break down in punishment for its crimes and errors." He began to give the conferences at the University of Padua. Professors and students attended his lectures in big crowds, attracted by his logic and the simplicity of his talks. After World War II, Father Lombardi felt the necessity to leave the university to preach to the great masses of people. First he spoke in lecture halls in the leading Italian cities but, as his fame spread, these became too small. Then he lectured in theatres, and later in large stadiums to huge crowds. Sometimes from one hundred thousand to three hundred thousand people were present; on one occasion, in 1948, in the Campidoglio of Rome, over five hundred thousand men came to hear him. In Milan, speaking over a microphone, his voice was heard in fourteen churches at the same time; in Turin twenty-five churches; in Genoa fifty-two and in Rome itself two hundred churches. It has been claimed that the defeat of the communists at the 1948 general elections was to a very great extent due to him.

In 1949 Father Lombardi started his conferences abroad — in Vienna and other Austrian cities. Then he went to France where he preached in the cathedral of Paris, in June 1949. He delivered his sermon in French. From France he went to Belgium and in September, 1949 he sailed for the United States. While he spoke to Italian-Americans in their native tongue, after one month in the United States, he was able to make himself understood speaking in English.

In 1950 Father Lombardi traveled through central Europe and preached in about one hundred cities in Germany, Holland, Switzerland, Belgium, Austria and even in the Russian zone of Berlin. For each sermon there were from ten to twenty thousand persons present. In 1951 he went on a preaching tour of Latin America.

After his great journey, in December, 1950, he preached the "Crusade of Love" over all radio stations of Italy. On one occasion the Pope celebrated Mass and Father Lombardi preached to the twenty-four thousand people who were present from several Italian parishes.

For some years Father Lombardi confined his literary activities to the official organ of the Italian Jesuits' periodical, *Civilta Cattolica*, of which he is now editor. Since his favorite field is philosophy, he wrote many articles for the philosophical section of the *Civilta Cattolica*. His articles have also appeared in many other reviews.

His books in Italian are: *La salvezza di chi non ha fede*, 4ª ed. (1949); *La storia e il suo protagonista*, 3ª ed, (1947). *La dottrina marxista* (1947); *Una mano tesa minacciosa*, 10ª (1945); *Radiorientamenti*, 4ª ed. (1948); *Per una mobilitazione generale dei cattolici*, 3ª ed. (1948); *Squilli di mobilitazione*, 3ª ed. (1948); *Crociata della bonta* (1949); *Per un mondo nuovo* (1951).

In German: *Es kommt das Zeitalter Jesu—Lombardi spricht zu uns* (1950); *Die erste Botschaft vom Kreuzzug der Liebe* (1950); *Die Versöhnung der Herzen* (1950).

In Dutch: *De Boodschap van Pater Lombardi.*

In Norwegian: *Hjertenes Forsoning* (1951) and in Japanese: *Ai no Jujigun* (1951).

Two of his books, *La salvezza di chi non ha fede* and *La storia e il suo protagonista* will be published in English by The Cima Publishing Company. His new book, *Per un mondo nuovo* (1951) will be translated into all languages, and therefore into English.

Father Lombardi writes that the "Crusade of Love" took root while sitting at his desk and meditating upon Jesus and His doctrine of fraternal charity — His love for the suffering and the poor.

As Father Lombardi speaks to the multitudes he uses the eternal words of the Gospel and observes how Christ's words still move people. "As Jesus also looked after the daily exigencies of men and thus found a way to their hearts," says Father Lombardi, "so we must try to bring about social justice; we must concern ourselves about the poor." Father Lombardi believes there was never such an opportune time in history as today for the sower. The field is well prepared. We must sow good seed and carry out God's mission so that souls may be saved. Such is the theme of Father Lombardi's teaching.   M. A. H.

Reverend Joseph Adam Lortz
1887–

Joseph Adam Lortz was born in Grevenmacher, Luxemburg, on December 13, in 1887. Owing to the early demise of his father, his mother took charge of his education. "The Catholicism in which I was brought up," he writes, "was decidedly a most narrow-minded one. At school we never had the chance to get a deeper, or even a somewhat sufficient knowledge of ancient, medieval or modern history." One day a professor uttered a phrase that Joseph Lortz would never forget, "and that," he says, "accompanied me through my life." The phrase became the slogan for his subsequent career as historian: *Il faut ouvrir les formules.*

Having decided to be a priest, Joseph Lortz went to Rome to study at the Gregorian College. He attended there before this famous college was modernized by the decree of Pius XI. He became interested in the history of art, and began to accumulate a knowledge of early Church history. This research led him to write his first essay on *Die Seelenlehre Tertullians*, published in *"Der Katholik"* (Mainz 1910). "An external influence," he remarks, "made me turn to the works of Tertullian. And so it has remained to this day: all my books were written under the influence of something outside me."

He continued his studies at the universities of Fribourg (Switzerland) and Bonn and finished them by taking the doctorate degree in philosophy and theology. In 1917 Professor Joseph Greving of Bonn University invited him to the post of "scientific secretary" at the "Corpus Catholicorum" (1917–1923). His former studies on Tertullian were carried on and grew into a book of two volumes: *Tertullian als Apologet* (1927–1928). Soon after he was called to the chair of Church History at the "Staatliche Akademie in Braunsberg," Professor Lortz composed his *Geschichte der Kirche in ideengeschichtlicher Betrachtung* (1st ed. 1930; 15th–16th eds. 1950 — the last editions were dedicated to the late Cardinal von Galen; English translation 1938). In this book the author tries to give not only the facts, but above all the underlying principles and main *ideas* determining the development of ecclesiastical history. Two years later, Professor Lortz was asked to prepare a conference for the commemorative day of Cardinal Hosius, the great counter-reformer. His conference became a book: *Kardinal Hosius* (1932). More and more his enquiries were directed into the Reformation period, and step by step with his scientific progress and his important academic appointments there grew his effort to solve the problem of the division of Christianity and to open the way to the unity depicted in the sacred words (John 17, 21): "That they all may be one." Being asked by the publishing house of Herder for a paper on the Reformation, Professor

Lortz's contribution grew into two volumes: *Die Reformation in Deutschland* (1st ed. 1939–1940; 3rd ed. 1949). By this historical and theological review of the Reformation, Professor Lortz tends "to give a solution for the modern crisis of the world based on history." The picture he gives of Luther and his activities is quite different from that given by Denifle and Grisar. He frankly admits the faults of those within the Church, lay and clerical. Viewing facts to our discredit that cannot be denied and that it is useless to attempt to veil, he calls on us to face realities and to learn from them. It is an open, sincere, earnest, and extensive discussion of the problems arising out of the Reformation between Catholic and Protestant theologians, such as had not taken place in the last four hundred years. The next two books, *Thesen zur Handreichung bei ökumenischen Gesprächen* (1st ed. 1941; 3rd ed. 1945) and *Die Reformation als religiöses Anliegen heute* (1948), concentrate on the relevance of the problems already discussed in the earlier book to the conditions of the present day.

In 1950 Professor Lortz was (together with Professor Fritz Kern) appointed director of the recently founded "Institut für Europäische Geschichte" in Mainz. The chief task of this Institute lies in the study of the history and theology during the 14th, 15th, and 16th centuries, that is, during the period of the later middle ages, the Reformation and the Counter-Reformation.

Through his books, as well as by a great number of discourses and lectures, Professor Lortz became one of the most remarkable advocates and preachers of the *Una Sancta* in Germany.

Reverend Henri de Lubac, S.J. 1896–

Since 1929, Father Henri de Lubac, a Jesuit of the province of Lyons, France, is a professor of the history of religions on the Faculty of Theology of Lyons.

His most recent work in English, *Catholicism* (1950), is a translation of the 1947 French edition. Father de Lubac aims in it to refute Renan's hoax that Christianity is a religion made for the interior consolation of a few chosen souls. The book proves that the Catholic Church is social in the deepest sense.

In *The Drama of Atheist Humanism* (1950), Father de Lubac studies the thought of Feuerbach (as the source of the Marxist view of religion), Comte and Nietzsche.

Father de Lubac's other works include: *Corpus Mysticum* (1944); *Surnaturel* (1946); *Proudhon et le Christianisme* (1946); *Histoire et esprit* (1950); *De la Connaissance de Dieu* (1948); *Paradoxes* (1947); *Le Fondement théologique des Missions* (1945); *Affrontements mystiques* (1950); *Aspects du Bouddhisme* (1951).   M. A. H.

Barbara Lucas. See *Barbara Wall*

Patricia Lynch   1898–

"I wrote," says Patricia Lynch, "before I knew how books were published, and if publishers had never been thought of, I would write stories to please myself." Even before she could write she told stories. Everything, "from my early childhood," was a story to her. Storytelling was in her blood and in the atmosphere of her quaint home, an old house on Fair Hill, in Cork City. "My mother," she tells, "was a fine storyteller and I had such a love for stories it was natural for me to write as well as to read them. I began by telling stories to other girls at the many schools I attended." At convent schools, where she attended classes, the nuns would ask her to sit on a table and tell stories while her companions were sewing. When she began to publish she would write as many as three short stories a week.

Everything Patricia Lynch writes seems to be a tale of fantasy, but also of truth. Even her autobiography, *A Storyteller's Childhood* (1947), is an example. A critic has written — "Miss Lynch tells this beginning of a life with a rare faithfulness to childhood vision undistorted by later adult judgments. The changing world of her travels has the bright detail of a magic toyshop, and the portraits of her own kin and of her friends, whether schoolfellow, nun, farmer, or shopkeeper, are drawn from the child's intuitive perceptions aided by a sure handling of dialogue. . . . The book is written with depth and understanding in spite of its simplicity. Suddenly we find in reading an autobiography of childhood, we are reading about friendship, about life and death." True to her art and her vocation Patricia Lynch sees things with a child's eyes. She is one of our great writers for children, and is ranked by critics with Hans Andersen.

Her medium is usually Irish folk-lore, and the conduct and thinking of Irish donkeys and geese. The reviewer (in *America*, July 1940) of one of her most popular stories, *The Grey Goose of Kilnevin*, wrote: "It is equally presentable to the big chief or the small child. It has four-star Irish charm. It is a direct importation from Eire. . . . You never met a goose like 'Betsy.' Beside her 'Donald Duck' is a double ache in the neck. 'Betsy' is sweet, kindly, innocent, dear. She reflects in her activities the naive love the Irish have for their animals. As she marches along in lost wandering through bog and town, hers is the veritable goose step. She makes no pretence at being a soldier. She has the way of friendliness and peace. She hobbles among humans like a baby girl among angels."

Patricia Lynch's first animal story, *The Turf-cutter's Donkey* (1934), secured the Junior Book Club's award (London), and was published in America (Dutton, New York). It was translated into French, German, and Irish and on several occasions Patricia Lynch's books have headed the poll in the BBC "Request Week" votings used in broadcasts in England and Australia. Others of her books have been translated into Swedish, Dutch, Malayan, and Icelandic. Her books have been brilliantly illustrated by such artists as Jack Yeats, Sean Keating, Harry Kernoff, Elizabeth Rivers, and Eileen Coghlan. When asked where her stories come from, she answers: "I was brought up on legends, my dreams are very real and persistent, and all around me is a world of wonder and magic."

Of her book *Knights of God*, a factual account and imaginative reconstruction of the lives and adventures of twelve Irish saints, she says: "I tried to show how the Irish saints were glorious adventurers, and if we cannot live such thrilling lives, we can look at life with their vision."

Patricia Lynch was born in Cork, Ireland, in 1898. Her folks were seafaring, of uncertain substance. Her father, who went to sea, died in Egypt while Patricia was still very young. Her grandfather was a kindly man of wide scholarship who boasted he had never *passed* a bookshop or a beggar in his life. . . . "He taught Greek and Latin to lads going up to the University and Irish to those who wanted the old language. If they were poor, grandfather wouldn't take any money at all, and they were mostly poor. In his spare time he was writing a poetic history of Ireland in Irish that was to make him famous. Then we'd all be rich and the family's debts would be more than paid."

Patricia went to school in Cork and later in London and Bruges (Belgium). In Bruges she lived in a boarding house with an English writer, a Miss Carmichael, who encouraged her to write. "I told Miss Carmichael how we were always trying to be rich. She asked question after question and I answered every one." 'Perhaps writing will be your gold-mine,' she said. "You mean I'll be a writer — like you?" I asked. 'It's a good life,' said Miss Carmichael. (*A Storyteller's Childhood*, p. 341.) Patricia set to work to write a story about the circus that came to Bruges and sent it to the continental *Daily Mail*. Alas! It was returned with the comment: "Try again when you're older."

Patricia showed, what she considered, this "encouraging" comment to Miss Carmichael, but she shook her head. "The most encouraging letter," she commented sagely, "isn't as good as the shortest acceptance, and you won't get that until you make them forget you are young." Soon there were acceptances for Patricia Lynch.

Among the published works of Patricia Lynch are the following: *The Cobbler's Apprentice* (1930); *Knights of God* (1930); *The Turf-cutter's Donkey* (1934); *The Turf-cutter's Donkey Goes Visiting* (1935); *King of the Tinkers* (1938); *The Turf-cutter's Donkey Kicks up his Heels* (1939); *The Grey Goose of Kilnevin* (1940); *Fiddler's Quest* (1941); *Long Ears, The Little Grey Donkey* (1943); *Strangers at the Fair* (1945); *A Storyteller's Childhood* (1947); *Brogeen of the Stepping Stones* (1948); *The Mad O'Haras* (1948); *The Seventh Pig* (1950).

Apart from her wider love of childhood and fantasy, Patricia Lynch holds in her heart a deep and abiding love of Cork City. To return there — if possible to return with so much gold as to be able to live in Blackrock Castle — such has been her dream. Cork is her ideal city. Dublin, where she lives, is good in her eyes, but "I still think," she sighs, "there isn't another city to equal Cork. It has everything — quays, hilly streets, a glorious river leading one way to the mountains, the other to the ocean, the glamor of Blackrock Castle and the music of Shandon."   E. B. B.

Stanislaus Lynch

The only Irishman to win a literary award at the 1948 Olympic Games or at any other Olympic Games is Stanislaus Lynch. He was awarded a *Diploma* for Epic Literature (with Honorable Mention) in the Arts Section of the fourteenth Olympiad, London, 1948 for his book, *Echoes of the Hunting Horn.* Sixty nations competed.

Stanislaus Lynch was born at Ballyjamesduff, County Cavan, Ireland and was educated at St. Vincent's College, Castleknock, County Dublin.

When living in Ballyjamesduff, Mr. Lynch kept his small private pack and rode, as well as exhibited, his own horses at local horse shows. He won prizes for horse-jumping, and has hunted with the majority of Irish hunts. He has also hunted with and has written about the Le Rallye Valleire, Le Pique Avant Nivernais, and Le Rallye Bonnelles Staghound Packs in France.

For the past five years Mr. Lynch gave running commentaries for Radio Eireann at the Dublin Horse Show on the Aga Khan Cup International Military Jumping Competition and World Championship Jumping Competition.

He won prizes on Radio Eireann's "New Verse Competition," and won the "Championship Contest" confined to "Prizewinners Only." The adjudicator was the distinguished Irish poet, Mr. Austin Clarke. The subject was optional in all the competitions, but Mr. Lynch's entries were all about horses, hounds and hunting.

Besides lecturing to the Blackrock Literary and Debating Society (Dublin) and to the Irish P.E.N. Club and giving technical advice to Pan-American Airways when filming "Wings Over Ireland," he is on the Executive Committee and is Honorary Treasurer of the International P.E.N. (Irish Centre). He is a member of the Society of Authors (London); member of the Horse Jumping Association and member of the South County Dublin Harriers Hunt Club. He is the first honorary member of the Sylvan Park Hunt, and an honorary member of the Naas Harriers Hunt.

He is the author of: *Rhymes of an Irish Huntsman* (1937); *Echoes of the Hunting Horn* (1947); *From Foal to Tally-Ho* (1948); *Hounds are Running* (1950), and *A Hunting-Man's Rambles* (1951).

Mr. Lynch is a contributor to *Country Life, The Field, The Tatler, The Sketch, Field Sports, Country Sportsman, Riding, Sport and Country,*

Horse and Hound, Pony, etc. in Great Britain; *Town & Country, The Chronicle* in the United States; *L'Eperon, Le Saint Hubert,* in France; *L'Annee Hippique Swisse* in Switzerland; *Hoofs and Horns* in Australia; *Tally-Ho* in New Zealand, and *Dublin Magazine, Irish Field, The Leader, Irish Digest, Irish Tatler and Sketch, Social and Personal,* and daily and weekly newspapers in Ireland.

His poems and essays have been published in *The Foxhunter's Bedside Book, 1,000 Years of Irish Poetry, The Country Life Reader* (for schools in Ireland); *The Irish Horse,* etc.

Mr. Lynch was invited to write a special article on "Hunting in Ireland" and to prepare, in addition, a comprehensive record of Irish sporting activities for the Holy Year Exhibition in Rome, 1950.

In other countries, particularly in the United States and France, the word "hunting" includes shooting, fishing, coursing and kindred sports. In Ireland, however, it has only one meaning: — the pursuit by a pack of hounds, hunting entirely by scent, of some beast of the chase. In the case of drag-hounds, the scent is laid artificially. Since there are over eighty recognized packs of hounds and scores of less important packs in Ireland — a small island 32,525 square miles in area, about the size of the State of Maine in the United States — Mr. Lynch's latest work has been the preparation of a condensed booklet on the subject for the Irish Government. This will be distributed over the world by the Irish Tourist Association.

In the main, Mr. Lynch's books have been collections of essays which portray vividly the clean wholesome pleasures of the chase among the hills, bogs, woodlands and green pastures of the Irish countryside that is so close to his heart. *The Field* (London) comments on his *From Foal to Tally-Ho:* "he succeeds in attaining the excellence of the old essay writers." *Horse & Hound* (London) says of his *Echoes of the Hunting Horn:* "his essays are reminiscent of the prince of all essayists on such matters, the late Wilfred Jelf." Mr. William T. Cosgrave, a former head of the Irish Free State, very graciously reviewed this book for *The Leader* and wrote: "Writing with a fine, easy style, a keen eye for detail and a rare sense of humour, Stanislaus Lynch packs all the clamour and music of the Chase into forty-three delightful essays." Perhaps one of the most noteworthy tributes to his work was paid when the fastidious *Dublin Magazine* (reviewing *From Foal to Tally-Ho*) wrote: "This prose is the equivalent to a poem for anyone who appreciates good writing."

When reviewing Mr. Lynch's most recent book, *Hounds Are Running,* Mr. M. J. MacManus, one of Ireland's most noteworthy present-day literary figures and the biographer of Mr. Eamon de Valera, wrote: "Through Mr. Lynch's eyes one sees more than the hunt. One sees the Irish countryside in all its fascinating variety — its green hills, its brown boglands, its shining lakes, its winding roads, its little boreens."

That, perhaps, is the most warm-hearted tribute of all; for it epitomizes the final goal of every sincere artist: — to depict faithfully the things that lie close to his heart!

Right Reverend Abbot Justin McCann, O.S.B.   1882–

In one of his letters the Venerable Bede excuses his remissness as a correspondent on the score of the exacting claims of his monastic duties. Dom Justin also is a Benedictine monk and his literary work has been achieved within a similar framework. Yet the "*retinacula* of the monastic service," of which St. Bede speaks, though responsible for some interruptions and intermissions, have permitted the production in the past half-century of an assortment of magazine articles, pamphlets, and books. Dom Justin's main interests have been St. Benedict and mysticism.

Born in Manchester, England, in 1882, Philip Justin McCann went for his schooling to the Benedictine college of Ampleforth in Yorkshire. In the year 1900 he was on the point of entering Manchester University to study for a medical degree, when he returned instead to Ampleforth, to offer himself as a Benedictine novice. He made his final profession in 1904 and was ordained in 1909. In the course of his pre-ordination studies he spent four years at the University of Oxford, in the Ampleforth house of studies (St. Benet's Hall), and in 1907 secured the coveted classical distinction of a "First in Greats" and his university degree. For twelve years thereafter he was an assistant master in the school of his abbey (Ampleforth College), and at the same time held various offices in the monastery, e.g. Junior Master, Librarian, Claustral Prior. In the year 1920 he returned to Oxford as Master of St. Benet's Hall, which post he held for twenty-seven years. Since 1947 he has been an assistant priest in the Benedictine parish of St. Mary's, Warrington, which is under the jurisdiction of the Abbot of Ampleforth.

Although he had already contributed regularly to the *Ampleforth Journal* and had been responsible for some minor publications, such as his *Self Discipline* for the Catholic Truth Society, it was in his period as Master of St. Benet's Hall that Dom Justin became a producer of books. The first two display those interests which have been mentioned. They were a translation from the French of Abbot Delatte's massive *Commentary* on the Rule of St. Benedict (1921 and 1950), and *The Confessions of Father Augustine Baker* (1922). This well-known mystical writer (1575–1641) having been a member of the same community as himself, during its period of exile abroad, Dom Justin's interest in him, which was manifested again in later books, is readily understood. Next came an edition from the manuscripts of the very remarkable English medieval treatise, the *Cloud of Unknowing* (1924). This book has been reprinted four times, and will presently appear in a completely-revised edition. Apart from minor publications, the next book was a short treatise on the *Resurrection of the Body* (1928), which was followed in 1929 by *The Spirit of Catholicism*, a translation from the German of Dr. Karl Adam. This book has appeared in many editions, of various format, and has been widely circulated. In 1931 came a translation from the French of Dom Roulin, a monk of Ampleforth, entitled *Vestments and Vesture* (reprinted 1932 and 1950). This was followed by two further translations from the German of Dr. Karl Adam, viz. *Christ Our Brother* (1931) and *Saint Augustine* (1932). Returning then to Father Augustine Baker, Dom Justin published in 1933 two books dealing with the history of his life and with his mystical writings. After a period occupied with articles and pamphlets, there came in 1937 two books on St. Benedict, viz. a life of the saint (twice printed) and an English translation of his Rule. The same year saw Dom Justin appointed Annalist to the English Benedictine Congregation, a post that entails a good deal of work which is not intended for general circulation. Some of this work has been printed; much of it remains in manuscript. As a consequence of this duty and of the parochial work in which he has been engaged since 1947, Dom Justin's literary work in recent years has been confined to articles contributed to the *Clergy Review*, *Downside Review*, and *Ampleforth Journal*. And there have been some pamphlets, e.g. *Saint Benedict* (for the Catholic Truth Society), *Saint Benedict by Saint Gregory the Great* (a translation of Dialogues, Bk. 2), and *Ampleforth Abbey, a Short History*. However, despite declining years, Dom Justin's production of books has not stopped entirely. Returning to his earliest love, he has produced (1951) an edition of the Latin text of the Rule accompanied by his English translation. Moreover, he has in the press a new translation of the *Imitation of Christ* and that revised edition of the *Cloud of Unknowing* which has been mentioned already.

In view of their pre-reformation history, the English Benedictines have from Rome the privilege of using the titles of some of the ancient English abbeys. The papal decree which accorded this privilege to the English Congregation announced that its purpose was twofold: (1) to preserve the memory of the ancient abbeys; (2) to reward the exceptional virtue or merit of monks of the English Benedictine Congregation. Among the titles thus put at the disposal of the Congregation is the title of Abbot of Westminster. The title does not confer any jurisdiction, but allows the recipient the use of the abbatial pectoral cross and ring. Since the Ampleforth community is able to claim lineal continuity with Westminster, the title is regularly assigned to a member of that community. At the English Benedictine General Chapter of 1949, on the petition of the Abbot and monks of Ampleforth, the title was conferred on Dom Justin, who is now therefore the titular Abbot of Westminster.

John Bernard MacCarthy   *1888–*

Born at Crosshaven, Co. Cork, Ireland in 1888, John Bernard MacCarthy began his literary career by writing verse after the tradition of Edmund Spenser, prompted by the fact that an ancestress of his, Elizabeth Boyle, was a first cousin of the Elizabeth Boyle who married Spenser at Cork in 1594. Later he took to miscellaneous journalism and play writing. Four of his plays, "Kinship," "The Supplanter," "Crusaders," and "The Long Road to Garranbraher" were staged at the Abbey Theatre, Dublin. He has published 40 plays, a book of poems, and contributed about 250 stories to different publications. One story of his, "Of Their Kin," was reprinted in O'Brien's "Best Short Stories of the Year" Series. Among his novels are: *Covert* (awarded a silver medal in 1928); *Possessions*, and *Exile's Bread*.

In 1931 he married Brigid, daughter of Dr. Edmond Walsh, M.O., of Mitchelstown, Co. Cork. They have one son, Walter Bernard, and a daughter, Finola Mary Breeda.

Reverend Vincent Patrick McCorry, S.J.   *1909–*

"I get a sinking sensation every time I think of starting a new book," writes Father Vincent McCorry. To date he has launched three books.

Born on May 8, 1909, in Union City, New Jersey, the son of Patrick and Mary (Hatton) McCorry, he is the youngest of seven children. He was educated at St. Augustine's Grammar School and Xavier High School in New York City. While at Xavier High School, he was a member of the Senior Debating Team, the editor of *The Xavier*, and the school representative on the Aloysian Pilgrimage to Rome in 1926. A year later, on August 14th, he entered the Society of Jesus. He made his noviceship at St. Andrew-on-Hudson, Poughkeepsie, New York from 1927–1929 and remained there for his juniorate, 1929–1931. Philosophy was studied at Woodstock College, Maryland, from 1931 to 1934. Then he went to Loyola College, Baltimore, Maryland to serve his regency (1934–1937). Here he taught sophomore Latin and English and was moderator of the debating society. He returned to Woodstock College in 1937 to begin his theological studies which he finished in 1941. He was, however, ordained June 23, 1940 by the late Archbishop Curley of Baltimore.

He served his tertianship at Port Townsend, Washington and Auriesville, New York.

From 1942 to 1944 he taught English and Religion at Canisius College, Buffalo, New York and was student counselor. The following years (1944–1946) he was a member of the New York Province Mission Band. For one year (1946–1947) he was a parish priest at St. Ignatius Loyola Church in New York City. In 1947 he was sent to Fordham University to teach English and Religion until 1949, when he was assigned to his present position, teacher of English at LeMoyne College in Syracuse, New York.

His first publication, *Most Worthy of All Praise* (1945), was very favorably received. It was written for nuns. Other books penned by Father McCorry are: *Those Terrible Teens* (1949), a book of essays for Catholic young women, and *As We Ought* (1949), a book of spiritual essays for religious.

Father Vincent Kienberger, O.P., in reviewing *As We Ought* for the *New World*, says: "Religious welcome a new book from the pen of Father McCorry. It is a trenchant pen, dipped into the inkwell of sanctifying grace. His style is scintillating and sprightly. His counsels spiritual and practical; his approach disarming and engaging."

Father McCorry is well-known as a retreat master, especially to nuns. On one occasion he was locked out of a convent where he was giving a retreat and was finally admitted by an imperturbable novice, after considerable pounding and ringing the door bell. He thinks Sisters are, by and large, the most wonderful people in the Church.

He states: "My two most acute ambitions are to travel and to write *the* great Catholic book, and I don't expect to do either."

M. A. H.

William Henry McDougall, Jr.
1909–

William McDougall was sent to the Far East as United Press correspondent to report on the war that was about to break, but his fate was to describe the sufferings of men in prison camps and their desperate efforts to survive hunger, sickness, and despair. As a prisoner of the Japanese (1942–1945), he lived a life of mixed heroism and misery at four dreadful internment camps. First at Palembang (S. Sumatra); then close to Palembang; next at Muntok, on Banka Island; and lastly at Belalau in the interior of Sumatra. He describes in his forceful and vivid book, *By Eastern Windows*, the lives and deaths of his English and Dutch companions. Humbly, soberly, and with spiritual insight he reveals the awful problems that face tortured starving men. His records include tales of wondrous charity, of deeds of daring, of surpassing endurance, of saintliness and faith. There are splendid nuns and priests in the picture; one of the latter, Father Bakker, who died as a result of his sacrifices for others, is Bill McDougall's hero.

During the greater part of his internment, Bill worked as a hospital helper, attending victims of beriberi and other diseases. From time to time he fell ill himself, and on one occasion it was so certain that he would die that a coffin was made ready for him. But as God delivered him from his hopeless position in the Java Sea ("my own private miracle" he calls that deliverance), He saved him again from cerebral malaria. Notable throughout his writings on the Japanese is the absence of any show of hate. Bill decided that man's great need is love for all, Christ's love. And soon after he was liberated, at the war's end, he found himself on Iwo Jima where he prayed, as he had been asked by Father Bakker, for mercy on the souls of Japanese.

Bill McDougall must have suffered very terribly from hunger, for on this subject he has written with deep insight — and strikingly. "Hunger," he says, "throws into bold relief a man's true self. It strips away the false front behind which hypocrites masquerade. From others it removes the mediocrity which disguised them as only ordinary men and reveals the hidden rock of noble character." Of many illustrations of what men do when hungry, one may be quoted.

"One of the Pangkal Pinang men uncovered a nest of newborn mice. 'How much will you give me for them?' he asked the Britisher. 'Two guilders and they aren't worth that, they are so small.' 'Three,' demanded the salesman. They compromised at two and one half. The buyer ate them raw because, he explained, 'They are too small to cook. They'd disintegrate.'"

Bill McDougall has made famous his "private miracle," as he calls his amazing escape from death by drowning in the Java Sea on March 2nd, 1942. The story is told in full in *Six Bells Off Java* (ch. 9). When his ship sank he found himself swimming in the Indian Ocean with nothing in sight save lifeboats, overcrowded, and pulling away from him. After desperate efforts he swam close to a crowded lifeboat, begging to be taken in. No one heeded him. He seized a rope that was trailing behind. "Someone in the boat yells, barks a command. The rope is jerked from my fingertips, oars bite the sea, the boat leaps forward away from me."

His thoughts turn to God. "At the end only two things concern a man; his family and his God." Grace works in his heart. "I do a lot of praying. First time I ever realize what prayer really is. The things which used to matter so much now matter not at all . . . Christ's words burn with new meaning. 'For what doth it profit a man, if he gain the whole world, and suffer the loss of his own soul?'" He finds: "Regret is more terrible than fear" and prays: "Please God, in the name of Your Blessed Mother, lend me some more time. I'll try to use it well." He recalls his mother's last words to him, spoken over the trans-Pacific telephone. "Don't forget, son, I love you." He thinks he hears a further message from her now, as he sinks or mounts in the ocean swell. "Keep swimming, son. I'm praying for you."

In the distance he sees another boat. He swims towards it but sees the crew have hoisted a sail. He prays God that the sail may collapse. It collapses. He has a few minutes more to get near the boat. Again the crew hoist the sail. Again, in answer to his prayer the sail collapses. Someone in the boat sees him and waves an arm. "Help save me." No one touches an oar to row in his direction. He struggles on. "I'm alongside now, choking, gasping, extending both hands. Two men lean over, seize my outstretched hands, haul me in. . . . Heaven must be something like the emotions inside me. . . . Gulping a deep breath I tell those in the boat: 'Thanks a million, boys, thanks!'"

Bill McDougall was born in Salt Lake City, Utah, in 1909. He was graduated in 1931 from the University of Portland, Oregon. The next year he went to Jackson Hole (Wyoming), where he helped start a weekly newspaper. From 1934 to 1939 he worked as reporter and in the "city room" for the Salt Lake *Telegram*. From there he went to Japan, and joined the Japan *Times* in Tokyo (1940). In October 1940, he became a United Press correspondent at Shanghai; his flight from that city was the start of his sufferings and adventures in a kind of war different from that which other war correspondents described. Looking back, he summarizes: "I had been in a different kind of a war, a battle of souls and minds instead of bullets and bombs. During the fighting I had explored the heart of my fellowman but, most important of all, I had searched my own soul and found myself. The missing years had not been a total loss."

On his liberation from prison and return to the United States he was awarded a Nieman Fellowship at Harvard University (1946–1947) which ranks as a high honor for excellence in journalism. Following his time at Harvard, Bill McDougall went to the Washington bureau of the United Press. His next step was to abandon journalism for theological studies for the priesthood at Catholic University, Washington, D. C. Bill McDougall's published works are: *Six Bells Off Java* (1948); *By Eastern Windows* (1949). His third book has not been published yet (1952) but appeared serially in various Catholic newspapers, being syndicated by NCWC under the title "Joe Johnson — Leg-Man, Reporter for Our Lady." It is a story of a sixteen-year-old high school boy, Joe Johnson, who is taken to Europe by his godfather, who is doing a book on shrines of Our Lady. The godfather injures his leg and is therefore prevented from visiting the shrines sufficiently to do the necessary leg-work. So Joe does it. The shrines are the Miraculous Medal in Paris, La Salette, Lourdes, Fatima in Portugal, and two villages in Belgium, Beauraing and Banneux, scenes of apparitions in 1932 and 1933.

Readers of Bill McDougall's books find (with the New York *Times* reviewer) evidence of "devout religious faith and courage." They also find a splendid moral tone and a telling exposition of Christ's doctrine of forgiveness and love. Bill learned much from Father Bakker's request made from his deathbed, to pray for the Japanese; and from Bishop Mekkelholt's plea for quinine pills for a sick man who had been an enemy both of the bishop and of McDougall. "Please give him the quinine, Mac! It is not for you or me to judge the value of a life." Not content with describing powerfully and movingly (as the *Times*' reviewer writes) the dreadful details and phases of war prisoners' camp life, Bill McDougall teaches what the reaction of a Christian should be to cruel jailers. He ends his story thus: "God, please help Seki and his interpreter — and have mercy on Tojo, too. . . . My private battle against hate is half won. The other half will be continuing in this prayer every day. When all the men of all the earth do that for one another there will be no more war. And until they do war is inevitable. There is no possible disarmament except in the hearts of men."

E. B. B.

Maeve Cavanagh MacDowell 1878–

Known as the poetess of the 1916 Revolution, Maeve Cavanagh MacDowell was born on August 28, 1878, the second youngest of her parents: Michael Cavanagh and Mary Murphy Cavanagh had ten children.

After her father and mother were married, they went to Terre Haute, Indiana, to live with an uncle of Maeve's father. Maeve's mother was not strong enough for this different life and climate; so the family returned to Dublin and opened a grocery store. When Maeve became of working age she was apprenticed as a milliner, the trade at which she has worked since.

In 1912, she was married to Cecil MacDowell, an engineer and artist. He joined the Republican Army and fought under De Valera. After the Rising, he was in prison in England for some time. An artist of great merit, his water colors of Clonfert Cathedral's famous doorway in Galway is now in the Irish museum. This drawing and also his water color of Cormac's Chapel are the standard pictures of this subject. Mr. MacDowell was baptized a Catholic by Father O'Reilly of Westland Row Church, who was hearing the confessions of the Republican soldiers while they were being bombarded by the British from Beggars Bush Barracks. He died in 1926 at Nice. Both he and Mrs. MacDowell were the holders of two medals each for their service in the revolution of 1916. Mrs. MacDowell's brother, Ernest, a cartoonist, was killed on Easter Tuesday of the Rising.

Mrs. MacDowell's first verse was published in the *Derry Journal* about 1908. She wrote constantly for *The Peasant* until it ceased publication sometime before 1916. After 1916 she wrote for *The Cross*, the monthly publication of the Passionists. She also wrote for the *Catholic Bulletin*, *America* and the *Monitor* — the latter two being American publications. Her verse was published in the *Southern Cross* in Argentina and in the *Freeman* in Sydney, Australia.

Her books of verse are: *A Flame from the Whins* (1912); *Sheaves of Revolt* (1915); *A Voice of Insurgency* (1917); *Soul and Clay* (1918); Passion Flowers (1918).

Her book, *A Voice of Insurgency*, was dedicated to James Connolly, one of the leaders of 1916, who was shot by the British. Two editions were sold out in two months. Mrs. MacDowell is proud to state that she was the trusted friend of Connolly, and wrote for his paper every week. Her last verses appeared in his paper the Saturday before the Rising.

Mrs. MacDowell also wrote plays. *In the Time of the Tans* (1925), a play in three acts, has frequently been produced successfully. It has been translated into Irish. Her play, *The Test*, though only in typescript, has been performed in the Gaiety Theater, Dublin and in the provinces.

Her songs include "The Fields of God," "The Prayer of Love," "The Men of '16," and "The Leprechaun."   M. A. H.

Sister Martha Mary McGaw, C.S.J. See under Martha

Reverend Fergal McGrath, S.J.
1895–

Father Fergal McGrath, S.J. was born in Dublin, in 1895, the only son of the late Sir Joseph McGrath, LL.D., Registrar of the National University of Ireland. If the literary bent is hereditary, it would seem to have come from his mother's side. One of her ancestors was R. R. Madden, the historian of the United Irishmen, and her brother, the late Alister McAllister, was well known in England about the 'twenties as a dramatist under the pseudonym of Anthony P. Wharton, and as a writer of detective fiction under that of Lynn Brock. He it was who typed out his nephew's first literary effort — at the age of six — a poem entitled "The Wreck of the Barentee."

In 1908 Fergal McGrath commenced his high school career at Clongowes Wood College, Co. Kildare, the oldest Jesuit school in Ireland. A poem on Joan of Arc, contributed when he was twelve to the school magazine, and a prize essay on the Unification of Germany were the only precocious signs of literary leanings. He entered the Society of Jesus in 1913, and in 1917 took his B.A. degree in the National University of Ireland with 1st Class Honors and the Browne Gold Medal in modern languages. Then came philosophy at St. Mary's Hall, Stonyhurst, and the usual Jesuit routine of teaching at Belvedere College, Dublin and Clongowes Wood. Before his ordination in 1928, Father McGrath had made a beginning at writing with a story for boys, *The Last Lap*, which was published by Benziger, in New York, and also in Ireland.

After a year spent in the Rhineland, Father McGrath was appointed Prefect of Studies at the Jesuit House of Studies, Rathfarnham Castle, Dublin. During his four years there he found time to publish another story for boys, *Adventure Island,* which was adopted by the Irish Department of Education as a reader for elementary schools, and a volume of sermons, *Christ in the World of Today,* and to co-operate in the Sheed and Ward volume, *The Irish Way,* with a biography of Mother Catherine McAuley, foundress of the Sisters of Mercy.

In 1933 Father McGrath found himself rector of his old school, Clongowes Wood. The eight years that followed were full of administrative cares, but he found time during them to publish a volume of collected short stories, *Tenement Angel,* and a biography of Father John Sullivan, S.J., who had been a member of the Clongowes community and died in 1933 with the reputation of sanctity. In 1941 Father McGrath was appointed superior of St. Francis Xavier's, Upper Gardiner Street, Dublin, but in 1944 his superior decided to replace him in educational work. He became a member of Campion Hall, Oxford University, where he worked for two years on a thesis for the Ph.D. degree dealing with the composition of Newman's *Idea of a University* and the efforts made by Newman to put his theories into practice in the Catholic University of Ireland. This work, which was based on a large number of unpublished letters of Newman, took four years to complete. In 1948 it secured for Father McGrath the Ph.D. of Oxford. He then was sent for a year to America to study educational methods there. He lectured in the School of Education of Fordham University, and visited numerous schools and colleges. On his return to Ireland in 1949, Father McGrath was appointed rector of the church and college of St. Ignatius in Galway. He is chairman of the Catholic Headmasters Association, and a member of the Irish Government Council of Education.

In March, 1951, his book, *Newman's University: Idea and Reality,* was published. Norah Hoult in *John O'London's Weekly* (March 30, 1951, p. 207) praises it as a "long, important and scholarly work." J. M. Hone in *The Irish Times* (March 24, 1951) remarked: "The story of Newman's rectorship of the Catholic University of Ireland has hitherto been chiefly known from Wilfrid Ward's biography of the Cardinal. The Irish chapters in that book could never be satisfactory. They ignored the historical background of the educational controversy here, an understanding of which supplies at least a partial explanation of Newman's difficulties. They were also insufficiently annotated in respect to the complicated skein of antagonisms, political and personal, in which Newman was so unwillingly involved during his rectorship. These and other defects have now been remedied by Father McGrath, whose work indeed will be an essential book of reference for any future historian of Ireland in the nineteenth century." *The Scotsman* stated: "Dr. McGrath's vindication of Newman is accompanied by marked fairness to all involved in the complicated episode, which he unravels with great skill. His study throws new light on Newman's life and at the same time adds a valuable chapter to the history of Irish education." *The Times Educational Supplement* commented: "Father McGrath's book . . . is one of those that will always be with us. Its scholarly use of new sources . . . and its fair and judicial approach mark it out as a standard work."

In addition to his literary activities, Father McGrath has always taken an interest in social problems. When in Clongowes Wood College, he founded and ran successfully for five years a summer school in Catholic sociology, and he was on the committee of alumni who ran the Family Housing Association for the housing of the working class in Dublin, and the Clongowes Club for working boys in the same city. He is at present chaplain to Our Lady's Club for working boys in Galway. Father McGrath has also been all his life an enthusiastic student of the Gaelic language, which he speaks fluently.

Reverend Arthur Raymond McGratty, S.J.   1909–

When inquirers ask Father McGratty about his "background," they are likely to be handed by the author a copy of his own book, *I'd Gladly Go Back* (Newman Press, 1951). "Statistical biographies," he says, "are ghastly things if they confine themselves to a series of dates, and this sort is of little or no interest anyway to the general public. What really counted in the far days of youth are the doings and incidents which make up *Go Back*."

The not very stimulating factual data of the author's younger years are not much in evidence in the book. "They wouldn't be of public interest. Nor would the McGratty family, as such, be either. Rather, the book is a series of reminiscences of what I hope is a large, typical Catholic family, with emphasis upon some light humor and easy satire."

Father McGratty was the third child of the seven children born to his parents, Edward and Helen McGratty. His father was president for fifty years of McGratty and Sons, Brooklyn, New York, a marble and natural stone business, and a member of the building trades industry of New York. Father McGratty was educated at St. Gregory's parochial school, Brooklyn Preparatory, and Holy Cross College, preparatory to his entrance into the Jesuit Order in 1930. During 1935 and 1936, he taught classics at Canisius College, Buffalo, New York. Ordination to the priesthood came in 1941. During World War II, he served as chaplain with the U. S. Marines in the Marianas and Okinawa engagements, then spent a year of occupation in Japan with the armed forces. In 1947 he became the National Director of the Apostleship of Prayer and League of the Sacred Heart.

Delegate to the International Congress of the Apostleship, Rome, 1948, Father McGratty was received by Pope Pius XII in audience, at which time he presented the Pontiff with the greetings of the six million American members of the League of the Sacred Heart. In the fall of 1949 he was chosen as priest escort of the great Relic of St. Francis Xavier (world patron of the Apostleship) for its national tour of the States. The trip included visits to 31 American dioceses, and ended when Cardinal Spellman received the Relic at St. Patrick's Cathedral in New York for the opening of the final triduum.

In 1942 Father McGratty's *Face to the Sun* (Bruce, Milwaukee) appeared. This historical novel, published in the "Science and Culture Series," gave through 600 pages what was called at the time "the *other*, the truer side of the bitter Spanish Civil War of the thirties." The author was not surprised, he said, that the book was criticized unfavorably by the editorial page of *The Commonweal*, nor that the reading desk of Warner Brothers, although liking the story, "dropped it like a hot cake" because the position he took was too "controversial."

The Jesuit's position as Apostleship and League director has resulted in the frequent contribution of articles to the *Messenger of the Sacred Heart*, official organ of the League. In the interests of League purposes he has, moreover, contributed columns to the New York *Catholic News*, and other publications. His three-act historical drama, dealing with Campion and Elizabeth and titled *Shadow of the Tree*, has had frequent production by both high school and college dramatic societies.

Favorite amongst the author's writings is, for him, the history of the Sacred Heart devotion, published by Benziger Brothers, New York, in the spring of 1951. Of this book, *The Sacred Heart Yesterday and Today*, he has written: "In September of 1948 it was the writer's privilege to offer the Mass of the Sacred Heart at the altar of the apparitions in the little Visitation chapel at Paray le Monial. Above this same altar Our Lord had shown His Sacred Heart to Margaret Mary, and given the saint that formulation and procedure in the devotion to the Divine Heart which we have in modern times. Then and there I resolved to try to tell, however inadequately, something of the history and meaning of devotion to the Sacred Heart, that devotion which Pius XI called 'the very epitome of our holy religion and the way to a more perfect life.' The book is an attempt to fulfill that resolve."

The book was immediately selected for its members by the Spiritual Book Associates. Public statements of endorsement were given by Francis Cardinal Spellman, Reverend Eugene Murphy, S.J. (producer of the Sacred Heart Radio Program), Reverend Francis Larkin, SS.CC. (National Director of the Enthronement), and Reverend Daniel A. Lord, S.J. (Director of the Knights and Handmaids of the Blessed Sacrament). Although there had been coming from the presses for some years a series of books, touching upon this or that phase of personality of the devotion, there was a need for an over-all historical study, done in popular style and aimed at the vast English-speaking audience. "This book," Cardinal Spellman declared, "is not merely the record of the devotion to the Sacred Heart. It is a history of Christ's own appeal for the love of mankind and the response to it by Catholics the world over."

Father McGratty has said, with regard to this book, "No author ever had a better subject to work upon. Especially when there was the added opportunity to include chapters upon the growth of the devotion to the Immaculate Heart of Mary, from the days of John Eudes down to the 1942 World Consecration by Pius XII at Fatima. Again, as we use the word 'devotion,' the Sacred Heart devotion remains, apart from the devotion to the Eucharist, the greatest of Catholic devotions. It couldn't be otherwise when we recall its *divine* origin, and its formal object which is the created and uncreated love in the Heart of Christ for His own. I may do further writing in the future, but I doubt if any of it will please me more than this book upon the Sacred Heart devotion."

R. J. K.

Mrs. Francis McHugh. See Dorothy Adams

Dorothy Mackinder
(Mrs. Charles T. B. Donkin)

Dorothy Mackinder was born at Selsey, Sussex. Both her parents were on the stage. When she was a few months old, she was taken to live in London, at Chelsea, and at five years old she went as a boarder to a convent in Hempstead. Later, owing to illness, she became a day scholar at a school in Chelsea. She started writing stories when she was seven and was greatly encouraged all through her youth by her maternal grandmother, a relation of Thomas Hardy. She was the widow of an artist who had intimately known many of the pre-Raphaelite artists, including Rosetti, who dedicated one of his poems to her. At sixteen, Dorothy Mackinder decided to become an artist and went for a year or so to a London art school, but soon after that she followed the rest of her family on to the stage. "I was a dismal failure in that profession," she says, and after a few years decided to return to her first love, writing, but though she worked hard at articles and short stories she could get nothing taken for twelve years, till finally her first article was accepted in a London daily paper. In 1938 her first book, *The Violent Take It by Storm*, was accepted by Sheed and Ward and was published also in America and serialized there. By this time she was living in a small cottage in the Cotswolds with her aunt (Grace Leigh), who had been a famous comedienne of the Edwardian stage. Her second book *Captain Cerise* was published by Hamish Hamilton at the height of the blitz, and was followed three years later by *Brief Was the Laurel*, which was published by Macdonald and Co., her present publishers. Her next book *Silver Fountains* was published in America by the Declan

X. McMullen Co., as well as in England, and was followed by *The Wandering Osprey*, also published in America by the Bruce Co. *The Wooden Statue* appeared in 1951.

She is sometimes asked why she so often makes France the locale of her books, and the reason she gives is the fact that Catholicism is indigenous to France, but still seems an alien growth in England. Many books about Catholicism in England seem to her to have a strained and unnatural air. She has never been in France, nor indeed out of England at all, but owing to being given the freedom of her grandmother's excellent library when she was very young, she was early acquainted with the classics of France and Russia as well as with the great English masters, and it is to this fact that she owes her life-long passion for literature. She was never allowed to read anything but the best. She later read many American authors. One of her favorites is the late Willa Cather, whose beautiful economy of phrasing and clean-cut characterization, particularly in *Death Comes for the Archbishop* and *Shadows on the Rock* influenced her more than any other writer of modern days at a time when her own style was till in process of forming. She dislikes over-lengthy novels, too heavily padded, too lush in style, and, owing to her passion for "sparseness," often has great difficulty in bringing her own novels up to the requisite length, which publishers say the public and especially the library public expect of their authors.

Her favorite hobbies are eating and sleeping.

When asked by Bruce Publishing Co. to describe her approach to writing fiction she replied: "One is seldom conscious of any particular reason or purpose behind the writing of fiction. Ideas develop slowly and somewhat nebulously in the mind: one begins dimly to apprehend a certain kind of place, a country, a town and a certain set of people, and very often they remain almost formless until the very moment when the book begins to be written. There are, no doubt, writers who think very deeply and clearly about their work before actually commencing upon the labor of writing, but I am afraid I am not one of them."

Bryan MacMahon   1909–

To readers in the United States, Bryan Mac-Mahon became well known almost overnight in the early part of 1949 with the publication of his first book, *The Lion Tamer*, a collection of twenty-two short stories. The reviews were most favorable. Critics saw in these stories a fresh-ness, a vitality, a richness of imagination and language which made them brilliant interpreta-tions of Irish life and spirit. It received the cover review from the *Saturday Review of Literature* of the 5th of February, 1949. The book is now in its fourth edition. As a result, Mr. MacMahon leaped at once into the front ranks of first-rate Irish writers.

The inspiration for these happy stories came mostly from the country round his native town of Listowel, County Kerry, where he was born on September 29, 1909. "Our house was actually on the market place and the horse fairs were held outside our door so that I could not avoid feeling the fresh impact of the countryside. I did my best to pick up the speech modes of the farmers and when I set them down on paper I found they were really beautiful." He was educated at the local National Schools, at the Classical School of St. Michael's College, Listowel, and at St. Patrick's College, Drumcondra, Dublin, a training school for teachers conducted by the Vincentian Fathers, where he is still remembered by the faculty as an outstanding student. By profession Mr. MacMahon is a teacher in the National Schools at Listowel. He was married to Kathleen Ryan in 1936 and has five children.

Mr. MacMahon is also interested in balladry and folklore. When acting as a collector for the Irish Folklore Commission, and taking down the stories just as they were told to him, he saw that the beauty of the diction which Synge discovered was still active and vibrant. He hopes to make further use of this English of the country people, heavily influenced as it is by the Gaelic idiom.

From 1939 to 1948 he ran a bookshop with his wife in Listowel and got a lot of fun out of it.

When *The Bell* was founded in 1940 under the editorship of Sean O'Faolain for the purpose of "letting Irish life speak for itself," MacMahon was welcomed by Frank O'Connor in "The Belfry," a section devoted to young Irish writers, as a new poet of quality. For several years he was a leading contributor of poems, stories, articles and reviews to that magazine.

Many of the MacMahon ballads have been sung by the traditional ballad-singers at the fairs in Southern Ireland. He admits that he experiences an immoderate satisfaction on hearing one of his ballads emerge triumphant above the clamor of a fair-day pub.

Later he abandoned poetry for the short story and in 1945 received the Bell Award for the best short story of the year with *The Good Dead in the Green Hills*, which is considered typical of his best work. The year before he was a runner-up in this contest with his story, *Yung Mari Li*. MacMahon is of the opinion that the Irish country town is virgin soil for a writer, as Irish literature up to now has come largely from the islands, the deep country, or the big city.

Besides fiction and poetry, Mr. MacMahon is also interested in drama. He has written a three-act tragedy, *The Bugle in the Blood*, which was produced in March 1949 by the Abbey Theatre in Dublin. He is the founder of a local (Listowel) drama group which has produced a variety of plays and won major honors at the famous Killarney Drama Festival with their presentation of Sean O'Casey's *The Shadow of a Gunman*.

Mr. MacMahon, in addition to all this, has had stories, plays and features broadcast over Radio Eireann and the BBC. One of his features, *I Was Born in a Market Place*, broadcast over BBC on December 26, 1948, attracted much attention, dealing as it does with color and drama inherent in an Irish market place.

In collecting his material, Mr. MacMahon maintains that he gets a valuable education at the forge and saddler's shop where he learns the proper thrust and parry of words and the delightful art of oblique reference. All his writings are influenced by the speech patterns of the locality and he hopes to develop these patterns in his future works. His first novel, *Children of the Rainbow*, "a story about a fabulous Irishman and how the news of his death affects the home villagers," was published by Dutton in 1952. He is obsessed by a sense of color in the Irish life around him in tinkers, ballad-singers, customs, sky, bog, fair and market place of a land so rich in beautiful backgrounds and racy, individual characters. All of which proves that Bryan MacMahon is one of literary Ireland's bright young men. American readers will want more of him. A book for children: *Jack O'Moora and the King of Ireland's Son*, a retelling of an Irish folktale, was published in the United States in September, 1950.

His stories have appeared in *Little Reviews Anthology* of 1944 and 1946; also in *Stories of Our Century by Catholic Authors* (Brunini and Connolly). He is represented in *A Thousand Years of Irish Poetry* by Hoagland, and he contributed to *Irish Writing, Mademoiselle, Argosy, Life and Letters, Partisan Review, The Sign, Nash's, Envoy,* and *Kenyon Review.* J. C. L.

Francis MacManus 1909–

The city of Kilkenny, in southeast Ireland, is second only to Dublin in historical and cultural importance. If Dublin be the Athens, Kilkenny might well be called the Corinth of the country. There St. Canice (d. 600 A.D.) founded a monastery which developed into a town. In the twelfth century the Norman Butler family, the Ormands, seized it, ruling it and walling it in and building up its trade. Often it served as the Capital, and there the famous "Confederation of Kilkenny" (1641) was held. Then came Cromwell's soldiery and destruction. In later times Jonathan Swift, Bishop George Berkeley, and a host of scholars and writers were educated there. Still an important city, still redolent of the past, names are to be seen over stores and shops which figure in medieval documents.

Kilkenny today has its Carnegie Library, where a boy, born in a nearby street, learned from "a quiet philosophic man, the librarian" to develop his interest in the city's past. He read widely; listened to old-time tales; studied the ancient buildings; and some twenty years later when his pen was seasoned by other historical novels, wrote *The Greatest of These*, a novel about Kilkenny, which told a touching story of a lovable, impetuous priest and his understanding bishop. Francis MacManus, with insatiable zeal delved deeper into Irish history, and

learned the language of his country so well as to be able to write stories
in it. Then he set himself to learn other languages, and literatures, in
particular that of Italy.

On foot or on a bicycle he explored the Celtic terrains of Wales,
England, Normandy and Brittany, adding to his store of memories of
people and places and folklore. Earning his bread at first as a professional teacher in Ireland, and later as radio broadcaster, and General
Features Officer of Radio Eireann, Francis MacManus has found time
to produce prolifically, verse, essays, articles, and novels, of every
genre, historical, romantic, and humorous. Some of his novels have been
translated into Gaelic, others into Dutch and French.

Francis MacManus was born in Kilkenny City, in 1909. His parents
on both sides came from farming families. He received his first education
in St. John's National School, and in the Christian Brothers' School in
the city. His knowledge of farm life, which is seen in many of his novels,
was gained on the farm of a maternal uncle. He loves Kilkenny. "Life
there," he says, "is close, warm, neighborly, full of traditions, some of
them going back to the fourteenth century." He went to Dublin for his
training as a teacher at St. Patrick's Training College and the National
University, where he took his degree of bachelor of arts.

At the age of sixteen he had begun to write verse. His verse was not
about love but about "romantic gloom." Warned off from this kind of
poetry he began to write short stories in Gaelic, only to find "that
good writing can be done only in languages heard from the cradle,"
and he was not, what is called, "a native speaker." His first serious
writing began with his intense study of Eighteenth Century Ireland —
a period of gloom and disappointment and persecution. A triology of
novels, *Stand and Give Challenge, Candle for the Proud*, and *Men Withering* dealt with the period. The second of the triology received the award
of the Irish Academy of Letters. Novels on farm-life followed, namely,
This House was Mine, Watergate, Flow on Lovely River, and after them,
The Greatest of These (1943).

Francis MacManus gives part of his time to book reviews, broadcasts, and to editing a sociological magazine devoted to the propagation
of Catholic principles. In 1939, he married and is the father of three
children. At the outbreak of World War II he gave up teaching to
take up his post at Radio Eireann, which includes directing, in the Irish
and English languages, radio talks, plays, verse broadcasts, short
stories, debates, and so forth.

Francis MacManus has published, in addition to reviews, articles
and poetry: *Stand and Give Challenge* (1934); *Candle for the Proud*
(1936); *Men Withering* (1939); *This House Was Mine* (1937); *The Wild
Garden* (1940); *Flow on Lovely River* (1941); *Statue For a Square* (1945);
Watergate (1942); *The Greatest of These* (1943); *The Fire in the Dust*
(1950); *Pedlar's Pack* (stories, sketches, essays, verse, 1944); *After the
Flight* (1938, historical essays); in biography, Francis MacManus
wrote *Boccaccio* (1947).

Francis MacManus has to content himself with "walking and
talking" as recreational habits. "I have had to give up membership in
all clubs," he complains, "because there are only twenty-four hours in

the day." His profession "by inclination" is novel-writing and the writing of biographies, but he has been forced into other occupations. "A writer living in Ireland (and dependent on the Irish book market) must work at another job to live." Of late, this gifted Irish writer has been "reading about America, the United States, and the South American Republics." E. B. B.

Neil MacNeil 1891–

For thirty-three years Neil MacNeil served on the staff of the *New York Times*. He joined its staff as copy editor in the spring of 1918 and retired in the spring of 1951 as assistant managing editor.

Born on February 6, 1891, in Dorchester, Massachusetts, he was educated in the Meeting House School in Dorchester and in schools in Nova Scotia. Later he was graduated with a bachelor of arts degree from St. Francis Xavier University in Antigonish, Nova Scotia in 1912.

Mr. MacNeil went into newspaper work soon after he was graduated. Working first as a reporter on the Montreal *Daily Mail*, the following year he became a reporter for the Montreal *Gazette*. In the fall of 1917 he was sent to New York by the *Gazette* and the Toronto *Globe* as their correspondent.

This assignment brought him in contact with the editorial offices of the *New York Times* and resulted in his employment by that paper. He left in June, 1918 to serve in the United States Army, running the trade test division of the personnel section at Camp Dix, with the grade of Sergeant Major.

The war over, he returned to the *Times*. In 1924 he was appointed assistant to the night telegraph editor and two years later was made foreign editor. From 1928 to 1930 he was night city editor, and then was elevated to assistant managing editor.

While with the *Times*, Mr. MacNeil headed the staffs that covered the political conventions from 1932 to 1948. He also headed the staff that covered the United Nations Charter Convention in San Francisco in 1945.

In its article on Neil MacNeil (April 17, 1951, p. 26) the *New York Times* states: "Mr. MacNeil is a close student of international affairs and in 1935, during a tour of Europe, he studied the League of Nations at Geneva at first hand. While World War II was at its height, he wrote a book, *An American Peace*, in which he urged the United States to use its economic power to get the kind of world Americans wanted to live in, thus anticipating to some extent the Marshall Plan and President Truman's Point Four Program of aid to backward areas."

Other books by Mr. MacNeil are: *Without Fear or Favor*, a study of the metropolitan press, widely used as a textbook in schools of journalism; *How to be a Newspaperman,* and *The Highland Heart in Nova Scotia.*   M. A. H.

Reverend Edward Mahoney 1888–

Born in 1888 of Michael and Sarah (nee Pleydell) Mahoney, Canon Mahoney was educated at St. Joseph's parish school, Chelsea, London; at St. Edmund's College, Ware; and at Fribourg University, Switzerland.

His ordination to the priesthood on August 2, 1914, by Cardinal Bourne in Westminster Cathedral, coincided with the outbreak of World War I, in which he served as an army chaplain in Flanders. In 1919 he was appointed professor of moral theology at St. Edmund's College, Old Hall, Ware, a post he has held ever since, except for a year (1921–22) spent at the University of Fribourg. There he completed his studies with the acceptance of his thesis "The Theological Position of Gregory Sayrus, O.S.B.," which was published at Ware in 1922.

In addition to his work as a professor he has engaged in pastoral work in the vicinity and has had some experiences in marriage trials as synodal judge. He became an honorary canon of Westminster Cathedral in 1935.

Before the founding of *The Clergy Review* in 1931, he contributed many theological articles to American Catholic magazines. He is now a regular contributor to *The Clergy Review.*

His books include: *The Secular Priesthood* (1930); *Christian Marriage* (1928); *Sin and Repentance* (1928); *Marriage Preliminaries* (1949); *Questions and Answers,* Vols. 1 (1946) and II (1949).

Clarence Emmet Manion 1896–

For eleven years Dr. Clarence Manion was dean of the College of Law at the University of Notre Dame. He resigned in January, 1951, because "the pressure of private business, together with a constantly lengthening schedule of writing and speaking commitments now makes it physically impossible for me to continue to administer the affairs of the law school."

Born at Henderson, Kentucky, July 7, 1896, the son of Edward and Elizabeth (Carroll) Manion, he was educated at Notre Dame Parochial and High School in his native city and at St. Mary's College in the same state. From the latter institution he was graduated in 1915 with an A.B. degree. From 1915 to 1917 he was a (Knights of Columbus) graduate fellow of the Catholic University of America, and received there the degree A.M. in 1916 and the degree Ph.M. (Master of Philosophy) in 1917. His theses were: *Origin of Political Parties in the United States*, and *Proximate Sources of the Constitution of the United States*. In recognition of his persistence in the "God in Government" campaign, the honorary degree *Juris Utriusque Doctor* was conferred on him by the Methodist institution, Boston University, in 1942. For two years (1917–1919) he served as second lieutenant in the United States Army. After the war, Dr. Manion studied law at the University of Notre Dame, Indiana, from 1919 to 1922, and received the degree, Doctor of Jurisprudence from that institution in 1922. While a student of law at Notre Dame, he taught American history and politics in the School of Arts and Letters. From 1922 until 1925 Dr. Manion engaged in the general practice of law in Evansville, Indiana.

In 1925 he returned to Notre Dame as professor of law. Known as a lecturer throughout the West, Clarence Manion is a popular speaker at schools and colleges. He is greatly interested in public affairs, in politics and in government and has used his oratory to advantage on several occasions. He was keynote speaker at the Democratic State Convention of Indiana 1932. From 1935 until 1940 he was the Indiana Director of the National Emergency Council. Dr. Manion has been repeatedly criticized by the legal teaching fraternity for stubborn adherence to a favorite theme, namely, that the God-given rights philosophy of the American Declaration of Independence is the basic principle of our American constitutional system.

In 1950 Dr. Manion was honored by the Notre Dame Club of Chicago, Illinois, when he was presented the Club's annual Faculty Award for outstanding contributions to the field of learning.

In his latest book *Key to Peace* (1951), Dr. Manion points out that the key to peace is to be found in our system of government. As one reviewer (Father Robert P. Nennan, S.J., *Catholic News*, March 31, 1951) puts it: "It is the unity from diversity achieved through the years of growth, by means of the basic principle, the personal God-given integrity of each free man. This key is the unique equality among men founded on the indestructible soul of each, whose source of life and rights is the Creator."

His other books are: *Sources of the Federal Constitution* (1917); *American History* (1926); *Catholics in Our Country's Story* (1929), and *Lessons in Liberty* (1939).   M. A. H.

Eduardo Marquina 1879–1946

The verse drama was the forte of Eduardo Marquina.

Born in 1879 in Barcelona, Spain, of Aragonese parents he made his secondary studies with the Jesuits. Later he pursued law, philosophy and letters at the university but left before completing these studies. While a student at the university he began to write a weekly poem for the newspaper *La Publicidad*. These poems and some others appeared in 1900 as a book under the title *Odas*. Friends paid the cost of publication. That same year (1900) he went to Madrid, where he was well received by literary critics. This encouraged him to devote himself to poetry.

At the age of twenty-four he married. His means of support was journalism and translating foreign works until 1909 when he produced *Doña María la Brava*. Then he was able to live from the profits of the theatre, as he himself says, "not always badly, nor, as some believe, always well. Thank God, the life of a writer in Spain is more difficult than in any other country. And I sincerely say 'thank God,' because this demands effort of us, and this effort is a constant education." Marquina was a family man and loved his home. He traveled extensively, however, all over Europe and America. He died in the arms of A Llopis de Olivares in the year 1946 at the Roosevelt Hotel in New York, while they were both attending the International Authors Societies annual convention.

Some critics hail Marquina as the best contemporary dramatic poet in the Spanish language. In *Odas* (1900), *Eglogas* (1902) and *Elegias* (1905), he followed the *modernista* tendencies of the day, which Rubén Darío had popularized more than any one else but he distinguishes himself from other modernist poets by his vigor and serenity. He also distinguished himself as a social poet in several compositions and, above all, as a representative of patriotic poetry in *Canciones del momento* (1910), which he began to publish in the daily press about 1905; in them he comments on the political and social questions of the day with patriotic optimism. The same patriotic sentiment animates *Tierras de España* (1914), a collection of poems on historical subjects.

To the theatre, Marquina had brought epical subjects. In 1908 he produced *Las hijas del Cid*, a drama in verse inspired by the medieval *Poema del Cid*, based on the third canto of this great epic poem. *Doña María la Brava* (1909) shows a more accomplished and polished technique than *Las hijas del Cid*. *Doña María la Brava* reminds us of the old Spanish romances. The best dramatic production of Marquina is *En Flandes se ha puesto el sol* (1910), which obtained for its author the prize of the Spanish Academy. The action takes place in Flanders at the time when the Duke of Alba was trying to suppress the rebellion of those Spanish dominions. Other dramatic works in verse are: *Las flores de Aragón* (1914), on the marriage of Ferdinand and Isabella, the future Catholic rulers; *El Gran Capitán* (1916), which deals with the great deeds of the most famous captain of the XV century, Gonzalo de Córdoba, victor over the French and the Italians; *Don Luis Mejía* (1925), a drama in which the protagonist is the rival of Don Juan Tenorio; *Fruto bendito* (1927); *Salvadora* (1929); *Fuente escondida* (1931); *En el nombre del padre* (1936), and others. In addition to lyrical poetry and dramas, Marquina has also produced a number of comedies and novels such as: *Cuando florezcan los rosales* (1914), *La extraña* (1921), *Maternidad* (1916), *La Dorotea* (1935), *Teresa de Jesus* (1933), *La Santa Hermandad* (1937), and *El estudiante endiablado* (1942). His latest work, in manuscript, was donated to A. Llopis de Olivares, the United States Representative of the Sociedad General de Autores De Espana, by his family in appreciation for his kindness to Eduardo Marquina.

As Peman says, "Eduardo Marquina never lost his faith in Spain; although a Catalonian by birth, he felt the totality of the country; as poet, he sang to love and goodness; as a man, he felt in himself the wounds of the Redemption. Because of this, the great metaphysical and Catholic import of all the past glories which he evoked is fused in all his works with the Christian sentiments of mercy and forgiveness, of love and charity."   G. D.

Sister Martha Mary McGaw, C.S.J.
1915–

Sister Martha Mary McGaw was born in Sedalia, Missouri, on January 31, 1915. It was there she received her early education at Sacred Heart Grade School and Smith Cotton High School. She attended the College of Saint Teresa, Kansas City, Missouri; De Paul University, Chicago, Illinois; Dayton University, Dayton, Ohio; and Fontbonne College, Saint Louis, Missouri, where she received her bachelor of arts degree. In 1950 she received her master of arts degree in literature from the University of Hawaii, Honolulu. She is a member of the honor society, Phi Kappa Phi.

Sister Martha Mary entered the Congregation of the Sisters of Saint Joseph of Carondelet, Saint Louis, Missouri, in September 1933. After her profession in March 1936, she began her teaching career at Saint Viator's School, Chicago, Illinois. At present she is teaching at Saint Theresa's School, Honolulu.

Always interested in literature, Sister was the co-foundress of the Catholic Library Society of Hawaii. "The primary purpose of this organization is to provide good reading material for children who are unable to attend Catholic schools." The use of portable libraries has made it possible to reach many children living in outlying districts in the Islands.

A combined interest in Father Damien, the famous leper priest, and in Robert Louis Stevenson led Sister Martha Mary to do research work concerning the visits of the author to Hawaii.

When asked how she became interested in Stevenson she replied: "As far back as I can remember, I have been devoted to Father Damien. Both my mother and father admired him greatly, and though we were far removed from Hawaii and I never dreamed of ever living here, I listened with awe whenever they spoke of him and his self-sacrificing labors in Molokai. After I became a Sister of Saint Joseph, he assumed even greater prominence in my mind as a perfect example of one who led the mixed life and achieved the delicate and difficult balance between action and contemplation. When our community was considering taking this mission in Hawaii, I volunteered to come, believing somehow that I might be able to emulate Father Damien in some small degree. (Of course I knew I was not going to take care of lepers while I was teaching school. Still the very thought of Hawaii was linked with Father Damien's name.)

"Through the years I learned more and more about the heroic priest. As our former pastor, Reverend Athanasius Bous, SS.CC., who is dead now, and our present assistant, Reverend Philip Blom, SS.CC., both spent many years at the Leper Settlement, though long after the death of Father Damien, they were able to tell me many interesting details about Father Damien and his family whom they had known in Belgium. They also spoke of Father Pamphile, his brother, who came to work in Molokai for a short time after Father Damien died. Father Philip has a marvelous photograph album of pictures of Father Damien and of the translation of his body to Belgium in 1936. I also knew Sisters Leopoldina and Benedicta, two elderly Franciscan Sisters who worked with Father Damien. Both are now dead. All of these contacts interested me immensely, yet seemed not to lead anywhere in particular until I started studying for my master's degree at the University of Hawaii.

"When the time came to choose a topic for a thesis, I had no particular subject in mind, but I had decided it would have to be something Catholic. It would be unbearable to spend hours on end doing research on some subject entirely unrelated to God. One day Doctor A. Grove Day, who is the Chairman of the English Department and the author of several books on Hawaiian history, said very casually, 'It is too bad that no one has ever taken the trouble to find out what Stevenson really did while he was in Hawaii. There is such a fusion of fact and fiction regarding his two visits that unless someone separates the wheat from the chaff soon, it will be almost impossible to do it.' Immediately the thought came to me, 'Stevenson — Father Damien!' I knew I had my thesis topic.

"Everything went smoothly from that time on. The topic was approved, I buried myself in the Territorial Archives, and the work progressed.

"The bombshell that I would have to rewrite the thesis for popular consumption fell later. The editors felt that it should be made to have appeal for everyone and not just research students. The deadline of publication was November 13, 1950, for the University wanted to use it as its contribution to the centenary celebration of Stevenson's birth. 'How can I?' I thought. 'The time is too short.' That it *was* done is due chiefly to the assistance of Our Blessed Mother, and the book is dedicated to her under the title of Our Lady of Peace, Patroness of the Hawaiian Islands.''

Gregorio Martinez Sierra
1881–1948

The Spanish novelist and dramatist Gregorio Martínez Sierra was born in Madrid, Spain in 1881.

In his twenty-fifth year, he said: "Mere happenings in life have never interested me. I have no other personal history than that which is found in my books. I was at the point of becoming a lawyer at the University of Madrid, but this was frustrated by my failure in historical criticism, no doubt because of my horror of battles. My intimate friends are the following: words, air, light, water, some poets and my wife. I am absolutely spiritual despite my love of nature. I possess the pride of my dreams, but not the vanity of my works. I daily marvel at my own happiness.''

Gregorio Martínez Sierra began to write in 1898. A year later (1899) he was married to Maria de la O Lejarraga. From then on he wrote largely in collaboration with his wife. Their joint efforts resulted in an admirable and uncommon combination of masculine and feminine qualities to produce works worth while. He brought his first work, *El poema del trabajo* (1899) to Jacinto Benavente, who gave him encouragement. Critics see in his early works the temperament of an epical-lyrical impressionist and feminine poet, to whom the smallest things speak and open their secrets. Later he produced poetical novels, of greater feeling but less color than his early works; they were less descriptive but more human.

In his novels, as in his early poems, there stands out the fresh and delicate feeling and the refined description of landscape and nature of one who knows how to put his soul into the landscape. He has been described as a poetical optimist. Martínez Sierra's love for the landscape explains his friendship for and collaboration with the poet and painter of gardens, Rusinol, his principal teacher after Rueda.

It is as a dramatist, however, that Martínez Sierra distinguished himself. He began his career as a dramatist in 1905 with *Teatro de ensueño*, a collection of sentimental scenes. Then followed *Vida y dulzura* (1908), a comedy, in collaboration with the Catalan dramatist Santiago

Rusiñol. Two other comedies *Juventud, divino tesoro* and *Hechizo de amor* also appeared that year. The following year (1909) he produced *La sombra del padre*. This comedy shows the author as a finished dramatist. A more successful play was *El ama de la casa* (1910).

The plays that have made the name of Martínez Sierra particularly known in the English-speaking world are: *Cancion de cuna* (1911), English translation — *The Cradle Song* (1917); *El reino de Dios* (1915), English translation — *The Kingdom of God*, in *Plays*, Vol. II (1923), and *Sueño de una noche de agosto* (1918), English translation — *The Romantic Young Lady*, in *Plays* Vol. II (1923).

Canción de cuna (*The Cradle Song*) is Martínez Sierra's masterpiece. None of his other plays is so representative of his art. The action takes place in a nuns' convent. One day someone left a little baby girl on the revolving dumbwaiter of the convent. This unexpected guest is reared among the good and simple nuns, filling the holy house with laughter and joy, until she leaves to marry. The author portrays various feminine types such as the discreet Abbess, the severe Mother Vicar, the sweet and gentle Sister Juana de la Cruz, and the guileless and merry novices in an atmosphere of serene peace and of holy joy and purity in the convent. It was played in New York in 1921, and in London in 1926 (109 performances). In 1927 it was again played in New York, with Eva Le Gallienne. There were 125 performances. Later (1933) it was made into a movie.

In *El reino de Dios* (*The Kingdom of God*) the author describes the career of a nun, Sister Gracia. It is a picture of charity towards the unfortunate; of the Sisters of Charity, who devote themselves in the spirit of self-sacrifice to take care of and console the aged in asylums, fallen women, and orphans. It was played in London in 1927 and Ethel Barrymore starred in it in New York in 1928 in the theatre named for her.

Sueño de una noche de agosto (*The Romantic Young Lady*) is an amusing play. Another outstanding play is *Navidad* (1916), one of the best mystery plays of our day.

Gregorio Martínez Sierra died in 1948.

G. D. and M. A. H.

Gustavo Martinez Zuviria (Hugo Wast)   1883–

Some seven years before the present century began, Gustavo Martínez Zuviría (later he used the pseudonym Hugo Wast) at the age of ten, wrote his first book, on the blue lining of a sugar box. He was destined to be the most-read Argentine writer that his country has seen.

Not content with writing, the little lad read widely and studied hard. But for decades he experienced neglect and failure. No one paid any attention to his stories. At the age of twenty-two (1905), he published his first novel, *Alegre*, and none read it. Two years later he tried again with his novel, *Novia de vacaciones*. This, too, was ignored. In 1911 he tried for a third time, writing *Flor de durazno* (Peach Blossom), and for seven years it remained unsold on the shelves of book-stores. Then, one day, the author himself bought a copy. Later he bought a second copy and still later a third. It may be that these secret sales started things moving. Somehow the tide of ill success turned, and today over 188,000 copies of *Flor de durazno* have been sold. And, of the other eighteen or twenty novels from Gustavo's pen that followed, eighty translations of them have been made, 353 editions have been issued, and of the Spanish printings alone more than 2,000,000 copies have been sold.

His phenomenal success as a writer in no way restricted Gustavo's output of energy. Far from being merely a writer, he is, or has been, a distinguished university professor, a brilliant lawyer, a cattle-rancher on a large scale, a newspaper editor and publisher, a politician, legislator, and the Director of the National Library at Buenos Aires. His influence in public life in his country has been large and uniformly patriotic. As Minister of Justice and Public Instruction, he introduced, on December 31, 1943, the teaching of the Catholic religion in all the colleges and universities of the country. The teaching of religion had been abolished in 1884. It was severely forbidden to pronounce the name of Christ in the Argentinian schools, despite the fact that the national constitution recognizes the Catholic religion as the religion of the State. The public schools of Argentina for sixty years had been secular and godless. For this law his country is deeply in his debt.

Gustavo Martínez Zuviría was born in 1883, of noble parentage, in the old city of Córdoba, Argentina. He was educated at the College of the Immaculate Conception and afterwards at the University of Santa Fe. There he took the degree of Doctor of Law and Social Sciences, and in due time was appointed Professor of Political Economy. Entering politics, he was elected to represent Santa Fe in the National Congress (1916–1920). In 1908 he married and became in time the father of four sons and eight daughters, all still living and married. He has already twenty-one grandchildren. In order to avoid embarrassing confusion between literary and other interests, after his two first novels in 1910, he adopted the nom de plume Hugo Wast. The appellation is an anagram derived from his first name *Gustavo*.

In 1916 Hugo Wast published *La Casa de los cuervos* (*The House of the Ravens*) which won the $10,000 prize award of the National Athenaeum, and sold over 150,000 copies. It was followed in 1918 by *Valle negro* which was awarded the Gold Medal of the Royal Spanish Academy. The Academy forthwith incorporated into its dictionary many Argentine idioms on the literary authority of Hugo Wast. Year after year, new novels appeared under his name, each one a success, until in 1925 *Desierto de piedra* won the Grand National Literary Award of 30,000 pesos.

In 1931 Gustavo Zuviría was appointed Director of the National Library of Buenos Aires, an office which he still holds, and in the same year he was nominated by the Government as member of the newly-founded Argentina Academy of Letters. He is also correspondent of the Royal Spanish Academy, and of the Colombian Academy of Letters. He has been a member of the National Committee of Culture, of the National Committee for Intellectual Co-operation and of the Argentine-Uruguayan Cultural Institute. Highest among the honors showered upon him is that of Knight-Commander of the Order of Gregory the Great, bestowed by His Holiness Pope Pius XI.

When in 1941 there was trouble in the Province of Catamarca, Zuviría was appointed "Interventor Federal," until the province's officials were duly and freely elected. In 1943, as we have seen, the religious education law was passed on his initiative. Under this law parents have the right to demand that religious instruction be given their children in the public schools. On the passing of the law 97 percent of Argentina's parents signified their desire for Catholic instruction in school for their offspring. At once, the Catholicism and democratic spirit of Zuviría was justified.

The novels of Hugo Wast are over twenty-four in number. For the most part they have to do with the social and economic problems of rural and urban Argentina. Interwoven in the stories are magnificent descriptions of Argentine scenery and apt illustrations of the customs of different types of his countrymen. The plots move swiftly and hold the reader's interest. Sometimes he has been accused by critics of a tendency to melodrama, a fault that is noticeable in the work of Blasco Ibanez by whom he has been influenced. A trilogy of his novels, *Miriam la conspiradora, El jinete de fuego*, and *Tierra de jaguares* are historical and are based on incidents of Argentina's fight for independence. Hugo Wast's popularity has not been confined to his own country, or to countries of Spanish speech. More than half his novels have been translated into foreign idiom, and have appeared in English, Italian, French, German, Dutch, Polish, Hungarian, Russian, Czech and Portuguese. More than eighty American colleges have adopted, as texts for the teaching of pure and classical Spanish, four of Wast's novels: *La casa de los cuervos; Desierto de piedra; Pata de Zorra*, and *El Camino de las llamas*.

The genius of Hugo Wast has been devoted to the service of his Catholic Faith in several of his later books. In 1931 appeared two volumes under the title: *Aventuras de Don Bosco* in which the life of the great teacher-saint is vividly recounted. In 1941, *El 6 sello (The Sixth Seal)*, on Biblical prophesies, was issued. In 1944, Hugo Wast wrote of priestly celibacy, under the title *Esperar contra toda esperanza* and the following year he wrote of Catholic marriage, under the title, *Lo que Dios ha unido*. In 1948 he published the life of Father Joseph Vespignani in two volumes, the first being called *Alma Romana* and the second *Su segunda patria.*

It goes without saying that several of the novels mentioned above have been adopted for the stage, screen and radio. Some of them have given rise to public excitement and controversy, as for instance when in 1919, his book, *Ciudad Turbulenta Ciudad Alegre* appeared. In two stories which appeared in 1942, *Juana Tabor* and *666*, Hugo Wast projected himself into the future, and wrote of the year to come, 2000 A.D. He has given wise advice to would-be-writers in his book, *Vocación de escritor* (1931), and has written character sketches in autobiographical vein in *Las espigas de Ruth* (1926). In *Vocación de escritor (Writing as a Vocation)*, Hugo Wast has collected his experiences of forty years as a writer and publisher. Not being able to find any publisher willing to publish his first book he was forced to publish and advertise it himself at his own expense. Since 1905 Hugo Wast has been his own publisher. He calls himself the smallest publisher in the world, because his catalogue contains only one author — himself. In *Vocación de escritor*, he teaches how to write but especially how to publish books and how to gain millions of readers, when an author does not have the good fortune to find an intelligent and generous publisher.

Among Hugo Wast's published works are the following: *Alegre* (1905); *Novia de vacaciones* (1907); *Flor de durazno* (1911); *Fuente sellada* (1914); *La casa de los cuervos* (1916); *Valle negro* (1918); *Ciudad Turbulenta Ciudad Alegre* (1919); *La corbata celeste* (1920); *Los ojos vendados* (1921); *El Vengador* (1922); *La Que no Perdonó* (1923); *Pata de Zorra* (1924); *Una estrella en la ventana* (1924); *Desierto de piedra* (1925); *Las espigas de Ruth* (1926); *Miriam la conspiradora* (1926); *El jinete de fuego* (1926); *Tierra de jaguares* (1927); *Sangre en el umbral* (1927); *Luciá Miranda* (1929); *15 días sacristán* (1930); *El camino de las llamas* (1930); *Vocación de escritor* (1931); *Aventuras de Don Bosco* (2 vols., 1931); *Oro* (1935); *El kahal* (1935); *Naves, oro, sueños* (1936); *El 6 sello* (1941); *666* (1942); *Juana Tabor* (1942); *Esperar contra toda esperanza* (1944); *Lo que Dios ha unido* (1945); *Aventuras del Padre Vespignani* (2 vols., 1948). Among the books translated into English are: *The House of the Ravens; Peach Blossom; Black Valley; Stone Desert* and *The Strength of Lovers*. A great artist with a high moral purpose in his writing; a great and influential citizen whose patriotism is not merely a natural but a Christian virtue, Gustavo Martínez Zuviría well deserves a niche in the Hall of Fame of his beloved fatherland, Argentina.

E. B. B.

Francesca Marton. See *Margaret Bellasis*

Vera Laughton Mathews

In two world wars Dame Vera Laughton Mathews worked for the W.R.N.S. (Women's Royal Naval Service). Her association with the Wrens began in 1917, the year of its formation. She joined it in December of that year, and in January 1918 was put in charge of the W.R.N.S. in H.M.S. Victory VI, R.N. Depot at the Crystal Palace, where eventually three hundred Wrens were stationed. As their Principal (First Officer) she was then Miss Vera Laughton. In *The Wren* (April 1945) tribute is paid Dame Vera by a Wren who served under her in those early days.

She writes: "We respected and loved our Principal for her great devotion to duty, for her uprightness (she detested evil, but was always on the side of the sinner), for her kindness and labour for our welfare, and above all for her fearlessness. It was this gift which so impressed us at that time and helped many a Wren to tackle a job which at first sight looked impossible — she expected you to do it and you did it! She inspired us with confidence." When the W.R.N.S. unit at the Crystal Palace was disbanded in 1919, Miss Laughton was made a member of the Order of the British Empire. Soon after her demobilization, she published a record of the W.R.N.S. under the title "The Wrens, being the story of their Beginnings and Doings in Different Parts."

When the Association of Wrens was formed in 1920, Miss Laughton became a member of the first committee. It was under her auspices that the magazine The Wren came into being in February 1921. She served as editor until 1924. On April 24th of that year she sailed for Japan and on her arrival was married to Mr. Gordon Dewar Mathews in the Roman Catholic Church at Kobe. They have three children, one of whom is now a student for the priesthood in the English College in Rome. Mr. Mathews died in 1943. Ever public-spirited, she accepted an appointment as Commissioner for British Guides in Japan. In 1927 she and her husband returned to England, where she continued to show an interest in the Guide Movement, and other activities up to the most outstanding of her achievements, her appointment as Director W.R.N.S. in 1939. The Service had been entirely demobilized and Dame Vera had to create it anew. At the peak of the war there were seventy-five thousand women and girls serving in over a hundred different categories of work. Their Director was awarded the C.B.E. in 1942 and the D.B.E. in 1945.

The Navy is in Dame Vera Laughton Mathews' blood. Her father, the late Sir John Laughton, was the well-known naval historian; her brother died while serving in the Royal Yacht Victoria and Albert, her half-brother, is a well-known archaeologist and writer; two nephews were in the navy, one a navigating officer on a destroyer and the other a naval air pilot, and her daughter Elvira served under her as a Wren. After nearly eight years of service as Director, Dame Vera retired from the post at the end of 1946. She is now Chairman of the Association of Wrens (old Comrades Association).

Her present (1951) work is connected with the Ministry of Fuel and Power. From July 1947 — since the Council was instituted — until December 1950, when she resigned, she was the Chairman of the Domestic Coal Consumer's Council set up under the Coal Nationalization Act. She retains her membership of the South-Eastern Gas Board, in which appointment she was the first woman in gas management. She is also Adviser on Women's Affairs to the Gas Council and President of the National Smoke Abatement Society.

Another interest that claims Dame Vera's attention is the women's movement. She has always been a staunch feminist. She has served on the executive committee of St. John's Social and Political Alliance (formerly the Catholic Women's Suffrage Society) and was its chairman for seven years, from 1932 to 1939. She is now International President of the Alliance.

In addition to her other gifts of mind, Dame Vera possesses artistic gifts particularly in the realm of music. She was also a very good all-round athlete — she captained her college at hockey and played for London University; she was a very good tennis player, a very fine swimmer, and she now possesses a small motor yacht which, apart from her piano, is her main hobby.

Before joining the W.R.N.S. in 1917 she had been the subeditor of *The Ladies Field,* and in May 1920 she launched the magazine *Time and Tide.*

Her only book thus far is *Blue Tapestry,* the story of the W.R.N.S.

M. A. H.

Right Reverend Olivier Maurault
1886–

Translations into other languages are commonly made of literary works but bilingual books are most unusual. Monsignor Jean Léon Olivier Maurault, a Sulpician Father presently rector of the University of Montreal, is the author of two such books, *Among the People of Louisiana (Aux Louisianais)* and *Mexico of My Memories (Le Mexique de mes souvenirs)* published in 1943 and 1945 respectively.

This distinguished Canadian prelate who enjoys a reputation as a "sacred orator, a fine literary man, a tenacious historian and a progressive educator" was born January 1, 1886 at Sorel in the Province of Quebec. His parents were Elias and Lucy Boucher Maurault. He received his first schooling at the kindergarten conducted by Mademoiselle Alain in his own town, his primary and commercial courses at École Olier and École du Plateau in Montreal and his classical course at the College of Montreal, where, in 1907, he received his B.A. degree. He was ordained July 25, 1910 after making his theological studies at the major seminary in Montreal where he also obtained the degree of bachelor of theology. He became a member of the Sulpician Institute after a year of novitiate at Issy-les-Moulineaux near Paris and took a two-year course in letters at the Catholic Institute of Paris before returning to Canada in 1913. He was a professor at the College of Montreal for two years and then was assigned as assistant at St. James Cathedral, Montreal, which post he held for eleven years.

During these years (1915–1926) he published his first historical works: *The Minor Seminary of Montreal (Le Petit Séminaire de Montréal)* (1918); *St. James of Montreal (Saint-Jacques de Montréal)* (1923), and *St. Francis of Assisi of Long Point (Saint-Francois d'Assise de la Longue-Pointe)* (1924).

When he was appointed pastor of Notre Dame in 1926 the centenary of its building was about to be celebrated. He organized these celebrations and *The Parish (La Paroisse)* and *The Centenary of Notre*

Dame (Centenaire de Notre-Dame), both published in 1929, are the literary fruits of that labor. These historical works associated him with the Historical Society of Montreal and with the school of Tourism. He eventually became a vice-president and finally president of the Historical Society. During his pastorate at Notre Dame he also published *Brevities (Brièvetés)* (1928), and when he became superior of the Classical Day School of St. Sulpice in 1929, he wrote *Marges d'Histoire*. This is a three volume work of which Vol. I, *L'Art au Canada*, and Vol. II, *Montreal*, were published in 1929, and Vol. III, *Saint-Sulpice*, in 1930.

In 1934 he returned to his own alma mater, the University of Montreal, as its rector and in 1937 he was made a domestic prelate by His Holiness Pope Pius XI.

Monsignor Maurault has represented his university in England, France and Italy, in the United States, Mexico and South America as well as in most of the provinces of Canada. Because of his literary, educational and historical activities he has been the recipient of numerous honors, among them doctorates from many universities, membership in the Royal Society of Canada, Prior of the Holy Sepulchre Chapter, medals of George V and George VI of England, Companion of the Order of St. Michael and St. George, the Kornman medal of the French Academy and other decorations from France, Belgium, and Haiti.

Although burdened with many duties as rector of a large institution, Monsignor Maurault is continuing his literary work. Since assuming the rectorship he has published besides the two bilingual volumes of his experiences in Louisiana and Mexico, *Our Gentlemen (Nos Messieurs)* (1936); *Talks and Portraits (Propos et Portraits)* (1941); *Harvest of Ville-Marie (Moisson de Ville-Marie)* (1943); *By the Ways and Roads of the Air (Par voies et par chemins de l'air)* (1947) and *The Polytechnic School of Montreal (L'École Polytechnique de Montreal)* (1948). He has also written for magazines, for the *Transactions of the Royal Society of Canada*, for the fifteen issues of the *Cahiers of the Ten Historians* (Cahiers des Dix), a yearly publication, and several other collaborations, among which is an illuminating chapter of "French-Canadian Backgrounds" published by Queen's University in Kingston, Ontario.   M. B. H.

Peter Maurin 1877–1949

Peter Maurin was the founder of the Catholic Worker Movement and co-founder of the *Catholic Worker*, a monthly newspaper, dedicated to Catholic social principles. He was called the "peasant of the pavements."

Born of French peasants at Oulet, Languedoc, France, on May 15, 1877, he was one of his parents' twenty-three children. At the age of fourteen, he went to a school near Paris run by the Christian Brothers and returned five years later to teach there.

After some years of teaching he sailed for Canada where he farmed for a while and then got jobs in work gangs. With one of these gangs he illegally entered the United States in 1911. Here, too, he worked on back-breaking jobs but devoted his leisure moments to the study of economics, philosophy, and history. To gain further knowledge he engaged strangers on buses, in the city streets or in parks, in conversation. His purpose was to transform modern society so that "it would be easier for people to be good." To spread his doctrine he realized he needed a medium — a newspaper. Lacking journalistic ability himself, he looked around for someone who could write and who was interested in social reform. He found the writer he wanted in Dorothy Day, who at the time was writing for *The Sign* and *The Commonweal*. In 1933 they met and decided on the paper. With the money Dorothy Day received from the sale of her articles, the first issue of *The Catholic Worker* was launched. "I am an announcer," Peter Maurin said, "of a new social order, and not a denouncer. We must create a new society within the shell of the old, using an old philosophy, a philosophy so old that it looks like new." *The Catholic Worker* has attained a circulation of 65,000.

Later he took up lecturing. His technique was not to get on a soap box and preach, but to engage someone in the crowd in what he called an easy conversation. "I will give you a piece of my mind, and you will give me a piece of your mind, and then we will both have more." The discussions in Union Square would last all through the night and Peter was never at a loss for words no matter which way the discussion went.

Peter Maurin was completely detached from all worldly goods and personal glory or fame. For many years he never had a room or bed he could call his own. On one occasion he was invited to a dinner. When Peter arrived, dressed in his shabby clothes, the people thought that he had come to read the gas meter and sent him down to the basement. He was obedient and stayed there until the host returned and corrected the mistake. It gave him an opportunity to read.

On another occasion when he was introduced from a lecture platform as Dr. Maurin, he was asked from what university he was graduated. Peter Maurin replied: "Union Square."

He died as he had lived — in poverty of this world's goods but rich in charity for others. As Dorothy Day says, "He was another St. Francis of modern times." (*Catholic Worker*, June, 1949, p. 1.)

After a lingering illness of five years, he died on May 15, 1949, at Maryfarm, Newburgh, New York, on one of the thirteen farming communities he had helped to found. He wore for a shroud a suit that had been sent in for the poor, and the grave was donated by Father Pierre Conway, a Dominican. Peter Maurin lived to see his work spread to England, Canada, Australia and India.

He is the author of only one book, *Easy Essays*. Since people would not take time to listen he decided to write down his ideas in an essay style and mail it to them. It was in this fashion that Peter's famous *Easy Essays* was born. S. V.

Sister Maria Serafina Mazza   1900–

Sister Maria Serafina Mazza is one of Mother Seton's Sisters of Charity. She was born in Italy, the daughter of the late Giuseppe and Rosa (Talarico) Mazza, on January 13, 1900, and came to the United States in August of 1904.

After graduating from the Indiana State Normal School of Pennsylvania (1919), Miss Mazza taught in the public schools of Allegheny County until 1923, when she entered the novitiate at Seton Hill. As a public school teacher, she was very active in the Missionary Confraternity of Christian Doctrine, conducting week-end classes in religion during the school year, and daily classes throughout the summer vacation. As a religious, Sister Serafina still finds herself in the Confraternity, along with her academic duties and literary interests. She has been teaching languages since 1925, and, like most teachers, she has been a student nearly all her life. She holds the degree of Bachelor of Arts from Seton Hill College (1930); Master of Arts from McGill University (1935), Montreal; and Doctor of Philosophy from Columbia University (1947).

Sister Serafina, who is chairman of the department of Italian at Seton Hill College, is interested in Italian authors who are militant Catholics and also militant writers — literary men who strive to keep high the standards of Catholic literature. She has been writing about those zealous Catholic laymen of the Frontespizian movement (Bargellini, Casnati, Fenu, Giordani, Giuliotti, Lisi, Manacorda, Papini, and their associates), and about the Catholic Frenchmen of the past century (De Maistre, De Bonald, Barbey d'Aurevilly, Veuillot, Hello, Bloy, and others), who had directly or indirectly influenced the Frontespizians. Most of Sister Serafina's writings about these authors can be found in *Not for Art's Sake* (1948), the story of that vigorous literary monthly with a keen appreciation of artistic values, which was published in Florence during the years immediately preceding World War II. Writing about this book in the *Osservatore Romano*, the scholarly critic Don Giuseppe De Luca commends the author for being the first to devote an entire volume to the story of *Il Frontespizio*, a periodical that earned for itself a place in the history of the Italian literature of our day, even though it was discontinued at the close of its twelfth year.

Sister Serafina is among the contributors to the *Columbia Dictionary of Modern European Literature* (1947), and occasionally writes for current publications.

Reverend Denis Meehan   1914–

Born in Castlebar, County Mayo, Ireland in 1914, Denis Meehan was educated in Sligo Diocesan College and in Maynooth College and was graduated in 1940 with an S.T.L. degree. In 1942 he was awarded an M.A. degree in Ancient Classics, his degree dissertation being *Saint Gregory of Nazianzen and the Emperor Julian*. He was appointed Professor of Ancient Classics in Maynooth in 1943, and librarian at the same institution in 1947. He is a priest of the Elphin Diocese. He is honorary secretary of the Maynooth Union, an association of Maynooth priests which is quite world-wide, and has during the fifty years of its existence sponsored many cultural and religious enterprises in Ireland and abroad. Archbishop Mannix was the first secretary.

In 1949 he visited the United States and traveled very extensively there, visiting Catholic institutions at university level in East, Central and West America.

Since 1941 he has been a contributor to the *Irish Ecclesiastical Record* on topics of current interest and on patristics, and to various other Irish journals.

His first book, *Window on Maynooth,* a complete historical guide to Maynooth College, was published in 1949.   M. A. H.

M. M. Merrick (Mother Cecily)

Writing under the pseudonym M. M. Merrick, Mother Cecily says that she is not at all an author, but a hard-working principal of a training college, with no time save holidays in which to follow her hobby. This is not writing in general, but mere working for the English martyrs, of the 1535 to the 1681 period. All her private work is done for that cause.

Her name in religion is Mother Cecily, and she is a Sister of Mercy belonging to the Endsleigh Community of Hull, England. It is the mother house of the Sisters of Mercy of the Middlesbrough Diocese, and to it is attached the only training college administered by the Sisters of Mercy in England.

Mother Cecily was born and brought up in Dublin, but was educated in England. She holds an honors degree in English language and literature from Oxford University, and also one from London University in psychology. These qualifications are some twenty-odd years old, and she is prouder of the fact that she has been a nun for thirty years. She considers that all her research has not equalled what she has learnt from her community.

Before she became a nun, she used to write songs and verses, and make some metrical translations from Gaelic into English. She did not consider writing a serious business, but loved her real work of teaching in a slum school of a mission conducted by the Benedictine Fathers.

As a nun, Mother Cecily discovered a fund of old books and prints once owned by her predecessor, Mother M. Stanislaus, a great English-woman and lover of the martyrs. This find stimulated Mother Cecily to yet further discoveries, and ended in a long dedication to their some-what neglected histories and cause. She has lectured up and down Eng-land on their stories, with a collection of pictures, books and icons, all illustrating her themes. She has also written short articles for periodi-cals, such as the *Sacred Heart Messenger* and the *Grail Magazine*, as well as the more serious reviews, *Blackfriars* and *Life of the Spirit*.

She is the author of *James Duckett*, the story of a man who died at Tyburn in 1602 for a cause we would now call "the freedom of the press." Then followed *Thomas Percy, Seventh Earl*. *The Catholic Herald* (London) says of it: "This book fills a gap which has long needed filling in the ranks of our modern books on the English martyrs. . . . It is one which no Catholic bookshelf should be without."

Her other books are *The Jesus Psalter* and *Memoirs of the Martyrs*. She is now working on a life of Blessed Philip Howard.

James J. Metcalfe   1906–

A patchwork of experience preceded James J. Metcalfe's rise to prominence as the author of verse of every-day philosophy that has brought comfort, inspiration and happiness to millions.

Born in Berlin on September 16, 1906, of an Austrian father and an American mother, he came to this country at the age of seven. He received his early education at the University of Notre Dame, including two years of prepara-tory schooling in Holy Cross Seminary. His sister is a Holy Cross nun.

Financial reverses in the family caused him to leave Notre Dame and go to work in Chicago. There, while he pursued an assortment of jobs, such as soda dispensing, theater ushering, clerking and typing, he at-tended night law school at Loyola University. Both in high school and college he won many oratorical honors. In 1929 he received his law degree. The following year he was admitted to the bar of the Supreme Court of Illinois and in 1935 to the Supreme Court of the United States.

The practice of law, however, was not meant to be Mr. Metcalfe's career. Instead he became a special agent of the Federal Bureau of In-vestigation in 1931, and during his four years in that service he was largely instrumental in the capture of such desperadoes as John Dillinger, Baby Face Nelson, and the Karpis-Barker mob. He was there, gun in hand, the night Dillinger was killed in front of the Biograph Theater in Chicago.

In 1935 he became an investigator for the United States Department of Agriculture, and two years later he left to join the staff of the Chicago *Times*.

Mr. Metcalfe's first assignment as a reporter was to make an undercover investigation of the German and German-American Bunds. He became a uniformed storm trooper, drilled and marched with the Nazi army in the United States, and by gaining the confidence of its leaders, learned their innermost secrets of espionage and sabotage. On September 9, 1937 his exposé of Hitler's puppet army was published by the Chicago *Times* and appeared in newspapers from coast to coast. This won him the National Headliners Club award for distinguished journalism.

It was while on the newspaper staff, as reporter, feature writer, rewriteman, and assistant picture editor, that he yielded to the urge to compose verse. His first effort, at the age of fourteen, was published in the Notre Dame *Scholastic*. Versifying became a hobby, and he continued to write until he entered government service. Then he dropped it until in June 1938 he began his daily column, "Portraits," in the Chicago *Times*. The *Times*, incidentally, was the former Chicago *Daily Journal*, which in 1929 had awarded him its annual poetry prize.

After two years in newspaper work Mr. Metcalfe returned to agricultural investigation duties for the government but he continued to write his daily verse for the Chicago paper. In 1945, this feature was syndicated, and now, through the Chicago *Sun-Times* Syndicate, it appears in thirty-five states, the District of Columbia, Canada, and Ireland.

In his senior college year the author of "Portraits" married Lillian Hammer, a native of Norway, and they have three children. Their home is in Dallas, Texas, to which city they moved in 1940. It was in Texas, as a boy of eight years, that Mr. Metcalfe lived on his grandfather's farm.

At present (1952) he devotes his time to writing his daily newspaper verse, his books, and greeting card sentiments, and to giving lectures throughout the country.

Poet Laureate of the Fraternal Order of Eagles, he is the author of the following books: *Poem Portraits* (1948), a collection of verse published in newspapers; *Garden in My Heart* (1949), a volume of Catholic and friendly verse; *Poems For Children* (1950), *More Poem Portraits* (1951), and *My Rosary of Rhymes* (1952).   E. L.

Peter Michaels. See *Carol Jackson*

Ernest Milton 1890–

Born in San Francisco on January 10, 1890, Ernest Milton has spent most of his life in England and is a British subject. In 1926 he was married to Naomi Royde Smith, the distinguished writer (q.v.). In 1942 he was received into the Church and owes a debt of gratitude to his friend, Robert Speaight for an intervention at the most critical period of his conversion. This took the form of an introduction to Father Steuart, S.J. (of blessed memory) who gave Milton his final instruction and received him.

Ernest Milton is above all an actor. His most notable work has been done with the famous Old Vic Company which he joined at the invitation of Lilian Baylis, its great founder. There, in addition to a few of the small parts, which it is customary for all actors in that organization to do, he played most of the great Shakespearean leads including Hamlet, Romeo, Shylock, King John, King Lear, Leontes, Macbeth, King Richard II, Benedick, Biron, Parolles, Don Adriano de Armado, as well as juveniles like Orsino, Sebastian, Prince Hal, — and excursions into eighteenth century comedy such as Joseph Surface in *The School for Scandal*. He is probably the first male actor of modern times to have appeared in the title role of the mediaeval morality play *Everyman*, the earlier protagonists within living memory having been star actresses like Constance Crawley, Edith Wynne Matheson and Dame Sybil Thorndike. He is one of the few actors who have done Hamlet in its entirety. He has appeared with the Old Vic Company in Brussels and more recently, in 1950 — Holy Year — in Italy, when the crowning moment for some of its members was the private audience accorded them by the Pope. Milton had an outstanding success as Malvolio in *Twelfth Night* during the Company's triumphal tour of the major Italian cities. He has also played in Shakespeare, in Egypt, under the direction of Robert Atkins.

Milton has been actor manager at the Queens and St. James's Theatres, London, appearing in and directing "Othello," Pirandello's "Henry IV" and "Night's Candles," an English version of Musset's *Lorenzaccio*.

In the modern drama his outstanding successes have been in "Loyalties," "Rope" (in which he appeared in New York, where it was called "Rope's End"), "Grand Hotel," "Victoria Regina," "Death Takes a Holiday," "The Brothers Karamazov" (Father Zossima) and more lately "The Compelled People." He has appeared in two plays by his wife: "A Balcony" and "Mafro."

During the War he toured (with the Old Vic) the mining villages of County Durham in northern England playing Shylock, Svengali, King John, Macbeth, Aguecheek, etc.

Milton is, in addition, a well-known radio artist.

His writings include a play in verse, *Christopher Marlowe*, written at the age of eighteen and published many years later by Constable & Co. Ltd., of London, with a most gracious preface by Walter De La Mare — *To Kiss the Crocodile*, a novel of colorful adventure in the life of an adolescent, brought out by Harper in America and Messrs. Duckworth in England; two plays "Paganini" and "Mary of Magdala," in both of which he has appeared, the latter being published by the Society for Promoting Christian Knowledge. He has just completed a new play which was produced in the winter of 1951, and he is planning a book on the theatre which will be largely autobiographical in character.

He has lectured to various societies on Shakespearean and other theatrical subjects and has, on three occasions, been honored by invitations to speak to the senior boys at Downside Abbey School.

In all his undertakings he has found his wife his best critic.

Mrs. Ernest Milton. See Naomi Royde Smith

Joseph Cardinal Mindszenty   1892–

When peace and freedom return to Hungary, a person who will be remembered and revered will be the patriot Archbishop of Esztergom, Joseph Cardinal Mindszenty. In virtue of his addresses and pastorals as well as his books, the one-time peasant boy, Joseph Pehm, deserves a place among great writers, not indeed for any unusual grace of style, but for the authority and terrible directness of his writing. He was striking blows against the enemies of the Church and the Hungarian nation, and they were hard blows and deft. The deftness and strength of his blows constituted his style. He used no shield; he disdained to take shelter; he exposed his person as he struck. He knew martyrdom lay ahead and he did not shrink from it. If the Church was to be stricken, his should be the honor, for he was Cardinal Primate, of being the first victim. "One day," says *Newsweek* (February 14, 1949), "as he was riding through Budapest, followed by several other priests, the car bearing his entourage was stoned by the Communists. Mindszenty immediately stopped his own car and wrathfully approached the Red mob. 'I am the Church,' he cried. 'If you want something of the Church, stone me!'"

When the Communist Government confiscated the schools, Cardinal Mindszenty issued a Pastoral Letter (June 19, 1948), in which he denounced the Government's action as robbery. Without fear of consequence, he went straight to the point. A few passages will reveal, better than any analysis, the power and incisiveness of his pen. "That which we, the Bishops of Hungary, wished to spare our country, bleeding from a thousand wounds, has become a fact. Our schools and educational institutions have been confiscated. We solemnly protest against this measure in the name of the natural rights of the parents, the educational rights of the Church, and in the name of the freedom of religious instruction. Conscious of our duty, we cannot renounce our rights to our schools and institutions, and we shall not fail to demand, by every legal means, the restoration of that of which *we have been robbed.*"

The Pastoral concludes in a characteristic and revealing way. It shows the profound faith and the deep patriotism of the Cardinal, who was fighting for Christ and for his nation. "We ask you now, beloved in Christ, priests and faithful, to pray to Our Lord continually, that He may grant us steadiness and endurance so that we may be able to bear the ever increasing number of crosses of life. Do not forget what the Catholic schools have meant to the nation for centuries. Do not forget the eternal salvation of the souls of your children. *We, the Shepherds of your souls, declare once more that we wish to and shall continue to serve the Hungarian people and the Hungarian homeland in loyalty to our mission of Christ.*"

The Church annals of Hungary were presenting to the Catholic world the most inspiring of all public figures, a strong leader, who was at once a Patriot Bishop, and a Man of God. "I stand for God, Church and my country," he said in his last Pastoral. "This historic duty is bestowed upon me by the service of my people — the most orphaned people in all the world. When compared to the sufferings of my country, my own fate is unimportant.

"I am not accusing my accusers. If, from time to time, I must cast a light upon conditions, it is only a revelation of my country's surging pain, its welling tears, its truth crucified. I pray for a world of justice and brotherly love; I pray for those, too, who, in the words of my Master, know not what they do. I forgive them with all my heart."

Cardinal Mindszenty gave a living example of true democracy. From the day in 1921 when he was appointed parish priest of Zalaegerszeg, he loved and protected the poor. He gave to them; he fought for them; he lived as one of them. "Every Wednesday," recounts Bela Fabian (*Cardinal Mindszenty*, p. 57), "he invited seventeen guests to dinner — seventeen of the poorest of his parish — and served them exactly what he himself ate on the other days." His bread, his clothes, the milk of his cows, the carpets from his floors, was theirs as much as his. His charity knew no limits. The Jew was his child, his brother, as much as the Christian. It was only injustice, tyranny and deceit that he hated. The pseudo-democracy of the Reds angered him. "We must not," he wrote, "have the kind of 'democracy' that replaces one ruthless, power-hungry clique with another. . . . Do not be frightened by the threat of the sons of evil. The less opposition it finds, the stronger will tyranny grow."

The public, all the world over, knows that when the Reds imprisoned this great priest of God, they found a way of hurting and incapacitating his brain without actually killing him. "They had not let Cardinal Mindszenty die. They had arranged a more bitter martyrdom for him. . . . How the Communists managed it no one in the West knows. Somehow they broke this man of burning courage. Somehow they made him say things he had denied with the utmost vehemence, and with full knowledge of the consequences, until his arrest" (*Newsweek*, February 14, 1949).

Joseph Pehm was born in the village of Csehimindszent, in 1892. His father, John Pehm, was descended from a German family that had come to Hungary three hundred years previously. He had been mayor of the village and was much respected, raising a large family on a small farm of wheat, grapes and apples. Barbara Pehm, née Kovacs, is Joseph's mother, to whom all through life, he remained tenderly attached, and for whom he wrote his first book, *Motherhood*, when he was twenty-five years of age.

Joseph Pehm was sent to the Latin School of the Premonstrants at Szombathely in 1902 and continued there, through grammar and high school, and after that for his course in theology. He was ordained priest in 1915. He taught religion at the State School of Zalaegerszeg (1917–1919), editing *The News of Zala County;* publishing a pamphlet *Beware of the Newspapers;* and completing his book, *Motherhood*. In 1919 he was arrested and imprisoned by the Béla Kun Communists.

In 1921 came the turning point in Father Pehm's life with his appointment as parish priest of Zalaegerszeg. He at once set about organizing his parish and erecting churches and schools. He was a model, if stern pastor. If a curate complained of the work being too hard, he would reply, "The priesthood is not play. It is duty. It is work. If a life of ease is what you wanted, you should have chosen another vocation." As his influence grew in the county he came to be called "the Pope of Zala." He raised the Church taxes so as to improve the condition of the social work of his parish. He was a stern disciplinarian, a fighter, honest, "a tough fellow," independent, progressive.

A thousand stories are told of his humor and homely peasant ways. He was a true Hungarian; one of the people who loved and worked the soil. When he discovered the existence of the Nazi "Arrow and Cross" society in Zala County and that it was out to persecute the Jews, he fought it tooth and nail. In 1944 he was consecrated Bishop of Veszprém, and soon after, when Hitler's forces came, he was thrown into prison. In 1945, being liberated from prison on the arrival of the Russians, he was appointed Archbishop of Esztergom (October 2nd, 1945). The following February he received from the hands of His Holiness, Pius XII, the Cardinal's hat, becoming Primate and Prince Cardinal of Hungary. From then on he fought the Communist Government until his arrest in December 1948.

Apart from his addresses and pastorals and pamphlets, Cardinal Mindszenty published two books: *Motherhood* (1917); and *The Life and Times of Martin Padányi Biró* (1934). *The Face of the Heavenly Mother*, in preparation before his solitary confinement, appeared in 1951.

Cardinal Mindszenty combines in his person and in his philosophy two apparently irreconcilable characters; he is strongly progressive; he is resolutely conservative.

His progressive spirit was revealed in his dispute with the wealthy and powerful Count Batthani who objected to the contributions that Cardinal Mindszenty, then parish priest of Zalaegerszeg, demanded for his social works. "In what age has it not been demonstrated," wrote the then pastor, "that insuring the welfare of the people is the sole function of the nation? There is one way, and one way only, in which the healthy life of the Church and of the State can be furthered; *uplift the masses!* Allow the people to sink in misery and ignorance and you destroy both Church and State. . . . Whoever does not understand this, whoever opposes it, belongs to the Dark Ages!" One of his constantly repeated sayings was: "*Poverty must not be tolerated!*"

But when it came to interfering with the Catholic principles of the education of the young, or the administration of the Church, Cardinal Mindszenty was uncompromisingly conservative. This aspect of his character is portrayed by Lily Doblhoff in *The Commonweal* (January 21, 1949). "He did not want to compromise since he believed firmly . . . that no understanding could be reached with the forces of evil, of tyranny, and that the teaching of Christ, with the profound importance it gives to the individual's soul and the individual's approach to religion, is in fundamental opposition to materialistic theories and Marxist principles."

The Cardinal took a bold, uncompromising, fighting stand against the Red alien government of Hungary, because he knew better than others the thoughts and wishes in the deep soul of his country. The kind of leadership the soul of Hungary yearned for, he supplied.

E. B. B.

Margaret Theodora Monro   1896–

Margaret Theodora Monro is a Scotswoman, born in 1896 at Ranaghat, Bengal, India, where her father was a medical missionary of one of the Anglican missionary societies. He was Charles George Monro, M.B., Ch.B., and her mother Eliza Stuart (Rattray) Monro; from them she considers that she had about the best religious upbringing possible outside the Catholic Church.

In 1904 she was sent home, along with younger brothers and sisters, for education, until her parents came home for good and settled in Edinburgh.

The most notable figure in the family background was her grandfather, James Monro, "the most just man I have ever met" by the testimony of all who knew him. After rising to be a judge in the Indian Civil Service, he was brought home to London to become "the best-loved chief the Metropolitan Police have ever had," according to the historian of Scotland Yard. He had the unravelling of the "dynamite" plots of the 'Eighties. Miss Monro was thus brought up on true detective stories, and feels that in one sense her life has been a detective story, ending with the discovery of the Church Christ founded — a quest in which she owes much to all her grandfather had taught her of the laws of evidence.

Until the age of eleven she was educated at home by governesses. From 1907 to 1910 she attended St. Margaret's School, Aberdeen, then till 1913 she was a boarder at St. Michael's, Limpsfield, Surrey, a school for the children of missionaries of the mission to which her father belonged. After a further year as a day pupil at Wimbledon High School, London (1913–1914), she studied privately at home for a year in Edinburgh, before completing her education at Girton College, Cambridge (1915–1918) where she obtained First Class Honors in the Medieval and Modern Languages Tripos in 1918, her subjects being English and French language and literature. Her linguistic bent found further outlet when in 1919 she went as a missionary to Palestine. In 1920 she transferred to Cairo, remaining till 1933, save for a break in Palestine from 1925 to 1928. While in Egypt she learned to speak Arabic fluently and to read enough to cope with the editorial work of the mission in that language. Save for two years of school teaching, her life as an Anglican missionary was given to publication work.

During these fourteen years in the Near East, she found herself, like many of her generation, driven to make a complete re-assessment of the religion in which she had been brought up. Her environment was helpful. Living among a number of distinguished personalities, American as well as British, she was also living in the lands of the Bible and of the Early Church, with direct contact with every variety of Protestantism and of Eastern Orthodoxy. Christian re-union, and what was called "the restatement of doctrine" occupied much of her thoughts. By the time she was invalided home in 1933, she had recast much of her childhood beliefs in more modern molds. But not until she was settled in Scotland did she discover what "modernism" was doing to religion, and so found herself started on a new quest, in search of a firm foundation. "What most impressed me," writes Miss Monro, "was the spiritual debility of my country — and it was in the attempt to understand how it had come about that I first really learned anything about the Reformation." Her readings in Church History had long given her a more sympathetic appreciation of the Early and Middle Ages, than she had acquired from family tradition. "For years, however," she says, "I had assumed that the Catholic Church was moribund, a back number, though even before leaving the East three great modern Catholics had impinged on my horizon — Charles de Foucauld, Mother Janet Erskine Stuart, and Baron von Hügel. As it came home to me that my 'modern' position was failing to meet the needs of 'modern people,' it gradually became clear that I had to come to terms with the Catholic Church, if only to get an obsession out of the way and let me get on with my work. Once under instruction, however, the situation rapidly cleared up, and I was received into the Catholic Church on May 23rd, 1937." Looking back, she sees how all her life led up to this. Since then, the sister with whom she makes her home has also become a Catholic.

While in the East, longstanding deafness had grown steadily more serious, so that writing now offered the best hopes of earning a livelihood. At first she was drawn into the Scottish Renaissance Movement, and worked on plays on Scottish history — part of an effort to rescue Scots from the condition of a disintegrating dialect and give it literary status once more. Two of these plays were produced, "Greenside" by the Scottish BBC in 1936 and "The Winnock" by the Curtain Players, Glasgow, in 1937.

In 1938, a year after her reception into the Catholic Church, a road accident left her without the power to write plays. But she was already thinking of turning her energies in another direction. "The war in 1939," she writes, "precipitated on to paper ideas that had been growing up for many years." The result was her first saints' book: *Seeking for Trouble*, with the subtitle *Saints for Christian Civilization*.

Her published works are: *The Path Divides: A Story of Egypt*, a missionary study circle book, (1932); *Breaking out of Prison*, a book for the deaf and their friends, (1934); *Mother Forbes of Craiglockhart*, semi-privately published in Edinburgh, (1940); *Seeking for Trouble* (1941); *A Book of Unlikely Saints* (1943); *Enjoying the New Testament* (1944); *Margaret Clitherow* (1945). A verse play, *A Stream on Mount Olympus*, was printed for private circulation in 1949.

Miss Monro has a special interest in the lives of the Desert Fathers, whose Egyptian background is personally known to her. When she herself began to be gravely deaf, it was from them that she received the best help in making a constructive use of her limitation.

P. B. L.

Right Reverend Monsignor Edward Roberts Moore   1894–

Only two others among the four hundred pastors in the archdiocese of New York share with Monsignor Edward Roberts Moore the accidental distinction of returning as pastor to the parish where they had started as assistants. In 1919 Father Moore was sent as a curate to St. Peter's Church on Barclay Street; since 1937 he has been pastor of St. Peter's.

He was born in New York City, on January 9, 1894. His mother was a convert from the Church of England; his father was a Catholic. He attended St. Augustine's Academy in the Bronx, the Morris High School, and then Fordham College and Fordham University. He received his A.B. in 1915, his A.M. in 1921 and his Ph.D. in 1923. He studied for the priesthood in St. Joseph's Seminary, Dunwoodie, New York and hoped that he would be among those selected after the first or second year for study abroad, generally at Rome or Louvain. World War I dissipated the hope of going to Europe but kept open a chance of going to the Catholic University for post-ordination study. Great was his joy when at the end of his third theology year, Monsignor Chidwick, then rector of the seminary, informed him that he was selected by the Faculty to go to the Catholic University. About ten days after he was ordained a priest, came the day when the newly ordained priests were to meet their Archbishop, then Archbishop Hayes, and receive from him formally and officially their assignments. Father Moore with the others met the Archbishop at eleven o'clock in the morning. He had made arrangements to leave for Washington immediately after meeting the Archbishop. He had reserved his room at the university, sent his trunks and books there and had his tickət. Then came the bombshell. Instead of being sent to the university, "my lifetime dream," he had been assigned as an assistant at Old St. Peter's on Barclay Street! From 1919 to 1923 he labored there as a curate. His experiences at this oldest Catholic Church in New York are told in his most recent book, *Roman Collar* (1951), published by the Macmillan Company. The book was written to give the normal daily routine of the life of a priest. By the end of his four years as an assistant he knew practically everyone living in the parish.

Then came his appointment to membership on the staff of the Catholic Charities of the Archdiocese of New York, the central Diocesan Charitable Agency that had recently been established by Archbishop, later Cardinal Hayes. He went to live at St. Gregory's Rectory from 1923 to 1929. When he reported to the Reverend Robert F. Keegan, Executive Director of the Catholic Charities of the Archdiocese of New York one day in September, 1923, Father Keegan appointed him Director of the Division of Social Action of the Catholic Charities of the Archdiocese of New York. "It took two lines on a calling card. It was most impressive." Father Moore held this position until 1941. From 1924 to 1938 he was a professor of Community Organization in the Fordham University School of Social Service. He has also been a member of numerous organizations, committees and boards. He worked with the C.Y.O. (Catholic Youth Organization), Boy Scouts and the Legion of Decency. He was diocesan contact man with the New York Province of Newman Clubs and for ten years was Chaplain of the New York University Newman Club. In 1933 he became a member of the Slum Clearance and Low Cost Housing Committee of the City of New York, and in 1939 a charter member of the newly created New York City Housing Authority. At the end of his second five-year term he asked Mayor La Guardia not to reappoint him. He wanted to get back to the purely spiritual work of his priesthood.

In 1937 he became pastor of St. Peter's where he had come as an assistant fresh from the seminary. St. Peter's, located as it is in downtown New York, has only a handful of people present at the Masses on Sundays. On week days, however, the business people who work in the neighborhood throng the church for the eight o'clock, the eight-thirty and midday Masses. The beautiful church that seats eight hundred overflows on Holy Days. Because of the unusual situation there, a varied

and useful schedule of activities is carried on. First, a Catholic Lending Library was established and then Forums and Round Tables.
Courses are given on the Mass, the Liturgy, Liturgical Music, the
Teachings and Practices of the Church. There is an active Legion of
Mary and "Approved Workmen," a men's group aiming at personal
santification through the knowledge and practice of the liturgy.
"The Followers of Fatima" is a young business girls' organization
devoted to Our Lady of Fatima. These and a whole series of other
activities are publicized through a little paper called the *Barclay
Street News.* In 1941 Father Moore was made Private Chamberlain of
the Papal Household of Pope Pius XII and in 1949 he was made a
Domestic Prelate, with the title of Right Reverend Monsignor.

Monsignor Moore's first book was *The Case against Birth Control,*
published by The Century Company in 1931. Asked what prompted
him to write the book he replied: "In the two or three years immediately
preceding *The Case against Birth Control,* a powerful effort was made
by the Birth Control League of America, now the Planned Parenthood
Association, to modify the then and now (1951) existing legislation in
the State of New York in such a way as to remove practically all restrictions on the manufacture, distribution, advertising and display of
birth control material.

"Much of the organization in opposition to this unhappy program
had fallen to my lot. When the smoke of the battle had cleared, we
approached His Eminence, Cardinal Hayes, then Archbishop of New
York, with the proposal that we make a scientific study of that much
vexed question, dealing with such matters as population trends, trends
in public opinion and the medical aspects, etc. His Eminence approved
the project and made available a considerable sum of money to carry
it out. It was arranged that a committee of which I would be chairman
would be set up under the auspices of the National Conference of Catholic Charities. The committee secured the services of Dr. Constantine
McGuire, research expert of Brookings Institute, and did, I think I
may say, a fairly good job. The results of this study were published
in five successive articles in *The Commonweal.* These articles were subsequently expanded into full book length in *The Case against Birth
Control.* Ever since then I have been attempting to live down the op-
probrium of being the Catholic Church's 'expert on birth control.'"

Monsignor Moore is hoping that his second book, *Heart in Pilgrimage* (1948), written in collaboration with Evelyn Eaton, may, in
preference, result in his name being associated in people's minds with
that lovely soul and dynamic leader, Elizabeth Ann Bayley Seton.
His interest in her was a natural one. Elizabeth Ann Bayley Seton was
born and lived much of her life in the neighborhood of Barclay Street,
and, what is more important, was received into the Church in Old St.
Peter's. "As pastor of St. Peter's," remarks Monsignor Moore, "I
could not but be deeply interested in her life and her prodigious works
of piety."

His third work, *Roman Collar,* appeared in 1951. It is a revealing
account of the multivaried activities of a priest.   M. A. H.

Reverend Thomas Hendrick Moore, S.J. 1898–

It is not without cause that Saint Bernard has said, "No man enters easily into the mind of Christ." There have always been, however, Catholic theologians who have reverently and successfully studied the mind of Christ as it is revealed in the life, teachings, and revelations of the Redeemer. Father Moore belongs to this number. His writings, in the words of the Dominican, Father Kienberger, "radiate Christ . . . and, with deft strokes and magnificent imagery, have coded a message of power."

With regard to the background to his writings, Father Moore says, somewhat wryly, "I suppose it adds up to neither more or less than the usual item-by-item background of the average member of the Society of Jesus."

Born in Buffalo, New York, on January 22, 1898, the son of Thomas Francis and Elizabeth Victoria (McClure) Moore, he spent his boyhood in Syracuse, where his parents had moved when he was six months old.

After finishing high school in Syracuse, he entered Holy Cross College in 1915 with the intention of becoming a diocesan priest, but a year later decided to enter the Society of Jesus. His classical studies in the Society were made at St. Andrew-on-Hudson, Poughkeepsie, New York, followed by philosophy courses at Woodstock College, in Maryland. At Woodstock he obtained the A.B. degree in 1922, and the A.M. in 1923.

From 1923 to 1926, Father Moore was instructor in physics at Georgetown University. Four years of theological studies followed at Woodstock, and he was ordained priest in 1929. It was from the Gregorian University in Rome that he received his S.T.D. degree in 1930. From 1931 to 1934 he was professor of physics at St. Joseph's College in Philadelphia, Pennsylvania.

In 1935, Father Moore entered that phase of his career, still continuing to the present, which associated him much more formally with distinctly religious activities. Between 1935 and 1941, he was associate professor of Religion, Student Counsellor, and Director of the Parthenian Academy at Fordham University. Thereupon, under his direction as Spiritual Director of the Laymen's League for Retreats at Mt. Manresa, Staten Island, the men's retreat movement made forward strides in both numbers and effect throughout the metropolitan New York area. He held this position from 1941 to 1948. It was in 1949 that he was appointed to his present position, one giving wider scope to his message, as editor of the *Messenger of the Sacred Heart*. The magazine, which he edits from the New York office, is the official organ of the Apostleship of Prayer, going out every month to some hundreds of thousands of readers.

"Editing this magazine now, with more than eighty years of publishing behind it," Father Moore has pointed out, "is a welcome challenge and opportunity to an editor. It's a challenge inasmuch as it offers itself as a medium to bring first-rate devotional and spiritual reading to Catholics across the country. Its opportunity lies in the fact that it is the only magazine which features in first position, month after month, a careful analysis of the needs of the Church as they are identified by by the Roman Pontiff in those intentions which he commands to the world apostleship."

Besides his continuing articles in the *Messenger*, Father Moore has written several spiritual volumes. These include: *I Also Send You* (1937); *Beyond the Altar Rail* (1939); *Heart of the King* (1945); *The Darkness is Past* (1946); *Heart of the Queen* (1949); *The Risen Dead* (1951), and *Morning Offering* (1952). His compilation of prayers and devotions, gathered for men retreatants in the Mount Manresa Book (1946), has been used as a model in numerous houses of retreat.

Father Moore's writings have been called, not without cause, "purposeful." This characteristic is seen, for instance, in his exposition of the *meaning* of the Mass in *Beyond the Altar Rail*. Few writers, if indeed any, have better succeeded in setting forth in intelligible and "popular" exposition the celebrated theory of de la Taille concerning the Sacrifice of the Mass. Thus the author, instancing the official decrees and canons of Trent respecting the Mass, reminds readers that "there are yet many important questions which have not been authoritatively settled by the Church. Such questions theologians are free to discuss. *How* is it possible for the Mass to be a true sacrifice of the Body and Blood of Our Lord? *How* can Christ, now glorified in heaven, be the Victim of this Sacrifice? *Why* should there be a sacrifice at all, since the Sacrifice of Christ redeemed once and forever them that are sanctified?"

The same inquiring mind sets itself to work in the pages of *I Also Send You*, with its able apologetic pages. The divine claim of Christ, the authenticity and integrity of the Scriptures, the various "missions" of the Apostolic Church, an analysis of the separated churches, these and other questions fill the book with readable, practical material.

It is in the study of the Life of all living, that of the Redeemer, that Father Moore prefers most to concern himself and his talent. In his continuing series in his magazine, as well as in the books from his typewriter, he brings Christ to the general reading public.

The meaning of the new dispensation, following the groping darkness of paganism, Father Moore finds heralded in Paul's joyous "The darkness is passed and the true light now shineth." In the book bearing the first half of this quotation as title, he expounds one of his pet theses: "The supermen of this world are the adopted sons of God."

A. R. McG.

Adolf Morath   1905–

The photographer Adolf Morath is a British subject and a member of a large German Catholic family from the Black Forest, Germany.

Born in Wallasey, Cheshire, England on June 23, 1905 he was educated by the Christian Brothers in Liverpool, and by the Marist Brothers at St. Joseph's College, Dumfries, Scotland.

At the age of twelve his father bought him a Brownie box camera, and he then commenced his photographic work by photographing his school friends and landscapes in the South of Scotland.

Upon leaving school he went into his family's watch making business, but after a short while he found that this work did not agree with him so he left it to take up work as a professional photographer. Year after year he increased his artistic and technical skill until today he is looked upon as one of the most outstanding photographers in Europe.

Mr. Morath's first book is *Faces Before My Camera*. It is primarily intended as a guide for those who wish to take portrait photographs above average. *The British Journal of Photography* comments: "This book should prove a storehouse indeed of ideas on posing, lighting, and above all understanding one's sitters. From this standpoint it is the most notable and outstanding book on portraiture that has been published in this country, and Adolf Morath is to be most sincerely congratulated." *Photography* says of it: "As a guide to those aspiring to do good work like this, the book is invaluable. As a book full of pictures just to look at, it is a treasure."

His second book was *Children Before My Camera* and the third, *Pets Before My Camera*. His latest book is *Portrait of Ireland*. To produce this book, Mr. Morath, in 1948, made a four-month tour of Ireland in his car to photograph a full cross-section of Irish faces as well as landscapes and pictures illustrating the whole of the life of Ireland. The great painters and poets, the leaders of the Church and State, the great fighters for Irish freedom, the politicians, the stage, etc., have been portrayed as well as representative types of Irish faces from town, from the country and from the sea — fishermen, farmers, railway workers and all types of Irish workers, both men and women. Dublin, the scenery in County Kerry, Donegal, the Blasket Islands, the Aran Islands, in fact every county has been covered with his camera.

Mr. Morath found the Aran Islanders most unresponsive to photography. The women ran behind doors, and the children scampered off at his appearance. Having managed to overcome this shyness he discovered a commercialized outlook. One old woman whom he approached told him bluntly that she could be photographed only if he paid her 2/6. "And if you want to take a picture of the chimney you'll have to pay 7/6," she added. He has to date nearly a thousand black and white photographs as well as some beautiful color photographs. Mr. Morath remarked: "I can truthfully say that I have not only captured the 'face of Ireland' but its spirit and soul as well."

Speaking of Ireland he said: "When weather conditions are good, no country in the world presents such wonderful stuff both for the camera artist and the painter. I have seldom encountered anything like it in any other part of the world."

Mr. Morath is a bachelor. He will not marry unless he finds a wife who is also a strict vegetarian like himself, and "has a brain radiation approaching his own, and has other qualifications not usually found in women looking for husbands."   M. A. H.

Sylvanus Griswold Morley
1883–1948

"Morley," writes Alfred Vincent Kidder, the internationally famed archaeologist, in *El Palacio* (September, 1948), "will always be best known as a Mayanist. His name will rank with those of Stephens and Catherwood, Maudslay, Bowditch, and Tozzer. His contribution was three fold: through his own discoveries, studies, and scientific publications; through his wide popularization of the Maya by lectures and magazine articles and by his last book, *The Ancient Maya.*"

Sylvanus Griswold Morley was born in Chester, Pennsylvania on June 7, 1883, the son of Benjamin Franklin and Sarah Eleanor Constance (de Lannoy) Morley. His father was professor of chemistry and vice-president of Pennsylvania Military College, and insisted that Sylvanus study engineering at that college. After graduating with the degree C.E. in 1904 he went to Harvard, where he hoped to study Egyptology, for he was curious about hieroglyphics. Professor Putnam, Director of the Peabody Museum, convinced him, however, that there was little new to be learned as to Egyptian writing but that the Maya glyphs were still for the most part undeciphered. Morley gave up the idea of studying Egyptology, once he started courses under Tozzer. Three years later he received his A.B. degree and was awarded a research fellowship in American archaeology. His A.M. degree was received in 1908. That same year he married Alice Galtinger Williams and was later divorced. In 1927 he married Frances Louella Rhoads.

His first archaeological expedition was in the Southwest under Dr. E. L. Hewett of the Archaeological Institute of America. "One thing about Morley's life in the Southwest should be recorded," writes A. V. Kidder in *El Palacio*, "for perhaps few people realize how much he did to make Sante Fe architecturally what it is today. What happened was this. When he took a position with the newly-founded School of American Archaeology and in 1909 came to live in Santa Fe, he bought a semi-ruinous adobe on a little knoll at the foot of Fort Marcy. It had a lovely portal with posts and corbels. Instead of tearing the house down, or "modernizing" it, as was then the regrettable practice in such cases, he kept the portal as it was and replaced the rotten vigas of its rooms with fine old carved beams. . . . The success of his house led others to follow his lead."

In 1915 he was appointed Research Associate of the Carnegie Institution of Washington and continued in this capacity until his death. Thus began "the long series of explorations in all parts of the Maya country that resulted in more than doubling the then known number of hieroglyphic inscriptions and in the discovery of many new cities, most important of which was Uaxactun in the jungles of northern Peten, Guatemala," writes A. V. Kidder in *El Palacio*. Mr. Kidder also states: "I know he covered an amazing amount of most difficult country; on muleback, by canoe, afoot. He certainly put to his credit more leagues of bush travel than any other Mayanist has accomplished, or is ever likely to again." He was often down with malaria and amoebic dysentery. . . . Yet he went back again and again. Mr. Kidder further states: "He had a genuine love for Yucatan and the people of Yucatan both native and Latin. There was, indeed much of the Latin in his makeup. He possessed their real courtesy, their quickness of mind and flashing intuition as to situations and persons, their lack of hypocrisy. He liked them and they liked him. They also liked to hear him talk Spanish, for his Spanish was as unique as everything else about him; unbelievably fluent, unbelievably indifferent to mood, tense and gender. He and I and the eminent archaeologist Alfonso Caso once lectured in Mexico City before the Sociedad Antonio Alzate. In summing up, Caso said: 'This, fellow members, has been a memorable evening. We have had addresses in three languages: English, Spanish and Morley!'"

His first literary work was accepted by the Smithsonian and published under the title, *Introduction to the Study of Maya Hieroglyphs* (1915), still a standard text-book. Then followed *Inscriptions at Copan* (1920); *Guide Book to the Ruins of Quirigua* (1935); *The Inscriptions of Peten* (1937). His last book, *The Ancient Maya* (1947), has been called the definitive work on the subject.

In his sixty-fifth year, Dr. Morley was received into the Catholic Church by Archbishop Edwin V. Byrne of Santa Fe, New Mexico. He died on September 2, 1948, soon after his reception into the Church.

M. A. H.

Daphne D. C. Pochin Mould
1920–

Although Miss Daphne Mould lived in Scotland for several years, she is actually English, having been born in Salisbury in Wiltshire in 1920. In fact, she did not cross the border into Scotland until after she had learned to drive an automobile and went there in 1938 on her first motoring holiday. She found herself so immensely attracted to Scotland that she returned in 1939 to enter Edinburgh University, graduating B.Sc., with First Class Honors in geology in 1943. That same year she was also awarded the Falconer Memorial Fellowship at Edinburgh to do research in geology. She held this for three years, graduating Ph.D. in 1946.

These years at Edinburgh were those of World War II. She was not called up for the forces as she was not physically fit then. From 1940 onwards, however, she did part time Civil Defense work, first as "a sitting case car driver" in Air Raid Precautions, and later (from 1942) in the Volunteer Car Pool. Edinburgh never experienced any raiding to speak of, but the Volunteer Car Pool was kept busy doing routine runs for government departments, the blood transfusion service and so on.

Doctor Mould's thesis for her Ph.D. was on "The Geology of the Foyers Granite and Surrounding Country," and it was published in the *Geological Magazine* for December 1946. Foyers is near Fort Augustus, a typical Highland district, and as yet she says "unsurveyed by our Geological Survey, so that my mapping was almost completely pioneer work, the old small scale map being inaccurate. More important, I got to know the Highlands and the Highlanders, and to realize some of their problems — the difficulty of transport, depopulation, the picture of ruined croft houses and neglected fields invaded by brackens and rushes."

She had always meant to take up writing seriously. She had written articles and poems for her own amusement "as far back almost as I can remember," and when she finished writing her Ph.D. thesis she started writing about Scotland and succeeded in selling some articles. She regards article writing, however, as unsatisfactory: "no sooner does one get really started on a subject when it is time to leave off — anyway, here in our paper-rationed papers — so I started work on my first book."

Meantime, she moved north again, to Fort Augustus, a good centre for her intended writing about the Scottish Highlands and their problems. The house in which she lived has four acres of land attached and having been empty many years, the whole was completely derelict and overgrown. "Obviously," she says, "it is no good writing about

Highland problems without some practical experience: the average Highlander, for instance, is highly suspicious of anybody with a theory but no experience of the job itself. Accordingly (and also because I like growing things), I set to and cut down brambles and got the ground into cultivation, and have been successfully growing fruit and vegetables, both for our own use and for sale. It appears that all kinds of soft fruits do well here: the problem which is killing the Highlands is transport, the difficulty and high cost of getting any surplus over and above what can be consumed locally away to market."

In 1947, she collected the material for her first book, *The Roads from the Isles*, which was published in 1950 by Oliver & Boyd of Edinburgh (the long delay between the getting of the material and publication is due to the many difficulties of labor and supply affecting the publishing business in Scotland at the moment). This book is a study of the Northwest Highland drove roads and tracks, the routes by which cattle used to be driven from the Hebrides across Scotland down to the big markets in the Scottish Lowlands, a trade which was the mainstay of Highland economy before the glens were evicted, first to make sheep walks and later deer forests. The book describes the old routes, their present condition (Dr. Mould went over all of them herself both on foot and, when possible, by car), their relation to the underlying geology and the history and archaeology connected with them.

After *The Roads from the Isles*, it was natural to look across the Minch to the Outer Hebrides and plan a book about them. She therefore visited all the Outer Hebrides, from Lewis to Barra, over a period of two years and wrote her second book, *West-over-Sea: The Outer Hebrides*, about them. This book describes each of the islands, its history and archaeology placenames, problems, and also includes a special study of the archaic beehive-vaulted huts which still survive in some of the islands. These beehive huts resemble those built by the Celtic Church, which still survive in some of the Hebridean islands and in Ireland; the interesting part about the ones in Lewis is that they were kept in repair and used as summer shielings by the local people almost to the present day.

Having completed this second book — also to be published by Messrs. Oliver & Boyd, in the not too distant future — she began to follow up a suggestion that she write about the Inner Hebrides, about Mull, Coll, Tiree and Lismore. This is how she came to be a Catholic. Iona is just off the coast of Mull and the whole area is very rich in associations with the Celtic Church. She thought the sites of the churches founded by the Celtic saints and the routes they followed (which can be traced by placenames) would be a good basis for a book about an otherwise rather disjointed district. She could correlate sites with primitive agriculture, routes with geology and archaeology, the work of the different saints with early Scottish political history. "Except for a brief interlude of about three years," she says, "when I had some belief in the Church of England, I had always been agnostic: I intended to write about the saints as people who had used their religion (which, being reasonable men, they knew to be false), as a means to gain political power and their own advancement. I did not get very far with this idea. At the least, I thought, I should find out what the Church did believe and why, before attacking her. Just over a year ago, I started to make enquiries into the matter; to my utter astonishment I found that Christianity was reasonable and true. I am therefore in the somewhat peculiar position of having begun to write a book about the Celtic Church in the West Highlands and Islands, as an attack on the Church and the faith, and ending up by becoming a Catholic and getting the Catholic imprimatur for the MS!"

Miss Mould is now living in Co. Galway, Ireland, in one of the cottages on the grounds of Kylemore Abbey, which belongs to the Benedictine nuns who have a school and guest house there. She writes: "It is a most attractive part of Ireland, snuggled in amongst the Connemara mountains and about 50 miles from Galway town — where I am in contact with the University College for books and information generally."

Her third book, also to be published soon, is *Scotland of the Saints;* about the Celtic saints in Scotland. In preparation is *Ireland of the Saints.*   M. A. H.

Reverend Jean Claude Mouroux
1901-

Jean Claude Mouroux was born in Dijon, France on March 16, 1901. After finishing the secondary school there, he entered the local seminary.

Ordained a priest on June 29, 1926, Father Mouroux was sent by his bishop to study at the Catholic University of Lyon. Upon his return to Dijon in 1932, he was appointed professor of the minor seminary in Flavigny and then he was appointed professor of fundamental theology and dogma in the major seminary. When he became superior of the major seminary in 1947 he retained his position as professor.

Amidst all his work, he finds time to write on intellectual and spiritual problems. His favorite subject is the problem of faith and religious experience. On that theme he contributed the articles "Sur la nation d'experience religieuse" published in the *Melange de Science Religieuse* (XXIV, 1949, p. 29); "L'experience de L'Ésprit chez Saint Paul" (ibid. V, 1948, p. 38), and "L'experience de l'Ésprit chez Saint Jean" *(La Vie Spirituelle* 1947).

On the problem of faith he wrote "Sur la genèse de la certitude morale" *(Revue Apologetique,* LIX, 1934, pp. 689–712); "Discernement et discernibilité de miracle" (ibid. LX, 1939, pp. 938–962); "Remarques sur la foi dans Saint Paul" (ibid. LXV, 1937, pp. 129–148; 281–299); "Structure personelle de la foi (XXIX, 1939, p. 39–107), an article which was rewritten in a completed form in the work *Je crois en toi mon dieu* (Paris 1949), and "Sur la conscience de la foi" (*Recherches de Science Religieuse*, XXXVI, 1949, pp. 422–494).

The book which gave him considerable fame is *Sens chrétien de l'homme* (1949). It was translated into Italian, German and English. The translation into English was made by A. H. C. Downes and was published by Sheed and Ward under the title *The Meaning of Man*. The book is divided into three sections. "The first, called Temporal Values, deals with man's relationship to the created order. The second, Carnal Values, deals with the body, its nobility, its misery, and finally its redemption. The third and longest section, on Spiritual Values, deals with the human person, spiritual liberty, Christian liberty, love, charity and the sacred character of man."   G. B.

Reverend Senan Moynihan, O.F.M. Cap.

As editor of Capuchin periodicals, a series of reviews — *The Capuchin Annual, The Father Mathew Record* and *Bonaventura* — published at Dublin, Father Senan is one of the most vital influences not merely in the Catholic journalism of the contemporary world but more immediately in literature and the arts in present-day Ireland.

Born in County Kerry some fifty years ago, he was educated at the local national school, at Saint Brendan's Seminary, Killarney, later at All Hallows College, Dublin, at University College in the same city, with the Capuchins at University College, Cork, and in their house of studies at Rochestown. In those years he manifested a special feeling for literature in both Irish and English, and scored occasionally a heartening distinction. Having been ordained priest at Holy Trinity, Cork, in 1928, he took up duty, a few weeks later, at the Capuchin friary in Dublin, where he was put in charge of what was then the only Irish Capuchin periodical, *The Father Mathew Record*, named after the famous Irish Capuchin Apostle of Temperance. With Father Senan as editor it was inevitable that the *Record* should gain in dynamism and in influence. Even so it was far from exhausting the young priest's energy and initiative and in 1929 he founded *The Capuchin Annual*.

What the *Annual* has become today and the various stages of its development as the years have gone on are known to practically every reader of the *Annual*. *The Capuchin Annual* is a lively compendium, at once grave and gay, representing Irish life in poetry, in fiction, in *belles-lettres*, in criticism of the fine arts and of music, illustrated by drawings, by reproductions of pictures, ancient and modern, and by photographs of the contemporary scene.

Bonaventura was founded by Father Senan in 1937. Published quarterly, it sustained a perhaps more consistently "high-brow" note than *The Capuchin Annual*, though perhaps we should say only in so far as was consistent with the true Franciscan spirit. Owing to shortage of paper supplies during the Second World War, publication of *Bonaventura* had to be suspended in the course of the 1940's, but the *Record* and the *Annual* go on perennially.

At home Father Senan is active in many spheres outside that of his literary work. He is a Governor and Guardian (appointed by the Irish Government) of Ireland's National Gallery, which is one of the more important picture galleries of the world. He is also a member of the advisory board of Dublin's municipal gallery of modern art. In 1945 he took the initiative in organizing a loan exhibition of the works of Mr. Jack B. Yeats, the *doyen* of contemporary Irish painters and now recognized as one of the modern world's greatest artists. The 1945 exhibition was an act of homage from the Irish nation to its most representative great artist in which the government, leading churchmen and citizens of all denominations joined.

Father Senan also effectively drew attention to the work for Irish music of the late Carl Hardebeck and it was to help his activities in that particular instance that a great concert of Hardebeck's music was given in New York in 1944, the year before the great musician died. The help and encouragement that Father Senan has given to younger writers, artists and musicians is a story that has no end.

With all these activities it might seem that he has little time for study or for writing himself, but his knowledge of even minute details of Irish history is enough to make the mouth of any professional historian water. His recent book *Angelic Shepherd* — a study of the life and activities of our present Holy Father, Pope Pius XII — is an exemplar in its own domain and has won the highest encomiums.

It may be noted that Father Senan's elder brother, the Very Reverend Francis Moynihan, who died a few years ago, was for many years the distinguished editor of *The Advocate*, Melbourne, Australia.

K. MacG.

Reverend Hermann Muckermann
1877–

Father Hermann Muckermann, the anthropologist, was born on August 30, 1877, at Bückeburg (Schaumburg-Lippe), Germany. After attending several German gymnasia, he entered, in 1896, the novitiate of the German Jesuits in Blyenbeck, Holland. After two years of application to the humanistic studies, he studied rhetoric at Exaten, Holland, for two semesters.

In 1899 he was sent to the United States in order to study philosophy at the old Jesuit University in Wisconsin at Prairie du Chien, then called the College of the Sacred Heart and incorporated on August 20, 1881. He remained there for six semesters. The teachers were German Jesuits and their courses of instruction were the same as in the Ignatius College of Valkenburg, Holland. His final examination for the Ph.D. degree took place on June 21, 1902. His thesis was: "The essential difference between the human and animal soul, proved from their specific activities."

In the fall of 1902 he was ordered to teach mathematics and natural sciences in the above named college for four years. At the same time he contributed articles to the *Scientific American* and the magazine of the North American Jesuits — then called *The Messenger*.

In the fall of 1906 he returned to Holland to study theology at the Ignatius College of Valkenburg. Besides, he was also professor of biology and published a *Grundriss der Biologie* (*A Compendium of Biology*) and contributed to the *Catholic Encyclopaedia* in the United States, and to magazines.

He was ordained a priest by the Bishop of Poona, India, on August 28, 1909, in the private chapel of the college. After another year of theology, his superiors sent him to Tronchiennes, Belgium, for his third year of probation and then to Louvain in order to study biology for four semesters. At the same time he did research work in cytology at the Institut Carnoy and took his final examination in histology, anatomy, embryology, animal psychology, systematic zoology, biogeography and palaeontology.

On August 15, 1913, he made his solemn profession.

From 1913 to 1916 he held the office of director of the authors affiliated with the Jesuit periodical, *Stimmen der Zeit*; moreover, he was also editor of the aforesaid magazine. In 1916 he was able to work again in his special field of anthropology; his main interest then was matrimony and the family in its biological, ethical and supernatural aspects. From this study he published his book, *Kind und Volk* (*The Child and the Nation*). This book of 600 pages was published in fifteen new editions. In addition, he averaged more than one hundred lectures a year in many cities all over Europe. He also preached in the cathedrals and in many churches.

As Father Muckermann progressed in his scientific work he conceived a plan to found a new scientific institute. To be more free to devote himself to this work he applied to the Church authorities for permission to become a secular priest. This request was granted. He became a priest of his home diocese, and was granted all the liberty necessary for the continuation of his work. In 1927 he accepted a call from the Kaiser-Wilhelm-Gesellschaft zur Förderung der Wissenschaften to the new institute, founded at his suggestion, and which was called Kaiser-Wilhelm-Institut für Anthropologie, menschliche Erblehre und Eugenik, at Berlin-Dahlem. The doctorate which he had obtained abroad was approved by the Prussian Ministry of Public Instruction and Worship, after they had examined his thesis. The same board allowed him to assume the title of professor, and acknowledged his professorial work.

As head of a division of the institute he did much research work on applied anthropology which was published in scientific periodicals. He also contributed to other magazines and reference works and gave many lectures all over Europe.

When Hitler came into power, Father Muckermann was dismissed from his office, due to the opposition he displayed to National Socialism. Father Muckermann also had to resign from the Prussian Board of Health.

Through the help of the German bishops he was able to continue scientific work in his house in Berlin. This activity consisted especially in the synthesis of his science with the kindred sciences. He also had the opportunity during this period to write or complete his books: *Der Sinn der Ehe, biologisch, ethisch, übernatürlich; Vererbung und Entwicklung; Eugenik; Rassenforschung und Volk der Zukunft; Eugenik und Katholizismus; Grundriss der Rassenkunde; Die Religion und die Gegenwart; Von den sieben Sakramenten; Von der Wiederkehr des Welterlösers,* and some smaller books. Soon after their publication, however, they were banned by the Nazis. In addition to his books being forbidden, Father Muckermann was also forbidden to lecture and preach, because he tried to tell the truth and to refute Nazism. In 1937 his passport was taken away so that it would not be possible for him to lecture in other countries. At the risk of being sent to a concentration camp, he secretly spread the truth.

Even after the collapse of Nazism, Father Muckermann had to wait some time before he was free to lecture. Only his sermons he began at once. They have been continued Sunday after Sunday till the present day. Moreover, he used this time to prepare some of his formerly proscribed literary productions for reprinting. The first work to be published was *Die Familie.* The first edition of 20,000 copies was soon sold out. A new edition appeared in 1952. A second work was *Vererbung und Entwicklung* (355 pages), a third work: *Feiertag und Feierabend* (416 pages).

On September 6, 1946, he was called back to Dahlem, but there was at first no possibility of establishing the former institute. He was authorized, by the French military government on October 29, 1946, to continue his research work at Berlin-Frohnau, located in the French sector. On March 19, 1947, he was given a professorial chair for applied anthropology at the Technical University in Berlin-Charlottenburg.

In the meantime work had been going on for the renovation of the former institute at Dahlem. On November 20, 1947, the American occupation force invested Father Muckermann with full powers for the inauguration of the Kaiser-Wilhelm-Institut für angewandte Anthropologie. The official authorization was forwarded to him by the municipal council of Berlin on December 1, 1947. The title to be given to the Institute was to express by name the three sciences concerned: anthropology, human heredity, eugenics, in a way that no misunderstanding would be possible. Before it was realized, however, three problems had to be solved: (1) the building of the institute; (2) the list of officers, and an inventory; (3) a careful selection of the staff of fellow scientists.

The negotiations were retarded by the medical department of the University of Frankfurt that wanted him to accept a call to their university; the rector and senate of the University of Frankfurt as well as the minister of culture of Hessen sanctioned the call. He declined, because he did not want to leave Berlin in the days of distress. Instead he accepted an ordinary professorship of applied anthropology and social ethics at the Technical University of Berlin on April 1, 1948.

A suitable building in Berlin-Dahlem was placed at his disposal for the institute in October, 1948. The empty building was soon adapted and equipped so that scientific work could be started on January 3, 1949. The budget problem was also solved by the magistrate of Berlin. In 1952 the institute was connected with the Max-Planck-Gesellschaft zur Förderung der Wissenschaften which replaces the former Kaiser-Wilhelm-Gesellschaft.

The scientific work to be stressed at this institute is the reorganization of anthropology and the application of its principles in the human community. Attention will be given especially to hereditary cytology of man, to hereditary psychology, to hereditary phylogeny, to hereditary demography, and to the application of all knowledge on the ethical and social-ethical transformation of our world.

Since 1949 Father Muckermann is also a guest professor at the newly created Free University in Berlin-Dahlem and since January 1, 1950, honorary professor at the same University.

Since October 1, 1950, he was selected as a member of the International Union for the scientific study of the population problem.

The first results of the new research work were published in various periodicals and as separate publications. The principal work in preparation is a book on a new anthropology that considers the different sciences referring to man from the *personality* of man, which is the foundation of the dignity of man and of the partnership of all men in family and in all social communities and in the united nations of the whole of mankind.   W. B.

Reverend Albert Muntsch, S.J.
1873–

Beginning his teaching career as an instructor in languages, Father Albert Muntsch of the Society of Jesus turned next to sociology and finally anthropology. His reasons for his "conversion" to the latter are first, his interest in languages, more especially primitive languages. This implied some devotion to the study of primitive culture. In giving his second reason, he said: "I realized very fully when starting out in teaching sociology, that a knowledge of

primitive social institutions was necessary for a more complete understanding of social conditions like marriage, the family, private property, and especially religion."

Albert Muntsch was born in 1873 in St. Louis, Missouri. He attended St. Joseph's parochial school and received both his high school
and his college education in St. Louis University in his native city,
receiving the A.B. in 1897 and the A.M. in 1898. On July 16, 1891 he
entered the Society of Jesus in St. Stanislaus' Seminary, the Jesuit
novitiate in Florissant. He was ordained to the priesthood by the late
John Cardinal Glennon in St. Francis Xavier's (College) Church
on June 26, 1906.

In 1898 he began his teaching career as an instructor in French,
German and Spanish at St. Mary's College, St. Marys, Kansas, where
he remained until 1902. The following year (1902–1903) he held a
similar appointment at the University of Detroit. Then he returned to
St. Louis University for his theological studies (1903–1906) and remained there to teach. The year 1917–1918 he devoted to special
private study in sociology and ethnology. From 1919 to 1929 he was
professor of sociology at St. Louis University. He attended the Chicago School of Civics and Philanthropy the summer of 1919, the Judge
Baker Foundation, Boston in the summer of 1924, and the University
of Chicago in the summer of 1923, the latter primarily to secure a
methodology; he was a graduate student in anthropology at the University of California, 1929–1930 and then had definitely turned to anthropology. From 1930 to 1942 he was professor of anthropology at St.
Louis University. Since 1942 he is engaged chiefly in literary and lecture work.

For six months during the years 1936–1937, Father Muntsch
did field work in British Honduras and Guatemala among the Mayas
and Caribs. He had also spent extensive periods living with the
Iroquois of Canada, the Plains Indians and the Pueblos of the United
States.

Frequently Father Muntsch has been called upon to address meetings and conventions of Catholic societies. His favorite themes are:
The Christian Family, Capital and Labor, and Christian Social Reform. Early in his life, as a Jesuit, he contributed papers on social and
economic topics to the *Central Blatt and Social Justice* and to the now
defunct *Fortnightly Review*. A turning point in his career came in 1921
when Doctor Koppers published his book, *Die Anfänge des mensch-
lichen Gemeinschaftslebens im Spiegel der neueren Völkerkunde.*

Being eager to spread the "new gospel" of social origins to other
workers in the field, Father Muntsch published *Evolution and Culture*
in 1923, based largely on the researches of the "Vienna School" of
Schmidt and Koppers.

In 1928 still feeling that the new points of departure for the study
of social origins were not sufficiently appreciated, he published in
collaboration with Reverend H. S. Spalding, *Introductory Sociology.*

With the publication of *Cultural Anthropology* (Bruce Publishing
Company, 1934) his "conversion" from sociology to cultural anthropology was complete.   M. A. H.

Gerard Murphy 1901–

Gaelic is the special study of Gerard Murphy. He had inherited this interest in Irish from his father, the late Henry Murphy, who as a boy in Dublin and later as a solicitor in County Monaghan, had interested himself in the Irish language even before the foundation of the Gaelic League. Gerard Murphy's father could speak no foreign language well, but he read and loved German, French, Spanish, and Italian poetry, and had studied the grammar of several other languages. He had learnt Old Irish and Modern Irish from books, without a teacher, and imparted a smattering knowledge of Gaelic to Gerard and his other sons. Although Gerard did not begin to study Irish seriously at school until he was fourteen, he always remembered the little his father had taught him and cherished the hope he would be able to read the books of Irish poetry he saw his father reading. To Mr. Francis Ormsby, his teacher of classics and Irish at Mount Saint Benedict, Gorey, Gerard Murphy owes the real foundation of his knowledge of Modern Irish. To Dr. Osborn Bergin, Professor of Old and Medieval Irish at University College, Dublin, he owes his knowledge of the older phases of the language.

Born on May 2, 1901, in Clones, County Monaghan, Ireland, Gerard is the second son of Henry Murphy, now deceased, and Mary Frances (nee Donnelly) Murphy, who is still living. He was educated from 1915 to 1918 at the Benedictine boarding school, Mount Saint Benedict, Gorey, County Wexford, a school which is no longer in existence. In 1918 he went to University College, Dublin, a constituent college of the National University of Ireland where he studied Latin, Greek and Old Irish. He was awarded a B.A. degree in 1922 and a M.A. degree in 1931. From 1922 to 1929 he served as an assistant librarian in the National Library of Ireland, and during this time (1923) he married Mary O'Neill. They have two children, Ann Barbara Murphy and Daniel Lonan Murphy.

Mr. Murphy's books in English are: *Tales From Ireland* (1947) and *Glimpses of Gaelic Ireland* (1948).

Besides his edition, with English translation, of Part II of *Duanaire Finn* ("the poem-book of Finn") in the Irish Texts Society's series, and several articles (in Gaelic and English) on literary and linguistic aspects of medieval and modern Irish in various periodicals, Mr. Murphy has edited Domhnall Bán ó Céileachair's *Sgéal mo Bheatha* in 1940, and since 1941 he has been editor of *Eigse*, a journal of Irish studies, published for the National University of Ireland. Mr. Murphy is at present professor of the history of Celtic literature in University College, Dublin.   M. A. H.

Reverend James George Murtagh
1908–

The Advocate, Australia's oldest Catholic newspaper (founded 1868) and official organ of the Archdiocese of Melbourne, has taught Reverend James Murtagh, M.A. many things during his fifteen years in charge of its editorial staff. Perhaps the most important, he thinks, for sound Catholic journalism are two simple rules: first, when in doubt, leave out; secondly, always understate your case. Father Murtagh has been associate editor, feature writer, book reviewer, editorial writer and commentator on Australian affairs since 1936.

Born in New Plymouth, New Zealand, on July 21, 1908, he was educated by the Marist Brothers in their college, Kilmore, Victoria, Australia, and at Corpus Christi College, in Werribee, Victoria. He was ordained to the priesthood in July 1932. He also attended the University of Melbourne in Australia and the Catholic University of America, in Washington, D. C., in America, where he studied the social sciences during the years 1941–42.

He is assistant secretary of the Australian Catholic Truth Society, a chaplain to the Catholic Evidence Guild and former National Secretary of the Pontifical Mission Aid Societies. He occasionally gives lectures and radio talks on the Melbourne "Catholic Hour."

In 1945, he wrote his first book, *Democracy in Australia*, a study of Australia's social and political structure in the light of Christian principles, with suggestions for its development according to the papal plan for the organic reconstruction of society. Then followed *Australia: The Catholic Chapter*, in which he tells the fascinating story of Australia's development from a penal colony to its present highly industrialized state. Of particular interest is the discussion of the Church and the social problem. Father Murtagh traces the social roots of Australia's development to a clash between two early traditions, the one conservative, deriving from the "plantation frontier" of New South Wales (the convict system), the other radical, thrown up by the "camp frontier" of Victoria (the gold rushes). This is expressed today in a conflict between liberalism (without doctrines) and socialism (without doctrines). The only group which has made a sustained and united impact in terms of values is the Catholic Church.

In 1951, the jubilee year of Australia, Father Murtagh published his third book, *Catholics and the Commonwealth*, which tells the story of the Catholic part in the making of the Australian Federation. He is also the author of the following pamphlets: *A Catechism of Communism; Why be Moral?; The Story of Antigonish*, and *Christianity and National Patriotism*.

Elizabeth Myers (Mrs. Littleton Powys) 1912-1947

Elizabeth Myers was born in Manchester, England on December 23, 1912. Her father, George Myers, belonged to a distinguished Yorkshire family. His branch were manufacturers; her mother was of Irish descent.

Both her parents were Catholics, and so the little girl Elizabeth was sent to St. Michael's School, over which, fortunately for Elizabeth, Miss Ann Lee, a very cultured lady, presided as headmistress. Miss Ann Lee recognized her gifts and kept in touch with her after she left school. When Elizabeth was eleven she won a scholarship to the Notre Dame School, but had to leave at the insistance of her father when she was fourteen and a half years old. Her mother, however, insisted on her continuing her education at the Gregg Commercial College, and in a short time she passed the examinations and received her diploma.

Her first position, as a private secretary, was in the Cleveland Petroleum Products Co., Ltd., and she worked for them in Manchester, then in Preston (Ribbleton), and finally in London in 1931 when she was in her nineteenth year.

Throughout these years, she never swerved in her determination to be a writer. We hear of stories having been written when she was twelve. Her first novel, at fifteen and a half, was praised but considered too immature for publication. Elizabeth found London just the place to carry out her scheme of self-education and writing. Not a moment of her spare time was wasted; she made a study of music, art, the film world, and the ballet; she went to London University to hear lectures on history, philosophy, psychology, and literature. Meanwhile she read books of every kind, gladly making full use of the public libraries. Her first story was published in *The Countryman*. From then on, story after story appeared in magazines and papers.

The strenuous life she was living impaired her health. In 1938, when she was twenty-five, she was sent to a hospital and spent fifteen months there before going to a sanatorium. In the quiet life of the sanatorium she did much thinking and much writing of short stories. In 1940 she was at work again as a secretary in Fleet Street. This was the year of the heaviest bombing of London, yet back and forth she went to the office, and returning home she would resume her writing. She then tried her hand at a novel and in 1942 finished *A Well Full of Leaves*. On this occasion fortune smiled upon her, for she was introduced to Arthur Waugh, ex-chairman of the board of Chapman & Hall. He at once recognized her ability and her charm and they became great friends. He read her novel and recommended it with great enthusiasm for publication.

In the year 1943 her doctor forbade her to do any more office work. Nevertheless, this year was her *annus mirabilis* because she was awarded the Tom Gallon Prize for Literature. Her first novel was published and had a remarkable reception. She visited Sherborne and there met Mr. Littleton C. Powys, whom she married in August. During the next three years, while in Sherborne, she finished *The Basilisk of St. James's;* she wrote *Mrs. Christopher*, and made a selection of twenty-seven of her short stories to be called *Good Beds: Men Only* which was published after her death.

She regarded her responsibility as an author very seriously, as the following "Cycle of E. M's Work" found by her husband after death shows:

1. The least thing, i.e., the necessity for personal happiness, *A Well Full of Leaves.*
2. Romantic love, *The Basilisk of St. James's.*
3. The higher achievement, without which all the foregoing have no significance, i.e., Love of God, *The Governor.*

She did not live to finish the last book; so, acting according to her instructions, her husband destroyed what she had written of it.

In 1947 she and her husband decided to go to Tucson in Arizona in the hope that the warm, dry climate might benefit her health, but it did not have the effect hoped for, and although they had a very happy time together in Tucson and during the twelve days they spent in New York, three weeks after their return to Sherborne, she had a series of heart attacks and on May 24 died. On her death her husband received the following letter from Nowell C. Smith, ex-chairman of the executive committee of the English Association: "I am very grateful to you for having brought me into contact with her. I have never known anyone who impressed me with so unmistakable a stamp of genius, of both intellectual and moral strength; and her warmth and the largeness of heart were equally exceptional. She radiated love and intelligence. She has joined the band of geniuses dying young, and what a loss not only to you and her intimates but also to the world."

The Letters of Elizabeth Myers was published in November, 1951, by Chapman & Hall. In the Foreword, Mr. Littleton C. Powys, her husband, writes: "I am offering to the public my late wife's letters . . . as a tribute to her memory.

"It was by one of those marvelous acts of Providence that we came to know each other. To me it was a rare privilege to have for three and a half years the close companionship of so choice a spirit.

"It is not for me to sing her praises as I should dearly love to; the letters will do that unconsciously and far more effectively." L. C. P.

Takashi Nagai   1908–1951

Dr. Takashi Nagai, the researcher in "atom bomb sickness," was born in 1908 in Matsue, the capital of Shimane Prefecture in Western Honshue, on the coast of the Japan Sea, where Lafcadio Hearn had made his Japanese home. Dr. Nagai's father was also a physician, a general practitioner among the people of a suburb of Matsue.

Takashi Nagai completed his high school and college in Matsue and then entered Nagasaki University in 1929. When he was graduated three years later (1932), he was appointed to an assistantship in physiotherapy and to a lectureship in 1937. In the meantime (1934), he became a Catholic and shortly after married Marina Midori Moriyama, a home economics teacher in a girls' high school in Nagasaki, and one of whose 17th century ancestors had been among the earliest Japanese converts to Christianity.

In 1940 Dr. Nagai became an associate professor, and in 1946, a full professor. In the thirties he was twice called to service in the armed forces, first during the Manchurian Incident, and then during the China Incident. In 1944 he took an advanced research degree corresponding to our Doctor of Medical Science.

During the Second World War (1945), because of the scarcity of civilian doctors, he overworked himself as a roentgenologist, and contracted "radiation sickness." He was a member of the staff of a hospital near Urakami, a Catholic settlement outside of Nagasaki, the site of the world's second wartime atomic bomb explosion.

Returning to his home after the blast, Dr. Nagai found the charred remains of his wife and the beadless chain of her rosary. His son (Seiichi) and daughter (Kayano) survived. The children had been visiting elsewhere while the bomb took a toll of 8,000 victims in Nagasaki. His first book, *The Rosary Chain*, recounts what he found in his home on his return the evening of the bombing.

Since 1945 Dr. Nagai had been slowly dying. He kept a scientific record of the progress of his disease watching himself die through his own medical eyes. In spite of his suffering, he opened a clinic for radiological victims, and treated hundreds of patients, until the radioactivity effects of the bomb invalided him for life.

All day streams of visitors came to talk to him in his one-room cabin, built for him voluntarily by the carpenters of his parish, until he became too weak to receive them. Among the prominent visitors were His Imperial Majesty, the Emperor; Cardinal Gilroy of Australia; and Archbishop de Furstenberg, Apostolic Delegate to Japan. Tokens of regard came to him from Pope Pius XII, who had imparted a special blessing along with an autographed photograph and a rosary. Madam Perón, wife of the President of Argentina, sent a plaque of Our Lady of Lujan. Giving his days to visits, he wrote nights.

Lying prone on his bed, he wrote by hand on a tablet fixed to one side. His solitary electric light bulb, which could be seen across a darkened valley, told the story of his midnight labors.

His books treated the postwar problems of the Japanese — family griefs and losses, parents' sorrow for lost sons, shattered and impoverished homes — always viewed through the light of Catholic faith and hope.

Once, afraid that his life would end uselessly in the loneliness of an empty night, Dr. Nagai decided to write his children a book, *Kono Ko Wo Nokishite* (Leaving These Children) — a delicate testimonial to a love for his children and his faith in God. *Yomiuri,* one of the three largest dailies in Japan, selected it as a best seller. *We of Nagasaki* presents first-person accounts by six adults and three children who survived the atomic blast on August 6, 1945. His other books are: *The Bells of Nagasaki; The Stream of Life; The Flowering Hill;* and *Psychology of an Atomic Battlefield,* which was published posthumously.

Dr. Nagai's writings are effective because all Japan knew the author himself was in the front rank of the bomb sufferers, practicing what he preached. The film version of *Bells of Nagasaki,* a portrait of his life, widened his influence.

As his life ebbed away he wrote: "Through the atomic bomb, all that obstructed my right way of living has been cleared away. I was able to taste the true happiness, which is a gift of God. Even death, now waiting at my door, is the greatest gift of love, which Our Heavenly Father, of Infinite Love, is extending to me. Therefore, all the sufferings of the mind and all the pains of the body which I still have to endure before leaving this world are necessary for the final revelation of the glory of God. I am facing these with a joyful heart."

At the very end in a clear voice he called out, "Seibo Maria," invoking the intercession of the Blessed Virgin. Then he said: "I want to pray, send for Father Nakashima." Father Nakashima is pastor of the parish church in Urakami. With these words, he took the crucifix from his son's hand and holding it to his breast he breathed his last at 9.50 P.M., May 1, 1951.   P. J. O'C., W. A. K., D. S., and P.

Reverend Robert Nash, S.J. 1902–

Since 1934 the principal work of Father Robert Nash has been giving retreats to priests, religious, college students and also giving public missions to people in the parishes. Most of the material for his books and pamphlets is gathered from experiences gained on his rounds as a missioner and retreat master.

Born in Cork, Ireland on April 23, 1902, Father Nash received his early education at St. Munchin's College, Limerick, and Redemptorist College, Limerick. On September 1st, 1919 he entered the Society of Jesus at St. Stanislaus' College, Tullamore, Ireland. As a junior he pursued the usual course of studies at Tullamore; his philosophical studies were made in Milltown Park, Dublin. Then he taught for three years (1925–1928) at Xavier College, Kew, Melbourne, Australia. In 1928 he returned to Milltown Park to begin his theological studies and he was ordained in 1931. Another year of theology and tertianship followed which ended in 1934. Since that time, as it was stated above, he has been giving retreats and missions. He has also lectured in theatres and auditoriums. He is particularly interested in lecturing on the Life of Our Lord, which he illustrates with beautifully-colored lantern slides. This he has given a few hundred times to widely different audiences.

Father Nash began to write in 1921, when as a young student, he preached in the Jesuit refectory a twenty minute sermon on "The Sower." Afterwards the superior and students congratulated him and suggested that he ought to try to have the sermon published. When he consulted his superior in private, the superior encouraged him to send the manuscript to the *Homiletic Monthly and Pastoral Review*. Acting on the suggestion, he sent it to the periodical mentioned and it was accepted. He received a handsome check as an honorarium. Later he sent four or five sermons, all of which were published.

While in Australia, he tried a few biographical sketches for the Catholic papers. These also were accepted. Then he began writing an occasional pamphlet for the Australian Catholic Truth Society. Now devoted to "the apostolate of the pen," he has published over seventy pamphlets; he has contributed regularly every month, for many years, to *The Irish Messenger of the Sacred Heart, St. Anthony's Annals, Little Flower Monthly, Madonna* and others; he has written six books.

Missions and retreats stimulate him to write. His pamphlets are made available on these occasions and people are eager to buy them. "The object of this," he says, "is to try to ensure that 'the fruit may remain' of the good work done by the spoken word. Many of the ideas heard in the pulpit are to be found in the pamphlets and we point out that these can be perused when we are gone and that they will serve to keep alive the resolutions."

Father Nash's first book, *Send Forth Thy Light*, was published in 1946. It contains subject-matter for mental prayer. It was a selection of the Spiritual Book Associates. Then followed a similar volume under the title *Thy Light and Thy Truth*. Published in 1948, these meditations are meant to encourage souls when they are tempted to slacken their prayers after they have become disappointed with the result. *The Priest at His Prie-dieu* appeared in 1949. These fifty-two meditations were designed principally, though not exclusively, for priests and aspirants for the priesthood. This is the book Father Nash likes best. "For," he says, "one of my strongest convictions is that there is no greater need for the priest than a deeply interior life flowering into the active works of the apostolate. Prayer is his bulwark of defence, his source of light in his difficulties and problems, his inspiration in his preaching and teaching. Without prayer, whatever natural gifts he may have and utilize, whatever spectacular results (buildings, funds, organizations, etc.), there may be, he is only sounding brass

and tinkling cymbal. The world today, says Chesterton, is like a huge
lunatic asylum; it can be brought back to sanity only by those who
draw near to the Source of light and learn how to guide it aright, i.e.,
by those who live lives of union with God in prayer."

Father Nash is the author of: *The Nun at Her Prie-dieu* (1950).
Over eight thousand copies of this book were sold in about six months.
Is Life Worthwhile? (1950) was also published in the United States,
but under the title *Living Your Faith.* His latest book is *The Seminarian
at His Prie-dieu* (1951). In preparation is *Challenge to the Catholic
Church,* an expansion of six lectures he gave in Lent, 1951, in the Church
of St. Francis Xavier, Dublin.   M. A. H.

Thomas Patrick Neill 1915–

Born on January 19, 1915 in Telluride, Colorado,
Thomas P. Neill is the son of Harry G. and
Marian (Cuthbertson) Neill. His grandmothers
were both Irish Catholics and his grandfathers
both marriage converts, one from Presbyterianism, the other from Anglicanism.

Since his parents had to move a good deal,
Thomas attended twelve different schools, both
public and private, in eight years. In 1929
his parents finally settled down in St. Louis, Missouri. There he went to
the Christian Brothers high school and then to St. Louis University,
receiving his A.B. degree in 1937. He majored in economics. The following two years he spent at the University of Notre Dame, specializing in apologetics and political theory and was awarded the A.M.
degree in 1939.

In the summer of 1939 he and his friend, Emerson Hynes, went to
Europe. They covered all Ireland on foot and bicycle and as much of
England and France as they could before their money gave out.

Two years later (1941), Thomas Neill married Agnes Weber of
Denver, Colorado. At the present time (1952) they have six children.

His Ph.D. degree was earned in 1943 at St. Louis University,
majoring in modern European history and political thought. He was
the last student to finish up under the late Father Raymond Corrigan,
S.J. Since then Dr. Neill has devoted himself exclusively to university
teaching. Except for two years at Aquinas College (1941–1943) he has
been teaching at St. Louis University. His major interest is modern
European intellectual and social history, "a subject," he says, "which
leads one to a serious consideration of the Church and its deposit of
truth."

Dr. Neill has never looked upon writing as an avocation; nor
has he made it a vocation. It is a part of teaching. He writes, "I am
convinced that good popular writing is a method of teaching and I
do not believe that scholars can afford to neglect it. My articles and

books have all grown out of my university courses or out of lectures I have been asked to give in the Midwest."

His published works thus far are three: *Weapons for Peace* (1945); *Makers of the Modern Mind* (1949); and *They Lived the Faith: Great Lay Leaders of Modern Times* (1951). At the present time (1952) he is writing a book on Liberalism since the French Revolution.

Dr. Neill has also contributed frequently to *The Catholic World* and to *Columbia* and occasionally to *America, The Commonweal, The Historical Bulletin, Journal of the History of Ideas* and the *Quarterly Journal of Economics.*

He is a member of the American Historical Society, the Catholic Association for International Peace, and the Catholic Commission on Intellectual and Cultural Affairs.   M. A. H.

Jean Nesmy. See *Henry Surchamp*

May Nevin (Mrs. Canice Whyte)
1909–

May Nevin was born on Wednesday, August 11, 1909, in Dublin, Ireland. She trained to be a Pitman's shorthand teacher, after qualifying for a position as shorthand-typist, but — "Aren't you very young looking?" dogged her everywhere she went.

Her early success with short story writing lured her from a commercial career. Hundreds of her short stories, articles and serials appeared in all religious and several secular magazines. Her articles also appeared in Dublin dailies and weeklies. Some of her short stories appeared in *The Catholic World, Sacred Heart Messenger, Ave Maria, Orphan's Messenger* and other magazines in the United States. From time to time she conducted a Children's Department and Household Corners for such publications as the *Father Mathew Record, Assisi* and *Drogheda Independent.*

At the age of twenty-four she wrote her first novel, *The Girls of Sunnyside.* Asked how she came to write that novel, she replied: "The story caught me in that white heat of inspiration enjoyed by most young beginners. The plot and characters unfolded clearly while listening to the playing of the late Mr. Wilfred Brown, organist in the Vincentian Church, St. Peter's, Phibsborough — my native district. Before evening devotions in May and October he played magnificently. I submitted the first seven chapters to the late Mr. P. J. Fogarty, editor of *The Irish Catholic.* After leaving the manuscript for his Christmas number, he rushed his subeditor after me on the street to ask whether the serial was nearly finished as he was anxious to get it started for he had never read anything as attractive." When it appeared as a serial under the title "Cloone Abbey," letters came pouring in urging her to have the story printed in book form. She submitted the manuscript to the Talbot Press. When the publisher sent for her, his first greeting was: "Aren't you very young to write a book?" In desperation she replied: "But readers won't bother about my age as long as they like what I write." He laughingly consoled her by saying: "Oh you'll grow out of it."

The publisher immediately accepted it, but suggested the change of title from "Cloone Abbey" to *The Girls of Sunnyside*. Two years later (1935) she published her second novel *Over the Hills*, which was favorably received by the Australian press in which country part of the scene is laid. The Father John Collins mentioned in the second novel is really her first cousin. She took the liberty of transferring to Australia his parish life in California. The verses quoted in this book as written by one of the characters are efforts of the author which won prizes from time to time in Irish newspapers.

Since 1941, May Nevin is married to Canice Whyte, a Dublin man, and is the mother of two daughters and one son.

While still contributing short stories, serials, etc. to magazines, May Nevin is trying to find time "to concentrate on a really worthwhile novel, but concentration is not always easy for a housewife with children. They and my home come first but literary work still holds an important place in my life. Ideas come and just have to be used up like breathing air."   M. A. H.

Reverend Albert J. Nevins, M.M.
1915–

The editor, author, and foreign missioner, Father Albert J. Nevins, was born in Yonkers, New York on September 11, 1915. He attended public elementary school; Gorton High School; Cathedral College, New York City; Venard College, Clarks Summit, Pennsylvania; and Maryknoll Seminary, Maryknoll, New York. He was ordained a priest at Maryknoll, New York, on June 21, 1942.

Before entering Maryknoll, Father Nevins was employed in the editorial department of the Yonkers *Herald*, the Yonkers *Statesman*, and the Yonkers *Herald-Statesman*. Following ordination, he was assigned to editorial work by Maryknoll. At present he is assistant editor of *Maryknoll — The Field Afar*, director of press relations for the Maryknoll Fathers; assistant director of the Maryknoll Bookshelf; director of the Maryknoll Photographic Service; and director of World Horizon Films. This last is an organization engaged in producing films on mission countries which will have an educational and promotional value. Father Nevins has written and produced the film "The Miracle of Blue Cloud County" (China). In filming it practically everything that could possibly happen to cause confusion, happened. First, the project was planned in days when equipment was short. A schedule was drawn up, a script written, and everything planned to begin in Hong Kong on a particular day. A search was begun in New York for necessary equipment, but nothing could be turned up for less than the price of the Empire State Building. A trip to Rochester and a sales talk to some Eastman executives produced the filming equipment even though some of it had to be taken from product display cases. Next a shipment of film was lost. Again there was a hurried drive to Rochester. Finally, the film and equipment were shipped in time to catch a ship in San Francisco. The producer breathed a sigh of relief.

Then came a cable from Hong Kong. The ship had arrived with no equipment. A cable caught the ship in Manila. It was searched but no equipment was aboard. No one remembered it. Father Nevins then began to trace the shipment down. Time was at a premium. The rainy season in South China was close at hand. The shipment was traced across the country to San Francisco. Father Nevins found the express-man who carried it from the train to the exporter. He traced it through longshoremen to the dock. It was no longer on the dock so it must have been put on the boat. Cables were sent to all ports of call. No equipment. By this time the ship was back in San Francisco. Its cargo was examined and the boat was searched from stem to stern. Finally, when all hope was abandoned, the equipment turned up in a warehouse in Hong Kong, where it had gone by mistake.

During the actual filming many other things happened. A boat carrying photographers and equipment broke down and drifted out into the China Sea. It was finally rescued by a junk and towed to shore, but only after valuable time was lost. On another occasion, the photographers were trapped by a flood — the biggest flood ever recorded in that section of South China. In the house where they were staying, they retreated from the first to the second floor, and then to the roof. They spent the night on the roof, listening to the crash of mud houses all about them and expecting at any moment to be plunged into the swirling waters. It would have made wonderful pictures but the camera and equipment were ten miles away — completely out of reach.

On the way back to Hong Kong the photographers were on a boat attacked by pirates. The boat finally outran the pirates but one of the photographers had his leg smashed by a bullet.

When the film arrived back in the United States there was trouble with customs, trouble with the laboratory (a strike), trouble in recording and editing. When "The Miracle of Blue Cloud County" was finally released everyone connected with it knew that the title was inspired. It was a miracle that it was ever completed. Father Nevins also wrote and produced "The Kid Down the Block" (China); "Kyoto Saturday Afternoon" (Japan); "Indian Street" (Bolivia), and "The Story of Juan Mateo" (Guatemala). This latter film was also photographed by Father Nevins. World Horizon Films produces two films a year for television and national distribution.

Father Nevins would like to make a motion picture about making motion pictures.

He was one of the founders of the Catholic Institute of the Press, and served on the executive board of that organization for three years. A member of the executive board of the Catholic Press Association of the United States for the years 1949–1952, he was also treasurer of the Catholic Press Association of the United States for the term 1950 to 1952.

He first broke into print at the age of seven with an article about a friendly chipmunk. The story appeared in a daily paper. "I suppose the pleasure of seeing one's own words recorded left a taste for more," remarks Father Nevins. At fourteen he became editor of his monthly high school paper. During this time he gathered all the high school publications of a county adjacent to New York into an inter-scholastic press association.

In addition to numerous articles and pamphlets, he wrote *The Catholic Year* (1949) and *The Adventures of Wu Han* (1951, Dodd, Mead & Company).

Asked how he came to write *The Adventures of Wu Han* he replied: "Dorothy Bryan of Dodd, Mead & Company called me on the telephone one day and said she was looking for a juvenile on Korea and was there anyone at Maryknoll who could write such a book. I assured her that there was and that I would call back in ten minutes and give all the details. Two days later I was still hunting for someone to write it. Since we had committed ourselves to Miss Bryan, there was nothing to do but write it myself."

He sketched out a plot line, read everything he could find on Korea and then began to write. As soon as a chapter was written, it was duplicated and sent to twelve priests and Sisters who had worked in Korea. This board of advisors were responsible for the authenticity of the book. They came up with such observations as that turnips are not yellow but white in Korea and so on.

Since the book gives us an understanding of the Korean people, their heritages, their family relations, their unique way of living, it is especially timely now (1952) with war being waged in that country.

Because of the success of *The Adventures of Wu Han*, Father Nevins has signed a contract to do another book on the same pattern on Japan. After that he has one in mind on Guatemala. He left for Central and South America in January 1952.   M. A. H.

Mrs. Darcy Niland. See *Ruth Park*

John Frederick Nims   1913–

Like a number of other poets, John Frederick Nims is also a university professor, partly no doubt because teaching provides him with a regular income but also because he likes teaching. Yet, unlike most poets and professors, he came rather close to being a tennis star, for in his freshman year at De Paul, he won the university championship, losing only one game. Subsequently — and this was after he had proved himself a poet — he traded his tennis racket for a Colt Woodsman and a .38-Super — but has now given up his pistols for a set of golf clubs. This last he suspects may be a sign of approaching senility, though such unsedentary activities probably make him all the better and fresher a poet.

He was born at Muskegon, Michigan. On his father's side he is descended from a French Huguenot family that settled in Massachusetts in the 17th century and from the Brewsters of Plymouth colony; the parents of his mother, Anne McDonald, were from Ireland. After attending the parochial school in Muskegon up to the sixth grade, he completed that phase of his education at St. Cyril's School in Chicago, and graduated from Leo High School. Two years at De Paul were followed by another two at Notre Dame University, where he took his A.B. and A.M., subsequently obtaining his Ph.D. at Chicago University in the field of comparative literature, working in Greek, Latin, French and English tragedy, studies that have put some mark upon his poetry.

He had early begun to write, though, as he admits, without much certainty as to what he wanted to do, and, as is natural with the very young, in a somewhat magniloquent manner. Fortunately for his muse, his doctor decided, when young Nims was about nineteen, that he was overtaxing his strength at tennis and ordered him to stop completely. This gave him more free time, which he used by studying Keats and Spenser with a friend and trying his hand at verse in their vein, along with triolets, villanelles and such things. Some of his first pieces were accepted by the Chicago *Tribune* and the *Daily News*, to his wild excitement; but not until some years later did he discover modern poetry, developing enthusiasm for poets as varied as Yeats and Dylan Thomas and T. S. Eliot, the result being a wider range, a more mature note and acceptance by such magazines as *Accent*, the *Partisan Review*, the *Saturday Review of Literature*, *Harper's*, the *Kenyon Review*, *Spirit* and *Poetry*. After winning prizes in three successive years offered by the last named of these magazines, he became one of its editors in 1944.

During the year 1936–37, he taught in a high school at Portland, Oregon, and, after his graduation from Notre Dame, was given a teaching position there, which has been interrupted only by a year when he served on the faculty of St. Michael's College, Toronto. While teaching he obtained his doctorate in Chicago University. Teaching at Notre Dame was a fortunate assignment for him, for he married in 1947 a graduate of the adjoining St. Mary's College. This was Bonnie Larkin, who is probably the only girl who attended that institution who was class president for three out of her four scholastic years. After her graduation she wrote copy for an advertising agency in Chicago, until her marriage in 1947. She and her husband now live at Niles, Michigan, only a fifteen minutes' drive from Notre Dame University; they have two sons. Bonnie shares John's interests, even to the extent of keeping two Irish setters, named after the famous Irish whiskeys, Bushmill and Jamison. When the dogs ranged too far afield to be conveniently kept in a city, they were replaced by a handsome Hamlet-like collie named Apple, who seemed more likely to stay put. The only trouble with Apple is that he is gloomy when guests arrive and embarrassingly delighted when they get up to go.

Mr. Nims' first book, *The Iron Pastoral*, was published by the William Sloane Associates in 1947, and was described by the *New York Times* review as "often witty and brilliant, at times unpolished, always refreshing to the eye and ear." Previously, about thirty-five pages of his verse were included in *Five Young American Poets*, brought out by New Directions in 1944, and the promise these gave was fulfilled by *A Fountain in Kentucky*, published by the William Sloane Associates in 1950.

In this, as in most of his later work, Nims shows himself inclined to the modern mode, though not excessively so. But in such pieces as "The Quiet Night," "First Date" and "The Weeds" he proves that he has now all-but-lost lyricism at his command, however austere may be its expression. And his translation of Horace, while retaining the ancient forms, has a direct ruggedness which comes rather nearer to catching the true spirit of the Poet of the Sabine Farm than most of the thousands of mellifluous renderings of his odes that have been attempted. We need not take too seriously the lines of "One Crumpled Valentine":

> "Flutters my soul, half angel and half goat.
>   Always at parties I posture, a scholarly cad" —

unless these are intended as a description of somebody else. From what has been already said, it must be evident that John Frederick Nims is not at all that kind of a professor. That as a professor he is entirely free from professional humbug appears in what he says of his classes. Only 4.8 per cent of his students fall asleep; he charitably thinks that "the rest whose eyes are closed and shaded are sunk in a contemplation so profound it is frequently quite impossible to distract them." His optimism appears in his venturing to have taught in a number of writers' conferences. His versatility appears in his skill with his hands. He and Norbert Engels — a Notre Dame colleague — panelled the poet's study at Niles shortly after Mr. Nims had taken possession of his house there. In short, he is not at all like the conventional picture of a poet but is fascinated by all aspects of human activity, and finds his subjects anywhere and everywhere. As he is still only thirty-nine, his hearty humor and sanity, joined as they are to considerable powers of expression, put him among the American poets who are best worth watching.   T. M.

Willis Dwight Nutting   1900–

Places that have influenced Willis Dwight Nutting were Iowa City, his home-town, where he attended the State University; next, Antigua (British West Indies), which he visited with his father when he was eighteen years of age; then, Oxford University (England), where he studied as a Rhodes Scholar; after that, Athens (Greece), where he made researches and organized relief for impoverished Greek exiles from Asia Minor and lastly Evergreen (Colorado), where he labored for five years as a clergy-man. Of these five places, in view of the subsequent development in his life, Antigua was the most important, for it was there, as he confesses, that he experienced the moment "that was the turning point of my life." There, this grandson of a Presbyterian clergyman, attending an Anglican service in a church "filled with black people singing the psalms . . . had a firm conviction that I was at home and that my future would be with these people."

To the grief of his parents, young Willis determined to abandon Presbyterianism and to embrace Episcopalianism. He made the change with such ardor as to hurt his relations with his father, whose religion he did not hesitate to belittle. Back at college he became one of a little group of Anglicans who set out, *pronto*, to conquer the world. "We had a superabundance of zeal and went fiercely to work opening up abandoned little wooden churches in the small towns of Eastern Iowa and holding services before the three people that we could per-suade to come . . . the results were small but that was unimpor-tant. We had all the *esprit de corps* of young Athanasiuses against the world. Never have I worked so hard." (*The Road to Damascus*, p. 174.) For twelve years the suddenly acquired faith in Anglicanism lasted. Then, at the age of thirty, Willis Dwight Nutting found the hitherto unknown "depth of understanding of the meaning of the worship of God," and "depth of participation in that worship" which could not exist elsewhere than in the Catholic Church.

Born in Iowa City, in 1900, the son of Charles C. and Eloise W. Nutting, Willis Dwight Nutting's ancestors on both sides were teach-ers and ministers. His parents, Presbyterians, were, he says, "praying and hymn-singing people of the sober and dignified variety." His father was for over 40 years head of the department of zoology at the State University of Iowa, and it was natural that Willis should attend there. Winning a Rhodes Scholarship, he went to Oxford University in the fall of 1921 to study theology in Keble College and to associate with leaders of the Anglo-Catholic movement. In order to write his thesis for his B.Litt. on "Popular Religion in the Orthodox Church of Modern Greece," he went to Athens in the winter (1923–24) and was at once confronted with the misery and destitution of the fugitives from Turkish cruelty. Organizing a Relief Fund, he spent himself in assisting the distressed, while in so doing he had to neglect his research.

Willis Dwight Nutting was ordained an Anglican clergyman before leaving Oxford, and after a brief period spent in the West Indies, he settled at Evergreen, Colorado. While there, his loyalty to Anglican authorities, and to Anglican doctrines, was gradually weakened. By 1929 he found himself recognizing no authority other than his own judgment. He recognized that, in truth, he was his own church: "L'Église, c'est moi!" Leo XIII's encyclical on Anglican Orders and Newman's *Essay on the Development of Doctrine* helped to clarify his mind. In July, 1930, having resigned his ministry, Willis Dwight Nutting was received into the Church.

Foreseeing that he would have to teach and to write, Willis Dwight Nutting returned to the University of Iowa in 1931, and took his Ph.D. degree in 1933, writing his thesis on the philosophy of a German Catholic, Joseph Geyser. The next year he married Eileen Barry. He taught first (1933–36) at St. Theresa's College, Winona, Minnesota, and in 1936 joined the faculty of the University of Notre Dame. "Before coming into the Church," says Professor Nutting, "I was not at all interested in writing anything, not even letters to my relations and friends. The only thing I did during that time was a thesis for the B.Litt. degree at Oxford. Since that time I have become genuinely interested in writing. It is creative work that seems to be worth-while. It gets ideas 'off my chest,' and though it seldom convinces anybody, it does help very much in clarifying my own thinking." But for Professor Nutting writing is no easy matter. "I have never developed any fluency," he adds, "and most of the stuff has to be written over and over again before I stop in exhaustion."

What he calls "his apostolate" is his work with his pen, his voice and his spade, in "the revitalizing of the fundamental units of society, the family, and the neighborhood community." In his able and thoughtful book, *The Reclamation of Independence*, Professor Nutting deals with the economic side of his *revitalizing* program, namely "the increase of local self-sufficiency." He advises a form of "back to the land" movement and himself, together with his wife and three children, with spade and hoe, work a small farm. "It would be the height of arrogance for me," he says, "to advocate what I was not living."

His program of *revitalizing the fundamental units of society* has also educational and religious sides. The educational side throws emphasis on "the family as a school, and on the school as a community"; the religious side stresses "corporate liturgical worship . . . and taking part in parochial life." About these latter aspects of *revitalizing* society, he has written many articles.

His published works are: *How Firm a Foundation* (1939), and *The Reclamation of Independence* (1947). His Oxford thesis was entitled *Popular Religion in the Orthodox Church of Modern Greece* (1924).

Professor Nutting is a man of strong views and able gifts of mind. But his views are not more strong than his honest determination to practice what he preaches. His search for truth, to find and know God, which lasted for fifteen years, revealed his genuine sincerity and strength of will. Now, in the economic field, with no less resolution, "he endeavors daily to realize more fully the ideal of independence and economic family self-subsistence that is the central thesis of his book, *Reclamation of Independence.*" E. B. B.

Most Reverend Eris Michael O'Brien 1895–

Besides his rank of titular Archbishop of Cirro, Most Reverend Eris O'Brien is a dramatist and an outstanding compiler of both secular and ecclesiastical history in Australia.

Born on September 29, 1895 in Condoblin, New South Wales, he was educated at Jesuit schools, and holds a doctor of social and political science degree from the University of Louvain (Belgium) and a master of arts degree from both the University of Sydney and the National University of Ireland. He prepared for the priesthood at the diocesan seminaries at Sydney, Australia and was ordained to the priesthood in 1918. In 1940 Pope Pius XII made him a domestic prelate and in 1948 he was appointed bishop. Early in 1951 he was elevated to be titular Archbishop of Cirro. He is a fellow of the Royal Historical Society of London 1935 and fellow of the Royal Australian Historical Society 1949. He lectured in modern history at the University of Sydney in 1947. He was a member of the Australian Government Delegations to the United Nations Assemblies at Paris in 1948 and at New York in 1950.

When asked how he came to be interested in Church history, he replied: "Realizing that historical writing is best when based on original research and that Australia is too far removed from the treasures of European documentation, I decided to concentrate on the Australian subjects for which ample documentation is available locally." That determination, however, did not deter him from spending more than a year in the Public Records Office at London and other depositories and libraries in Europe in preparation for his work on the *Foundation of Australia.*

He is the author of: *Foundation of Catholicism in Australia* (1922), 2 vols.; *Dawn of Catholicism in Australia* (1928), also in two volumes; *The Hostage, A Miracle Play*, in three acts (1928); *Foundation of Australia* (A Study of Penal Colonization and Criminal Law Reform in the Nineteenth Century, 1936).

Archbishop O'Brien is an associate author of Hartley Gratten's *Australia* (1947), and a contributor to *Australian Encyclopedia,* Eyre's *European Civilization,* as well as magazines. He also lectures on the radio.

M. A. H.

Cathal O'Byrne

The singer, poet and writer, Cathal O'Byrne, was born in Belfast, Ireland and was educated at St. Malachy's and St. Joseph's schools. After further studies privately, he went into business for eight years. He studied singing with Doctor Keoler, the city organist of Belfast, and with Professor Carl G. Hardebeck, Dublin. Specializing in Irish folk songs, he gave concert recitals in Ireland, Scotland, Paris, Brussels, Dresden and Prague. He toured America twice. He did invaluable work for Ireland all over the United States in the years of Ireland's resurgence. During his first six months in America he made more money for the Irish White Cross Relief Fund than any other living Irish singer. On a Sunday afternoon at the Metropolitan Opera House, New York, his concert cleared seventy-five thousand dollars, one thousand of which was donated by the Archbishop. In four nights at the Opera House in Philadelphia, his concerts cleared twenty-two thousand dollars. In one night in Buffalo, New York, he made eight thousand dollars for relief in Cork City, and so on until Mr. O'Byrne had cleared over one hundred thousand dollars.

His recital in Minneapolis prompted James Davis to write in the Minneapolis *Tribune*: "He may rightly be called an Irish minstrel, for the songs he brings are culled from the rich treasury of Irish music. How fertile Ireland has been in the realm of folklore and folk songs we are just beginning to realize, and no more exquisite tunes can be found anywhere than the hundreds that are part and parcel of the lives of the people of Ireland. Mr. O'Byrne has made many of these his own. He entered into the character of each of his pieces with naturalness, simplicity and fine appreciation of every varying mood, and no doubt there are many more such songs in his repertoire as those sung with such charm last night."

Writing in *The Catholic World* (February, 1930, p. 586) Marie Antoinette de Roulet remarks: "Cathal O'Byrne's unique minstrelsy is important, not only for the impetus it lends to the spread of Irish culture, and the enthusiasm it arouses in its behalf, but chiefly for the realization it affords of the habiliments and principles of a civilization more spiritual than our own. Nevertheless, his literary work possesses a more tangible value, since an art that can perpetuate itself only in the memory of the artist's contemporaries does not permit of such accurate evaluation as one that is definitely committed to some physical medium."

Mr. O'Byrne's earliest poems were published in the *United Irishmen*. Others appeared in the *Freeman's Journal, Southern Cross* (Buenos Aires, Argentina), the *New World* (Chicago), *Ave Maria* (Notre Dame, Indiana), and *America*.

Some of his verses were set to music by the composers Sir Hamilton Harty, Professor Carl G. Hardebeck and others.

He is the author of three books of poems: *The Lane of the Thrushes; The Grey Feet of the Wind* (1928), and *Wayfarers*. His prose works include: *As I Roved Out*, historical sketches of old Belfast; *From Far Green Hills*, short stories selected in the United States as the Catholic Book-of-the-Month; *Pilgrim in Italy*, sketches of a tour through Italy; *Ashes on the Hearth* (1948), short stories of old Dublin; *The Gaelic Source of the Brontë Genius* (1935), a study of the Irish Brontës (Grandfather Hugh Prunty was a Gaelic shanachie or storyteller. Prunty was the original family name. The father of the novelists changed the spelling of his name when Nelson became the Duke of Brontë). *Where Memory Dwells* deals with reminiscences of distinguished people and cities and places of note; *From Leprechaun Land* is a volume of Irish folk tales, and *Writing up Mary Ryan* is a book of Irish sketches.

Some of his poems appear in the Dublin Book of Irish Verse and all worth-while anthologies of verse. M. A. H.

Reverend John O'Connell 1888–

The primary interest of Father John O'Connell is the liturgy and all his books deal with some phase of it. He became interested in the liturgy soon after his ordination to the priesthood and chiefly through his friend, the celebrated Dom Lambert Beauduin, O.S.B., of Louvain, the founder of the modern liturgical movement in Europe, begun in Belgium in the early years of the century.

Born in Mallow, Ireland, in 1888, Father O'Connell is the son of Doctor James O'Connell and Minnie Josephine (Wallace) O'Connell. He was educated by the Jesuit Fathers at the premier Irish College, Clongowes Wood, and took an M.A. degree, with honors, in philosophy in the Royal University of Ireland (the predecessor of the National University of Ireland). From 1910 to 1913 he attended the Irish College in Rome and was ordained in 1913.

After serving as an assistant and rector in several places of the diocese of Menevia, Wales, he became Professor of English in the college of St. John Eudes, Vire, and in St. Mary's College, Caen, France, until obliged to flee before the German advance in June, 1940.

From 1940 to 1945 he was pastor of a church in Cardigan, Wales and also acted as temporary chaplain to United States troops stationed in the parish. He is now parish priest of Builth Wells, Breconshire, Wales.

Father O'Connell is the author of: *Rubrics of the Forty Hours'
Prayer* (1927 and 1949); *The Nine First Fridays* (1934 and 1949); *The
Sacrament of Confirmation* (1934); *A Simple Explanation of Low Mass*
(1934, 1936, and 1944); *The Celebration of Mass*, a study of the rubrics
of the Roman Missal in three volumes, written for the Bruce Publishing Company (1940, 1941) and also published in separate editions
(1940–1942 and 1949) by Messrs. Burns and Oates of London. Of
this work the *Ecclesiastical Review* (March, 1941) says: "This is probably the most complete and comprehensive work on the subject in
English."

Father O'Connell has also edited a "Benedictionale" for use in
the United States, Great Britain and Ireland (1930 and 1932) and was
the editor and reviser of Fortescue's *Ceremonies of the Roman Rite
Described* (1930, 1932, 1934, 1937, 1943, 1948). In 1933 and again in
1936 he edited and revised *Directions for Altar Societies and Architects*, first issued by Cardinal Vaughan.

In 1950 Sheed and Ward brought out a new Latin-English *Missal*
which he and H. P. R. Finberg edited. "The translation of the prayers
is the work of the joint editors; that of the scriptural passages throughout the volume is by the Right Reverend Monsignor R. A. Knox."

M. A. H.

Armel O'Connor   1880–

After thirty-eight years as music master of
Ludlow Grammar School, Armel O'Connor retired in 1950. Ludlow Grammar School is the
oldest grammar school in England and is situated in Shropshire. It was a Catholic foundation, though now in Protestant hands. Our Lady
and St. John are on the coat of arms and the
school antedates St. Edward the Confessor.

The *Ludlovian*, the Ludlow Grammar School
publication, in an appreciation states that he was the most distinguished
member of their staff and pays tribute to him for his patience, his
untiring zeal as well as his influence in molding the characters of the
students entrusted to his care.

Born in 1880, the son of John O'Connor, he was educated in
France and at the Benedictine school of Ampleforth Abbey. He was
received into the Catholic Church when sixteen years of age. He served
in Palestine and Syria in the First World War with the ½ East Anglian
Field Ambulance and later with the Australian Cavalry Division.

On December 24, 1908 he married Violet Bullock-Webster (con-
sult *Catholic Authors: Contemporary Biographical Sketches, 1930–1947*).
After Mrs. O'Connor's death in 1946, Mr. O'Connor stayed on at
Mary's Meadow, the house they lived in, near Ludlow, and was looked
after by his daughter, Catherine. When she died in a few days, after
an accident, Mr. O'Connor decided to sell the house and to live with

his son, Aelred, a doctor, now a Surgeon Lieutenant Commander in the navy. Since he came to London, Mr. O'Connor has started again to teach and to serve as housemaster and form master. He has composed music for orchestra, violin and piano. He has also composed songs.

Mr. O'Connor loves travel. He knows most of North Africa, Palestine, Syria and Egypt. He has visited Italy many times and he has traveled in Spain, Belgium and Holland. For years he lived in France.

While he loves literature, art and music, his greatest enthusiasm is for the young. His chief interest is for their future.

Mr. O'Connor is the author of *Poems*. *The Times Literary Supplement* in its review of this work states: "Mr. O'Connor is a Christian mystic; . . . his poetry reveals the choice and ordered gaiety of spirit which is the mystic's privilege; . . . he shows the rare faculty of writing lightly and gaily about the profound mysteries; his is a choice mind that makes choice poetry." Mrs. Meynell, in the *Tablet*, says of his book *The Exalted Valley:* "When — as happens at long intervals — a freshness does indeed come into the world of poetry and life, it is not readily recognized, for it is simple — it makes no boast; it is single. . . . Such a vitality, such a novelty does Mr. Armel O'Connor reveal. . . . His verse is the very freshness of art."

Of his book, *A Singer in Palestine, The Catholic World* comments: "A message heavy with love and consecration. . . . Like everything that comes from Mr. O'Connor's hand, the pages are impressed with fastidious literary taste."

His other works are: *Life of St. Peter of Alcantara* (1915); *Boyhood of a Priest* (1920); *A Lovely Time* (1921); *The Happy Stillness* (1920); *Lilies of His Love* (1920); *A Knight in Palestine* (1921); *The Little Company* (1925); *Poor Man of Assisi* (1921) and *Candles in the Night* (1946).   M. A. H.

John O'Connor   1921–

Born at Drumcairne, Armagh, Ireland, in 1921, John O'Connor is the son of John and Catherine (Rafferty) O'Connor. He attended St. Patrick's public elementary school but left at the age of fourteen to go to work. His first job was delivering telegrams. Then he became a fruit harvester, clerk, laborer, a soldier in the Irish Army (1940) in that order. During World War II he worked in a munition factory in London, through the "Blitz." In 1946 he returned home to Armagh where he has lived ever since.

He has always been interested in writing. His first success came while he was in school. He won a fountain pen for his essay, "The Tyranny of Time."

About 1944 he began to write short stories. "Soon," he writes,

"I had a collection of rejection slips representing about every magazine in the British Isles. But a few of the stories struggled through to print and one of them, 'The Boy and the Stone' was judged the best short story of the year in Sean O'Faolain's magazine, *The Bell*. But it was only a flash in the pan, and soon the rejection slips were flowing in merrily once more. Seized with despair I threw my pen aside, thinking that I had had enough. But it was too late; the poison had set in, and soon I was writing away as hard as ever."

John O'Connor's first novel, *Come Day — Go Day*, was published in 1949. Benedict Kiely called it a "minor masterpiece." Bryan Mac-Mahon in *The Standard* remarked that the author was "a promising young writer."

Mr. O'Connor's stories have appeared in *Argosy, Chamber's Journal, Irish Digest*, and have been broadcast by BBC and Radio Eireann.

At present, 1951, Mr. O'Connor is busy at his book which will describe his bicycle tour through France, Switzerland, Italy, Spain and Portugal in 1950. M. A. H.

Right Reverend John Joseph O'Connor 1870–1952

Popularly known as the original of G. K. Chesterton's famous "Father Brown" stories, Monsignor John O'Connor was also the inspirer of Chesterton's poem "Lepanto." Father O'Connor met Chesterton for the first time in 1904 at the house of a friend in Keighley, Yorkshire.

The story of how the idea of the detective priest first dawned is told on page two hundred and fifty-two of Maisie Ward's *Gilbert Keith Chesterton*. "On their second meeting Father O'Connor had startled, indeed almost shattered, Gilbert, with certain rather lurid knowledge of human depravity which he had acquired in the course of his priestly experience. At the house to which they were going, two Cambridge undergraduates spoke disparagingly of the 'cloistered' habits of the Catholic clergy, saying that to them it seemed that to know and meet evil was a far better thing than the innocence of such ignorance. To Gilbert, still under the shock of a knowledge compared with which these two Cambridge gentlemen knew about as much of real evil as two babies in the same perambulator, the exquisite irony of this remark suggested a thought. Why not a whole comedy of cross purposes based on the notion of a priest with a knowledge of evil deeper than that of the criminal he is converting? He carried out this idea in the story of 'The Blue Cross,' the first Father Brown detective story. Father O'Connor's account adds the details that he had himself once boasted of buying five sapphires for five shillings, and that he always carried a large umbrella and many brown paper parcels."

"The idea of 'Lepanto' came to Chesterton," states the *Scottish Catholic Times* (December 1, 1950) "as the two friends were lunching together. G. K. C. had promised a poem to his brother, Cecil Chesterton, but had not written it. As the day was the anniversary of the battle of Lepanto, Father O'Connor recalled the significance of the battle in the history of Europe and the Church. Immediately after lunch, G. K. C. began to write, completing the poem at a sitting, while a messenger of the *New Witness* waited impatiently in another room."

It was Father O'Connor who had the happiness, in 1922, of receiving Chesterton into the Catholic Church. When in 1936, Chesterton died, it was Monsignor O'Connor who sang the Requiem Mass.

Monsignor John Joseph O'Connor was born December 5, 1870, in Clonmel, Ireland. After three years of education by the Franciscans and two years with the Christian Brothers he transferred to the Benedictine school of Douai, where he won a scholarship. He says: "I cannot be too grateful for the Benedictines. They never crammed, as some other schools did for Intermediate Examinations. They gave things to assimilate, such as the *Dream of Gerontius*, the Antigone of Sophocles, the letters of Cicero, and the Prometheus of Aeschylus, and above all a taste for things liturgical."

In 1889 he went to the Venerable English College in Rome and while there took the famous mission oath. Ordained a priest on Passion Eve in the basilica of St. John Lateran in 1895, he read his first Mass at the tomb of St. Peter. His first parish work was in Bradford. In 1937 he was elevated to the rank of Monsignor.

Monsignor O'Connor has written a simple elucidation of Francis Thompson's unique and matchless poem, "The Mistress of Vision." He translated into English, Paul Claudel's *Satin Slipper*. He had printed privately a number of his sermon notes and sketches called *A Month of Sundays or The Foolishness of Father Brown*. Half the edition was destroyed by the German Nazis. In 1937 he published *Father Brown on Chesterton*. His most recent book is on Savonarola which he said is "not for edification but for information."

He comments: "In the intervals of being Holy Church's doggerel bard I have built two places of worship, one with the altar in the middle, the only possible beginning of Liturgical Reform."

He died on February 6, 1952.   M. A. H.

Joseph O'Connor 1877–

(Jeremiah) Joseph O'Connor was born on September 25, 1877, although his birth certificate states November 25. His mother had been severely reprimanded by the registrar for not having registered the birth of her first child, Elizabeth, within the statutory time. When her eldest son was born, she again forgot to notify the authorities, and when she remembered, postdated his birth by two months to evade another scolding. After that, this same son relates, "she had good practice: children came every year and a half, until she had completed the dozen. She reared them all to maturity, and beyond." Jeremiah, or Joe, as his mother called him, was born in the South of England, but later his family went to live in Dingle, Kerry, where he attended the Christian Brothers School. It was in Dingle that he picked up the fluent Gaelic he was to find so useful later. From Dingle he went to St. Brendan's College in Killarney, and thence to Maynooth, where he remained until 1898, when he discovered "that my real vocation lay outside its walls." But although *"ad vota saecularia transivit,"* he spent his lay life preparing others for the priesthood, including his own son, the Very Rev. Donal O'Connor, of Uttoxeter.

Dr. Coffey, Bishop of Kerry, in 1898, had "a soft spot in his kindly heart" for Joe O'Connor, and when he heard he was doing an art course at the Metropolitan School under Sir William Orpen, he suggested he return to teach drawing and the classics at St. Brendan's. O'Connor "jumped at the proposal and came back."

He remained at St. Brendan's for twenty-six years. During this time the Gaelic revival began, which, as he says "developed into our War of Independence." His knowledge of Gaelic was a great help towards the recovery of the native language in Killarney. He introduced it as a subject of study in the college, and went about the country, unearthing forgotten MSS., and bringing unknown Gaelic speakers into the light. After the War of Independence was won, he was summoned to Dublin to assist in formulating a Gaelic programme for the schools of the country, and was appointed an inspector of schools to supervise its operation in the new dispensation. He spent twenty years as inspector, watching, as he puts it, "a unique experiment in the making, a national endeavor to revive a beloved language which was almost *in articulo mortis*. It has proved almost superhuman, with ultimate success not yet in sight. But, as Mr. O'Connor's brother in Chicago, home after an absence of twenty-five years, remarked, "It is hard to believe that the Ireland I knew can have become the contented well-fed, well-housed Ireland of today."

Mr. O'Connor has written much in Gaelic, to supply a need in the language: textbooks on art, on artistic geometry, and one of the folklore of Killarney. He has written also short stories in English, published in *The Irish Bookman, The Capuchin Annual,* and other organs of the Irish press.

He has also written a full-length novel, The *Norwayman,* published by the Macmillan Company in the United States, where it was the Catholic Book choice, and in England by Faber and Faber. It is the story of Mike and Maire McGillicuddy, newly wed, who live on Shark Island just off the Irish coast. The bay in the story "might be anyone of the hundred salients the Atlantic has thrust into the land between Shannon and Fastnet. The people of Manistir are anyone of the separate communities walled off from each other by the coastal mountains." Mike and Maire find a Norwayman, half drowned in an open boat: they save him, and though Maire falls in love with him, and though Mike is plagued by man-crazy Mai Hogan, there are no triangles. The story is leisurely, rich, "a joyous and moving affirmation of human dignity and faith."   A. F.

Patrick O'Donovan   1918–

For over three years Patrick O'Donovan has been stationed in the Middle and Far East as a successful journalist for *The Observer.* When he was in Singapore in the summer of 1949, his publishers approached him about writing a book. His reply by cable was: "Accept. Writing. Astounded. O'Donovan." When he returned to England for a stay, he wrote *For Fear of Weeping.*

Patrick O'Donovan was born in Richmond, Surrey, England in 1918, the son of a skin specialist in Harley Street, and one of the leading Catholic laymen in England. He was educated first by the Benedictines at Ramsgate and later at the Benedictine Abbey at Ampleforth, Yorkshire. From there, following the conventional path of English "upper class" education, he went to Christ Church at Oxford. This was immediately before the war and the older universities in Britain knew little of austerity. He says he did not do much work, and played at politics most of the time, though on paper he was studying law. Of this he can remember nothing. He was elected treasurer of one of the most famous debating societies in the world, The Oxford Union, which has numbered amongst its officers such men as Hilaire Belloc, Gladstone, Lord Birkenhead, Mr. Asquith, several archbishops of Canterbury, Msgr. Ronald Knox, and an astonishing list of British prime ministers, cabinet ministers, viceroys and writers. He was also President of the University Conservative Association.

World War II broke out at the end of his second year at the university and almost immediately he was commissioned in the Irish Guards and served throughout the war with the Second Battalion and at the divisional headquarters of the Guards Armored Division. Serving as a

tank officer, he went through France, Holland, and Belgium and into
Germany. He was wounded, mentioned in dispatches, and was demobilized with the rank of major in 1945. "On the whole," he says,
"it was a most enjoyable experience, for the Irish Guards have a habit
of making themselves comfortable, even luxurious under the most
impossible circumstances. They chose to give, at least, the impression of
not taking the process of war too seriously. It is the only regiment in
the British army that habitually has a Catholic chaplain for its battalions."

Like many others, after the war, there arose the problem of finding
a job without any particular qualification for any. "Two idle years at
Oxford do not impress possible employers." The obvious answer seemed
to be journalism. He therefore went to Fleet Street, which is the heart
of journalism in Britain and was offered a trial run by *The Observer*,
spending most of his time reporting in the provinces. To gain experience
he was sent to the industrial city of Manchester, where for a few months
he reported weddings, church socials and fires for a local evening paper.
On his return, because no one else was available, he was sent to Palestine as a foreign correspondent at a time when the British were beginning to give up their mandate. He remained behind, after the departure
of the British troops and officials, to cover the war between the Jews
and the Arabs. Since then, he has remained primarily a foreign correspondent, maintaining a slightly amateur attitude to his work which
is an advantage, at least when dealing with British officials. He went
to Greece for the war against the Communist rebels and then after a
brief stay in England was sent to the Far East at the height of the great
and tragic change that has come over that part of the world. He visited
the civil wars in Indo-China, Indonesia, Malaya and lost his laundry
in Nanking and Canton as, successively, those cities fell to Chinese
Communists. As a result of this tour he wrote *For Fear of Weeping*
and began to broadcast frequently on the BBC. His writing is careful,
even "Mandarin." He concentrates as much on the people, their
clothes, their poverty, their attitudes, as on the hard politics of any
given situation because he believes all these to be interwoven.

In 1951 he returned to England after a year spent visiting the
British dependencies in Africa of which there are over a dozen, as well as
Ethiopia, South Africa and Liberia. As a result of his experiences in the
Far East, he has become interested in that great upsurge of nationalism
which has affected most countries of the world that are in any way
backward. All his writings are directed toward finding a way of satisfying this emotion on a democratic and just basis; for the alternative to
such a solution is now quite clearly Communism for these people.
When he was young, like many Irishmen, he was a keen Irish national-
ist, but other interests have taken the place of the early fervor. He is
at present (1952) completing a second book, a travel book, which will be
largely devoted to the working of nationalism in Africa. This, he believes, is now an emotion that could one day present the West with
the same sort of problem that it failed to meet in the Far East.

Reverend John M. Oesterreicher
1904–

Father Oesterreicher's writing career began, much to his bewilderment, in his twentieth year, just a few weeks after his baptism. As he sat studying in the library of the Society of Christ the King, a modern religious institute, Father Max Josef Metzger, its founder and his godfather (who, under Hitler, was to become a martyr for peace), entered, dropped a collection of files on the table, and declared: "Now you are editor of *Der Missionsruf (The Mission Call)*." Stunned, the young convert saw to the publishing of this monthly, which labored to restore all things in Christ, for a radical Christianity in the spirit of the papal encyclicals, and that all Christians might be one.

John Oesterreicher was born on Candlemas, 1904, in the little town of Stadt Liebau, then Austria, and he was to attest to Our Lady's special patronage when he added "Maria" to his name. This came about through one of God's little ironies. While browsing around a bookshop, there fell under his eye a secondhand copy of Houston Stewart Chamberlain's *Words of Jesus*. Must not the Lord have smiled when a book by a hater of Jews and denier of Christ's divinity led a Jewish youth to the Gospels, whence he came to know and love Christ?

A year or two passed. John Oesterreicher, now a medical student, had read Kierkegaard and Dostoevski, and found himself a fervent believer in Christ, an equally assured disbeliever in the Church. But Newman's *The Grammar of Assent* and *The Development of Christian Doctrine* proved his match. This last he opened still certain that the Catholic Church was the arch-falsifier of the simplicity of the Gospel: he closed it, conquered and convinced. It was, he often remarks, an intellectual illumination whose like he has not known since, showing him that the doctrines of the Church are to the words of Christ as the full-grown tree to a mustard seed. And he came to see her teaching as being architectural, as in a great cathedral, in which stone rests on stone, each supporting each, each essential to the whole.

Swiftly there followed baptism, transfer from medical school to theological school, and, only three years later, ordination. Among Father Oesterreicher's first assignments as a young priest was the co-editorship of *Der Pfarrbote (The Parish Messenger)*, published by one of the deaneries of the Archdiocese of Vienna. An article by Father Oesterreicher in this weekly, calling for civil peace during the 1931 disturbances in Austria, attracted international attention, being reprinted as far afield as England.

Hitler's rise brought Father Oesterreicher to a realization of his destined apostolate. In 1934 he founded the Opus Sancti Pauli, a missionary institute which appealed to the Jews to see, behind Hitler's hateful persecution, Christ's loving pursuit. He was sure that once a Catholic has understood that the Jewish question is a mystery of faith, once he has grasped the marvel of Israel's election, guilt and hope, he will never be able to condone the heresy of racism. Father Oesterreicher also established and edited *Die Erfuellung* (*The Fulfillment*), a bi-monthly review dedicated to the same vision, to the yearning that the Jews may meet the Person and message of Jesus Christ, and Christians the mystery enfolding the people of Israel. The venture was welcomed enthusiastically by many European bishops. Jacques Maritain admired "the prudence and courage of *Die Erfuellung*," and Dietrich von Hilde-brand wrote: "I know of no other Catholic journal in German on so high an intellectual plane, nor of any so utterly pervaded by a supernatural spirit." The Dominican theologian, Father Franziskus Stratmann, de-clared that "in our times of anti-Christian pride, *Die Erfuellung* saves the honor of Christ's name."

With Hitler's invasion of Austria in 1938, Father Oesterreicher had to flee. After spending some time in Fribourg and Rome (where he re-ceived the Holy Father's blessing on his apostolate), he lived for two years in Paris. With one threat of the concentration camp behind him (and another to come), he nevertheless continued his weekly broad-casts as the "Voice of Austria," exposing Nazism as an ugly hodge-podge of all the modern heresies, as the first mass attempt at the aboli-tion of man; he denounced it as a devilish effort to twist man's mind and will so that he would no longer seek truth and love, an effort to turn him from a creature *capax Dei*, open to God, into one that is dead to Him.

While in Paris, Father Oesterreicher wrote a book on *Racisme, Antisemitisme, Antichristianisme*, which has since been reprinted in New York. In it are collected the many condemnations of Hitlerism by bishops and Catholic thinkers, and the thesis is developed that Hitler's hatred of the Jews was not merely an economic or political device, but, deep down, a hatred of Christ. It was a protest against the people who, at Sinai, were appointed by God as herald of the Decalogue, for they were a symbol of conscience his soul could not endure. With the instinct of Cain, who struck at grace when he slew his brother, he sought to annihilate the Jews, who had brought forth Christ, and with them the Church, the bearer of His spirit.

Forced to flee France, a few days before its fall, Father Oester-reicher came to New York, not without some dramatic escapes. Though he arrived in this country knowing not one word of English, less than half a year elapsed before he preached his first sermon. Many a sermon of his since has become well known. An address he gave at a mass con-firmation of converts in Brooklyn gained much attention when, at the wish of the Archbishop, it was printed on the front page of *The Tablet*; from there it went to the first page of *Our Sunday Visitor* and then to pamphlet form as *The Sacrament of Strength*.

The next to last day of the Church Unity Octave is devoted to the conversion of the Jews, and for a number of years in succession, Father Oesterreicher preached on that evening. Some of these sermons have been gathered into a book, *Seeds of Hope*, of which Donald McDonald asked, to Father Oesterreicher's dismay: "How long has it been — since Newman — that we have had sermons with the doctrinal depth and literary style worthy of preserving in written form?" Another reviewer described its prose as "strong enough, full of passion enough, to equal Gertrud von Le Fort's *Hymns to the Church*."

Other publications include: *The Apostolate to the Jews*, a study syllabus for seminarians; *The Blessed Virgin and the Jews*, and articles in *Thought*, *The Thomist*, the *Dublin Review*, *Theological Studies*, *Cross and Crown*, *The Commonweal* and *Orate Fratres*, of which he is an associate editor. Indeed, Father Oesterreicher has a special interest in the liturgy, which, combined with his devotion to the apostolate to the children of Israel, led him to do research on the Good Friday intercession for the Jews. "Pro Perfidis Judaeis," his paper on it, is credited with a part in the decision of the Sacred Congregation of Rites to approve a more accurate translation of this beautiful prayer, for it showed that in it, the Church does not speak of "the perfidious Jews," but of "the Jews (still) unbelieving (in Christ)," begging, with tender affection, that the veil may be withdrawn from their hearts. In another liturgical study, *The Elder Brother*, the reader is guided through the Church year, finding in prayer and parable the Church's authentic attitude towards the Jews.

The age-old conspiracy of silence which has kept the Jews from Christ is a frequent subject of Father Oesterreicher's lectures. He feels that in our day, Jewish writers, scholars, painters, etc., are speaking His name again, a sign of an underground stream of water moving beneath what looks like dry and barren ground. Father Oesterreicher has completed a book on seven modern philosophers of Jewish origin and their discovery of Christ and the Church. Bergson, Husserl, Reinach, Scheler, Landsberg, Picard and Edith Stein show that *Walls are Crumbling*. In this, as in all his writing, Father Oesterreicher reveals a special respect and love for the human word, for he regards it as a mirror of the divine Word — a respect and love that have earned the critical title of "literary asceticism."

In addition to directing convert work at Old St. Peter's, the mother-church of the Archdiocese of New York, Father Oesterreicher is Research Professor of Sacred Theology at Manhattanville College of the Sacred Heart. His retreats and lectures are known in many parts of the country, on subjects from "Our Lady in the Old Testament" to "An Answer to Mr. Blanshard," from "Worship in Mid-Century" to "The Philosophy of Persecution." He is a member of the Catholic Theological Society of America and of the Liturgical Conference.   M. R. B.

Kathleen O'Flaherty   1916–

Enniscorthy, a little country town in the southeast of Ireland, is the birthplace of Kathleen O'Flaherty. Up to her fourteenth year she was educated privately. In these early days she got the bare minimum of formal instruction. In her home, however, there was a well stocked library. Urged on by intellectual curiosity, and a father, who, besides an extremely wide range of interests, had a profound classical culture and a rare capacity for communicating his knowledge, her informal education was fairly extensive. The Ursuline Convent, St. Mary's, Waterford, managed in three years to fill up many of the lacunae. Then a year at the Sacred Heart Convent in Lille, France, where she attended the Catholic University, opened up for her a new intellectual field — French thought and literature.

Having returned to Ireland, she became a student at University College, Cork, and after three years graduated from the National University of Ireland, with a Double First in French and English in 1938 and was awarded the French Government Gold Medal. The following year she obtained her M.A. degree for a thesis on A. E. Housman. She won the Travelling Studentship of the National University of Ireland in Modern Languages in 1941. World War II prevented her from going abroad. Therefore, she spent two years preparing a Ph.D. thesis on the pessimism of Chateaubriand. This first extensive work of research revealed her originality, her penetrating critical judgment and a remarkable knowledge of the French romantic background.

In 1943 she was appointed a member of the French department of University College, Cork, and some years later, became, in addition assistant editor of the Cork University Press.

The controversy about the efforts to rehabilitate Voltaire had excited a lot of interest in Cork which explains why her first book, *Voltaire, Myth and Reality* (1945) was of a somewhat polemical nature. The first edition was sold out in a few months, and a second enlarged edition was then published. In its review of the book, *The Times Literary Supplement* stated: "The intention is laudable, and the resulting exposure of Voltaire's attitude to truth, of Voltaire as relentless enemy and false friend, warmonger, snobbish pseudo-democrat, incompetent scientific popularizer and philosophical fraud, and as the hater and foe of Christianity, could not well be more complete."

France, which, except during the war years, she has never ceased to revisit, interested her since "there the great modern Catholic writers seemed to have found a solution to the very difficult problem of integral intellectual Catholicism. While their yard measure, their whole philosophy was deeply Christian, they were not self-conscious and neither did they make the mistake of turning the world into a sacristy peopled with plaster statues." The result of this interest was Kathleen O'Flaherty's second book, *Paul Claudel and " The Tidings Brought to Mary,"* (1947). Here, in studying Paul Claudel's best known play, she has attempted by numerous and apposite references to his other plays to show, for English speaking people, the main characteristics of the French dramatist's work. An American edition was published by the Newman Press.

Miss O'Flaherty is a contributor to various Catholic periodicals in which she deals mainly with modern French Catholic writers.

Y. S.

Terence O'Hanlon 1887–

Terence O'Hanlon belongs to the early environment of Brian O'Byrne, better known as Donn Byrne, whose mind was steeped in the folklore and traditions of northeast Ireland. Terence lived as a boy on the same poor land as Brian, heard the same old Gaelic tales, "glimpsed the same distant hilltops," attended the same feiseanna where prowess in song and dance and storytelling was displayed. And the romance of it all, that made Donn Byrne great, lingers in his ear. He tells:

"Though distance shuts the gate of song,
    I hold thereof the key,
And hear the warblers still among
    The hills of memory."

Terence's parents, though strict, were "just and considerate." "They must have observed early," he relates, "that I had neither taste nor talent for farm work, for after school hours I was given the freedom of the friendly hills, with a dog and a book for company. I loved the solitude of those airy heights and the brooding stillness, broken only by singing birds or the drumming of a snipe or the lonesome cry of a peewit."

Terence was born at Lislea in County Armagh (Ireland) in 1887. His father, a farmer, was John O'Hanlon; his mother's maiden name was Anne McKeown. He went to the local National School, and completed his education by wide reading in English literature and Irish history.

At school he had a remarkable teacher, "terribly cross," but for whom to teach was "the breath of his nostrils." For fifty years this devoted scholar travelled each morning, on foot, up "three miles of hilly road from his home at Camlough to the school at Lislea and back again in the evening, yet never seemed to eat a lunch. At playhour he would draw from the recesses of his swallowtail coat a cutty pipe and a plug of strong tobacco. Then, and then only, would those stern features relax a little as he wreathed himself in a rancid cloud of smoke." When, soon after a long-deferred retirement, he died, he willed that his grave be dug "close to the back wall of the school (where there was a churchyard) that he might still hear the boys at their lessons."

In a brief biography written for *The Capuchin Annual*, Terence O'Hanlon tells with inimitable charm of the scenes and personages that were familiar to him in his early days. Among others, he tells of Captain O'Hagan, a retired seaman, who yarned away the hours at a cross-roads tavern, "sitting under a tree with his jug of ale and his pipe." From him he learned of a Derry bookseller, a Scotsman, who acquired cheap a bankrupt stock of Protestant Bibles. He offered the Bibles for sale in his store window at two-and-nine (two shillings and ninepence) apiece. As a sales-promotion effort he composed and hung on a placard, a verse:

> "Holy Bible, book divine,
> Very cheap at two-and-nine —
> Satan trembles when he sees
> Bibles sold as cheap as these."

Sternly and thoroughly schooled, Terence O'Hanlon began work at seventeen as reporter for the *Dundalk Democrat*. From this position he advanced to the staff of the Dublin daily, the *Irish Independent*, and thence to the editorial staff of the Dublin *Evening Herald*. He was twenty-five and getting ahead, and recently married (1912) to Mary Hally, from Clonmel, County Tipperary, when tragedy struck. He had a stroke, which left him permanently an invalid.

"The outlook," he says, "was bleak as could be. . . . The decision of the doctors was that I could not even hope to resume staff work on a newspaper again. There was nothing for it then but to try my fortune as a free lance. As I could no longer guide the pen with my right hand I quickly acquired the knack of writing with my left. This was my first encouragement. Keeping firmly in mind the inspiring words of Thomas à Kempis: 'Do what is in thy power, and God will be with thy goodwill' — I resolved to specialize in the class of literary work that would interest the common reader and at the same time, directly or indirectly, further the cause of Catholic truth."

He began to write serialized sketches on aspects of the Faith in Ireland, on saints and scholars of the early ages, of the monasteries, and of religious persecution. Many of his sketches appeared in *Our Boys*, a magazine published by the Irish Christian Brothers.

In 1929 he published an anthology of patriotic Anglo-Irish poetry, *The Minstrel of Erin*, dedicated to the memory of the dead who died for Ireland. Pursuing his researches into Irish history, Terence O'Hanlon accumulated material on famous Irish highwaymen, heroes of the undercover war that was waged unceasingly for centuries against the English. Among his own kindred was one, Count Redmond O'Hanlon, whose land the invading Planters seized.

"Instead of following his ruined kindred to moil for existence in the stony wastes around Slieve Gullion," Terence tells us, "Redmond O'Hanlon packed a blunderbuss and took to the highway. As captain of a squad of outlaws, and with a tempting reward on his head, he led the Planters of Armagh, Tyrone, Down and Monaghan a lively dance for fully twenty years, 'giving their roofs to the flame and their flesh to the eagle' when chance offered. They got him in the end and spiked his poor head on the portals of Downpatrick Jail."

Basing himself on history and local tradition, Terence published his volume of historical sketches, *The Highwayman in Irish History* (1932).

Terence O'Hanlon is well known as a book reviewer and writer. The charm of his style in storytelling is exemplified in "Wisps of Memory," the autobiographical sketch already referred to. Proud father of three sons and a daughter happily launched on their careers, he finds "distant hilltops can send his spirits soaring" — but they must remain distant! For nearly forty years Terence has had to suffer "stuffy bondage," due to his illness. But it is a bondage over which his soul has triumphed.

E. B. B.

Mary O'Hara (Mrs. Mary Alsop Parrot Sture-Vasa) 1885–

There were two outstanding personalities in the early life of Mary O'Hara Alsop; her grandmother, "a fascinating grandmother — a really beautiful and wonderful and thrilling grandmother"; and her father, "a strikingly handsome man," and great scholar, clergyman, a broadminded man, to live in the same house with whom "was to receive an education of the rarest kind."

Her grandmother used "to descend upon our Brooklyn home every so often . . . and pick up the small fry — four of us — and take us to Europe. In her opinion school didn't matter; languages and music and travel were the important things." Sometimes Mary was taken by this marvelous lady to her Pennsylvania country home where she learned to know and love ponies and horses. Meanwhile her father taught her to use words correctly and to attend to his sermons in such wise that she could mentally make and then repeat aloud an intelligent résumé of them. Other times, of an afternoon, he would call from the hall of their home: "Who will walk over the Brooklyn Bridge with me?" And Mary would go, telling stories to her father, who would appraise them. She would a'so recount to him the novels she had read. "The esplanade of the bridge was paved with wood and sprang pleasantly underfoot. The wind blew. The big ships and little tugboats moved in endless panorama of beauty and interest below and on either side of the bridge. I loved to hear the boat whistles . . . conversation never lagged. . . . I told him many stories of my own invention. Looking back, I see that this was all fine literary training." [3,750,000 copies of her novels have been sold.]

Her grandmother encouraged Mary to devote herself to music. She provided the best teachers for her wherever they traveled. In London, Mary was taught harmony and composition. In other foreign cities she had piano and violin instructors. Later, in memory of the good times

she had in her grandmother's country home, she composed her delightful collection of juvenile piano studies, "Summer Days" and had the
satisfaction of seeing it published and of using for the first time her
(permanent) nom de plume "Mary O'Hara."

Travels in northern Africa provided the little girl with a host of
new impressions, the Sahara Desert, small oases and sign language
conversations with strangely dressed Arab women, a race between a
smart young French officer on a magnificent Arab horse and an Arab
on one of the famed racing camels — ("the camel won — just walked
away from the horse"), dancing girls with heavily painted faces, French
Zouaves in full red trousers.

Of all that she saw on her travels she wrote long descriptive letters
home to her father. "Mary's letters, Mary's diary" were considered
remarkable by the older members of her scholarly family before she
had reached her teens.

This free and unconventional education undoubtedly prepared the
mind of Mary O'Hara to produce the marvels of her descriptions of
Flicka, Thunderhead, and the state of Wyoming where, in later life,
she found "such emptiness, such solitude, such vastness."

Mary O'Hara Alsop was born in Cape May Point, New Jersey, in
1885. The winter home of the family was in Brooklyn Heights. Her
father was the Reverend Reese Fell Alsop, an Episcopalian clergyman
of Quaker descent; her mother, Mary Lee (Spring) Alsop. Mary's
grandmother was Mary O'Hara Denny of Pittsburgh who married
Walton Spring, son of the Reverend Gardiner Spring, famous pastor
of the Brick Church, New York, writer and scholar.

Mary's first school was Packer Institute (Brooklyn Heights) and
later she spent two years at a finishing school in Connecticut. Unlike
her brother and sisters she never went to college but made up for this
by wide reading of those subjects which interested her, metaphysics,
music, art. In 1905 she married Kent K. Parrot by whom she had two
children. A divorce terminated this marriage and it was in the lonely
years following that she began to write professionally.

Hers is not the usual story of final success after long and dogged
pursuit. "For the most part my work sought me. We were living in
Hollywood. Because of my association with literary people, and my
background, I was asked to have a try at doing the job of 'reading' in
a motion picture, important work because it influences the selection
of material to be filmed." An immediate success at this, she was asked
to do adaptations, and then chosen as staff writer for a famous director.

She won a "name," a repute for having "the human touch" and
acquired invaluable training in dramatic construction, editing, word-
painting.

But the work, she confesses, was impossibly arduous. "One wrote,
not to suit one's own artistic conscience, but to suit the star, the director, or the producer, or all three and all different."

Her second marriage in 1922 provided a welcome escape and took
her to a Wyoming ranch. "Here at the ranch," she says, "I have done
many things. I brought all my furniture and my Mason and Hamlin
grand piano from Hollywood and I did a great deal of composing. Quite

a little of it was published. I helped with the horses. I ran a dairy and delivered milk in Cheyenne all through one blizzardy winter."

Serious writing was suspended for a time, but automatically she collected material. Everything she saw, experienced, thought or imagined must be written down. It was not only the habit of a lifetime but a positive addiction. So the stacks of paper — "Mary's diaries" — were periodically burned; they took up too much space. No sooner was one burned than she began the next. And she gradually admitted to herself that it was foolish to write so much and publish nothing, and if she was through with screen-writing she must find a different market. It occurred to her that possibly, with not too much time taken from her activities on the ranch, she could catch the "slant" of magazine fiction. So she went to New York, talked to fiction editors, got an agent, wrote half a dozen short stories.

How the enthralling story of Flicka came to be written was both commonplace and exciting. Mary O'Hara, in 1939, was working at a story. It was difficult and complicated, and she told herself that a "good story ought to come easily," for instance, "a simple little story about an animal — the sort of thing I tell people and they always seem to like so well."

She thought of a little filly she had, named Flicka. She thought Flicka should have a little boy as owner. The character of Ken (not her own boy who was then at West Point) walked into her mind. "The story flowed just as easily and naturally as I had wanted it to." It was written, in the short form (five thousand words) in two days, and a year later accepted for publication by *Story Magazine*.

Now another opportunity sought her out. The publishing house of J. B. Lippincott asked her for a novel similar to the short story of "My Friend Flicka." Never having dreamed of writing a novel, Mary O'Hara demurred, they persuaded; she doubted, hesitated, held off, and finally took the plunge. Making a novel out of the short story took five months time. "But," she says, "I had a lifetime of training for it."

The screen rights were sold; both book and picture were so successful that *Thunderhead* and *Green Grass of Wyoming* followed. Mary O'Hara had won her place among America's distinguished novelists.

Meanwhile Mary O'Hara continued to compose her musical pieces. In 1942 the famous choir of the Paulist Fathers (New York City) produced a Christmas carol she had written. Two years later, Mary O'Hara was received into the Catholic Church. "From childhood," she says, "I leaned toward mysticism and made a personal discovery at an early age that the motto of our family, *Sine Deo Quid* was true for me. I was an avid reader, and the writings of St. Augustine, St. Thomas, St. Teresa, inclined me toward Catholicism. For ten or fifteen years I had been attending Mass. Heretofore I had belonged to the Soul of the Church. When my marriage tangle was straightened out, I was received into the Body. I could always take fire from the writings of the Saints. If I came upon a quotation I would follow it to its source, and so I found St. Augustine, or shall I say he found me?"

Mary O'Hara's published works include, piano compositions:

Summer Days at Deercreek; Novelette in G; Idle Moments; When the Wind Blows; Little Girl Dancing, and others. Books: *Let Us Say Grace; My Friend Flicka* (1941); *Thunderhead* (1943); *Green Grass of Wyoming* (1946) and *The Son of Adam Wyngate* (1952).

Mary O'Hara's portraiture of ranch life is intensely American . . . "a pattern of American living" . . . "homey family life" . . . "down to earth, true to family life" are phrases that reviewers have justly used. In fact both her life and her ancestry justify her personal statement that, "I feel as if no one could be more American than I am. If I have presented a typical American way of life, it is the most natural thing in the world."

Lady Mary O'Malley. See Ann Bridge

James Milton O'Neill   1881–

Law had been the career James Milton O'Neill had planned for himself. When he was graduated from Dartmouth in 1907, he decided to teach for a few years, for financial reasons. After teaching two years as an English master at Hotchkiss School, in Lakeville, Connecticut, he was called back to Dartmouth to teach. "I had such a good time and prospered so in promotions, that I decided, in 1912 when I accepted the Chairmanship of Public Speaking in the University of Wisconsin, definitely to be a teacher, rather than a lawyer," writes Mr. O'Neill.

Professor O'Neill was born on December 17, 1881, the son of John and Margaret (Spellescy) O'Neill. As was stated above he did undergraduate work at Dartmouth; he did graduate work in law at the Universities of Chicago and Harvard. On September 17, 1918 he married Edith Winslow. They had six children — John, James, Margaret, Hugh, Richard and Paul. John, a Marine captain, was killed in action when the marines took Bougainville, in the Second World War.

Mr. O'Neill began his teaching career in the district school of Vine Valley, New York in 1900 but taught there only one year. For two years, 1907–09, he was English master at Hotchkiss School, Lakeville, Connecticut. From 1909 to 1911 he was instructor in English at Dartmouth College and assistant professor of oratory from 1911 to 1913 at the same institution. Then he accepted a professorship at the University of Wisconsin and remained there until 1927. After eight years (1927–1935) as professor of speech at the University of Michigan, Professor O'Neill accepted a position at Brooklyn College. Here he has been since as Chairman of the Department of Speech from which he is now retiring in June, 1952. He has published thirteen books in the field of speech before turning to civil liberties and the relation of American Catholics to our American system. He was the first President of the American Speech Association, and the founder and the editor, for its first six years, of the professional organ *The Quarterly Journal of Speech*.

From 1936 to 1948 he was a member of the Committee on Academic Freedom of the American Civil Liberties Union. From 1944 to 1948 he was Chairman of that committee. "My experience on this committee," he writes, "demonstrated to me that most people had a very hazy idea of the American doctrine of civil liberties, or the origin, purpose, or effect of the Bill of Rights. I wrote an article on the meaning of the First Amendment which was published in the Jewish monthly *Commentary*, and it attracted so much attention of one kind or another, that I decided to expand it into a book, which would give me an opportunity to prove the positions I had taken in the article, and in which, of course, evidence and documentation was not possible. The result was *Religion and Education Under the Constitution*, published by Harper & Brothers in 1949."

The book's purpose is to establish a better understanding of civil liberties. It challenges the recent Supreme Court opinions in the Everson Bus Case and the decision in the McCollum Religious Education Case. Professor Edward S. Corwin of the Department of Politics, Princeton University, says of it: "Your attack on the McCollum decision is well developed and relentless; it is in short, simply devastating. My congratulations!" Dean Luther A. Weigle of the Divinity School, Yale University, writes: "I have read it with great interest and with hearty approval. I hope that the book will get a wide reading."

When Paul Blanshard and Bishop Bromley Oxnam took to the rostrum to try to mislead Americans that Catholics were opposed to civil liberties and seek to establish Catholicism as the national religion, Professor O'Neill wrote a book to correct their misstatements. It was published by Harper in 1952 under the title, *Catholicism and American Freedom*. This book is an answer to Paul Blanshard's attack on American Catholics.

In recent lectures Professor O'Neill traced American history, illustrating how religion and the state have worked hand in hand for the good of the republic, since President Washington first asked Congress for an appropriation to finance missionaries to Christianize the Indians. He also pointed out that Congress voted to pay salaries to chaplains in both Houses of Congress out of public funds only three weeks after the adoption of the Bill of Rights.

Professor O'Neill's latest book, *Catholicism and American Freedom* continues the work of his previous book *Religion and Education under the Constitution*, in attempting to distribute accurate information to replace antique prejudices. In giving the facts of American history and proving how Paul Blanshard "points out only those parts of Catholic sources which he can distort and ignores the plain statements of endorsement of the American Constitution made by the leaders in the Church," Professor O'Neill has done a service for truth.   M. A. H.

Joseph O'Neill   1886–

"How often do we misconceive of our friends. They turn a shining side of their character to us and we think that is what is best in them and we imagine no other depths. About Joseph O'Neill, whom I knew as the efficient head of a great Public department of the Irish Free State, with heavy burdens placed on him, how was I to know, for all the torrent of picturesque speech and prodigality of humor, that within that long head and long body, there were other creatures than those he exposed to me? For he had so vividly imagined Dublin as a city ruled by Norsemen that, when I read his novel, *Wind from the North*, I felt as if I almost remembered being there in some past life, so freshly did the winds of that ancient world blow on me. And how was I to know that he had it in him to imagine and write *Land under England*, a satire so original and so profoundly felt on the totalitarian evil of our time? I feel, as I read O'Neill's great work that I could be one of an army fighting for the soul whose virtue it is to be free. There have been times in the past when humanity has fallen into servitude, but never has the prison-house been so menacing to such wide ranges of humanity as today.

"It is because O'Neill evokes all that is spiritual in us to fight against that inhuman despotism that his work is of such moment at the present time." Such was the estimate of A. E. (George William Russell, Irish poet and painter) of Joseph O'Neill in the decade before World War II and the estimate holds with even more truth today.

Joseph O'Neill, a west-of-Ireland man, was born in December 1886, the son of Martin O'Neill and Mary Quigley O'Neill. In 1912 he married Mary Davenport O'Neill (the author of Prometheus and other poems).

Mr. O'Neill has had what might be described as a triple career; a research worker, an administrator, and a writer. He was educated at Queens College, Galway; Victoria College, Manchester; University of Freiburg, Baden, Germany; and he is an honors graduate of the Royal University of Ireland.

Before he entered on his university career proper, he spent two years at Maynooth College reading Catholic philosophy so that his university work might be based on the deepest foundations.

His first work was in the field of Old Irish Scholarship and included publications from early middle Irish manuscripts, chief of which was the editing and translation of the very difficult *Rule of Ailbhe*, which remains the fundamental source of our knowledge of life in the ancient Columban monastic foundations.

At this period Joseph O'Neill was lecturer in Celtic in the University of Manchester and had done research work in philology under Professors Thurneysen and Kuno Meyer. The field of education had however always held special attractions for him and, when in 1907, he was offered a post as inspector of primary schools he found it impossible to refuse. Within two years he was appointed to the still more responsible position of senior inspector of secondary schools, in which he proved so successful that, when the Irish Free State was established in 1922, he was appointed head of the first Irish Ministry of Education. It was a time of profound reconstruction of administration with few highly-trained men available to do the work, and O'Neill was selected by the new Irish Government to fill many of the highest posts, such as the Chairmanship of the Primary Education Commissioners, the Chairmanship of the Secondary Education Commissioners and the control of the Technical and Vocational Branch of Education. In addition, in 1923, he was called on to act as civil service commissioner, a position in which it was his duty to make all appointments to the civil service of the new Irish Free State, and from 1926 to 1946 he was Local Appointments Commissioner, which gave him control of the appointment of all medical, legal, and other professional officers under local authorities throughout Ireland.

It was an arduous life on the highest administrative plane. Yet it was during this period of intense administrative activity that O'Neill wrote the novels of which A. E. has spoken above. In later years, novel after novel flowed from his pen. *Philip,* a picture of the last days of our Lord, as seen through the eyes of a young Jewish-Greek doctor, is so poignant that it has been used by many preachers giving retreats. Another book, *Day of Wrath,* was a forecast of the last war in novel form, a terrifying book and yet no more terrifying than the reality. His last book, *Chosen by the Queen,* is a study of the utter demoralization of English society in the final phase of Elizabeth's reign, when the Reformation had uprooted all the moral standards of England's Catholic days.

As regards dates of publication, his first book, *Wind from the North,* was published by Jonathan Cape of London in 1935, with a foreword by Sigrid Undset, the Nobel Prize winner, who was profoundly taken by the book. This novel won the Harmsworth Award for the best Irish novel of 1935 and was translated into German and published in Berlin in 1939. The German edition was followed by one in Irish in 1940. Selections from the book are prescribed as part of the English Course for Matriculation in the National University of Ireland and a special edition is in use as a reader in the highest classes of Irish primary schools.

The second novel, *Land under England,* was published in England by Victor Gollancz, and in the United States of America by Simon and Schuster in 1935, was serialized widely in America, England and the British Commonwealth, and was generally acclaimed as a work of genius. A French edition, under the title, *Le Peuple des Ténèbres,* was published by Gallimard in Paris in 1939 in the *Editions de la Nouvelle Revue Francaise,* and received a special review on the front page of *Le Temps* in August of that year as one of the most important books of the century.

The other books were published in the following order: *Day of*

Wrath (Gollancz, London, 1936); *Philip* (Gollancz, London, 1940); *Chosen by the Queen* (Gollancz, London, 1947). All have been acclaimed by the English critics and the sales have been so rapid that they are now difficult to get, although they ran through several editions.

In addition to his novels, Joseph O'Neill is the author of various articles contributed to high-class Catholic journals such as the Jesuit quarterly, *Studies*, the final quarterly issue of 1949 of which contains a most searching examination by O'Neill of the whole course of Church and State control of education from the earliest times to the present day. As one of the most important Irish writers of the day, he is a member of the Irish Academy of Letters and of various other literary bodies. Amongst his close friends he has counted W. B. Yeats, Lady Gregory, and other famous authors at home and abroad. When his work receives its final assessment in the future, it is possible that his chief achievement may, as A.E. has pointed out in the passages quoted above, be his war on behalf of the human soul against secularist totalitarianism, no matter what form it takes or under what shape it rears its evil head.   M. A. H.

Alfred O'Rahilly 1884–

The versatility of Dr. Alfred O'Rahilly, the President of University College, Cork, Ireland, is a matter for awe. In addition to his duties as head of a well-known institution of learning and author of several books, he has published some five hundred articles on philosophy, theology, scripture, sociology, science, history, biography, finance, politics, apologetics, ethics, and other subjects.

Born at Listowel, Co. Kerry in 1884, of a gifted family, he was educated at Blackrock College, Dublin, where he was an Intermediate Exhibitioner and a Medallist in Modern Languages; and at University College, Dublin, where, in 1904, he won a Mathematics Scholarship, in 1907 a first class honors degree in Mathematical and Experimental Physics, and in 1908, a first class honors M.A. degree in the same subjects. From 1908 to 1911, he did a complete course in Scholastic Philosophy at St. Mary's Hall, Stonyhurst, England, and in 1919 he obtained the Papal Degree of Doctor of Philosophy. It might be said justly of Dr. O'Rahilly that he ate and drank learning with the gusto that gourmets give to fine foods and wines. But the learning was not devoured for mere egoistical ends. Early in his career he began to make his presence felt in Irish public affairs. He lectured and wrote about the principles of politics and the nature of statehood, and in everything he wrote and said he manifested a mature and ardent democratic spirit. During the War for Independence (1916–1921) he argued publicly for the rights of the new Irish State, born in war. He was imprisoned by the British, first in Cork Gaol and then in Spike Island. On the day after the murder of Lord Mayor MacCurtain by the Black and Tans he was leaving college early when the milkman told him of the murder. Dr. O'Rahilly at that time was a member of the Corporation and his story of what happened is: "I went down to the City Hall and ordered that it be closed and put up a notice saying that it was closed because of the brutal murder of the Lord Mayor of Cork. I then went to the City Library and did the same, and then I wondered if there was anything else I could close." In 1921 he was Constitutional Adviser to the Irish Plenipotentiaries in London, and in 1922, he was a member of the Constitution Committee. On three occasions he was chief Irish Government Representative at the International Labor Conference in Geneva, and he was chiefly responsible for the International Convention on the Abolition of Night Work in Bakeries, as well as for important changes in the procedure of conferences. In 1927 he spent a year at Harvard University where he studied social and political theory. He was instrumental in introducing the subject of sociology into the curriculum of University College, Cork, and became the first lecturer there on sociology. Even with all these activities, he has found time to have been a member of the Irish Parliament (Dail Eireann) for Cork City, a member of Cork Corporation, and a successful arbiter in many trade disputes for which work he was honored, in 1943, with a life membership of the Cork Chamber of Commerce.

The life of action and the life of contemplation were commingled in him. One of his earliest and best-known books is his lengthy biographical study of the saintly Jesuit, Father William Doyle, who was a chaplain with the Allied Forces during the First World War. One of his least known but weightiest works is his massive tome on Electro-Dynamics (1939), by which he secured from the National University of Ireland the degree of Doctor of Science. By that time he was already a Doctor of Literature (*honoris causa*). In 1942 he published one of his most brilliant and controversial works, entitled *Money*, which has become an arsenal of argument for Irish citizens who are interested in financial reform. In between studying and writing books and lecturing, he has engaged in controversies in Irish and British journals, magazines and newspapers, and has become renowned for the clarity of his reasoning and for his hard-hitting. His motto in controversy is: "Have plenty of ammunition," and his ammunition, gathered by wide and deep study during his lifetime, is organized in a magnificent filing system devised and maintained by himself.

The subject dearest to his heart is a study of the New Testament. He has projected a twelve-volume work on the Life of Our Lord, the first volume of which, *The Family at Bethany*, was published in 1949 by the Cork University Press, and was acclaimed by students of scripture and by professors of Irish colleges and seminaries. One of the byproducts of this study has been a closely reasoned, heavily documented monograph on the Holy Shroud of Turin.

From 1914 to 1916, he was assistant lecturer in mathematics at University College, Cork, and in the latter year he was appointed Professor of Mathematical Physics. He became Registrar in 1920. Since

1943 he has been President of University College, Cork. As a member of the Cork faculty and as chief, he has founded and fostered a movement for education of the Irish workers which has issued in workers' courses in Cork, Carlow, Galway and other Irish towns.

Socially, there is nothing of the dry-as-dust bookworm or academician about Dr. O'Rahilly. Following Aristotle's maxim, he thinks high and speaks the language of the people. It is brilliant, witty, rapid language, impelled by swift thought, charming with its Kerry accent and full of the warmth of fellowship. He is short in stature, and alert and quick in his movements as a sparrow. His sense of humor, and more predominant than that, his acute sense of irony, lighten his lectures and writings about the most abstruse subjects. His handwritten manuscripts are a joy to editors for his handwriting is neat, clear and fluently cursive.

It is only when some valiant student undertakes and concludes a bibliography of Dr. O'Rahilly's writings that the breadth and depth of his knowledge will be adequately sketched. His influence has been incalculable in Irish life — religious, social, political and economic, and above all, cultural. It is a perpetual mystery how he, in the midst of the very busy life, devoted to administration at University College, Cork, Ireland, has succeeded in writing so much. Five of his books have been published since his appointment as President.

His chief works are: *Father William Doyle, S.J.: A Spiritual Study* (1920); *Electromagnetics* — A Discussion of Fundamentals (1938); *Money* (1941); *The Burial of Christ* (1942); *Religion and Science* (1948); *Aquinas versus Marx* (1948); *Moral Principles* (1948); *Social Principles* (1948); and *The Family at Bethany* (1949).

He reads detective stories for recreation but never takes exercise. He was once quoted in a New York paper as having said, "The true test of education is the power to resist jargon."   F. M.

William Aylott Orton   1889–

A wound suffered on the Somme during the First World War occasioned the change of fortune that made of William Aylott Orton a distinguished writer and professor in the field of economics. From active service in the field he was called to serve on the Intelligence Staff of the War Office (1917–19). He was thence transferred to the Ministry of Labor (1919–22), where, as he says, "had close experience of industrial relations in troublous times and good training in the testing out of various social theories." Digging deeper into economics he was, though still an Anglican, "much impressed with the essential sanity of papal teaching in this field."

Meanwhile the great quest "to find a meaning for life" impelled him. "For me, as for many non-Catholics," he writes, "this quest split up into two puzzles; a meaning for my life as an individual, and a meaning for the life of society in historical and political terms. I was professionally challenged by the latter, privately by the former; but many years ago, I conceived the logical solution that the two answers might be one. Logic, however, was not enough. In experience I owe much to the chapel of the Sacrament in Westminster Cathedral and to the rite of Benediction. But it was simply too good to be true that the divine love would give me a blessing that I am sure I never earned. There you have the mystery of Faith — or a bit of it. But on the objective side, the more I studied, the more I was impressed by the essential rightness of Catholic teaching, and the sureness of it in so many historical crises."

William Aylott Orton was born in 1889 at Bromley, Kent, England. His education was first at University College School, and subsequently at Christ's College, Cambridge, where he received post-war degrees, B.A. (1919); M.A. (1922). At the University of London he received his M.Sc. (1921), and obtained the Doctorate of Science in Economics in 1946. Boston College honored him with its LL.D. in 1948.

His first writings were essays in the *Westminster Review* (London) on Walter Pater, Ibsen, and Alexander Smith. Occasionally he wrote for the *New Age* and in 1920 he won the national essay prize offered by the *Athenaeum* (London) for a study of English literature during the war.

In the fall of 1922, Orton came to America as Professor of Economics at Smith College. He has been visiting lecturer at the University of California, Amherst, Williams, and other institutions. He is a member of the American Economic Association, the American Academy of Political Science, the Executive Board of the Catholic Historical Association, and the Board of Trustees of the University of Massachusetts.

Among his works are the following: *Labor in Transition* (1921); *Prelude to Economics* (1932); *America in Search of Culture* (1933); *The Last Romantic* (1937); *Twenty Years' Armistice* (1938); *The Liberal Tradition* (1945); *The Economic Role of the State* (1949).

Professor Orton does a good deal of extramural lecturing, now mostly to Catholic audiences. He is keen, he says, "to make people realize there is a solid and coherent social philosophy alternative to that of the 'commies' and materialists, if they would take the trouble to get acquainted with it; and a true internationalism that will really work if they can rise to it."

Looking back over his writings and finding implicit in them "the great quest," thankful for the divine solution found in the Catholic Church, Orton writes: "Like all converts I am still humbled and overwhelmed by the knowledge. I still feel that the Faith is almost too good to be true. And who doesn't?" E. B. B.

Reverend Augustine J. Osgniach, O.S.B. 1891–

From section gang to eminence as author, missioner, lecturer, and retreat master is the new version of the American success story, experienced by the Reverend Augustine Osgniach, O.S.B. of St. Martin's Abbey, Olympia, Washington.

Father Augustine was born on June 23, 1891, in Osgnetto, Italy, in that part of the province of Udine which is almost entirely inhabitated by Slovenians. His parents were Pietro Osgniach and Teresa Sibau. After completing his elementary education at San Pietro al Natisone, in 1901 he entered St. Francis' Preparatory School at Cherso (Cres) Dalmatia. In 1907 he joined the novitiate of the Minorite Conventuals of St. Francis at Padua. At this time, however, various family misfortunes prevented him from pronouncing the religious vows in that community. In consequence of this, he left the Franciscan Order after six months of novitiate, for only by returning to the world could he offer assistance to his parents in their financial difficulties. But the hope that more favorable circumstances would later permit him to pursue his religious vocation was always kept alive.

With this end in view, Father Augustine came to the United States of America in 1908 when he was eighteen. He began his new adventures in the State of Washington, working first on a section gang 10 hours a day for $1.25. He also labored in mines, dug irrigation ditches, and slept in a box car with other immigrants. He pursued this line of work for over three years, contributing his earnings to his parents' support. No doubt, these experiences proved very valuable in his latter life. There remained only one sad recollection. The majority of his working companions, who came with him from Italy, gave up the practice of their religion. They soon fell victims to the anticlerical and socialist spirit with which the earlier immigrants were imbued. The latter waged constant war against the Church and capitalism which in their views were closely allied. All this offered the young man ample opportunities to discuss religious, political, and economic problems. In such circumstances he found consolation and enlightenment in the two books he always carried with him and read in his spare moments: *The Imitation of Christ* and Dante's *Divine Comedy*.

Upon the betterment of his family's financial conditions, Father Augustine decided to pursue his religious vocation. A Jesuit Father advised the young man to contact Father Sebastian Ruth, O.S.B., who was then Director of St. Martin's College. Through the services of Father Sebastian, the young man was accepted as a candidate for the Benedictine Order in 1911. Hence one year after leaving the section gang, Father Augustine was studying philosophy at St. Martin's.

Reverend Augustine J. Osgniach, O.S.B. 420

Joining the community of St. Martin's Abbey in 1913, and after completing the course of theology, he was ordained to the holy priesthood in 1916. He became a naturalized American citizen in 1917.

Because of his knowledge of many foreign languages (Italian, Slovenian, Slovak, Polish, Croatian, French, and Spanish) the newly ordained priest was immediately appointed pastor of Roslyn, Washington, a mining town of many nationalities. This offered him additional opportunities for studying the social and economic conditions of the working classes, especially since this town was at that time a very nest of radicalism and communism. These first hand experiences were later on utilized when Father Augustine wrote his two books dealing with socio-economic problems: *The Christian State* and *Must It Be Communism?*

In 1920 Father Augustine was recalled to St. Martin's to serve as professor of philosophy. His interest in philosophy was engendered by the study of Dante's *Divine Comedy*, which is Aquinas in verse. He became so fascinated by this subject, that at the early age of twelve he committed to memory the whole of Inferno and many cantos of Purgatorio and Paradiso. His philosophical pursuits were spurred on by the Virgilian motto: *Felix qui potuit rerum cognoscere causas.*

In 1921 he attended the University of Washington in Seattle, doing graduate work in philosophy, English, and psychology. He studied philosophy under the nationally known professors, William Savery, C. J. Ducasse, and Ralph Blake. While the study of philosophy in our state universities may be a dangerous undertaking for those who are not well grounded in Scholasticism, it was very beneficial in Father Augustine's case. For, as dogma is crystallized by the study of heresy, so Thomistic thought becomes more resplendent by the study of other philosophical systems. In many public debates on philosophical subjects, Father Augustine successfully defended the teachings of Aquinas thus giving his fellow students and his teachers an opportunity to acquaint themselves with the doctrines of the Schoolmen. He obtained his Master of Arts degree in 1922. The next four years were devoted to teaching at St. Martin's and to the pursuit of the postgraduate work for the doctorate in philosophy which he received from the same university in 1926. His doctoral dissertation is intitled: *The Scholastic Doctrine of the Categories.*

After serving as professor of philosophy and dean of liberal arts at St. Martin's for five years, Father Augustine was transferred to St. John's University, Collegeville, Minnesota in 1931. Here he was head of the department of philosophy for nine years. He took an active part in the programs espoused by the Institute of Social Studies, which was established by Father Virgil Michel, O.S.B., contributed a number of articles dealing with socio-economic questions of the day and represented St. John's University at several national conventions of the American Catholic Philosophical Association. In his spare time he wrote his first work: *The Analysis of Objects* (Wagner) which was published in 1938. Recognition has been given his outstanding reputation as a philosopher by mention of him in *Who's Who in Philosophy.* During his residence in Minnesota, he likewise assisted various pastors in their parochial duties, preached missions and conducted retreats.

On his return to St. Martin's in 1940, Father Augustine resumed the teaching of philosophy and working on another book: *The Christian State* (Bruce), published in 1943. This book was named by the American Library Association as one of the fifty most outstanding religious books for 1943. The same book also made the select list of 100 books chosen by the *Saturday Review of Literature* as outstanding in the field of solutions for postwar problems. His latest work: *Must It Be Communism?* (Wagner) was published in January, 1950. Father Augustine has also contributed articles and book reviews to the *New Scholasticism* and other magazines. He is now at St. Martin's College where he is gathering material for another work in the field. He is a member of the American Catholic Philosophical Association, of the American Benedictine Academy, and is mentioned in the *American Catholic Who's Who*, in *Who's Who on the Pacific Coast*, and in the *Directory of American Scholars*. In January 1951 he was elected to honorary membership in the *International Mark Twain Society*, and was named to the *Gallery of Living Catholic Authors*. In addition, Father Augustine has at different times given missions in English, Croatian, Slovenian, and Italian, in the States of Washington, Wisconsin, Minnesota, and British Columbia. His life may be summed up in the Benedictine motto: *Ora et labora.*

Reverend Denis O'Shea   1904–

Denis O'Shea was born under the shadow of the old cathedral of Mullingar, Westmeath County, Ireland in 1904. He matriculated in the diocesan seminary of St. Finian, took his B.A. degree with honors in the National University of Ireland, and was ordained in St. Patrick's College, Maynooth, in 1929. After working for four years in London, England, he was recalled to his native diocese of Meath. He is now a country curate in Tang, a purely rural parish containing more cattle than Christians.

He lives in a little house between the parish church and the school. There is no village, no electric light, no telephone, no police station, no cinema, no garage, no medical dispensary in the parish, and there are no funds available for the erection of even a tiny parochial hall, where the young folks who have not yet emigrated might enjoy some legitimate recreation. During the day the priest's little car penetrates the long lanes and bumpy "boreens" to the houses where his parishioners dwell in the seclusion of their fields and raise cattle for the English market. When the rain persists and the river Shannon rises, many acres are flooded and wheeled traffic is impeded. In every house there are pictures of the Sacred Heart, Our Lady and St. Joseph, and every household kneels round the hearth at night to recite the family rosary. Indeed many of these humble homes are edifying in their resemblance to the Holy Family of Nazareth, and there are only two families of non-Catholics in this parish of a thousand souls.

Although Tang has been rated as the Siberia of the diocese, it has
its literary associations. It is the homeland of both a minor and a major
poet. Leo Casey wrote, "In leafy Tang the wild birds sang," and Oliver
Goldsmith here found his inspiration for *The Deserted Village*. "Sweet
Auburn" remains deserted and only one crumbling wall remains of the
"modest mansion" of his father.

> "The never failing brook, the busy mill,
> The decent church that topp'd the neighb'ring hill."

The busy mill alas! is gone, but its millstone is embedded in the threshold of "The Three Jolly Pigeons," the inn made famous in Goldsmith's
play, *She Stoops to Conquer*.

So even Tang has its inspirations, and its compensations too,
chiefest of which is the leisure to study, meditate and write on the
grandest subject in the world, the Holy Family. When the Stygian
blackness of the long winter nights descends upon the wet fields around,
Father O'Shea lights his lamp and burns the midnight oil. In his little
study, warmed by the turf provided by his kindly parishioners, he works
in lonely silence, unbroken save by the clatter of his typewriter or the
peremptory knock that heralds an urgent sick call. Dante's inspiration
was the gracious memory of his Lady Beatrice, of whom he determined
to write "what has never before been written of any woman." The
Blessed Virgin Mary is an even nobler ideal, and Father O'Shea tries to
discover the factual details of her life on earth, and write her story as it
has never been written before.

Curiously enough, his name first appeared in print as the author of
a short detective story entitled "The Black Box." He was then only
sixteen, and before he was twenty he had published tales of adventure,
ghosts and humor. In the diocesan seminary of Mullingar he founded
and edited the short-lived *College Review*, with the collaboration of his
school-fellow, John Kyne, who is now his bishop. The flow of these
productions of his boyish fancy necessarily ceased during the studious
years of his preparation for the priesthood in the stone halls of Maynooth, and also during his busy years on the London mission. Back in
Ireland once more he took up his pen, this time to write of Jesus, Mary
and Joseph. As curate in the town of Tullamore, he was given charge
of the flourishing men's Confraternity of the Holy Family. Based on
sermons preached to these good men, he published two series of Eucharistic hours entitled *Twelve Hours, A Second Twelve Hours, The Fifteen
Mysteries of the Rosary*, and *The Fourteen Stations of the Cross*, all
blessed with success in Ireland. Many other sermons were reported in
the local newspapers. While reading for the preparation of these works
he became aware of the striking fact that while devotional works on
Mary and Joseph abound, there was no historical biography of them in
existence. So he set himself to supply the need, and after years of
research he produced, in 1944, *The Holy Family*, the first work of its kind
in English, and had the honor of receiving a letter of approbation from
His Holiness Pope Pius XII. His method is thus described by Mr.
Francis MacManus, novelist and critic, in a review broadcasted from
Radio Eireann.

"To be candid, when I first looked at this book, I thought it was, well, just another book that wouldn't gather dust on any layman's shelf because no layman would bother about it. But the first bad impression became of no account as I read Father O'Shea's book. It is unique as a study. It is also unique among recent religious biographies in its manner. It is the manner achieved by a man who has gone on working year after year in a labor of love to make his book fulfill his plan with complete satisfaction. His plan, it appears, was to give as fully a detailed a picture as possible of the life and times of the youth of Our Lord from the first Christmas Eve until that day when He went down to Nazareth and was subject to His parents; his plan was not to expound but to represent. He succeeded in accomplishing his design, I think. His picture is convincing; it seems accurate; at any rate, it is impressive. He builds up the picture detail by detail. He does not forget anything of the landscape of the Holy Land which he seems to know so well. The architecture of the houses, the food, the weave of the clothes, how the ground is ploughed and the seed sown, — nothing escapes the attention of this imaginative biographer; and the details are backed up by authorities or by credible surmise. His book must be recommended warmly as a difficult work splendidly done."

Since then Father O'Shea has delved deeper into the mine of research to extract the precious ore of authentic information. In 1949 Bruce of Milwaukee published his *Mary and Joseph, Their Lives and Times*, a work of almost 200,000 words. Now for the first time there is brought within reach of the general reader much interesting matter hitherto obtainable only in learned tomes and works of reference. The Irish *Daily Independent* thus reviewed the book on the 10th of September 1949 under the heading of Irish Priest's Fine Work. "Here is a book which an author might give the best years of his life to write, and his readers among the best days of their lives to read. Father Denis O'Shea rightly claims for his book that it is unique in being 'the only considerable documented biography in English of Mary and Joseph.' We in Ireland have reason to be proud that it fell to an Irish priest of the diocese of Meath to write it (and to an Irish Bishop to receive its dedication), though America has had the honor of publishing it. Immense labor and devotion must have gone to the achievement the book represents. Father O'Shea has aimed not only at telling the story of Mary and Joseph, but at bringing us back with him over nineteen and a half centuries to the Palestine which made and formed them, and the materials for this enormous task of reconstruction he has drawn not only from the Gospel narrative, and (with due reserve) from the Apocrypha, but from the works of Josephus and Philo, the Talmud, the classical historians, the early Fathers, the great modern commentators, and the best results of later day scholarship."

Richard O'Sullivan   1888–

Richard O'Sullivan, a well-known member of the English bar and lecturer in law at The Inns of Court and at University College, London, was born in Cork, Ireland in 1888. He is the eldest son of Richard O'Sullivan of Cork and Mary Fleming O'Sullivan of Goresbridge, County Kilkenny; and a descendent of the O'Sullivan family of Berehaven. In 1942 he married Dorothea Close, daughter of Lieut.-Colonel A. C. Borton D.L. J.P. Cheveney, Kent.

He was educated at Our Lady's Mount, in Cork, London University, and at the Inns of Court where he was a prizeman in Constitutional Law (1912) and Common Law (1914), and received a Certificate of Honor in the Bar Final Examination. Called to the Bar (Middle Temple), in 1914, Mr. O'Sullivan read in Chambers from 1914 to 1915 with H. A. McCardie, afterwards Mr. Justice McCardie. From 1915 to 1919 he served in the Royal Artillery. With Sir Leonard Costello, as joint author, he wrote his first book, *The Profiteering Act* (1919). Two years later he wrote on *Military Law and the Supremacy of the Civil Courts* (1921).

Since 1928 he has been Honorary Secretary of the Thomas More Society of London. In 1934, with the late Professor Edward Bullough of Cambridge, he presented the National Petition to Pope Pius XI for the canonization of Saints Thomas More and John Fisher. He was President of the Aquinas Society of London from 1928 to 1937, and Chairman of the Sword of the Spirit from 1941 to 1944. At present he is Chairman of the Executive Committee of the Catholic Social Guild.

Mr. O'Sullivan became King's Counsel in 1934 and Recorder of Derby in 1938. Since 1939 he has been a member of the General Council of the Bar, of which he is Chairman of the External Relations Committee, and since 1940 he has been one of the Masters of the Bench, Middle Temple.

During the war years, 1939–45, he acted as Chairman of the Regional Advisory and Home Office Advisory Committees. He served also on the Departmental Committee on the Imposition of Penalties by Marketing Boards; on the Hops Marketing Board Committee; and on the Law of Defamation Committee from 1939 to 1948.

Besides translating Jacques Maritain's *Le Regime Temporel et la Liberte* (1935) and editing Gatley on *Libel and Slander* (1938); *The King's Good Servant* (1948); *Under God and the Law* (1949); he published *Christian Philosophy in the Common Law; Three Broadcast Talks on the Common Law of England*, with a Foreword by Viscount Jowitt, Lord High Chancellor; and *The Inheritance of the Common Law* (1950).

Mr. O'Sullivan has contributed to *Transactions of the Grotius Society, Dublin Review, Modern Law Review, Nineteenth Century, Clergy Review, Blackfriars, Tablet*, and the *Times Literary Supplement*.

He is in constant demand as a lecturer.

In 1949 he lectured at the University of Notre Dame, the University of Chicago, Fordham University, Providence College, Rhode Island, and elsewhere in the United States.   M. A. H.

Gretta Palmer 1905–

"When you are a professional writer as I have been," says Gretta Palmer, "you can't afford the luxury of becoming interested 'in a special field'; you have to become interested in whatever some editor will pay you to write about." Going on to illustrate this "discipline" she says, "I remember snarling with some bitterness at my editors when I was writing an assigned article on sinusitis. It was in the midst of the war. I had just returned from a European theatre of operations with a bagful of facts I felt the American public ought to know, and there I was, forced to turn my energies to work on the assumption that the most interesting thing in the world to my readers was a hole inside their own cheekbones."

Nevertheless, Gretta Palmer, in recognition of her extraordinary ability as a free lance reporter, received assignments of the utmost importance and interest. One such was to investigate political influences within the Federal Communications Commission for the *Reader's Digest* — an assignment which led to her being herself subpoenaed by one of the congressional committees as an expert witness in 1944. In the same year she was sent to Italy as a war correspondent for the same magazine and, as she put it, "Invaded Europe from Corsica in a Piper Cub" on D-day — some four weeks before women correspondents were supposed to join in that South France invasion.

In 1945, Gretta Palmer shifted from the Mediterranean Theater to China, where she remained until V-J Day and after. Her most notable writings from this period were a definitive article on General Albert C. Wedemeyer, which appeared in the *Reader's Digest* and won his enthusiastic praise, and the first chapter in a book, *Deadline Delayed*, published by the Overseas Press Club of America, of which Miss Palmer is a member and former governor. In her contribution to the anthology she recounts her eye-witness experiences at Hanoi, Indo-China, in the turbulent months immediately following the war, when the city was in the hands of Ho Chi Minh's revolutionary government and the whole fate of that little country hung in the balance — with only three correspondents from the press of the whole world in attendance. Miss Palmer foresaw that the Annamites would not permit the French to return without much bloodshed, and in this her predictions have been borne out by years of civil war. She hoped that the United States or the new-born United Nations would give the Indo-Chinese people an alternative to the radicalism of Ho Chi Minh and the sovereignty of the French and, in this hope, hurried back to America to press the urgency of the matter in Washington and in the press. In this matter she signally failed. And she is still uncertain as to whether success then would have won a friend for free government in Ho Chi Minh (with whom she had had frequent discussions at Hanoi) or whether he was, even then, and in spite of his denials, pledged to the Marxist views which he has since espoused.

Within a year of Gretta Palmer's return to New York came the amazing, factual, tale of her battle for Faith. The long hard fight to escape atheism, to grope for revealed Truth, to re-orient her whole mind and soul, and that tale, as recounted in *The Sign* (November–December 1947), will seem to many readers far more thrilling than her previous writing. This article comprises one chapter of the book, *The Road to Damascus*, compiled by Father John A. O'Brien. In *The Sign*, September 1951, pp. 26 et seq. ("4 Years Later"), she tells of her first four years in the Church.

From "Faith in Freud and in a mystical, unproven principle of life called 'progress'" she came to know that "every act of the day can be sanctified and turned into a prayer in the economy of supernatural belief." Through labor and sacrifice she had reached the goal. In her victory there was a human tinge of pathos. "My most painful sacrifice, intellectually and emotionally," she writes, "was the surrender of the belief in man's perfectibility. I did want to think that an extension of good will and a development of knowledge would enable all of us, here and now, to become happy and whole forever. It is the ideal of our century — the belief in unaided achievement of the Brotherhood of Man without a Father. It is the dearest fallacy of our times."

There is something refreshingly "hard-boiled" about the way Gretta Palmer faced the problem of her doubts and uncertainties, and brazened it out with the Church's answers. She confesses that she was on the alert for any attempt "to put one over on her." She came to see in time that it was not Monsignor (now Bishop) Fulton Sheen who was "converting" her. As Bishop Sheen told her: "Priests don't convert. They merely hoe the earth a little bit and make the growing easier. . . . God will come, if you watch for Him. . . . Read the Gospels. Very slowly."

Since her conversion (1946), Gretta Palmer finds the scope of her journalistic adventures limited. She confesses: "It takes a certain amount of nimble-wittedness in this generation to make a fat living off the magazines without writing outright heresy and nonsense, such as puffs for psychoanalysis or misty, uplift pieces urging the Brotherhood of Man with no theological backing." Her first effort to write a creative book, is *God's Underground* (1949), in which she recounts the startling experiences of "Father George," a Croatian priest who fought the Nazis in Dalmatia and later entered Russia to visit and encourage Russian Catholics.

Gretta Palmer was born in St. Louis, Missouri, in 1905. Her father was August Brooker, her mother Marie Louise, nee Morphy. She graduated in 1921 from Mary Institute, St. Louis, and then went to

Vassar College where she took her A.B. degree in 1925. Her earliest writing was reviewing books for the *St. Louis Post-Dispatch*, after gaining experience as an editor of the Vassar College *Miscellany News*. A year after she left college, she secured a position on the *New Yorker*, through a letter to Harold Ross (the editor), which contained suggestions of new features for the magazine. Her marriage to Paul Palmer had occurred the previous year.

In 1928, Gretta Palmer joined the staff of the New York *Sunday World*. Three years later she transferred to the New York *World-Telegram*, where she became a columnist and editor of a woman's page. An account of her work as an editor appears in *Ladies of the Press* by Ishbel Ross. In 1934 she began free lance journalism and reporting, combined (for a time) with commentating over the Mutual Broadcasting Company Stations. When war broke out, she received two assignments as war correspondent, first to the Mediterranean Theatre in 1944, and next to the China-Burma-India Theatre in 1945. As magazine writer she has contributed to *Collier's*, *The Ladies' Home Journal*, *Liberty*, *Life*, *Coronet*, *Good Housekeeping*, *Saturday Evening Post*, *Look* and *Reader's Digest*. For four years, she has written a column, *The Top of My Mind*, syndicated to Catholic newspapers by the NCWC. She had done much lecturing to Catholic groups. Apart from reviews and articles she has published: *Murder* (with Evelyn Johnson, 1928); *Shopping Guide to New York* (1930); *God's Underground* (1949) and *God's Underground in Asia* (1952).

Gretta Palmer is first and foremost a reporter. She has proved her capacity to inform, and in part to form, public opinion. She writes clearly, pungently, and caustically. At times she writes with great power and eloquence, and this was particularly noticeable in her writing, already referred to, about her conversion. She is convinced of the high destiny and moral purpose of the press. On this high vocation she sheds light: "Sometimes great and tragic events occur with no correspondents at hand or no telegraphic communications for them to use. Then history turns out quite differently. Then public opinion, cut off from its source, ceases to be a factor with which men in power must reckon. Then dark little deals are quietly made, with nobody the wiser. Then men who died for an ideal lose the place they have rightly earned in history, because their martyrdom lacked witnesses. Then the lack of newspapermen on the spot becomes the cause of a whole series of unnecessary deaths and avoidable treacheries."   E. B. B.

Reverend Pascal P. Parente   1890–

Pascal P. Parente was born at S. Giovanni (Benevento) Italy, on September 18, 1890, the son of Giovanni Parente and Elisabetta Lepore.

His first education was received at the Collegium Marianum Tiburtinum in Tivoli, conducted by the Salvatorian Fathers, where he also acquired perfect mastery of the German language. He began his philosophical studies at the Pontifical Gregorian University in Rome, in the fall of 1908, and three years later, he received the degree of Doctor of Philosophy. In the fall of 1911, he was drafted for military service during the Italo-Turkish War for Tripoli. When released from duty, at the end of that war, he began his theological studies at the Gregorian University in Rome. On May 22, 1916, he received the Doctorate in Sacred Theology, having been ordained priest on May 3, 1915.

In July 1916, he was drafted once more for military service, this time during the First World War. Because of his knowledge of the German language, he was assigned as military chaplain to the Austrian prisoners of war in Italy. In that capacity he had to travel extensively visiting the various concentration camps on the islands of Sardinia and Asinara, and in the northern zones of Milan, Treviso and Venice, bringing the comforts of religion to the poor prisoners and acting as their interpreter and mediator with the military authorities. He had the satisfaction of receiving into the Catholic Church some Jewish and some Protestant prisoners.

He was released from duty early in 1920. In the fall of that year, he came to the United States of America to teach sacred theology at the request of the head of the Salvatorian Seminary of St. Nazianz, Wisconsin, where he remained till 1926, when that religious seminary was transferred to Washington, D. C. Because of his health, he came East and was engaged as curate in several parishes of the diocese of Trenton to which he now belongs.

In June 1937, he was invited by Bishop Joseph Corrigan, D.D., to teach ascetical and mystical theology at the Catholic University of America in Washington, D. C. He began his lectures there in the fall of 1938, having been given the rank of assistant professor. Because of the quality of his teaching and the acclaim of his publications, he was finally promoted to the rank of full professor in the fall of 1947. In the same year he was elected member of the academic senate.

Dr. Parente's first publications were in Latin, a language he has cultivated with predilection. He is the author of a book of Latin verses, *Roma Inoccidua* (1939), for which he received the honorary membership of the Eugene Field Society. He composed and read the Latin *Carmen* at the convocation for the jubilee of the Catholic University, November 13, 1939. Later he published his Latin lectures, *Cursus Asceticae et Mysticae Theologiae* (1940) and the scholarly work, *Quaestiones de Mystica Terminologia* (1941).

Of still greater importance are his publications in English. Besides a number of articles in various Catholic periodicals, he has contributed an article to the *Encyclopedia Britannica*. His books include *The Ascetical Life* (1944); *The Mystical Life* (1946); *The Well of Living Waters* (1948). They are clearly written, informative explanations of ascetical and mystical theology. The third volume is a rich mine of short and practical quotations from the scripture, the Fathers of the Church, and other saints and writers. The title well describes it. It is a well, and a cup of its water will revive the tired spirit of the reader. During the Holy Year, 1950, he published a very practical volume on *Spiritual Direction* and a biography with the title, *Susanna Mary Beardsworth*.

Dr. Parente was elected as member of the Gallery of Living Catholic Authors in the fall of 1948. At different times in the past he has given retreats in Italian, in German and in English. He became an American citizen in Washington, D. C. on March 4, 1930.

Ruth Park (Mrs. Darcy Niland)

The novelist, Ruth Park, was born in Auckland, New Zealand, and christened Rosina Ruth Park, but she never uses her first name. Her grandparents were all immigrants — Irish, Scots and Swedish. "I find this significant," she says, "for every one of them was a storyteller, and while I grew up in the new world, my mind was mostly developed by the traditions of the old."

Her father was a contractor, thrusting out roads through the wild and desolate King Country (stronghold of the Maori "king" or sovereign chief). She and her mother went with him, camping by waterfalls in old deserted farmhouses, in the silent bush. She could read well but the family library contained only three books: the *Bible, Banjo Paterson's Poems,* and *The Three Musketeers.* Parts of them she read hundreds of times. When she was seven she went to school in Te Kuiti where the Sisters of St. Joseph had a little convent. She played mostly with Maori children, and grew up knowing the Maori character well. She cannot remember when she started to write but was eleven when she had something published. She received a guinea for a patriotic essay entitled, "My Own Country." Encouraged by this success she went to her teacher and said: "How do I become a writer?" The teacher replied: "First you must be educated." "That nun practically beat me over the head to win a scholarship at an age so tender they had doubts about admitting me as an entrant. She coached me, browbeat me, and I have no doubt pestered the saints so furiously that at last they gave in. This scholarship gave me secondary education. I was educated practically by force at the hands of priests and religious.

For years nuns were saying to me: 'Come on Saturday at 8.00 A.M. and we will run over some history.' Or priests were stopping me in church porches and saying: 'It is time you got some more books from the presbytery library.' When I wanted to read Daniel Lord, they gave me Newman, Wiseman, Manning. All this time I was writing, sprouting in all directions and wanting most of all to write poetry. My greatest ambition was to have a religious vocation. My friends went off to convents in droves, but I was left standing. In deep despair, I joined a newspaper staff instead, on the Auckland *Star*," writes Ruth Park. She was still in her 'teens when she left school to enter journalism.

She read proofs by day and attended the university at night. When she was eighteen, she became editor of a children's page on the *Zealandia*, a Catholic paper. She describes this experience as "wonderful," and learned so much that she became competent to take over the editorship of the *Star's* children's pages, a colossal job.

During this time she began to do slum welfare work, mostly among children and old-age pensioners. In 1941 she went into general reporting, and had the usual journalistic experiences. Realizing that she needed wider experience, she went to Sydney, Australia, to take a job on *The Mirror*. When she got there she saw that the job would not be of any use to her, and so she tried free lancing. She did radio plays, children's stories, general articles, short stories, paragraphs, gag scripts, in fact everything, with moderate success.

Then, in 1942, she married Darcy Niland, a journalist and one of Australia's most outstanding radio playwrights. He is also a novelist in his own right and won a major prize in a *Herald* competition. The Nilands have five children.

In 1946 she decided to write a novel for the *Morning Herald's* competition. She won the two thousand pounds prize with her story *The Harp in the South*. It is a story about a tenement family of Irish extraction, living in the slums of Sydney. She chose this subject because she knew it best. F. H. Bullock in her review (New York *Herald Tribune Weekly Book Review*, Feb. 22, 1948, p. 4), writes: "The most sustainingly beautiful novel that has come my way in many a day. And its fresh and supple graces both of style and inmost content are the perfect reaffirmation of a too-frequently overlooked fact, that the deep poetic quality which is characteristic of many truly fine novels does not depend upon the natural beauty of the materials used. It is fruit of the novelist's creative gift." Seymour Krim in his review (New York *Times*, Feb. 22, 1948), says: "Miss Park's novel has a weight and a solidity that puts fancier books to shame." This book has appeared in Sweden, Denmark, Germany, Spain and is being translated into Braille. It was also published as a Penguin.

Her second book, *Poor Man's Orange*, was published in 1950. It appeared in the United States under the title, *12½ Plymouth Street*. It is a sequel to *Harp in the South* which continues the story of the Darcy family, living in the slums of Sydney. Reviewing this book for the Chicago *Sunday Tribune* (Feb. 11, 1951, p. 2), Richard Sullivan says: "Few writers of our time have the knowledge, compassion, humor and skill to do this sort of thing. Ruth Park has done it twice."

Besides her two books, Miss Park has done considerable writing for newspapers and periodicals, including a syndicated column through Australia and New Zealand.

She likes writing poetry, and writing for children best. She does a great deal of the latter, mostly for radio sessions, kindergartens, school broadcasts, etc. She can devote only two hours a day to writing because of her duties in the home.   M. A. H.

Reverend Pius Parsch, Can. Reg. Lat. 1884–

One of the great innovative movements within the Catholic Church in Austria is the popular Liturgical Movement (Die Volksliturgische Bewegung) which originated at Klosterneuburg, having as founder and leader Father Pius Parsch, a canon regular of the Abbey of Klosterneuburg which was founded about 1106.

Pius Parsch was born in Olmütz, Moravia on May 18, 1884, of parents "not very religious, but friendly to religion." He had an uncle who was a pastor, with whom he spent most of his vacation. Here his love for religion began and also his inclination toward the liturgy. With other children he could "play priest" in a room in the attic. They had an altar, vessels and vestments to "celebrate Mass." From childhood on Pius Parsch fostered the desire to become a priest. While he was at the gymnasium he had the opportunity to meet priests.

Since the Germans were a small minority in the boarding schools of his German-Slovakian homeland of Olmütz, like most of the Germans, Pius Parsch preferred to go to an Austrian monastery. He entered the monastery of Klosterneuburg on August 28, 1904. Here he made his first acquaintance with the liturgy. He recalls that he requested a commentary on the psalms from the library of the abbey; he found it unbearable to recite the psalms without understanding them. In the course of his theological studies his interest in the Divine Office became so great that he resolved to write a commentary about it. At the same time he acquired a great love for the Bible.

In 1905 Herder published the five-volume set of Wolter's *Psallite Sapienter*, a liturgical commentary on the psalms. Pius Parsch received it in installments. He remarks: "I remember that I swallowed the books literally."

When the time of his ordination drew near, his uncle gave him sufficient money to buy a bookcase. Pius, however, bought the fifteen volumes of Gueranger's *The Liturgical Year* with the money. He believes this set might be the basis of his later liturgical studies.

After his ordination in 1909 he was made an assistant in the big parish Church of Maria Treu in Vienna. Most of his time was taken up with the pastoral care of souls. He spent hours every day in the confessional; devoted himself to club work and at the same time obtained his doctorate in theology. All through these years his interest in the liturgy lagged.

When obedience called him back to his monastery in 1913 to teach, he had his choice between pastoral theology and the New Testament. His preference for parish work prompted him to take pastoral theology. He was also to assist in training the novices. It was then that his interest in the liturgy was revived. The instructions he had given the novices comprised principally explanations of the psalms and the breviary. These activities were brought to an abrupt end at the outbreak of World War I. He volunteered as a chaplain and in May 1915 went with the army to the Front and remained in it until the end of the war.

The years of military life he found rich in experience. There among officers and soldiers he learned to know people better; he learned to know the psychology of the simple man; he learned to know of the soldiers' spiritual needs. He came to the conclusion that man needed more healthy spiritual food than the "sweet and subjective piety of the prewar years." This cleared the way for new ideas based on the Bible and the liturgy.

One day he was appalled at the little knowledge he had of the life of Christ. He had a commentary on the Gospels sent to him and made a thorough study of Christ.

Then he realized with sorrow that the soldiers knew so little about the Mass. On the other hand he had become acquainted with the active participation of the Greeks in the Mass in Galicia and Bukovina. Now and then he would request a priest to read Mass while he would explain the Mass to the soldiers.

When the war came to an end, Father Parsch returned to his monastery by mid-November to resume his post as teacher of pastoral theology and his work with the novices. A few months later, Father Schmidt, a chaplain he met at the Front, visited him to tell him that his *High Mass Magazine* was ready for publication. Father Parsch volunteered his services to help distribute it. The magazine appeared every Sunday and holy day and was sold at the church doors.

In 1919 Father Parsch started to give Bible classes at Klosterneuberg. Both these classes and his Lenten sermons in the cathedral that year stressed the life of Christ. After about a year, a Bible group of more than one hundred persons was formed. The following year this group requested that the Mass be explained to them. Realizing how little the people knew about the Mass, he taught a liturgical class once a week.

Next he introduced the *Missa Recitata* in the church of St. Gertrude and this little parish was to become the cradle of the Liturgical Movement. A regular liturgical mission began for Father Parsch. He gave liturgical weeks in about twenty churches where he explained the Holy Mass and finished with the introduction of the choral Mass. In most of the churches it did not go beyond the attempt but in the Gersthof parish it has become a regular Sunday custom. This prompted a suitable textbook. At first, a four-page pamphlet was printed with the varying parts of the Mass; later on an eight-page textbook followed; and still later a sixteen-page pamphlet, which eventually led to the book form.

In 1936 his book, translated into English by Frederic C. Eckhoff, was published by B. Herder Book Co. under the title *The Liturgy of the Mass*. Some of his main works are *Das Jahr des Heiles* (translated into French, Italian, Dutch, Hungarian, English and Spanish); *Volksliturgischer Wochenabreisskalender* (every year since 1930); *Direktorium* (a church calendar, every year since 1930); *Das Stundengebet der heiligen Kirche* (1. Auflage: 1923; 2. Auflage: 1926; 3. Auflage: 1931); *Die Heiligen des Messbuches* (1. Auflage: 1927; 2. Auflage: 1930); *Das heilige Wort Das Leben Jesu; Die Heilige Schrift des Alten Bundes* (1934); *Kinder suchen den Advent* (1938); *Kleine Brevierschule* (1939); *Fastenmessen für den Gemeinschafts-gottesdienst* (1939); *Volksliturgie: Ihr Sinn und Umfang* (1940), *Die liturgische Predigt*, 6 Vols. (1946–1950) and *The Breviary Explained* (1952).

                                                                                    G. H.

Howard Rollin Patch   1889–

Howard Patch's many academic honors and his brilliant researches in medieval literature, which were duly recognized by the important professorships opened to him, pale in significance before the great event of his career, his conversion to Catholicism. It was an event long impending.

Already at Hobart College, before his entrance into Harvard, he began, in discussion and argument, his religious quest. He had been confirmed as an Episcopalian at old St. Paul's Church, Shelton Square, in Buffalo, and now, at Hobart he had to defend his faith, in discussion with one of his teachers, John Archer Silver. "On Sunday evenings," he writes, "several of us students went to Professor Silver's house, where we had cake and coffee and argued about many things — but often religion (since he was a professed 'unbeliever') — until very late at night."

Soon after entering Harvard (1910), he made the acquaintance of Lawrason Riggs. He writes, "One summer, Lawrason Riggs and I went to Europe together and spent some weeks in Munich. We argued religion the whole way over and back; for the first time, as far as I know, I entered a Catholic Church; I was still a faithful Episcopalian and I believed the differences with 'Rome' were only on the surface. Riggs himself was a Catholic and later became chaplain to Catholic students at Yale. Without knowing it I was forever afterwards searching for the Catholic Church."

By 1917, when associate lecturer in English at Bryn Mawr, he found his way into Anglo-Catholicism, and with his wife began to attend the Good Shepherd Church at Rosemont, where "an imitation of historic Christianity" was preached. "It was like a marvelous modern bit of sculpture," he says, "reminiscent, let us say, of a statue of Our Lady at Chartres or Rheims. God blessed our sincerity but time showed over and over again that what we were cherishing were our own ideas."

While at Smith College, as Professor of English, he published a novel, biased in favor of Catholicism, and admits that "several times he was shaken in his loyalty towards the Episcopal Church and tottered Romewards," only to be held back from the logical step by the influence of such men as Chauncey Brewster Tinker at Yale, Chandler Rathfon Post at Harvard, and Robert Kilburn Root at Princeton. For five years more, while knowing what he should do, he gave himself every test to forestall any false move. Then, he says, "the recent action at Lambeth, on top of the thousand and one other forms of evidence, left no doubt in me anywhere. And, once having decided, how easy all the rest of it was! Looking over the whole terrain now the map is quite clear, and how I wish I could gather in all Anglo-Catholics and say to them: 'Struggle no more! Here is God's Church! God wants you to use that energy of yours for something beside what we may call the battle of the sects.'"

Howard Rollin Patch was born at Lake Linden, Michigan, in 1889. His father, Maurice Byron Patch, was a mining engineer; his mother's name was Emily Isabella White. One of a family of five, his early years were spent amid considerable hardships. In time his father moved to Buffalo (New York) and Howard Patch attended private and public schools. At Lafayette High School he won the Jesse Ketchum medal for excellence of scholarship in the ninth grade. From high school he went to Hobart College and after that to Harvard for graduate work. At Harvard he took his A.M. degree in 1912, and his Ph.D. degree in 1915. He was made an Hon. Litt.D. of Hobart in 1924.

Meanwhile he had married Helen Louise Kennedy in 1916 and begun his teaching career, first at Harvard as assistant in English (1912–15), next at Harvard University and Radcliffe College (1915–16), and later at Bryn Mawr and then Smith College, where he became Professor of English in 1924. Professor Patch is a Fellow of the American Academy of Arts and Sciences; member of the Medieval Academy of America; the Modern Language Association of America; the Modern Humanities Research Association; the Dante Society; Phi Beta Kappa; and Kappa Alpha.

Among his published works are the following: *The Goddess Fortuna in Medieval Literature* (1927); *The Tradition of Boethius* (1935); *On Re-Reading Chaucer* (1939); *The Cupid on the Stairs, a Romance in Rococo* (1942); and *The Other World* (1950). In conjunction with President W. A. Neilson, Professor Patch edited *Selections from Chaucer* (1921). He has also contributed to philological journals.

Having lived so long and so fruitfully with the great writers and thinkers of medieval times, to be a Catholic means something more to Professor Patch than to many another. "What gives me special joy," he says, "is to be in the communion with all the men I have so long known well: Boethius, Thomas Aquinas, Geoffrey Chaucer, Dante, Thomas More and so many others."   E. B. B.

Richard Pattee   1906–

Formerly with the State Department, Richard Pattee is at present (1952) a traveling observer and Consultant for the National Catholic Welfare Conference, Washington, D. C.

Born in Arizona, in 1906, the son of Samuel L. and Eva (Sanborn) Pattee, he is of French and Irish origin. His early education was received locally. After receiving his A.B. degree in 1926 from the University of Arizona, he attended the Catholic University of America where he received his A.M. degree, in 1927. For the year 1931–32 he studied at Louvain University in Belgium. He also did work at the University of Coimbra in Portugal.

His career as a teacher began in 1927 at the University of Puerto Rico in the West Indies, as instructor and assistant professor of history. From the latter part of 1927 through 1930, he travelled extensively through Hispanic America, beginning with the West Indies. He covered the interior of South America from the mouth of the Amazon up the Madeira River to Bolivia and hence through the interior of Bolivia via the famous Franciscan missions of Guarayos to Paraguay. He spent many months in the jungle in the conviction that most specialists in Hispanic American affairs never see anything but coastal cities and airplanes. He did most of Bolivia on foot and muleback concluding the journey from Santa Cruz de la Sierra to Cochabamba with a fifteen-day trek afoot.

His interest in Hispanic affairs dates from childhood. During that entire period he was in constant contact with the Hispanic world through residence on the Mexican border of the United States and contact with the Spanish language. His father cultivated in him a great love for France, the land of his ancestors, and between the two he became increasingly devoted to French and Spanish culture and languages.

As we have seen above, his first teaching post was in a Spanish-speaking country and from there he was able to satisfy a boundless curiosity to know that world as thoroughly and completely as possible. As a matter of fact, since the age of twenty-one, with the exception of a five-year period in the Department of State, the rest of his life has been spent in Spanish or French speaking countries. Equally at home in Spanish and English he has written more in Spanish than in any other language and he looks upon it very much as a mother tongue — at least by adoption. He also speaks French, Italian and Portuguese.

In 1934 he married Ana Mariá Marquez of Puerto Rico. They have four sons. His children speak both Spanish and French fluently.

Mr. Pattee has taught and lectured in Mexico, Cuba, Ecuador, Peru, Dominican Republic and Haiti.

In 1938 he worked for the United States Department of State, first in the Division of the American Republics and later as Assistant Chief of the Division of Cultural Relations, remaining until 1943.

Having no vocation for government work, he became affiliated with the National Catholic Welfare Conference in Washington, D. C., first in Mexico, where he lived for some time during the year 1943–44, and later in Europe, where he has settled at Fribourg in Switzerland as Consultant in International Affairs for the NCWC.

Besides teaching at the University of Puerto Rico he had also taught at the Catholic University of America; three summer school sessions (1939, 1942, 1943) at Middlebury College; Université Laval, Quebec; the National University of Mexico; the Université d'Haiti, and the University of Fribourg, Switzerland.

During the past seven years he lectured on forums and at colleges. In 1945 he delivered twenty lectures in Cuba under the auspices of Cuban Catholic Action. In 1947 he lectured in most of the Spanish universities. He also lectured at the University of Fribourg in Switzerland and at university centers and to other groups in Ireland, England, Scotland, Netherlands, France and Italy.

In 1948 he received the Christian Culture Award Medal of Assumption College, Windsor, Ontario, Canada, given annually to some outstanding lay exponent of Christian ideals. He is a former president of the American Catholic Historical Association.

He is a member of the Academies of History of Ecuador, Venezuela, Panama, Colombia, and Nicaragua, the Geographical Society of Lisbon, as well as the Franciscan Academy of History in the United States.

At the San Francisco conference of the United Nations he was consultant to the American delegation.

Since 1947 he is a member, for the United States, on the Vatican Commission on UNESCO with a seat in Paris.

Mr. Pattee is the author of: *The Negro in Brazil* (1938) (translation from the Portuguese of Arthur Ramos); *Gabriel García Moreno y el Ecuador de su tiempo* (1940), (a detailed study of the great Ecuadorean Catholic statesman); *El catolicismo en los Estados Unidos* (1945) (the first Spanish language study of the history and development of American Catholicism with attention to the contemporary scene); *Introduccion a la civilizacion hispanoamericana* (1945) (a textbook for university use on Hispanic civilization); *An Introduction to Hispanic America* (1945) (a textbook for Catholic secondary schools in the United States); *Informe sobre España* (1949) (a collection of articles on Spain today, published in Mexico City). His latest book is *This is Spain* (1951).

He has also published pamphlets on the religious revival in Mexico, Catholicism in the West Indies, Protestantism in Spain, and several others.

From St. Bonaventure University he received the Catholic Action Medal for 1951.   M. A. H.

José María Pemán   1897–

Poet, orator, dramatist and prose writer, José María Pemán is very popular in Spanish speaking countries. Keeping aloof from movements and groups, Pemán has followed, for twenty-five years, a very individualistic and independent life.

Born in Cadiz, the southern part of Spain, on May 8, 1897, to John Gualberto and Mary (Fallecido) Pemán, he pursued his college studies at the Colegio San Felipe, under the Marianists of Cadiz, then studied law at the University of Madrid. From the latter institution he received his doctorate with the thesis, "Ensayo sobre las ideas filosófico-jurídicas de la Repúblicá de Platón." (Essay on the Philosophico-Juridical Ideas of Plato's Republic.) He practiced for two years as a penologist, but he soon abandoned his profession to devote himself entirely to literature.

At the age of twenty-three, he was named a member of the Spanish-American Academy of Cadiz. A year later, on March 8, 1922 he married Mary del Carmen Domeiq Rivero. They have nine children.

In May, 1936, under the regime of the Spanish Popular Front, he was unanimously elected a member of the Spanish Royal Academy. In 1944, he was elected President of the Royal Academy and filled this chair until 1947, when he voluntarily resigned in order that it might be occupied by the illustrious philologist Don Ramón Menéndez Pidal.

During the Spanish Civil War, he was one of the most ardent defenders of National Spain. Franco conferred on him the honorary title of second lieutenant and appointed him President of the Cultural and Educational Commission of the Provisional Government in the first month of the Civil War.

Impelled by patriotism he had presented his name as a candidate to congress from Madrid in the political struggle of 1936.

A master of oratory, he obtained the special privilege of speaking in the Cathedral of Madrid to appeal for funds for war relief, which were dispersed by Pope Pius XII during World War II. Ramiro de Maeztu called him "The first orator of the Spains."

He was influenced in his literary career by the works of Gabriel y Galan. In 1923 he published his first book, *De la vida sencilla,* and in 1925, the second, *Nuevas poesías.* Soon after he began his work on the newspaper *El Debate* and won success with his Andalusian portraits and stories.

In 1933 his play *El divino impaciente* (Saint in a Hurry) won the "Cortina" prize of the Royal Academy. Two years later (1935) he received the "Mariano de Cavia" prize for his article "Nieve en Cádiz." His work *El Viatico* obtained the prize "Flor Natural" (Natural flower) in the literary game called "Juegos Florales" of Sanlúcar de Barrameda.

His books number over eighty. Some of his works have been translated into English, French, Flemish and German. Among his books of poetry are: *De la vida sencilla* (1923); *Nuevas poesías* (1925); *A la rueda rueda* (1929); *El barrio de Santa Cruz* (1931); *Señorita del mar* (1931); *Elegía a la tradición de España* (1931) (8 editions); *Salmo de los muertos del 10 de agosto* (1933); *Poesía* (Antología) (1937); *Poema de la bestia y el ángel* (1938) (perhaps his best work); *Por Dios, por la Patria y el Rey* (1940); *Poesía sacra* (1940); *Las musas y las horas* (Antología) (1946) and *Las flores del bien* (1946).

The prose works include: *Cuentos sin importancia* (1927); *Romanza del fantasma y doña Juanita* (1927); *Inquietudes de un provinciano* (1930); *Volaterías* (1932); *La vencedora* (1933); *San Pedro* (1933); *Fierabrás* (1935); *El vuelo inmóvil* (1936); *Atención, atención!* (1937); *Historia de tres días* (1939); *La historia de España contada con sencillez* (1939); *El paraíso y la serpiente* (1942); *Señor de su animo* (1943); *Un laureado civil* (1944) and *Ocho ensayos religiosos* (1948).

Some of his plays are: *El divino impaciente* (1933) (12 editions); *Cuando las Cortes de Cádiz . . .* (1934); *Cisneros* (1935); *Almoneda* (1938); *De ellos es el mundo* (1938); *Metternich* (1942); *Juan sin versos* (1942); *El testamento de la Mariposa* (1942); *Como el primer día* (1943); *Hablar por hablar* (1944); *Si me quieres o me dejas* (1944); *Yo no he venido a traer la paz* (1945); *Diario íntimo de la tía Angélica* (1946); *Antígona* (1946); *La casa* (1946); *En tierra de nadie* (1947); *Vendimia* (1947); *La verdad* (1947); *Lo que debe ser* (1948); *Semana de Pasion* (1948); *Hamlet* (1949); *Electra* (1949); *El viejo y las niñas* (1950); *El gran cardenal* (1950); *Paca Almuzara* (1950); *Por el camino de la vida* (1950); *La muerte de Carmen* (libreto de ópera, para música, de Ernesto Halfter — 1949).

El divino impaciente was translated into English, under the title *Saint in a Hurry*, by Hugh de Blacam. It is a story of Saint Francis Xavier.

Many of his comedies and dramas have been produced hundreds of times all over Spain.

He has given innumerable lectures in Spain and has lectured in Rome, Paris, Lisbon, Argentina, Peru, Chili and Uruguay. His thought is always Christian and he has been acclaimed, "A torrent of inspiration and enthusiasm." He can speak French, Italian and English fluently.

Peru granted him the Grand Cross of the Order of the Sun.

M. A. H.

Francesco Antonio Perri 1885–

Francesco Antonio Perri was born on July 15, 1885, of a modest old family of farmers in Careri, a little village in the southern province of Calabria, Italy.

He completed his first studies at the bishop's seminary in Gerace. Upon his father's death in 1897, Francesco continued his studies but only at the cost of many sacrifices. He was obliged in 1908 to accept a job at the local post office at moderate pay. With the money he earned, he studied law at Turin University, where he obtained the degree of Doctor of Law. Then he went to the University of Pavia to study philology.

In 1916 he volunteered to serve in the army. He participated in the battles of Carso, Bainsizza and Tonale as a lieutenant in the artillery. At the end of the war he became a staunch enemy of fascism. After the liberation he was called upon to edit and direct a newspaper in Genoa and then in Rome.

During the struggle against the monarchy he was the editor of the *Voce Republicana*. He was a candidate for the "Consituente" but did not appear before his electorate because he did not want to be drawn away from his studies and his literary work by any political activities.

In 1925 he published his first novel, *I Conquistatori (The Conquerors)* in which he described the savage occupation of the agricultural Po Valley, the Lomellina region, by the fascist troops. All the copies of the book were instantly seized, and Perri was placed under surveillance by the police. Now he was without a job, and he had four children to feed. Undaunted, he wrote his second novel, *Emigranti*, which in 1927 received the Mondadori Prize for prose at the Academy. It was translated into English and published by Brentano in the United States and by Geoffrey Bles in England. At the same time it was published in Russia and Holland.

Then in 1935 he began a trilogy which he calls "Iromanzi della Fede" ("The Triptych of the Faith.") The first part was published in 1946 under the title *Il Discepolo Ignoto (The Unknown Disciple)* and has been translated into eight languages. The English translation is by H. T. Russell and is published by the Macmillan Company.

The Unknown Disciple "portrays in the dramatic style of a historical novel the birth of Christianity during the time of Tiberius. The Hebraic world, Imperial Roman world, and early days of Christian ethics and faith are the background against which the prominent figures, Emperor Tiberius, Pontius Pilate, Jesus, the Greek Megacles, Mary Magdalene play their influential parts."

The second work of the trilogy at which he is working at present will have the title *Epicari* and will describe the first struggles of Christianity under Nero. The third part will be called *La Morte de Roma* and will give the story of the end of paganism and the final victory of Christ's message over the barbarians.

The author writes: "I hope that God will grant me the time and energy to complete this plan." He adds: "Our society and civilization is saturated with devilish ideals and, for many, Christianity has become external and formal like the religion of the Pharisees. We exalt the authentic spirit of Christ, his divine understanding of human sufferings, his teaching of fraternal charity and love without which all our teaching is null and void. Literature itself is an expression of demoniac forces and teaches only perversity. It is against these forces that I pledge myself to fight as long as I have energy. We are living in a very troubled age and have to cry out to Christ: Domine mane nobiscum, quoniam vesperascit."   M. A. H.

Reverend Henri Perrin, S.J. 1914–

In 1943, when only twenty-nine years of age Father Henri Perrin went to Germany as a volunteer workman. The Nazis would not allow chaplains to accompany the French workers. Consequently, on July 5th of that year, he applied for work at the Erlan factories in Leipzig and entered the National Centre of Apprenticeship in the Rue Dedieu. His purpose was to bring the comforts of religion to the workingmen and to enliven the faith in the fallen-away and negligent Catholics. His experiences there, from late August, 1943, until late April, 1944 are set down in diary form and were published by Sheed and Ward in 1948, under the title *Priest-Workman in Germany*.

Henri Perrin was born in Cornimount (Vosges), France, on April 13, 1914, the son of J. B. Perrin and L. Voinson Perrin. He was ordained a priest in 1938 at Saint Die (Vosges). In 1940 he joined the Society of Jesus. From 1940 to 1943 he continued his studies in the Jesuit Society. Then he undertook his arduous duties among the laborers, working with them, praying with them and saying Mass for them.

In 1945 he became a chaplain in the Repatriation's Mission in Germany (British Zone). Two years of further studies followed.

Upon his return to France, Father Perrin undertook the same work he did in Germany. It was a long time, however, before he was employed in a plastic factory in the district of Paris. Only a few people knew he was a priest. "I decided," he writes, "to try the experience of silence, first of all for myself, to be more definitely one of them, to get in their rhythm, their thought, into their way of seeing things.

"Later on, I believed that the moment had come to reveal that I was a priest; from each side they persuaded me, saying how little we can imagine the distrust and the resentment of the heart of the people against priests and how little they are supposed to believe in our disinterestedness.

"The reaction of my companions was at first some surprise, some curiosity, but there were no lively reactions or problems. Some believed that I must have been defrocked; others thought that I was forced to earn my bread; on the one side there was discreet reserve and distrust, on the other hand sympathy because of the companionship which had sprung up between us. It was only very slowly that my position was understood and confidence was given me, which was normal enough because this presupposes an occasion to explain myself and the occasion doesn't come up every day. Two kinds reacted more clearly on learning of my priesthood. The Christian sort, practicing Christians, the C.F.T.C., have received with joy and treated as a grace the presence of a priest in their midst. On the other, the Communists, except for a few militants among them, who have all of a sudden become very sympathetic, have treated me for a long time with reserve and distrust." (*The Catholic Worker*, May 1949).

Since then he has worked in a sheet iron factory and in an automobile factory. Everywhere he finds the war between capital and labor. He confesses that he still does not have a complete understanding of the problem, *but* he has revolted against "the inhuman attitude of the bosses who inspect the workers as one inspects a room full of machines."

Father Perrin is firmly convinced that "it is normal and necessary for a priest to be in this factory as a simple workingman." Understanding mutual problems, he can instill in both workingman and employer the Christian principle of social justice.

Father Perrin is a member of the "Action Populaire" — Vanves, the Jesuits' Social Institute.   M. A. H.

Reverend Emery E. Petho   1918–

Being the son of an ex-minister and the direct descendant of Hungary's greatest poet, Alexander Petofi, it is natural for Father Petho to turn to things religious and poetic.

Born in old Delray, Detroit, Michigan, on the 21st of November in 1918, Father Petho was the fourth child of six children, born to his parents Peter and Margaret Hornyak Petho. They made their home in the west section of Detroit, then called Delray. Father Petho attended Holy Cross School there which is under the direction of the Viennese Sisters of Charity.

Perhaps nothing encouraged his love for things artistic more than the musical and literary background of both his parents. His father was the director of the Delray Brass Band: and his mother was court-interpreter for the Balkan peoples who lived within the densely populated section of the auto metropolis.

From Holy Cross, he entered the Sacred Heart Seminary. After he had received his bachelor of arts degree from there he continued his studies at Mt. St. Mary's Seminary in Norwood, Ohio. He was ordained at Blessed Sacrament Cathedral in Detroit, December 19, 1943.

He was first stationed as assistant at Wyandotte; but since September 1949 he is living in the beautiful Irish Hills where the Shrine of St. Joseph on Highway 112 is a great inspiration to all passers-by.

While at Sacred Heart Seminary he was encouraged to write by his English teachers, Monsignor Donnelly and Father Leo Ward. After a few attempts of submission to the quarterly school magazine, the constant rejections of the editorial staff made him try an outside market.

His first try was very successful. He sent two of his efforts to the *Catholic Extension* and both were accepted for publication. Bolstered by this triumph he sent poems to the magazine *Meanjin* in New Zealand and *Poetry* in Australia. Both "Surf Song" and "The Word" were accepted. These were submitted under the pen-names of "Amerigo" and "Emmerich."

While yet a seminarian he wrote to Sister Edwardine for literary advice. She encouraged him to collect his verses for publication; and suggested that he try Bruce Humphries of Boston as publisher. Not being proficient with the typewriter, his classmates undertook to prepare the manuscript. After the collection of the forty-one lyrics was finished, Ben Musser wrote an introduction. The publication of the first volume, *Of Bitter Grapes* (1942) was followed by *As the Swift Seasons Roll* (1947) and *Alien in the Land* (1950).

The reviewer of *Of Bitter Grapes* in *Spirit* says, "His work is distinctly original and worth watching."

He turns to nature and the praise of creation. He concentrates on the unpretentious charm and beauty about him. He is conscious of the seasons, the landscapes and elements. He is a sound theologian, sharp imagist and a deft craftsman.   SR. M. P.

Henry J. Petiot. See *Henry Daniel-Rops*

Reverend Henri Petitot, O.P.
1880–1934

As a young professor of philosophy and later of theology at the Biblical Institute of Jerusalem (1906–1914), Father Henri Petitot published there two major books, now out of print: *Introduction á la philosophie traditionnelle ou classique* (1914), an original treatment of the nature, method, and aim of the traditional Catholic philosophy, and *Pascal, sa vie religieuse et son apologie du christianisme*, "a discussion as to the orthodoxy or heresy of the Pensées. Although

Pascal received absolution on his deathbed, Father Petitot believes he was a Jansenist to the end." (*Catholic World*, Vol. 93, p. 833, Sept. 1911.)

Henri Petitot was born in Armentières, France, on August 2, 1880 and was educated at the Institution Saint-Jude in his native city. He was ordained to the priesthood in July 1903.

When the First World War broke out in 1914, Father Petitot returned to France and was mustered into the army. He was seriously wounded at Verdun in 1916. After his recovery he was sent to Amiens. For his service he received the médaille militaire, with a magnificent citation. After he was honorably discharged he lived first at the convent at Amiens, then at Nancy and in 1924 returned to Amiens to assume the duties of prior. In 1927 he was assigned to the monastery of Saint-Honoré, in the center of Paris.

His postwar years were replete with a variety of activities such as writer, speaker, and spiritual director. People still remember the talk he gave in the monastery chapel at Amiens on the occasion of the condemnation of the *Action Française* by the Holy See and on the philosophy of Charles Maurras. He enlarged this material on that subject, and almost finished a book, which unfortunately remains unpublished. In Paris, for three consecutive Lents, he preached sermons on the spiritual, ascetical, and mystical life, and drew considerable crowds to hear him.

At the same time he served as a confessor and spiritual director. His confessional always drew big crowds.

Notwithstanding these activities he did not neglect his literary work. During these years he wrote *Mlle. de la Rochetiere en religion Mère Marie de Jésus, fondatrice de l'Institut de Marie Thérèse: sa vie et son oeuvre* (1928); *Ste. Jeanne d'Arc* (1921); *Vie de Saint Thomas Aquin; Vie de Saint Dominique* (1925) and the one which made him famous, *Vie de Sainte Thérèse de Lisieux*. An abbreviated edition of this latter work was published by Burns, Oates & Washbourne, Ltd. in English under the title *St. Thérèse, the New Omen* (1933).

In all his works he proved himself a most accurate historian and critic and had the spiritual experience to penetrate into the personal sanctity of his characters. But above all he was a spiritual writer. The study of the mystical theology of St. Theresa and of St. John of the Cross, his spiritual contacts with souls, all contributed to the development of his spiritual doctrines and teachings, which he published in numerous articles but especially in his two books: *La Doctrine Ascétique et Mystique Intégrale* (Labergerie, 1930), and *L'Introduction à la Sainteté* (Cerf. 1934). In these works he shows the way to sanctity, which he wanted to follow and on which he wanted to lead souls to salvation. His doctrine is to unite in a vital and harmonious synthesis all the riches of nature and grace. He balances reason and intuition, human activity and grace, body and soul. Those who knew him testify that this doctrine — traditional and at the same time original — is the perfect expression of his personality. Petitot had a strong and burning temperament. While he was a religious of faultless regularity, he practices his strict austerity without ostentation.

A sudden stroke suffered during the summer of 1931 crippled him for life. Handicapped in many ways, he still continued to dictate his books. As he was expiring on October 4, 1934, he struggled for breath and then uttered his last words: "Lord Jesus, I put all my confidence in Thee." J. V. D. and E. O.

Josef Pieper 1904–

In the very small Westphalian village of Elte, Germany, Josef Pieper was born on May 4th, 1904. Not even a local train connects this lonely spot in the middle of the heath with other towns of Westphalia; at that time whoever wanted to reach the next station had to cross a river in a small ferry-boat. Josef Pieper's father was the only teacher at the only school of this village.

Josef Pieper went to the Gymnasium Paulinum in Münster, one of the oldest German schools, which has existed for more than eleven hundred years. Now his son is taking up that tradition as a pupil of this old institution, the buildings of which, however, were completely destroyed during World War II.

A teacher of this school, a priest, induced Josef Pieper to read the works of Thomas Aquinas. "At that time," Josef Pieper writes, "I was foolishly fond of Kierkegaard, whom we used to devour, my friends and I, naturally without quite understanding him; and it was this paternal friend and teacher, who directed me — with a sort of violent, ironical, and humorous intensity — to St. Thomas' *Commentary to the Prologue of St. John's Gospel*. Being a youngster of eighteen, I set about reading this work and, in fact, finished it, of course, again without understanding it perfectly. But from that moment the work of St. Thomas has accompanied me through life." Years later he translated this *Commentary to the Prologue of St. John's Gospel*, into German (*Das Wort*).

In 1923 Josef Pieper went to the University of Münster and later on to Berlin. The plan of his first book — which he ultimately submitted to the university in order to obtain his doctorate in philosophy — was born during a lecture on Goethe and Thomas Aquinas, given by Romano Guardini at the Jugendburg Rothenfels on the Main in 1924; the lecture was entitled "About Classical Spirit." Dr. Pieper's first book, *Die Wirklichkeit und das Gute*, based on St. Thomas' works, tries to show that the good is nothing else but what is in accordance with the reality of things.

From this path of "pure philosophy," Dr. Pieper deviated for some time; the social problems fascinated him so much that he applied himself to the study of law and sociology. He became an assistant at the Institute of Social Research at the University of Münster. When, in 1931 the papal encyclical Quadragesimo Anno was published, Dr. Pieper wrote a few booklets explaining the fundamental idea of the

"Entproletarisierung." Dr. Pieper says he would have devoted himself entirely to the social sciences if National Socialism had not come into power. From 1934 on, it became impossible for a Christian author to speak in public about the problems of social life. Fortunately, he was forced to take up his former theme: the attempt to build up from the elements of Western tradition, as it has been formed especially by St. Thomas Aquinas, a philosophical and ethical doctrine of man, which might be comprehensible to modern people. Therefore, he wrote, in 1934, a small book about the virtue of fortitude, *Vom Sinn der Tapferkeit*. "At first," writes Dr. Pieper, "the manuscript was refused by all editors (later on, this fact proved to be a good example for explaining to my children, what a boomerang is) till at last one editor, Jacob Hegner (Leipzig), who made known in Germany the works of Claudel, Yeats, and Bernanos, accepted the book and at the same time asked me to treat in the same way all seven virtues."

Pieper next wrote about hope. The small book was published in 1935, being just in time for the day of his wedding. During the years preceding World War II, two other works were published: one about the first cardinal virtue, prudence (*Traktatrüber die Klugheit*) and the other about the fourth cardinal virtue, temperance (*Zucht und Mass*). "To write about justice was quite impossible then in Germany," writes Pieper, "yet, in any case, I had put aside this treatise until later, for it seems to me just as difficult as that about love and up to now I have not yet written it."

During the first year of World War II, he brought out only a little biography of his hero, St. Thomas Aquinas.

Then he joined the army and during the time he was in service, a volume of the *Summa Theologica* or the *Quaestiones Disputatae* always accompanied him, and in the course of these years he succeeded in putting together two breviary-like collections of short sentences, chosen from the whole work of the Angelic Doctor, but they were not published until the end of World War II. One of these "breviaries," the more philosophical one, was published both in England and the United States under the title, *The Human Wisdom of St. Thomas*.

His other scientific work, which he also finished during World War II, is rather extensive. It deals with the idea of "veritas rerum" and its history. This work was of special use to Pieper after the war in procuring a professorship at the university which, under the Nazi régime, had been impossible for him. In 1946, Dr. Pieper became lecturer of philosophy at the Pedagogical Institute of Essen (Ruhr), at the University of Münster, and later on professor. The result of the experiences with afterwar university-life and of those first years of instruction finds expression in two small books. The first one, *Musse und Kult*, develops two theses: first, that culture is founded on leisure, secondly, that leisure has its roots within the region of cult. The second book, *Was heist philosophieren?* draws the consequences of these theses for the study of philosophy. These two books were published in English by Pantheon Books, Inc., New York City. The primer for Christians, containing short essays on Catholic dogma and ethics as well as on the history of the Church, written in collaboration with Heinz G.

Raskop, appeared in August 1951 under the title *What Catholics Believe*, with an introduction by Reverend Gerald B. Phelan, and in November of the same year, *Leisure the Basis of Culture*, with a preface by T. S. Eliot.

"St. Thomas is still my hero," writes Dr. Pieper. "I think his work is inexhaustible and his affirmative way of looking at the reality of the whole creation seems to me a necessary correction modern Christianity cannot do without. Yet my admiration of Plato is likewise growing continually. And one theme not expressly treated by St. Thomas and the whole scholastic school is becoming more important to me than ever: the philosophy of history."

A recent book by Dr. Pieper deals with the idea of antichrist and Christian hope (*Über das Ende der Zeit*).

In 1950 Dr. Pieper was invited to teach one semester at the University of Notre Dame, Indiana. And at the 24th annual meeting of the American Catholic Philosophical Association at St. Paul, Minnesota, he read the Annual Association Address on "The Condition of Philosophy in the Modern World." Dr. Pieper is one of the regular contributors to the *Review of Politics* and of *Orate Fratres* (now *Worship*).

M. A. H.

Armand Pierhal   1897–

Armand Pierhal was born in Salonica, Greece, in 1897. He spent his early life in Switzerland where he studied engineering at the University of Lausanne. Abandoning engineering for music, he went to Geneva, where he studied under Émile Jaques-Dalcroze. From Geneva he went to Paris to continue his music studies under Blanche Selva and Nadia Boulanger. In Paris, at the age of 27, he became private secretary to Jacques Rivière, director of the Nouvelle Revue Française, and began his career in literature. On the death of Jacques Rivière, in 1925, he became literary secretary to the painter and writer, Jacques-Emile Blanche.

At this time he began to write for many French periodicals; the *Nouvelles Littéraires*, the *Annales*, *L'Aube*, *L'Art Vivant*, *La Nef* and *Le Figaro*. In 1935 he went to the congress of the Nazi Party at Nuremberg as a representative of *Le Figaro*. Being a gifted linguist, Armand Pierhal became foreign language editor for several publishing firms that covered English, German, Italian and Spanish literature. He himself translated more than twenty volumes from German, English and Italian into French. After the liberation of France, he became literary critic for the Catholic weekly, *Temps Présent*. As director of the *Pavillons* collection, he published in France all the great novels of Graham Greene, and others by Henry James, Evelyn Waugh, Ellen Glasgow, Hersey, Marquand, Schulberg, etc. In addition he writes critiques of art and is the musical critic for the Catholic daily *La Croix*.

In 1938, Armand Pierhal published his first novel, *Jeunes Morts chéris des Dieux*. Meanwhile, in preparation for his projected great work, in twelve volumes, *Science without Conscience* he collected a vast store of material. For twenty years he continued to collect figures, facts and ideas. Then, in 1947, the first volume, *De Dieu Vivant* appeared. It is the story of a return to the faith, a conversion to God, of a mind which, because of its scientific training, was enabled to see and recognize the limitations of science. Published in New York, 1950, by Harper & Brothers, as *The Living God*, it is described as "a dialogue between two protagonists, the educated unbeliever and the author who speaks as a member of the Christian Church — a discussion of the manifestations of God's existence and immortality." The second volume of *Science without Conscience*, called *Le Combat de Poitiers* (1949), is in praise of democracy, and a refutation of rightist and leftist totalitarianism. The third volume, called *L'Antimachiavel*, appeared in 1951. He comments on the words of John Locke: "Honesty is the best policy" and includes a discussion of Machiavelli's *Il Principe*, Hitler's *Mein Kampf* and James Burnham's *The Machiavellians*.

To date, Armand Pierhal's strongest claim to recognition as a writer of consequence rests on his book, *The Living God*. In France it was widely read and discussed and warmly welcomed by the Catholic literary world. In it, Mr. Pierhal, who describes himself as "a Catholic who writes" rather than a Catholic writer, gives an extraordinary account of faith in operation. Much impressed by the book, François Mauriac wrote the author: "You do much good with this book. One cannot 'prove' God's existence, but this book proves that God has touched you."   E. B. B.

Catharine Plummer 1919–

Catharine Plummer was born in New York City, September 6, 1919, the oldest of five children. While she was still an infant, her parents moved to Long Island. There she started school with the Dominican nuns. When she was eight, the family moved to Boston where they lived first in Jamaica Plain, then in Roslindale, and later in Waltham. Here she was graduated from St. Mary's where the Sisters of Notre Dame de Namur taught. While she was still a student at Simmons College in Boston, her family moved again, this time to western Massachusetts, living first in Pittsfield, and then in Dalton.

She can not recall when she did not want to write, but she does remember the struggle she had in high school wondering whether she could be both an artist and a writer. She began painting under the Sisters while still in grade school, and later, when in high school, went into classes at the Boston Museum of Fine Arts. But in the end, she decided that if she were going to be a good writer she could not be a good artist, too, and so she went to college instead of art school.

Two years later, when her family moved to Pittsfield, finances took such an alarmingly downward plunge that instead of going back to school she went to work. After a succession of short-lived jobs, she was hired at General Electric Company as an inspector in the factory. She held the job a half day and then became a clerk and later a secretary. During this period she wrote a number of short stories. They were of such an experimental nature that she sent very few of them out, and these inevitably came back with the usual form rejection slip.

In September, 1943, the General Electric plant where she was working and which was also headquarters for a number of other plants, decided to start a weekly newspaper to cover the whole division, and she was selected to help with it. Two weeks later, the man who was named editor left for another job, and she became the first woman in General Electric to edit such a paper.

Though she did no writing of her own for the next two years that followed, the job was exactly what she needed. It gave her the discipline of meeting a deadline, of writing whether she wanted to or not, and in learning to express other people's ideas, she learned to express some of her own. In addition, it gave her an opportunity to do a certain amount of traveling and to meet and talk with all kinds of people.

When she began in December of 1945 to spend her nights writing from her own material, she found that a big change had taken place, and that she was able to let go and express some of the things she wanted to say. She made slow headway on a novel, because in a way, it was a complete voyage of discovery, and she was finding out the answers to many things that had been puzzling her for a long time. The result was that in August of 1948 she had finished the first draft of an enormous manuscript which, "now that I view it," she says, "was a hodge-podge of everything. But at least I had finished it. I made some minor revisions on it, and began sending it around to publishers in March of 1949."

In the meanwhile she began the manuscript entitled *The Rose on the Summit* which she intended to be a simple thing, a long short story which she expected to finish within a few months. Once started, it began to grow, and nine months later it was completed. She then decided to send it to Scribner's where the first manuscript, though it had been rejected, had been kindly received. *The Rose on the Summit* had hardly gone out when she received her eighth rejection slip on the first manuscript. Accompanying the manuscript, however, was a most kind and encouraging letter from Theodore M. Purdy who was then editor at Appleton-Century-Crofts.

She put the first manuscript away, resolving "to send *The Rose on the Summit* to Mr. Purdy, if Scribner's should reject it. Unfortunately, it took six months to be rejected, and by the time it was on its way to Appleton-Century-Crofts, Mr. Purdy had already become editor-in-chief at another publishing house. The manuscript came back in five weeks, and I decided to try just once more before putting it away with the first manuscript.

"*The Rose on the Summit* went out again in July 1950, and I forgot all about it as I immersed myself in the new work which I had already begun. In September, I had a letter asking me if I would be willing to come to New York to talk about some revisions with the editor and the editor-in-chief. By some inexplicable stroke of luck, the manuscript had gone to Putnam's where Mr. Purdy had been named editor-in-chief. The memorable meeting took place on the 29th of September and I was in a complete daze when I left."

By November the revised manuscript which she had completed with the help of encouraging letters from Mrs. Marjorie M. Mayer who turned out to be the kind of editor she had always dreamed about having, was back at Putnam's. She waited impatiently to hear the results.

She could not have been more surprised, when shortly after, she had a letter telling her that they had decided to take the book and that a contract was being forwarded. The contract was signed on January 10, 1951. Then began a process of minor revisions and last-minute changes and finally the galley proofs.

When asked how she came to write *The Rose on the Summit* she replied: "I hardly know what to reply in answer to why I wrote *The Rose on the Summit* except at that particular time I became fascinated by the universality of the passion of Christ, and how the resurrection was truly a symbol of a new life. It seemed to me that the more I looked around the more it was being re-enacted and in all states of life — that a suffering and a death to the old life was inevitable whenever a change took place. I thought perhaps I could put this idea into very simple words and ordinary events so that everybody would understand it, and after I had been writing a while, it seemed to me that I really had nothing to do with it, except to sit and listen and write down what I heard."

Miss Plummer lives at home in Dalton with her family (or rather what is left of it, since everybody is married, except her brother who is a student at Holy Cross), and she still works on the paper for General Electric. Her youngest sister, Rose, is her severest critic, and although she has a big room, she prefers to write in the pantry which is cozy and right in the middle of the house where she cannot miss any of the excitement. "I should also like to say that I am most grateful to an uncle, Francis Plummer, who is himself author of a novel, a science book, and a number of detective stories, for the encouragement he gave me from the very beginning. He was for a long time my only audience, starting way back in my teens when I used to bring him an occasional story which I thought was not too bad. I think the biggest thrill in my life was when my mother (who was always a staunch and loyal admirer of my writings without ever having read any of them — as mothers often are, no matter what their children do) stayed up until two o'clock in the morning reading an advance copy of *The Rose on the Summit*."

Count George Noble Plunkett
1851–1948

George Noble Plunkett was born on December 3, 1851, a collateral descendant of the martyr Blessed Oliver Plunkett, at whose beatification he represented the family. He went to school at the Petit Séminaire at Nice, then lately ceded to Italy by France, at Clongowes, and at Trinity College, Dublin, taking the degree of B.L. He soon became eminent as a scholar with a profound knowledge of the Christian art and culture which he so zealously promoted. An ardent patriot, he fought for the cause of Gaelic and of Ireland's freedom. A devout Catholic, he strove for the beauty of God's house and the replacement of shoddy commercialism by true sacred art. His logical mind, French-like in precision, could not endure compromise, which for him spelt betrayal, and so he felt bound to maintain the continued existence of the First Dail Government of Ireland long after it had ceased to function, on the ground that the nation had never deposed it, although the Holy See had recognized its successor. Statesmanship, into which the troubled years, 1914–31, had drawn him, was not his calling, but he was greatest as a patriot, scholar and artist; yet all must admire his heroic courage in danger and his Christian resignation in heart-rending sorrow, when his son Joseph, also a poet and scholar, gave his life for Ireland's freedom, being executed for his part in the Easter Rising of 1916. His later years were largely given to the Academy of Christian Art in Dublin, of which he was founder and president.

Made member of many learned societies, such as the Belle Arti of Florence, the Virtuosi al Panteon and the San Luca of Rome, he became President of the Society of Antiquaries in Ireland and the Society for the Preservation of the Irish Language and the Director of the Science and Art Museum, Dublin (1907–16), Vice-President of the Irish Academy (1907–14); besides other cultural honors, Leo XIII made him a Papal Count. In 1884 he married Josephine Cranny, a highly-cultivated lady whose outlook was in fullest accord with his, and a charming hostess. It was an ideally happy marriage. In 1916 he was banished for some time to Oxford by the British authorities. From 1917–27, he was Member for North Roscommon; under the Dail he was Minister for Foreign Affairs and for the Fine Arts. In his advanced old age he lost in quick succession his devoted wife and his son George, a man of exceptional courtesy and charm, thrown from his trap in an accident. Count Plunkett himself died in his home at 42 Upper Mount Street, Dublin, on March 12th, 1948, in his ninety-seventh year.

In 1894, together with the late Father E. J. Hogan, S.J., he edited *The Jacobite War in Ireland* and in 1911–15, Margaret Stokes's *Early Christian Art in Ireland*. In 1900 he published a monograph on *Sandro*

Botticelli, in 1903 *Pinelli,* in 1908 *Architecture of Dublin* and in 1921 *Arrows* (Poems).

Since his books are not easily accessible, two passages from his letters sent to the writer of this sketch, are here quoted. On July 24, 1935, he wrote: "Your praises of Oxford, in verse and prose, interested me oddly, for I spent most of a year in exile there (when we were deported). The Bodleian gave me a genial forgetfulness, at times, when I got lost in the Middle Ages. What an escape one makes, on opening an ancient book, like a door — into the Infinite! or a glimpse of it: as someone has spoken of the stars 'piercing the veil.' Mrs. Concannon has just issued a new life of the Blessed Oliver Plunkett. It gives the living human spirit, his thoughts and feelings and desires, his misery, borne with humor, his self-denial and stringent endurance, and a tenderness of heart that made his passion a cry of sympathy for the dear fold. He was indeed a patient toiler for God."

On December 15, 1938, he wrote: "It is like your usual kindness to send me that lovely book on Chinese Art, that expresses in design what you have in mind. When will the Western world recover the sense of beauty and the consciousness of exquisite skill, with the fresh delight in both, which the East has never lost? Yet Europe had that receptivity and gift of expression, that sensitive understanding, when generations of a family or of a group wrought some church interior or exterior to completion. And now, thank God, Chinese Christians are devoting that gentle power to religion." Happily he did not live to see China the dupe or slave of Red Moscow. But the end is not yet.

Truly a great and what is more, an eminently good man, Count Plunkett, a ripe scholar, true patriot, and dedicated servant of sacred art, has left us work whose influence will bear increasing fruit in the days to come.   H. E. G. R.

Leo Politi 1908–

Leo Politi, the author-artist, was born in Fresno, California on November 21, 1908, of Italian parents. At the age of seven, he went to Italy with his family and lived near Milan. There he went to school. The Indian costume Leo had brought with him from America caused so much interest and excitement that the teacher had to ask his mother not to let him wear it to school.

At the age of fifteen, Leo, who made a practice of drawing everything he saw, was given a scholarship for the Institute of Monza (near Milan). "This art school," he says, "had at our disposal the gardens, the zoo, everything beautiful and convenient for outdoor sketching.

"I remember our good teacher, Ugo Zovetti, and how he took pride in showing us the great wealth of nature. He would take a small flower and gently open it to show us its beautiful lines, shapes and colors. When we were drawing birds and animals he taught us not to see them as static objects but to seek the inner life, which projected movement and rhythm."

Here he studied for six years. At the age of twenty-three he returned to the United States and settled down on Olvera Street, in Los Angeles. The little street and its Mexican people fascinated him and later he used this material in his books. In 1938, he married Helen Fontes. They have two children, Paul and Susanne.

"More than anything else," he says, "I love drawing children. In all my books I try to embody certain universal things — the warmth and happiness of family life; my love for people, animals, birds and flowers, and for the simple warm and earthy things."

His first picture book was *Little Pancho* published by Viking Press. Then followed the illustration of several books about the Latin-American countries, which he undertook "because of my love for the people of Latin America and my admiration for their arts and their great civilizations of the past."

One Christmas he sent a card with a small Mexican angel to Alice Dalgliesh, the children's book editor, at Scribner's. She wrote back to him to ask: "Why don't you make a book about that charming little angel?" A few months later to her surprise, a complete dummy for *Pedro, the Angel of Olvera Street* came to her. This was followed by other books. "These I was able to do," he says, "because of my love for California, its rich folklore and traditions."

The American Library Association awarded him the 1949 Caldecott Medal for his book *Song of the Swallows*. "This is a picture story book about the swallows of the San Juan Capistrano mission, and of the little boy and the old gardener who loved the swallows and waited for their return on Saint Joseph's Day."

Other books by the same author are *Juanita*, a story of Juanita's birthday party, and especially of the old Spanish custom of blessing all the animals on Easter Sunday; *A Boat for Peppe* (1950) tells how Peppe longed for a boat, of the storm in which his father's boat was almost lost, and of the festival of the Blessing of the Boats; *Little Leo* (1951) narrates how Leo, who first lived on a ranch in California, went back to Italy with his family on a visit. While attending school Leo wore his Indian suit to school and told the little Italians about the West. Then they all made themselves suits and played Indian.

M. A. H.

Dame Una Pope-Hennessy
1876–1949

The British author Una Pope-Hennessy is distinguished for her literary biographies of Dickens, Poe, and Kingsley.

Born in 1876, the only daughter of the late Sir Arthur Birch, K.C.M.G. (Knight Commander of St. Michael and St. George), she is a convert to the Catholic Faith. In 1910, she married Major-General Ladislaus H. R. Pope-Hennessy, C.B., D.S.O. (Companion of the Bath and Companion of the Distinguished Service Order).

During the First World War, Una Pope-Hennessy worked continuously in London and, for her services, received in 1920 a D.B.E. (Dame Commander of the British Empire). She was also made a Lady of Grace of St. John of Jerusalem.

When her husband returned from Mesopotamia, she accompanied him to Ireland where he was sent to command a battalion of his regiment during the Sinn Fein activities. She then went with him to Berlin where he held an appointment under the Allied Commission of Control. There she had first-hand experience of fuelless homes, half-starved children, and the generally hopeless demeanor of a conquered people.

Later she accompanied her husband to Washington, D. C., when he was sent there as military attaché. She loved America and her recollection of the kindness and appreciation she received there was always vivid. While at Washington, she wrote *Three English Women in America* and on her return to Europe edited the amusingly frank letters of Mrs. Basil Hall written from the United States in 1927–28.

Her last trip abroad was made in the summer of 1937 when she and her husband visited Russia. In 1938 she published *The Closed City*, a record of sightseeing in Leningrad.

During the so-called "phoney" period of World War II she completed two books mainly written before the outbreak of hostilities — *Agnes Strickland: Biographer of the Queens of England* and *Durham Company* both published by Chatto and Windus.

From the summer of 1939 to the spring of 1942, Mrs. Una Pope-Hennessy lived with her husband at a District Warden's Post, and shared in the experiences of a much-bombed area. These experiences included the blasting of her own home on a Christmas Eve of which she wrote an account for the New York *Herald-Tribune* (Feb. 9, 1941).

In the spring of 1942 Major-General Pope-Hennessy died suddenly of heart failure brought on by his devoted service in raids and out of raids to the A.R.P. (Air Raid Precautions). He was military expert on the *Evening News* and author of *Can Britain Attack?*

The two sons of Mr. and Mrs. Ladislaus Herbert Richard Pope-Hennessy are well-known writers. The elder son, John, was a Flight-

Lieutenant in World War II and is the author of monographs on *Giovanni di Paolo* and *Sasseta*. He is the editor of a *Sienese Codex of the Divine Comedy* (1949); author of *The Drawings of Domenichino in the Collection of His Majesty the King at Windsor Castle* (1949); the author of *A Lecture on Nicholas Hilliard* (1949); and editor of *The Complete Work of Paolo Uccello* (1950). The younger son, James, was a Captain in the Second World War and was the winner, with *London Fabric*, of the Hawthornden Prize.

Dame Una Pope-Hennessy's works are: *Madame Roland: A Study in Revolution* (1918); *Three English Women in America* (dealing with the visits here of Frances Trollope, Fanny Kemble and Harriet Martineau) (1929); *The Aristocratic Journey* (1931); *The Laird of Abbotsford* (an informal biography of Sir Walter Scott) (1932); *The Closed City* (Leningrad and vicinity) (1938); *Agnes Strickland: Biographer of the Queens of England* (1940); *Durham Company* (1941); *Charles Dickens* (1946); *A Czarina's Story* (1948), and *Canon Charles Kingsley* (1948).

Perhaps her most important work is *Charles Dickens* (1946). In her *Acknowledgments* she says: "I owe a deep debt of gratitude to the late Mr. Walter Dexter, editor of *The Dickensian* and prime authority on every aspect and detail of the life of Charles Dickens. He lent me books, he showed me unpublished letters, and, more valuable than any other form of help, discussed with me the problems that inevitably arose in dealing with the novelist's relations with his family and his contemporaries."

Charles Dickens was the April 1946 selection of the Catholic Book Club.

Mrs. Una Pope-Hennessy died on August 16, 1949.

Crawford Power   1909–

Born in 1909 in Baltimore, Maryland, Crawford Power was privately educated in the Gilman Country School. He spent his freshman year of college at Georgetown University, and the other three years at Yale. After receiving his A.B. degree he attended the Yale Architectural School for three years, and was awarded a B.F.A. degree.

For a number of years, Crawford Power was employed as an architect in various subdivisions of the Department of the Interior and later he worked in the Municipal Architect's Office in Washington, D. C. For a year or two, Mr. Power was a "builder," after which he practiced general farming on Goose Creek, Loudoun County, Virginia, where he now lives.

After the attack on Pearl Harbor, Mr. Power worked for Civilian Defense on Bomb-Shelters in Washington. For the last eighteen months of the war he was in the United States Navy, in the Department of

Ordnance, with the rank of Specialist X, First Class. Since the close of
World War II, Mr. Power devotes his time to writing and spends most
of the year on his farm.

In 1935 he was married to Mary Cornelia Hunt of Washington,
D. C. They have four children.

His first book, *The Encounter*, is a "novel describing how a priest
discovers his inhumanity to man in an encounter with a carnival diver
and his girl." Reviewing the book for the New York *Herald Tribune*
(*Book Review*, June 4, 1950, p. 5), Gouverneur Paulding writes: "Because Crawford Power writes well and because he is accurate and hard-
headed all the time, *The Encounter* is a fine achievement." The *New
Yorker* (June 17, 1950) remarks: "Mr. Power is a thoughtful and sometimes striking writer who presents his characters with such respect and
understanding that it is impossible to lay his book down until one discovers what the end is going to be."   M. A. H.

James Farl Powers   1917–

"As a boy, my favorite authors were James
Willard Schultz, Ralph Henry Barbour, and
Howard Pyle," Mr. Powers writes. "By the
time I reached high school, my interest in books
had fallen off; the one legitimate writer I cared
for was Washington Irving at Christmastime.
I was the real American boy, playing baseball,
basketball, football. I graduated from Quincy
College Academy in 1935 and went to Chicago,
where my family was living, and began to seek my fortune. It was a
bad time for it. I worked in Marshall Field's department store, selling
books, shirts, and even linoleum for a day. By 1936 there was not so
much of the American boy in me, I think. In fact, I had become a
writer in my own mind — which is the only place to become one.
For a month, I remember, I tried to sell insurance door to door. From
my profits, very nearly all of them, I bought a typewriter and a copy
of James Joyce's *Ulysses*. I traveled through the South and Southwest,
working as a chauffeur, and I took the typewriter with me. I had
some kind of idea that I needed it in my business — the only catch
being: what was my business? I know now that I was a writer then,
for better or worse. It was the only thing I cared about being."

J. F. Powers was born in Jacksonville, Illinois, in 1917, the first
child of James Ansberry and Zella (Routzong) Powers. He attended
public and parochial schools through the grades in Jacksonville, Rockford, and Quincy, all in Illinois, and Quincy College Academy, under
the Franciscan Fathers. He took courses in English at Northwestern
University while working as an editor on the Historical Records Survey
in Chicago. In 1946, he married Betty Wahl, another writer whose work
appears in *The New Yorker*. They have two daughters, Katherine Anne
and Mary Farl. For several years they lived in Minnesota near Avon

and in St. Paul. Mr. Powers taught creative writing for a brief period at St. John's University, Collegeville, Minnesota. For two years (1949–51), he taught courses in writing at Marquette University, Milwaukee, Wisconsin. He is presently (1952) on the staff of Doubleday.

Mr. Powers' first published story appeared in *Accent*, a quarterly. Other stories, articles, and reviews have since appeared in *The Commonweal, The Catholic Worker, Collier's, The Sign, Tomorrow, Renascence, The New Yorker, Partisan Review, The Month, Horizon, New Writing*. Of Mr. Powers' story, "Lions, Harts, Leaping Does," Dorothy Canfield Fisher, judging the O. Henry Prize Stories of 1944, said: "The characters are portrayed with air all round them. There is the added quality of unhurried, rounded spaciousness which gives the story depth and charm, noteworthy in these days of slightly breathless writing." In 1947, a collection of Mr. Powers' stories appeared under the title, *Prince of Darkness*, which was later issued in England, Italy, and France. *The New Yorker* described it as "written in delightfully firm and straightforward prose, in which Mr. Powers proves that he has few rivals at creating characters with more than superficial reality." Of the title story, Katherine Anne Porter said, "The story shows the after-thought of an extremely conscious mind with a real sense of form." Frank O'Connor, reviewing the book in England, said: "You don't often find me recommending collections of short stories (being in that line myself I have more sense), but *Prince of Darkness and Other Stories*, by J. F. Powers, is a book I shall keep." V. S. Pritchett said: "Mr. Powers is above all an intelligent writer, with a gift for recording natural speech: he is poetic without being poeticising, and he has a notably wide range of characters and a fine sensibility to atmosphere. He is sometimes obscure and over-allusive and he is hard-reading in stories where the scene cannot be filled in by the English reader; but he has, as a general rule, the indispensable gift of being unexpected in every line, without straining after literary effects." In *Books Abounding*, Abigail Quigley McCarthy wrote: "He knows his characters as an artist must know them, more thoroughly and more understandingly than they could know themselves. . . . He has said that he writes of priests because they are engaged in the only race worth running and that their failures and successes are, therefore, more truly stories."

Mr. Powers acknowledges his indebtedness to Charles Shattuck, an editor of *Accent*, who provided "invaluable criticism when it was hard to get anyone to look at my work. It is my humble opinion that neglect and hard times are more often an accident than a condition of the artist's achieving."

In 1948, Mr. Powers received a Fellowship in Creative Writing from the Guggenheim Foundation and a Grant from the National Institute–American Academy of Arts and Letters. His work has been reprinted in *The Best American Short Stories; O. Henry Memorial Prize Stories; Our Father's House; American Writing; Primer for White Folks; Accent Anthology; Cross Section; Short Stories: Tradition and Direction; Modern Short Stories; The Commonweal Reader; Stories of Our Century; The House of Fiction; The Story: A Critical Anthology; The Best of the Best American Short Stories 1915–1950.*

Mrs. Littleton C. Powys. See *Elizabeth Myers*

Reverend Ferdinand Prat, S.J.
1857–1938

From the time of Saint Bonaventure to the present day, there have been many literary presentations of the life on earth of the Saviour of the world. In 1950 there appeared in English a translation of Father Prat's monumental work *Jésus-Christ, sa vie, sa doctrine, son oeuvre.* Rendered by Father John J. Heenan, S.J., of Georgetown University, the translator, into *Jesus Christ, His Life, His Doctrine and His Work*, the work has been proclaimed by Biblical experts the best life of Christ in existence. The author, Father Prat, S.J., succeeded in combining Biblical exegesis with an interesting style to produce a book which awakens many to the setting and drama of the greatest story ever told.

Father Heenan devoted two years to the task of translating into English Father Prat's great work. Phillips Temple, in his review of the book in the *Georgetown Journal* states: "As a matter of fact he (Father Heenan) did more than translate it: anyone who takes the trouble to compare these volumes with the French original will discover that numerous Scripture references have been corrected; citations are given to English translations of books mentioned in Father Prat's footnotes; and a few are added that do not appear in the original, e.g. E. Allison Peers' translation of *The Complete Works of St. Therese of Jesus* (Vol. II, p. 28, note 5)."

In the village of de Lafretarie, in the south of France, on February 10, 1857, there was born to Ferdinand Prat and his wife, Anne Dujols, the fifth of 12 children, a son baptized Antoine Ferdinand. The Prat family was an old and respected one in the vicinity and among its members there were many who served in notable positions both in Church and state. The young Ferdinand was a precocious boy, who received his first Holy Communion at 9 years of age, much ahead of the age customary in those times. When surprise was expressed by an elder acquaintance that this should be so, the young Ferdinand answered, "But I know everything." At an early age he was placed in care of a paternal aunt, Marie Jeanne Prat, who inspired him with both devotion and a desire for learning. His early education was obtained at the Petit Seminaire Rodez, a few miles from his birthplace. While he was at this school the Franco-Prussian War broke out and every French boy shared the concern of the nation for the integrity of France. The boys of the seminary were no exception and were organized into two cadet corps, of one of which young Prat, then thirteen, was the captain. He formed a liking for the military life and after the end of the war, and after he had finished his studies at Rodez, he was called upon to choose a career. He said, "It will be either St. Cyr or the novitiate." St. Cyr is the French West Point and by the novitiate he meant the spiritual militia of the Society of Jesus.

In 1873 he entered the Society of Jesus in the novitiate at Pau and pronounced his first vows, September 17, 1875. Then he went to Toulouse for two years as a teacher of the classics. He took up studies again at the scholasticate at Vals in 1877 and in 1880 received the baccalaureate in letters. He had been noticed by his superiors and in the reports sent to the general of the Jesuits in Rome, Prat was noted as being of fine character, of great erudition, and of prudent judgment. This recommendation resulted in his being sent to Rome for higher studies. Since his tastes turned toward the Sacred Scriptures he was in 1884 transferred to the University of Beirut in Syria, which was conducted by the Society. Here he was ordained a priest, August 24, 1887 by Mgr. Bonfigli, Apostolic Delegate to Syria. While in the East, Father Prat made many trips to Palestine, familiarizing himself with the setting of his future work. The immediate fruit of this sojourn was his first published work, *La Bible de Sixte-Quint* (The Bible of Sixtus V), which appeared in *Études Bibliques* in 1890. Then came another year in Rome at the Gregorian University where he studied under the scholarly Cornely and Billot (later Cardinal). In 1888 Father Prat was sent to England, where at Ditton Hall he taught the young Jesuits then in exile from Germany. The year 1892–1893 was spent in Paris teaching and studying. From 1893 to 1925, when he was relieved of all professional duties to work on his book, Father Prat was professor of Scripture in the Jesuit colleges at Uclés, Vals, Toulouse and, after the expulsion of the Society from France in 1904, at Enghien in Belgium. Actually, however, he taught for only about 15 years. The many interruptions were not distractions, however. He was making a name for himself as a consultor on the Pontifical Biblical Commission and as a writer for and an editor of the *Etudes Bibliques*.

In 1903 Pope Leo XIII was interested in setting up the Biblical Commission for solving Scripture cases. There was much covert opposition in the Roman Curia both from "liberal" minded theologians and the more conservative members of the hierarchy. The Pope, however, went ahead with his plans and Father Prat was summoned in January 1903 to the Eternal City as a consultor. In July of that year the Pontiff died and Father Prat returned to France, not knowing what the policy of the next Pope would be. In 1904, however, Pius X recalled him and proved a friend and promotor of the Commission. Many of the decisions regarding "Modernism" leading up to its condemnation in 1907 were prepared in part by Father Prat. In 1907 Father Prat again went to the East, back to Beirut, this time as a professor. He again collected much material for his future work.

When the world was convulsed with war in 1914, Father Prat immediately volunteered in the French army as a chaplain. He served in the Battle of the Marne and all through the war, being mustered out only after the Armistice in 1918. For his heroic service and bravery under fire he won the coveted Cross of the Legion of Honor.

After 1919 most of his life was spent in the preparation and publication of his great works. What might be called his life work is the *Theology of Saint Paul*, published between 1908 and 1923. A most studious, thorough, and enlightening work, it has been translated into several languages and evoked a great interest in the life and teachings of the Apostle of the Gentiles. He wrote *Le Bible et l'histoire* (The Bible and History) in 1904; *Le Code de Sinai* (The Ten Commandments) in 1904; *Origène, Le Théologien et l' exégète* (Origen, Theologian and Exegete) in 1907. His last great work, *The Life of Christ*, appeared in 1933. At his death he left in manuscript form a work, *La Théologie de Saint Jean* (The Theology of St. John). Over a hundred articles in Biblical, scientific, and theological reviews are from his pen.

In November 1933 he met with a serious automobile accident and though painfully injured, he recovered but not enough to do much writing. A series of cerebral hemorrhages weakened his strength and he passed away among his brethren in Toulouse, August 4, 1938. A simple soul, at the same time a profound student of the Sacred Sciences, he left an ineffaceable mark on the present day theological literature.   K. M.

Mrs. Harry Rogers Pratt. See *Agnes Edwards Rothery*

Patrick Purcell   1914–

But for the grace of God, Patrick Purcell would have been a schoolteacher as were his father and mother and elder sister before him. However, after his primary education in his father's country schoolhouse he moved on to St. Kieran's College in Kilkenny, and thence to University College in Dublin, where he secured his B.A. in 1936, followed by his M.A. degree in 1937 in English literature. Just to be on the safe side he secured a high school teacher's qualification, the Higher Diploma in Education but successfully side-stepped the schoolrooms, and in 1938 became a subeditor on the staff of the *Irish Independent*, a national daily published in Dublin. While at University College, *The National Student* and *The National Rooster* introduced him to the fatal smell of printer's ink.

Two years later he left Middle Abbey Street to join the editorial staff of a large Dublin printing house and in 1948 became editor of the monthly *Irish Digest*, a magazine with which he had long been associated.

In September 1940 he wrote a romantic short story which he says "to my great surprise was published in *Woman's Life*. Thus encouraged, I began to write another similar story, but this story proved very obstinate and refused to come to an end when it should. I became just as obstinate and determined to keep on writing until I finished that story — even if it took me a lifetime. So I wrote and wrote and wrote, even in the most unlikely places — in trains and long distance buses, on the backs of envelopes, while my wife (only she was not my wife then) dressed for a dance, in a dentist's waiting room. . . . It took me eight or ten months before I bested those stubborn characters and brought their story to its long overdue conclusion." When a man of some importance on the *Limerick Leader* read the manuscript, he urged Purcell to have it published. "Well, I thought it over," Mr. Purcell writes, "and came to the conclusion I had nothing to lose, and, when I got back to Dublin, rewrote the whole thing in a somewhat more orderly fashion. I had it typed, by various friends, and sent a copy to two Dublin publishers. One of them accepted it. That was how *Hanrahan's Daughter* came to be born, and that was how I became an author." This first novel appeared in 1942. It is the love story of Joe Doyle, a small farmer in County Kilkenny, and Esther Hanrahan, the girl he met at the University in Dublin, and whose father was more prosperous than he. *Hanrahan's Daughter* quickly became one of the most popular books published in Ireland in recent years. G. P. Putnam's Sons published the book in the United States.

Patrick Purcell's second novel, *A Keeper of Swans* (1944), was also very popular in Ireland but has not thus far been published elsewhere. When this book appeared, a friend asked him how one of the characters, a retired teacher, came to live in a big house. "So I had to write *The Quiet Man*," remarked Purcell, "to satisfy my friend and myself on that point." G. P. Putnam's Sons brought the book out in the United States in 1946. This book has been his best seller thus far. It appeared also in translation in Germany, Holland, and Belgium. His fourth novel, a sequel to *The Quiet Man*, was published in Dublin in 1949.

Born at Carrigeen, Moocoin, County Kilkenny, on December 5th, 1914, Patrick Purcell was married in 1943 to Agnes Hourigan of Ballingarry, County Limerick. They have three children. The family lives in a Dublin suburb at the gates of the famous Passionist foundation of Mount Argus.

Despite his years in Dublin, his heart is still on the banks of the Suir, where he was born, as is evident from his novels.

Patrick Purcell at 38 (1952) is five feet ten inches in height and weighs one hundred and fifty pounds, and is proud of the fact that despite the assaults of his children he still retains most of his hair. A keen motorist, he hopes at some future date to write a travel book on Ireland, for he has travelled the country up, down, and crossways.

Patrick Purcell is the successor of Kickham and Canon Sheehan as the chronicler of rural Ireland. He writes in a romantic style, often reminiscent of the late Donn Byrne. Two great characteristics of his work are the raciness of his dialogue and the quiet humor that underlies all his characters and situations.

In addition to his editorial post and his novel writings, Patrick Purcell is also possibly Ireland's busiest literary critic as he runs a weekly column of reviews in the weekly *Irish Catholic* and a monthly book page in *Hibernia*.

As a sports writer, too, he is much in demand, when he has any time available, for he is an acknowledged authority on Ireland's national games of hurling and Gaelic football. In fact he is an inveterate sports fan and spends many evenings listening to American baseball and football games on his short-wave set. He admits to being a completely biased supporter of two teams which he has never seen, the Brooklyn Dodgers and Notre Dame.

One of the founder members of the Catholic Writers Association, Patrick Purcell is also honorary secretary of that organization.

Reverend M. Raymond, O.C.S.O. (Reverend Joseph David Flanagan) 1903–

Father Raymond's work is principally about contemplatives of his order and their struggle for sainthood. His remarkable success has been due, apart from his learning and literary skill, to the fact that he holds tenaciously the opinion that saints are for imitation more than for admiration. Saints, he believes, should be shown to be of common clay, humans with difficulties such as are experienced by all of us.

Father Raymond's career, first at college and subsequently as a son of Saint Ignatius, led up to the rare event of 1936 when he became a Cistercian of the Strict Observance. Then only, as he explains, in silence and in solitude has he been able *to live* all he learned under St. Ignatius and spend all his days and nights in the Society of Jesus. "Perhaps," he adds, "I'll become a cloistered contemplative in earnest only when cloistered in heaven and contemplating the Beauty 'ever ancient, ever new.'"

Born in Roxbury, Massachusetts, in 1903, he was baptized Joseph David, to which names he subsequently added "Stanislaus" through admiration of the Polish Jesuit boy-saint. His parents are Patrick J. and Mary B. Flanagan and he has not belied the Irish temperament implicit in the name. His first teachers were the daughters of Mother Seton, and his earliest enthusiasm for a book was for one written by a future teacher who influenced him greatly in subsequent years, Father Francis P. Donnelly, S.J. The name of the book was *Imitation and Analysis*.

At Boston College High School, Joseph David Stanislaus was known as "J.S." to distinguish him from another Joseph Flanagan who came to be called "J." In sports, where both "J.S." and "J" won distinction, they were known as "the Flanagan brothers."

Providence, in a remarkable way, prepared "J.S." for his future work as a writer. After entering the Society of Jesus in 1920, and finishing his novitiate, he had as teachers in literature, two very distinguished Jesuits, Father George Johnson and Father Francis Donnelly.

The former, as Professor of Poetry, developed Father Flanagan's imagination and emotions, the latter, as Professor of Rhetoric, gave him a true *ars dicendi*, a fine sense of rhetoric and expression.

Father Raymond claims that his greatest education came not from the schools he attended, but from their variety. He made his literary studies in New York, his philosophical course in New England, his theological course was completed in the Midwest, though his degree S.T.L. came from the Gregorian University in Rome. He completed his Jesuit training at the farthest point of the far West, at Port Townsend (1934–1935), where he attended the *Schola Affectus* of St. Ignatius, the tertianship. The greater part of his life has been spent among the classical authors of antiquity, but amongst the moderns his favorites are Leon Bloy, because of his power and prophetic insight, and G. K. Chesterton because of his penetration. The living authors who please him most are Fulton Sheen and Caryll Houselander, perhaps because of their devotion to the doctrine of the Mystical Christ.

From 1927–1930, Father Raymond (to anticipate his future name) held the Chair of Rhetoric at Holy Cross College, Worcester, Massachusetts. During these years he was Moderator of the Holy Cross Debating Societies and developed teams that achieved fame. His period as missioner and retreat master were at the end of his career in the Society of Jesus, and soon the cloister of the Abbey of Our Lady of Gethsemane closed around him.

Among the published works of Father Raymond are the following: *The Man Who Got Even with God; The Life of an American Trappist (Brother Joachim,* 1941); *The Saga of Citeaux (First Epoch) Three Religious Rebels, Forefathers of the Trappists* (1944); *The Saga of Citeaux (Second Epoch) The Family That Overtook Christ* (1942); *The Saga of Citeaux (American Epoch) Burnt Out Incense* (1949), and *God Goes to Murderer's Row* (1951). In addition he has written over twenty booklets.

Father Raymond's central idea in his religious philosophy is the beloved doctrine of the Mystical Body of Christ. In everything he has so far written, this doctrine is illustrated. He claims that it is not only the heart of theology but the only satisfying explanation of life, since it gives man his dignity, his destiny, and points out his duty.

In *Burnt Out Incense*, man's dignity and destiny, when he takes up the contemplative life, are justified. This story of the first hundred years of Trappist life in Kentucky moves the mind and heart profoundly. "The title of this work," writes Father John J. Campbell, S.J., "epitomizes almost perfectly its contents and expresses well what the Cistercians of the Strict Observance are doing for our land — giving their lives, burning themselves out that America may be holy as God wants it to be holy. . . . The reader is carried away by the story of heroic sanctity, of trials, of privations, and hardships that are as much the foundations of Gethsemane in America as the bricks and mortar that went into the building of the proto-abbey."

William Bernard Ready   1914–

William Bernard Ready was born on September 16, 1914 in Cardiff, Wales. He was the eldest child of John and Nora Hart Ready. John Ready was a dockworker, a coal trimmer, and was himself the son of a shipwright, William Ready. The great-grandfather of the author had come across to Wales from Tramore, County Waterford, around the turn of the mid-nineteenth century, and was among the first to hear the Mass publicly celebrated in South Wales, where it had been driven underground since the Reformation. The great-grandfather Ready was killed in the Morfa Colliery disaster of Easter Monday, 1890.

The long residence in Wales of the Ready family, along with thousands of other Irish families, did little to bring them into any sort of social accord with the Welsh people, although there were never any of the ugly racial and religious riots that accompanied Irish settlement in other parts of Great Britain. The Irish in South Wales were, for the most part, the laboring poor. The mother of the author, Nora Hart Ready, was born in Cardiff, of parents who hailed from Clonakilty.

William Ready went to the parochial school of Saint Alban, at the age of four, and at the age of eight years, his parents sent him to the newly-opened private school of Saint Illtyd, that the Brothers of the Christian Schools had brought into being at the invitation of the Archbishop, Francis Mostyn. In 1930, the school was inspected by the Board of Education and was accorded the status of a public high school.

In 1931, Ready, aged 16, began to work as an apprentice librarian in Cardiff Public Libraries, where he remained, with some years of leave of absence until he graduated with honors from the University of Wales, until 1939.

In August, 1939, he enlisted in the British Army and served until December 1945. For the first eighteen months of the war, he was a gunner in the anti-aircraft artillery. He saw a great deal of aerial bombardment. Early in 1941 he went overseas, as a troop sergeant, to the Middle East, where, until the Tunisian campaign's end, he soldiered as an enlisted man, from Syria right across the North African littoral, as a member of the British Eighth Army. By this time he was acting as Battery Sergeant-Major, which is in the British Army the senior noncommissioned rank in the organization of a battery.

From the fall of Tunis until October 1942, Ready was confined to Officer Training Camps, in the Canal Zone, in Acre, and in Sarafand. He was finally commissioned into the Royal Inniskilling Fusiliers. In October, immediately following his commission, Ready went to the Aegean, as a reinforcement. After several weeks aboard a caique, attempting to reach Leros Island, Ready, from Samos, managed to escape, taking with him some scores of German prisoners that he had been guarding, and after some adventures he landed back safely in Palestine.

After a rest, Ready joined the second battalion of the Inniskillings in Italy, and campaigned with them on the Geragliano line and on the Anzio bridgehead. Becoming incapacitated through enemy action at Anzio, Ready was hospitalized for many months around Naples and in Sorrento. Upon recovery he was down-graded because of the injuries caused to his left hand, and he became an instructor and the librarian at the New British Army University, which had taken over the property of the Universita per gli Stanieri, at Perugia, Italy, where he saw the war out safely and securely. It was at Perugia that Ready met his future wife, a Canadian nursing sister, stationed at the Canadian hospital there.

Upon his return to England in September 1945, Ready was admitted to Balliol College, Oxford, where he read Education and was awarded the diploma of the University. In 1946, he and his wife arrived in Canada. For two years they lived in Winnipeg. During this time, Ready taught in a private school and took a master's degree in history at the University of Manitoba. It was there that his first article, an essay on Plato, was published, followed by some articles on Canadian history. Then followed the publication of an account of his visit to the Pope, and in the fall of 1947 the *Atlantic Monthly* accepted his story "Barring the Weight" and encouraged him to keep on writing.

A teaching fellowship took the Readys to the University of Minnesota for two years, where his writings increased. He was fortunate enough to be noticed by Father Vincent Flynn, the President of the College of Saint Thomas, who gave him the opportunity of teaching creative writing and who also found a home for him and his growing family on the campus of the College.

The School of Librarianship of the University of California invited Ready to become a member of the faculty and Ready accepted, teaching Bibliography and Reference in the year 1950–51. In July 1951, Ready transferred to Stanford, where he is the Head of the Acquisitions Division of the University Libraries. A book of his stories, *The Great Disciple*, appeared in June 1951. His articles, reviews, and stories have appeared in *America, Atlantic Monthly, Books on Trial, The Sign, Catholic Historical Review, Saturday Evening Post, Tomorrow*, the *California Librarian, Education*, the *Library Review*, the *Library Journal* and *School & Society*.

He has three sons, Patrick, Vincent and Liam.

Kenneth Reddin 1895–

As District Judge for the County Dublin in Ireland, Kenneth Reddin seldom gets more than three hours a day to write. Of writing he says: "It is the most egotistical, engrossing and satisfying work a man or woman can possibly engage in. The sense that you have written a paragraph, a page, a chapter adequately and well, gives the deepest, the most intimate feeling of pleasure. I know no pleasure like it."

Born in Dublin, Ireland in 1895, Kenneth Reddin is the son of John J. Reddin, Clerk of the Dublin Port and Docks Board, and Teresa (Sheila) Reddin — both are dead.

Kenneth was educated in the Jesuit day school, Belvedere, from 1908 to 1912; in the Jesuit boarding school of Clongowes Wood from 1912 to 1914, and then attended St. Enda's College, under Padraig Pearse, who was executed after the Rising of 1916. Mr. Reddin had taken part in the Rising and was incarcerated in Stafford Prison for a short time. Upon his release he returned to the National University to continue his study of law. In 1918 he became a Qualified Solicitor and four years later, he was appointed Judge of the District Court, the position he still holds for the County of Dublin.

His interest in writing was encouraged by his mother. "My mother," he writes in *Eason's Bulletin*, "was an original subscriber to the Abbey Theatre. She knew Yeats, Lady Gregory and the great figures of the Irish Renaissance. She continually encouraged me to write. I would write a sketch or . piece of verse, read it to her, get her criticism, and stuff it away in a drawer. I never thought of it being published. I just started writing another sketch or piece of verse. At that time, I was a Sgoil Eanna with Pearse as Headmaster. In the library Pearse gave me advice. He indicated the kind of books I ought to read and the kind I oughtn't to. . . . Pearse was then preparing a new issue of *An Macaomh* (i.e. *Youth*), the college periodical. He asked the boys for contributions. I sent in a piece of verse. Pearse accepted it. I staggered around the school for weeks, drunk with pride and a sense of achievement."

Kenneth Reddin's one act play, *The Passing*, was awarded the Gold Medal in the Tailteann Games Literary Competition and was produced in the Abbey Theatre in Dublin. Another of his plays is *Old Mag*.

For three years he worked on his book *The White Bolletrie*. The story was pure phantasy. The introduction is by Padraic Colum.

His first novel, *Somewhere to the Sea*, appeared in 1936. "It is," he says, "an authentic record of my life in Sinn Fein during the Black-and-Tan days. I had to write it or I should have burst." The book went into a second edition and was serialized by the Dublin *Evening Mail*.

His recent novel *Another Shore* was sold out in three weeks. "It is set, almost entirely, in the streets of Dublin, which I pride myself I know pretty well." It has gone into a second edition. Recently it was filmed by Ealing Studios in London and published in the United States by A. A. Wyn, Current Books Inc., under the title of *Young Man With a Dream.*

Mr. Reddin has also a children's book *Mary Ann and the Old Party* which he says "came to be written out of deep emotion. . . . I sat at the fire and told the stories to my two children."

Some of his sketches and verse appeared in AE's *Statesman.*

M. A. H.

Douglas Reed   1895–

Douglas Reed is an English writer, born in London, England in 1895, who became a journalist by accident and an author in protest against the inhibitions of present-day journalism.

He was a bank clerk at the outbreak of World War II, throughout which he served in the infantry and air force, being twice wounded and cited for gallantry. At its end he went through the familiar difficulties of readjustment and after some hard times gained employment as a stenographer with *The Times* (London) in 1921. From this he was promoted to reporter (1926) and then to foreign correspondent (1929). In the next ten years he became one of the newspaper's leading foreign correspondents, first in Berlin (1929–1935) and then as its Chief Correspondent for Central Europe, covering Austria, Hungary, Czechoslovakia, Yugoslavia, Bulgaria, and Rumania, with special missions to Moscow and other places.

Thus he was in the midst of the great events which led to the 1939–1945 war and to the situation in which it has left the world today. By chance he was near the German Reichstag when it was fired in 1933. He wrote a book, *The Burning of the Reichstag* (1934), about this event (which he considers the starting-point of the whole present chaos) and the trial which followed it. In 1938 he was caught in Vienna by Hitler's invasion, and in 1939, in Prague by Hitler's second invasion; he returned to England just before the second war began, and may have been fortunate not to have been caught by it in Europe, for his name was on Hitler's "Black List," discovered in the Chancellery after the fall of Berlin in 1945.

After the Agreement of Munich in 1938, which surrendered Czechoslovakia to Hitler, he resigned from *The Times*, believing that the public could not be enlightened through daily journalism, and since that time, with two brief intervals (one as war correspondent in Normandy in 1944), has withdrawn from newspaper-writing and devoted himself to books about current affairs. The first of these, *Insanity Fair*

(1938) foretold the Second World War and the dangers of National
Socialism and had a very large circulation in England, the United
States and throughout the world. In the next book, *Disgrace Abounding*
(1939), he began to perceive and draw attention to the likelihood that
the coming war might be used to promote two causes, Communism and
Political Zionism, which he thought as dangerous, in their ways, as
National Socialism. This book was not published in the United States,
a contract for it being repudiated at sight of the typescript. In several
subsequent books he has elaborated this argument with growing conviction and, since the war's end, with the added force which its outcome, by justifying his warnings, has given. None of these books has
been published in the United States, but they have had a very large
circulation in all other English-speaking countries. They are: *A Prophet
at Home* (1941); *All Our Tomorrows* (1942); *Lest We Regret* (1944), and
From Smoke to Smother (1948).

In 1948 he went to South Africa "to look at the world set-up from
a new angle" and continued his portrayal of the world, as it was left
by the war, in *Somewhere South of Suez* (1950). In 1949 he came to the
United States, believing that "the decisive third act of the twentieth
century melodrama" would be shaped chiefly "between New York
and Moscow." This journey completed a range of travel, research, and
experience rare among living writers, and he put the results of it in
what he considers to be a culminating book, *Far and Wide*. After
travelling the United States from New England to New Mexico, from
the Carolinas to California, from Los Angeles to Boston, and from San
Francisco to Salem, he felt he had, in twenty years, completed the circuit of what he calls "the political dust-bowl of the world." By this he
means the area, with its rim running from the eastern edge of Europe
to the Pacific coast of the United States, in which, as he considers,
"the answer to the riddle of the twentieth century will be written."
He avowedly believes that the convulsive struggles of this century have
a definite core and purpose: namely, the destruction of the Christian
era, the erasure of the memory of Christianity, and the re-infliction
of paganism and slave-status on the white peoples. That he holds to
be "the pattern" behind the chaos, and he has seen many of the con-
flicts of this century, of the men who made them, of the forces behind
them, and of the places in which they have raged.

He stepped aside from this long and turbulent journalist's journey
to write several novels: *The Next Horizon* (1945); *Galanty Show* (1948);
Reasons of Health (1949), and *Rule of Three* (1950).

John Cowie Reid 1916–

John Reid was born in Auckland, New Zealand, on January 4, 1916, and has lived in that city all his life. He was educated by the Marist Brothers at Vermont Street Primary School and Sacred Heart College and later at Auckland University College. He graduated Master of Arts with honors in English and French in 1939.

As he left school in the early years of the economic depression which hit New Zealand hard, he was unable to attend the university as a full-time student. Consequently, he took lectures in the evenings while working by day in factories, stores, offices, and eventually as a clerk in a government department. In 1940 he entered the teaching profession and became English master at the Auckland Grammar School, the largest public high school in New Zealand.

Since 1940, also, he has conducted courses in modern literature for adult education classes, save for the years he spent on active service. He became a part-time lecturer in the English Department of the Auckland University College in 1940. In 1947 he was appointed a full time lecturer at the University, a position he, at present, holds.

He entered the New Zealand Armed Forces in May, 1942, where he remained until February, 1946. After being commissioned, he was appointed Assistant Director of the newly-formed Army Education and Welfare Service in 1943. In this position, he helped to organize the educational work for the three services in the Auckland military district and conducted classes in the evenings in literature, music, and current affairs.

Among his other interests, apart from writing, are dramatic production and acting. He produced the official play to celebrate the Catholic Centenary in 1938 and has also produced and played in plays by Shakespeare, Shaw and Ibsen. In 1944 he was responsible for the formation of the Combined Services Operatic Society (still a flourishing Society), and produced operas by Gilbert and Sullivan and by Lehar, which toured New Zealand with considerable success. Since 1945 he has done a good deal of radio broadcasting, chiefly literary talks. At present he broadcasts a fortnightly book talk from Station 1YA, and is Chairman of "The Critics" discussion panel.

Mr. Reid is President of the New Zealand Film Institute (which is the combined body of Film Societies), President of the District Court of Convocation (the official body of graduates of the university), and vice-president of the Auckland Recorded Music Society, and President of the University Catholic Society of New Zealand.

He was married in 1939 and has six children: Christopher, Bernard, Piers, Gerard, Miriam and Godfrey.

His earliest published efforts were stories and poems for children's papers. In 1938 he founded and edited *View*, a monthly journal designed to carry the Catholic viewpoint on current affairs and social principles to non-Catholics. *View* ceased publication when he entered the Army. While in training camp he founded a soldiers' monthly magazine *Guerilla*, which he edited from 1942 to 1945 and which circulated throughout New Zealand and the Pacific.

During his student years, he edited several University publications and wrote much material for these, winning prizes for prose and poetry. His chief writing has been literary criticism and his first serious study of this nature was a paper on Gerard Manley Hopkins, published in a university annual in 1937.

His chief publications have been: *Live Rounds,* a collection of light verse; *The Secret Years,* verse; *Creative Writing in New Zealand,* a critical history of New Zealand; and *Catholics and the Films,* a historical and critical survey. He has also published several shorter studies: *Gerard Manley Hopkins, A Centenary Essay; Catholic Readers and Writers; Educational Change in Soviet Russia,* etc. He has had several plays published and produced, e.g.: *The Road from Damascus; A Letter from Rome; The Eternal Door.*

Since 1944 he has written a weekly literary article for the *New Zealand Tablet.* He is a regular contributor of studies of French, German and English literature to *Twentieth Century* (Australia), *The Advocate* (Australia), *Catholic Review, Zealandia* and other New Zealand Catholic papers. These have included assessments of Kafka, Rimbaud, Bloy, Bernanos, Péguy, Claudel, Wassermann, Gide, Graham Greene, Evelyn Waugh, Gabriela Mistral, Manzoni and Papini.

He writes a monthly literary article for the New Zealand equivalent of *Time, Newsview,* and radio criticism for the New Zealand *Listener,* and contributes to other New Zealand secular papers. He wrote a survey of the literary history of Otago for the official publication celebrating the centenary of the province in 1948.

He has developed a particular interest in foreign literature (possibly as a compensation for not having left New Zealand) and has a knowledge, recognized in New Zealand as specialized, of the literature of contemporary France, Latin America and Germany. He has published several translations from modern French writers in various reviews and journals. Mr. Reid has a particular love for modern French Catholic writing, which was inspired by reading Leon Bloy's *La Femme Pauvre* as a young man.

On the academic side, he has a special interest in the Victorian period, with emphasis on the Catholic writers. He is at present working on a detailed study of the poetry of Coventry Patmore, which he hopes some day to publish.

Kurt Frank Reinhardt   1896–

Kurt Frank Reinhardt was born on November 2, 1896 in Munich, the capital of Bavaria, Germany. A few years later his parents moved to Mannheim in the German Grand-Duchy of Baden, where he attended public elementary school and nine years of a secondary school which combined certain essential features of the German humanistic gymnasium with scientific and technical education. It was named after G. E. Lessing, the German eighteenth century rationalistic writer and critic. From 1916 to 1922 he attended the German universities of Munich, Heidelberg, and Freiburg and took his Ph.D. degree at the latter institution in 1922 "magna cum laude." His special fields of study were German and general literature, philosophy, history of art, and medieval history. His course of studies was interrupted for about a year and a half by a severe attack of tuberculosis of the lungs and a stay in a sanatorium in the Swiss mountain resort of Arosa. Late in 1919 he returned to Heidelberg to continue his studies. "This period of grave illness was spiritually the most fruitful of my life. It brought me from the almost total paganism in which I had grown up to the Catholic Truth. It stimulated my interest in philosophy and theology and made me choose, after my recovery, a dissertation subject dealing with some of the basic problems of Christian mysticism (*Mystik und Pietismus*), published in Munich in 1925," he writes.

After the completion of his academic studies he was employed by the Herder Publishing Company in Freiburg in Breisgau as one of several editors who compiled the encyclopaedia *Der Kleine Herder* (published 1925), and he translated for Herder's series of Papal Encyclicals both the Thomas and Josaphat Encyclical from Latin into German. In his spare time he taught in the Freiburg *Volkshochschule* (university extension center) and did editorial work for the Freiburg daily newspaper of the Center Party, the *Freiburger Tagespost*.

In 1925 he became editor-in-chief of the Catholic illustrated weekly *Der Feuerreiter*, a new and unique venture in Germany. This periodical was published in Cologne, but as the printing plant was located in Zurich (the paper was financed by Swiss capital), he moved from Germany to Switzerland. In Zurich he met his future wife, Miss Bertha Bollinger, whom he married in 1926. In 1927, they went to Canada with the intention to stay in the New World in case he should be able to find suitable employment. They stayed in Winnipeg in the Province of Manitoba the greater part of the year they spent in Canada, but they took several longer trips in Canada as well as in the eastern part of the United States. He was engaged in newspaper work for German, Austrian, and Swiss publications, and in order to gain some broader experience he accepted a temporary position as Secretary of the Swiss Consulate in Winnipeg.

In 1928, the University of Oregon at Eugene, Oregon, offered him a position as assistant professor of German and as lecturer in the School of Architecture and Allied Arts. He accepted, and stayed at Eugene until the summer of 1930, when he received and accepted a call to Stanford University, California, to teach in the Department of Germanic Languages. Alongside with his teaching at Stanford he has been conducting extension courses in scholastic philosophy and related fields for the University of California's San Francisco Adult Education Center.

His major publications include the following books: *Mystik und Pietismus* (Munich, 1925); *The Commonwealth of Nations and the Papacy* (Bruce, Milwaukee, 1939); *A Realistic Philosophy* (Bruce, 1944). This work deals with the metaphysical principles of Thomistic thought and their application to the moral, political, and economic problems of the present age. *The Main Problems of Philosophy* (Bruce, 1946) is a translation of the *Propedéutica Filosófica* of Dr. Oswaldo Robles, Professor of Philosophy at the National University of Mexico and one of the foremost Thomist thinkers of the western hemisphere; *Germany: 2000 Years* (Bruce, 1950), is a comprehensive political and cultural history of Germany (illustrated with 36 plates and numerous maps) and represents the fruit of many years of study and teaching. It may therefore perhaps be said to reflect best the range of his interests and preoccupations. A book dealing with the problems and the history of atheistic and Christian existentialism and entitled *The Battle for Man* is his latest book. Aside from writing articles and book reviews for various North American periodicals, he contributes, regularly, articles in Spanish and English to *Universidad Pontificia Bolivariana*, the bi-monthly journal of the Catholic Pontifical University at Medellin, Columbia. He holds at present the rank and title of Professor of Germanic Languages at Stanford University.   M. A. H.

Reverend Hans Anscar Reinhold
1897–

The liturgy is the prime interest of Father H. A. Reinhold. The seeds of this study were sown by Father Reinhold's pastor when he encouraged him to read *Hochland*. "The big push to the liturgy cause came while I was at the University of Freiburg," writes Father Reinhold. Later at Innsbruck he was influenced by his teacher, Father M. Gatterer, S.J., and in Germany by Romano Guardini. His most significant training was in Maria Laach (1920–1921) and Rome (1928–29).

Father Reinhold was born in Hamburg, Germany, on September 6, 1897, the son of Bernard and Johanna (Schulz) Reinhold. He was educated at the Johanneum in Hamburg until September 11, 1914. Then he joined the German army, and was discharged by the Workers' and Soldiers' Council on December 19, 1918. For two semesters he studied philosophy at the University of Freiburg, which was followed by two more years of philosophy at the University of Innsbruck. Then came the year at Maria Laach (1920–1921), followed by a year of travel in Europe, Indonesia, Sudan, Greece, and Spain. His first two years of theology were studied at the University of Münster, the last two years at Osnabrück.

For two and a half years he was a chaplain among migratory Polish workers in the states of Oldenburg and Mecklenburg. Then he studied for two semesters at the Pontifical Archeological Institute in Rome. He did extensive travel in Italy, Austria, Germany and France.

On April 30, 1929, he became the General Secretary of the Catholic Seamen's Mission of Germany, which he had founded. He is a co-founder of the International Body of the AMIC and served as chaplain in Hamburg and Bremerhaven.

When he was expelled by the Gestapo on April 30, 1935, he went to London and arrived there on May 2nd. From July 1935 to August 1935 he did parish work in London. Next he served one year as an assistant at Interlaken, Switzerland, and field man for the new Catholic Refugee Committee in the United States.

On August 20, 1936, he arrived in New York to try to establish the refugee committee. "The hierarchy accepted the plan," writes Father Reinhold, "but at the request of Cardinal Hayes, warned by German agents, I was excluded from this work."

Father Reinhold then studied for two semesters at Columbia University under Dr. Carlton Hayes. He resided in Brooklyn. From September 1937 to June 1938 he taught Dogma and Exegesis at Portsmouth Priory in Rhode Island and at the same time studied archaeology and Eastern Orthodox art at Harvard University. From June 1938 to August 1938, he visited London, Paris and Switzerland. Upon his return to the United States he became seamen's chaplain in Seattle, Washington for three years. This was followed by two years in Yakima as an assistant. During the months June, July and August, 1943, he taught at Assumption College in Windsor, Ontario. Then he went to New York as the guest of Father Ford, the pastor of Corpus Christi Church, and stayed there until June 1944. In the meantime (April) he became a United States citizen. In September he was appointed pastor of St. Joseph's Church, Sunnyside, Washington.

Father Reinhold has taught at the University of Notre Dame, Xavier College, St. Mary's College, Notre Dame, Indiana, and has lectured at Berkeley Divinity School, Marquette University, St. John's University and many other places. In 1951 he was awarded an honorary D.D. degree by St. John's University. The June issue of *Orate Fratres*, pp. 324-325 states: "For nearly thirteen years Hans Anscar Reinhold has been writing the monthly column for *Orate Fratres* which most readers turn to first of all when opening the magazine. Taking over the 'Timely Tracts' after Father Virgil died, he has proved a worthy successor in the catholicity of his outlook, in his concern for the wider social problems of Christianity, and in his forthrightness. The liturgical movement in America owes him a great debt of gratitude for helping preserve it from a mere sacristy mentality, and for coming to grips in realistic fashion with everyday life. As a mark of grateful esteem, St. John's invited him to give the baccalaureate address to its graduating college students of 1951, and conferred upon him the honorary degree of doctor of divinity. The citation reads: 'In recognition of his merits as a frequent and stimulating contributor to more than a score of European and American periodicals, both on the scholarly and more popular level, who brings sacramental theology to bear significantly upon the social and cultural problems of our time; in tribute to his tireless priestly activities as a co-founder and director of the International Apostolate of the Sea, as chairman of Industrial Conferences, as lecturer at Catholic and non-Catholic universities on theology and liturgy, on Christian art and architecture, as editor of the first English anthology of mystical literature, as seamen's chaplain and parish priest; and more particularly, in gratitude for his contribution of a 'Timely Tract' every month since the death of Father Virgil Michel in 1938 to St. John's own magazine, the liturgical monthly *Orate Fratres* — St. John's University, upon recommendation of the faculty, presents Father Hans Anscar Reinhold, in this year of his own and *Orate Fratres'* silver jubilee, for the degree of doctor of divinity, *honoris causa.'"

He began to write for publication in 1926 with a contribution to *Jahrbuch für Liturgiewissenschaft* (Odo Casel) and then for *Der Seelsorger* (Vienna), *Die Seelsorge* (Breslau) and in this country for *The Catholic World* and *The Commonweal*. In England, in 1938, Victor White asked him to contribute to *Blackfriars*. Soon he was writing for *Orate Fratres*, *Architectural Forum*, *Choirmaster*, *Liturgical Arts*, *Priest*, and several other publications.

He is one of the founders and the first advocate, after the late Father Virgil Michel, O.S.B., of the movement for more use of the vernacular in the liturgy. He called the first meeting in October 1946, the second meeting in August 1947 in Portland, Oregon and the "constituent meeting" in Chicago, in July 1948. His first articles and papers on this subject appeared in *Clergy Review*, *Orate Fratres*, *The Commonweal* and *The Priest*. He is more proud of this achievement than any other.

Father Reinhold is the author of *Soul Afire: Revelations of the Mystics* (1944) and *Our Parish* (Paulist Press). Peter Anson's book, *Churches*, was provided with footnotes and an introduction for the American edition by Father Reinhold.   M. A. H.

Marie René-Bazin (Mother Marie St. Justin) 1883-

The fourth child of the celebrated Catholic novelist René Bazin (See *Catholic Authors: Contemporary Biographical Sketches, 1930-1947*), Marie René-Bazin received her inspiration to write while reading some portraits of nuns in her father's last work. She decided to write sketches that would make her religious family better known. Strongly encouraged by her superiors, she went to Paris and submitted her first essays to her father who was then critically ill. Her father expounded to her his own methods and took a keen interest in the enterprise. One may even say that it was the supreme interest and joy of René Bazin's remaining days. He himself gave the title to his daughter's first book: *Quelques-unes de mes Soeurs*, translated into English and published by P. J. Kenedy & Sons, under the title *Some Sisters of Mine*. The French work was crowned, in 1933, by the French Academy.

Marie René-Bazin was born in Angers, France in 1883. Amid the growing popularity of her father's name as a novelist, both René Bazin and his wife were eager to preserve, in their offspring, a strong spirit of faith, of love for the Church, of esteem for countries outside their own, and above all an extreme simplicity of life. Like her sisters, Marie was educated as a boarder at the Convent des Oiseaux in Paris, under the care of the Regular Canonesses of St. Austin. Her religious vocation, which she had felt as a young child, was fostered there. She was strongly determined to devote herself to the service of the poor. In the meantime, she received at home the title of "Captain of the Juniors" on account of her love for childish games, and of her reluctance to relinquish these when time arrived to be "grown up."

When her father was elected a Member of the French Academy, the family took up its residence in Paris; the summer months, however, were passed at Les Rangeardières, near Angers. René Bazin was thus able to perform his duties at the French Academy and at the same time teach at the Catholic University to which he was strongly attached. It was here at Les Rangeardières, Marie recalls that her father welcomed such illustrious visitors as Brunetière, Paul Bourget, Georges Goyau, Henry Bordeaux, Maurice Barrès and a galaxy of others. It was there, too, that René Bazin composed most of his novels. Often at night-time when the younger children were asleep, and his wife had been reading aloud to the eldest or playing music with them — he would suddenly enter the drawing-room and offer to submit to their criticism the pages he had just written. Marie says: "He read like a poet enamored with his dream, or rather like an apostle afire with love for souls and eager to communicate his flame."

Marie called Les Rangeardières, her "earthly paradise," but left it at the end of 1907 to enter the novitiate of the Helpers of the Holy Souls. The two things that influenced her in choosing this order were: its work among the poorest of this earth, and the virile training of St. Ignatius' Rule. At the end of her juniorate (period of probation following that of the novitiate), she was sent to London. Her religious life, up to 1947, was given to apostolic labors in London and in Edinburgh: catechism classes in populous districts, clubs for girls, and the instruction of converts. Then, in 1932, came the idea to write. Upon the success of her first book, she published, in 1936, a second series of sketches of Helpers: *Au Carrefour des trois Eglises* (*My Sisters Pass By*), which was likewise crowned by the French Academy. In 1948, a biography of the Foundress of the Society appeared, entitled: *Celle qui vécut son Nom, Marie de la Providence* (*She Who Lived Her Name*). To these books which were published simultaneously in English and French, Marie René-Bazin added two books which she translated: *Life of Mother St. Dominic* written by Mother St. Austin under the title: *Fixty-six years a Missionary in China* and *Le Creuset de L'Amour* from one of the unpublished manuscripts of the same author on purgatory.

As may be seen, all the literary activities of René Bazin's daughter are centered round her religious Society or on the spirit which animates it. The Foundress of the Helpers of the Holy Souls loved to enjoin her first companions "to help in all manner of good." Marie René-Bazin shows us that even literary writing is considered by her Institute as one of the high-ways or by-ways in the service of the living and of the dead.

Mother St. Justin is now stationed at the motherhouse, in Paris.

H. S.

Right Reverend Giuseppe Ricciotti Can. Reg. Lat. 1890–

Joseph Ricciotti, titular Abbot of the Canons Regular of the Lateran, is described as "broad, neither too stout nor too thin, blond hair, brown eyes, swarthy complexion, humble, plain and humorous." He was born in Rome in 1890, and made his religious profession in the above mentioned congregation in 1906. He was ordained to the priesthood in 1913, and elected Abbot in 1938.

A Doctor of Sacred Theology and a Consultor to the Sacred Congregation of Religious, he was from 1935 to 1946 Procurator General of his Congregation.

Early in his career he studied Oriental history and literature. On various archaeological and historical missions he has travelled through Asia, from Palestine to China.

From 1924 on, he has been Professor of Hebrew, and later of

Semitic languages and oriental Christian History at the University of Rome. He contributed articles on oriental subjects to the Italian Encyclopedia.

Besides writing for European magazines and American publications, Abbot Ricciotti gives conferences in many Italian cities and also on the radio. In 1949 he was invited to Brazil, Argentina and other South American countries to give a series of lectures.

His books mostly concern oriental history, especially Hebrew history. Among these the trilogy consisting of *The History of Israel, The Life of Jesus Christ* and *St. Paul the Apostle* are the most important. *The Life of Christ* has been translated into sixteen languages. The idea came to write this book (*Life of Christ*) during World War I, in which he served as chaplain of the D'Annunzio regiment. In his Preface to *The Life of Christ* he writes:

"I had been carried to a field hospital set up in a wood of fir trees in a valley among the Alps. For some time I hovered between life and death, and I was much closer to the latter than the former. Night and day the valley shuddered with the crash of grenades, the wounded were screaming around me, I could hear the death rattle of the dying, and the stench of gangrene sickening the air seemed a forecast of the cemetery. As I lay awaiting my fate, it suddenly came to me that if I should live I might write a life of Christ; His Gospel, in fact, was on the straw mattress beside me, and its pages, with splotches of blood crossing the Greek letters like rubrics, seemed a symbolic pattern of life and death.

"When I was well and back in normal life again, instead of being attracted by the idea of writing a life of Christ, I was terrified, and the more I thought of it, the more afraid of it I was. But not only did the thought never leave me, it became a kind of spiritual necessity. And as we instinctively do with frightening necessities, I began to walk around it, as it were, as if to fool myself. I began to publish studies on Hebrew and Syriac texts; I produced a *History of Israel*, and then *The Wars of the Jews* of Flavius Josephus. But the real citadel was still there unassailed among them despite all my circuitous activity; I did not touch it because I was afraid of it. The persuasion of friends and the urging of persons of authority made no impression on me; I invariably answered that my strength faltered before a life of Jesus Christ.

"Later, however, I unexpectedly gave in. But that was because after so many years the agony of that little field hospital began all over again and in much worsened circumstances. When I realized that the tempest of another war was gathering over humanity and that Europe was again to be drenched with blood, then it seemed to me that not only my own body but all mankind, all of so-called civilized humanity, lay dying with a Gospel splotched with blood beside it.

"This image became so compelling that I was forced to obey. Since blood was again flowing over the world, then the Gospel must return to it again too. And so the present volume was written while Europe was the prey of war, that is, of the thing which is the most complete denial of the Gospel."

The works by Abbot Ricciotti are: *Dalla Bibbia* — Antologia

Letteraria. Versioni critiche dai testi ebraici, aramaici e greci, con introduzione e note (1922); *Il Libro di Geremia* — Versione critica dal testo ebraico con introduzione e commento (1923); *Le Lamentazioni di Geremia* — Versione critica dal testo ebraico con introduzione e commento (1924); *Il Libro di Giobbe* — Versione critica dal testo ebraico con introduzione e commento (1924); *S. Efrem Siro* — Biografia, Scritti, Teologia (Torino 1925); *S. Efrem Siro Inni Alla Vergine* — Tradotti dal siriaco; 2a ediz. (1939); *Afraate O Il Sapiente Persiono* Le Piu belle pagine tradotte dal siriaco (Milano 1926); *S. Afraate Il Sapiente Persiano* — La Dimostrazione della fede, la Dimostrazione dell'acino. Tradotti dal siriaco con introduzione e note (Roma 1927); *Il Cantico Dei Cantici* — Versione critica dal testo ebraico con introduzione e commento. Premio Rezzi 1925 dell'Accademia della Crusca (Torino 1928); *Bar-Hebreo Nomocanone* — Fonti per la Codificazione Canonica Orientale (Roma 1931); *L'Apocalisse di Paolo Siriaca* — I. Introduzione, traduzione e commento; II. La cosmologia della Bibbia e la sua trasmissione fino a Dante. Premio Rezzi (1930 dell'Accademia della Crusca (Brescia 1932); *Apocalypis Pauli Syriace* — iuxta codices vaticanos nunc primum edita. In Orientalia, Nova Series vol. II. 1–2; *Roma Cattolica E Oriente Cristiano* (Firenze 1935); *Il Cantiere Di Hiram* — Materiali per costruzioni spirituali (Torino 1936); *Flavio Giuseppe Tradotto E Commentato* — I. Introduzione; II. III. IV. La "Guerra giudaica" (Torino 1937); *Storia D'Israele* — I. Dalle origini all'esilio; II. Dall'ésilio al 135 dopo Cristo; 4a ediz. (Torino 1944).; *La Religione D'Israele*, nella Storia delle Religioni diretta da P. Tacchi-Venturi; ristampa della 2a ediz. (Torino 1944); *Bibia E Non Bibbia* — 4a ediz. (Brescia 1946); *Paolo Apostolo* — 4a ediz. (Roma 1951); *Le Lettere Di S. Paolo* — tradotte e commentate 2a ediz. (Roma 1951); *Vita Di Gesu'Cristo* — 14a ediz. (Roma 1951).

In preparation is *Gli Atti Degli Apostoli*.

Abbot Ricciotti's *Life of Christ* was translated into English by Alba Zizzamia. She is now translating his *St. Paul the Apostle*.

M. A. H.

Reverend Joseph Rickaby, S.J.
1845–1932

Father Joseph Rickaby's long life, which extended a little over 87 years, began at Everingham in Yorkshire on November 20, 1845. This by a coincidence was the year of Newman's reception into the Church, and of him and his writings Father Rickaby was later to conceive a profound admiration. This discipleship, as it may almost be called, led him not merely to read every one of the great Cardinal's works but to undertake the task of compiling an index based upon them all. And among his more notable sermons was that he preached on Cardinal Newman at the opening of the Birmingham Oratory. But this is to anticipate. Joseph was a frail boy and consequently was not allowed to go to school at Stonyhurst till his tenth year. Even when studying philosophy at St. Mary's Hall as a young Jesuit he weighed no more than 6 stone. And as it was feared that he would not live long, he was ordained in 1877, earlier than he would otherwise have been. From then on, he averred, his health and strength improved. This improvement was caused, or at least fostered, by his love of nature's beauties and devotion to the exercise of walking. He had a saying that it is a good thing every now and then thoroughly to tire the body; and it is on record that when Professor of Ethics at St. Mary's Hall, where he spent the years 1879–1896, his walking expeditions as to the sources of the Hodder and the Trough of Bowland were of a length that has deterred many a younger and stronger man.

His intellectual ability was early manifest. In 1862 he took the first place in Classical Honors at the London Matriculation examination. In the B.A. examination he headed the list, though J. S. Reid, the well-known classical scholar of Cambridge, was among the candidates. In the M.A. examination, however, the positions were reversed; Reid was first and he was second. His London examiners judged his papers to be of quite exceptional worth. His alertness of mind and felicity of style marked by a love of short, crisp sentences remained with him to advanced old age. Some of his books were written during the closing period of his life, 1926–1932, which he spent at St. Beuno's College, crippled by rheumatism and obliged to use a wheel chair.

His diminutive stature and frailty of frame debarred him from excelling or even taking much interest in games — at school he was described as a "shrimp of a boy." Despite this boyhood disability his cheerful and affectionate disposition won him close friends among his fellows, the most intimate being William Constable-Maxwell, second son of the 10th Baron Herries. When, in 1862, he entered the Jesuit novitiate at Manresa, Roehampton, whither it had been but recently removed from Beaumont near Windsor, he found among his companions Sylvester Hunter, later to be widely known by his three-volume *Outlines of Dogmatic Theology*. As a "philosopher" at St. Mary's Hall, for the course of Special Metaphysics he sat at the feet of the celebrated Father Bayma. When he returned there later to teach in his own turn, in addition to his office as Professor of Ethics and Natural Law he held also during the whole of his stay the responsible post of Spiritual Father.

In 1896 he moved to Oxford where he was entrusted with the same post of Spiritual Father at the newly opened Clarke's Hall, which now has the permanent name of Campion Hall. Here he remained, with a short interval at London, 1897–1899, till 1924. His conferences and retreats were in wide demand, and for many years Father Rickaby paid a monthly visit to Oscott College. A professor there at the time has put his memories on record: "It is difficult, almost impossible, in a few words, to convey an impression of the influence exercised by Father Joseph Rickaby on the students of Oscott during the years in which he was Spiritual Father. The keenness with which we looked forward to the monthly recollection, the exhilaration of those talks, the profound and abiding impression on our minds and lives, is remembered and cherished, but cannot be described." He also gave courses to the Catholic undergraduates. These were printed in several volumes and some may be read in *The Lord My Light.*

His intellectual interest apart from the classics, to which he was devoted, were almost entirely religious. In illustration of his love especially of the Greek writers may be quoted his whimsical remark that "if proof of my death were needed, my failure to show any vitality in the presence of a 'Liddell and Scott' would be enough to certify me for burial." This, however, might suggest that his scholarship was of the dry-as-dust brand. This was far from the truth. Ideas were the life-blood of his mind, which was original, supple, and inventive. He was deeply rather than widely read. Among his favorites were St. Augustine, St. Thomas Aquinas, and St. John Chrysostom, of the last-named of whom, at least, he had read the entire literary remains. St. Augustine he used to read with Dr. Headlam, sometime Regius Professor of History and later Anglican Bishop of Gloucester.

By disposition Father Rickaby was shy. On a memorable occasion Father Charles Plater, who at the time was his Rector, happened to meet him at the railway station at Bletchley. After some remarks had passed between them Father Rickaby said, "I'm afraid I don't know you." In his shy way he had probably not looked his companion in the face. He was simple in his tastes, careless of his dress and of his appearance in general — a trait sometimes found in men habitually absorbed in the things of the mind.

When he left Campion Hall in 1924 he retired to St. Mary's Hall, which he left in 1926 for his last home at St. Beuno's College, N. Wales. There he completed the toll of his considerable literary output. In addition to some sixty articles in *The Month,* to which he contributed from 1870 to 1930, he wrote a number of pamphlets and no less than some thirty books. After a short illness he died on December 18th, 1932 and was buried at Pantasaph near Father John Rickaby, his brother and fellow-Jesuit.

Among his works are: *Moral Philosophy* (1890); *Aquinas Ethicus;* or *The Moral Teaching of St. Thomas* (with notes. 2 Vols.) (1892); *Of God and His Creatures* (1905); *Political and Moral Essays* (1902); *Free Will and Four English Philosophers: Hobbes, Locke, Hume, & Mill* (1906); *Waters That Go Softly; or Thoughts for Time of Retreat; Notes on St. Paul; Corinthians, Galatians, Romans* (1898); *The Lord My Light* (1915); *Ye Are Christ's: 84 Considerations for Boys* (1903); *Four Square, or The Cardinal Virtues: Addresses to Young Men* (1908); *Further Notes on St. Paul: Ephesians, Philippians, Colossians, Philemon* (1911); *Old Man's Jottings* (1924).   E. F. S.

Right Reverend (Andrew) Romanus Rios, O.S.B. 1891–

Abbot (Andrew) Romanus Rios was born at Corella, in Spanish Navarre, in April 1891. In 1903 he entered the Benedictine Priory of El Miracle in Spanish Catalonia, near Montserrat, as an aspirant for the Benedictine Abbey Nullius of New Norcia in Western Australia. After completing his humanistic studies at El Miracle in 1907, he was sent to the Abbey of San Giuliano d'Albaro at Genoa for his year of novitiate. On the same day that he made his monastic profession, October 29, 1908, he left for St. Anselm's College, the international Benedictine college in Rome, where he spent the next five years studying philosophy and theology and obtaining the licentiate in the latter. In October 1913 he arrived at New Norcia where he was ordained priest in September 1914. From 1915 to 1917 he was professor of Biblical Exegesis, Hebrew and Greek in the Australian seminary of St. Patrick's, Manly, near Sydney. On his return to New Norcia he was appointed prior and vicar-general of the Abbey Nullius, working at the same time as pastor of several stations, and as professor of theology and Scripture for the clerics in the monastery. He held these offices until his election as conventual prior of El Pueyo in Spain in May 1925.

As prior of El Pueyo, Dom Romanus had under his care a group of some fifty students who were being prepared for the Abbeys of New Norcia and Manila, as well as for the community of El Pueyo itself. He took an important share in their humanistic training and at the same time superintended the rebuilding of the priory, which had fallen into a state of dilapidation. This was no easy task as the monastery was, and still is, exceedingly poor.

With the establishment of the new Republican regime in Spain in April 1931, the prior found himself, along with most other religious superiors, in a very difficult position. As a consequence of the strain, his health broke down, and realizing that he could not work any longer for the welfare of the priory, he resigned and obtained permission from his Benedictine superiors to transfer his stability to Ramsgate in England, where, without the burden of responsibility, he could still help the community in teaching and preaching.

Two years after his departure for England (April 1934) the Catholic Church in Spain was the victim of a bloody persecution. The monastery of El Pueyo, being situated close to Catalonia, between Barbastro and Huesca, suffered more than any other Benedictine house in Spain. No less than nineteen of the community, most of them quite young, were martyred for Christ at Barbastro, during the months of July and August 1936. Abbot Rios has described their death in his book, *Benedictines of Today*.

The other publications of Abbot Rios may be conveniently divided into three groups: Latin, English and Spanish. In Latin: *Beda Noster Est* (1935), a dramatic play in honor of the centenary of his death; *Corona Sanctorum Anni Benedictini* (1948), a Benedictine menology; and a great number of Latin poems, in several Australian, Spanish and English reviews, from 1920 to 1950. In English: *A Heroine of the Mission Field*, Mother Mary of the Heart of Jesus, Foundress of the Institute of Our Lady of the Missions (1944). A German translation of his book, *Benedictines of Today* has been published, and it is being translated also into French, Italian, Spanish and Dutch. In addition to the above a very large number of articles and historical studies have been published by Dom Rios in various English, Australian and American reviews. In England he has contributed in recent years to several periodicals, especially monthly articles on liturgical studies to the *Clergy Review* (1944 and 1945). In Spanish: *Canciones y Leyendas Monásticas* (1926); *Florecillas Bíblicas del Año Litúrgico* (1927); *El Libro de la Cautividad* (1928); *Historia de New Norcia* (1930); *Historia del Monasterio del Pueyo* (1930); *Con flores a María* (1931); *El Cantar de los Cantares* (1933); *Cluny* (1934), and others. From 1925 to 1934, Dom Rios was also the founder and editor of the *Boletin de Información Benedictina*.

In November, 1947, Dom Rios was elected Abbot Visitor of the English Province of the Congregation of Subiaco. In 1946, he was granted by the Abbot General of his congregation the diploma in theology which is equivalent to the doctorate.   M. A. H.

Reverend Francis J. Ripley, C.M.S.
1912–

"If you think I have any zeal for souls," says Father Francis J. Ripley, "give credit for it to two people, my father and Mr. Frank Duff, the founder of the Legion of Mary." When they married, the future priest's parents were both officials of what would now be called associations of Catholic Action in the parish of Windleshaw, St. Helens, Lancashire, England. The district has long been famous for the sterling faith of its Lancashire yeomanry, who defied the persecutors during the darkest penal days. In 1912 Francis Ripley was born, and he began to grow from babyhood to childhood in a thoroughly Catholic atmosphere, his father being a national vice-president of the Catholic Young Men's Society. Tragedy came in 1916 when Mrs. Ripley died suddenly, leaving behind her three children, of whom Francis was the eldest. Her place was taken by her husband's two sisters, who continued to maintain the home in the same spirit of Catholic fervor. Having matriculated with honors at the local Catholic grammar school, under the Christian Brothers, Francis decided to enter the novitiate of the Society of Jesus, and was admitted at Manresa House, Roehampton, London. Although supremely happy there he was dogged by ill health. In spite of every care and several months at home, this did not improve and eventually an eminent London specialist gave his considered opinion that young Mr. Ripley would never be able to complete the studies necessary for the priesthood. He returned home, after making the complete Spiritual Exercises.

Several months elapsed before he applied for admission to the Capuchin Order and was allowed to enter the noviceship at the lovely friary of Pantasaph, North Wales. He completed the period of probation and studied philosophy for three years with distinction at Olton, Birmingham; but at the end of this time he and his superiors agreed that he would be more suited to the life of the secular priest. Having thus proved his ability to study, he was admitted to the Liverpool archdiocesan seminary at Upholland in 1935 and for three years in succession carried off the first prize in dogmatic theology. In June 1939, he was ordained a priest and immediately appointed to Rome for a postgraduate course in moral theology and canon law at the Gregorian University. World events intervened with the outbreak of war, and Father Ripley found himself appointed as curate to St. Cecilia's parish, Liverpool. During the five years he labored there, he was encouraged and helped by the grand example of Father John Casey, one of the most saintly and zealous of priests. In September 1940, a bomb fell within six yards of Father Ripley, but failed to explode. That was just one incident of many experiences during the severe German air attacks. In spite of war-time conditions, the young priest found an outlet for his zeal for the conversion of those outside the Church. Already, even as a student, he had become a well-known figure on the outdoor platforms of the Catholic Evidence Guild; now he continued that work and extended it. Apart from courses of sermons in the church, he lectured at the Liverpool Catholic Action College and taught Catholic social principles to the boys at St. Edward's College.

It was during this period that he was able to increase his contact with the Legion of Mary and to form a close personal friendship with its saintly founder, Mr. Frank Duff, which has been one of the major formative influences in his priestly character. He was now a regular contributor to the leading Catholic journals of the country and in 1944 published his first booklet, the now famous "A Blue-print for Lay Action." This was followed, at Mr. Duff's instigation, by "Calling All Apostles" and "A Plan of Campaign."

In 1944 Father Ripley offered his services as a military chaplain and enlisted in the Royal Air Force with the rank of Squadron Leader. Here he gained valuable experience, and as a result, wrote two small books on marriage, "Letters to Muriel" and "Letters to Molly," both of which have since sold over 10,000 copies. He was immediately co-opted as a lecturer on the famous Moral Leadership Courses, founded by the late Monsignor Beauchamp, a work he continued until the end of 1950. As a result of these courses, *Flarepath*, the Catholic magazine of the R.A.F., came into being and Father Ripley was appointed its editor, a post he held until his return to civilian life in 1947. In its last number, Father Ripley wrote an article entitled "This is Stalin," which aroused the ire of the Communists to such an extent that their then member of Parliament, Phil Piratin, raised the matter in the House of Commons.

It was during his days in the Air Force that Father Ripley completed two other works, the first an account of the history and work of the Legion of Mary, entitled "Terrible As An Army," and the second, a major work, "Souls at Stake." The latter consists of several chapters by Father Ripley himself, together with others he edited and adapted from speeches and articles by Mr. Frank Duff, who assumed the pen name of F. S. Mitchell. These latter form the major part of the work, which has now become a standard volume on Catholic Action.

Anxious to widen his experience, our author spent his leave before returning to Liverpool, in attending the great Marian Congress at Ottawa and in visiting many centers in the United States, from New York to California, lecturing under the auspices of the Legion of Mary. He also stayed for some time with his relative, Dean Hugh Stott Taylor, F.R.S.E., Chairman of the Department of Chemistry, Princeton University.

Early in 1948 Father Ripley was appointed to St. Gerard's parish, Liverpool, as senior curate. In addition to his labors for the good people of this poor dockside area, he began a series of twice-weekly talks for non-Catholics, under the auspices of the Legion of Mary, at the Cenacle Convent. Apart from bringing in over a hundred converts in three years, these enquiry classes set a headline for the rest of the country and in a fairly short time similar ventures had been undertaken in many other places, with the result that this is now an established method of winning converts. After he had repeated the entire course several times and in response to many requests, Father Ripley published his talks under the title, *This is the Faith*, with a preface by his own archbishop. While working at St. Gerard's he also published a smaller work on the spirit of the Legion of Mary, called *Holiness Through Mary*, which has already gone into a second edition.

Apart from his primary interest in the re-conversion of his country, Father Ripley is a capable organist and a competent exponent of the liturgical music of the Church. He is a lover of the beauties of nature and a keen photographer. During 1949 and 1950 he undertook two tours into the Hebrides and the Highlands of Scotland on behalf of his beloved Legion of Mary. At the beginning of 1951 he joined the Catholic Missionary Society, an association of secular priests specially chosen for the task of preaching the Faith to non-Catholics and specializing on the establishment of enquiry classes as a result of their "missions" and courses of lectures.

Henry Morton Robinson   1898–

Poems, short stories, essays, histories, magazine articles and novels have flowed from the pen of Henry Morton Robinson.

Born in Boston, Massachusetts on September 7, 1898, the son of Henry Morton and Ellen (Flynn) Robinson, he was educated in the public schools of Malden, Massachusetts. Shortly after he was graduated from Malden High School he enlisted in the navy and served on the U.S.S. Aylwin, and rifle ranges during World War I. Most of these twenty-two months in uniform were spent "vainly searching our Atlantic Coast for German submarines." He was honorably discharged as a gunner's mate, Third Class.

In 1919 he matriculated at Columbia College and soon distinguished himself in poetry. He became editor of *Varsity*, the campus literary magazine, and president of Philolexian, the debating society founded by Alexander Hamilton. In 1923, his senior year at Columbia, he published his first volume of poetry, under the title *Children of Morningside*.

Upon receiving the A.B. degree in 1923 he was awarded the Phi Beta Kappa Key and the Moncrieff Proudfit Fellowship in Letters for 1923–24. The following year he earned his A.M. degree, and for his thesis on the poetry of Alan Seeger he was given the James S. O'Neal Poetry Prize.

From 1924 to 1926 while acting as instructor in English at Columbia, he published three volumes of verse, and contributed, at the same time, to the now defunct *Century*, *Bookman* and *North American Review*.

On October 18, 1926 he married Gertrude Ludwig. They have three children. They have lived for the last twenty-two years at Woodstock, New York.

From 1925 to 1927, he was editor of *Contemporary Verse* and then became a free lance writer until 1935. For the following five years he was associate editor of *Reader's Digest* and senior editor of the same publication from 1942 to 1945. He is now a roving editor.

Mr. Robinson rises at dawn and is in his studio to start work at 8.30 A.M. According to a booklet sent out by his publisher, Simon and Schuster, "he works in a square, long-windowed room heated in winter by a woodburning drum stove. There are no pictures on his walls to distract him; his worktable is flat and cluttered; his chair, hard and straight. He writes on a portable typewriter and his paper is the traditional 'yellow seconds.' Standard equipment for the day's work includes several pipes, a canister of 'Three Nuns' tobacco, a thermos bottle of coffee, and a bar of chocolate."

He considers *Fantastic Interim*, a history of the United States between the wars, his best non-fiction work. His first novel *The Perfect Round* was published in 1945.

In 1950 appeared his novel, *The Cardinal*. Writing in *Cosmopolitan* he says, "I wrote *The Cardinal* out of sheer biologic necessity. If pen and ink hadn't been available, I'd have scratched the story on the bark of trees, on rocks, or the parchment of my own skin." This story about a young priest advanced to the cardinalate took three years to write. Although Robinson himself never aspired to the priesthood, he was impressed "with certain shining exemplars of priestliness and became determined to sing the praises of priests in a novel. . . . "The courses in scholastic philosophy I attended (and later gave) at Columbia University," he writes in *Cosmopolitan*, "familiarized me with the thinking of Catholic theologians, Dante, Augustine, Theresa, and Bernard of Clairvaux — to mention only a few of the greatest mystics — charged me with their intensely spiritual voltage. Added to these were a lifelong interest in the details of ritual ('poetry addressed to the eye') and a deepening sense of the profound symbolism underlying the Mass. Imperfect and partial though my knowledge was, I made it serve me as a writer." He adds: "I shall probably never write about the Catholic Church again. . . . I am not a propagandist or a proselytizer — but merely a writer. My vocation is not with the *Word* but with words."

His other books include: *John Erskine, A Modern Acteon* (1928); *Buck Fever* (1929); *Stout Cortex* (1931); *Science vs. Crime* (1935); *Second Wisdom* (1936); *Public Virtue, Private Good* (1937); *"D.W."* (1940); *A Skeleton Key to Finnegan's Wake* (1944) (with Joseph Campbell); *The Great Snow* (1947); *The Enchanted Grindstone* (1952). M. A. H.

Reverend Aloysius Roche 1886–

Described as "a writer who has the gift of making saints fascinating," Father Aloysius Roche has published twenty-one other interesting books besides his five on the Blessed in Heaven.

Born in Dundee, Scotland, in 1886, Aloysius was the youngest of ten sons. His father, Edward Roche, a native of Tullamore, King's County, had to leave Ireland in the "bad" times and settled in Dundee, Scotland. His mother Elizabeth (Richards) Roche is a native of Shropshire, England. Besides the ten sons, Aloysius' parents had six daughters. Four of the sons became priests.

Aloysius did his preparatory studies at the parish school of St. Mary's, Lochee, Dundee and his higher studies at St. Mary's Monastery, Kinnoul, Perth, from 1908 to 1914. He continued his education at the Redemptorist House of Studies in Perth, Scotland. In 1917 he became affiliated with the Diocese of Brentwood as a secular priest, and has been parish priest of Billericay, Essex, England since 1918.

During the early years of his priestly life, much of his time was spent giving retreats to children and these retreats "led to my first excursion into the field of literature with a book of instruction entitled *Talks for Girls* (1932)." Since then he has published twenty-six books, half of which developed out of sermons and lectures delivered mainly in the churches of London. He writes: "I possess no literary gifts or propensities. Whatever success I have achieved with books has been derived from my experience in the pulpit. My own partiality is for works addressed to young readers while my best work is undoubtedly the one I hope to write someday."

Father Roche is the author of *Practical Hints on Preaching* (1933); *Sermon Matter for the Year* (1934); *A Bedside Book of Saints* (1934); *The Light of Other Days* (1935); *Apologetics for the Pulpit* (3 vols.) (1935–1936); *The Splendor of the Saints* (1936); *Talks for Young Women* (1938); *Fear and Religion* (1938); *Religion and Life* (1938); *The Boyhood of a Priest* (1938); *Is it all True?* (1938); *These Animals of Ours* (1939); *A Night of Adventure* (1940); *The Things That Matter* (1941); *Knots and Crosses* (1942); *A Bedside Book of Irish Saints* (1942); *The First Monks and Nuns* (1943); *All Aboard the Centurion* (1945); *Between Ourselves* (1945); *A Bedside Book of English Saints* (2 vols.) (1948); *Under the Rainbow* (1950); *Mystery Man, or The Catholic Priest Explained* (1950).

M. A. H.

Very Reverend Theodore Roemer, O.F.M.Cap. 1889–

Father Theodore Roemer acquired his interest in the study of American Church history from the late Monsignor Peter Guilday, his major professor at the Catholic University of America. After twenty years of research and writing in various fields of this subject, this interest has found its culmination in the publication of *The Catholic Church in the United States*, a textbook for seminaries and colleges.

Father Theodore (baptized Edward) was born January 19, 1889, at Appleton, Wisconsin. His parents were Henry and Frances (Quick) Roemer. After the elementary courses in the local parish school of St. Joseph, he started his preparation for the priesthood at St. Lawrence College, which is a minor seminary conducted since 1860 by the Capuchin Fathers at Mount Calvary, Wisconsin. Upon completion of this course he entered the Capuchin Order, July 14, 1906, in Detroit, Michigan. After one year he pronounced the simple vows, and after three more years the solemn perpetual vows. He pursued the courses in philosophy and theology at the Capuchin clericates (seminaries) in Milwaukee, Wisconsin. He was ordained to the holy priesthood, July

13, 1913, in the Church of St. Francis of Assisi, Milwaukee, by the late Most Reverend Sebastian G. Messmer.

Although he saw intermittent parochial service in various parishes, Father Theodore's principal field of labor has been in the educational sphere since 1915, when he was sent to teach at St. Lawrence College, Mount Calvary, Wisconsin. In those days the preparation for the priesthood was considered a sufficient foundation for teaching in a minor seminary. As time went on, he began to realize the necessity of a firmer footing in history, his principal branch. With the permission of his superiors he entered the Catholic University of America in 1930 to study under Dr. Peter Guilday. Under his guidance, he soon became convinced of the possibilities and the necessity of research in the field of the mission-aid societies. The consequent dissertation, *The Leopoldine Foundation and the Church in the United States (1829–1839)*, earned for him the degree of master of arts.

Dr. Guilday advised him to continue his studies at the Catholic University of Louvain, Belgium, which is known for its historical studies. During this year, his views on the European background were broadened, but he also discovered an unexplored treasure trove of mission history pertaining to the United States in the archives of the Ludwig-Missionsverein at Munich, Bavaria. Upon returning to the Catholic University of America he used this archival material for the dissertation, *The Ludwig-Missionsverein and the Church in the United States (1838–1918)*. It procured for him the degree of doctor of philosophy, and also filled him with the desire to make the charity of the French, Austrian, and Bavarian mission-aid societies better known. This was partly accomplished in the publication of *Pioneer Capuchin Letters* (1936), and *Ten Decades of Alms* (1942).

Upon returning to Mount Calvary in 1933, Father Theodore was plunged into a very full schedule of history classes. Yet he found time to write articles for Catholic periodicals on his European experiences and on the mission-aid societies. These endeavors were greatly hampered during the three years (1936–39), in which he was occupied as the guardian of the friary at Mount Calvary and as a provincial definitor. Relieved of these duties, he set about collecting material on the large amount of alms that had been sent to America by the Society for the Propagation of the Faith, the Ludwig-Missionsverein and the Leopoldinen-Stiftung. In the midst of this work he was stricken with a cerebral hemorrhage, which kept him confined to the hospital for almost five months. Doctors ascribed his recovery to prayer. As soon as he had recovered sufficiently he returned to his writing desk by collaborating with Father Louis Biersack, O.F.M.Cap., in the publication of *The Saints and Blessed of the Third Order of St. Francis*. He next set about writing the history of his home parish, which resulted in the three-hundred page book, *Saint Joseph in Appleton*. Sensing the necessity of a textbook for his classes, he amplified his lectures into *The Catholic Church in the United States* (1950), the only available textbook on the subject for seminaries and colleges.

In consequence of his interest in the educational problems of his Order, Father Theodore has been the chairman of the Scholastic Council of the Province of St. Joseph of the Capuchin Order in the United States since its foundation in 1943, and has been instrumental in having the educational institutions of the province affiliated with the Catholic University of America. He has taken part in the sessions of the minor seminary section of the National Catholic Educational Association. Since 1934 he has been an active member of the executive board of the Franciscan Educational Conference and since 1941 has been an associate editor of *Franciscan Studies*. During the year 1942 he was the second vice-president of the American Catholic Historical Association. He is also a member of the Wisconsin Historical Society, and is one of the charter members and a director of the Fond du Lac County Historical Society, a branch of the state society. In 1949 he was accorded corresponding membership in the Academy of American Franciscan History. In 1950 he was received into the Gallery of Living Catholic Authors. He is the present editor of *The Alumni News*, the official organ of the St. Lawrence College Alumni Association.

Heinrich A. Rommen 1897–

For two clearly written, timely books, Heinrich A. Rommen is particularly known. They are *The State in Catholic Thought* (1945) and *The Natural Law* (1947).

Heinrich Rommen was born on February 21, 1897 in Cologne, Germany. He studied at the Universities of Münster, (Dr. rer. pol.), Munich, Bonn (Dr. jur. ubr.) from 1920 to 1929.

He was a member of the Centralstelle des Volks-Verein, M'Gladbach and Director of summer courses in Economics and Politics at Brandts-Hitze Haus M'Gladbach, for the Adult Education Center. He was founder and secretary of the Institute for Social and Economic Order up to the dissolution of the Volks-Verein by the Gestapo in 1933. Then until 1938 he was a free lance writer and worked in the legal department of a Berlin corporation.

In 1938, with the help of the Episcopal Committee for Catholic Refugees, he came to the United States to teach economics at St. Joseph's College in West Hartford, Connecticut. Since 1946, he is professor of political science and political philosophy at the College of St. Thomas in St. Paul, Minnesota. He received a LL.D. (honoris causa) from Boston College in 1950.

On October 8, 1929 he married Martha Tolksdorf. They have three children.

His first important book, on Suarez, was the effect of the attacks of conservative Catholics and writers "against popular sovereignty and the theory of political revolution, the constant confusion of the latter with Rousseau, practiced by these conservatives against the modern democratic constitution, especially against the Weimar Constitution."

Der Staat (1935), a political philosophy book, and *Die Ewige Wieder-kehr des Naturrechts*, on natural law, were written against the Nazi philosophy and its "abuse of venerable terms for their propaganda purposes. These attacks had to be worded carefully and often camou-flaged by using the 'Red' form of totalitarianism as examples. Many letters from readers proved that they understood quite well whose doctrines were meant."

Dr. Rommen's other publications are: *Die Kirche und ihr Recht* (1930), (a small volume against an all too spiritual conception of the Church by contemporary German writers and those in the Youth Move-ment); *Grundrechte Gesetz und Richter in U.S.A. und anderen Common Law Ländern* (1931); *Die Staatslehre des Franz Suarez* (1927) (Spanish trans-lation, 1951); *Der Staat in der katholischen Gedankwelt* (1935). *Die Ewige Wiederkehr der Naturrechts* appeared also in French translation.

Dr. Rommen has contributed articles to *Hochland, Der Katholische Gedanke, Soziale Kultur, Review of Politics, Notre Dame Lawyer, Pen-samiento* (Madrid) and *Nova et Vetera* (Fribourg). His main interests are social, political and legal philosophy; history of ideas, and the relations between philosophy and politics and economics.   M. A. H.

Very Reverend Myles V. Ronan
1877–

An American correspondent who recently "cov-ered" Dublin reported with exclamations of wonder that "from the very first, Dubliners impress the visitor with their vigor, their enter-prise, energy, humor and initiative." This led at least one reader to regret that the cor-respondent did not meet the Very Reverend Myles V. Ronan, P.P., D.Litt., M.R.I.A., F.R. Hist. S., who embodies all these characteristics.

Father Ronan is pastor of St. Michan's parish, named from the Welsh cleric who went to Ireland toward the end of the fifth century, and set up a religious hostel at the very ford from which Dublin received its early name, Ath Cliath, or Ford of the Hurdles. The modern St. Michan's parish goes to the northern bank of the River Liffey which the ancient ford traversed. When Father Ronan was assigned to the post in 1941 he was peculiarly qualified for it. He was born in 1877, the son of Myles and Margaret Ronan of Dublin. He was educated at the O'Connell Schools and Clonliffe College, Dublin, and at Propaganda College, Rome, where he was ordained in 1900. From 1901 to 1903 he was curate at Rathdrum, Co. Wicklow, and then after a year at St. Michan's he went to the Pro-Cathedral. In 1906 he was secretary to the Most Reverend W. J. Walsh, Archbishop of Dublin, and remained curate of the Pro-Cathedral until 1922 when he became curate at St.

Michael's, Dun Laoghaire, where he remained for twenty years till given St. Michan's parish.

The list of his honors indicates the acuteness of his intelligence: winner of scholarships under the Intermediate Education Board (Ireland), 1892–93; first place and medallist in dogmatic theology and Gregorian chant, Propaganda University, Rome, 1899; licentiate of theology, Rome, 1899; member of Royal Irish Academy; vice-president of Royal Society of Antiquaries, Ireland; vice-president of Academy of Christian Art, Dublin; fellow of the Royal Historical Society, London; member of the Historical and Heraldic Society of France; trustee of the National Library of Ireland; Honorable Treasurer of the Leinster College of Irish (1910–1951), and honorary D.Litt. of the National University of Ireland.

His major publications include: *The Reformation in Dublin 1536–58* (1926); *The Reformation in Ireland 1558–80* (1930); *St. Anne, Her Cult and Her Shrines* (1927); *Irish Martyrs of the Penal Laws* (1935); *'98 in Wicklow* (1938); *Erasmus Smith Endowment* (1937); *An Apostle of Catholic Dublin* (1944), a life of Father Henry Young, (1787–1869), a curate in 1814 at St. Michan's; and many contributions to such scholarly publications as the *Transactions of the Royal Irish Academy*, *The Journal of the Royal Society of Antiquaries*, Ireland, *Archivum Hibernicum* of Maynooth College, the *Journal of the Academy of Christian Art* (of which he was editor) and the *Irish Ecclesiastical Record*. He has also written many pamplets for the Catholic Truth Society, Dublin, and *Messenger of the Sacred Heart*, and has contributed articles ("European Civilization"), to *Encyclopedia Britannica* (1934), and *Dublin Historical Record*, and an article on "Irish Schools and Schoolmen of the Middle Ages" for the *Encyclopedia Americana* (1951).

With his profound scholarship, Father Ronan combines a zest for research and unfailing wonderment and delight at every new contribution to human knowledge which keep him from falling into the category of dusty antiquarian. The possessor of many rare manuscripts, he is most generous in making them available to others, and besides numbers of his own countrymen, many Americans who have gone to Ireland to do research have been given the benefit of his advice, his superb library, and his cordial and inspiring friendship.

Since going to St. Michan's he has recovered and identified some precious relics belonging to the old church which had become mislaid through the centuries. One is an ivory crucifix of 17th Century French art, brought to Ireland by a predecessor 250 years ago. It goes almost without saying that he has written a brief but comprehensive history of his parish, which was published in 1948. In 1904, when a curate in St. Michan's, he wrote for the *Irish Rosary* a series of articles on the history of St. Michan's parish, which was the beginning of his literary career. At his Golden Jubilee in 1950 his parishioners gave him, among other things, a promise to pay for the redecoration of his beautiful old church (1817) which is currently engaging part of his energies. The people supply him with 30 pounds weekly until the cost is paid off. Another occupation is a booklet dealing with the James II period, and the bid of an Irish bishop, Dr. O'Mollony of Killaloe, for an Irish republic against the pretensions of the king. It is chiefly based on a manuscript collection of James II's secretary, Lord Melfort, which Father Ronan discovered in the British Museum in 1939 and copied *in extenso*. Father Ronan hopes to publish in the near future at least the MS. portion of Melfort's correspondence. He has recently published in the *Irish Ecclesiastical Record* an article on George Browne, Henry VIII's first Protestant Archbishop of Dublin, containing Cardinal Pole's absolution of Browne (Municipal Archives, Douai, France), which he copied among other absolutions of Irish bishops by the Cardinal Delegate. The most interesting point is that Elizabeth deprived him of his canonry in St. Patrick's Cathedral, and that he remained steadfast and died a Catholic and was buried a Catholic near the Barnewall House at Turvey Donabate, North, Co. Dublin. So, Henry VIII's first archbishop of Dublin, an English Augustinian, went down into Irish soil a confirmed papist. Until Father Ronan discovered in Cardinal Pole's Registers this absolution of George Browne, and found in the register of St. Patrick's Cathedral that he was deprived of his canonry by Elizabeth, no historian had been able to throw any light on what became of Browne in the end of his days on earth.

Another interesting article of Father Ronan's, on the "Catholic Schools in Old Dublin," from the Anglo-Norman Invasion (1170) up to the Emancipation (1829), was published in the August number of the *Dublin Historical Record* (1951).

All these activities are of only secondary importance to the direction of a parish numbering twelve thousand souls.   H. L.

Reverend Henry Edward George Rope   1880–

Father Henry Rope was born in Shrewsbury on October 23, 1880. His father, Henry John Rope, Fellow of the Royal College of Surgeons, was a doctor, as was also his mother's father. His parents were intensely devout Christians with a horror of compromise. From childhood, Henry Rope was surrounded by Catholic influences. "The heroic Christian consistency of my parents," writes Father Rope, "was of Catholic origin. My father's watchword was that one must follow one's conscience at all costs; he died in 1899 in unshaken belief in the Church of England. My mother's mind and outlook were Catholic and she was received into the Church in January 1901. In childhood she taught us to love and venerate St. Thomas More. Her eldest sister, soon followed by two others, had become a Catholic about 1883, and gave me my first lessons in ancient history, chiefly in 1887–89. Under God I came to the Faith through the prayers of my mother, which I do not hesitate to compare with those of St. Monica in agony for the salvation of her unbelieving son. My mother died a saintly death on December 10, 1948." Father Rope, her son, had come into the Catholic Church in 1907.

Father Rope adds: "There were other influences to help me. Our old home was probably within the old precincts of the Collegiate Church of St. Mary, our later one certainly within those of the Austin Friars, Shrewsbury. St. Mary's is one of the most beautiful old churches in England and was enriched with old glass, mostly from the Continent. I well remember, in later childhood, a vague yet real sense of something, I knew not what, lacking in this church, something that had been there before, haunting it like half-forgotten music. I gladly bear witness to the goodness and sincerity of the Anglican clergy, whom I knew, but they could not help me in my difficulties and I dwelt rather upon Christianity than the Church of England, in which I had lost all real confidence before I was fully aware of it, about the age of seventeen. I did not understand the Anglican Eucharistic teaching and concluded it was a sin against Faith to search into it. The Catholic Church seemed remote as the Middle Ages, but I never doubted that England had been as 'Roman Catholic' as France or Spain before the Reformation, about which I knew little enough. I took it for granted that the change must have been justified, but never could doubt that it was a great change.

"Just about this time a wicked book, Kingsley's *Westward Ho*, turned my hazy, but not invincible, prejudice into anti-Catholic bigotry. To this was added my first meeting with unbelievers at Oxford. I began to read Huxley's antichristian sophistry and the like. Youthful pride and the wish to escape from the pricks of conscience undermined what religion I had left. Agnosticism *sounded* intellectual, but in my case, and, I am convinced in most others, spelt intellectual laziness and inflated self-conceit. Any lingering belief in the Anglican Church was shattered when I saw it complacently following, instead of trying to lead, public opinion, in the Boer War, in which my convictions were those of Chesterton. I remember flippantly referring to the Church of England at the time as 'military on earth and rather dubiously triumphant in heaven,' but it is only fair to add that too many Catholics in wartime are content to be guided not by the Holy See but by very secular and interested *propaganda*. It is strange that Kingsley harmed me so deeply, for I was utterly disgusted with his jingo hero, Sir Richard Grenville, who never appeared without thanking God that he was not as other men or even as these Spaniards and papists. Again, while I dreaded the notion of her success, I saw that the Catholic Church had every right to strive to recover her lost position in England. The Catholic confessional called up Browning's slanderous poem, but the Anglican claim to hear confessions made me angry, this new assumption of a monstrous authority. I knew that the Catholic claim, terrible as it was in my imagination, was *not* new and was accepted by the Catholic body.

"Meanwhile there were happier influences. My love of the old churches grew. I loved the Middle Ages, and somehow the Mass was a part of them. I read Ruskin eagerly, who proved an antidote to Kingsley, and gradually convinced me that the true heritage of Christian civilization was a Catholic one. From him, I passed on to the reading of

Newman. I also met Catholics at Oxford (and elsewhere) including some Jesuit students who disconcerted me by being the very opposite of my Kingsleyan notions of a Jesuit, frank, manly, open-hearted, healthy Englishmen, all of them. Then there were first experiences of Catholic countries, Freiburg in Breisgau in 1900 and a corner of Brittany in 1901. But above all and through all there were the constant unconquerable persistent prayers of a saintly mother, now I believe, a special friend of St. Monica in heaven."

Henry Rope was educated at Shrewsbury School from 1894 to 1898 and at Christ Church, Oxford, from 1898 to 1902, taking second class honors in English. From 1903 to 1905 he was on the staff of the Oxford English Dictionary, under Sir James Murray, and again from 1908 to 1910, under Dr. (later Sir William) Craigie. From October 1905 to July 1907 he was lector in English at Breslau University in Silesia. On Epiphany, 1907, he was received into the Catholic Church.

He tried out his vocation with the Benedictines at Erdington, Birmingham, 1910–11, and then entered in 1911 the Beda College in Rome. He was ordained at the Lateran in February 1915, and served missions at St. Werburgh's, Chester, Ellesmere Port, Crewe, Plowden, Market Drayton, and Mawley in the See of Shrewsbury from 1915 to 1937. In October, 1937, he became archivist to the English College, Rome. During World War II he was a convent chaplain in England. In 1945 he rejoined the English College and returned to Rome in October, 1946.

Since 1907 he has been an occasional contributor to various periodicals, mostly Catholic, and editor of the *Catholic Review* from 1917–1918 and the *Ransomer* from 1932–1934.

He has published four small volumes of poems between 1916 and 1926: *Religionis Ancilla* (1916), *Saul's Belfry* (1919), *The City of the Grail* (1921), and *The Hills of Home* (1926).

His works in prose are: *Fisher and More* (1935); *Pugin* (1935); *Matthew Parker's Witness against Continuity* (1931); *Forgotten England* (1932); *Benedict XV* (1940), besides editing *Flee to the Fields* (1934); also a few pamphlets and prefaces.   M. A. H.

Agnes Edwards Rothery (Mrs. Harry Rogers Pratt)   1888–

Best known for her twenty-odd books of travel (which include half a dozen for young readers in a Roundabout series), Miss Rothery has written several novels, a play, essays and two autobiographical books.

Born in Brookline, Massachusetts, she is the daughter of John Jay Elmendorf and Rosamond Dale (Pentecost) Rothery. In 1909 she was graduated A.B. from Wellesley and in 1912 took a special course at Radcliffe. Five years later

Agnes Edwards Rothery (Mrs. Harry Rogers Pratt)   494

(September 24, 1917) she married Harry Rogers Pratt, associate professor of music and dramatic art since 1927 at the University of Virginia. Both are converts from the Episcopalian Church.

Her literary career began in 1909 with the *Ladies' Home Journal*, where she was engaged in editorial work. Then she became editor of the woman's page on the Boston *Herald* and later was appointed literary editor of the same paper. She contributed many popular essays under the title "Agnes Edwards' Morning Talks." She was also a contributing editor to *Youth's Companion* and the *House Beautiful*, of which she later became Travel Editor.

Her travel books are unlike the usual books in the category since they are neither a rambling chronicle of personal anecdotes nor a mere compilation of facts. They are never written in the first person, as her purpose has been to give the reader information about the country rather than about herself. She has imparted information she would have liked to have been told before visiting a new country. The books are excellently constructed, having a beginning, middle and end, and they progress not only geographically and historically but also thematically. For this reason they have been very popular over a long period. Some of them have been reprinted in England and translated into French. They are in all public libraries and many of them are used as supplementary reading in schools and colleges.

During World War II she was commissioned by the United States Army to write booklets on Norway and Denmark. These were distributed to the armed forces in those countries. The King of Denmark gave her a decoration for the booklet on that country.

In 1937 the Association of American Publishers donated two hundred books to the White House Library as a nucleus for a permanent national library. She was the only author to have three books in this collection. The three books were on Denmark, Finland, and Sweden. In 1946 she published for children, grades five to eight, *Scandinavian Roundabout*. In two parts, one devoted to Norway, the other to Sweden, she tells of "Leif Ericson, of the Viking burial mounds of kings and queens, of Norwegian fishing and forestry, Swedish mines and match factories, the grandeur of the land of the glaciers beyond the Arctic Circle — and of the Swedish Christmas which is celebrated for a month." A review of the book in *Kirkus* (March 1, 1946, p. 128), states: "A wealth of delightful and curious material on Norway and Sweden."

For grades six to nine, she wrote, in 1947, *Maryland and Virginia Roundabout* in which she gives information about these two states, with emphasis on "history, places of historical interest, legend, and people of the past, industries, characteristic foods, and customs."

Her next two books were on Iceland, *Iceland, New World Outpost* (1948) and *Iceland Roundabout* (1948); in which are described the "physical features of the country, the government, the customs, the cities, arts and crafts," as well as the social, economic, and cultural history.

In 1949 she brought out a book of essays on gardening, *Joyful Gardener*. This book won for her from some reviewers the praise of being the most graceful living American essayist.

In 1950 appeared *Rome Today*, a series of essays on the Eternal City, suggesting to the reader what he might find to be interesting. A travel book on Italy for boys and girls, aged ten or older came out also in 1950, *Italian Roundabout*.

One of her autobiographical books, *The Fitting Habitation*, was re-issued in January 1951 in an enlarged and revised edition. The other autobiographical volume *Family Album* is still very popular.

Her latest book is *New York Today* (1951).

Most of the books of Agnes Rothery have been made possible because of her extensive traveling. Her husband, a professor at the University of Virginia, spends, with her, the three months of summer vacation visiting other countries and collaborates in furnishing the photographs for his wife's books.

For twenty-five years the Pratts have lived in Charlottesville, Virginia.   M. A. H.

Corinne Rocheleau Rouleau
(Mrs. Wilfrid Rouleau) 1881–

The large convent-school of the Sisters of Providence in Montreal, Canada, for deaf girls has influenced the life of Corinne Rocheleau Rouleau. There she spent her most fruitful years as a student. There she returned year after year to visit her old teachers, to build up her spiritual strength and get mental solace in their affection and understanding. There, after having served as normal instructor and lecturer and written much for the school, Mrs. Rouleau has lived since the death of her husband, in 1940, still busy doing research and publicity work for the deaf — an affliction she herself has endured so many years and largely conquered.

Corinne Evangeline Rocheleau was born in 1881 in Worcester, Massachusetts. In her ninth year, deafness developed and soon grew complete. For several years she attended various schools for children who had good hearing, but she could not follow the usual program. She then spent four years at the school for deaf girls conducted by the Sisters of Providence in Montreal, Canada, where, under the guidance of a saintly old priest, Canon Trépanier, wise in child psychology and the teaching of the deaf, which he had studied on two continents, young Corinne received private lessons from three nuns — one for French, one for English, and the third who taught her to regain her lost voice and to become an expert lip reader. Then she was sent for a year to a private school in Worcester (the Dalzell School, later merged with the Bancroft School). She also attended drawing lessons under Philip Hale at the Worcester Art Museum. Much later, there was a year of travel and study in Europe. And ever since, which is to say practically all her life, she has been an omniverous reader in two languages, and developed an appreciation for the finer things of life. "The thought that I do not have a college degree in crackling parchment to prove that I had been 'finished off' does not disturb me. It is consoling to know that I can go on studying and learning on my own," she says. Corinne Rocheleau, during her childhood, had also learned to play the piano. Her mother was a church organist in Worcester; two of Corinne's sisters were accomplished pianists and one of them an excellent violinist, and so Corinne, before losing her hearing, had also gained a knowledge and appreciation of good music. This, too, served to enrich her life, even though being deprived of the enjoyment of music has been, especially at first, a sore trial.

Corinne, while still in her teens, lost both her father and mother. Later, when an elder sister married, Corinne kept house for seven years for two younger sisters, still at school. When these sisters went on to higher studies, Corinne, after attending business college a few months, for a refresher course, presented herself for civil service examinations. She passed and was accepted as clerk in the research department of the Census Bureau, Washington, D. C., where she stayed two years. When the climate of Washington injured her health, she reluctantly resigned and returned to Worcester, Massachusetts. There her brother, H. Oscar Rocheleau, asked Corinne to run the office of one of several clothing stores, then owned by the Rocheleau family, which she did faithfully, but "without much enthusiasm," for seventeen years. Then in her forties, Miss Rocheleau went back to her convent school in Montreal for another refresher course — lessons in speech and voice culture, "since it is necessary for people totally deaf to give as much care as professional singers to such matters, for a good many years, if they are to acquire and retain a good speaking voice." This time she was advised by Bishop Deschamps, who had been for years Canon Trépanier's successor, and was then Auxiliary Bishop of Montreal. He directed her in research work on the subject of the education of the deaf and the deaf-blind, which had already led Miss Rocheleau to write a biographical study of Ludivine Lachance, a peculiarly difficult case. This book was written in French and published in 1928. The following year it was crowned by the French Academy. Many magazine articles, in English or French, have followed. Also lectures in various cities — Washington, New York, Philadelphia, Milwaukee, Montreal, etc., on educational or historical subjects.

In August, 1930, Miss Rocheleau was married in the cathedral of Montreal, to Mr. Wilfrid Rouleau, a retired chief examiner for French and Spanish work at the Government Printing Office, Washington, D. C., where they returned to live. "Those years in Washington," she says, "were the happiest of my life. The Capital's wonderful architectural beauty, its fragrance and flowery charm, the fabulous treasures of its libraries and museums were explored and enjoyed under the guidance of one who had watched them grow for nearly forty years."

Along with some housekeeping, she did considerable work as chairman of a committee of the Volta Bureau; made translations and did proofreading for the Department of the Interior and the Pan-American Union (now the Bureau of American Republics). She also contributed to magazines.

When Mr. Rouleau died in 1940, Mrs. Rouleau returned to "the one sure, quiet haven of by-gone years: my Montreal convent school, where the Sisters also maintain a sort of French-style 'pension' as an annex." Here she lives now, still busily at work on manuscripts of a forthcoming book, and frequent magazine and newspaper articles.

She has already published a novel, based on the peaceful and picturesque way of life led by the well-to-do French Canadian country folk just before the turn of the present century. Its title is *Laurentian Heritage* (Longmans, Green & Co., 1948). The preface erroneously states that it is a translation from the French. This work has been in use in high schools in Ontario and elsewhere as "recommended reading." As yet (1952) there is no French version of it. Her other books are: *Françaises D'Amerique* (1915), a series of short historical sketches; *Hors de sa Prison* (1927), the story of the rehabilitation of little Ludivine Lachance; *Those in the Dark Silence* (1930), in collaboration with Rebecca Mack, a volume primarily for teachers of the deaf and the blind. The last, or rather latest, of Mrs. Rouleau's published works (she intends to keep on working) is a reprint of a thirty-page article which appeared in the December 1950 number of *La Revue d'Histoire de l'Amérique Française*, a magazine sponsored by the University of Montreal. This long article, illustrated and re-issued in booklet form (August 1951), is being sent out by the Social Service department of Mrs. Rouleau's school. It gives a concise account of the education and care of the deaf, from remote times to the present. This booklet is under the distinguished patronage of the Most Reverend Paul Emile Leger, Archbishop of Montreal, and of the Honorable Omer Coté, treasurer of the Province of Quebec.   M. A. H.

Gabrielle Roy
(Mrs. Marcel Carbotte)

Born in St. Boniface, Manitoba, Canada, Gabrielle is the youngest child of Léon Roy and Mélina (Landry) Roy. She attended St. Joseph's Academy, now known as St. Joseph Collegiate Institute, under the direction of the Sisters of the Holy Names of Jesus and Mary. After graduating, she went to the Normal School in Winnipeg and then taught for some years at the academies of St. Joseph and Provencher — the latter is a school for boys, in St. Boniface. While teaching she became interested in dramatics and achieved fame as an actress. She played on several occasions with "Le Cercle Molière," a local troup of high repute throughout Canada. When she had twice taken part in the Canadian Drama Festival, she decided that acting was more interesting than teaching.

With the money she saved, she went to London in 1937 to study dramatics at the Guildhall School of Music and Drama. While in London, Miss Roy contributed articles on Canadian life to the French weekly, *Je Suis Partout*. After taking a walk along the Mediterranean, from Menton to the Spanish border she made up her mind to go back to Canada to try her hand at free lancing. Back in Montreal in 1939 she made her living writing stories and feature articles for the Canadian papers and magazines; she did articles on fishing in the Gaspe, boatbuilding on the lower St. Lawrence River, goldmining in Northern Quebec; she wrote about the Hutterites of Manitoba, the Doukhobors of Saskatchewan, and the Mennonites of Manitoba. She also wrote a series of stories on Canadian life for *Le Bulletin des Agriculteurs*, but each year she managed to spend two or three months on her first novel, *The Tin Flute*.

In recalling the beginnings of that novel she says: "I remember one stormy spring evening when I found myself for the first time in Saint-Henri Place, Montreal, street car bells clanked, a train was tearing full speed right in front of the big church; cars, trucks and people were held back by the railroad gates on either side of the square; the wind carried from below the narrow streets the melancholy whistle of a barge. The smoke from the locomotives hovered over the little wooden houses. Then, suddenly, throughout all this broke simultaneously the ringing of the bells from countless domes and steeples. As far as I can remember it was at this spot and on this wild evening of wind and tumult that the characters of *The Tin Flute* came to life."

It took Miss Roy three years to write the novel. It is a book she felt she had to do. Referring to that "one stormy spring evening," she says, "I saw a group of people who had suffered the worst effects of depression and unemployment and to whom war meant a way out, a better living, perhaps adventure, in any case a job." After finishing it, she says, "My trouble was to forget the characters I had described." She likes the character Daniel best in *The Tin Flute* "because he so wanted to have his coat finished so that he could go back to school."

The Tin Flute was first published in French, in June, 1945, under the title *Bonheur d'Occasion*. The first edition of 3,000 copies was followed by a new printing of 4,000 the next November. By February, 1947, 13,000 copies, an almost unheard of amount for a French language book in Canada, were in print. It won awards from the French Academy and the recently formed French-Canadian Academy.

After Mrs. Miriam Chapin, the sister of the late Curtice Hitchcock, read the story while on a trip to Canada she sent it immediately to her brother, who sent it to Hannah Josephson, the wife of Matthew Josephson, to translate. It was published by Reynal and Hitchcock in 1947. Under its American title, *The Tin Flute*, the Literary Guild of America chose it as its selection for May. It thus had a guaranteed minimum distribution of 625,000 copies. Universal-International Pictures bought the screen rights.

After her great success she became a member of the Royal Society of Canada — the first woman to become a member of the French section, and was awarded the le Prix Femina.

In 1951 she brought out a book about her native Manitoba, *Where Nests the Water Hen*. It is a story of the large Tousignant family living on a lonely island in the wastes of northern Manitoba.

Gabrielle Roy was married to Dr. Marcel Carbotte in St. Emile Church, St. Vital, Canada. After their marriage they went to Paris where Dr. Carbotte took a post-graduate course. They are now back in Canada.

Reverend Leslie Rumble, M.S.C.
1892–

The names Rumble and Carty, of Radio Replies Press, St. Paul, Minnesota, are known far and wide throughout America and overseas for their many publications explaining and defending the Catholic religion. The two names link America and Australia, Father Carty, of St. Paul, having established in that city his center for a nation-wide apostolate of Catholic literature; Father Rumble co-operating from far-off Sydney, Australia, by supplying a constant stream of books and pamphlets.

Leslie Rumble was born in Sydney, New South Wales, Australia, on August 24, 1892, and was duly christened in the Church of England, to which both his parents belonged. When he was but three years of age his parents moved to Perth, in Western Australia, at the other end of the continent. There he completed his primary studies in State schools, which were committed to a policy of "free, compulsory and secular" education, and which are contributing to a widespread driftage from religion amongst the Protestant section of the Australian people. Catholics in Australia have, from the very beginning, established and maintained their own system of Catholic primary and secondary schools, with a resultant fidelity to religion amongst the Catholic population, which is the envy of other churches.

Leslie Rumble himself drifted to almost complete irreligion in practice, but some years after leaving school and commencing work as a professional photographer he became a convert to the Catholic Church. In 1913 he decided to become a priest and returned to Sydney in that year to enter the Congregation of the Missionaries of the Sacred Heart (M.S.C.). After twelve years devoted to secondary studies, novitiate, philosophy and theology, he was ordained to the priesthood in Sydney on July 26, 1924. Sent to Rome for a postgraduate course in theology at the International Pontifical University of the Angelico under the Dominicans, he obtained the Doctorate of Sacred Theology (S.T.D.) in 1926. After his return to Australia in that year he was appointed professor of dogmatic theology at the Sacred Heart Monastery, Sydney,

N.S.W., the center of philosophical and theological studies for the congregation to which he belongs.

Two years later, in 1928, the International Eucharistic Congress was scheduled for Sydney, and Father Rumble was called upon to help prepare the general public in advance by a series of weekly radio talks during several months. After the Congress, a Catholic Radio Station, 2SM, Sydney (named after St. Mary's Cathedral), was established under a special license from the Government. From this Station, Father Rumble at once began conducting a "Question Box Session" of a full hour's duration every Sunday from 7 P.M. till 8 P.M., dealing with all types of enquiries, not to speak of objections, on religious and moral topics submitted by listeners. That session has been on the air for twenty-two years (a record for any one-man session of such duration) and is still one of the most popular features of the Catholic radio program. As a result there is scarcely a parish in the Eastern States of Australia without its convert family, due to listening to the "Question Box Session" from Station 2SM.

The development of an overwhelming correspondence with prospective converts by mail compelled Father Rumble to abandon the teaching of theology in 1932; and since then he has devoted himself entirely to radio work, missions to non-Catholics, retreats, specializing in the comparative study of religions, and in the constant writing of apologetic literature. During the past twenty-six years he has regularly contributed articles to the weekly papers, *The Freeman's Journal* and the *Catholic Weekly;* to the monthly devotional magazine *The Annals of Our Lady of the Sacred Heart;* and to the clerical quarterly, *The Australian Catholic Record.* His books include; *Cobblestones and Catholicity* (1929); *Correspondence Course in Catholic Doctrine* (1929); *The Catholic Lineage* (1932); *Radio Replies* (1934), a collection of queries and answers given over the air during the first five years of his radio session; *The Unavoidable God* (1937); *The Ten Commandments of God* (1945); *The Mass and the Sacraments* (1946).

In 1937 the Rev. Charles Mortimer Carty, Diocesan Missioner at St. Paul, Minnesota, wrote to Father Rumble to suggest an American edition of the book *Radio Replies,* and collaboration with himself in an apostolate of Catholic literature. Father Rumble agreed, and the book was edited for American readers by Father Carty, appearing in 1938 under the title *Radio Replies,* by Fathers Rumble and Carty. So great was the demand for this book that Father Rumble visited the United States in 1940 to prepare two further volumes of *Radio Replies,* based on the six years of radio matter accumulated since the publication of the first volume in Australia in 1934. The three-volume work has attained to a circulation of 2,000,000 copies.

During the latter part of his year in America, 1940, Father Rumble gave many lectures in the Northwestern and Eastern States of America, and then returned to Sydney to resume his radio work, which a confrere had continued on his behalf each Sunday evening during his absence. But ever since his visit to America, Father Rumble has been writing for the apostolate of Catholic literature, conducted by Rumble and Carty, numerous "Quiz Booklets" on Christian doctrinal and moral teachings, together with pamphlets on the major Protestant denominations and on many other subjects. Meantime he continues his efforts as vigorously as ever to spread the Faith by voice and pen in Australia.

M.A.H.

Mariadas Ruthnaswamy 1885–

An outstanding Catholic leader in education, Mariadas Ruthnaswamy was born of Catholic parents in Madras, India, on August 15, 1885. Since he was born on the feast of the Assumption, his parents gave him, at baptism, the name of Mariadas which means servant of Mary.

He was educated first at St. Anne's School, Secunderabad (1890–1895), then at St. Joseph's School, Cuddalore (1896–1903), St. Joseph's College, Trichinopoly (1903–1905) and at Nizam College, Hyderabad (1905–1907) where he took the B.A. degree of the Madras University. He went to Cambridge University for the years 1908–1910, where, at Downing College he took a Second Class in the Historical Tripos. He was called to the English Bar at Gray's Inn.

Returning to India he was appointed Assistant Professor of English at Baroda College (Bombay University), and taught there from 1913 to 1918. From 1918 to 1937 he was professor of history at Pachaiappa's College (Madras University). Although a Catholic he was appointed principal of this Hindu college and held this position from 1921 to 1928. The Madras Government called him to the principalship of the Law College in 1928 at which he served until 1930. For the years 1923–1926 he was a member of the Madras Legislative Council and was elected their president by the votes of a Hindu majority. From 1930 to 1942 he was a member of the Madras Public Service Commission and then was appointed to the leadership of the Annamalai University, which was founded by a wealthy Hindu. He served for a term of six years (1942–1948).

He took up writing early in life, about 1918, convinced that "reading without writing is mere lotus-eating." He began by writing unpaid articles for Catholic papers like the *Catholic Friend* and the *Catholic Watchman* of Madras. The new political life opening out to Catholics in the twenties induced him to start a paper of his own, *The Standard*, which lasted only eighteen months, in which he tried to acquaint the Catholic public of India with Catholic principles in politics, economics, and social reform. He has been doing this work ever since in the *New Review* of Calcutta and the *New Leader* of Madras and other Catholic papers. He is also active in this work as President of the Catholic Indian Association of Madras and of the Catholic Union of India.

His first book, *The Political Philosophy of Gandhi*, reminded one Hindu reviewer of the tourneys of the Middle Ages for the chivalrous courtesy the author showed to the subject of his criticism, eulogizing the Indian leader's moral purpose and religious fervor in politics but criticizing his strange economic theories and anarchic method of civil disobedience. His next book was a collection of college lectures in politics and law. It was published in 1932 by Williams and Norgate of London under the title, *The Making of the State*. In this book was realized the patriotic purpose of all his studies in politics and the art of government, which, as he put it, in the preface to this book, was to find answers to the question which he was asking in all his studies: "How will this fact or idea or institution help or retard the making of India?" The book was favorably received in England. *The Times Literary Supplement* headed a column-and-a-quarter review with the words: "This is a striking book." His next effort was a historical study of the British Administrative System in India, which grew out of the William Meyer endowed lectures at Madras University. It was published in 1939. His latest book is *India from the Dawn*, a popular history of his country published in 1949 by the Bruce Publishing Company, in the United States. With this book the author hopes "to arouse general interest outside India in the history of a people whose experience has been unlike that of any other. It is a people that has suffered as no other people from burdens imposed on her by her own children as well as by strangers, and whose efforts to shake off these burdens must evoke the admiration and sympathy of her more fortunate fellows among the nations of the world."

Mr. Ruthnaswamy having retired from the Vice-Chancellorship of the Annamalai University spends his time writing articles for the Indian and foreign press and is preparing material for new books on Christianity and Democracy in India. He is, since October, 1950, editor of a weekly journal called *Democracy* which seeks to disseminate the ideas and practices of true democracy in India.   M. A. H.

John Julian Ryan   *1898–*

John Julian Ryan, teacher, lecturer, and writer, was born in Houston, Texas, October 5, 1898. His family moved to Boston when he was fourteen, and he was graduated from Harvard in 1921. After having studied for a few months at the Harvard Graduate School of Business Administration, he spent some years with various business firms and then returned to Harvard to teach in the English department for nine years. During the same period, he began to teach philosophy, psychology, and logic, as well as English, at the Chamberlayne Junior College (for girls), conducting these courses for about ten years. In 1940, he joined the English Department of the College of Holy Cross, Worcester, Massachusetts, where he became an Assistant Professor. After a year out, for writing, he became a member of the English Department of the Boston

College School of Business (1946–1949). In 1950, he and his family moved to Conception, Missouri, where he joined the staff of the Seminary conducted by the Benedictine monks of Immaculate Conception Abbey.

In 1945, he wrote *The Idea of a Catholic College*, as an indirect result of which he was made General Adviser to the Catholic College Workshop at Catholic University. His second book, *Beyond Humanism*, is largely the product of his experience with this workshop. As these books show, his basic educational beliefs are: — that sin is the main obstacle to education; that grace is the main source of education; that everyone is called, each in his own way to fulfill, in God's plan for the cosmos, the fourfold functions of priest-prophet-maker-ruler; that Christian practicality, not mere busy-ness or utilitarianism, is the integrative principle of liberal education; that our schools should be schools of liberal arts, not merely schools of science and letters; that they should be conducted primarily by artists-in-residence and secondarily, though no less certainly, by scholars; that the cultivation of the intellectual virtues is not assured by the simple process of neglecting two of them — prudence and art; and that, whether virtue can be "taught" or not, discipline and asceticism are as much a requirement for general education as they are for military.

Mr. Ryan is the husband of Mary Perkins (See *Catholic Authors: Contemporary Biographical Sketches, 1930–1947*, author of *At Your Ease in the Catholic Church; Speaking of How to Pray; Your Catholic Language; The Sacramental Way*, and *Mind the Baby*). They have three boys.

Very Reverend Dom Idesbald Ryelandt, O.S.B. 1878–

Born on July 24, 1878 in Bruges, Belgium, Dom Idesbald Ryelandt was the fifth son of his father, Louis Ryelandt, a lawyer, and his mother, Marie Casier Ryelandt. For eight years Dom Idesbald was a student at the cathedral college of Bruges and for four years, as a monk, he studied theology at Mont César Abbey, under the direction of Dom Columba Marmion, O.S.B., the professor of dogma. Then he spent two years under Dr. Joseph Gredt, professor of philosophy at St. Anselm's College, the International Benedictine College in Rome, where he received a Ph.D. degree.

Dom Idesbald was professed a Benedictine monk at Maredsous Abbey in the presence of the Right Reverend Hildebrand de Hemptinne on August 15, 1899. Four years later (1903) on August 30, he was ordained a priest.

From 1906 to 1910 he was professor of philosophy at Maredsous and from 1910 to 1937, master of novices, save for the period, 1916–1918, when he was a prisoner of war, having been condemned by the German Council of War for having aided a British soldier to return to the front. Dom Idesbald had been in three prisons, Namur, Bonn, Siegbourg. His neighbors in the prison cellblock at Siegbourg were Cardinal Mercier's secretary and a German assassin. They suffered hunger day and night. Throughout the three years, however, they received from the American government and later from the Spanish government a package of biscuits each week. Despite this great trial, the morale of the Belgian and French political prisoners was on the whole very courageous. All were conscious of having done their duty. Much time was devoted to prayer. There were about twenty priests among the prisoners and under the supervision of the prison chaplain they were allowed to celebrate Holy Mass on improvised altars in the chapel and sacristy.

From 1923 to 1937, Dom Idesbald was prior of Maredsous. It was the wish of Dom Marmion, a native of Dublin and Abbot of Maredsous, to found a Benedictine Abbey in his native land. All monasteries had been destroyed in the reigns of King Henry VIII and Queen Elizabeth. A short time after Dom Marmion's death, the Archbishop of Cashel appealed to Maredsous to make a monastic foundation. The invitation was accepted in 1927, and Glenstal was the site chosen. Dom Idesbald was sent there in 1938 to take up the duties of prior. In 1932 a secondary boarding school was opened at the request of the Archbishop. This was an immediate success and continues to flourish. In 1949 a hostel was opened in Dublin to accommodate alumni and others attending National University.

When the war was over (1945), Dom Idesbald returned to Maredsous to resume his duties as prior there. In the beginning of the twentieth century in Belgium, the Liturgical Movement gained headway among the clergy and faithful. Dom Idesbald wrote many articles on the Mass and the Eucharist for the *Revue Liturgique et Monastique*, edited at Maredsous. From these articles sprung his little book *Pour Mieux Communier* which was translated into English by Dom Matthew Dillon, O.S.B., under the title *The Mass and the Interior Life*.

As master of novices, Dom Idesbald tried to learn the moral physiognomy of St. Benedict. He had studied the Holy Rule, the Dialogues of St. Gregory and established a parallel between St. Benedict and St. Francis de Sales; both dominated by the desire to do everything with discretion. Hence his book, *Essai sur la physionomie morale de St. Benoît*, translated into English under the title, *St. Benedict, the Man* (1950). Struck by the need which each man has, whatever his age or state in life, to overcome the griefs, discouragements, obsessing ideas and passions he used the articles which appeared in the *Revue liturgique* for his book *Nos forces de réaction dans la vie spirituelle*. This work was also translated into English by Dom Matthew Dillon, O.S.B., under the title, *Self-Discipline and the Interior Life* (1945).

Besides writing many articles on the spiritual life, he has collaborated with Dom Raymond Thibaut, O.S.B., in editing the book, *Le Christ, Idéal du Prêtre*.   M. A. H.

Edward Charles Sackville-West
1901–

The Honorable Edward Charles Sackville-West is descended, in the male line, from the family of De la Warr (of which the 3rd Baron was the first Governor of Virginia); in the female line, from the Norman family of Sackville, of which Thomas, first Earl of Dorset, cousin of Queen Elizabeth and Lord High Treasurer, was the first member of the Sackville family to own the great house of Knole, in Kent, now the home of his father.

Born November 13, 1901, Edward Sackville-West was educated at Eton and Christ Church, Oxford. While at Oxford he contributed musical criticism to the (Oxford) *Fortnightly Review,* and his career as a fiction writer began with the publication of short stories in the Oxford *Outlook.* After leaving Oxford he contributed to the *Spectator,* and in 1926 joined the staff of the *New Statesman* as assistant to the literary editor, Desmond MacCarthy. His first novel, *Piano Quintet,* was published in 1925, his second, *The Ruin,* in 1926. In 1927 he went to Germany, to study music, the language and the people, spending six months in Dresden and six months in Berlin. Three more novels, *Mandrake Over the Water-Carrier, Simpson* (a fictionalized biography of his old nurse), and *The Sun in Capricorn,* appeared in 1928, 1931, and 1934 respectively. A critical biography of Thomas de Quincey, entitled *A Flame in Sunlight,* followed in 1936. This book marks the temporary abandonment of fiction for critical writing, the less ephemeral part of which was published in *Inclinations* (Secker & Warburg, 1949 and Scribner's, 1950). During World War II, Mr. Sackville-West was employed in the Features and Drama section of the BBC, where he was entrusted with the bulk of the poetry broadcasts. An off-shoot of this period was *The Rescue,* a poetic drama on the subject of the Odyssey, written especially for radio and furnished with an elaborate orchestral score by Benjamin Britten. This was first broadcast in 1943, again in 1947, and in 1946 by the Radio Fusion Française (in French). Mr. Sackville-West has for many years devoted much time to reviewing gramophone records, for the *New Statesman* and *The Gramophone.* He is deeply interested in the art of recording, and in musical activities of all kinds. He is at present a director of the Royal Opera House, Covent Garden. He was received into the Catholic Church in September, 1949.   A. F.

Blanaid Salkeld   1880–

"Story-writers usually seek after adventure, travel, perpetual change," writes Blanaid Salkeld. "But the poet," she continues, "is more inclined to sit and saunter and sit again. As for change — all change savors of death to me. The same house (in Dublin), the same chair, the same corner by the fire — I wish they had always been mine. My great solace here, in Morehampton Road, is that I can see from my bedroom window — up beyond the intervening roofs — a wind-charger that stands in the garden where my small brother and I played during our earliest years."

Blanaid Salkeld was born in Chittagong, India — now Pakistan — on the 10th of August, 1880, the daughter of Lieutenant Colonel Jarlath ffrench-Mullen. He was a doctor in the Indian Medical Service. Her mother was a Byrne. It was from her mother's mother that she learned to love her country, Ireland. Her grandmother prayed every night that she might live to see Ireland free.

Blanaid Salkeld was only two and a half years old when she left India for Dublin with her parents. "I know nothing about my birthplace," she says, "except what the map tells me — that it is east of the Bay of Bengal, and west of Burma, with Assam well to the north. I notice that seven-tenths of the population are Buddhists. Chittagong was ceded to the East India Company in 1760, by Nawab Mir Kasim Ali."

When Blanaid was six years old, her father came home from India and introduced her to poetry — and John Keats. "I was very precocious," she says, "and could read and write at three." Some years later she read Keats with delight. "It is strange," she remarks, "how a child will put wrong meanings on words, and still enjoy a poem. I just put what meaning I liked on the long, long words, and it was not until I was many years older that I found out my mistakes. Of course, I started writing verse myself, and after my father's return to India, I would enclose the latest small composition in my weekly letter."

Blanaid's education was at first by governesses. At thirteen she went to Alexandra School, Dublin, for a year. At fourteen, she went to the convent of the Holy Child, St. Leonard's, England. At eighteen, she left the convent for India. A year later she became engaged and returned to Dublin with her parents. When she was twenty-two, she sailed to India and was married to Henry Lyde Salkeld, of the Indian Civil Service — "in a Catholic Church in Bombay — straight off the boat."

At her husband's death, when she was twenty-eight, she returned with her two sons, Cecil ffrench — now a well-known artist, and Laurence, who passed into the Indian Civil Service and was killed six months later, in an accident, playing polo.

In 1916 Mrs. Salkeld drilled with Cumann na mBan, but when the Rising came she happened to be with her small sons in a cottage on Howth Head. She tried to get into Dublin but failed.

"For many years," she says, "my writing was too desultory to be of any account. Since I have become immersed in poetry, I trust I have been more successful. My first volume of verse was brought out by Elkin Mathews, in 1933." She has written a great deal since. These works include: *Hello, Eternity* (1933); *The Fox's Covert: a poem* (1937); *Engine is Left Running* (poems) (1937), and nine verse plays. Of the latter, only one has been produced: *Scarecrow Over the Corn* — by the Dublin Drama League, in 1941. Several of her poems and reviews have appeared in various periodicals. Two volumes of her verse are in the hands of her publisher.

                                                                M. A. H.

Nelle Margaret Scanlan

The popular novelist, Nelle Scanlan, was born in Picton, the lovely little seaport of Marlborough in the South Island of New Zealand, "when the church bells were ringing on a summer Sunday evening," so her parents told her. It was mid-January to be exact, and January is mid-summer in the southern hemisphere. Oddly enough she was born within a few miles of New Zealand's best poet, Eileen Duggan.

Her parents were both Irish, her mother came from Cork and her father, Michael Stack Scanlan, was born in Kerry. Nelle was educated at the convent of the Sisters of Mercy, in Blenheim, the capital of Marlborough Province, a pleasant market town surrounded by rich agricultural lands of the Wairau Valley, and big hilly sheep stations farther back.

While she was no prize-winner at school, she was adventurous. When old enough to revolt against the annual holiday being spent with relatives or at the seaside, she set off to see something of the beauty and grandeur of her native land. She climbed Mt. Egmont (about 9000 feet) and she tramped the magnificent Milford Track to Milford Sound, sixty miles, with her pack on her back, fording streams and climbing the Pass, and she learned something of the foothills of their highest mountain, Mt. Cook (13,000 feet), but she did no serious climbing there. She has sailed for days in and out of the Marlborough Sounds, those miles of quiet waters, with myriads of land-locked bays, with bush-clad hills to the water's edge. And it was about these happy journeys that she first wrote. Sketches and short stories followed.

When the First World War came, she replaced a soldier and became a general reporter on a morning daily newspaper in the North Island, where she had then gone to live. She became subeditor and cable editor. After the war, she made her first venture abroad. She was

New Zealand correspondent at the first Limitation of Arms conference held in Washington in 1921, after which she remained two years in the United States, travelling slowly from coast to coast three times, writing for American papers and magazines as well as for New Zealand and Australian publications. She was in demand as a speaker at women's clubs.

Then she went to London and the Continent and included English publications in the list of journals she wrote for.

For over twenty years she made her home in London, returning to New Zealand five times during that period and remaining a few months or a year. When the Second World War started, she was in New Zealand, where she was obliged to remain several years. A year before the war ended, she managed to get a passage back to England, sailing across the Atlantic in convoy from Panama. After nearly five years in England "seeing the end of the war and the beginning of the doubtful peace, I returned to New Zealand early in 1949, and hope to remain here for some time," she writes.

During the past twenty years she has travelled in France, Switzerland, Italy, Germany, Austria, Czechoslovakia, Norway, Sweden, Finland, Denmark, Scotland, Ireland, South Africa, Australia, Java, Malaya and she also got "a brief look at Russia." Most of this time she was working as a special correspondent for newspapers and magazines, and contributed to others.

Her first piece of fiction was written on her slate in school at the convent and she was punished for it. "The general public," she writes, "has not been quite so hard on me as the nuns were."

To date (1952) Miss Scanlan has written fourteen novels, many of them set in New Zealand, including the four Pencarrow books, a saga of New Zealand. All of them have been published in England, and some of them in America also.

Her books are: *The Top Step* (1931); *Primrose Hill* (1931); *The Marriage of Nicholas Cotter* (1937); *Leisure For Living* (1938); *A Guest of Life* (1938); *Ambition's Harvest* (1935); *Pencarrow* (1932); *Tides of Youth* (1934); *Winds of Heaven* (1934); *Kelly Pencarrow* (1939); *March Moon* (1945); *Kit Carmichael* (1947); *The Rusty Road* (1948); *Confidence Corner* (1950).

Besides writing, Miss Scanlan has given several hundred talks. While she was in New Zealand during World War II she gave a series of 200 broadcast talks under the heading "Shoes and Ships and Sealing Wax," a title which gave her a wide field. Most of these talks were based on her travels and gave a background to the war news.

Now back in New Zealand, she found the housing shortage acute, so she handed the problem over to St. Jude, the Patron Saint of Lost Causes and Hopeless Requests. He found her a charming cottage by the sea, which is now known as "St. Jude's Cottage," which is at Paraparaumu Beach, thirty miles from Wellington. In this pleasant and peaceful spot, she is now engaged in writing her next novel.

M. A. H.

Most Reverend Joseph Henry L. Schlarman 1879-1951

The Most Reverend Joseph Henry L. Schlarman was born in Breese Township, Clinton County, Illinois, the tenth child of Bernard Joseph and Philomena (Keyser) Schlarman, February 23, 1879. He was educated at St. Francis Solanus College (now Quincy College), Quincy, Illinois; at the University of Innsbruck, Austria, and at the Gregorian University, Rome. From the latter university he obtained the degree of Doctor of Philosophy and Doctor of Canon Law.

On July 1, 1907, he was appointed assistant at the cathedral of Belleville, Illinois, and secretary to the bishop, and upon the death of the Reverend H. J. Hagen, Bishop John Janssen of Belleville appointed Father Schlarman rector of the cathedral and chancellor. During the night of January 4, 1912, the cathedral of Belleville was gutted by fire. Because of advanced age, Bishop Janssen left the matter of reconstruction in the hands of Father Schlarman, thus giving him, early in his career, building and executive experience. He kept his promise to his bishop that the cathedral would be sufficiently restored to permit the burial of Bishop Janssen, who died, July 1913.

Between the years of 1915 and 1923 Father Schlarman underwent more than a dozen serious operations, but the robust constitution he had inherited from his parents and his strong will power aided the surgeons, and he finally recovered fully. He was made a Domestic Prelate of His Holiness in September 1921.

Monsignor Schlarman was appointed Bishop of Peoria, April 19, 1930, and consecrated in the cathedral of Belleville, June 17, 1930, by His Eminence George Cardinal Mundelein, Bishop Henry Althoff of Belleville, and Bishop Edward F. Hoban, then Bishop of Rockford, being the co-consecrators. Bishop Schlarman was enthroned as Bishop of Peoria by His Eminence George Cardinal Mundelein, June 24, 1930. He was named Assistant to the Pontifical Throne on November 7, 1950. In 1951 he was honored by Pope Pius XII with the personal title of Archbishop.

His first care as bishop was the adequate protection of his priests, and he announced the establishment of the Clergymen's Aid Society the very day of his enthronization and contributed the first thousand dollars for that purpose. The next objective was a sound business administration of parishes and institutions. In accordance with the instructions of the Sacred Congregation of the Council of August 10, 1911, Bishop Schlarman established parish corporations and a diocesan corporation. Adequate protection of church properties against the hazards of fires, wind, and boiler explosion with extended coverage was next in line. The buildings were appraised by a competent agency, and all buildings covered up to 80 per cent against loss from any source.

An adequate and efficient chancery office was installed in rebuilt quarters on the ground floor of the cathedral rectory. The Peoria *Register*, which was introduced Easter 1934, was also housed in quarters at the chancery office, and is now located at 409 North Monroe Street.

The interior of the cathedral was thoroughly renovated according to plans by Ralph Adams Cram, now deceased. A complete set of new windows depicting in twenty-four panels the spread of the faith to all races and nations is the work of Wilbur H. Burnham of Boston. They are in glass of the fourteenth century technique, and form part of the restoration of the cathedral.

The Catholic Charities was thoroughly reorganized and modernized and set up in a special building. In the course of Bishop Schlarman's administration a two-million dollar debt on the several parishes of the diocese was liquidated. During the summer of 1945 the Bishop asked for one million one hundred twenty-five thousand dollars, to be raised by a drive, for diocesan purposes, such as the enlargement of the orphanage, and a building of a new home for the aged. The pastors and people added an equal amount for their own parish purposes and thus raised a total of $2,500,000. Great efforts have been made to teach the catechism to every child in the diocese. To reach those rural children not in Catholic schools the Peoria-Aledo Plan was started with the encouragement and financial aid of the bishop. It is part of this plan to spot Sisters in strategic places and have them contact the Catholic children once a week on released time or in any other way that may befit the area. Five such centers are now functioning and more will be opened as Sisters become available.

Between 1946 and 1947, twelve classrooms were added to Spalding Institute; the Schlarman High School was opened in Danville, and the Central Catholic High School was set up in Ottawa. The $1,250,000 Alleman High School for the Rock Island-Moline area was opened in September of 1949. Since 1935 the National Convention of Catholic Charities, The National Catholic Rural Life Conference, and the National Catholic Press Conference were held in Peoria.

The extra-diocesan activities of Bishop Schlarman may be summarized as follows: In 1936 he was chairman of Governor Horner's Commission for the Study of Prison Problems and, in that capacity he and the commission visited and studied the penal institutions of Illinois for a period of five months, and during the summer of 1936, Bishop Schlarman studied prison systems in Italy, Austria, and England. From 1943 to 1945 he was President of the National Catholic Rural Life Conference, and in that capacity visited Mexico and seven countries of South America with the Right Reverend Monsignor Ligutti, Executive Secretary of the NCRLC, for the study of rural problems.

Bishop Schlarman is the author of several books and numerous brochures and pamphlets. *From Quebec to New Orleans, The Story of the French in America*, was published in 1930. *Catechetical Sermon Aids* is a method of treating all the subjects of the catechism in a three-year series. Published in 1942, it has passed through several printings. *Why Six Instructions?* presents a plan of instructing the contracting parties to a mixed marriage. This pamphlet was very extensively used by chap-

lains during the late war and has had sixteen printings. B. Herder &
Co., St. Louis, are the publishers of both. *Why Prisons?* summarizes
the Bishop's Commission of the Study of Prison Problems. *Mexico: A
Land of Volcanoes*, from Cortes to Aleman, Bruce Publishing Company,
April, 1950, and the Spanish edition: *Mexico, Tierra de Volcanes*, JUS,
Mexico City, August, 1950 are very popular.

Archbishop Schlarman died on November 10, 1951, at the age of
seventy-two.

Reverend Mark Schmid, O.S.B.
1901–

A man of varied interests is Father Mark
Schmid. As librarian of Mt. Angel College and
Abbey libraries, he has made a collection of in-
cunabula and manuscripts, and has devoted
much time to research in this field. He has given
several lectures at the State University Oregon,
and to college librarian groups on books printed
before 1700. His knowledge of six languages helps him to read old books.

Library work gave him the urge to learn bookbinding, which at
first he began as a hobby, but now he can do the work of a first-rate
professional. He and an assistant do all the bookbinding for the Mount
Angel Abbey and Seminary of St. Benedict, Oregon.

Strange as it may seem, since his dominant field was philosophy,
he has, for more than ten years, studied biology. He has collected several
thousand items of biologic and zoologic interest to fill two special
museums. He has mounted nearly every conceivable animal from a
bear to a hummingbird; and collected nearly all the invertebrate fauna
of the Oregon, Washington and California coasts. In connection with
this work he has edited several monographs, such as *The Problem of
Evolution* and *The First Origin of Life*. He also wrote two papers for
the National Educational Convention in 1937 and in 1938, and published nine pamphlets ranging in size from 32 pages to 64 pages.

In 1942 he published *The Solution is Easy*. It is an explanation of
the main human problems of life. In a popular style he gives an interesting picture of scholastic philosophy. His latest book, published
in 1951, is *The Story of an Oregon Countryside*. It throws light on the
history of the state.

Father Mark was born in Jordan, Oregon, in December, 1901, the
son of Matthew and Bernadine (Rosegarden) Schmid. He was educated
at Sacred Heart Academy, Salem, Mt. Angel College, St. Benedict,
Oregon and at Saint Anselm's College, the International Benedictine
College in Rome, where he received a Ph.D. degree. He did graduate
work also at the University of Washington, Seattle. In 1922 he entered
the Benedictine Order and was professed in 1923. He was ordained a

priest in 1928. From 1929 to 1934, he was editor of *St. Joseph Magazine*, and since 1934 he is professor of philosophy and head librarian. From 1940–1945 he was dean of the summer school at St. Mary's, Beaverton, Oregon.   M. A. H.

Reverend Philibert Schmitz, O.S.B. 1888–

In the beginning of the nineteenth century, after the Napoleonic era, the historic Order of Saint Benedict, in point of numbers and influence had diminished to a very low degree. As a result of the French Revolution, the abbeys of this Order had all well-nigh been destroyed, save for a few in Germany and Switzerland. One of the phenomena of the Church's history in the nineteenth century was the revival of the ideals and life of the monks claiming sonship of the great Saint Benedict, Patriarch of Western Monasticism. Stemming from the revival initiated by Dom Gueranger in France, came the Congregation of Beuron and from this congregation arose the Abbey of Maredsous in Belgium. From this centre have issued many representative leaders of Benedictine thought and activity in fields spiritual, historical and liturgical. Not the least of these has been Dom Schmitz, who latterly has thrown great light of the civilizing influence of Benedictinism down through the centuries by the publication of his monumental work, *L'histoire de L'ordre de Saint Benoit*.

Dom Philibert Schmitz was born at Brussels, Belgium, September 15, 1888. After brilliant classical studies with the Jesuits, he entered the Benedictine Order at the Abbey of Maredsous in 1906. After his profession and the completion of his philosophical studies, he was sent to pursue theology in the International Benedictine College of St. Anselm in the Eternal City. He was ordained to the priesthood in 1912. In 1913 he received his doctorate there presenting as his thesis "The Doctrine of Rupert de Deutz on the Holy Eucharist."

In 1911–1912 the Anglican monks on Caldey Island had been converted to the Catholic Church. Dom Schmitz, now a young priest, was engaged to go to Caldey to teach theology for two years to those of the monks who were destined for the priesthood. This work finished, he was made professor of the classics in the school of his own abbey of Maredsous, a post which he held till 1919. At the reopening of St. Anselm's in Rome after the First World War, Dom Schmitz returned to his Alma Mater to teach Church History, a field in which he was becoming ever more engrossed. Forced by ill health to quit Rome in 1924, he returned to Maredsous and devoted himself to Benedictine history and became a collaborator on the *Revue Benedictine*, of which he was appointed Director in 1928, and the successor of the noted Dom

Berlière. He published in this periodical, from 1924 on, a *Bulletin of Benedictine History* (gathered into 2 volumes in 1932 and 1941) wherein is written up, and often analyzed and criticized, all the books and articles which appear in the world concerning any point at all of the history of the Order of St. Benedict. This bulletin constitutes an indispensable repertoire for historians, particularly mediaevalists. At the same time Father Schmitz was librarian of the very important library at Maredsous. In 1947 he supervised the construction of a new and modernly equipped library. It now contains 135,000 volumes and 30,000 brochures.

Dom Schmitz has also published a critical and practical edition of the Latin text of the *Rule of St. Benedict*. To this rule, based on manuscripts of the "textus purus," specializing in ecclesiastical and Benedictine history, he has added a concordance of each word used in the text.

Prepared by a long period of research, Dom Schmitz published (1942 to 1949) a monumental history of the Order of Saint Benedict in six volumes. Paradoxical as it may seem, this work offers the first somewhat complete history of the Benedictines and their civilizing work. Called by critics "definitely masterful," this work fixes the reputation of the author as an unrivalled master of Benedictine history in our times. The history is now in process of being abridged and translated into English.

He contributed articles on the Benedictine Order to the *Dictionnaire d'Histoire et Géographie ecclésiastique* (Paris); *Biographie nationale de Belgique* (Brussels); *Lexicon für Theologie und Glaube; The Catholic Encyclopedia*; and diverse periodicals such as *Revue Mabillon; Revue d'Ascétique et de Mystique*, etc.

If the steady growth in numbers of those pursuing the monastic life, both Benedictine and Cistercian, may presage deeper knowledge of the roots of this great ideal in history, Dom Schmitz may well be considered as a pioneer in this field.   K. M.

Reinhold Schneider   1903–

"History is the evolution of a nation in relation to God. Everything that men accomplish must be measured in terms of eternal values. In the course of history, Eternity makes ever varying demands on mankind for decisions which will become their destiny." This quotation from "Das Inselreich" by Reinhold Schneider sets the theme for all the work by this prolific author of modern Germany.

Reinhold Schneider was born in Baden-Baden on May 13, 1903. His Protestant father was the proprietor of the Hotel Messmer, a famous hostelry frequented by the King of Prussia, later Emperor William the First, for over forty years. His mother was a Catholic, and

Reinhold was baptized in this religion. It has been said that "happiness in the family during his formative years made Schneider the harmonious, well-balanced person who speaks to us in all his works."

Travel has influenced him to a great degree. An opportunity to travel in Spain and Portugal was the birth of his literary work but the death of his career as a businessman. He had been sent to Dresden, when he finished his schooling, to be trained in business but he endured this "imprisonment," as he called it, only seven years. In Portugal, in 1930, he wrote his first book, *The Life of Camoëns* (*Das Leben des Camoes or Untergang, und Vollendung der Portugieschen Macht*) (1930).

He lived in Potsdam for several years. During 1934–35 he visited England. His travels about the countryside and in cathedral towns prompted him to write *Das Inselreich: Gesetz und Grösse der britischen Macht* (1936), a history of England from the landing of Caesar to the death of the elder Pitt. Some consider this book his masterpiece.

He wrote books on German history: *Die Hohenzollern* (1933), *Auf Wegen Deutscher Geschichte* (1934) and *Kaiser Lothars Krone* (1937). Here his underlying theme, *Die Tragic der Macht*, was again apparent.

In 1937–38 he wrote one of his most important books, *Las Casas vor Karl V*. This work, which was about the philanthropist Las Casas who became a bishop in Mexico during the reign of Charles V, analyzed the conflict between man and the state and the task of a Christian in that conflict. It caused the Nazis to suppress Schneider's writings. Words of Las Casas to Karl V: "It is certain that judgment will fall on this land. For he who fails to fulfill the highest duty bears the heaviest guilt. . . . God does right if he destroys the might of this land. Terrible punishment follows terrible crime" were too pointed for Hitler and his henchmen! This book was published in English, under the title *Imperial Mission*, in 1947, by Gresham Press in New York.

After the suppression of his works, Schneider found a publisher in Alsace and continued his writing. He prepared numerous periodicals, among them *Das Vaterunser, Das Gebet in der Zeit* and *Weihnacht der Gefangenen*, and circulated them secretly. 500,000 copies of his anonymous pamphlet "Our Father" were distributed. During 1940 he contributed a collection of compositions under the title "Macht und Gnade." He also wrote many poetical works at this time which were secretly distributed from person to person. Sonnets from this period appearing in collections later were *Sonnet* (1939) and *Jetzt ist des Heiligen Zeit* (1943). Others he published in small volumes, *Die letzten Tage, Die Neuen Tuerme* (1946) and *Apokalypse* (1946). In a letter he says, "My activity at the time of Hitler shows in a modest way what ought to have been done by many. It was an attempt to protest against the regime, and to offer help where it was most needed." He was under suspicion and in 1943 accused of defeatist writings. The charge was dropped apparently but only the collapse of Germany in 1945 saved him from a serious indictment.

After the collapse of Germany he wrote a collection of short essays, "Gedanken des Friedens," to encourage the defeated nation. His own words, from a letter, describe best what he attempted: "Since the collapse we tried to advocate the idea that only atonement combined with a religious and moral renaissance can help the Germans and gradually bring them again into the family of nations." Atonement he describes as "the attitude of a man who remains conscious of his dignity — although it is impaired — and endeavors to restore it completely."

He is concerned about the re-education of German youth and is critical of literature as taught in German schools and universities. He throws down a courageous challenge to "literary judgments sanctified by tradition" in his *Faust's Rettung* and *Dämonie und Verklärung*. Here he criticizes Goethe's *Faust*, Schiller's *Wallenstein* and plays by Heinrich von Kleist because he feels their fluctuating moral values subtly poison German youth, and that lust for power, arrogance, and false sentimentality glorified in these works give Germans the wrong characteristics to imitate.

His solicitude for German intellectual life starved by Nazi book-burning and library destruction is shown by his most recent project. He has founded a new library of the Occident ("Abendländische Bücherei") in conjunction with Herder in Freiburg where he has lived since 1938. He is choosing the works he considers most valuable in European literature and publishing them with the originals on the left and the German on the right. To each volume he is writing a preface in which he shows its direct relationship with present-day Germany. Sixteen volumes have been published already and more are to follow. ("The library is meant for young people, not only to give them the pleasure of learning a foreign language, but also to show them a mirror of that international outlook to which they should aspire." Marie Heynemann. Nov. 1949).

Writing essays and giving addresses on the lives of several church dignitaries, St. Francis, St. Ignatius, Cardinal Newman; contributing a preface to a collection of letters from concentration camps by Catholic and Protestant clergymen ("Sieger in Fesseln, Das christliche Deutschland 1933–45"); writing numerous religious booklets like *"Die sieben Worte am Kreuz"*; these are some of the other activities carried on by Schneider. That he is in constant pain from an incurable disease has not stopped the steady flow of literary, historical and religious works from his pen. Only in *Herz am Erdensaume*, a collection of poems in free rhythms, do we catch a glimpse of his insight into suffering.

From his early historical novel to his more recent works, *Mensch vor dem Gericht der Geschichte*, *Weltreich und Gottesreich*, *Und Petrus steig aus dem Schiff*, Reinhold Schneider has tried to fulfill the literary mission he has set himself, viz., to interpret the historical events of his time in relation to God. "No need, however great, must drown the voice of truth; no power can give peace and protection if men do not think in terms of peace." (*Gedanken des Friedens.*)

His book, *Die dunkle Nacht* (*The Dark Night*), a story book which first appeared in 1942, was greatly praised by a priest who sent his letter of congratulation to the author just a few hours before he was beheaded. *Stern der Zeit* (*The Star of the Time*), his latest collection of sonnets, was published in 1947. Recently Mr. Schneider has been occupied with dramatical works. In 1940 he brought out the drama, *Der grosse Verzicht* (*The Great Resignation*), dealing with the contrast between Pope Peter Celestine V and Boniface VIII. Three other dramatical works were published in the fall of 1951.

"It is my plan," Mr. Schneider says, "to give up the psychological drama, and to bring before the public concrete historical topics; better than anything else I like to show the conflict between the world and truth, the truly Christian tragedy which lies in the commandment to accomplish the truth in the world, although that truth is not of this world. I am anxious about writing a Christian record in dramatic guise. Furthermore, I am preparing the publication of a collection of essays and sonnets under the title, *Rechenschaft (Justification)*, in order to explain my political attitude in 1950 and in 1951."

In June, 1951, Reinhold Schneider, a staunch opponent of Nazism during the war, caused considerable surprise by contributing an article to the magazine *Aufbau*, a Communist publication in Berlin. The editor of *Catholic Authors* wrote to Mr. Schneider for an explanation. Mr. Schneider sent a clipping from the *Der Christliche Sonntag* entitled "Eine Erklärung von Reinhold Schneider" in which he defends himself by saying "militarism is incompatible with Christ's love. . . . To my thinking, universal compulsory military service, by imposing on men an oath of incalculable consequences, is an unchristian and inhuman law. . . . There is only one peace: that which is based on the Christian conscience, and its liberty. On behalf of this truth I wrote, this spring, two articles for the East when warning and protesting still seemed to be imperative." (Only a part of the article is quoted.)

In another letter to the editor of *Catholic Authors* he said: "Although I don't think that any proof is required to show that I am a sworn enemy of communism, I assure you of it expressly. In all my books, from the first to the last, I have tried to prove that all values, hopes and power of this world will come to nothing on the other side. A doctrine which concentrates on the meaning of life on this side is not tempting to me at all. In those two essays written for the East in the beginning of this year (1951), I made a clear confession of my Christianity; they are the only essays written for the East and they will not be followed by any others. One must take into consideration the tragic conditions of life the Germans are in: the danger of self-destruction by fratricidal strife is threatening us. I believe that under circumstances like those, one would have to do one's utmost to be a mediator. Those two essays were written to negotiate a peace. I do not want to become a regular contributor, but all I wanted to do was to discuss two points in question: armament and war, relationship of Christians and non-Christians, of the West and an atheistic power. In those two writings I did not deny my faith. I have never done that in any of the books I had printed in the West. Only the methods used by the West against incredulity did not seem appropriate to me because they were lacking in that radical Christianity which alone might, one day, convince the others."

M. B. H.

William Greenough Schofield
1909–

William Greenough Schofield has had an intense and varied career as reporter and feature writer since his college days at Brown University, where he contributed to the *Brown Herald*, the *Brown Jug* and the *Literary Quarterly*. Intermittently he has written five novels that failed to sell and five novels that sold, culminating in *The Deer Cry*, a romantic tale woven around the apostolic figure of St. Patrick. During his literary career, circumstances made him at varying times, a stevedore, a waiter, a night-club singer, a laborer, a naval gunner, a public relations officer for the navy, and a student of the Catholic religion, to which Faith he submitted in 1943.

An early literary adventure brought him to Mexico; later work as columnist and feature writer for the Boston *Traveler,* brought him to London, Rome, Madrid, Lisbon, Paris, Berlin, and to Dublin, where, New Englander though he was, he found the atmosphere attractive and congenial. "I visited Ireland several times during the war and liked it," he tells us. "I flew back there for a visit *en route* to Rome in 1946, and by that time had become interested in Ireland's ancient history. That, of course, led to deep interest in St. Patrick and a desire to write a novel about him in a way that might attract today's average reader."

Though an experienced and brilliant writer of news stories, William Schofield confesses to the temptation to quit news writing. "I may leave newspaper work some day," he says, "and concentrate on full-time creative writing, but in a way I hesitate to do so. Newspaper assignments have taken me on all types of stories from strike-bound coal fields to overseas broadcasts and the privilege of three Papal audiences, and I'll miss the life when I leave it."

William Schofield was born in Providence, Rhode Island, in 1909 of Protestant Episcopalian parents. He was confirmed in that church and played saxophone accompaniment for the choir. "The neighborhood," he says, "was strongly anti-Catholic but I still don't think they were using the saxophone as a weapon for religious feuding."

After high school at Cranston (Rhode Island), he went to Brown University, Class of 1931, still playing the saxophone but in clubs and dance halls now instead of a choir. He joined the Alpha Tau Omega fraternity, sang and played in the musical clubs and college band. "I played lacrosse," he says, "and ran with the track team, but not fast enough to win."

Nudged by the depression, Schofield left college to do newspaper reporting for the old Providence *News*. He then went South by freight train and truck to New Orleans. He wrote for New Orleans papers, then, in company with a Guatemalan political exile he went to Mexico to write a biography of Manuel Estrada Cabrera. "It was a good book," Schofield claims, "but nobody cared about dead Guatemalan presidents, so it never sold."

Working his way, Southwest and Middle West, he found himself at last in New York City where he wrote another novel that failed to sell. In 1934 William Schofield married Blanche Hughes at St. Michael's Catholic Church in Stonington, Connecticut. Miss Hughes, a Catholic, had had considerable success in writing poetry, her work appearing in *America* and *Extension Magazine*. After nine years of married life, and the birth of three children, Elinor, Michael and Peter, William Schofield joined the Catholic Church. "Conversion," he says, "is a rare personal gift and should be regarded humbly and gratefully."

Meanwhile he had worked on the Providence *News Tribune*, now defunct, the Cape Cod *Colonial*, the Providence *Journal and Bulletin* and lastly, 1940, he joined the staff of the Boston *Traveler*. Schofield still wrote novels, but not until he had finished five did he have success. Then *Narragansett Night* appeared in *Redbook Magazine*, and later was published in book form as *Ashes in the Wilderness*. It is a story of New England in the time of King Philip's war, when the colonists were nearly wiped out.

War now supervened and William Schofield joined the navy in 1942, being promoted in the course of the war from lieutenant, junior grade, to lieutenant commander. War duty included eighteen months on convoy service as a gunnery officer in all theatres of war. He was in combat several times but escaped unharmed. After the war he rejoined the Boston *Traveler* and covered many important stories, including the treason trials of Douglas Chandler and Robert Best, and the elevation of Cardinal Spellman. He also wrote more novels, of which *The Deer Cry* has been the most popular. To date William Schofield has written: *Ashes in the Wilderness* (1942); *The Cat in the Convoy* (1946); *Payoff in Black* (1947); *The Deer Cry* (1948); *The Keeper of the Inn* (1949), published in London. *The Cat in the Convoy* was republished in Paris after its American run, and *Payoff in Black* was republished in London.

In the fall and winter of 1948, Schofield took up lecturing. "I tried," he says, "to draw a parallel between civilization's crisis at the time of St. Patrick and the crisis of today — in each case, with clouds of an oncoming Dark Age threatening the civilized world, and only the Catholic Church standing as an active barrier to the spread of barbarism and anti-Catholic doctrines." By way of hobbies, Schofield likes to see a baseball game, to cross swords in argument, or to pack his bag and travel.   E. B. B.

Kurt von Schuschnigg 1897–

The former chancellor of Austria, Kurt von Schuschnigg, has been professor of government at St. Louis University since June, 1948.

He was born on December 14, 1897, at Riva on Lake Garda, where his father, the late Artur von Schuschnigg, served as a captain in the Austro-Hungarian army. The territory then belonged to the Austrian province of Tyrol; it was given to Italy after the Second World War. His mother was the late Anna (Wopfner) von Schuschnigg. Both parents were of Tyrolean stock, of families which had originally come from Carinthia. Kurt von Schuschnigg attended the grade school in Vienna during the reign of Emperor Francis Joseph, while the Christian Socialist, Karl Lueger, was mayor. Thus he grew up in the atmosphere of old Austria, and learned to think along lines of Central-European integration. This means that he was from his earliest childhood a convinced anti-Nationalist. This basic attitude has not changed in after life.

In 1908 he entered the Stella Matutina school in Feldkirch, Austria, conducted by the Jesuit Fathers of the German province. Originally barracks, the school buildings at Feldkirch were given to the German Jesuits when their members were driven from Germany by order of Bismarck. This school was sometimes described as an exclusive social institution. "It was, on the contrary," Mr. Schuschnigg says, "a wholesome democratic place of learning, with a student body recruited from all the different strata of the population, poor and wealthy alike, and stemming from different nationalities."

After he was graduated in 1915, he joined the Austrian army and served, during the rest of the war, on the Italian front, namely, the part between Gorizia and the sea, known as the Carso sector. He fought in all the battles on that front until the armistice in 1918. He was released from a prisoner of war camp near Naples on September 1, 1919.

After the war the family moved to Innsbruck, and he attended the law school of the university there from 1919 to 1922. Then he practiced law for a short time before opening up his own law office. In 1927 he was elected a deputy of the Tyrolean Constituency of the Viennese parliament, as a member of the Christian Socialist Party. In 1930 he was re-elected, and specialized in constitutional questions. It was during this time that he published some pamphlets about the Austrian constitution (Vienna, Tageblatt-Bibliothek). In January, 1932, he became minister for justice in the coalition government of Chancellor Dr. Karl Buresch. He remained in the cabinet under Chancellor Dr. Engelbert Dollfuss, in charge of the Ministry of Public Education. After the assassination of Dollfuss, he became chancellor and served in that position until the last day of the independence of Austria,

March 11, 1938. During his term of office he had the privilege of negotiating an Austrian Concordat with the Holy See, which was represented by the then Secretary of State, Cardinal Eugenio Pacelli, the present pope. "I shall never forget my negotiations with the Cardinal Secretary of State," Mr. Schuschnigg says. "His lofty spirituality and priestly dignity were most impressive."

When political affairs became very tense in Austria, Kurt von Schuschnigg planned to hold a plebiscite. On March 11, Hitler called him on the telephone and said: "You are planning to hold a plebiscite. It must be called off. You must resign. A man of my choosing must be put in your place. If this is not done, the German army will march into Austria. You have sixty minutes to decide." Schuschnigg tendered his resignation to the council, but the president refused it. Then, in turn, he called London, Rome, and Paris. They would do nothing. With only ten minutes left, Mr. Schuschnigg spoke to the Austrian people and made it clear to them that he must cancel the plebiscite and resign to avoid bloodshed. Walking out of the room where he had spoken, he was seized by Nazi officials and put under arrest. From March, 1938 to May, 1945, he was a political prisoner of the Nazis under the name of Dr. Auster. Nobody was supposed to know that he was in the concentration camp of Sachsenhausen, yet he could hear the SS men in trucks shout "Schuschnigg" derisively as they roared passed the camp. In February, 1945, he was transferred to the concentration camp at Flossenburg, and in April he was sent to Dachau. The following month he was taken to the Hotel Pragser-Wildsee, high in the mountains of southern Tyrol, south of the political border of the Brenner. It was there, on May 4, 1945, that he learned he was free. An American detachment took over the hotel.

In 1927 Mr. von Schuschnigg was married to Herma Masera. She was killed in 1935 in an automobile accident. Three years later he married, by proxy, his present wife, Countess Vera Czernin, according to the provisions of canon law for emergency cases. Mr. von Schuschnigg's brother led Vera Czernin to the altar; his father and a sacristan were the witnesses. The ceremony was performed without the knowledge of the Gestapo in the parish church of the Dominican Fathers on June 1, 1938.

Besides his articles in *Schweizer Monatshefte, Furche, Wissenschaft und Weltbild* (Vienna), *Social Order* (St. Louis University), and other periodicals, he is the author of two books: *My Austria*, published in 1937 in German, French, Spanish, Hungarian, Italian, and English. The American edition appeared in 1938 with a Preface by Dorothy Thompson; and *Austrian Requiem*, published in 1946 in German, Italian, Swedish, Czech, and English.

His honors include: Grand Cordon of the Order of Pius, Grand Cordon of St. Gregory, Grand Cordon of the Legion of Honor, Grand Cordon of the Cross of the South (Brazil), and Grand Cordon of the Order of Malta.   M. A. H.

Ildephonse Cardinal Schuster, O.S.B. 1880–

Frail looking, yet a powerhouse of spiritual and physical energy, Cardinal Schuster of Milan was born in Rome on January 18, 1880. His parents, Johannes and Maria (Tutzer) Schuster, had him baptized at the Lateran two days later with the names of Ludovico Alfredo.

His early education was received from the Daughters of Charity. At the age of eleven he entered the school of the monastery of St. Paul in Rome. On November 12, 1898, he began his novitiate. A year later, on November 13, he made his simple profession. From 1900 to 1902 he attended Saint Anselm's, the International Benedictine College in Rome, founded by Pope Leo XIII, where he obtained the degree of Doctor of Philosophy. On November 13, 1902 he pronounced his solemn vows in the Order of St. Benedict. He was ordained a priest at the Lateran on the 19th of March, 1904 by Cardinal Vicar Respighi.

Abbot Giovanni Del Papa of St. Paul's Monastery appointed him master of novices on May 15th, 1908. In 1911, Father De Sanctis of the Society of Jesus and founder of the Higher Institute of Sacred Music called him to the chair of Sacred Liturgy in the same Institute and he was chosen as a Consultor of the Sacred Congregation of Rites. In 1914 he took part in the General Chapter for the revision of the Cassinese Constitutions. A year later he was appointed prior of the monastery. On the death of Abbot Del Papa, he was elected to succeed him in 1918. The election found favor with Pope Benedict XV who esteemed him as one of the best Roman prelates. Pope Benedict entrusted to Abbot Schuster the presidency of the Oriental Institute until this Institute passed into the hands of the Jesuits at the earnest request of Pope Pius XI. He also held the presidency of the Commission for Sacred Art. Later he received diverse commissions from the Congregation of Religious and of Seminaries. He made the Apostolic Visitation of the seminaries of Lucania and Calabria, and other places, and afterwards of those of Milan, and of the whole of Lombardy.

On the 15th of June, 1929, Abbot Schuster was made cardinal priest, and on July 21, 1929, he was consecrated Archbishop of Milan by his Holiness Pope Pius XI in the Sistine Chapel, and took possession of his see in September of the same year.

The literary activity of Cardinal Schuster began in 1901, when he was only twenty-one years of age. He started with archaeological studies in preparation for the writing of the history of the monastery of Farfa, for which he had a great love. His interest in the liturgy grew, as he occupied the chair of liturgy, which he later diverted to archeology from the liturgical point of view.

In 1924 his *Liber Sacramentorum* was translated from the Italian into English by Arthur Levilis-Marke and published by Benziger Brothers in five volumes. It contains historical and liturgical notes on the Roman Missal. The notes were originally intended for the use of his own pupils at the Pontifical Higher School of Sacred Music and later at the Pontifical Oriental Institute in Rome. He was persuaded, however, by influential persons, to have them printed. As he tells us in the Preface: "To bring out clearly the subject matter in its historical and archaeological aspect, by rapid but accurate touches, to illustrate it by expressive comparisons, to point out the theological authority for its most important statements, whilst at the same time drawing attention to the artistic beauty of its mystical aspect — such has been the aim that I have kept in view."

Orate Fratres (July, 1951, pp. 376–77) states: "Ildefonse Cardinal Schuster, famous as a liturgist . . . has become equally famous since the war for his leadership in the social problems burdening his see city of Milan. In his Easter pastoral letter he called upon the government to legislate for a more equitable distribution of wealth, and to eliminate the just causes for resentment of workers against employers. 'How can we dare celebrate Easter,' he writes, 'when the unemployed and homeless die of hunger, or are forced to live without decent clothing and without the joy and dignity to which a Christian has a right?'"

Besides his books in Italian, he has contributed more than two hundred and forty articles to such periodicals as *Arte Cristiana, Révue Bénédictine, Revista Diocesana Milanese, Rivista Liturgica, Rivista Storica Benedittina.*

Among the many books he edited are: *Historia S. Pauli de Urbe; Historia S. Benedicti et eius saeculi; Commentaria in Regulam S. Benedicti: Meditationes quotidianae in Regulam S. Benedicti:* and *Historia S. Ambrosii.*

In 1951 B. Herder Book Company published his *St. Benedict and His Times.*   G. D.

Father Senan, O.F.M.Cap. See *Reverend Senan Moynihan, O.F.M.Cap.*

(Margaret) Elizabeth Sewell   1919–

Elizabeth Sewell was born in India, a typically English beginning to life in those days (1919) when India was still in the British Empire. "Apart from my exotic start to life, however," she says, "we are English on both sides of the family way back, one of the few English families, I think, who are not Welsh or Scottish or Irish anywhere, just plain Anglo-Saxon, my mother's family coming from Sussex, my father's from Dorset, so that India and the South of England divided my childhood between them. My elder sister and I grew up half in one, half in the other, with all the uncertainty that a rootless life brings with it. I developed a passion to settle down in one place for good; but life has turned out very differently.

"We were thrown back very much on our own company, and I find it hard to remember a time when I could not read or take pleasure in books. As soon as I could hold a pencil and make reasonable shapes for letters, I began to write verse. No one suggested this to me, and none of the rest of my family writes, in a literary way, though I have a great-great-aunt, of the same name as myself, who was a successful novelist in Victorian times, though since forgotten. But I began with poetry, and with the conviction that it was my job to write it. My attempts were preserved in a black folder by my surprised family; I now own the folder, and delve into it occasionally, for my own amusement or mortification. My avowed classic is on the subject of Saints Simon and Jude, a combination of names culled from the Anglican Prayer-book, no doubt during sermon time. I don't think I shall ever produce a work that will give me more pleasure than those eight lines. From this time on I produced a steady stream of verse, with occasional stories, until I was grown up.

"My later childhood was a troubled time in various ways. My mother died when I was twelve, and owing to ill-health I had a very chequered school career, changing schools often with rather odd results on my education, such as, for instance, my complete ignorance of English history after 1640. By the time I was eighteen, things settled down a little. My father had bought a house in Cambridge. I decided to go to college and study Modern Languages, and entered Newnham College, Cambridge, to read French and German in October 1939, just after the outbreak of war. There followed three packed, troubled, hungry years, and I emerged in 1942 with a B.A., First Class Honours, a Research Scholarship which was to be deferred until peace-time, and a great cloud of bewilderment and uncertainty in my head. We were at once drafted into National Service, and mine took the form of three years in the civil service, the Ministry of Education in London. There I learned a certain amount about the minor processes of administration, a great respect for my professional colleagues, learned, too, during three years of bombing, that I am much more of a coward than most people, an opinion I have not had to revise since.

"In 1945 I went back to Cambridge to start research in French for a Ph.D. After three years away from academic work my brain seemed to have gone to sleep altogether. I spent a miserable eighteen months achieving nothing, and then decided, arbitrarily and madly, that I would pretend no one had ever thought about my subjects (language and poetry) before, and to start thinking on my own. The results were astonishing, for the work suddenly came to life in very unexpected fashion. By the end of a year I was in trouble first with my college and then with the university for my unorthodox way of working, but intent on finishing the job, or letting it finish me, for the process seemed to be mutual. After two years I was receiving instructions prior to being received into the Church as a result of my work, an odd but good way in which to arrive. After three years I had a Ph.D. degree but also the conviction that I had better work in other places than Cambridge from this time forward. My first full-length piece of work to be published was brought out by Routledge and Kegan Paul in London, in February, 1951, under the title *The Structure of Poetry*.

"At the same time I was completing my first novel. Efforts to sell this failed, so I dismissed it from my mind, and went, in the summer of 1948, to London, where I cooked for a family in return for my keep, and wrote short stories. These began to sell to London journals, to my pleasure and surprise. About this time I conceived the idea of going to America to do my next piece of work, and after writing dozens of letters to all kinds of educational institutions in the U.S.A., I found myself in the spring of 1949 the holder of the Howald Research Fellowship at Ohio State University, and went there in August to study "The Structure of Nonsense, with special reference to the work of Edward Lear, Lewis Carroll and Nursery Rhymes." 1950–51 saw me back in London again, with enough dollars saved to live for one year and write full time, a short book on Paul Valéry which is to appear in England and America in the early part of 1952, finish the Nonsense book which Chatto and Windus, London, will publish next year, together with a collection of short stories, and to write a long poem and a certain amount of other stuff.

"Meanwhile the novel had come to light again. It had been mentioned casually in an interview in a local Ohio newspaper. A representative of Doubleday who happened to be in the university bookstore that day saw the reference, and sent it to headquarters. The result was that Doubleday asked to see the manuscript, which was now gathering dust in England, and accepted it with a good deal of enthusiasm some months later. The book, *The Dividing of Time*, was published in America in March, 1951, and in England in July, where it was chosen Daily Graphic Book Find of the Month.

"Late 1951 finds me visiting lecturer in English at Vassar College. Next year I expect to be back in England again, writing, a children's book, a second novel, a book on Poe and Pascal, perhaps something on education, a third novel, and as always, poetry and more poetry."

Don Sharkey 1912–

The urge to write came very early in the life of Don Sharkey. In fact he can scarcely remember a time when he was not interested in writing. In high school, he and a friend published a four-page humorous publication called *The Weakly Searchlight*. At the University of Dayton he contributed an article every month to the campus literary magazine, *The Exponent*, and was editor of the magazine in his senior year.

Don Sharkey was born on August 31, 1912, the son of Dr. Bryan Sharkey and Gertrude (O'Donnell) Sharkey in Middleton, Ohio. He was educated at Holy Trinity School in his native city for nine years; the Catholic High School of Hamilton, Ohio, for one year, and graduated from Middletown High School in 1930. For the following four years he studied at the University of Dayton and received his A.B. degree and also a certificate to teach high school which he never used. In 1944 he received his M.A. from the same university.

Soon after he was graduated in 1934, he joined the George A. Pflaum Publishing Co. One of his first tasks was to read manuscripts for *The Young Catholic Messenger*. It used a short story and a chapter of a serial each week, and it had difficulty getting them. Most of the manuscripts were pretty poor at that time. It occurred to Mr. Sharkey that he would be able to write a better serial than the ones they were receiving in the mail. He then began to write *The Lost Prince* in his spare time at home. He submitted it to the lady who was then the editor; and she accepted it. Later he clipped the installments from the *Messenger* and mailed them to Benziger Brothers. They published the book.

When he wanted to write something else, it seemed natural for him to use the same characters; so he wrote a sequel, *Nicholas, the Boy King*. By the time he had completed this story he had become editor of *The Young Catholic Messenger* and did not wish to run his own story. Besides, he had made a rule that no serial should run more than six installments. *Nicholas, the Boy King* would have been twenty installments. Finally he sold the story to *Ave Maria*. They ran it in the magazine and brought it out in book form — but before it appeared in book form, he had several other books out.

When Pope Pius XI died and the cardinals met to elect his successor, the editor of the *Messenger* asked Sharkey to do a series of articles about the Pope and the Vatican. This series was suggested by one of the girls on the staff. The girl was Martha Louise Shea. She had come there to work as copy reader after her graduation from Mt. St. Joseph's College in 1937. Mr. Sharkey married her on June 7, 1939. They have four children — John Bryan, Gerald Shea, Nicholas O'Donnell and Mary Anne.

Later his wife suggested that he clip the four articles and send them to the Bruce Publishing Co. to see whether they would be interested in publishing a book on the Vatican. Having received an affirmative answer from William C. Bruce, Mr. Sharkey spent two years on the research and the writing of that book, *White Smoke Over the Vatican*. When it came out in 1944, the entire first edition of 6,000 copies was sold out in two weeks. It was a choice of the Catholic Literary Foundation, and was on *America's* list of Catholic best sellers for several months. It is now in its fourth printing. A British Isles edition was published in 1950.

His next book, *After Bernadette, The Story of Modern Lourdes* (1945), was prompted by Werfel's book, *The Song of Bernadette*. It is a story of Lourdes since the time of Bernadette. It was a co-selection of the Catholic Literary Foundation and sold well.

Mr. Sharkey's research for *After Bernadette* aroused his interest in the Blessed Mother and the role she plays in our redemption. "Hitherto," he says, "I had taken her pretty much for granted. The more I read, the more I became convinced she is especially active in our own day. I asked Bruce whether I might do a book on this subject, covering the period beginning with the Miraculous Medal in 1830."

In the meantime Mr. Sharkey became concerned about the fact that the words of Our Lady at Fatima were not more widely known. It seemed to him that *The Young Catholic Messenger*, of which he was editor, was an excellent medium for spreading the story of Fatima. *The Young Catholic Messenger* at the time had a circulation of more than half a million and went into more than 90 per cent of the Catholic schools of the country. He decided to devote one whole issue to Fatima; it would be impossible for school children and teachers to overlook it. He also knew that many parents looked at their children's copies of the *Messenger*. So he wrote the story and devoted the entire issue of October 1947 to it. That year was the thirtieth anniversary of the final apparition. So many requests poured in for extra copies that the material was printed in booklet form. The booklet has sold about 250,000 copies so far and is still selling very well. It was revised in 1949 to bring it up to date.

In this same year he brought out a study club booklet on the Blessed Mother at the request of Monsignor Leon A. McNeill, of the Catholic Action Bookshop.

By 1949 Mr. Sharkey realized he was more interested in writing than in editing; so he resigned from Pflaum's. He then made an arrangement with the W. H. Sadlier Co. to do a series of United States histories, with the understanding that he was to have time to do other work. The need for the histories has been so urgent, however, that he has not had time for much else. The histories will be used in Catholic elementary schools throughout the country. The seventh grade history, *A New Nation*, appeared in November 1951. His latest book is *The Woman Shall Conquer* (1952).

Although most of his time is spent on the histories, he manages to contribute to such magazines as *The Sign, Columbia, Catholic Digest, Information, St. Joseph's Magazine* and *The Catholic School Journal*.

Mr. Sharkey is a member of the Gallery of Living Catholic Authors, consulting editor of *Catholic Boy*, and contributing editor of *Our Lady's Digest*. He is a member of the advisory board of the *Marianist*, and treasurer of the Guidance Center for Dayton and Montgomery County.   M. A. H.

Clare Consuelo Frewen Sheridan
1885–

The sculptor, traveller and author, Clare Sheridan was born in London, in 1885, the eldest daughter of Moreton Frewen. Her mother and the mothers of Winston Churchill and Shane Leslie were the three well-known Jerome sisters of New York. Clare Frewen was educated at the Convent of the Assumption in Paris and at Darmstadt. Her husband, Wilfred Sheridan, was killed in France, in September, 1915. Ever since his death, Mrs. Sheridan has earned her living as a sculptor. "It may be remembered in the United States," she says, "that I embarked on a lecture tour in 1921 as a result of having molded the heads of Lenin and Trotsky and others in the Kremlin. It was a great scoop, if an unpopular one. To me it was a great adventure but it labeled me Bolshevik. My cousin, Winston Churchill, whom I love as a brother, was furious with me at the time. He didn't speak to me for a year."

Her portrait busts include Senator Marconi, Lord Oxford and Asquith for Oxford Union, Lord Birkenhead, Winston S. Churchill; Lenin, Trotsky, and others for the Soviet Government; the Archbishop of Galilee, Mahatma Ghandi, Count Keyserling and others. In 1921 she made a trip to Mexico to model President Obregon, but failed to get a sitting. Obregon, however, granted her an interview which appeared in the New York *World* and the *Metropolitan Magazine*. In 1922 she became European correspondent for the New York *World* and interviewed Mustapha Kemal, Mussolini, Stamboulisky, Primo de Rivera and others.

Her travels took her to Russia, Turkey, Germany, Czechoslovakia, Poland and Algeria.

"The Second World War broke literally over my head," she writes, "when I was living in broken-hearted seclusion in my home at Brede in Sussex. I had just lost my son, who was my 1915 war baby, born six days before his father was killed. When I had recovered from this staggering blow in 1937, I began to devote my art to religious subjects. This form of sculpture was in a way a substitute for prayer, a substitute too for tears."

Her first statue was carved from an oak tree. She had visualized Our Lady and Child as a memorial to her son. "In creating images of

Our Lady with the divine Child," she writes, "my Catholic devotion dating back to my school days at the Convent of the Assumption in Paris was renewed in me. I had wanted to become a Catholic when I was sixteen but parental opposition and later, the lures of the world interposed. My resolve was shelved. The time seemed now to have come. I was in that spiritually battered state when one turns to religion."

Before she could fulfill this plan however, the Battle of Britain raged. Her house was requisitioned by the military authorities and she was obliged to relegate herself to a cottage in the park. "But the old fourteenth century house had a chapel which I had restored," she writes, "and when there were any Catholics in the billeted unit, their padre celebrated the Mass in that chapel and I was permitted to be present. Mass had not been heard within those walls since the Reformation."

Mrs. Sheridan came into the Catholic Church a year after the war ended when she was able to get to Italy — to Assisi. "Down into the dark crypt where the beloved saint's tomb is floodlit," she went to confide to him the reason for her coming. The details of her experience there are told in her article "Into the Church Through Art" in *Liturgical Arts*, May 1949, pp. 79–85. "Unknown, unplanned, unexpectedly, on the fifth day of my arrival, on the feast of Saint Clare, I, Clare, was baptized in that same Church where Clare, too, was baptized."

Mrs. Sheridan's publications include: *Russian Portraits* (1921); *My American Diary* (1922); *In Many Places* (1923); *Across Europe with Satanella, A Turkish Kaleidoscope* (1926); *Nuda Veritas* (1927); *Arab Interlude* (1936); *Redskin Interlude* (1938); *Without End* (1939); *The Mask* (1942) and *My Crowded Sanctuary* (1943).   M. A. H.

John Desmond Sheridan   1903–

Like many other authors, John Desmond Sheridan learned to write the hard way. For five years he labored without a single acceptance. To date the total sales of his books are over 60,000 copies. His first success was with the *Irish School Weekly*. This heartened him so much that eight years later he became editor of the journal. By that time he was thirty-one, and in the meantime he had qualified as a primary teacher.

Born in Glasgow, Scotland, of Irish parents, Mr. Sheridan jocosely remarks: "I left that city as soon as I came to the use of reason," and he has lived in Dublin since his early childhood. He was educated by the Irish Christian Brothers at the famous O'Connell Schools, North Richmond Street, Dublin; St. Patrick's Training College, Dublin; and the National University of Ireland, of which he is an Honors M.A. in Educational Science.

John D. Sheridan began to write poetry, essays, sketches, and short stories for very exclusive magazines at the age of seventeen, and by the time he was twenty-two he had worked his way down to the daily newspapers — without a single acceptance.

As was mentioned above, his first success was with the *Irish School Weekly*. Between 1928 and 1935 he contributed verses to *Everyman, The Commonweal, The Sign, The Catholic World,* and *The Capuchin Annual*. (His first collection of poems was published in December 1949 under the title *Joe's No Saint*.)

"Finding that poetry did not pay dividends, either in fame or in money, I turned to light essays," writes Mr. Sheridan. Although he claims to be a serious person at heart, he quickly made a reputation as a humorist.

His first collection of humorous essays, *I Can't Help Laughing* (1944), has run into seven impressions, and he has followed it up with four others: *I Laugh to Think* (1946); *It Stance to Reason — the Intelligent Rabbit's Guide to Golf* (1947); *Half in Earnest* (1948); and *My Hat Blew Off* (1950). Many of his humorous pieces have a family flavor, and he has been called the apologist of the common man.

He has also written four novels, two of which, *Paradise Alley* and *The Magnificent MacDarney*, were published both in Ireland and America. *Paradise Alley*, which is based on Mr. Sheridan's experiences in a Dublin dockland school, has been translated into Dutch, and was chosen as the Book of the Month by the Catholic Literary Foundation.

In addition to essays, novels and poems, Mr. Sheridan has written and compiled many educational texts — including works on arithmetic, English, Gaelic, mathematics (which he took for his degree course) and geography.

As editor of the *Irish School Weekly*, he represented the Irish National Teachers' Organization at the first meeting of the World *Conference of the Teaching Profession*, which was held at Endicott, New York, in August, 1946. In his opening address to this body he contradicted a previous speaker who had said that the first teachers' training college was founded in New York "a hundred years ago." The first teachers' training college, Mr. Sheridan pointed out, was founded in Palestine — nearly two thousand years ago: and its diploma was worded: "Go you therefore, teach all nations." He also struck the headlines with the epigram: "Teachers are born, not paid."

Mr. Sheridan is a Council Member of the Irish National Film Institute, and takes a keen interest in the documentary film. He has written scripts for two short documentaries filmed in Ireland under government auspices: *A Nation Once Again* and *The Life of William Butler Yeats*.

His other published works include the two novels, *Vanishing Spring* (1937) and *Here's Their Memory* (1941). He has also written a biography, *Life of James Clarence Mangan* (1939).

Mr. Sheridan is well known, too, for his Saturday morning essays in the *Irish Independent*.   M. A. H.

Walter Shewring
(Hayward Francis) 1906–

Walter Shewring was born in Bristol, England on January 1, 1906. His early upbringing, though suburban, was leavened by contact with the Cotswold country from which his family originally came. His religious background was Protestant, partly Low Church, partly Nonconformist. From 1917 to 1924 he was at Bristol Grammar School under a headmaster of genius, J. E. Barton, who imparted to a long succession of pupils something of his own taste and zest for literature and the visual arts. Greek and Latin studies throve at the school, and in December, 1923, Shewring won the senior scholarship of the year at Corpus Christi College, Oxford.

Reading, reflection, and the first glimpses of mediaeval art had by now detached him from his Puritan beginnings and moved him towards High Anglicanism. Going up to Oxford in October 1924, he soon became an advanced Anglo-Catholic, and was influenced by the Anglican community at Cowley, especially by their most famous preacher, Father Waggett (a friend of Chesterton). Hitherto, Shewring had met few Catholics; Father Martindale he admired, but distantly, as a brilliant university lecturer on Roman poetry. But an undergraduate friend introduced him to the Ampleforth Benedictines at Benet Hall, and, through friendships here, he began to grow familiar with the claims and character of the Catholic Church. The two points of unity and authority proved decisive. He was instructed by Dom Justin McCann, O.S.B., and received into the Church in June 1926.

His academic life was congenial and successful as far as pure classics went. He gained a First Class in Classical Moderations, a Craven Scholarship and the Chancellor's Prize for Latin prose. On the other hand he took slight interest in the subject matter of "greats," in which he was fortunate to get a Second Class. Ancient history appeared uniformly dull, and the chief effect of Oxonian philosophy was to give him a distaste for philosophy in general, which for years he failed to overcome.

In the interval he had made many Catholic contacts and friendships. At Bristol he met Desmond Chute, and through him Eric Gill. At Oxford he came to know Father Ronald Knox and Father Martin D'Arcy, S.J. He spent his first Catholic Christmas at Rome, his first Holy Week at Downside. His early writings appeared under Catholic auspices. Hilary Pepler, at Ditchling, printed privately a small book of his verse, *The Water Meads*, later enlarged and published as *Hermia*. Algar Thorold encouraged him to contribute reviews and poems to the *Dublin Review*. Stanley Morrison commissioned two works to be inset in his magnificent journal the *Fleuron* — a Latin essay on printing and a translation of the *Passion of St. Perpetua* which was illustrated by Eric Gill and printed in the type now known as "Perpetua."

In September 1928, Shewring took up his present position as a lay-master at Ampleforth College near York, teaching principally classics but also some French and English; Italian was added later. Some of his work for pupils has reached published form in *Greek and Latin Versions* (1938) and *Italian Prose Usage* (1948). At the beginning of his teaching career he was chiefly known as a specialist on Greek and Latin prose-rhythm, on which he wrote in the *Classical Quarterly* and later in the *Oxford Classical Dictionary*. Between 1929 and 1931 he published *Meditations on Our Lady* from Thomas à Kempis, a version of the *Golden Epistle* of Abbot William of St. Thierry, and a revised *Perpetua* with a Latin text. These translations had their use in bringing forward neglected treasures of Christian history and doctrine; but in them, as in the Psalms and prayers translated for the Ampleforth *Benedictine Hours* (1934), the effect is weakened by the use of an archaizing style which the author himself would now deprecate.

Meanwhile many visits to Eric Gill at Pigotts had had their effect intellectually. Shewring began to discard the scholarly aestheticism which had once contented him and to become aware of the social, moral, and intellectual problems of our time. He began to study St. Thomas seriously. He corresponded with Dr. Coomaraswamy, in whom he saw one of the noblest minds outside the Catholic Church. From about 1935 onwards, his writings in the Dominican monthly, *Blackfriars* and the Distributist *Weekly Review* show the gradual change in his ideas. In *Topics*, a book of essays published in 1940, he appears as a confessed disciple of Eric Gill. The *Westminster Hymnal* of the same year has a group of his hymns, original and translated.

In 1941 Shewring interrupted his teaching to work on Mrs. Gill's farm at Pigotts. In 1946 he returned to Ampleforth with much new experience behind him and with much work already done on his two most important books, both published in 1948: the *Letters of Eric Gill* and *Rich and Poor in Christian Tradition*. In the latter, his knowledge of languages and his experience in translation are made to serve the social enthusiasm of his later years.

Outside reading and writing, he finds his chief pleasures in staying with friends in England, Italy, and Holland; in visiting mediaeval churches; and in playing historic organs. The following quotations may serve to illustrate his characteristic views. "Book-learning, the natural means of education for a small clerical class, has become a conventional means of education for everyone; a particular instrument has been turned to general uses, and much of its aptness has been lost." "Learning and wisdom have often been divided; perhaps the clearest result of modern literacy has been to maintain and enlarge the gulf." "Narrow didacticism may be the devil, but didactic art in an ampler sense embraces the noblest works of mankind." "The normal theory of art applies to the sphere of making what theologians tell us about the sphere of doing. Where ordinary actions are perfectly done, holiness can look after itself; where ordinary things are perfectly made, culture can look after itself."

Gregorio Martinez Sierra.   See under Martinez

Paul Kwang Tsien Sih   1909–

Previous to his present position (Director of the Institute of Far Eastern Studies of Seton Hall University), Dr. Paul Sih was Legal Consultant to the Washington Office, Ministry of Communication of the Chinese National Government. He arrived in the United States in 1949. He entered the Catholic Church in Rome in 1948 when he was Minister Plenipotentiary of the Chinese Embassy in Rome and concurrently Chief Delegate of the Chinese Delegation to the United Nations Special Committee on the Balkans.

Born on November 7, 1909, in Kiangsu, China, Dr. Sih studied law at Soochow University, Shanghai, China and was awarded an LL.B. degree in 1933. Three years later he earned a Ph.D. degree in political science at the University of Rome, Italy.

From 1931 to 1934 Dr. Sih was Secretary of the Bank of China in Shanghai. For the year 1935–1936 he was an attaché at the Chinese Embassy in Rome. From 1936 to 1943 he was technical counsellor of the National Resources Commission of China responsible for the rural rehabilitation and industrial development of China. At the outbreak of hostilities with Japan in 1937 he served with the Ministry of Communications, first as technical counsellor, senior secretary and later as Deputy Director General of the National Highway Administration which also supervised the transportation on the Burma Road, chief artery into China during World War II. At the time when the Burma Road was disrupted, the desperate shortage of fuel nearly paralyzed the whole structure of motor transport. It was Dr. Sih who first introduced the establishment of a nation-wide "Stage-Transportation" system and he himself was made chairman of that Planning Board of that new administration.

In spite of his heavy burden with public duties during the war, Dr. Sih devoted part of his time in the year 1943–1944 to teaching law at his Alma Mater, Soochow University, Chungking, China. At that time Chungking was China's war capital.

As soon as World War II was over, he joined the Ministry of Foreign Affairs as technical counsellor and then was appointed chargé d'affaires with ministerial rank of the Chinese Embassy in Italy. In his diplomatic career he participated in several postwar important international conferences including the Council of Foreign Ministers at London in 1945 and the Peace Conference at Paris in 1946. During the Peace Conference, China played an important role in the task of giving due recognition to the effort of the democratic elements of the Italian people in overthrowing the Fascist regime. As a result of this, Italy could in some way enjoy rights as a co-belligerent and not be treated entirely as an ex-enemy country.

His connections with the United Nations are worthy to be mentioned. More than once he acted as advisor of the Chinese delegation to the General Assembly and in 1946 he went to Greece as the Chinese deputy delegate to the United Nations Investigation Commission in Greece. He spent six months in Greece, Bulgaria, Yugoslavia, Albania investigating border incidents and met and talked with many statesmen in these countries.

For his considerable working experience with the problem in the Balkans he became Chief Delegate of the Chinese Delegation to the United Nations Special Committee on the Balkans in 1947 and played an active part with the American Delegate, Admiral Alan Kirk, and the British Delegate, Sir Horace Seymour, in bringing the United Nations' goodwill to the world's most troublesome spot.

When Dr. Sih was in Rome in 1948, he cultivated an intimate friendship with Dr. John C. H. Wu, who was then Chinese minister to the Vatican. It was Dr. Wu's little book, *The Science of Love*, which gave him the earnest desire to embrace Catholicism. "In it," he says, "I found the true conception of the One Church and the great spiritual force of love, the fundamental aspect of Christianity. . . . The more I studied it (the life of the Little Flower) the more it fascinated me and the more I was united in love with the Church. This beneficial, tonic effect on the soul, enlivened by such intense love and enlightened by such magnificent inspiration, made me a Catholic. This fascinating force is so obvious that I wonder how Protestantism could have ignored altogether the affectionate devotion to the Blessed Virgin."

Laurence Scupoli's book, *The Spiritual Combat*, taught him how to conduct spiritual warfare through the practice of prayer. In his article, "From Confucianism to Catholicism" (*The Sign*, Jan. 1950, p. 29), Dr. Sih gives some instances of how prayer helped him. He writes: "Only since I became a Catholic have I begun to taste the ineffable happiness of shedding tears of joy, the infinite sweetness of reciting my family rosary, the feeling of complete emancipation after receiving Holy Communion, and the wondrous peace resulting from a devotional confession."

Dr. Sih is the author of: *The Banking System of China* (in Italian) (1935); *The Renascence of Italy* (in Chinese) (1936); *The Communication Administration System of China* (in Chinese) (1940); *The Stage-Transportation* (in Chinese) (1942); and his recent work, *From Confucius to Christ*, a story of his spiritual pilgrimage.

From 1939 to 1944, he contributed many essays, covering economic, social fields and international relations, to various Chinese daily newspapers and magazines.

Reverend M. Raphael Simon, O.C.S.O. (Kenneth Simon, M.D.) 1909–

The converted Jew and psychiatrist, Kenneth Simon, is now a Trappist monk at Berryville, Virginia, and is known as Father Raphael.

Born on August 6, 1909 in New York City, the son of Sidney K. and Saydie C. Goldgraber, he received the name of Kenneth. Since he attended public grade and high schools he had no religious instruction except his early religious training in a Reformed Jewish synagogue. After finishing high school, he entered the University of Michigan. Again he had no contact with religion or religious ideas. Then the idea struck him of spending his third collegiate year at a foreign university hoping to find what he sensed to be lacking in his education. He decided to study at the University of Berlin. During this year he was especially attracted by the course on the History of Philosophy. "Philosophy presented ideas about life, the soul, truth and justice — and through these ideas I caught glimpses of a secret kingdom."

When he returned to the United States in 1928 he completed his fourth year of undergraduate study at the University of Michigan and then entered the medical school there. It was only toward the end of these medical studies that he had an opportunity to study philosophy again. His friend at the university, Herbert Schwartz, had just obtained his Ph.D. in philosophy at Columbia University, and, remarks Mr. Simon, "I noticed his power of reasoning became more disciplined. Under his tutelage I entered upon that well-traversed road of philosophy which has led many to the Church of God." He received his A.B., M.A., and M.D. degrees at the University of Michigan.

From 1934 to 1936 Kenneth Simon studied at the University of Chicago. During this period he says, "I was forced to re-examine many of the ideas which I had taken for granted in my earlier education, e.g., concerning the origin of the universe and the human race, the nature of the mind, the existence of immaterial beings. . . . I was now able to appreciate the inadequacy of the materialistic account of human nature."

He continues: "At this time I realized that the Catholic Church alone laid claim to possessing the whole religious truth, that it alone claimed an infallible teaching authority. A religious society which has divine truth must claim that everything which contradicts its doctrine is erroneous and that every other faith which omits part of its teaching is incomplete. Otherwise it does not really believe that it has the truth, and that all parts of its doctrine are equally true. Likewise, I had come to realize that the word 'Catholic' means 'universal.' The Church held its faith to be objectively true and therefore true for all men. The

Protestants were divided into hundreds of disagreeing sects, the Jewish religion laid no claim to be other than a religion for Jews, while the Catholic Church proposed its religion as *the* single divine religion and it invited all men equally to accept it." (*The Glory of Thy People*, p. 31.)

Then Mr. Simon read the Gospels. "I recognized that their story was the account of the life and teaching of Jesus Christ." Convinced of its import, when the summer vacation began, he visited Father Gillis, the Paulist, in New York City and asked to be baptized. Since Mr. Simon was sailing for Europe that week, Father Gillis gave him some books to read and told him to report after his trip to Europe. On his return from Europe he again saw Father Gillis, who, when he learned that Mr. Simon had planned to return to Chicago in a month and therefore did not have sufficient time to receive instructions, advised Mr. Simon to report to the rectory of St. Thomas the Apostle Church. There he was instructed by Father Connerton. That period of instruction, he claims, was one of the happiest in his life. He said, "I came to appreciate more and more the unity of the Catholic faith. The same faith, the same doctrine taught by Christ and then by His Apostles is taught in every Catholic parish by every Catholic priest throughout the entire world."

His baptism took place on November 6, 1936. He felt free now to begin to work. He wanted to make some return to his parents for their love and affection. Consequently, he obtained an internship at the Oak Park Hospital, near Chicago, Illinois, on January 1, 1937, two months after his baptism. When his parents requested him to come East, he obtained an internship in the psychiatric division of Bellevue Hospital in New York City, beginning July 1, 1937. After completing this internship he received an appointment in the New York State Psychiatric Service at the Brooklyn State Hospital. After nine months he was invited by a Catholic institution, Lincoln Hall (the successor to the Catholic Protectory), which was just opening, to institute a psychiatric department. He left the school in December, 1940, to enter the Order of Cistercians of the Strict Observance, commonly called the Trappists. On May 31, 1947, he was ordained to the priesthood.

At the request of Miss Rosalie Marie Levy, the Jewish convert and author, and under the obedience of his novice master, he wrote the story of his conversion, *The Glory of Thy People*. It was published by the Macmillan Company in 1948.   M. A. H.

Liam C. Skinner   1908–

The lecturer, journalist, and author, Liam Skinner was born in Tralee, County Kerry, Ireland on July 25, 1908. His father was a foreman printer; his grandfather, a schoolteacher and a convert. Liam Skinner was educated at the Christian Brothers' School in Tralee and while there won a hundred pound Primary to Secondary Scholarship, and passed, inter alia, Matriculation and Leaving Certificate with honors.

He entered journalism as a cub reporter on the *Kerry Champion* in 1928 and in 1930 was sent to Killarney as staff correspondent. He contributed a weekly column which attracted some attention. While in Killarney he acted as correspondent for the *Irish Press* and the leading London news agencies and dailies. In 1932 he met Miss Doris A. Gladwell of Teddington, Middlesex, who came on a holiday to Killarney. They were married four years later and now have a family of four boys and two girls. Mrs. Skinner became a Catholic before the marriage.

In December, 1943, he was appointed subeditor of the *Irish Press*, and one of the staff which has successfully launched *The Sunday Press*.

Mr. Skinner has been an active Irish Republican from youth. As a member of the Fianna Eireann (boy scouts' auxiliary of the Irish Republican Army) he took part as a boy of eleven years in many activities during the Black-and-Tan War, and was on active service throughout the Civil War. He revived the Gaelic League Branch in Tralee, and re-organized the I.R.A., in which he continued a member until the De Valera Government took office in 1932, and was last Honorary Secretary of the Sinn Fein Club in Tralee. He re-organized the Gaelic League Branch in Killarney and founded the Killarney Progress Association, which promoted the Peace and Goodwill Festival there in 1941.

He has made a special study of national and international politics from his youth. He publicly advocated Ireland's participation, even as a partitioned Republic, in the Atlantic Pact, and the restoration of Ireland's territorial unity by force. He considers the existence of the Border dividing Ireland may prevent the nation playing its proper role in combatting Communism.

A life-long worker for the realization of Pearse's goal — an Irish-speaking, free Ireland — Mr. Skinner has long advocated and worked for the elimination of all foreign influences in such spheres as trade unionism and finance. He believes that a thirty-two county republic will become a close friend of Britain and a bridge linking the Western democracies with democracy's strongest champion, the United States of America.

Mr. Skinner began his career as a writer by winning a special prize in a short story competition held by the *Father Mathew Record*. He has written several short stories and special articles for newspapers and is the author of two books: *Politicians by Accident*, the biographies of the last De Valera Government, and *When Paths Divide*, a novel of the "Black-and-Tan" War.   M. A. H.

Henry Slesser   1883–

In a passage of self-revelation, in his autobiography, *Judgment Reserved*, Sir Henry Slesser tells us; "Though temperamentally delicate and nervous, I am, I think, lacking in that quality of caution which is sometimes unkindly called moral cowardice. Once I have been persuaded that a certain course of conduct is right, I cannot remember when I was deterred from following it by fear of consequences. I do not say this in self-praise; it was often a course of folly, but, regarding my life as dispassionately as I can, it appears to me to afford the clue to much of my history. Sometimes my actions have been in the highest degree unwise, sometimes they have brought me the confidence of others; rarely have they been restrained by apprehension of results."

It was certainly with "lack of caution" that Henry Slesser as an impecunious young barrister joined the Fabian Society (1907) and became one of its executive committee. Thus he found himself among the Socialists and founders of the English Labor Party. His honesty, modesty, and intelligent work won him respect and confidence. Important duties were thrown upon him as the new party grew and in 1924 he was made Solicitor-General in the first Labor Government. Meanwhile a deep and profound change was wrought in his soul, of which he tells in an article "Steps to a Conversion" which appeared in *The Tablet* (London, November 20, 1948).

In the year 1920, accompanied by two friends, one an Anglo-Catholic, Valentine Spalding, the other, a sceptic, the principal of an English University, Henry Slesser was walking from Oxford, along the Thames, and passing Shillingford Lock. The friends were discussing the basic sanction of morals, and the argument of Valentine Spalding seemed to be best. He showed that "in faith alone existed the sanction and authority for all that was right in action." "In a moment," writes Henry Slesser, "the whole of my past belief came back to me; how this happened, how much was the result of reason, how much of grace, I leave for others to determine; for myself the faith which then returned to me has never since departed, however inconsistent my behavior." This conversion, sudden and mysterious from a state of agnosticism as regards religion, was not at all a conversion to Roman Catholicism, in which at the time he had little interest, but a return to a vague and early "devotion to Christianity." Henry Slesser had still to study and struggle for twenty-eight years before he finally sought refuge in Rome.

Of Jewish descent, but never a member of that faith because his ancestors, ultra-liberals, rejected Judaism as a "particularist racial creed," young Henry had imbibed evangelical Christianity from his old nurse who had taught him "to believe in Judgment, Redemption, and Heaven, though, of course Purgatory was never mentioned, nor prayers for the departed." Of Our Lady he learned nothing, save that she was a Virgin, nor of the Church Visible. This early faith which Henry loved and clung to lasted until his wide indiscriminate reading of sceptical books led to "a state of agnosticism which lasted for twenty years," but which in turn gave way before the reasoned argument of Valentine Spalding by the Thames bank in 1920.

Once more a practicing Christian, Henry Slesser embraced fully and fervently Anglo-Catholicism in its most sacramental and ritualistic form. He studied and loved the early Fathers and warmly embraced the ethics and philosophy of St. Thomas. Soon he became acquainted with Bishop Gore, Lord Mamhead, G. K. Chesterton and all the most prominent and advanced Anglo-Catholics of the day, becoming chairman of the executive committee of their church union. As Solicitor General (1924), and later as Lord Justice of Appeal (1929), Sir Henry boldly introduced into his speeches and writings the principles of Thomism. When in 1924, he had to seek election for Parliament, he dumbfounded his Labor Party leaders by the tenor of his speeches. "I had read Belloc," he says, "and feared a Servile State, and in fact stood my election largely on the encyclical *Rerum Novarum* and the economics of St. Thomas. This was not as fatal to my chances as might appear — many of my supporters were Catholics — but when I was returned to Parliament I felt that I was free to approach economic and social problems from a Catholic standpoint, a liberty which I should not have enjoyed had I not made my position clear to my constituents." Meanwhile as an apologist for his faith, he argued and wrote. "I collaborated with a number of Anglicans of a like mind as myself in a symposium called "The Return to Christendom," written very largely under medieval inspiration. Dr. Gore furnished a Preface and G. K. Chesterton an Epilogue. I wrote "The Return of Dogma," which, I insisted, was a necessary step in the recovery of faith." Soon he was heart and soul in the widespread movement among Anglo-Catholics called "The League of the Kingdom of God." Sir Henry defined the scope of this league in his religious work *Religio Laici*. "We believe that all those who would proceed to alter the world, whether by Socialism, Collectivism, Liberalism, or any other plan which does not base itself upon a change in the heart of man, must fail. And we believe that the heart of man can only be converted on that vast and all inclusive scale which the Kingdom demands by the grace of Our Lord, the intercession of the saints, and the operation of the sacraments."

Until his elevation to the judicial bench in 1929, Sir Henry Slesser was an active, though not conspicuous figure, in politics and (from 1920 on) in church life in England. From the time, 1914, when he was rejected for the army owing to his poor health, his legal practice grew apace, and with it involvement in problems of the Labor Party. Often he had to draw up bills for Parliament, and on one occasion he drew up a bill of his own to prevent the removal of old buildings from England to the United States. Wrote a correspondent in *Punch:*

> The lamp of England's honor
> Shall never burn out clear
> Till Slesser's patriot bill be passed
> And our buildings anchored here.

On one occasion in delivering a decision in the Court of Appeal, he quoted St. Thomas' *Summa;* it was, perhaps, the first time since the Reformation that this was done. As a result he was denounced in Hyde Park as an agent of the papacy. It was one of the many examples which his public life afforded of that "lack of caution" which he claimed for himself as a characteristic.

Henry Slesser was born in London in 1883. He was the youngest son of Ernest Slesser, Gerrards Cross, Bucks. He was educated at Oundle and St. Paul's schools, and at London University and called to the bar in 1906. Taking "silk" in 1924, the same year he was made a Bencher of the Inner Temple. The following year, together with his friend Henry Game, the present censor of plays, he joined the Fabians. "My acceptance," he writes, "of Fabian doctrines and the Fabian life was enthusiastic and entirely uncritical; I doubt if there were a member of the Society who knew less of human nature at large or the reasons which had gone to produce our deplorable social conditions than I. . . . I took all the objections to Socialism to be the result of inaccurate or insufficient thinking." In 1909 he married Margaret Grant, daughter of Corrie Grant, K.C., a Liberal Member of Parliament. In 1924, due to his important services to Labor, he was appointed Solicitor General in the Labor Government. As yet he had no seat in Parliament, nor was he well known outside his own political party. As a result, a journal cartooned him adding the verse:

> Sir Henry Slesser seems to be
> A sort of unsolved mystery.
> A law adviser of the Crown,
> He has no seat — so can't sit down.
> And as he's not accounted for
> In "Who's Who" (1924),
> I leave this problem to each guesser,
> What really is Sir Henry Slesser?

Elected for S. E. Leeds, he represented that constituency for four years (1925–1929), when he was appointed a Lord Justice of Appeal. Retiring in 1940 to live in Devonshire, he was elected in 1946 a member of the Devon County Council. In 1948 he was received into the Catholic Church.

Apart from many articles, addresses, and contributions to the press, Sir Henry Slesser has published the following books: *Trade Union Law* (1922); *Religio Laici* (1929); *The Pastured Shire and Other Verses* (1935); *Law* (Heritage Series) (1936); *Judgement Reserved* (1941); *The Judicial Office and Other Matters* (1943); *History of the Liberal*

Party (1944); *Order and Disorder* (1945); *Through Anglicanism to the Church* (Catholic Truth Society Booklet) (1949); *The Middle Ages in the West* (1949), and *The Anglican Dilemma* (1952).

In concluding the account of his conversion, Sir Henry Slesser says: "I have found in the Catholic Church authority for the practices and beliefs which I have long held; my chief fault, as I see it now, was the long delay which kept me outside for so long, but in the sight of the Church, time is not of the essence." For nearly three decades he had hoped against hope to find in English "Catholicism," (Anglo-Catholicism) a sound and authoritative Church. But what he hoped for was not there. He made the same mistake that, he says, Cardinal Mercier made in carrying on negotiations for "union" at Malines with Lord Halifax in 1921. "Cardinal Mercier never appreciated the precarious and unrepresentative nature of Anglo-Catholicism." There was no substance to this "Church," it was only "a Brighton and South Coast religion!" The Lambeth Conference of 1948, and the Amsterdam Assembly which followed, convinced Sir Henry that the Anglican Communion did not seriously regard episcopacy as of the essence of Church government. He saw that the work of the Tractarians and Anglo-Catholics had failed. It only remained for him to take the road to Rome, and that road he took with faith and joy.   E. B. B.

Most Reverend Jan Olav Smit
1883–

The Most Reverend Jan Olav Smit, a Canon of St. Peter's Basilica in Rome, was born in the city of Deventer in the archdiocese of Utrecht (Holland) on February 19, 1883.

He made his gymnasium studies, philosophy and theology, in the seminaries of the diocese of Utrecht at Culemborg and Driebergen. After his ordination to the priesthood on August 15, 1906, he went to Rome and pursued further studies in the Gregorian University and in the Pontifical Biblical Institute. In 1907 he was awarded a Ph.D., and S.T.D. in 1909, and in 1912 a doctorate in Scripture. His thesis was: "De Daemoniacis in Historia Evangelica."

Soon after his thesis was published, he was appointed professor of Sacred Scripture in the seminary of the archdiocese of Utrecht (Rijsenburg) in Driebergen and for nine years he taught the Old and New Testament there. During this period he published various commentaries in Dutch newspapers and several tracts for the students of his seminary.

In 1922 he was appointed Vicar Apostolic of Norway and Spitzbergen and titular bishop of Paralus. He was consecrated a bishop in his native city of Deventer by the archbishop of Utrecht, van de

Wetering. Seven years later (1929) he was appointed canon of St. Peter's in Rome. There he is a Consultor of the Sacred Congregation of the Propagation of Faith, the Sacred Congregation of the Sacraments and of the Pontifical Commission on the Bible. He was also appointed (honoris causa) canon of the Cathedral of Utrecht and a Knight of the Lion of the Netherlands.

Besides his doctoral dissertation and various tracts on the introduction to the books of Sacred Scripture he is the author of *Het Vaticaan* (1932); *Naar Rome* (1933, 4th ed. 1951); *Rome III* (1936); *Ave Roma* (1940); *Bruids-paren bij de Paus* (Marriage-couples with the Pope) (1941, 2nd ed. 1944); *Herenigingspogingen in Verlegen en Heden* (The attempt of reunion in the past and present) (1941); *Roma e l'Oriente Cristiano* (1944); *Saint Peter's and the Vatican* (1945, 30,000 copies); *Paus Pius XII Feestpreken-Toespraken* (Panigyrica-Orationes) (1946); *Pastor Angelicus* (1949), translated into English by Father James Vanderveldt, O.F.M., and published by Dodd Mead and Company (New York) in 1950, under the title *Angelic Shepherd* and by Burns & Oates (London) in 1951 under the title *Pope Pius XII; O Roma Felix, Practical Guide for Walks in Rome* (1950); *Het Zilveren Jubeljaar* (Silver Jubilee Year) 1950; *Van en Opstanding van een groot Christen volk* (1950); *Het Eeuwige Rome* (1950); Blessed Pius X (1951); Uw Huwelijksgelvk (Your Marriage-happiness, addresses of Pope Pius XII; 1952).

Bishop Smit has known Pope Pius XII since his school days in Rome. A resident of the Holy City and a Canon of St. Peter's for more than twenty years he has been close to the events he describes in his popular American book, *Angelic Shepherd*. His Holiness honored the book by a special blessing to the English-speaking world over his own signature. The Apostolic Blessing, with the papal coat of arms reproduced in full color, is included on a special page.

M. A. H.

Helen Grace Smith *1865*

Miss Helen Grace Smith was born on December 15, 1865 at "St. Helen," Torresdale, Philadelphia, Pennsylvania where she still resides.

Her father, General Thomas Kilby Smith, had a distinguished career in the Northern Army in the Civil War. Her mother was Elizabeth Budd McCullough, a poet and musician.

Helen Grace Smith was educated at the Convent of the Sacred Heart, Eden Hall, Torresdale, Philadelphia, Pennsylvania.

She has devoted most of her time to literature, research, travel and charitable work. Her poems and essays were published in various magazines, notably *The Sign*, the *Atlantic Monthly*, *The Commonweal*, *America*, *Lippincott's*, *Belford's Magazine* and others. They have never been gathered for publication. Her brother, Walter George Smith, an eminent member of the Philadelphia bar, began to write the life of James Kent Stone, Fidelis of the Cross, Passionist. When this book was half completed, Walter George Smith died, and Helen Grace Smith finished the work, which was published by Putnam under the title, *Fidelis of the Cross: James Kent Stone,* and went through seven editions. It was afterwards published by the Knights of Columbus.

Theodore Dehon Smith, a second brother, became a Passionist, known as Father Maurice C.P., who died in Buenos Aires at the age of thirty-six. Helen Grace Smith wrote the life of this brother under the title, *A Knight of the Cross.* The first chapter of this book is a short history of the Passionist Order. Father Maurice's portrait hangs in the corridor of the monastery in Rome of Saints John and Paul. .

Walter George Smith had married Elizabeth Drexel, sister of Mother Katherine Drexel, and later became a member of the Indian Commission. Helen Grace Smith visited the Indian reservations with her brother and became familiar with Indian affairs. Through his legal knowledge he had become a great help to Mother Katherine in the foundation and management of her Order for Indians and Negroes, and Helen Grace Smith wrote constantly to interest the public in this great work of charity for both races and in the national problem of Interracial Justice. She also wrote and lectured for the Armenian cause, having gone with Walter George Smith, who was Commissioner for Near East Relief, to Constantinople and the Caucasus in the First World War.

M. A. H.

Naomi Royde Smith (Mrs. Ernest Milton)

Of mixed English, Welsh and French descent, Naomi Royde Smith was born in Llanwrst, Wales, the eldest daughter of Michael Holroyd Smith and Ann Daisy (Williams) Smith. Her father invented the traffic roundabout and was the first Englishman to take out patents for an electric tramway, an automobile and a heli-copter. He could trace his descent back to William Smith who, in 1600, was keeper of the Monk Bar Gate on the walls of York, and to Elkanah Holroyd who married the daughter of one of the Huguenot silk-spinners who took refuge in Norwich at the time of the Edict of Nantes. Miss Royde Smith's mother belonged to the same family as the Welsh poet William Williams of Pantycelyn (1717–1791), of whom it has been said: "The influence of his correct and fastidious muse remains to this day . . . it is not enough to say of him that he was a hymnologist, he is much more, he is the national poet of Wales." His hymn, "Guide me, O thou Great Jehovah," has been bowdlerized by the compilers of

Hymns Ancient and Modern but is sung in the original Welsh, *Arglwydd Arwain trwy'r Anialwch,* in Nonconformist churches and chapels all over the world. Miss Royde Smith's grandfather, the Reverend Ebenezer Williams, was educated at Trevecca, the theological college founded in 1768 by the famous Countess of Huntingdon. Miss Royde Smith's mother was only twelve years old when he died; she was devoted to him and was able to understand and remember his teaching and to continue to read his books and the wonderful letters he wrote to her and to Naomi's grandmother when he was away from them. There had been a good many clergymen and pastors in Naomi's father's family; so he and her mother had religion in their blood. "Oddly enough," remarks Naomi, "it was my father, the Yorkshireman, who was devout and who had at times mystical experiences; my mother's interest in religion was intellectual. She read Biblical criticism, discussed points of doctrine and conducted a Women's Bible Class in the little village of Warley on a hillside some miles out of Halifax where we lived. I can remember hearing discussions of a book of theological essays called *Lux Mundi* which made a stir in the 1880's and there was a great deal of talk about a restatement of the doctrine of the Atonement. I heard this without understanding very much about it: but it had the effect of making me — child though I was — decide that religion was a matter to be debated — not a belief that was beyond doubt. . . .

"My father — the Yorkshireman — was a pillar of the Congregational Church. My mother, an eclectic, kept a photograph of Cardinal Newman on her writing table; a copy of the *Imitation* at her bedside; went to church or to chapel or to Christian Science meetings as her mood or opportunity presented themselves and took me to hear Father Ignatius, Mrs. Besant, General Booth, the Reverend R. J. Campbell, Father Bernard Vaughan, and a Mrs. Boyle, who impressed me deeply by saying: 'Give me a child of four to teach and by the time she is fourteen, no priest or clergyman could possibly confirm her.'

"It was not until after my marriage (1926) to Ernest Milton, who, though born and brought up as a Jew, had Catholic ancestors on his mother's side, that both he and I found our way (1942) into the Catholic Church, and were received by Father Steuart, S.J., at Farm Street."

Her sister contributes to *The Tablet* (London) and *The Catholic Herald* under the name Julian Holroyd. She is a Catholic, as are her two nephews, John and Michael Royde Smith. One of her sisters is a Quaker, another a High Anglican, while a third remains, as she did for so many years, outside of any church. When in London, Miss Royde Smith goes to Mass with her husband at St. Ethelreda's Church in Ely Place, the only pre-Reformation Church in England which has been restored to Catholic use. Miss Royde Smith had been interested in the stage and thus she met the well-known English actor, Ernest Milton, whom she married.

In her childhood her family moved from Yorkshire to London. There she was educated, first at home and later in a private school. Then she went to Clapham High School in London and a private school in Geneva, Switzerland. Her childhood is described in her novel, *In the Wood.*

In 1904 Sir George Newnes made a place for her in the newly founded *Saturday Westminster Gazette*. At first she invented subjects for, and judged, the literary competitions which under the title "Problems and Prizes" attracted a great many well-known writers until the paper ceased publication in 1923. She was the literary editor from 1912 to 1922.

By this time she had become a reviewer and dramatic critic. Her first novel, *The Tortoiseshell Cat*, was published in 1926. Since then she has written a dozen novels — three of them, *For Us in the Dark* (1937), *The Iniquity of Us All*, and *Miss Bendix* (1938), being intentionally and explicitly Catholic.

Miss Royde Smith has also written biographies. One of these, *A Study of Julie de Lespinasse* (1931), grew out of her experiences immediately after the First World War when she and Rose Macaulay conducted a joint salon, which, she says, was always crowded with writers and artists. Her other two biographies are on Mrs. Siddons and Mrs. Sherwood. She has had three plays acted in London.

Miss Royde Smith is also the author of: *The Housemaid* (1926); *Skin-Deep* (1927); *John Fanning's Legacy* (1927); *Summer Holiday* (1929); *The Island* (1930); *The Double Heart* (1931); *The Bridge* (1932); *Pilgrim from Paddington* (1933); *Jake* (1935); *All Star Cast* (1936); *The Altar-Piece* (1939); *Fire-Weed* (1945). *The Idol and the Shrine* (1949) is a critical biography of Maurice de Guérin, French poet who died in 1839, with extracts from the journal of his sister, Eugenie.

Her two novels, *Mildensee* (1943) and *Love in Mildensee* (1948), deal with life in Geneva at the beginning of this century. Her latest novels are *The Iniquity of Us All* (1949), *Rosy Trodd* (1950) and a novel of contemporary life, *The New Rock* (1951).   M. A. H.

Vincent Edward Smith 1915–

Vincent Edward Smith was born in Lockland, Ohio, on August 15, 1915, son of Andrew G. Smith and Margaret McQueen Smith. His elementary education was at SS. Peter and Paul School, Reading, Ohio, operated by the Sisters of Notre Dame de Namur. He attended Roger Bacon High School, conducted by the Franciscan Fathers in St. Bernard, Ohio, and received his college education at Xavier University, Cincinnati, Ohio, a Jesuit institution.

His postgraduate work includes study at five institutions: University of Fribourg (Switzerland); Institutum Divi Thomae, Cincinnati and Palm Beach; Catholic University of America; Harvard; and Massachusetts Institute of Technology. He holds the Ph.D. degree from Catholic University.

During the war he served in the U. S. Navy. In the Pacific theatre, he was engaged in radar countermeasure work and received from Fleet Admiral Chester W. Nimitz a letter of commendation for developing a new detecting device to locate enemy radar. Following his work in the Pacific, he was assigned to the U. S. Naval Technical Mission in Europe, where his work consisted in exploring German advances in electronic, infrared, acoustical, and other allied detecting equipments.

Following the war, he taught for three years at Catholic University and was a member of the faculty in the School of Philosophy. He resigned his position in 1948 to do research and writing. In the fall of 1950, he joined the philosophy department at the University of Notre Dame.

In 1948, he was named editor of *The New Scholasticism*, quarterly journal of the American Catholic Philosophical Association. He has held this position since that time. He is a member of the Société Philosophique de Fribourg.

The following are his books: *Philosophical Frontiers of Physics* (1947); *Idea Men of Today* (1950); *Philosophical Physics* (1950); and *Footnotes for the Atom* (1951). Articles of his have also appeared in learned publications. He has lectured on philosophical subjects in this country and abroad.

In 1945 he married Virginia Beck. They now have three children: Christopher, Elizabeth Seton and Mary Velma Margaret.

There are several decisive turning-points in his life to be noted here. First of all, his parents taught him to take life seriously. They are deeply religious people, loyal to God above all other things, and when he later came to make a career of philosophy, they knew it was close enough to religion to be important and gave him constant encouragement. "Besides that," he says, "as I look back over my youth, I remember with thanks the training my parents gave me in being responsible. We always had chores to do and systems of rewards and punishments in our home where I was the eldest of five children. I think of the value of these tasks now as I read about the delinquencies among youth and the attitudes toward work that so many of our young folk seem to show. There is no better training in the psychology of being loyal, productive, ability to be counted on, than a frequent dose of work mixed in with the play of childhood.

"The second turning-point, for which I now thank God, was a case of osteomyelitis which laid me low for a whole year when I was thirteen. Though I obviously did not know then, I know now that this year, when I was unable to walk, gave me habits of reading and study that I had not previously cultivated. If I was an extrovert before, I became an introvert afterwards. I never had before, and I have not lost since, the incentives and the interests in books that developed during my year of illness.

"A third turning-point was the interest taken in me after college by the late Archbishop John T. McNicholas of Cincinnati. At the time I graduated from college, Archbishop McNicholas was inaugurating in his diocese a program to train laymen in graduate philosophy before they went on to professional schools. He therefore sponsored my graduate studies at the University of Fribourg, Catholic University, and the Institutum Divi Thomae. In high school, I was most influenced by Rev. Hyacinth Blocker, O.F.M., poet and preacher and later editor of *The St. Anthony Messenger*, and in college we had a literary club called the Mermaid Tavern, named after the famous rendezvous of Elizabethan literati. I wanted to be a journalist after these experiences but had already discovered that I needed philosophy to do any thought-provoking writing in the newspaper field. So I was thrilled to accept the favors of Archbishop McNicholas.

"The more I went into philosophy, however, the less journalism appealed to me, and, if I wanted philosophy as a lifework, teaching was the only career open. But I also saw the important fact that philosophy today, to be true to its mission, must be able to interpret modern science, the greatest positive achievement of the modern intellect that has flooded over learning and life. I therefore engaged in an intensive study of science for more than two years, at the Institutum Divi Thomae, Catholic University, Harvard, and Massachusetts Institute of Technology. The more I studied science, the more I learned about philosophy. The more I discovered about the metaphysical vacuum of the scientific method, the more and more insight I gained into the fullness of vision that is the philosophy of Thomas Aquinas. I never really appreciated St. Thomas until I saw a system, from within, that was not Thomistic. I never learned philosophy until I knew physics. My major work in philosophy, as my writings indicate, is to explore the borderland territory between Thomism and modern science. This is more than a life's work. It is the work of generations. But I am convinced that the vocation of philosophy today is to work toward a new *Summa* that will expand the wisdom of the past to embrace, within an organic and integral vision, the scientific achievements of the modern world. We are not Thomists by repeating St. Thomas; we must imitate him.

"The final and crucial turning-point was my marriage. My wife was an outstanding student in college, for whom writing was a first-love. She has written articles and stories for many Catholic periodicals, including *America* and *The Catholic World*. Our marriage is built upon a principle that I take to be absolutely essential in successful family life, the principle of friendship. She appreciates my work, the long hours and sleepless nights and disappointments which such work entails. She criticizes and corrects my articles, lectures, and books. Her hobbies, reading and writing, make it possible for us to have a normal and exceedingly happy family life, while both of us make constructive use of our time. The greatest entertainment in life is self-entertainment. Our movie-ridden and television-conscious generation needs most of all, in the psychological order, the habits and the hobbies of my wife."

M. A. H.

Anthony Joseph Stanley   1899–

It is not too fanciful to say that among the Irish medical profession there prevails a spirit kindred to that of the medieval guilds. They, the Irish doctors, are on the whole less mercenary, and more concerned with the spiritual as well as the bodily welfare of their clients than doctors of many other countries. And there are traditions that live amongst them that are noticeable and interesting. In sport, and they all enjoy sport, a great number fish. In respect of patriotism, they are (or have been) ready, in great numbers, to seize a gun at freedom's call. And lastly, there are not many of them but have an addiction to some form of culture, be it painting, writing or archeological research.

In Anthony Joseph Stanley, a distinguished physician of Mullingar, County West Meath (Eire), we have an exemplar of the traditions referred to. As a young medico he took an active part in the Irish War of Independence, fighting the Black and Tans. He was a member of the old I.R.A. (Irish Republican Army) that bore the brunt of the fighting under the heroic "Mick" Collins. As a sportsman he takes his rod and rows out to fish on the peaceful and beautiful Lough Owel, in his home county. As an exponent of culture he has written dramatic works, notably *Troubled Bachelors* and *Family Secrets,* and is chairman of the Mullingar Little Theatre.

Anthony Joseph Stanley was born in Mullingar in 1899. His father was Patrick J. Stanley an accountant; his mother was Mary Connell of Cullionmore near Mullingar. His primary and early education was with the Irish Christian Brothers, at St. Mary's College, Mullingar; his secondary education was at St. Finian's College, in the same town.

From St. Finian's, Anthony Stanley went to the famous college St. Patrick's, Maynooth (County Kildare), where he studied arts and philosophy. He took first class honors in Irish and French in his B.A. degree (1919). Then, in 1920, he went to Dublin to take up his medical studies, at University College, where he qualified in 1926. In the same year he married Margaret Carlyle, a native of Offaly County. They have four sons, one of whom entered the Order of Friars Minor in 1948.

Dr. Stanley, besides his private practice as physician, holds an appointment in the County Hospital, as physician and obstetrician, and in the County Home, as Medical Officer. He is also District Medical Officer to the Railway Transport Company.

Among his published works are: *Troubled Bachelors* (play); *Family Secrets* (play); and *Deliver Me From Blood* (a novel, published 1948). Dr. Stanley's novel had considerable success at home but its sales across the channel, in England, were prevented by a British ban on books published in the Irish Republic. His early short stories and articles have appeared in the *Father Mathew Record, Columban Record (Irisleabhar*

Muighe Nuadhat), college magazine of Maynooth and local papers. Dr. Stanley is a member of the Catholic Writers' Association (Ireland), a member of the Authors' Guild of Ireland, and many other Catholic societies. In his literary work (and in his professional work, too) Dr. Stanley states he depends upon the help and encouragement of his very efficient and understanding secretary, Miss Peggy Hanrahan, a Laoigh's girl from Kyle, Rathdowney, who prepares all his manuscripts for the publisher. He is fond of music and singing and for many years has been a member of the cathedral choir of his native town.

E. B. B.

Francis Stanley. See *Reverend Francis Stanley Crocchiola*

Karl Stern   1906–

When one becomes a Catholic, the event is greeted with surprise by a few non-Catholic friends and sometimes with hostility. To clear away the misunderstanding, converts often write their Apologia Pro Vita Sua. When Karl Stern informed a girl he had known in Germany in 1932 and met again in America in 1946, that he had become a Catholic she said simply and shortly: "Oh!" It is about this "Oh" that prompted Karl Stern to write his book, *The Pillar of Fire.*

Karl Stern was born of Jewish parents in Bavaria, Germany, in 1906. Several of his ancestors were rabbis. He received his first schooling in a kindergarten, conducted by nuns. Up to that time no Jewish child had ever been sent to the Catholic kindergarten. "We had no catechism," he says, "but we were entertained with stories from the Bible, particularly from the New Testament, which were illustrated with colored pictures on the wall." Soon he moved on to public school. Throughout his schooling everything "personal, spontaneous and improvised stuck much better in my memory than those things which correspond to the official curriculum." At the age of ten he went to Ebenburg, "a drab industrial town in the east of Bavaria," to attend the high school there. After one year, he was sent to Munich and lived with an orthodox Jewish family. At this time he became fascinated by music. This love became a decisive factor in his life. He stood in line early to attend an opera.

When he had just finished high school, his mother died, and he had to make a decision about the future. He chose medicine as his career and studied it at the universities of Munich, Berlin and Frankfurt where he took a degree in 1930. After graduation, he worked as an interne in

Berlin, in the neurological department of the Moabit Hospital, one of the large municipal hospitals of that city, situated in the middle of one of the slum districts.

Then he developed a passion for chamber music. It was on a visit to the Erich von Baeyer home to hear some that he met a daughter of the family, Liselotte, who was later to become his wife.

From 1931 to 1932 he was resident physician in the medical university clinic in Frankfurt under Professor Volhard. Here he became lecture assistant. It was the duty of the lecture assistant to prepare the daily lecture in internal medicine. He had to select the patients according to the diseases which were to be discussed. In the summer of 1932 he went to Munich to work as a Rockefeller fellow at the German Research Institute for Psychiatry, the first institute for psychiatric research, Dr. Stern believes, anywhere in the world. Dr. Stern was made an assistant to the head of the department which was devoted to the microscopic study of the sick human brain. His main duty was to instruct the research fellows. When Hitler came into power, he was the only Jewish physician of his age in a non-Jewish institution in all Germany who was not affected by the Aryan laws. "This," he says, "was due to the fact that at the time of the 'Big Change' I was holding a position under the Rockefeller Foundation." After abandoning himself to Schopenhauer's philosophy, Kant's rationalism, Hegel's dialectic and "its particular offspring the dialectic materialism of Karl Marx," Dr. Stern returned to the orthodox synagogue. He became "convinced of the profound significance and central position of the Messianic idea in Jewry. I began to believe in the truth of a personal Messiah."

In 1936 he went to London where he obtained a research scholarship from the Medical Research Council at the most famous neurological center in the English-speaking world. "A Jewish family which had founded that particular research scholarship had made a provision that a German-Jewish refugee was to have it.

"My little address book had the names of all those whom I knew to have emigrated to London before me. One of the names was Liselotte's, who studied bookbinding and then had left her bookbinder shop in Heidelberg. At the time when I came to London she was working as a bookbinder at the Warburg Institute."

He met her at the Cumberland Hotel for lunch. Inter alia, he had told her he had discovered a new Judaism and that it was Christianity. After he had finished, she said: "Never mind, it *is* The Cloud and you *are* crazy," but she added later, "If I ever were a professing Christian, I would be a Catholic." Later they married. In 1939 the Sterns left for Montreal, Canada, with their infant son Antony, arriving there on June 24. Here he obtained a position at a mental hospital on the outskirts of the city. In the meantime he was still unsettled in his mind about religion. He thought there was one man in the Church who would have an answer to many of his questions and that man was Jacques Maritain. By chance he was introduced to him. Maritain had come to Montreal to lecture. They met about a week later. But it was Mrs. Stern who preceded the doctor into the Church. It was not until two years later that Dr. Stern made the decisive step.

It was late autumn, 1943, that he went to see Father Ethelbert, an old Franciscan friar in Montreal, to ask him to receive him into the Church. He was formally received on the Vigil of Saint Thomas the Apostle, December 21, 1943.

His book, *The Pillar of Fire*, tells the story of his conversion. It also tells the struggles and vicissitudes of his life.

Dr. Stern is now working at the Allan Memorial Institute of Psychiatry, and is director of one of the research laboratories at McGill University where he is also an assistant professor of psychiatry. He also has a private practice.   M. A. H.

Richard Leroy Stokes   *1884–*

The journalist, Richard Leroy Stokes, was born in Rockville, Indiana, on November 30, 1884.

From an early age, he showed a decisive inclination for study and reading; at the age of twelve, during the holidays, he taught himself Latin and mastered Caesar single-handed. His mother took a great interest in his work and they both decided he would be a poet, some day. On leaving Indiana public school, he went to Harvard University for one year (Class of 1904).

Tempted by journalism, he joined the St. Louis *Post Dispatch* in 1914 as a reporter: became, in turn, rewrite-man, feature writer, book reviewer, music and dramatic critic. In music, he was also self-taught. From St. Louis, he moved to New York where he became music critic of the *Evening World* from 1926 to 1931. He travelled a good deal at that time and for eight years roamed over Europe, particularly France, Germany, Italy and Austria.

In 1937, he returned to America and joined the Washington Bureau of the *Post-Dispatch*. He specialized in economic articles and later military preparedness. In 1944, he volunteered to go to Europe as war correspondent for the *Post-Dispatch:* he took part in the Normandy landing and wrote the first on-the-scene account of fighting on Omaha Beach. He was assigned to General Patton's Third Army and rode in the great swing around the German rear from Avranches to Paris, then to Rheims and Verdun. He took part in the Battle of the Bulge and rode with spearheads of the Fourth and Sixth Armored Divisions in the invasion of Germany through Thuringia and Saxony to the meeting with the Russians on the Elbe River.

After V-E Day (the day of victory in Europe for the allies in World War II, May 8, 1945), he returned to America and covered the atom bomb story at Los Alamos, New Mexico. Back in Europe again, he reported the war guilt trials of the Nazis, 1945–46, at Nuremberg, a city in South Germany, in Bavaria. He was there from start to end, except for a month in Rome where he reported on the 1946 Consistory.

In Nuremberg, his attention was violently arrested by the discovery of the secret protocols of the Russo-German non-aggression pact, one of history's most important events, that passed unnoticed. The *Post-Dispatch* files, in later years, have often been consulted by writers of all categories who peruse these exclusive articles.

On his return to Washington in 1947, Mr. Stokes was assigned to the press section in the State Department, specializing on foreign policy, for two years. In July, August and September 1948, he was in Berlin, at the height of the tension over the blockade. He witnessed, in the midst of it, the famous riot of September 9, where anti-Communist Berliners, unarmed except for fists and paving stones, charged into the pistol fire of the Soviet police, put them to flight, and then tore down and burned the Russian flag over the Brandenburg Gate.

Puritanism had no appeal for Richard Stokes, and a great part of his life was dominated by indifferent agnosticism. Notwithstanding, he always said that if he acquired a religion, it would be Catholicism. He kept within himself the poignant memory of a winter evening, during his Harvard year, upon which he entered a Catholic Church. It was close upon Christmas and an exquisite boy soprano was soaring on the notes of "Adeste Fideles"; he never forgot that hour of peace.

Henry Adams' books, with their eulogy of Gothic cathedrals erected by faith, and his sincere Protestant tribute to the Blessed Virgin and her profound influence on the Middle Ages, impressed him deeply. The civilization of chivalry to the Hallowed Mother, as opposed to the mechanic age, struck him forcibly. Then a climax was reached by an unforgettable interview in Rome, at the time of the Consistory, with His Holiness, Pope Pius XII, whose saintliness overwhelmed the writer. Added to this the great lessons in suffering taught by the war, and the meeting in Paris with a French Catholic woman (Mlle. Anne-Marie du Pontavice), whom he was ultimately to marry in August, 1950, in St. Mary's Abbey Church, Newark, New Jersey, made God's call audible at last. After a time of struggle and reflection, Richard Stokes received, in 1947, the sacrament of baptism from the hands of Father Jean-Baptiste Argaut, in St. Matthew's Cathedral, Washington, D. C. His confirmation deeply impressed him as a member of the militant Church, and he realized the responsibilities of a Catholic writer in these present times of confusion and subversion: "Who is not with Me is against Me." Two years after his baptism, he resigned on July 1, 1949, from the *Post-Dispatch* to devote himself to Catholic journalism, seemingly, to him, the best vehicle for truth. His approach to the Church has been more intellectual than emotional. The edifice of the Catholic Church in its structure — social as well as dogmatic — appealed to everything that rang true in his mind and quieted all his longings. But all of his poetic instincts were also quenched by witnessing the rendering of the greatest Act of Love ever performed, the daily Sacrifice of the Mass. He has found great delight in reading the English Catholic poets: Francis Thompson and especially Gerald Manley Hopkins.

In April and May 1950, he was a guest of the Chinese Ministry of Information, on a trip to Manila, Formosa and Japan. A survey of the defenses of the island and of military Chinese forces was extensively made. In June and July of the same year he was in Germany, for *The Catholic Digest*, and was present at the parade of East Germany's Communist youth. He went to Bonn and interviewed government officials on the Franco-German pool.

Mr. Stokes' greatest aim, in his literary career, was always poetry. He is the author of three books of dramatic poetry. *Merry Mount* was used as the libretto for an opera produced at the Metropolitan Opera House, season of 1933–34, with the musical score by Doctor Howard Hanson: the preacher hero, Wrestling Bradford, a bitterly repressed Puritan, bears the stamp of Richard Stokes' memories as a child, in severe Methodist surroundings. *Paul Bunyan*, a folk-comedy, used the familiar giant-hero as a vehicle for a satire on American mores. *Benedict Arnold* is a tragedy in heroic couplets. In the Congressional Library lie the manuscripts of a libretto on *Mozart, The Music Robber*, produced in Cincinnati; a libretto on Marco Polo, and a movie-script on Sheridan. He also published the first full-length biography of Leon Blum, the French Socialist Premier, with special emphasis on his fifteen years war against Communism (1936).

At present, Mr. Stokes is engaged in writing a book that discloses some past events he feels the country must know about as soon as possible. M. A. H.

Reverend Anselm Stolz, O.S.B.
1900–1942

Great hopes had been placed in the young theologian, Father Anselm Stolz, O.S.B., whom death called at the early age of forty-two.

He was born in Erkrath, near Düsseldorf on January 28, 1900. His father, the head of a school, was from the Saar region; his mother was a Rhinelander. One of his brothers, Father Benedict Stolz, is stationed at Dormition Abbey in Jerusalem.

At the age of eighteen (1918), he entered the Benedictine Abbey of St. Joseph of Gerleve, in Westphalia, where his brother, Father Benedict, had preceded him into the monastic life. Invested as a novice on March 22, 1918, he was shortly afterwards inducted into the army. All his life he remembered vividly the retreat which followed after November eleventh of that year. He was forced to march on foot from Malines to Düsseldorf. With joy he returned to the quiet and peace of the Abbey of Gerleve. On February 29, 1920, he made his monastic profession. Soon afterwards, his superiors sent him to Maria Laach Abbey to study philosophy, and later (1921) to Saint Anselm's College in Rome. He was ordained a priest in Gerleve on August 6, 1924. In 1925 he obtained the S.T.D. degree from Saint Anselm's. His superiors then sent him to the Gregorian University to continue his studies under Father de la Taille, S.J. Later he attended the University of Münster.

Upon his return to his monastery, he taught philosophy but a few months when (1928) the Abbot Primate of the Benedictine Order called him to Rome to teach dogma at the International College of the Benedictines. His favorite themes were the Holy Trinity and mysticism. He had a special love for the Blessed Virgin. He spoke several languages fluently.

His work under E. Peterson inclined him more and more to patristic studies and towards a renewal of the theology of antiquity. Deciding to devote his life to this work, he spread this interest to his students. With one of his former students, Dom Hermann Keller, he conceived a course of theology following his new principles. Most of the work he did himself, in six booklets, which appeared from 1939 to 1941.

In 1933, at the request of the Abbot Primate of the Benedictine Order, he began the *Studia Anselmiana* with the publication of his *Glaubensgnade und Glaubenslicht nach Thomas von Aquin*.

He planned to write a commentary on the *Summa*, which he read four times, but the doctrine of the Holy Trinity attracted him to the study of the Fathers. Dom Anselm collaborated in the *Deutsche Thomas Ausgabe* for which he made notes in parts two and three. He also wrote many articles, the most noteworthy of which appeared in French reviews; in the *Katholische Gedanke* of Augsburg; in the *Benedicktinische Monatschrift* of Beuron; in the *Theologie und Glaube* and in *Catholica* of Paderborn, as well as *Questions liturgiques et paroissiales* of Louvain and in *Irénikon*. The first volume of the collection *Gestalter des Christlichen Abendslandes* was entrusted to him. In it he traced the life and work of Saint Anselm. The French edition of his book, *Théologie de la Mystique*, which appeared just as the war broke out in 1939, was exhausted in a few months and printing difficulties prevented its early republishing. The English translation was done by the Right Reverend Aidan Williams, O.S.B., S.T.D. The book is an exposition of Christian perfection as held in the early Church before the time of St. Augustine.

In July 1939, Dom Anselm gave the spiritual conferences for the retreat to his confreres of Amay, whose monastery had lately been transferred to Chevetogne. His conferences, based on original theology, which he applied to the religious life, appeared in the *Morcelliana* at Brescia under the title *L'Ascesi cristiana*. This was his last work — and it was published posthumously.

During the last years of his earthly career, Father Anselm devoted much of his energies to the spiritual guidance of religious, both men and women. The Benedictine nuns at Sorrento owe much to him. It was here that he also took care of the spiritual needs of the German soldiers who passed through southern Italy at that time. It is believed that it was this contact with the soldiers which communicated to him the germ of his final illness. He was taken down with typhoid fever. When he was already feeling sick, but not yet knowing the character of his disease, he was scheduled to give the retreat to the Camaldolese monks at Camaldoli. He wanted to cancel the retreat but yielded to their insistent request. From this retreat he returned a very sick man and died at St. Anselm's in Rome, October 19, 1942, called to his reward in the midst of his work. His last word was "Christus."

                                                                          M. A. H.

Reverend Benedict Stolz, O.S.B.
1895–

Living in Jerusalem since 1924, Father Benedict Stolz, O.S.B., remarks: "The Holy Land produces very many privileged souls, most of them hidden in convents. The future will show them to the astonished eyes of the world." Their lives have become his special study.

Benedict Arno Stolz was born on January 6, 1895, in Erkrath, near Düsseldorf, Germany. Two members of the family became priests, and three became authors. One of them, Father Anselm, died in 1942. The future Father Benedict made his early studies at Duisburg and from 1910 to 1913 was educated by the monks of the Abbey of Seccau (Steyermark). Then he applied for admission to the monastery. That same year, on August 10, he began his novitiate. One year later (August 11, 1914), he made his profession in the Order of Saint Benedict. From 1914 to 1916 he studied philosophy at Maria Laach Abbey and from 1917 to 1920 he studied theology at St. Joseph's Abbey in Gerleve. He was ordained on February 25, 1920. The following year he attended St. Anselm's College in Rome, Italy. In 1921 he went to Beitgiala near Bethlehem, as professor of theology, philosophy and church history in the seminary of the Latin Patriarchate. From 1922 to 1923 he was again in Rome to study for his doctorate in theology which he received in 1923. The following year he returned to Palestine and has been there ever since. From 1924 to 1932 he was prefect of discipline in the seminary and was professor of church and profane history and taught other subjects. From 1932 to 1947, he was master of novices. For four years (1940–1944) he served as subprior and for five years (1944–1949) as claustral prior of Dormition Abbey.

Father Benedict's favorite study is the lives of the saints. In Palestine and Europe he met many people with "mystical gifts." Some of these are Theresa Neumann whom he visited three times; Father Pio Di Foggia; M. Josephine Rumèbe, and Mother Mary Alphonsus of the Rosary.

One of his works translated into English by Natalie Bevenot is *Handmaid of the Rosary, Mother Mary Alphonsus of the Rosary, First Foundress of an Arab Congregation.* This is the life of an Arab Christian girl who, at 15, became a Sister of St. Joseph, and later, at the direction of Our Blessed Mother, founded a Congregation for Arab girls.

His other books are: *Mirjam von Abellin (Sr. Maria von Jesus dem Gekreuzigten* (1928), a stigmatized Carmelite Sister of Bethlehem; *Rosenkranzperlen* (1932); *Rosenkranzgedanken* (1934); *Das Grosse Rosenkranzgebet* (1938); *Im Lichte der Regel St. Benedikts, (Examples to the Rule of St. Benedict).*

His latest publication, being translated into English, is *Die*

Stimme des Geliebten. Aufruf an alle Braeute und Opferseelen Jesu Christi (1951). It contains writings of a hidden mystic, now living in the Holy Land. It will be followed by a series of similar publications.

M. A. H.

Geoffrey Stone 1911–

Geoffrey Stone was born in New York in 1911. He had, he declares, "no schooling worth mentioning." In, or around, 1928 he started to work for *The Bookman,* for which he later regularly did reviewing, as he also did for the New York *Sun, The Commonweal,* and the New York *Times.* When *The Bookman* was succeeded by *The American Review,* he became assistant editor of the new magazine and contributed extensively to its pages. At about the same time, he served as reader for the Macmillan Company, a position that was terminated, he explains, when a novel he had rejected was announced as winner of the Atlantic Monthly Prize. In 1938 and 1939 he edited and published a quarterly of his own called *The Examiner.* He has also published articles and verse in *Transition, Hound & Horn, Thought, Blackfriars,* and a number of the transient little magazines. His verse has appeared in two anthologies, *An Anthology of the Younger Poets* (1932) and *Ten Introductions* (1934); "but," he says, "I am certainly no longer young and, so far as production goes, I am probably no longer a poet either."

After 1939 he engaged in dairy farming in Bethlehem, Connecticut, where he still lives, and wrote nothing until 1947, when he went to Italy with the notes for a biography and critical study of Herman Melville. This was published in the fall of 1949 by Sheed and Ward as *Melville.* The book is an attempt to relate Melville's personal experiences to his writings; to consider these writings in their formal achievements as works of literature; and to examine their larger implications in the light of the combination of Calvinism and romantic idealism, with Manichean tendencies, that Stone finds characteristic of Melville's attitude. Newton Arvin, himself the author of a study of Melville, calls the book "valuable for the distance it maintains, in the right sense, from its subject, and for the purely critical distinctions it succeeds in making."

Geoffrey Stone was received into the Church in 1947. "I was raised," he says, "in a Presbyterianism that had no doctrinal or dogmatic outlines that I can remember. At sixteen, without any struggle or parental opposition, I became a disciple of Elena Petrovna Blavatsky, and this was very quickly followed by a period of normal, if unfortunate, adolescent Nietzscheanism. Fairly shortly I came, guided by that strange and brilliant man, Seward Collins, under the influence of the writings of Irving Babbitt, and for a long time my position was what I suppose might be called Aristotelian humanism. Here I held religion, by which

I, of course, understood Catholicism, to be intellectually worth assent but, in some way that I now find obscure, not applicable to myself. Private experience perhaps more than any line of reasoning in time convinced me that there could be no purposive human action when one lacked a teleology, and Catholicism alone offered a viable one. There remained only, with the intervention of grace, to become a Catholic." A. F.

Reverend Francis Maria Stratmann, O.P. 1883–

Over twenty-five years ago, Father Francis Stratmann of the Dominican Order acquired fame through his book, *Weltkirche und Weltfriede* (World-Church and World-Peace). This book, now out of print, has been translated into several languages and through it Father Stratmann became the leader of the Catholic Movement for Peace in Germany.

Francis Stratmann was born in Solingen (Rheinland), Germany, on September 8, 1883. His baptismal name is John. After he graduated from the gymnasium of Saarbrücken, he furthered his studies at the University of Lausanne (Switzerland). In October 1905, he entered the Dominican Order in Venlo, Holland, but studied at Düsseldorf. He was ordained to the priesthood at Cologne in August 1912. Two years later he was appointed chaplain of the students at Berlin University and held this office until 1923. From 1924 to 1926, he was in Cologne and then returned to Berlin as a curate of the Church of St. Mary of Victory. In July 1933, he was arrested by the Gestapo and put in prison in Berlin, Spandau and Frankfort on the Main. From 1933 to June, 1938, he was a penitentiary in the Church of St. Mary Major in Rome. Then he returned to the monastery of the Dominican Fathers in Venlo, Holland, where he worked for the Utrecht Committee for the Victims of the Persecution by the National Socialists. In February 1940, he was deprived of his German citizenship by the Nazi Government. During the Second World War, he hid himself in the convent of the Dominican Sisters at Bethania in Ghent, Belgium. In August, 1947, he returned to Germany where he now (1952) resides at Walberberg, near Cologne and is still devoted to peace.

When asked by the writer of this sketch, how he became interested in pacifism, he replied: "My work for peace may be explained by the experiences I had in the First World War. Then the truth dawned upon everybody that all the butchering was senseless and immoral, and never could be reconciled with the spirit of Christ. It became clear that such a modern devastating war never will do any good to any state (as many people had believed) but is always morally if not materially harmful to it even if it ends with military success. I was first of all impressed by the voice of Pope Benedict XV and furthermore by the writings of Frederick William Foerster, especially by his book *Weltkrieg und Weltgewissen* (World-War and World-Conscience). Therein I found for the first time an application of the Christian moral law to politics. From that day on, I myself was deeply interested in those problems. Since I was a well-known opponent of militarism and nationalism, I was one of the first German priests to be arrested in July, 1933, after Hitler came into power, and I was detained in several prisons. I was released in November of the same year without any trial."

Father Stratmann's first article in print was entitled "Federation of the German Catholics for Peace" in the magazine *Der Friedenskämpfer* (Fighter for Peace). He gave many lectures on this subject and wrote many essays. His book, *Weltkirche und Weltfriede* (World-Church and World-Peace) appeared in 1924. It was translated into Dutch and English. His book *Church and War: A Catholic Study on Peace* was published in 1929. *Peace and the Clergy* appeared in 1937. While Father Stratmann was in Bethania, Belgium, he started his book *Die Heiligen und der Staat* (The Saints and the State). For this work he had access to the books at Louvain and the library of the Bollandists in Brussels. The first volume is entitled *Jesus Christus;* the second volume, *Petrus, Paulus, Die Martyrer, Helena* (1949); the third volume, *Athanasius, Ambrosius, Johannes Chrysostomus, Augustinus* (1950). Three other volumes are to follow to complete the set. Once Father Stratmann jokingly called this work his "Apologia pro Vita Mea" — because he was called a traitor to his country. In his *Die Heiligen und der Staat* he examines the lives of many of the great saints and Our Lord Himself to show they were innocent victims of such an accusation and had to pay with their lives for crimes they did not commit.

His other books are: *Regina Pacis: Eine lehre vom Frieden, dargestellt am friedenreichen Wesen und Leben U.L. Frau* (1927); *Betrachtungen über die Psalmen des Officium Marianum* (1937); *Bethanien predigt (Vom Geiste des Pater Lataste)* (1946) and *Krieg und Christentum heute* (1950). The last mentioned book deals with the perplexing problems which arose with the totalitarian war and which must be solved by the Church and Christian conscience. It also considers the problem of conscientious objectors to military service.   M. A. H.

Charles Stanley Strong   *1906–*

Charles Stanley Strong, traveler, author, lecturer and explorer, was born on November 29, 1906 in Brooklyn, New York, the son of Charles Warren and Rosella Agnes (Bradt) Strong. Baptized at St. Gregory's in Brooklyn, he received First Communion at St. Matthew's in Brooklyn, and was confirmed at the Holy Child Jesus Church, Richmond Hill, Queens.

Educated in the public schools of the City of New York, he won a scholarship in accounting and law at Pace Institute (1924–1925), now Pace College; and completed his education at the Royal Frederick University in Oslo, Norway (1925–1929).

Mr. Strong has traveled extensively, both as a means of gaining source material for his stories, articles and books, and in connection with work as an advertising representative and author of booklets and literature for various railroads, steamships, air lines and publicity bureaus.

For five years he did special correspondence work in Europe for various American newspapers and also conducted the American-Scandinavian News Bureau, which had its offices in New York City, Oslo, Stockholm, Helsingfors, Copenhagen, and Reykjavik. During this time he traveled extensively throughout Europe and North Africa, and in the north Atlantic islands of Iceland, Greenland, and Jan Mayen Land, and made several trips to Spitsbergen and Bear Island in connection with reporting work on the Byrd, Amundsen, Ellsworth, Nobile and other Polar expeditions. He spent a season with the Norwegian, Swedish and Finnish Lapps in the highlands just below the north coast of Europe.

Returning to the United States and Canada in 1930, Mr. Strong continued his work with Scandinavian groups, and visited many of the Scandinavian colonies in the United States and Canada, and subsequently went into more general work in the writing field with Canada and particularly the Canadian Arctic and Alaska as his special interest.

In 1934 he was married to Ida May Brower of Brooklyn, New York, and is the father of Charles Robert and Ida Leona Strong. Following his marriage, his wife and children accompanied him on a number of his trips throughout the United States and Canada, to Alaska, to the West Indies, and northern South America.

Mr. Strong has done a good deal of pioneering work in aviation during the past twenty years, and articles on this phase of his career have appeared in *The Sportsman Pilot* and *National Aeronautic Magazine*, covering his experiences on the Amsterdam to Java route, from London to Capetown, South Africa, into the jungles of British, Dutch and French Guiana, and in the Arctic and sub-Arctic of Canada and Alaska. He also made numerous trips with the air ambulance service in Lapland during his career in Scandinavia; and out over the Arctic Islands north of Europe while taking part with one of the search parties for Roald Amundsen in 1928.

The author's lectures have taken him to a number of colleges and universities in the United States and Canada, and he has appeared on numerous radio and television programs, and before Kiwanis and other service groups. He was selected by the International Association of Tourism of The Hague, Holland, to compile their authentic book of European travel, *Europe Calling*, which was published in thirteen languages for a number of years before World War II.

For the past fourteen years, Mr. Strong has been connected with Standard Magazines, Inc., Better Publications, Inc., See Publishing Company and Popular Library, Inc., and is now supervising editor. During the same period, however, he has managed to continue his traveling and lecturing, and has written a number of books, magazine articles and stories.

During the past thirty years, Charles S. Strong has written almost a hundred novels, more than two thousand stories and articles published in the United States, Canada, England and a number of other foreign countries, and has been elected to a number of societies and organizations for his work.

He was vice-president of the Catholic Writers Guild of America, Inc., is a member of the American Polar Society, associate member of the Arctic Institute of North America, of the Society for the Advancement of Scandinavian Study, the American Scandinavian Foundation, and similar organizations.

His present home is at Manhasset, New York; and he has a summer home at Purling, Greene County, in the same state. He is active in civic and social affairs in his community, and is president of the Manhasset-Lakeville Fire Department, one of the largest and best equipped completely volunteer fire departments in the United States. His interest in fire fighting also extends to other parts of his county and the state, and he is a member of the Nassau County Firemen's Association, the Firemen's Association of the State of New York, and has represented his department as a delegate at a number of annual conventions.

For the past ten years most of Mr. Strong's books have been in the action and adventure fields, and he has produced eight Royal Canadian Mounted Police books under the pen name of Charles Stoddard; numerous Western action novels under the name of Chuck Stanley; and two widely celebrated dog stories, *Ranger, Sea Dog of the Royal Mounted* and *South Pole Husky*, under his own name. *Ranger* was awarded the Gold Medal of the Boys' Clubs of America in 1949.

Some of the other books he wrote are: *The Spectre of Masuria* (1932); *Betrayed* (1935); *Beauty Racket* (1936); *Cruise Hostess* (1936); *Army Wife* (1937); *Professional Model* (1938); *Private Secretary Plus* (1938); *Flying Lovers* (1939); *The Winter King Killings* (1939); *Confessional* (1939); *Information Girl* (1940); *Very Private Chauffeur* (1941); *The Training Camp Murders* (1941); *Hat Check Girl* (1942); *Tropical Rapture* (1943); *The Trapper of Rat River* (1944); *Killer of Fort Norman* (1944); *The Timber Beasts* (1945); *Killer of Sheep River* (1946); *Show-*

down Guns (1946); *Tolliver on the Trail* (1947); *Larabee of Big Spring* (1947); *Prairie Peril* (1947); *Red River Crossing* (1948); *Top Hand* (1948); *Frontier Scout* (1948); *Buckskin Men* (1949); *Cayuse Courier* (1950); *Buckskin Beau* (1950); *Rio Patrol* (1951); *Mountain Men* (1951).

Mrs. Mary Alsop Parrot Sture-Vasa. See *Mary O'Hara*

Emmanuel Celestin Cardinal Suhard   1874–1949

A beloved figure in Paris since May, 1940, having been transferred there from the Archdiocese of Rheims, to be Archbishop of Paris, Cardinal Suhard so endeared himself to the French people that on his death the headline, in heavy type, of a French newspaper, read, "The Cardinal, our Father is dead."

Cardinal Suhard was one of those dignitaries who rose from the ranks. He was born in Brains-sur-les-Marches on the boundary of Mainz and Normandy in France, April 15, 1874. His parents were poor humble peasants. As a child, the Cardinal longed to be a priest. The rural pastor took an interest in him and taught him the studies preparatory to the minor seminary, which he entered at Mayennes. His progress was so marked in the major seminary that he was chosen to study at the French College in Rome. Upon completing his studies there, he was ordained to the priesthood on December 18, 1897, at the age of twenty-four. He then returned to France where he was appointed a professor in the Laval Seminary, a post he held for thirty years. In 1928 he was named Bishop of Bayeux and Lisieux. During his two years there, he did much to build the famous shrine of Ste. Thérèse the Little Flower, in Lisieux.

In 1930, he was elevated to the Archbishopric of Rheims, a position he held for ten years until he was named Archbishop of Paris. He had received the Red Hat in 1935.

During the war, the French government, fearful of Cardinal Suhard's life, urged him to leave Paris, but he declined. It was only after the liberation of Paris in 1944 that it became known that the Nazis had searched his home and confined him temporarily. When he was interrogated by the Nazi leaders, the Cardinal replied: "As a bishop I have defended imprescriptible rights. As a French bishop I have done my duty towards my country. No one can make me express regret for having defended these rights or fulfilled these duties."

A writer, Anthony B. Atar, who interviewed the Cardinal twice, described him in the Brooklyn *Tablet* (June 18, 1949) as "an unforgettable personality. A tall and strong looking man, he was slightly bent by age. But his benign and cheerful smile was of someone who, because of wisdom and knowledge of life, has become ageless and part of marching history."

The Cardinal "headed the drive in France to spread and improve the teaching of the catechism; championed the rights of workers; pleaded the cause of suffering children; demanded the economic redemption of the proletariat; and constantly insisted on basic reforms," writes a reporter for the National Catholic Welfare Conference.

The Cardinal was well known for his pastoral letters. One of these has been published as a book, *The Church Today: Growth or Decline* (1949). This document has become of international importance to the whole Catholic world. As Claire Huchet Bishop says of him in *The Commonweal* (July 15, 1949, p. 340), "He was a sign of unity. And what made him so was the fullness and perfection of his obedience to the Church, obedience made, not of servility, but of plenitude of faith."

This distinguished churchman died on May 30, 1949. More than 70,000 people had paid their last respects to the Cardinal, whose body had lain in state in the archiepiscopal palace. He was buried in the thirteenth century cathedral of Notre Dame.

The Cardinal's red hat was hoisted high up in the nave where, according to tradition, it will remain until it falls to the ground in dust.   M. A. H.

Mark Sullivan   1874–

Mark Sullivan tells us in his autobiography, *The Education of an American*, of his fidelity to his vocation as newswriter, master critic, and strategist in the country's politics. "Excepting the period I spent at Harvard, and the few years of my youth when I was a publisher myself, the career, beginning when I was not yet sixteen, has been lifelong and uninterrupted." In that vocation he earned his bread. "Fifty dollars is the only payment I ever received from the law or from any other occupation or source except writing."

Writing was in his blood, and the smell of printer's ink was in his nostrils from his days at normal school (1888–1892) when he contributed to the *Moore Gazette*, a school paper, and helped found another, the *Amulet*. In a fantastic sense "printer's ink" was a *motif* in his makeup. Mark tells how in later years he was walking along an old street in Antwerp when "a sense of pleasure and homesickness, of alertness and longing" came to him. There was, he felt, something in the air, he knew not what. He began to search here and there among the streets and alleys and found a smell "that hardly one person in a thousand would have noticed." He continued to search "like a hound upon scent" till he discovered a hidden court and "felt like a traveller who in a strange land comes miraculously upon blood kin." There, confronting him, was the oldest printing establishment in the world, the Plantin Museum!

Mark Sullivan was the youngest of seven sons of Cornelius Sullivan and Julia Gleason Sullivan, Irish immigrants. His father was a small farmer in Avondale, Pennsylvania. He had come from Kanturk, County Cork, with his fiddle and a store of Irish songs. It may be that the tenderness and sensitivity that Mark Sullivan was capable of in his many friendships and associations was derived from paternal influence. "My father," Mark says, "would take his fiddle and, for his solitary ear, play and sing one of the most poignant tunes of lonesomeness ever heard:

> Shool, shool, shool, a gradh
> I wish I were on yonder hill,
> 'Tis there I'd sit and cry my fill
> Till every tear would turn a mill . . . etc.

Mark's mother, who hailed from near Macroom, also in County Cork, brought with her some dear fancies and legends of the old land. Banshees she had heard, she told Mark, many a time and she would not let him make light of them. Like Cornelius, her husband, she spoke Irish, and when the parents wished to conceal something from the children, they would speak together in Irish.

The family was deeply Catholic, and Celtic-like knew how to combine gay, old-time ways with religion. It was an Irish Catholic home, redolent of folklore and customs. "After dinner," writes Mark, "there was playing of the fiddle and dancing, my mother the only woman, and, later, talking until after midnight and finally the Rosary, all kneeling, my father leading, the rest of the family responding." When the hour came for Mark to leave home, as his six brothers had in turn done before him, "as my father drove me to the station, my trunk in the back of the wagon, he gave me parental advice, with emphasis, that I should 'take care of my soul.' He knew that he was launching the last of his brood from the nest and forever."

Like many a good Irish parent, Mark's father saw to his education, first at the local school when he was eight, and later at the normal school when he was fourteen. There, Mark read widely and began to write and *to talk*, or rather reporter-like, to cultivate wide contacts. Writing home at the time he said quaintly: "I am on speaking terms with every boy here." While at normal school he tried twice for West Point but was turned down on each occasion on account of physical disability. On the second occasion *defective vision* was discovered. Looking back, years later, after brilliant "muckraking" exploits, Mark wryly notes: "my eyes turned out to be able to see a good deal."

At normal school he made friends with Edwin L. McKinstry, a senior fellow student who on graduating took a position on the West Chester *Morning Republican*, and was destined to remain in West Chester journalism for fifty years. When Mark graduated, McKinstry gave him a job as a reporter. To McKinstry, therefore, Sullivan is indebted for his start in newspaper work.

When Sullivan was a little fellow, working on his father's farm — and he worked hard — his mother used to love to hear her little son say, on coming in at evening-time: "I been a-workin', an' a-workin', an' a-workin' all day!" Now his long life as a keen and able journalist was to begin and with it an "a-workin' all day."

After a year on the *Morning Republican*, Sullivan went as partner with a young member of the staff, John Miller, in the purchase of a rundown paper in Phoenixville, the *Phoenixville Republican*. For three years the two young publishers developed their business. Then fate would have it that a very beautiful young lady, Miss Hope Cox, should come to the town with her mother to visit her fiancé, an engineer. Mark met Hope Cox and was strongly attracted by her charm. He heard for the first time "On the Road to Mandalay" played by her.

Hope, interested in the young editor, took it upon herself to advise him. Her advice was excellent and changed the course of Mark's life. "She told me," Mark reminisces, "I must go to college, I must go at once, the coming fall, and I must go to Harvard — no other would do!" Mark took the girl's advice.

At Harvard (1896–1900) "I learned to like learning" — and in an other-world Irish way, dallied with the idea of living a hermit's life among books. "I went," he says, "through the college catalogue and found that the total number of courses, including remote ones about the history of Syria, and of the Bagdad Caliphate, was roughly two hundred. To take all these courses at the rate of four a year would consume fifty years; and I thought it would be a nice way to spend one's life, living in a college room and covering the whole world of learning." But Mark was destined to be an intrepid writer rather than a sedate scholar.

Shrinking from "the routine and complexity of a publisher's life" which a return to Phoenixville would mean for him, Mark sold his interest in his paper and planned to pursue a law course at Harvard after taking his A.B. degree (1900). Meanwhile to help pay expenses he wrote occasional articles for the Boston *Transcript*. Immediately before entering the Harvard Law School he held a post for a short time on the *North American* (Philadelphia) in the news department. There he had a dramatic meeting with Archbishop Ryan to whose gentleness and saintliness he pays tribute.

It was while at Harvard Law School (1900–1903), that he wrote his first politically important article. It appeared in the *Atlantic Monthly*, anonymously, under the title "Ills of Pennsylvania." It was the first of many magazine articles he was to write. It began a new era in political penmanship. Judge Pennypacker made an issue of the article, claiming that "Pennsylvania had no ills that are worthy of mention." But Mark Sullivan had discovered *something* to do. To use his own words: "where politics and business met . . . there were conditions and practices that invited exposure."

Having left law school, and abandoned any inclination to practice law, Mark Sullivan accepted work from Edward W. Bok (1904) on the *Ladies' Home Journal*, which at the time belonged to Cyrus H. K. Curtis. Bok needed a cool-headed, factual-minded investigator of the patent-medicine business. He gave Mark Sullivan a free hand to track down and discover evidence. The investigation culminated in a sensational revelation of conspiracy between quack-mongers and the press. In an article entitled "The Patent Medicine Conspiracy against the Freedom of the Press," Mark Sullivan revealed his sensational findings. The article was too long for *Ladies' Home Journal* and appeared in *Collier's*, of which Norman Hapgood was editor, and R. J. Collier, owner and publisher.

Norman Hapgood "had a special appreciation of any writing about a public matter that was austere and factual, which made its effect, not by emotion, but by massing of facts." In Sullivan's article the facts were striking, abundant, and well presented. The article caused considerable stir, and soon, Collier and Hapgood, who "belonged in the very highest journalistic level of the America of that time" invited Mark to join their staff. Now, at last, his career had an impressive start.

Perhaps the biggest event in Mark Sullivan's life was the initiation of his own quasi-editorial page in *Collier's* called "Comment on Congress" (1910). He was given a free hand in making his own polemics, and he was not slow to direct his fight against the privileges and powers of the big corporations. "Corporations," he writes, "had come to have, in American life, politically and economically, a power that was intolerable." And in the Republican Congress of the time, there were two great figures, Joseph G. Cannon (Republican Speaker of the House), and Nelson W. Aldrich (Republican Leader of the Senate), whose political skill and political and economic conservatism worked to preserve the status of "big business."

Mark Sullivan now took up his pen to overthrow Cannon and Aldrich. An immense — an almost hopeless fight — was before him, but his courage never failed, nor did his skill. He began by explaining in his page the political art of Cannon as exemplified in his manipulation of House Committee rules — how he could prevent any legislation that he disliked. He did not call Cannon dishonest — but he denounced him as a "stand-patter" who prevented all progress, all reform. Sullivan publicized the patriotism of the dozen Republican "progressives" in the House and he taught the people how to use their power in elections by demanding "pledges" from candidates. Mark, at thirty-six, was now a national figure. His energy was amazing. He attempted, he tried every literary art in his fight against Cannon. He was even, he admits, "blatantly partisan." If there was any possible device of polemic journalism that escaped my ingenuity," he writes, "I did not know then what it could have been and cannot think now." But, always, Mark kept his self-restraint, and played down over-zeal. He could never forget an incident of his days at normal school.

It was a baseball game between his school and another, and he was letting himself go "in spasms of ululant vociferation." He was "the leading fan for his team, at least the most conspicuous." Then, as he confesses in his autobiography, "I noticed two young men, disinterested spectators, gazing at me. One of them said to the other, 'Will you look at that mouth.' . . . There it was borne in on me that my zeal for achieving a maximum of noise might diminish my favor in the sight of spectators. In that moment, I consciously added to my personality an ingredient of restraint which for a lifetime wholesomely diluted my impulses towards unreined enthusiasm."

Joseph G. Cannon was defeated by his own party in the House, thanks in large measure to the skill with which Sullivan had worked up opposition to him. Thereafter the Progressive Party waxed strong and Sullivan's longstanding friendship for Theodore Roosevelt was established.

After many years with *Collier's,* and the dissolution of the unity between Hapgood, Collier and himself, Mark Sullivan joined the New York *Evening Post* (1919), still writing political columns. Later he worked for the New York *Tribune* (1923), now the *Herald Tribune.* Honorary degrees from Brown University, Dartmouth, Washington and Jefferson, Bates, were later showered on him. From 1928 until 1934 he was Overseer at Harvard.

Long a familiar figure at White House press conferences, Sullivan reached the peak of presidential association in the days of Herbert Hoover, whose "deep well of good will" he acclaimed and with whom he had "a myriad associations."

Apart from innumerable political articles, Mark Sullivan wrote *Our Times — The United States* (1900–1925), at the invitation of Scribner's: a six-volume history of the nation from 1900 until 1925. "I was moved," he says, "by a feeling I had about the writing of history, to the effect that most history puts undue emphasis on politics." His second book, *The Education of an American,* an autobiography, appeared in 1938. Therein he gives an idyllic picture of his early days and proceeds to discuss factually the outstanding events and interesting associations of his busy life up to the early thirties. In writing his story, especially when he had to recall his early experiences, he tried "to wall out the present" and seek a "spiritual saturation, a deep immersion in the scene he was evoking from the past."

About his success as a professional writer, Mark has interesting things to say. "To ask for a job is not the best way of getting one . . . my way was not to ask an editor for anything but to present him with something. If a writer is to acquire any right to consideration by an editor he must be able to know for himself what the editor is likely to want." On one occasion Noel Coward asked Mark to see the motion picture "Cavalcade," that Coward had written, but had not had an opportunity of seeing. The experience proved a kind of shock to Mark. It was, he thought, a wonderful film and he marvelled over the art by which its remarkable effects were achieved. "Here am I," reflected Mark, "a writer engaged in the business of conveying ideas to the public, and here, while I have been laboriously pushing pen across paper, has arisen a new method of conveying ideas, a method in many respects more flexible, more direct and more effective than mine. I felt as if I were one of those old monks, the scriveners, who continued to copy manuscripts by hand long after printing had been invented." Mark advises young writers to "learn the art of writing, of course, but to learn also the art of the motion picture and the radio."

In his life, Mark Sullivan exemplifies his own formula for success: "to find a career to which you are adapted and then to work hard at it." He adds that "when the right career has been found . . . hard work is not hard work at all." As a philosopher, he is an individualist, "a sheer individualist, perhaps a naive one . . . believing in self-help . . . believing that America continues to offer opportunity as abundantly as ever." In temper he is Irish, more so even than he realized when admitting that "in myself I can recognize many qualities that are Irish by blood."   E. B. B.

Henry Surchamp (Jean Nesmy)
1876–

Henry Surchamp was born on July 11, 1876, at March la Tour, Correze, France, of humble parents. His father was a village schoolmaster.

He made his secondary school studies at Brive, in the province of Limousin, France, and then attended a school of agriculture and a school of forestry.

Until his marriage to a girl of Champenois, he spent his whole life in Champagne. All his life was spent as a state employee in the Department of Conservation of Water and Forests in which he became a conservator (top rank in the regional "hierarchy"). He is now retired and is on pension.

He wrote under the pseudonym of Jean Nesmy. His two sons, twins, entered the Benedictine Abbey of Pierre qui Vire. One of these took as his own name in religion his father's pseudonym and is now Dom Claude Jean Nesmy, the other kept the family name and is Dom Angelico Surchamp. These two monks are very active at their abbey. Dom Claude inherited his father's literary gift; Dom Angelico is an artist.

Henry Surchamp depicted the beauty of Limousin, his native section in his poems. He is the poet of woods and forests and that is what he describes in his different poems such as the ones entitled in English "The Four Seasons of the Woods," "The Fairy of the Forest," "The Novel of the Forest," "The Alphabet of the Forest" and in French, "Au Coeur Secret du Bois." He sometimes wrote in the style of Alphonse Daudet and imitated him in depicting the simple and sometimes rude village life of the peasants.

One of his books, *A Parcel From Heaven*, was translated into English by E. M. Walker and was published by Sands & Co. in 1916. *Limousin Folk*, translated into English by W. M. Daniels, was published in 1930 by Heath Cranton Limited. He also brought out *Nouveau Couter de la France contemporaine* (Fifteen stories of French life, war and adventure) — chosen and annotated by W. M. Daniels.

M. A. H.

Reverend Edmund Felix Sutcliffe, S.J. 1886–

Father Edmund Sutcliffe was born in 1886. His native place is Stowmarket, a small country town in Suffolk, England, though the family, like all of the same name, is of Yorkshire origin. "The Hollies," as his father's house was called, was mentioned in the thirties by *The Times* as having been acquired to be converted into the central post office of the town. Both parents had been received into the Church before his birth. Both had been staunch members of the Church of England. His mother, Catherine Willis before marriage, was a daughter of the then vicar of Trimley, Suffolk, and his father was himself a curate at St. Nicholas, Great Yarmouth, which has the distinction of being the largest parish church in England — in those days the number of curates ran into double figures. But he remained in the ministry of the Church of England only from the close of 1877 to the first months of 1879. "I certainly was distressed, when every new thing in doctrine swept unopposed over its pulpits. . . . I was still more distressed when, in pastoral work, grievous errors against some tenet of the faith opposed themselves, and I felt that my Church gave me no rod of power wherewith to combat them. Most of all was I distressed when in my own case doubts arose as to whether this or that opposing view were the true teaching of the gospel, and my Church blew her trumpet with a very dubious and uncertain sound, and I, who should have been the guide of others, knew not how to steer my own course." So he wrote in a little book, still full of interest and instruction, entitled *Prove All Things — A Letter to the Parishioners of Great Yarmouth* (1881). A turning-point in his thought was reached with the perusal of Father Gallwey's *Lectures on Ritualism* (No. vii, The Faith of St. Leo the Great). Many friends sent him Dr. Littledale's, *Plain Reasons against Joining the Church of Rome*. The study of it convinced him that "there is but a choice of alternatives possible for the author of this book: untruthfulness or incapacity." Incidentally it is amusing to record that this same book played a decisive part in forwarding the reception into the Church of the late Canon William O. Sutcliffe, uncle of the subject of the present sketch.

Kindly lessons in the arts of reading and writing from the Ursuline nuns, then in the Worple Road, Wimbledon, opened for Edmund Sutcliffe a prolonged career of often weary discipleship pursued first at Wimbledon College, then at Mount St. Mary's College, and later at

Oxford University and the Biblical Institute at Rome besides the seven years customarily devoted to philosophy and theology in the Society of Jesus. He entered the Society in 1903 and when in 1926 his own turn came to lecture on the Old Testament at St. Beuno's College, N. Wales (then the theologate of the English province), the memory of these long years engendered a sense of sympathy with his auditors which the passing of time has not dimmed. This professorial activity was interrupted when the theologate had joined with the faculty of philosophy at Heythrop College, Oxfordshire, by one of the outstanding blessings of his life. This was a sojourn during the calendar year 1927 in the land where the patriarchs had tended their flocks and received promises from heaven, where the prophets had striven to keep the people true to God and had foretold the coming wonders of the Messianic Kingdom, where the theocratic kings had for the most part betrayed their trust, and above all where those ancient foretellings received their world-shaping fulfillment in the doings, the sayings, and the silence of our Divine Lord and His Blessed Mother. It will be remembered how strongly St. Jerome, the master of all who study the Bible, recommends this pilgrimage: "Sanctam Scripturan lucidius intuebitur qui Judaeam oculis contemplatus est."

An article in *The Month* for June, 1906, proved to be the prelude to many others which have appeared in *Biblica, The Journal of Theological Studies, The Catholic Biblical Quarterly* and elsewhere. Two articles, reprinted as pamphlets, on *Who Perished in the Flood?* defending the view that not all men were destroyed in that catastrophe and on *The Six Days of Creation*, explaining Genesis, Chapter I, as an artistic schematic presentment of the fundamental fact of creation, have been adjudged to have had considerable influence in shaping opinion. Besides some translation, he has edited books by the Jesuit Fathers, John Donovan, Robert Hull, and Eric Burrows. In a notice of one by the last-named contributed by the late Dr. Vacher Burch to *The Dublin Review* he was described as "the ideal editor." He has also published three books. His *Grammar of the Maltese Language* (1936) is a textbook in the Royal University, Valletta, and is now in a second edition. Maltese is a form of Arabic, incidentally the only one which has developed in a Christian community, and every student of the Old Testament must extend his interest beyond Hebrew into the wider field of the Semitic languages. *A Two Year Public Ministry* (1939) defends the view that Our Lord's public ministry comprised three Paschs only. *The Old Testament and the Future Life* (1946; 2nd ed. 1947) traces the ideas of Israel from the early nebulous notion of mere survival to the developed belief in future rewards and punishments attested in the last centuries before Christ. Professor H. H. Rowley of Manchester University writing in *Theology* called this book "an important study (which) will command the attention of the scholar as well as of the general reader" and spoke of its "valuable contributions on disputed questions." Both these books appeared in the Bellarmine Series of which the author has been the general editor from its inception.

A Catholic Commentary on Holy Scripture, a one-volume commentary, is his latest work. The preparation of this extensive work which runs to about a million and a half words, has absorbed his time and energies for some years both in the writing of his own contributions and as editor of the Old Testament articles and individual commentaries. The editors have been fortunate in securing the collaboration of scholars in various parts of the English-speaking world belonging both to the secular clergy and to many religious orders and congregations.

Reverend Francis Sweeney, S.J.
1916–

Father Sweeney's maternal grandfather was a shepherd in County Tyrone, Ireland. His father's father came from County Cork, and the famous family of MacSuibhne, son of Suibhne, meaning the "well-going." From time immemorial, love of nature has been a characteristic of the Irish people, and so too has been their felicity for words. From the fifth century on, they have been fervent in their devotion to God and His Church.

With this triple heritage, undiminished by distance from the hills of Ireland, Francis Sweeney was born, the youngest of six children, on February 19, 1916, in Milford, Massachusetts. It was a home in which love of learning and the "sure companionship of books" came second only to the love of God. It had been a tragedy for Patrick Sweeney when he had been forced to leave high school at the end of his second year to help his father in the family market business. He had begun at sixteen the task of educating himself, going to night school to learn French, reading economics and history and the English poets after the long bone-wearing day on the market delivery cart. When he died at fifty, he left a memory of instinctive love for the finest things in the world, and an example of union with God which his children would always recall with astonishment and humility.

Francis Sweeney attended the Milford parochial schools, and at an early age began to patronize the local public library. An article he wrote for the February 2, 1946, issue of *America*, "Books and Doors," relates his literary progress from Thornton Burgess and Percy Keese Fitzhugh to Gerard Manley Hopkins, Cardinal Newman and others in the adult world of letters. Strangely enough, as a child he distrusted and disliked poetry, except that of James Whitcomb Riley and Edgar Guest. He was won over to it by the poems his mother found for him in magazines. Many of them he still has by heart, "all the more precious because woven with the verse fabrics are the tones of my mother's voice as she read them to me on quiet, lamp-lit evenings long ago."

Two of his childhood years were spent in Newark, New Jersey. Returning to Milford, young Francis Sweeney went to St. Mary's High School, where much of his outside reading was of a religious nature.

The first indication of his vocation to the priesthood came to him then, and his four years at Holy Cross confirmed it, and directed him to the Jesuits. His college years also saw the beginning of his career as a writer. He reported campus news for the New York *Times*, and in 1937 that paper printed on its editorial page his poem, "Temples." In his senior year he was editor of the Holy Cross literary magazine, *The Purple*.

He graduated in June 1939, and went on a brief students' tour of Europe. In September he entered Shadowbrook, the Jesuit novitiate at Lenox, Massachusetts, and it is this Berkshire town, and the cities he had seen in Europe just before the war, which are the main scenes of his poems. Then he studied philosophy at Weston College for two years, and the next year he taught English and Latin at Cranwell, the Jesuit preparatory school also at Lenox. His term of teaching was shortened by illness, and in the autumn of 1945 he returned to Weston College for his four years of theology. He was ordained June 19, 1948.

His poems have been published in *The Atlantic Monthly*, *America*, *Spirit*, *The Commonweal*, and *Thought*, and in three anthologies, *The Holy Cross Anthology*, *The Golden Book of Catholic Poetry*, edited by Alfred Noyes, and *From One Word*, an anthology of poems from *Spirit*. In April, 1951, his first book, *Baroque Moment*, was published by the Declan X. McMullen Company, Inc., and has won praise from outstanding critics such as Daniel Sargent, Thomas Merton and Sister M. Madeleva. Father Harold Gardiner, S.J., literary editor of *America*, has likened the poems to steel and song, saying that Father Sweeney, like all students of scholastic philosophy, is immersed in the brave and shattering truths that vivify sound philosophy, and make lovely, profound theology. He himself, in the poem, *Modern Poetry*, speaks of

> "The sure word, metal and music in the soul,
> The image struck coin-clear, like a Gospel phrase."

To this, one should add an all-pervading love and charity which warm and enrich the whole fabric of his writing, wisdom freshened with originality, and, as a fourth Celtic heritage, an acute sense of humor. Humility and modesty being dominant virtues with him, he decries all comparison with other priest-poets, but inevitably the names of his fellow-Jesuit, Gerard Manley Hopkins, and his friend, Thomas Merton, come to mind as talents liberated from worldly distractions. Father Sweeney's achievements and promise are great enough to justify linking the names.

His second book, *Bernardine Realino, Renaissance Man*, appeared in 1951. It is the first biography in English of this recently canonized Jesuit saint.

Father Sweeney does book reviews for the *New York Times*, *The Commonweal*, and *America*. He is now teaching English at Boston College, for whose library he was able to obtain one of the two type-scripts of Thomas Merton's, *The Seven Storey Mountain*.

Circumstance has kept him from participating in some of the more strenuous sports, but that he is no recluse or bookworm is demonstrated by the fact that his hobby is maritime Boston, and that he spends much of his free time along the waterfront. His family has always summered at the shore, and from childhood he has loved beaches, the sea, ships, and sea-faring men. Also, he has "sworn a terrible Gaelic oath" to take up again horseback riding, which he enjoyed when he was young.

H. L.

James Johnson Sweeney   1900–

The writer, lecturer and museum director, James Johnson Sweeney, was born in New York on May 30, 1900, the son of Patrick M. and Mary Johnson Sweeney.

From Georgetown University, Washington, D. C., he received his A.B. degree in 1922. From 1922 to 1924 he was a student at Jesus College, Cambridge, England. He spent the year 1925 at the Sorbonne, Paris, France, and the following year at the University of Siena, Italy. On May 17, 1927, he married Laura Harden. They have five children — Ann, Sean, Siadhal, Tadhg, Ciannait.

From 1924 to 1930 he contributed verse art criticism to AE's *Irish Statesman*, to the *New York Times*, and *Cahiers d'Art*, Paris, France. For the year 1931–1932 he was New York correspondent for the Chicago *Evening Post* and *Art World*. Then he directed exhibitions of twentieth century painting and sculpture at the University of Chicago. From 1935 to 1940 he was lecturer on fine arts, Institute of Fine Arts (Graduate School of Fine Arts) of New York University.

Then he was sent to Europe by the Museum of Modern Art, New York, to select and collect exhibits for an exhibition of African Negro art. In 1935 he directed and installed an exhibition of African Negro art at the Museum of Modern Art. In 1941 he directed the exhibition of art by Joan Miro and two years later (1943) an exhibition of sculpture and constructions by Alexander Calder. He directed the exhibition of *Photographs by Alfred Stieglitz* and the Alfred Stieglitz Collection in 1947, both were at the Museum of Modern Art in New York City.

He was director of the department of painting and sculpture at the Museum of Modern Art, New York for the years 1945–1946. The summers of 1946 and 1947 he went, as visiting lecturer on American Art, to the Harvard Seminar and on American Studies in Salzburg, Austria.

In 1949 he directed the exhibition of paintings by Pablo Picasso, in the art gallery of Toronto, Canada, and a year later the Virginia Biennial Exhibition of American Painting, Richmond, Virginia, and also that year an exhibition of sculpture by Alexander Calder, at the Massachusetts Institute of Technology.

In 1950 he was visiting lecturer at Richmond Area University Center and resident scholar at the University of Georgia, 1950–1952.

Mr. Sweeney has given lectures at museums and universities throughout the United States and Canada on art and literature.

Since 1948 he has been vice-president of the International Association of Art Critics, Paris, France, and a director of the Edward Mac-Dowell Association for the year 1950–1951.

For the years 1935–38, he was associate editor of *Transition* and advisory editor of *Partisan Review* since 1948.

He gave a fortnightly radio broadcast on art, literature, and theater topics over Radio Eireann, Dublin, Ireland during the year 1950–1951. Asked how he became interested in art, he said: "I imagine I was always interested since childhood. At least I can not recall when I was not. My mother painted. I grew up regarding painting much as I regarded talking, writing, or dancing, as a normal, natural activity. While I never aspired to be a painter myself I always drew for my own pleasure and was always interested in how painters produced their work. Possibly my interest in contemporary painting, sculpture and architecture grew out of my interest in what contemporary poets, prose writers and dramatists were attempting to do with their media. Perhaps, it was only a natural outgrowth of an interest in what the older masters had attempted to do and how they had worked towards their ends. For this reason it is very difficult for me to say 'how' I became interested in art; in looking back I can see no point at which any violent change of direction took place — in fact any turn, or even change to this direction whatsoever."

Besides contributing articles on art and literature to European and American periodicals, he edited with a critical introduction *Three Young Rats* (1944), a collection of traditional children's rhymes.

Mr. Sweeney is the author of: *Plastic Redirections in XXth Century Painting* (1934); *African Negro Art* (1935); *Joan Miro* (1941); *Alexander Calder* (1943); *Stuart Davis* (1946); *Marc Chagall* (1946); *Henry Moore* (1947); *Antoni Gaudi* (with José-Luis Sert) (1951).

At present (1952), Mr. Sweeney is working on a study of T. S. Eliot's poetry for Harcourt, Brace and Company; a study of Georgia O'Keeffe's painting for the Museum of Modern Art, and a study of African Negro Art for the Bollingen Press.   M. O. H.

Christopher Hugh Sykes   1907–

Orville Prescott in his review of Christopher Sykes's book, *Character and Situation* (New York *Times*, October 10, 1950), writes: "Christopher Hugh Sykes, who is not yet so well known in this country as he deserves to be, is a suave and sophisticated English writer of uneven but substantial talents. Like Evelyn Waugh and Graham Greene (see previous volume of *Catholic Authors*, ed.), he is a Roman Catholic, with, as far as his writings go, a strong interest in the brittle problems of worldly people."

Born on November 17, 1907, he is the second son of the late Sir Mark Sykes, Bt. Sledmere, Yorkshire, England. He was educated at the English Benedictine Abbey at Downside, Christ Church, Oxford, and La Sorbonne, Paris.

From 1928 to 1929 he was Hon. Attaché to the late Sir Horace Rumbold, British Ambassador to Berlin, followed by a very brief and inconclusive career as an accountant in the city of London. During 1930–1931 he was Hon. Attaché to the late Sir Robert Clive, British Minister, H.M. Legation at Teheran. The following year was spent studying at the School of Oriental Studies under Sir E. Dennison Ross. He then returned to Persia and Afghanistan to study the campaigns of the 1914–18 War in the interior of Persia and Central Asia. He was *Times* correspondent in 1934. A year later, he attended the Conference on Persian Art in Leningrad and Moscow as a delegate.

He married Camilla Georgiana, the daughter of Sir Thomas Russell Pasha in 1936. They have one son.

From 1936 to 1939 he was a contributor to the *Spectator* as critic of Oriental and travel books, and for the year 1937–38, assistant editor of the *Geographic Magazine*.

The outbreak of the Second World War found him serving as an officer in the Green Howards. He was in turn staff officer serving at the British Headquarters in Cairo, and Second Secretary to the British Legation at Teheran, prior to his return to England in 1943 where he rejoined the army as a commando. He took part in parachute operations in the Vosges, France, was mentioned in despatches, and received the Croix de Guerre.

With the return of peace, he joined the Associated Newspapers as a comic draughtsman, but the old wanderlust soon asserted itself and he was off to Persia as special correspondent for *The Daily Mail* where, with Cliff Daniels of the *New York Times* and Curtis of the Associated Press, he succeeded in scooping the brief Azerbaijan campaign in 1946. As no scooping openings were considered available by Associated Newspapers, he left them to take up the temporary post of deputy controller to the BBC Third Program. At the conclusion of this contract he took a permanent post with the Features Department of the BBC besides continuing to serve on the Third Program Committee.

He has broadcast many times, usually critical studies on well-known historical personalities, such as Cardinal Manning, Talleyrand and Palmerston. Two of his popular programs, "Freedom Our Ideal" and "The France We Love," have been highly praised.

But when his interesting and varied career has been forgotten, he will probably be remembered as a novelist and short story writer of more than ordinary talent. *Character and Situation*, Mr. Sykes's fourth book to be published in America, is a collection of six of his witty, entertaining short stories. They reveal a depth of penetration and a sympathy with his characters which make it one of the few collections of short stories published in recent years, acceptable to the reading public as well as to literary critics. In the Introduction to this book, Evelyn Waugh writes: "If I had to name the particular qualities of his work I should put this, Variety, first. There are many writers who confine themselves to one narrow milieu and fret away, book after book, with its problems. Not so Mr. Sykes. Secondly, I should put Independence. He is obviously not writing for a particular market — the vice that has enervated so many modern writers. Thirdly, I should put something which it is not easy to define in a single word. It is almost the gift of seeing events 'sub specie aeternitatis.'" Of his novel, *Answer to Question 33*, John Betjeman, one of the leading English critics, has this to say: "Until I read a good novel like *Answer to Question 33* I am apt to forget how moderate most modern novelists are."

Christopher Sykes is at present engaged in research and writing for his forthcoming work, *Studies in Virtue*. His books include: *Innocence and Design* (1935); *Wassmuss, the German Lawrence* (1936); *Strange Wonders* (1937); *High Minded Murder* (1944); *Four Studies in Loyalty* (1946); *Answer to Question 33* (1948), and *Character and Situation* (1949).

He also contributes regularly to the *Observer*, the *Yorkshire Post*, and the *National and English Review*, of which he is literary editor.

P. B. L.

Mrs. Zygmunt Szatkowski. See *Zofia Kossak*

Allen Tate 1899–

"Tate is one of the four or five best American poets of the century, and at his best he is with Hart Crane, although for entirely different reasons, the most powerful," writes Frederick Morgan in the *Hudson Review*, Summer, 1948, p. 266.

The critic and poet, Allen Tate, was born in Winchester, Kentucky, on November 19, 1899, the son of John Orley and Eleanor (Varnell) Tate. His early education was received at home. At the age of nine he entered a private school in Louisville where he astonished the teacher by reciting "The Chambered Nautilus" and Poe's "To Helen." Then he attended Georgetown Preparatory School, and Vanderbilt University. From the latter institution he received his A.B. (magna cum laude) in 1922. "After I had left Vanderbilt, my brother gave me a job in his coal office in Eastern Kentucky; in one day I lost the company $700 by shipping some coal to Duluth that should have gone to Cleveland, and my business career was over." (Twentieth Century Authors.) On November 3, 1924, he married Caroline Gordon, the novelist. They have one daughter, Nancy Meriwether (Mrs. Percy Wood, Jr.).

After graduation from college he was, along with Robert Penn Warren, John Crowe Ransom, and Donald Davidson, a member of the famous group of Southern poets known first as the "Fugitives" and later as the Agrarian-Distributists.

In 1924 Mr. Tate became a free lance writer and received Guggen-

heim Fellowships, 1928–1930. He was the Phi Beta Kappa orator at the
University of Virginia in 1936 and the Phi Beta Kappa poet at the
College of William and Mary in 1947. In 1948 the University of Louis-
ville conferred on him the honorary degree of Litt.D., and in the same
year he was given an award of $1000 by the National Institute of
Arts and Letters, of which he was made a member the next year.

From 1934 to 1936 he was lecturer in English at Southwestern
College, Memphis, Tennessee, and in 1936 was special lecturer in poetry
at Columbia University. From 1937 to 1939 he was professor of English
at the Woman's College of the University of North Carolina, and then
he became resident fellow in creative writing, with the rank of professor, at Princeton University until 1942. He was the incumbent of the
chair of poetry at the Library of Congress for the year 1943–44. From
1947 to 1951 he was lecturer in Great Books at New York University;
in 1948 he became a permanent fellow of the Indiana School of Letters
and was visiting professor of humanities in 1949 at the University of
Chicago. In 1951 he was lecturer on the Candlemas Foundation at
Boston College. Since 1951 he has been Professor of English at the
University of Minnesota. He is an occasional lecturer at Columbia,
Cornell, Harvard, Chicago, Minnesota, Yale, Illinois, Vassar, Vanderbilt and other universities.

In 1950 Allen Tate joined the Catholic Church.

In answer to the question put to him in 1940 why he became a
writer, Mr. Tate replied: "I simply could not put my mind on anything
else. As far back as I can remember, I was wondering why the people
and families I knew — my own family particularly — had got to be
what they were, and what their experience had been. This problem,
greatly extended, continues to absorb all my study and speculation,
and is the substance of my novel, *The Fathers*."

He was Southern editor of the *Hound and Horn* from 1931 to 1934,
and for the years 1944–47, Mr. Tate was editor of *The Sewanee Review*.
He has contributed to that publication as well as to *The Yale Review*,
The Criterion, *The New Republic*, *The Nation*, *The Kenyon Review*, *The
Southern Review*, *The American Scholar*, *The Hudson Review*, *Partisan
Review*, *Les Cahiers du Sud*, and many others.

Robert Fitzgerald in his article "Poetry and Perfection" in *The
Sewanee Review*, Autumn 1948, p. 696, writes: "I come to Allen Tate's
poems with a sense that they, at any rate, are 'imperishable if time is'
and are at the best inexhaustible, works that sheer literary power has
enabled to secrete energy like radio active substances. As examples,
rather than as a necessarily exclusive selection, I should name 'The
Mediterranean,' 'Aeneas at Washington,' 'Ode to the Confederate
Dead,' 'Ode to Fear,' 'The Traveller,' 'The Wolves,' and 'The Eagle.' "

Frederick Morgan, reviewing Allen Tate's *Poems 1922–1947* in
The Hudson Review, Summer, 1948, pp. 258 and 264 states: "Allen
Tate with a writing career of twenty-five years behind him, has to a
large extent been successful, in his battle with the angel of poetry, in
giving his work scope and dimension; his *Poems 1922–1947* brings together all of his best verse into a book of major importance. . . . Mr.
Allen Tate has been for years considered one of our leading men of let-

ters; his new book, *Poems 1922–1947*, is a collection of all the verse which he wishes to save . . . that Mr. Tate's work forms a durable and permanent contribution to letters there is no need to insist on now. The present volume should establish what one has long felt to be true: that Mr. Tate has done more than add a few very good poems to the language, fine though this achievement is and few enough the poets in any age who succeeded to it; this poetry has attained the stature at which it must inevitably be assessed in its totality, at which even the less successful poems take on importance for the understanding of the whole."

And William Elton reviewing Tate's collected *Poems 1922–1947* for *Partisan Review*, May, 1948, p. 601, writes: "The fact that Tate is a leader of a corps of critic-poets who have risen out of an intensely felt need, in a time of disorder, to defend our perilously-placed culture helps to explain his poetry, its tone, and the form it takes. Early in his career Tate decided that 'Poetry does not dispense with tradition; it probes the deficiencies of a tradition,' and he is, ironically, a propagandist in verse, much of his work being a variation on a theme in 'Dover Beach.' . . . Tate is like Jonson, a poet's poet and a critic's poet, functioning as guide and assimilator of sensibility; there is a rightness about his best work, reminding us that he is not only one of the finest poets of our age but that he probably corresponds to what Delmore Schwartz has called T. S. Eliot, a culture-hero."

And Dudley Fitts in the *New York Times* (March 7, 1948) in his review of *Poems 1922–1947* says: "Allen Tate's new book of poems is a literary event of the first importance."

He is the author of the following books: *Stonewall Jackson: The Good Soldier* (1928); *Mr. Pope and Other Poems* (1928); *Jefferson Davis: His Rise and Fall* (1929); *Poems: 1928–1931* (1932); *Reactionary Essays on Poetry and Ideas* (1936); *The Mediterranean and Other Poems* (1936); *Selected Poems* (1937); *The Fathers*, a novel (1938); *Reason in Madness, Critical Essays* (1941); *The Vigil of Venus* (1943); *The Winter Sea* (poems) (1944); *The Hovering Fly* (essays) (1949); *Poems: 1922–1947* (1948); *On the Limits of Poetry: Selected Essays, 1928–1948* (1948). He and his wife, Caroline Gordon, have collaborated in *The House of Fiction* (1950), an anthology with critical commentaries.

M. A. H.

Mrs. Allen Tate. See *Caroline Gordon*

Frank Sherwood Taylor   1897–

Frank Sherwood Taylor, an eminent authority on the history of science and Director of the Science Museum, the National Museum of Science and Industry, London, England, was born at Bickley, Kent, on November 26, 1897. His ancestry is in part American. His great-great-grandfather was Judge Jarvis of North Carolina, where the family had lived (at Curreytuck) since the seventeenth century.

He was educated at Sherborne School and at Lincoln College, Oxford. Chemistry was his special subject. During World War I he left his studies to serve in the war as a private, and was wounded. At the end of the war he returned to Oxford to finish his studies. Upon leaving the university, he taught chemistry in various public schools and at the same time studied the history of science. In 1933 he received his Ph.D. degree from London University for a thesis on Greek alchemy.

In 1933 Dr. Taylor was appointed assistant lecturer in inorganic chemistry at Queen Mary College (University of London); in 1940 he succeeded Dr. R. T. Gunther as Curator of the Museum of the History of Science at Oxford, and in 1950 he was appointed Director of the Science Museum. For twenty years before his conversion in 1942, Dr. Taylor had given thought to religion and philosophy, though remaining in that materialistic or at least agnostic position which characterizes so many scientists. Becoming, however, more and more critical of materialism, he had given much time to the examination of the Christian and especially the Catholic position. In 1941 he had been reading the Confessions of St. Augustine, and one day in a London street he heard an interior voice saying, "Why are you wasting your life?" This wrought in him an instant conversion: only later did he learn that the day, August 28 was the feast of St. Augustine. He at once sought instruction and was received into the church on November 15, the feast of St. Albert, patron saint of scientists.

Since his reception into the Catholic Church in 1942, Dr. Taylor has written three works on the relations of religion and science. *The Fourfold Vision* was published in 1944, *Two Ways of Life — Christian and Materialist*, and *Concerning Sciences* were published in 1949. *Man and Matter* appeared in 1951. He has translated from the Flemish, Blessed John Ruysbroek's *Seven Steps of the Ladder of Spiritual Love* and from the Latin he translated Hugh of St. Victor's *The Soul's Betrothal Gift*.

His earliest works were textbooks of chemistry and these are still widely used in Great Britain. His other books include: *The World of Science* (1935); *Galileo and the Freedom of Thought* (1939); *The Alchemists* (1949), and the *Short History of Science and Scientific Thought* (1949). Harrison Hale in his review of this book in the *Chemical and Engineering*

News says: "This is no ordinary history of science. . . . This is done so clearly and definitely that the story is fascinating."

Dr. Taylor is one of the original members of the Society for the Study of Alchemy and Early Chemistry (founded in 1936), and has edited its journal, *Ambix*, since its inception in 1937. His principal subjects of research have been the history of scientific instruments and the elucidation of the theories and practice of the alchemists.

M. A. H.

Right Reverend Monsignor Patrick J. Temple   1889–

Right Reverend Patrick J. Temple, S.T.D., was born at Shannon Harbor, Offaly, Ireland, on June 1, 1889. His father was an American citizen; his great-grandparents had emigrated to America in 1840 and had settled at Kingston, New York. For his scholastic training, Monsignor Temple attended St. Mel's College, Longford; All Hallows College, Dublin, and for his theological studies, St. Joseph's Seminary, Dunwoodie, New York. He was ordained by Bishop Cusack at St. Stephen's Church, East 28 Street, New York City on September 20, 1913.

After his ordination, Monsignor Temple pursued a postgraduate course of theological studies at the Catholic University, Washington, D. C., and there obtained the doctorate of theology. He served as assistant pastor at St. Bernard's Church, West 14 Street, New York City and at Holy Family Church, New Rochelle, New York. In 1929 he was appointed pastor of Our Lady of the Rosary, State Street, New York City. There he served as director of the mission for Irish immigrant girls and as chaplain at Ellis Island, Governors Island and as chaplain to the U. S. Custom officials' Holy Name Society. In 1939 he was appointed pastor of St. Gabriel's Church, New Rochelle, New York and he was made a domestic prelate by Pope Pius XII in 1950.

Monsignor Temple's first book *The Boyhood Consciousness of Christ* was in partial fulfillment of the requirements for the doctorate of theology at the Catholic University. It was published in 1922 by the Macmillan Company, New York City. His book, *Pattern Divine, or Our Lord's Hidden Life,* was published in 1950 by the B. Herder Book Company of St. Louis, Missouri. He founded *Old Castle Garden* in 1930 and every issue of this periodical contained literary contributions from his pen. Also he has written articles for the Conference Bulletin of New York Archdiocese and for the *Catholic Biblical Quarterly.* He is an active member of the Catholic Biblical Association of America.

His brother, Right Reverend Monsignor Thomas F. Temple, is pastor of St. Francis de Sales Church, East 96 Street, New York City.

Reverend Dom Raymond Thibaut, O.S.B. 1877–

Up to 1940 Dom Raymond Thibaut was the editor of the *Collection Pax*, which he created and directed. It contains forty volumes, two of them by Dom Raymond himself on the history of monks and monastic doctrine. Dom Raymond is also internationally known as the editor of Dom Columba Marmion's works.

Born on October 15, 1877, he attended St. Roch Seminary, Liège, Belgium. On October 1, 1896 he entered the monastery of Maredsous. Two years later (1898), on March 20, he was professed. After two years (1898, 1899) of philosophy at Maredsous, he went to Louvain to study theology, from 1899 to 1903, under Dom Marmion. He was ordained a priest on August 24, 1902. From 1903 to 1914 Dom Raymond served as librarian and director of the *Revue Bénédictine*. From 1910 to 1914 he taught church history and from 1914 to 1918 he taught philosophy. For six years (1922–1928) he was director of the *Revue Liturgique et Monastique* and from 1924 to 1936 he was chaplain of the Benedictine nuns of Faremoutiers, France.

Among the spiritual conferences of the Abbot of Maredsous that he edited are: *Christ, the Life of the Soul* (1917); *Christ in His Mysteries* (1919), and *Christ the Ideal of the Monk* came from the press in 1922, a few months before Dom Marmion's death. The spread of these works was extraordinary. *Christ the Life of the Soul* soon reached its seventy-fifth thousand in the French edition. It was translated into nine languages. *Christ in His Mysteries* and the other two volumes were likewise translated into several languages. These works were crowned by the French Academy. Dom Raymond also published three volumes of excerpts from Marmion's works: *Words of Life on the Margins of the Missal*, *Face à la souffrance*, and *Consécration à la sainte Trinité*.

In answer to the question how he became the editor of the works of Dom Marmion he said: "Dom Columba Marmion had given conferences to the clergy and religious communities from 1897 to 1922, and January of 1923. In 1902 the Carmelite nuns of Louvain, whose spiritual director he was, asked Dom Marmion to publish his conferences. He refused, saying 'there was nothing in them that could not be found in the Fathers or St. Paul.' He was too humble to write them. He not only was disinclined to write them, he had no leisure. The requests, however, multiplied. In 1914, the prior of Maredsous, Dom Robert, asked me to prepare the editions. He gave me some reasons: first, I was Dom Marmion's student in philosophy and especially in theology (two years of philosophy; four years of theology); secondly, I had been under the direction of Dom Marmion at Louvain, and after Marmion's election as Abbot of Maredsous in 1919, I had followed all his spiritual conferences (two a week), retreats, etc. for thirteen years. With the four year spiritual conferences at Louvain, there were seventeen years in all. Dom Robert was so insistent that I gave in. I had no text, no writings from Dom Marmion himself, but I had collected a great number of notes which I took myself, as well as notes taken by confreres, the Carmelites, the Benedictines, etc. — truly a virgin forest. In reading and rereading these documents I had gathered them under three headings and had filled three volumes with notes — i.e. *Christ, the Life of the Soul* gives and explains the simple and majestic plan of the spiritual life; and in the second, *Christ in His Mysteries*, the plan of the spiritual life is applied and developed in the light of the mysteries of Jesus; in the third, *Christ the Ideal of the Monk*, sets forth the claims and rulings of perfection — asceticism." The titles of the books were selected by Dom Thibaut. The coordination of the chapters after the plans of the retreat are Dom Marmion's. The style of writing is Dom Raymond's but he had been very careful to keep as close as possible to the thought, form and expression so characteristic of Dom Marmion. Dom Marmion did not write anything but read all his "works," when written, correcting in pencil or putting the thought, sometimes, in more precise terms. More often the corrections were confined to details, and Dom Raymond had no greater joy than that of hearing Dom Marmion say on returning the pages for the printer: "That's just me!" By this, he conferred on the volumes the character of authenticity.

Dom Thibaut's own works are: *Abbot Columba Marmion: A Master of the Spiritual Life* (1858–1923) (1929), crowned by the French Academy; *Union with God according to the Letters of Direction of Dom Marmion* (1934); *Melanges Marmion* (Studies and Documents) (1938); *Dom Marmion, Sa vie, sa doctrine son argument* (1938); *Pensées de Dom Marmion*, a collection of testimonies, documents and studies on his life and teachings, and *L'Idée maitresse de la doctrine de Dom Columba Marmion* (1946). For a long time Dom Raymond worked on *Le Christ ideále du prêtre*, which he finished in 1951. This volume completes the other three works of Dom Columba Marmion.

Dom Thibaut was made a Knight of the Order of King Leopold II of Belgium in 1948. M. A. H.

Reverend Newton Thompson
1882–

Newton Thompson was born in 1882. He studied at Harvard University (1901–1904); Dunwoodie Seminary (1904–1908); Columbia University (1905–1908), and the Roman University (1908–1910), where he received his S.T.D. degree. Previous to his present position as literary editor of the B. Herder Book Co., Doctor Thompson taught Holy Scripture at Maryknoll Seminary in New York and Church history at the Conception Abbey Seminary in Missouri.

For his editorial work, Doctor Thompson rises at three o'clock every morning and is at his desk at 3:30. He said he would be stumped unless he carried out that rigid program. He works until twelve noon, allowing time for Mass and his spiritual exercises. He goes back to work after lunch and works until 3:00, at which time he takes a walk. Since 1934 Dr. Thompson has been literary editor of the B. Herder Book Co.

In an interview, Father Thompson remarked that it has been his experience as editor that a first class scholar is always grateful for corrections in his manuscript. "The Herder Company," he says, "is interested in books of lasting value, nothing ephemeral. They do not ask: 'Will it have a big sale?' but 'Is it a contribution to Catholic scholarship?'" Father Thompson in trying to compose rules for his own guidance in the use of commas, ended up with fifty-eight rules. He says, "I couldn't get along with less." He also wrote a pamphlet on how to make an index.

In preparing his *Complete Concordance to the Bible*, written with the assistance of Raymond Stock, ninety thousand sheets of typewriting paper were used. It took two years to alphabetize the eight hundred thousand entries of the Concordance.

Father Thompson is also the author of *The Gospel Narrative, Verbal Concordance to the New Testament, Harmony of the Gospels* and has been a contributor to the *Homiletic and Pastoral Review*.

He translated Branchereau's *Meditations for Seminarians and Priests* (6 vols.): Ke Roy's *Religion of the Primitives;* La Vergne's *Good Cardinal Richard;* Lagrange's *The Gospel According to St. Mark;* Rose's *The Gospel According to St. Luke;* Fillion's *The Life of Christ* (3 vols.); Mourret's *History of the Catholic Church* (6 vols. thus far). His latest work is *A Handy Guide for Writers.*

Since 1937 Dr. Thompson has been living at a Benedictine monastery (Conception Abbey, Missouri) where, he says, association with scholarly men, an excellent reference library, the regular routine, the quiet and tranquillity, the liturgical observances and the sense of God's presence, combine to form an atmosphere ideally suited to literary work.   M. A. H.

Reverend Francis Beauchesne Thornton 1898–

Francis Beauchesne Thornton was born in 1898 and grew up in a small Wisconsin town, Chippewa Falls. His life there was the ordinary life of the age. He was third in a family of ten, went to a Catholic school and was normal enough to have a report from one of his teachers to his father which said, "You need not be afraid that Frank is in any danger of drowning, because he was born to be hanged."

During those first years of discontent with school, young Francis was stuffing his mind with literature of a sort — dime novels. Mr. Lund, the engineer in the sawmill near the Thornton home had stacks of these. By the time Francis was eleven or twelve, he knew Young Wild West or Dick Slater of *The Liberty Boys of '76* as well as he knew his own brothers and sisters. At this stage, the creations of the dime novelists had more imaginative meaning than real people had.

In the sixth grade Father Thornton started to write doggerel verse. This was an outgrowth of reflective hours spent in the pine woods and hills about his home. Everything sensuous in nature made a deep groove in his consciousness. Doggerel verses served as a good outlet for his ebullience through the remainder of the grades and high school.

In his dime novel days Frank had learned to "gulp" books. He now turned this appetite into the public library, where he literally devoured every book he could find — novels, history, poetry and natural history.

The Thornton children were always called in from play at dark. The long winter evenings were happy times. Seated about the dining-room table they pursued their tasks or interests, mostly in silence. Mrs. Thornton was always the center of the group, keeping order through love. She participated in games, or gave gentle advice, popped corn and made molasses candy or sang the "tear-jerker" songs of her youth such as, "The Letter Edged in Black." Sometimes the children all sang together, generally two-part songs. The big room would be filled with a gush of pure melody.

It was in these evenings that Father Thornton widened his reading interests far beyond his years. Poetry was particularly fascinating. The *Golden Treasury* proved to be his constant companion and delight. Imaginative power grew in great advancing spirals. This growth had both its pains and delights. Father Thornton remembers reading a story of a vicious king cobra at this time. Such was its imaginative power, that the young boy concluded the tale sitting on the top of the dining-room table, long after everyone had gone to bed. He was almost too frightened to come down from his perch, and when he had done so, cautiously ascended the staircase putting down his feet with terror on every shadowed step.

During high school years, Francis filled many copy books with verse. Much of it was religious. His teacher in second year high, Sister Mary Cleopha, S.S.N.D., encouraged him materially in his writing. Among other favors she set to music some verses Frank had written on the Feast of Our Lady of Lourdes. He had found his first real audience.

Along with the young man's growth in literary disciplines was a keen appreciation of games. He played football and basketball, learned to ski and skate, and was noted among his fellows as a wit or half-wit. He also became president of every society in his class.

It was Sister Mary Cleopha who played a major part in helping Francis find his vocation. In attempting to realize it, after completing high school, he went first to the Paulist Fathers. At the house of studies in Washington, D. C., the novice read omnivorously in the splendid library, wrote many children's stories for *The Leader* and saw his first verses published in *The Catholic World*. The kindly encouragement received from Father James Gillis was of tremendous importance to his writing career.

Upon leaving the Paulist House, Francis taught for several years in the public schools of North Dakota. He wrote a number of successful musical plays which were produced by his students, read widely in philosophy, and literary criticism, and wrote verse incessantly.

While on a summer holiday at Lake Louise, in which he did considerable mountain climbing, Francis decided to return to the seminary. It was on Mt. Rundle at Banff, to be exact, that he finally made up his mind. On the first part of the ascent of this peak which looks very much like the Prudential advertisement, the guide had a mild heart attack. Francis was determined to proceed toward his objective, and with a rude map, hurriedly drawn on an envelope, he left the guide and pushed on toward the summit. The last thousand feet were terrifying but enthralling. The path proceeded over a narrow ridge covered with loose shale. Below the climbing figure were sheer walls of rock; above the pure limpidity of the summer skies. Seated at last on the summit the triumphant man ate two Hershey bars in mild celebration. Far below the sinuous coils of the Bow River were chartreuse green among the solid-looking, black pines. Peaks and glaciers sparkled on every side. The mind of the young man seemed saturated with light and exaltation. He quenched his thirst with mountain snow.

Coming down from the summit, he missed a turn on the crude map and was lost for hours. He slipped and slid down dangerous slopes, keeping one point of the Bow Falls clearly in his sight. Rounding a grey escarpment of rock he came upon a huge, brown bear. The bear took one look and crashed off through the undergrowth. Finally, by sheer luck, Francis blundered on the switchback trail and safety.

In September, Francis entered the St. Paul Seminary. During the three years before ordination he wrote much poetry, directed plays, and made a circle of friends whose cultural interest were the same as his own. A number of his verses were accepted by *The Commonweal, America,* and *The Catholic World.* One of the poems, written at this time, and published by *The Commonweal,* was later chosen for the poetry column of the *Literary Digest.* It was made up of notes from several people Francis had known in his childhood, and, as such, is a bit of genuine Americana.

> With laughter all the village folk
> Would watch her pass —
> Old Mary Polk in flowered gown
> And clicking beads of glass.
> She, once so drab in all the years
> Her father lived, now glowed —
> A rose — a cabbage rose —
> A melon flower full blown.
> Poor fools! We tapped our heads
> Quite numb
> To her awakened soul that shone
> After eclipse

Not one
Could plumb
Her spirit's ecstasy,
Where dim lanes
Flung out bridal streamers —
Lanes long gloomed
With winter,
Where, at length,
The lilac bloomed.

For two years after ordination Father Thornton was stationed at St. Luke's parish in St. Paul. His life continued to be a sandwich of sports and literature. He managed the baseball team and St. Luke's Summer Camp and published two books of verse, *On Wings* and *Bitter Wine*. Overnight, he became poet laureate of St. Paul.

Archbishop Dowling, who was Father Thornton's greatest hero, sent the young priest for graduate studies to Notre Dame, Columbia and Oxford.

At Notre Dame, Father Thornton was an ardent member of the Scribblers Club and he won the Meehan Medal for a comparative essay on Baudelaire and Poe. His memorable companions were Charlie Phillips, Rufe Rauch, and Frank O'Malley.

The Columbia years were notable for acquaintance with Mother Grace Damman, R.S.C.J., and the incomparable Mother Stevens of the Pius X School of Liturgical Music. William Thomas Walsh lived next door.

The following Oxford days were also rich in people. Bede Jarrett, Ronald Knox, Hilary Carpenter, C. S. Lewis, Leonard Rice-Oxley, Martin D'Arcy, Thomas Gilby, and Hilary Pepler were more influential than they would have thought, or Father Thornton would have been willing to admit at the time. He produced a volume of mature poetry (still unpublished) and completed his research for a life of Alexander Pope.

In the holidays Father Thornton traveled on the Continent and upon one occasion had the pleasure of sailing on the same boat with George Bernard Shaw. Father Thornton came aboard at Tilbury and saw the flash bulbs popping. Pushing up to the barrier he saw the great man, a tall, bony figure in a mauve silk suit. The "beaver" was out-thrust like a sword into the welcome glare of the limelight. Behind came a meek Mrs. Shaw — carrying the baggage. This one incident cast a humorous light on Mrs. Shaw's large bequest to found an institution for teaching manners to the Irish.

On holidays spent in London, Father Thornton was often at Palace Court. There the delightful Meynells and Lucases were the center of a sparkling literary circle.

The time abroad ended all too soon. Busy years followed. Father taught at Duquesne University in Pittsburgh, was assistant editor to *The Catholic Digest*, and later a senior chaplain in the Canadian Army.

The Oxford years had helped Father Thornton in forming his prose style as an instrument of communication. He had also acquired a practi-

cal outlook on the field of letters. He wanted to make a fairly complete
anthology of the Catholic Revival. This desire produced *Return To
Tradition* (Bruce, 1948). With its emergence Father sensed the need
for a book on reading which should be wide enough to be of service to
those who are reluctant to read. In his conception of this task he cal-
culated an approach to the subject which would have universal appeal.
The result was, *How to Improve Your Personality by Reading* (Bruce,
1949). It was meant to be a glimpse into the learning of the past and
present. Half the modern discontent with reading sprang from the
rabbinical method of studying books, as Toynbee pointed out in his
Crisis of Civilization. Father Thornton strove for a Greek concept of the
printed word as an aid to the spoken word, and the unspoken thought.

In March, 1950, the Macmillan Company published *King Doctor
of Ulithi*. This book tells the amazing but true story of a navy doctor
who became king of a Pacific atoll.

During the summer of 1950 Father Thornton returned to the staff
of *The Catholic Digest* as book editor.

Since that time he has completed the following works: *Alexander
Pope: Catholic Poet* (Pellegrini & Cudahy, 1952) and *How's Your Catholic
I.Q.* (P. J. Kenedy, 1951). Also in preparation are: *Four Immortal
Chaplains*, *A Catholic Mother Goose*, A study of James Joyce and a criti-
cal estimate of Georges Bernanos, a Biblical novel, and an atom bomb
reader.

Felix Timmermans   1886–1947

The popularity of this Belgian author, Felix
Timmermans, began in 1916 when he published
his book *Pallieter*. "Either as a verb or noun the
word 'pallieter' was used to indicate and describe that healthy sentiment which in the days
before the war we used to call the joy of living."
(Hendrick Van Loon). Jan Albert Goris, the
Commissioner of Information of the Belgian
Government, in his booklet *Belgian Letters* says
of the book that "It was a paean to life, describing the idyllic existence
of a literary idler in a paradisiac environment in Flanders. The hero of
this book enjoys mystic poetry as well as fresh cranberries, the lyric
poems of Gezelle (Guido Gezelle, 1830–1899, the mystic poet of Flanders), as well as pigs' feet and early rain in his garden. By right he ought
to be a pagan; a decided conformist he prefers to be a sensual Christian
with occasional weaknesses. *Pallieter* was published at a time when the
occupation (German) was starving the Belgians. It sounded like a message from Eden. It reminded them so well of the cornucopias of Jordaens
and Rubens that they took the book to their hearts. Timmermans'
further books were more or less decorative: he used and abused the elements of the Flemish primitives and of Breughel to garnish the meager

Felix Timmermans

586

plots of his novels. In details he has an extraordinary power of suggestion: the world exists for him and he wants to enjoy it."

Pallieter, written between 1911 and 1914, is a book born out of the vacillations of Timmermans' soul, "of a soul longing for liberty, beauty, joy." *Pallieter* in its first edition had passages in it to which the Church authorities objected. These were expunged by the author. The first edition brought him an offer from an anti-religion group but instead he strengthened his Catholicism.

Felix Timmermans was born in 1886 in the small place of Lier, situated on the river Nethe in Belgium. He was one of fourteen children of his parents, who sold laces to make a living. Felix himself had to work at this trade. From his parents, Felix inherited a deep-rooted godliness. This manifested itself when he was attending the Academy of Lier. He did not like to draw Roman gods or goddesses; he liked to paint Jesus with His saints, wandering through Flanders, which was his Holy Land.

His interest in painting was aroused by a visit to the picture gallery of Antwerp with its priceless paintings of Rubens and Breughel. He could not get enough of Breughel "who is the incarnation of the Flemish soul." Because of this enthusiasm, young Timmermans went to the Academy of Lier for technical training. Coming to the conclusion that he did not have the patience to become a painter, he turned to writing. He became the best representative of his nation who drew modern Europe's attention to Flanders. His first collection of stories is entitled: *Schemeringen van de dood* (1910), (*Dusk of Death*), which is all about ghosts and spooks.

When the First World War broke out, Flanders became one of the main battlefields. Since the town of Lier was right in the war zone, the Timmermanns family suffered terribly. The family had to leave their home for some time but found comfort in praying the rosary. Timmermans wrote then *Het Kindeken Jezus in Vlaanderend* (1917) (The Little Infant Jesus in Flanders). Flanders, not Palestine, was the stage and background of this popular life of Jesus. His deep feeling for everything Flemish made Timmermans write about the trials of his countrymen. *Juffrouw Symforoza*, "a plain, touching, delicate tale," was written in Lier amidst the fury of war, when Timmermans, as a grocer, sold candy, cigarettes, etc. to the people.

For a very short time Timmermans dabbled in occultism but kept up his devotion to the Blessed Virgin. He soon became "his former self of a humble Christian, jubilant in the Lord."

Mr. Timmermans married Marie Janssens on October 12, 1912.

Hatzfeld in his biography of Felix Timmermans describes him as a man of "big gay-face, bushy hair, intelligent-looking eyes, a wide and tightly closed mouth, if there was not a pipe in it, just not quite looking the writer he really was."

"His workshop," writes Hendrick Willem Van Loon, in the preface to *Pallieter* (1924), "is in a corner of the old Beguinage of Lier and his neighbors are the quiet little Beguins whose life he has described with such wonderful understanding."

His works have been translated into German, French, Swedish, Polish, Hungarian, English and other languages. *Pallieter* (1924) was

translated into English by Mrs. C. B. Bodde with an introduction by
Hendrick Van Loon; *Droll Peter* (1930) was translated into English by
M. C. Dornton and W. J. Paul, and *The Triptych of the Three Kings*
(1936) by H. L. Ripperger. *De Harp van St. Franciscus* was translated into
English by Raphael Brown under the title, *The Perfect Joy of St. Francis*
(1952). Perhaps his most famous work was *Boerenpsalm* (1935), *(Peasant Psalm)*, a novel of peasant life.

Felix Timmermans died in 1947 in the small Flemish town in which
he was born (Lier), and which, through his books, had become known
throughout the world.   M. A. H.

Mari Tomasi   1911–

Before entering upon her career as a novelist,
Mari Tomasi did considerable work as a free
lance writer. Her first novel, *Deep Grow the
Roots*, published in 1942, was named one of the
ten outstanding first novels of that year.

Mari Tomasi is a native of Montpelier, Vermont. Her parents, Bartholomew (deceased) and
Margherita (Contratto) Tomasi were from Lo-
cana (Turin) Italy, but were married in Barre,
Vermont, early in the nineteen hundreds. Her father, who had travelled
extensively in North and South America, selected Vermont for his home
because he felt it resembled the Piedmont country of northern Italy.
He operated a general store on Main Street and ran a small cigar factory.

Miss Tomasi was educated at St. Michael's grammar school, taught
by the Sisters of Mercy. A double hip dislocation prevented her from a
very active life up to the age of ten, and, "it was," she says, "probably
at that time that I began taking delight in words and childish writings."
She was graduated from Montpelier High School and then attended
Wheaton College, Norton, Massachusetts for her freshman year and
Trinity College, Burlington, Vermont for her sophomore year.

Her professional writing began with the Montpelier *Evening Argus*
during the Second World War. She was an editorial writer and city
editor. She has also done considerable work for Vermont's state departments, formerly editing the quarterly *Vermont Social Welfare*, and currently (1951) compiling and editing for the fourth session the biennial
legislative yearbook, *Vermont — Its Government*. Governor Ernest W.
Gibson appointed her to serve as Montpelier representative to the
general assembly for the year 1950. She has done substitute teaching in
high school in her state, and during World War II she did volunteer
work in the local hospital as a Red Cross nurse's aide. She is historian
for the Burlington Diocesan Council (statewide), National Council of
Catholic Women.

Miss Tomasi lives at home with her mother; her sister Marguerite,
a nurse; a brother, Bert, a steward for the American Legion Club; a

second brother, Dr. Ernest Tomasi, lives next door. Her oldest brother, Andrew, is an American Red Cross director.

Two of her short stories were cited as outstanding in O'Brien's *Best Short Story Anthology*. In 1941 she was awarded a fellowship by the Breadloaf Writers' Conference (in connection with Middlebury College) for her first novel, *Deep Grow the Roots*, a story of village life in northern Italy.

The second novel, *Like Lesser Gods*, was awarded the Bruce Fellowship in fiction. It is a novel based chiefly on the lives of granite workers in her Vermont granite district. It was a book of the month selection of the Catholic Literary Foundation. She did not have to search for material. "It has been staring me in the face for years," she says. "Despite the fact that Vermont's 9528 square miles of idyllic valleys and rolling hills are predominantly agricultural, near my home and close to Vermont's geographic center, lies the Barre granite belt which provides about a half of our country's monumental granite.

"By the time I was a high school freshman, the granite quarries and finishing sheds were familiar scenes. Years have not lessened the fascination of standing at the rim of a vast quarry to peer to its floor, hundreds of feet below, to watch quarriers dislodge a huge block of granite from its wall and to see the block swing upward through the air by derrick power. Nor have years lessened the fascination of watching the sculptor pouring his talent into a memorial for someone whose days of work are over. Perhaps I subconsciously created the characters for this novel, at least in their beginnings, in early childhood.

"My father's store was halfway between home and school, and after school hours it was a treat to be allowed to sit for a few minutes behind a counter and listen to colorful worlds opened to me by the chatter of customers, especially the local stonecutters.

"They spoke of their dramas — marriage, birth, death. But they seldom voiced the fear that was always with them — the tragedy of dusty lungs and stonecutters' T.B. which had already taken so many of their fellow workers. . . . No doubt there are many stories that will come from these granite hills and from these men who have worked the granite."

Miss Tomasi is now working on her third novel, whose chief character is the "Mister Tiff" of *Like Lesser Gods*. "I cannot honestly call this book," she says, "a sequel in the ordinary sense of the word, although it will contain a number of the same characters and also the Granitetown background."

Miss Tomasi's hobbies are oil painting and gardening, when she has time for them.   M. A. H.

Maria Augusta Trapp

It is quite unlikely that any other author in this book had the unique though unconscious experience of Maria Augusta Trapp of being born on a train. "I could not wait," she writes, "until my mother had got from the village in Tirol down to Vienna to the hospital, but I appeared on the train, the conductor helping my mother. Many times I have been teased about this because my life has turned into such almost continuous traveling.

"My mother died shortly afterwards, and my father died when I was six years old. I had no near relatives, so the court handed me over to a guardian. This guardian happened to be a passionate socialist. The socialists we had at that time in Austria were very close to the communists of today. As such, he was a violent anti-Catholic. So, although I was baptized, I grew up really outside of the Church, hearing nothing but hateful things about it, growing into the same hatred of God and divine things as my surroundings constantly emanated. In my 18th year, when I was a senior at the State Teachers College for Progressive Education, I was 'thrown off my horse' by a very special mercy of God. From then on, I went to the sacraments and wanted, with all my heart, to atone for my previous life. The best way to do this, so it occurred to me, was to give up my freedom (I was always a very independent and self-willed girl), and serve God in a convent. This idea had come to me while I was on a trip through the glacier region of my native Tirol. It was at sunset, and sunset among the glaciers is something unforgettable. I had never been near a convent before, and I had only very foggy ideas about 'nuns burying themselves alive,' 'people sleeping in their coffins,' and all that stuff with which I had been fed in my early youth. Now, I was overwhelmed with the thought that this was going to be the life I would embrace for the love of God. I could not wait until the next day. I said good-bye to the rest of the party and walked down, down, down until I came to a little country railroad station which took me to Salzburg. I had walked most of the night and arrived very early next morning. A policeman was standing on the platform. I went over, and asked, 'Please, can you tell me which is the strictest convent in this town?' 'I do not know,' he answered, rather astonished. 'Why don't you ask him?' and he pointed at a priest standing there waiting for the morning train. Having very little to do with priests, I said: 'Sir, can you tell me which is the strictest convent in this town?' He looked just as surprised as the policeman, but said: 'The cloistered Benedictine nuns at Nonnberg.' Back I went to the policeman: 'How do I go to Nonnberg?' This he knew and told me.

"An old portress with a very kind face let me into the parlor. I had told her I wanted to talk to the boss. Terms like prioress, abbess, Rev. Mother I had yet to learn. After a short time of waiting, the door on the other side of the iron grill opened, and a frail, small figure in black, with a golden cross, entered, the Most Reverend Mother Abbess. For a moment, we just looked at each other. What she looked at was a girl, dark brown, like chocolate; over the left shoulder, a rope, on the back, a heavy rucksack, in the right hand an ice pick. After a moment's waiting, this rather unusual visitor announced, 'I have come to stay here.' 'Oh,' Rev. Mother said, and her eyebrows almost vanished under her veil. 'Who sent you?' Now, it was my turn to be astonished. 'Sent me?' I repeated, with the utmost surprise, 'I would not be here if somebody had sent me. I have never obeyed anyone in my life.'

"And she let me stay, and took me in as a candidate. Very soon, I disturbed the routine and order of the novitiate so much that a special mistress of novices was appointed to take care of me alone: first to make a girl out of a boy, and then to make a postulant out of that girl."

Maria Trapp looked upon herself as the black sheep of the community. Often she was corrected for taking two and three steps at a time on the staircase, and for whistling.

But she liked her work teaching fifth graders. She liked, too, "the supernatural beauty of this most beautiful place on earth. Twelve hundred years had worked and helped to make Nonnberg, the first abbey of Benedictine nuns north of the Alps, a place of unearthly beauty."

It was like a bombshell, therefore, when one day the Reverend Mother told her, "it seems to be the will of God that you leave us . . . your headaches are growing worse from week to week. The doctor thinks that you have made too sudden a change from mountain climbing to our cloistered life, and he suggests that we send you away for less than one year to some place where you can have normal exercise."

At Nonnberg, Maria had learned that "the only important thing on earth was to find out what is the will of God and to do it." Reluctantly she left Nonnberg to become the teacher of Baron von Trapp's little daughter, who was of delicate health. Reverend Mother had seen to it that Maria had some place to go.

For years Maria taught not only the delicate child but also the six other children. The Baron was especially pleased to see that the new teacher was loved by his children and were learning to appreciate music. Those pleasant years Mrs. Trapp describes beautifully in her book, *The Story of the Trapp Family Singers.*

On November 26, 1927, she married Captain Georg von Trapp. In their Salzburg home the Trapps had a chapel and priests were invited to say Holy Mass. "At Easter, 1935," she writes in her book, "Professor D. had to make a journey and asked a priest friend to come and say Mass in his stead. Afterwards, at breakfast, the young priest, whose name was Father Wasner, said: 'You really sang quite well this morning, but . . .' and he explained in a few words several important things to us, and right then and there at the breakfast table, made us repeat a motet, conducting it from where he was sitting. None of us knew then just how lucky we were: this was the birth of the Trapp Family Singers."

Later Lotte Lehmann entered their names in a music festival. They won first prize. Their next appearance was at a great solemn reception that was given by Kurt von Schuschnigg, then Chancellor of the Austrian Republic, for all national and foreign dignitaries. Soon they were singing in Paris, London, Brussels, and other European cities.

In 1938 the Trapp Family came to America and lived in the Wellington Hotel, New York until preparations were made to tour the United States. Years later they went to Stowe, Vermont to settle down. They are there now but they still go on concert tours to delight audiences with their soothing, consoling, uplifting music.

                                                    M. A. H.

Reverend Leo Trese   1902–

Named after Pope Leo XIII, Leo John Trese (pronounced Tracy), was born in Port Huron, Michigan on May 6, 1902. His father, Joseph Trese, was of German descent; his mother, Mary Alice Byrth of Irish descent. His only sister, Sister Marie Arthur, S.S.J., is Dean and Registrar at Nazareth College, Nazareth, Michigan.

He was educated at St. Stephen's parochial grade and high school, Assumption College, Windsor, Ontario, and Mt. St. Mary of the West Seminary, Norwood, Ohio. Ordained February 13, 1927, he read his First Mass at St. Joseph's Church, Port Huron on February 20. From the University of Western Ontario he received an A.B. degree in 1928 and from the University of Detroit an M.A. degree in 1929.

His first assignment was to the Blessed Sacrament Church, Detroit, where he remained for five years. In 1932 he went to St. Vincent Archabbey in Pennsylvania to study to become a Benedictine. He was then interested in going to the University of Peking, which was started and conducted by the Benedictines. After spending a year in the novitiate and three years in vows, he returned to his diocese — the University of Peking, in the meantime, having been turned over, by the Pope, to the Society of the Divine Word. In 1936 Father Trese started a new parish at Marysville, Michigan. Five years later he was appointed pastor of St. Mary Magdalen's Church in Melvindale, a Detroit suburb. His bishop assigned him to the pastorate of St. Patrick's, Carleton in 1945. In 1950 he was appointed chaplain of the Vista Maria school in Detroit. This institution is conducted by the Good Shepherd nuns for girls with a problem. There he teaches religion and history and does counselling, in addition to his routine duties as chaplain.

Besides being in demand as a lecturer and retreat master, Father Trese is diocesan director of rural life, and a member of the National Commission on Religious Organizations of the National Council of Christians and Jews. He is also actively interested in promoting the lay apostolate, and is spiritual adviser for Marybrook Farm, a lay retreat house under auspices of the *Catholic Worker.*

Father Trese first wrote for publication at the age of eleven, and won a book as a prize in a contest held by the Detroit *Free Press.* He edited and contributed to high school and college publications but wrote nothing for professional publication until 1944, when, during a trip to Puerto Rico, he wrote an article about the island, which *The Commonweal* published. "That pulled the cork out of the bottle," writes Father Trese, "and I have been writing ever since, in such spare moments as I can find — mainly for *The Commonweal* and a priests' magazine called *Emmanuel,* with a scattering of other articles here and there as requested." Father Trese is also the author of a weekly column, "It Seems to Me," in *The Michigan Catholic,* a diocesan weekly.

His first book, *Vessel of Clay,* published in March, 1950, was a grand success. Up to February 1, 1951, between 25,000 and 30,000 copies were sold. In thirty-two short, good humored chapters Father Trese invites his reader to spend a full day with him in his rectory to give him an insight of the multitudinous duties which challenge the parish priest every day. Two European editions of *Vessel of Clay* have appeared in England and in Holland. His second book, *Many Are One* (1952), was the February Book Club selection of the Thomas More Association. It contains more than 50 essays.

Right Reverend Monsignor Francis Trochu 1877–

Known in the United States for his excellent biographies of *St. Jean Marie Baptiste Vianney,* the patron saint of priests, and *Jeanne Jugan,* the Foundress of the Institute of the Little Sisters of the Poor, Abbé Francis Trochu (not to be confused with Father Felix Trochu, 1868–1950, the founder of the periodical, *Ouest-Eclair*) was born on October 4, 1877, in Nort-sur-Erdre in the diocese of Nantes. He was ordained a priest in 1901 and prepared for his licentiate degree at Saint-Aubin-D'Angers. He was a professor at the college Saint-Joseph d'Ancenis and of Saint Stanislaus-de-Nantes. He was awarded a doctor of literature degree for his thesis "Cure D'Ars" (the psychology of a man, the psychology of a crowd) and "Cure D'Ars Predicateur Populaire." Both books were a huge success when published. They were translated into thirteen languages and hailed by Catholics all over the world. Over thirty volumes flowed from his pen. The most important of these are: *Saint François de Sales* (1567–1622) (2 vols.); *Le Bienheureux Theophane Venard* (1829–1861); *Martyr au Tonkin* (1929); *Saint Jeanne-Antide Thouret* (1765–1826); *Fondatrice des Soeurs da la Charité; La Servante de Dieu Jeanne Jugan* (1792–1879), *Fondatrice des*

Petites Soeurs des Pauvres; Le Bienheureux Pierre Julien Eymard (1811–1868), *Fondateur des Pères du Très Saint Sacrement; La Servante de Dieu Henriette Aymer de la Chevalerie* (1767–1834), *Foundatrice des Religieuses des Sacrés-Coeurs et de L'Adoration Perpétuelle: La Bienheureuse Jeanne Delanoe* (1666–1736), *Fondatrice des Soeurs du Sainte Anne de la Providence de Saumur; L'Ame du Curé D'Ars: Les Institutions du Curé D'Ars* (3 vols.)*; La "Petite Sainte" du Curé D'Ars, Sainte Philomene; Autour du Curé D'Ars; Pérégrinations* (Paray-le-Monial, Notre-Dame-du-Laus, La Salette Fourvière, Le village d'Ars); *Abbé Charles Foyer (1771–1842); Ancient Capitaine de Paroisse de la Guerre de Vendée, Fondateur des Soeurs de Sainte-Marie-de-Torfou; George Bellanger (1861–1902), des Frères de Saint-Vincent de Paul; Sainte Bernadette Soubirous* (1844–1879).

Some of his books have been honored by the French Academy. In all his works Abbé Trochu follows a strict historical method. In writing many of his books he uses unknown and unpublished documents such as the data of beatifications and canonizations. He tries to interpret the psychology of his personalities and then give a spiritual analysis.

He was made a monsignor in 1943. M. A. H.

Margaret Trouncer   1906–

The novelist and biographer, Margaret Trouncer, who specializes in stories and subjects with a setting in France, was born in Paris, before the First World War. She is the daughter of James Duncan Lahey of Virginia, United States of America and of Nina de Scalon of St. Petersburg, Russia. Her aunt is the bookbinder for the Morgan collection. She was baptized and brought up in the Greek Orthodox Church, as she is half Russian. She became a Catholic in 1930. She was educated by private tutors until she came to live in England in 1914. There she attended Derby High School and in 1924 went to St. Hilda's College, Oxford to read for the Honors School of English Language and Literature, and took her degree of M.A. in 1931.

While at Oxford she wrote a medieval Nativity play about the life of the Blessed Virgin, which, for three years in succession, was produced in the College Hall.

In 1926 she met Thomas Trouncer, her husband, who was then studying at University College and was the head of the Boat Club. Although they were engaged after a brief courtship, they postponed their marriage for four and a half years, as neither of them had any money.

She began to write in 1934, as she and her husband were in dire need. Her first book was a life of Louise de la Vallière, whose charm captivated her imagination during her yearly visits to Versailles. The book,

Courtesan of Paradise, won the Book Guild Recommendation for 1936, the year of its publication. Sir Shane Leslie wrote to her to say: "All yesterday I spent entranced by your book. It is like a bouquet, a girl's first offering to the Muses."

Then came *The Pompadour* (1937) which also was very successful. This book was chosen by the First Editions Club to rank among the hundred best produced books of the year, and was put on exhibition in the Victoria and Albert Museum. *The Times* (London) in its review stated: "Supreme elegance and exquisite taste in trifles, Margaret Trouncer has steeped herself in the color and atmosphere of the period . . . fluttering ribbons, billowing gauzes and brocades, rococo boudoirs." *The Saturday Review* said of it: "How well Mrs. Trouncer can write. She has a flair for reconstituting the historical scene in all its colorful detail. . . . The engravings add to the charm of the book." *The Times Literary Supplement* in its review remarked: "Mrs. Trouncer's excursion into eighteenth century history has all the freshness of a voyage of discovery through the pictures and the bibelots of the rococo period. She delights in reconstituting the exquisite *mise en scène* of that age. . . . Full of zest and telling detail. She succeeds to admiration."

In 1939 she started her first novel, *Go, Lovely Rose,* which was about a Frenchman in the nineteenth century by the name of Richard de Hautefontaine who learnt of contemplation through earthly love, and entered the Grande Chartreuse near Grenoble. She dedicated the book to her husband who was killed while flying in the Royal Air Force. Then came two novels in quick succession: *Why so Pale?* (1942) and *The Smiling Madonna* (1943). Next came *Oriflamme,* the life of the Chevalier de Boufflers. It had a record sale and enabled her to spend a delightful holiday. After this came *She Walks in Beauty, Madame Récamier* and *The Bride's Tale.* Margaret Trouncer says: "Writing is a vocation. Thinking of the way I shall have to account for my response on the Day of Judgment, I take it very seriously. It is almost as though one had to lead an austere and dedicated life, to give beauty to the world. I have been much influenced by Gerard Manley Hopkins; greatly through his theory of "inscape," I learned to look at material things in a new way. I tried to get to the essence — to the secret behind the appearance. The old gardener at Roehampton who used to watch Hopkins as a Jesuit novice said: 'You should see that Mr. 'Opkins the way he walks round and round looking at a dew-drop on a blade of grass from every angle.' Every year I myself, for instance, learn something new about the mystery of a chestnut leaf unfurling."

Mrs. Trouncer has been very much influenced by the movement and rhythm of English poetry: — Shakespeare, the seventeenth century metaphysical poets, particularly Crashaw, Donne and Herbert; and then the French religious writers such as Léon Bloy, Paul Claudel, Bernanos, Mauriac, Maritain and Etienne Gilson; the mystics, Traherne, St. Gertrude, St. Margaret Mary, St. John of the Cross and Blessed Angelo of Foligno.

Asked how she creates imaginary characters in a novel, she replied: "Strangely enough, after a chapter or two, they seize the bit between their teeth, assume independent existences of their own, trailing me in their wake, gasping with excitement and admiration! I fall in love with my own characters. I am deeply deprived and unhappy the day I hand them over to the publishers in the typewritten manuscript. Then comes the period of physical and nervous depletion which is the nightmare of every author: one has torn out one's own entrails; one's bones are emptied of marrow."

Mrs. Trouncer's aim as a writer is, she says: "to bring beauty and truth to the masses, although I never suppress the sordid side of history if it needs to be related. As to style, when I was a younger writer, I loved to experiment with rare words and unusual musical phrasing, but as I grow older, I am drawn to a crystal clarity."   M. A. H.

Right Reverend Pierre-Célestin Lou Tseng-Tsiang, O.S.B.
1871–1949

Today China stands on the crossroads. A struggle, perhaps not to be resolved in our time, goes on for the soul of China. Anti-Christian materialism and the forces of what is known as the Western World vie for the physical possession of China's territory. Yet the effort to bring this ancient land and people into the fold of Christ has been going on for centuries. One outstanding phenomenon of our own time has been the awakening of this great Oriental people to the sound of the march of Western civilization. It may seem at times that attraction to the material rather than the spiritual legacy of the West has been the lodestar of this awakening. In the life history of no one man has there been found a more complete picture of what the future promises to be than in the story of Lou Tseng-Tsiang, Chinese diplomat of the 'ancien regime' of the Manchus, foreign minister and premier of the first Chinese Republic, a leading statesman and, in later life, an interpreter of the Chinese way of life from within the Catholic Church, a priest, a Benedictine monk and abbot.

Lou Tseng-Tsiang was born in Shanghai, June 12, 1871. His father, Lou Yong-Fong and his mother, Ou Kin-Ling were from well-to-do families, fallen upon lean days and coming to know trials and poverty. Lou Yong-Fong had become a Christian and was a Protestant catechist, so when Lou Tseng-Tsiang was two years old he was baptized a Christian by Rev. Dr. William Muirhead of the London Protestant Mission Society. At the age of thirteen he entered into the School of Modern Languages at Shanghai, a step which brought upon his parents the odium of disloyalty from many of their fellow countrymen. While at this school Lou specialized in French under a zealous master, Mr. Alphonse Bottu. At eighteen years of age, his studies were interrupted for a whole year because of illness but later he left for Pekin to enter Tong-

Wen College, a school for interpreters attached to the Department of Foreign Affairs. After he received a diploma from this institution, he was appointed to the foreign service and attached to the Chinese Embassy at St. Petersburg. In all, he spent thirteen years in St. Petersburg (from 1893 to 1906) first, as interpreter, later, as secretary and finally as counsellor. It was the period of the Russo-Japanese War and Lou gained recognition as a diplomat of major rank. During his residence in Russia he met and married, in 1899, Mlle. Berthe Bovy, a relative of the Belgian minister and a Catholic. Of this period of his diplomatic career, Lou later writes that the Chinese ambassador "concluded with Russia a secret diplomatic treaty which attracted the attention of every chancellery and of which I only learned the text when I read it in the University of Foreign Affairs in Pekin on the day when I became the head of that department. China had authorized Russia to build the Trans-Manchurian Railway. This treaty brought us no military assistance, giving great benefits to Russia without any corresponding benefits to us." A sharp reminder of events then in the future!

In 1907, he was made minister to The Hague, where he presided over the Chinese delegates at the Second Peace Conference. In 1911, he was sent back again to St. Petersburg, this time as Minister-Plenipotentiary. Just at this time the revolution in China was displacing the Imperial Dynasty and setting up a republic under the presidency of Dr. Sun Yat-sen. Lou had long sympathized with the republican aims and took it upon himself to telegraph to the emperor that the dynasty had no foreign support and that he (the sovereign) should renounce the throne. This the emperor did on February 12, 1912. The first president of China, Sun Yat-sen ordered Lou back to Pekin making him Minister for Foreign Affairs, a post which he held from 1912 to 1920. During this time, at two periods, first in 1912 and again, from 1915 to 1916, he was prime minister. He headed the Chinese delegation to the Versailles Conference in Paris in 1919. He refused to sign the treaty in the name of his government and in this course was backed up by the authorities in Pekin. He thought China was not being fairly dealt with by the other powers. Wearied by the strain and stress of diplomatic life he left the government in December 1920. Later, in 1923, he accepted the Chinese ministry to Berne, Switzerland.

The doctrinal, moral and disciplinary unity of the Church of Rome had long appealed to the soul of Lou, steeped as he was in the philosophy of Confucius. Though he had married a Catholic, he was still a Protestant until 1911. He was drawn, too, towards the Catholic faith by the exemplary life of his beloved wife; so he was received into the Catholic Church in St. Petersburg on November 22, 1911, taking the surname Réné. While he was Minister to Switzerland, his wife fell sick of a malady which caused her death on April 16, 1926. He buried her in her native Belgium.

The year after his wife's death, Lou presented himself on Pentecost Sunday at the Benedictine monastery of St. André in Belgium. He asked to be received as an oblate, that is, a layman living the monastic life without vows under the protection of the Rule. While he was a guest at the Abbey, the Abbot and Lou's spiritual adviser urged him to enter the canonical novitiate of the Order, which he did. He was professed a monk on January 15, 1929. After six years of study of theology (during which time he records that he had great difficulty in mastering the Latin language) he was ordained to the holy priesthood in 1935. As a monk he was known as Dom Pierre-Céléstin.

Lou's philosophy always remained Confucian. His main idea was that the ideals of Confucius, being the ingrained method of thought of the Chinese people, prepare the way and the only way, for their ultimate adoption of the Catholic faith. He hoped that the Benedictine Order, so renowned for meditation and study would take root in China, and he prophesied a bright future for that land, when Confucianism, Christianized by the Benedictine ideals, would move his countrymen to the heights of thought and action.

He has left two principal works, *Souvenirs et Pensées* (1945), translated into English by Michael Derrick, under the title *The Ways of Confucius and of Christ* and a posthumous work *La Rencontre des Humanités et la Découverte de l'Évangile* (1949). Though he disclaimed the first as his "memoirs," saying that these must be written in his Chinese tongue, the book is a moving record of what he terms his "diplomatic and spiritual vocation." In the latter work, *La Rencontre des Humanités*, he makes a plea for the use of the Chinese language in the ritual of the Church in China. He feels that the Chinese are so used to their own tongue that Latin or, for that matter, any Western language will fail as a medium of spreading Christian faith and worship. His general idea is made clear by the English title of his works *The Ways of Confucius and of Christ*. His life was a heroic model of the possible reconciliation of the two.

In 1946 Dom Lou was signally honored by the Holy Father, Pope Pius XII. He was elevated to the Abbatial office and was given the rank of titular Abbot of St. Peter in Ghent. He was solemnly raised to the abbatial dignity in the Abbey Church of Saint André on August 10, 1946 by the Apostolic Nuncio, Msgr. Cento. Thus he became the first of his race to become an abbot of the venerable Order of St. Benedict, a harbinger, perhaps, of the transfer of the ideals of St. Benedict from Monte Cassino to China. His pious death occurred in the Clinique des Soeurs Noires at Bruges, January 15, 1949, the twentieth anniversary of his profession as a monk. Buried in the crypt of the Abbey Church of St. André, his remains await the day when they can be brought back to the country which he served so well as a leader and prayed for so hard as a monk.   K. M.

Walter Ullmann   *1910–*

Walter Ullmann was born on November 29, 1910 in Pulkau, Lower Austria, and was educated in the gymnasium (formerly the school of the Piarist Fathers) in Horn, Lower Austria, the universities of Vienna and Innsbruck, where he received his J.U.D. in 1933.

From 1933 to March 1938, he was a civil servant in the Austrian Ministry of Justice and a research assistant, first at Innsbruck and later at Vienna Universities. Then he left Austria for political reasons and made his home in England where he continued research in Cambridge.

From 1940 until 1942, he served in the British Army, when he was discharged with a heart ailment. Then he held the mastership in history at Ratcliffe College, Leicester, England, from 1942 to 1947 when he was appointed lecturer in medieval history at the University of Leeds, England. In the fall of 1949 he was appointed university lecturer at Cambridge. From 1944 to 1946 he was a part-time lecturer at the British Foreign Office (Political Intelligence Department). For the year 1947–48 he was Maitland Memorial Lecturer at Cambridge and he is a F.R. Hist.S. (Fellow of the Royal Historical Society).

He is married and has two sons.

His first book, *The Medieval Idea of Law*, was published in 1946. Two years later (1948), *The Origins of the Great Schism* appeared. The reviewer of the book for *The Times* (London) *Literary Supplement* (Saturday, March 26, 1949) says: "Dr. Ullmann, in this comparatively short study has had a triple aim: to examine critically the course of the election of Urban VI and the subsequent disclaimers of the cardinals; to give, in some detail, the attitude of the contemporary jurists; and to explain the significance of the Schism as leading to new expedients, both legal and metajuristic, for leading the Church out of the impasse even at the risk of establishing a conciliar regime hardly to be reconciled with traditional theology.

"In the first and least original of these aims he is most successful, and the book should establish itself as the most convenient and completely documented work of reference on its subject. In the second he has done valuable work in a field in which he has already proved himself a master."

His latest book, *Medieval Papalism* (1949), is based upon the Maitland Memorial lectures delivered by the author at Cambridge in 1948 and its purpose is "to call attention to the importance of canonical scholarship in the formation of the political theory, and the political practice, of the Middle Ages." He is also a contributor to a number of periodicals on historical subjects.   M. A. H.

Reverend James (Herman Anthony) Van der Veldt, O.F.M.   1893–

If the Dutch saying, that there is something of the schoolmaster in every Hollander, has any value, it seems to have come true in the case of Father Van der Veldt who has been "condemned" to teaching all his priestly life. He was born in Sloten (Amsterdam), Holland, March 15, 1893, the eldest of ten children, of whom three became Franciscan priests and one a Poor Clare. After completing his course at the gymnasium, he joined, on November 28, 1912, the Dutch province of the Order of Friars Minor. Following his ordination, March 30, 1919, he pursued graduate studies in philosophy and psychology at the Universities of Louvain (Belgium), Nÿmegen (Holland), and Milan (Italy). He obtained the Ph.D. degree from the University of Louvain in 1926, and the same school awarded him the title of Agrégé en Philosophie in 1928. He also holds the titles of Lector Generalis and Lector Jubilatus in the Franciscan Order.

In the summer of 1928, the Minister General of the Friars Minor called him to Rome to teach experimental psychology at the Pontifical Athenaeum Antonianum, where Franciscan priests of the various provinces of the Order complete their graduate studies in theology, philosophy, canon law, history, or missiology. In 1931 the Cardinal Prefect of the Holy Congregation de Propaganda Fide appointed him professor of psychology at the Athenaeum Urbanianum, the central missionary institution of the Catholic Church. Here Father Van der Veldt established a well-equipped laboratory of psychology, one of the first of its kind in the Eternal City. In 1934 he was elected Dean of the School of Philosophy at the Propaganda College. During his twelve-year stay in Rome, he went twice, upon invitation, on lecture tours in the United States.

When World War II spread through the Low Countries, he obtained permission from his superiors to leave Rome, and he arrived in New York in June, 1940. His intention was to go from there to London in order to put himself at the service of the Dutch government in exile. But it turned out once more that he should be a teacher. Cardinal — then Archbishop — Francis J. Spellman invited him to the Archdiocesan Seminary of Dunwoodie where he taught empirical and pastoral psychology for five years. During the summer vacations, he visited several times the Dutch possessions of Curaçao, Aruba, and Surinam to lecture to both civilians and the armed forces.

Since 1945 he has been teaching in the Department of Psychology and Psychiatry of the Catholic University of America and at Trinity College, Washington, D. C. During this period, the Consejo Superior de Investigaciones Cientificas of Madrid invited him twice to give a series of lectures at the Universidad de Verano in Santander, Spain. In 1949 Father Van der Veldt became an American citizen.

His scientific works include *L'Apprentissage du mouvement et l'automatisme* (1928); *Prolegomena in Psychologiam* (1938); *Cuestiones de Psicologia* (1947); *Psychiatry and Catholicism* (1952), and numerous articles in the Netherlands *Catholic Encyclopedia* and in American, Dutch, and Italian periodicals. Besides these he has published two books of a literary-historical nature: *The City Set on a Hill* (1944) which is the story of the Vatican, and *Angelic Shepherd, The Life of Pope Pius XII* (1950), an adaptation into English of Bishop Smit's *Pastor Angelicus* for which he received an autographed blessing from the Holy Father.

In 1951 the Holy See appointed him Counselor of the Sacred Congregation of Seminaries and Universities.   M. M. S.

Reverend Ferdinand Valentine, O.P. 1894–

Father Valentine says that priests should be so occupied with the souls committed to their care that they should not have time to write books. Yet, paradoxically enough, he himself has somehow found time to write at least nine. He is, in a sense, an author by accident. To further his apostolate, a public wider than the pulpit and lecture room afforded was necessary, and books were his easiest means towards that end. He belongs to that increasing number of priests, who, deeply conscious of the menace of the materialism of the press, radio and cinema, and of the difficulties confronting young people beginning their adult Christian life, are endeavoring by every means in their power to combat the evil.

Thus, when the late Holy Father, Pope Pius XI wrote in *Vigilanti Cura*, "The motion picture should not be simply a means of diversion . . . to occupy an idle hour; with its magnificent power it could and must be a bearer of light and a positive guide to what is good," Father Valentine was one of the first in England to bring home to Catholics the truth of this statement in a practical way by founding in 1934 The Catholic Film Society. Together with his little group of pioneers, they produced a number of 16 mm. films which were shown at convent schools and parish halls in many parts of England. The films were documentary in character — on the sacraments, the Mass, boys' retreats, and on the life and work of some of the religious orders. In 1938 he brought out a monthly publication, *Catholic Film News*, whose purpose was to help Catholics in their choice of good entertainment films. Unfortunately, the war ended the activities of the Catholic Film Society. It closed down in 1941, but *Catholic Film News* continued publication. The society was re-started after the war as The Catholic Film Institute and the paper, which has a large circulation today, assumed its present title — *Focus*. However, because of his many other activities, Father Valentine is not a member of the new society.

Another of his great interests in prewar days was the Catholic Juniors' Retreat Movement, of which he was director. This movement, begun in 1934, aimed at deepening the spiritual life of Catholic boys, and retreats were given to groups (ages 11 to 15) at special retreat centers in London and elsewhere. The movement filled a real need and still continues in a slightly different form.

Anyone who has read Father Valentine's books will have realized the great emphasis he places on worship and prayer. In the early '30's he published a leaflet, "How To Make Mental Prayer," to help Catholics make their prayer an integral part of their spiritual life. Thousands of this leaflet have been sold, and the demand still continues. At the request of a blind man he had it transcribed into Braille and circulated among many Catholic blind. This was the beginning of St. Cecilia's Guild for the Blind, which now supplies Catholic books in Braille to the National Library for the Blind in London.

Father Valentine is in great demand as a retreat master, especially for religious Sisters and for young girls in their last year at school or at training colleges. The "Theophila Correspondence," the general heading for five of his books, followed naturally from these talks to young girls. They consist of letters to an imaginary young girl leaving school on the sacraments, prayers and the Gospels. Another, and perhaps the best of his works to date, *Religious Obedience*, is the result of his wide experience as a spiritual director. His latest, *The Art of Preaching*, gives practical hints to seminarians on the do's and don't's of the pulpit.

As a writer he is often humorous, always readable, but above all, practical in what he suggests and states.

He was born in 1894 and brought up by a devoted mother in the mining district of South Lancashire. He grew to love the miners, many of whom are still his friends. He was educated by the Jesuits at Mount St. Mary's College, Sheffield, later entering the Dominican Order, where he came under the inspiring influence of Father Vincent McNabb, then Professor of Dogmatic Theology at Hawkesyard. He completed his theological course at Louvain.

Father Valentine's publications include: *Reading Between the Lines* (1947); *For Better, For Worse* (1948); *Calling the Upper School* (1950); *Whatever He Shall Say* (1946); *The Lord We Serve* (1950); *The Inside of the Cup* (1946); *Religious Obedience;* and *The Art of Preaching*.

P. B. L.

Reverend Dom Eugene Vandeur, O.S.B. 1875–

Dom Eugene Vandeur was born in Namur, Belgium on May 21, 1875. He began his high school studies with the Jesuits at Our Lady of Peace High School and completed them in the Abbey high school in Maredsous, under the Benedictines. He joined the Order of St. Benedict on September 10, 1892, and was professed on February 15, 1894. He went to St. Anselm's College in Rome, Italy for theology and was awarded the S.T.D. (Doctor of Sacred Theology) degree in 1900. Meanwhile (1899) he was ordained to the priesthood.

Upon his return to St. Benedict's Abbey at Maredsous he taught in the high school for nine years. Then on October 9, 1909, he was appointed prior of Mont César Abbey, Louvain, Belgium, succeeding Dom Columba Marmion who had been elected Abbot of Maredsous. During the fifteen years that he held this office he taught theology. In 1924 he returned to Maredsous and collaborated in the foundation of the Benedictine Convent of Our Lady in Ermeton, Belgium. Since Dom Vandeur centers all the piety of the Church on the knowledge and practice of Holy Mass, and he believes that one can find asceticism and mysticism therein, he conceived the idea of a convent of Benedictine nuns who would live this ideal profoundly; Mass would be for them the soul of their Christian and religious life. The convent was established first at Wépion-sur-Meuse and received ecclesiastical approval on March 25, 1922 on the Feast of the Annunciation of the Blessed Virgin Mary. It soon flourished and became a school such as St. Benedict spoke of, School of Divine Service, consecrated to the spreading of the knowledge and the love of the Holy Sacrifice of the Mass. The convent was transferred to Ermeton-sur-Biert in the same diocese in 1928. The community is large now and exerts a great influence.

Since 1933 Dom Eugene devotes his time entirely to preaching retreats and writing books, especially on the Holy Sacrifice of the Mass. It was Dom Gregory Fournier, who was the director of the *Petit Messager de St. Benoit*, who urged him to write on the Mass in 1900. Dom Gregory asked him to contribute about fifteen lines a month on that subject. The articles pleased the readers, so the author wrote further articles for four years. When Monsignor Callewaerts, President of the Grand Séminaire, visited Maredsous, he strongly urged Dom Eugene to revise the whole work, and publish it — which Dom Eugene did in 1906. It became popular at once and was in constant demand so that by 1946 the work reached its tenth edition. It has been translated into English, German and Flemish. The priests in Europe use it as a text book to teach their flock. The *Notes sur la liturgie de la Messe* explain the history of the Mass without neglecting dogma and moral. The author published the *Sainte Messe, échelle de la Sainteté* (1928 and 1946) which treats step by step the ordinary of the Mass based on the Blessed Sacrament. He comments likewise on many Masses, for young people and for young girls.

Some of his other books are: *La Messe de Ste. Thérèse* (1925, translated into Italian in 1930); *La Messe du Sacré Coeur; La Ste. Messe et nos malades* (1941); *Vous Serez mes Temoins; Essai de synthèse chrétienne; O Mon Dieu Trinité Que J'Adore; A La Trinité Par L'Hostie; Elevations sur la Messe de Chaque Jour* (3 Vols.); *L'Abandon A Dieu; Quand se Fait Lourde Notre Croix; Adoro Te; Je Meurs de Faim, Je Vais a mon Père; Aimez-vous les uns les Autres.* His books translated into English are: *The Holy Sacrifice of the Mass: Ladder of Sanctity* (1937); *Adoro Te* and *The Holy Mass, Popularly Explained.*

Since he specializes on the Holy Mass as the basic mystery of our religion, Father Vandeur has been called the Apostle of the Holy Mass.

P. P., K. M., and M. A. H.

Kees van Hoek   1902–

Kees van Hoek (Kees is an old Dutch peasant name which appears on his baptismal certificate, Latinized as Cornelius) was born at The Hague, Holland, on September 6, 1902, the son of an old family of well-to-do business people. He received his early education at a Catholic private school from which he went to the Jesuit College at The Hague. His early ambition was to join the Dutch East Indian civil administration and with that goal in view he studied law, economics and the Malay language. When, in an essay contest open to all high school and university students throughout Holland, he won the second prize only a quarter point behind the first prize winner, he decided to turn to journalism, having always been haunted (as he once put it in an interview to *Commentary*) "by an insatiable interest to find out the how and why of things that make the world go round." He joined the new Catholic democratic daily *De Morgen* as political correspondent, becoming the youngest journalist in The Hague parliamentary press gallery. A series of articles against the legal restrictions enforced against missionary activities in certain Dutch colonial territories won him a warm letter of approbation from the then Prefect of the Propaganda Fide in Rome, Cardinal van Rossum. Like every young Dutchman he had been conscripted into the army at the age of 18, but was exempted first, as a student, later, as a working journalist, to be suddenly called up at the age of 23. Immediately after completion of his service he left his country for good, "feeling like a square peg in a round hole."

After a few years in London and some extensive journeys throughout Canada (to investigate the prospects of Dutch mass emigration to that country) he came to New York in 1928 as correspondent of the leading Dutch daily *Nieuwe Rotterdamsche Courant*. At the same time he began writing in English; his first English article — a study on the Norwegian authoress Sigrid Undset — appeared that year in *America*. After some years he ceased writing in his native tongue.

In the early thirties he worked for some years as League of Nations correspondent in Geneva, then returned to London to edit a multilingual weekly, *European Herald*, which, originally founded by English and German industrialists to foster better Anglo-German understanding, had soon to be abandoned by its original German sponsors under pressure of the Berlin Government for not following the Nazi Party line. Van Hoek was able to rescue the venture by giving it a much wider scope, turning it into the first truly international newspaper with English, French, German, Italian, Spanish and Esperanto sections, until the times grew altogether too unfavorable for such an undertaking. For some time afterwards he was assistant editor of the British-owned *Balkan Herald* in Belgrade and then started out on free lancing, travelling the Continent, specializing in interviews. His interview with the then Austrian Chancellor, Kurt von Schuschnigg, appeared in the London *Daily Telegraph* in January 1937.

The outbreak of the war put a temporary stop to his continental wanderings in search of men that make news. In the meantime he had made his home in Dublin, Ireland. There he started a daily column in the *Irish Independent* under the caption "Leader Page Parade," which he wrote every day for six years without a break. It was a vivacious personal commentary on people and places "in the news" in Ireland.

After the war he went travelling again and in 1948 changed over to the *Irish Times*, for which he writes a twice-weekly column, "The Way of the World," dealing with foreign affairs and travel and once a week a vignette — profiles of prominent men and women in all walks of life and from every country, based on talks with his subjects in their own environment.

A busy journalist he regrets that his many assignments leave him no time to write the books he would prefer to concentrate on. His first book (1929) was an English appreciation of Jan Toorop, the famous modern Dutch master. It was followed in 1932 by his only book in Dutch, *Man en Macht* (Man and Might), a selection of encounters with people of importance, including Frank Kellogg, Charles Evans Hughes, Gatti-Casazza and Upton Sinclair.

His biography of the present Pontiff, *Pius XII, Priest and Statesman*, appeared in Dublin (1939) and subsequently in London and New York editions, and was translated into Spanish and Hindustani. Brought up to date for the Holy Year, it was then serialized in a number of American dailies, including the Washington *Post*. All his other books appeared originally as newspaper serials. *Kruger Days* (London, 1939) is a series of talks with Dr. W. J. Leyds, Kruger's Secretary of State and his envoy in Europe during the Boer War, originally commissioned by the Argus South Africa group of newspapers. It was later translated in Afrikaans as *Gesprekke met Dr. Leyds* (Pretoria, 1939).

Diplomats in Dublin (1943) created among the Irish people a wider and clearer awareness of Ireland's hard-won status in the ranks of free nations. *People and Places* (1944) is a collection of vivid sketches, of which the Dublin *Standard* wrote that it contains "some of the best work done by any columnist this side of the Atlantic."

In 1946, the year he became an Irish citizen, he wrote *Country of My Choice* (separately published in London as *An Irish Panorama*), an impressionistic description of the beauty, variety and vitality of Irish life. The first book published on Ireland since the Second World War, it depicts the vigorous young as much as the romantic old Ireland.

Kees van Hoek married, in 1937, the daughter of a Danzig newspaper director; they live in Rathgar, Dublin, Ireland.

N. O'C.

Reverend Dom Idesbald Van Houtryve, O.S.B. 1886–

Father Idesbald Van Houtryve was born on September 24, 1886 in Bruges, Belgium, and was christened Louis. He assumed the name of Idesbald when he entered the Order of St. Benedict. The mystical spirit of his native city, so full of historical monuments and landmarks, seems to have infused some of its touching and deep serenity and harmony into the work and personality of Dom Idesbald.

At the early age of four he lost his father and from then on he was brought up under the tender and pious influence of his mother. After finishing his studies of the humanities at the episcopal college of his native town, he entered the Abbey of Mont-César, Louvain, on September 24, 1904, his birthday. The monastery which he joined was founded on April 13, 1899 and could boast of three great persons at the time he entered. Towards each of these, Dom Idesbald wanted to express his deep admiration and grateful veneration. One of these persons was the Abbot Dom Robert de Kerchove, the head of the Abbey, "endowed with exceptional ability for leadership and with a rare nobility of heart." He died at the age of 96, in 1942. In his honor Dom Idesbald wrote a booklet in 1949 on the occasion of the golden jubilee of the abbey in which he described the characteristic qualities of the abbot. The second outstanding figure was Dom Columba Marmion, whose fame as a director in the spiritual life is universally known among Catholics — Dom Idesbald dedicated to him his booklet *L'Esprit de Dom Marmion*, and also an article in *L'Année Théologique* in 1948. The third person he felt himself attracted to was Dom Bruno Destrée, convert, poet, master of novices and brother of the socialist minister, Jules Destrée. Dom Idesbald collected all the documents which served Count Carton de Wiart to write his touching biography, *La Vocation d'Olivier George Destrée*.

As a young novice, Louis Van Houtryve received as patron saint, Blessed Idesbald, third abbot of the Cistercian monastery of Dunes who lived in the twelfth century and whose relics are in Bruges. After his vows on March 26, 1906, Dom Idesbald Van Houtryve spent two years of philosophy at Maredsous. Then he returned to Louvain to study theology. He was ordained on August 27, 1911 and was given various duties to perform in his abbey. For about ten years he gave retreats to young people. Soon he dedicated himself exclusively to works of spirituality, including retreats to priests and religious every year. These conferences gave birth to the book *La Vie Sacerdotale* (2 editions). Then followed a number of liturgical booklets: *Septuagésime* (1920); *Liturgie de Noel* (1921); *Toussaint* (1929); *Le mystère de Pâques* (1930). When some apparitions took place at Banneux in 1933. Dom

Idesbald made a personal inquiry on the spot and wrote: *La Vierge des Pauvres*. In this book he solidly established the authenticity of the apparitions in Banneux. Its third edition has a Preface by Monsignor Kerkhofs, Bishop of Liège, who officially recognizes the supernatural character of the facts given. He collaborated with the same bishop on his book *Notre Dame de Banneux*. In the meantime, Dom Idesbald contributed to the review *Questions Liturgiques* founded by Dom L. Bauduin and he wrote the article, "La Mediation de Marie dans la Liturgie," which appeared in the *Vie Diocesaine* of Malines, in July 1922. Originally, this article was the report he read before the Commission de Marie Médiatrice, instituted and presided over by Cardinal Mercier, of which commission Dom Idesbald was a member. He also published *La Vocation et la Mission de la Bernardine Reparatrice* (1938) and *Les Soeurs de la Charité de Namur* (1939). For the Flemish review *Tijdschrift Voor Geestelijk Leven* he wrote articles on "La Liturgie et la Mystique," "St. John of the Cross," and other subjects on spirituality.

World War II forced Dom Idesbald to go in 1940 to Haute-Savoie, to the castle of Tourronde, where the elder sister of ex-King Albert, Princess Henrietta of Belgium, the Duchess of Vendôme, was residing. Dom Idesbald has written his memoirs of the Duchess, his sojourn at Tourronde and the royal family, in a brochure entitled, "La Duchesse de Vendôme." There he had time to study the patron saint of the country, St. Francis de Sales, whom he always loved as his special friend in heaven. Dom Idesbald read not only the books on the saint but also the documents of his canonization preserved at the Visitation Convent of Annecy. He published the teachings of the saint in five volumes: *La vie intérieure; L'amour du prochain; L'Equilibre surnaturel; La dévotion humble et génereuse; Le Zèle pastoral.* Later he brought out two booklets: *Le secret de saint François de Sales* and *Saint François missionnaire ambulant.* A book, *L'ami de Dieu et des hommes,* has a more personal note which is taken from the thoughts of the saint and his biography. There is also a book on the personality of St. Francis de Sales, *Saint François de Sales peint par lui même.*

The books, however, in which Dom Idesbald reveals his erudition and his soul are: *Dans l'Esprit du Christ* (8 editions); *La Vie dans la Paix* (8 editions, 2 vols.); *Via Vitae* (2 vols.); *Le chant de la cité de Dieu* (2 editions); *Prières contemplatives* (5 editions); *Paix bénédictine* (2 editions). This work was translated into English by Leonard J. Doyle, O.S.B., and was published by The Newman Press under the title *Benedictine Peace.* Many of his books were translated into other languages.

Dom Idesbald feels that his literary works had their germ in the first year of monastic life. The seeds sown then in the quiet and spiritual light of the monastery, bathed in an atmosphere of prayer and of contemplation, have borne fruit in his later years. The foundation of his writings are theological and the framework is evangelical. There are no dry moralizations. The unction of the Holy Ghost seems to pervade his writings and they encourage prayer. His works have often been compared to the *Imitation*.   E. O. and M. A. H.

Reverend Fernand Emmanuel Joseph Van Steenberghen
1904–

Internationally known for his scholarly research in medieval philosophy, Father Fernand Van Steenberghen succeeded Maurice De Wulf in 1939 in the chair of History of Medieval Philosophy at the Higher Institute of Philosophy, University of Louvain, Belgium.

Father Fernand Van Steenberghen was born at Brussels, Belgium, in the "commune" or district of Saint-Josse-ten-Noode, on February 13, 1904. After studying the humanities at St. Peter's College, Jette (1914–1920), he entered the University of Louvain (1920) and got the degree Ph.D. at the Institut Supérieur de Philosophie in 1923. Ordained to the priesthood at Malines on December 26, 1926, he continued his theological studies at Louvain and earned his bachelor degree in theology in 1928. Appointed to assist Professor De Wulf in the field of medieval philosophy, he undertook a journey to Rome to study under the direction of Monsignor Pelzer at the Vatican Library (1928–1929). He was still in Rome when the Lateran Treaty was signed.

Then he went to Munich, Germany, to work in the Manuscripts Department of the "Staatsbibliothek" (the State Library), where he frequently met Monsignor Grabmann, and had the opportunity of asking him many questions about medieval studies. Later he studied at Oxford. On March 10, 1931, he received, at Louvain, the higher degree of Maître-Agrégé de L'École Saint-Thomas, for defending his dissertation: *Siger de Brabant d'après ses oeuvres inédites. Volume I. Les oeuvres inédites* (Louvain, 1931). A few weeks later, Easter, 1931, he began to teach at the University of Louvain: he lectured on the "principles of Thomism" (general metaphysics) and on "Philosophical Texts of the Middle Ages." Since 1933, he lectured also on "Texts of Saint Thomas Aquinas," and from 1939 on, he added the general course on the History of Medieval Philosophy.

In 1932 he was appointed *chargé de cours* and received the title of professor in 1935. Since 1929 he is the director of the scientific seminar devoted to research work on the philosophers of the Middle Ages. From 1929 to 1936 he had been Secretary of *Revue Néoscolastique de Philosophie*.

In the field of medieval studies, Father Van Steenberghen is known chiefly for his large work, *Siger de Brabant d'après ses oeuvres inédites* (2 vols. in 4° xvi–760 pp., Louvain, 1931–1942). This work not only reviews the problems respecting Siger but presents in a very new light the evolution of philosophical thought in the thirteenth century. Chapter II has been published separately: *Aristote en Occident. Les origines de l'aristotélisme parisien* (Louvain, 1946). A first redaction of Chapters III and IV won for him, in 1938, the prize of the Royal Academy of Belgium and it was published by the Academy in the "Mémoires Couronnés" series (Brussels, 1938).

From 1932 until 1947, Father Van Steenberghen assisted Maurice De Wulf in the elaboration of the sixth edition of De Wulf's, *Histoire de la Philosophie Médiévale* (3 vols. 1934-36-47).

Besides numerous articles and critical studies, Father Van Steenberghen has published two small booklets which are useful research tools for medievalists: *Directives pour la confection d'une monographie scientifique* (2ᵈ ed. 1949, Louvain) and *Philosophie des Mittelalters* (in the series: *Bibliographische Einführungen in das Studium der Philosophie* (1950) (Bern, Switzerland).

Recently he has published, together with A. Forest and M. de Gandillac, *Le mouvement doctrinal du IXᵉ au XIVᵉ siècle* (Paris, 1951), being the 13th volume of the well known *Histoire de l'Eglise*, edited in 26 volumes by A. Fliche and V. Martin. Father Van Steenberghen wrote the second part of the volume: *Le XIIIᵉ siècle*.

In the field of philosophy, Father Van Steenberghen published an *Epistémologie* (1945) (2nd ed. 1947) and an *Ontologie* (1946), both in the series: *Cours publiés par l'Institut Supérieur de Philosophie*. In these treatises, the fundamental themes of Thomistic Philosophy are presented in a personal way and in modern form, quite understandable for twentieth century minds. An English translation of the series is being published by Joseph F. Wagner, Inc., New York. *Epistemology* appeared in 1949. *Ontology* was published in 1951. Two of his other important smaller studies are: *Réflexions sur la systématisation philosophique* (*Revue Néoscolastique de Philosophie*, 1938) and *Le problème philosophique de l'existence de Dieu* (*Revue Philosophique de Louvain*, 1947).

Students are chiefly struck by the clearness, accuracy and method they find both in his lectures and in his writings. His personal ideal would be, as philosopher and as historian, "to rethink Thomism in the light of our problems of the day and to present it in terms easily understood by our contemporaries."

Asked why he chose philosophy as his favorite subject, he replied: "When I presented myself at Malines, in 1920, as a candidate for the priesthood, my superiors sent me to the Séminaire Léon XIII, Louvain, in order to study mathematics at the University; so I was destined to spend my life as a teacher of mathematics! But Canon G. Simons, who was a good friend of Cardinal Mercier and who knew me intimately, informed the Cardinal of the exceptional qualifications he found in me for philosophy and so I was appointed to study philosophy instead of mathematics."

In philosophy his preference was for metaphysics and when he had to choose a subject for his dissertation, he sought the advice of Canon N. Balthasar. Canon Balthasar assigned him a metaphysical study of *De unitate intellectus* of St. Thomas. This led Canon Van Steenberghen to medieval philosophy. When Professor De Wulf saw his doctoral dissertation, he wanted Canon Van Steenberghen as his assistant and to become his successor. And so it happened. Canon Van Steenberghen also became the assistant and successor to Canon Balthasar for the general course of metaphysics.

During the winter term of 1950, Canon Van Steenberghen was a visiting professor at the Pontifical Institute of Medieval Studies in Toronto, Canada. He is the founder and director of the series *Philosophes Médiévaux,* founded in 1948 in order to replace the series *Les Philosophes Belges.* He was the spiritual director of the Séminaire Léon XIII (Louvain) from 1936 to 1948. Since 1941 he has been an honorary canon of the diocese of Malines.

His honors include: Laureate of the "Concours universitaire" awarded by the Belgian government in 1925; Laureate of the "Prix Mercier" in 1931; Laureate of the Prix de l'Académie Royale de Belgique in 1938.   M. A. H.

Reverend Hubert van Zeller, O.S.B. (Hugh Venning) 1905–

Spiritual matters are treated with a light touch, but without any flippancy, in the writings of Dom Hubert van Zeller.

Born in 1905, the son of the late Francis van Zeller, in Suez, Egypt — "the land which for a time sheltered Abraham, Joseph, Moses and Jeremias," Dom (Claud) Hubert claims "the dry smell of the desert reaches my nostrils still."

He began his studies in Munich but because of ill health had to return home. Later he studied at Downside Abbey, England, where he is now a Benedictine monk. He received the Benedictine habit in 1924 and was ordained priest in 1930.

He is particularly interested in the Bible, an interest which has been kept alive since his nursery days. "The motive which urged me to follow it up," he writes, "was the desire to get Catholics to read the Bible."

An experience that occurred at his own abbey school (Downside) confirmed his belief that adults, too, needed Biblical instruction. "Abbot Trafford, during the period when he was headmaster before becoming abbot, was on one occasion showing the school to a lady who was thinking of sending her boy to us. Admiration was expressed at all she saw, but never did her appreciation reach such a height as when this somewhat worldly-minded woman allowed herself to dwell upon the thought that her little boy would be able to attend classes in the company of other little boys whose parents were of the highest nobility. 'I had heard so much about Downside,' she said as she took her leave, 'but it has exceeded my wildest hopes.' 'Which is much what the Queen of Sheba said, if you remember,' replied Father Trafford. 'Oh, did she send her boy here, too?' is the reputed rejoinder."

Dom Hubert began to write on the twelve minor prophets. The first book, *Prophets and Princes, Watch and Pray,* was published in 1935.

Two years later *Sackcloth and Ashes* came off the press. Then he became ill. In bed he wrote *Isaias: Man of Ideas* (1938). "This book," he writes, "was meant to be a feeler to see if the public was ready to take full length biographies instead of, as hitherto, snapshot impressions of people and periods. The reviews seemed to justify the belief that it was." Consequently, he wrote *Daniel: Man of Desires, Jeremias: Man of Tears* (1942). It was chosen as the book of the month by the Catholic Book Club. This was followed by *Ezechiel: Man of Signs* (1944); *Lord God*, a prayer book for boys; *Come Lord*, a book of prayers for girls and young women; *Liturgical Asides* (1939), a book of prayers for Sundays and various feasts. The manuscript for *From Creation to Christmas* was destroyed in an air raid during World War II. Dom Hubert had no notes and no carbon copy. Since he was under contract for Burns and Oates — and they were anxious to have the manuscript — Dom Hubert started on it three days after the raid and finished it within the month.

Under the pseudonym, Hugh Venning, he wrote the novel *The End*. This was written in bed. "I had been working on the Apocalypse," he writes, "and when delirious with pneumonia and pleurisy imagined the end of the world. When I was allowed to write, I put down my 'ravings' which became the last chapter of *The End*. I then wrote backwards to Chapter I." Of it, Father Martindale, S.J., said: "Literally for the first time I have enjoyed, laughed over, and been moved to pray, by a novel about the end."

The plays in *Kaleidoscope* and *Portmanteau* were asked for by over-worked producers at the Downside School, who wanted "clean plays which could be put on without a blush." *The King with Half a Crown* was written in eight days and was followed by a week in bed with a high temperature. *Up the Garden Path* was written in twenty-four hours — rehearsals starting on the day after the play was requested. This is a one-act play. *A Quiet Afternoon* is the result of someone saying he could not write a short story about Plato.

Other books by Dom Hubert are: *We Die Standing Up* (1948); *We Live With Our Eyes Open* (1949); *Moments of Light* (1950); *Old Testament Stories* (1950); *Famine of the Spirit* (1950); *We Work While the Light Lasts* (1950); *Family Case-Book* (1950); *We Sing While There's Voice Left* (1951); *Praying While You Work* (1951); and *Willingly to School*.

"When not writing or teaching or being ill," he says, "I paint pictures and carve stone." M. A. H.

Hugh Venning. See *Reverend Hubert van Zeller, O.S.B.*

Angela Verne (Mrs. Robert Capes)

Angela Verne was born the third child of a family
of four. Her father, John Lewis Verne, of old
Catholic Bavarian stock was artistic and musical
with the gift of craftsmanship in his fingers; her
mother, of great literary ability, was of nonconformist, Irish-Yorkshire descent and the
eldest daughter of Bernard Battigan Hackney
of the Middle Temple, Barrister-at-Law, of
Birmingham. From both she inherited gifts
which made her love to be both author and artist.

To save expenses and to provide health and freedom for the children the family moved to a small cottage overlooking the Hampshire
Downs near the estate of Sir Joseph Tichborne Bart. About 1914 the
family moved to a large Victorian house in Clapham Park, London;
this house had once belonged to Mary Martineau, the writer.

From here, Angela and her sister Margaret attended La Retraite
Convent, where the sister of the present Bishop Beck was one of their
classmates; but Margaret, being two years older, was sent on to boarding
school in Hampshire and then on to the local high school.

After following her sister for a short time to Perin's school in
Hampshire, Angela was sent to St. Mary's Convent, Bishop's Stortford,
Herts, where she was supremely happy under the superiorship of Mother
Mary Ursula, now the Mother Provincial at St. Mary's Convent,
Lowestoft, Suffolk.

After the convent days, a London County Council Scholarship at
Camberwell School of Art enabled Angela to take up free lance work for
children's pages of newspapers and magazines, and, except for a break
of six months, when she was sent to Paris to teach English in a private
family, she continued to contribute children's verses, and one or two
line-drawing portraits were accepted by the London *Bookman*. A poster
for a child's reader published by Messrs. Ginn and Co. brought her an
invitation to join a group at their art studio in Kensington, where Molly
Capes, a clever black and white artist and verse writer, knew Angela
Verne as the "niece of Adela Verne, the pianist."

In 1932 her first book *Telling Beads* was published by Messrs.
Burns, Oates & Washbourne, and on May 31st of the same year, she
married Robert Capes, M.A., barrister-at-law, who was in the secre-
tarial department of the firm of Dorman Long and Co. The Capes have
three children: John, Denis, and Andrew.

It was during the Second World War, while evacuated with her two
children, that Angela Verne's interest in writing was revived. Her first
book had been disappointing and unprofitable; her second one was a
compilation of the poems of an Irish doctor who had died in tragic circumstances in 1936; this was followed by a pamphlet in verse, published
at her own expense by Basil Blackwell, which had been a complete

financial loss. Despite this, a priest, whom she met, encouraged her to
write, but sickness prevented her from carrying out his suggestion at
that time. Some weeks in a Nursing Home gave her time to think.
"I have always loved the very thought of Our Blessed Lady," she
says, "since I received a mother-o'-pearl rosary at the age of ten. . . .
She gave me the idea to write about her. Day after day I would spread
out some bright magazines over the bed, and underneath would be my
note-book and fountain pen, so that the inquisitive nurses and doctors
would not see what I was at. But it was some time before the manuscript
was finished and accepted and published. The book appeared in 1948
under the title, *Glorious Threshold.* A copy of this book was sent to
Pope Pius XII. A few weeks later she received a delightful and informal letter dictated by the Holy Father, from his private secretary,
Monsignor Montini.

Now Angela Verne is at work on a biography of childhood, in conjunction with her sister Margaret, which they hope will be finished in
time to enter for the competition in 1952 offered by Messrs. Heineman.
Miss Verne still retains membership of the Authors' Society, and of the
National Book Council. In her private life she has started a little school
for Catholic children in her own home with the help of an Irish lady who
came to live with her in 1946. Together they are striving to train small
boys, especially those who have been deprived of the advantages of a
Catholic home, during their prep school days.

David Esdaile Walker   1907–

Via the London *Daily Mirror*, David Walker has
developed into one of the outstanding special
correspondents of modern times.

Born in Darjheeling, India, in 1907, he is the
only child of the late Major-General Sir Ernest
Walker, K.C.I.E., and of Lady Walker. He was
educated by the Benedictines at Ampleforth
College, Yorkshire, England, and subsequently
(1927–29) at Christ Church, Oxford. While at
Oxford he played on the rugby football team.

During his last year at the university, while lodging with Father
(now Monsignor) Ronald Knox, he was a regular contributor to the
Isis. At this time he began short-story writing for *Pearsons', Bystander,*
London *Evening News, Windsor,* and other magazines.

In 1932 he joined the staff of the London *Daily Mirror* as sports
writer. After becoming feature editor in 1935, he went abroad in 1938
to begin his successful career as a foreign correspondent, mainly for the
Daily Mirror but also for Reuters, *The Tablet, The Christian Science
Monitor* and the London *Times.* "He has covered many of the crises of
our day from the entry of Hitler into Austria to the overwhelming of
Yugoslavia when he himself was made a prisoner," states Duckett's

Register (July, 1949). For eight months in 1946, he toured the United States reporting on the American continent. He has now spent twelve years "in a suitcase" and still enjoys it. In January, 1950, he was appointed chief European correspondent of the London *Daily Mirror* and the *Argus* (Melbourne, Australia).

In 1943 he married Rosalys Campbell, the daughter of a former British consul in China.

His first book, a novel on life in a tuberculosis sanatorium, was published in 1932 under the title *Eat, Drink and Be Merry*. He was too busy to write another until 1939 when he brought out *Religion in the Reich*, a study of Hitler's persecution of the Catholic and Protestant Churches in Germany. Oddly enough, the entire stock of this book was destroyed in one of the first Luftwaffe raids in London, where the book was published. To avoid identification of informants inside Germany, the nom-de-plume Michael Power was used by the author.

Death at my Heels (1942), published by Chapman & Hall, describes his Balkan adventures and eventual capture in Yugoslavia after serving as a war correspondent in Greece. This book became a best seller in Sweden. Then followed, in the same year, a translation called *The Greek Miracle*, which appeared both in Great Britain and the United States. In 1943 he published *Civilian Attack*, a study of the relations between press and diplomacy in war time with special reference to the undermining of enemy morale. *We Went to Australia*, published by Chapman & Hall in 1949, was written after spending eighteen months as a reporter in that country.

In September, 1950, Walker was recalled from his European assignment to proceed to Korea with Britain's 29th Independent Brigade as a war correspondent. He had previously been a war correspondent accredited to the Greek army in the winter of 1940–1941 and had also been a war correspondent with the United States 9th Army under General Simpson in Europe.

Recalled again to London on December 30, 1950, he publicly protested against the quality of the news coming from Korea — a protest which was widely published and broadcast in America, and in other United Nations countries.

In January, 1951, he was re-appointed to his European post but with special reference to General Eisenhower's SHAPE HQ in France.

From their consulates in Paris, both Poland and Yugoslavia refused his requests to re-visit their countries.

He is a member of the Catholic journalist society, The Keys.

M. A. H.

Barbara Wall (Barbara Lucas) 1911–

Barbara Wall, who usually writes under her maiden name, Barbara Lucas, was born in 1911. Her mother was one of the daughters of Wilfrid and Alice Meynell, famous names, the first because Wilfrid Meynell, in addition to being a writer of distinction himself, fathered the poet

Francis Thompson and was largely responsible for the publication and spread of his work; the latter, because Alice Meynell is one of the poets of the English language. Mrs. Wall is a niece of the late E. V. Lucas, the essayist, and editor of *Punch*.

Barbara Wall, who was educated at St. Paul's Girls School in London, was early associated with the *Catholic Worker* movement in London and was one of the founders of the paper itself. After writing her first novel, *Stars Were Born*, she married the essayist and publicist, Bernard Wall. Two years after her first novel, in 1936, she published her second, *The Trembling of the Sea*. But it was her third, *Anna Collett*, published ten years later, which brought her a wider public. This novel was recommended by the Book Society in London and highly praised by the critics.

In addition to fiction, Mrs. Wall has written a religious essay, *And Was Crucified*, and various *Catholic Worker* pamphlets. She is also a translator from the French, her translations including Leon Bloy's *Letters to his Fiancée*, Francois Mauriac's *God and Mammon* and *The Life of Margaret of Cortona*, and Henri Talon's *John Bunyan*.

Mrs. Wall has two daughters.   M. DE LA B.

Bernard Wall   1908–

Bernard Wall, born in 1908, was educated at the English Jesuit College, Stonyhurst, at Oxford University and at Fribourg University in Switzerland.

He was interested in the *Catholic Worker* movement in London, and in connection with this work he met Barbara Lucas whom he married, and with her became a co-founder of the *Catholic Worker* newspaper.

Always interested in a fresh and up-to-date approach to the problems of Catholicism and contemporary culture, Bernard Wall founded and edited two remarkable reviews. In 1934 he started the *Colosseum* which, though a small production with an appeal necessarily limited to intellectuals with a special religious fervor, created a good deal of interest in the years preceding the war. Unfortunately, the war itself killed it, as it was growing and gaining interest with regular contributors like Christopher Dawson, Eric Gill, Gonzague de Reynold and Kuehnelt-Leddihn. Shortly after the end of the war, Bernard Wall began *The Changing World*, a review of a similar type, but now it was less easy to fix a definite message, and there seemed to be less constructive Catholic curiosity for fresh approaches to literary and philosophical questions. *The Changing World* was not destined to last, and came to an end in 1949.

Bernard Wall, as a Catholic figure in England, has always had a very special interest in the Continent and Continental Catholicism. But he writes rarely, being one of those philosophers with a special sensitivity for changing moods and nuances in contemporary thought which can rarely be pinned down in book publication. His books, however, include: *Spain of the Spaniards* (1937); *European Notebook* (1939); *These Changing Years* (1947). Interested all his life in Italy and Italian literature — he was stationed in Rome during some of the war years — Bernard Wall's most important book is likely to be *Italy: Life and Landscape*, a book planned for two volumes, one of which appeared in 1950. He has been a regular contributor to the leading periodicals and a regular broadcaster.   M. DE LA B.

Francis Wallace

The nationally-known author and journalist Francis Wallace was born in Bellaire, Ohio, and still has his home and workshop there. His other favorite living spots are Beverly Hills, California and New York City.

After graduating from St. John's High School in his native city, he enlisted in the naval air force and was awaiting the call to service when World War I ended. In 1919 he entered the University of Notre Dame to study law but changed later to philosophy. Attending Notre Dame at the time were such prominent athletes as George Gipp, the Four Horsemen, Frank Thomas and most of the Notre Dame men now in the coaching profession. He is a classmate and close friend of Father John J. Cavanagh, President of the University of Notre Dame. He was graduated in 1923. While at Notre Dame, Mr. Wallace had been appointed publicity director by Knute Rockne, an experience which proved invaluable. Direct from college he came to New York City to become night sports editor and assistant night city editor for the Associated Press in his first year. Thereafter, he was engaged in sports writing — baseball, football, and boxing on the *New York Post, News, Mirror* and the *World-Telegram.*

His first magazine article appeared in *Scribner's* in 1927; his first short stories were in *Liberty* and *Redbook* in 1928. Since then he has had articles and fiction (mostly sports) in *The Saturday Evening Post, Collier's, Cosmopolitan, Redbook, Look, Reader's Digest, The American* and the News-Tribune Syndicate. In May 1949 he became associate editor of *Collier's* magazine.

Mr. Wallace has been identified as a *Saturday Evening Post* writer since 1930 when "This Football Business" appeared. With three serials in eighteen months ("Kid Galahad," "Double Ride," "Razzle Dazzle"), and three *Saturday Evening Post* covers in five months, he had two unique distinctions in *Post* history. He is, perhaps, the first and certainly one of the few to have two by-lines in the same edition — a serial and an article featured on the cover — "Double Ride" and "I Am a Football Fixer." The latter article led to the "Pigskin Preview," which began in 1937 — the only annual feature in the *Post*. Since 1949 this feature appears in *Collier's* as "Francis Wallace's Football Preview."

Mr. Wallace has had wide experience through the years as a radio commentator (mostly ad lib) after big football games, heavyweight championship fights, Kentucky Derbies, etc., with Husing, McCarthy, Fields, Wismer and others. While a writer at M.G.M., he predicted football results on the Good News program.

He is also in demand as an after-dinner speaker and toastmaster in major and minor cities from New York to Los Angeles. Until recently, at the annual Baseball Writers Dinner of the New York Chapter, he performed as a ham actor and soloist.

About 1936 Mr. Wallace began to be seriously interested in domestic affairs and has been a student of politics since that time. His major interest has shifted from sports to politics and economics and toward industrial fiction and articles.

When World War II broke out he was in Hollywood and became involved in fighting the Communists there. He helped organize the M.P.A. (Motion Picture Alliance) for the Preservation of American Ideals. Upon returning to Ohio he was made County Industrial Chairman for the Seventh War Loan, and put on the only county-wide Labor Management Dinner in the history of the country. In 1950 he was an unsuccessful candidate for the Republican Congressional nomination in the 18th Ohio district.

In 1925 he married Mary Heath of Bellaire, Ohio. They have one son, John Francis, Jr.

Most of Mr. Wallace's books have been in the field of sports. Of the seven that have been sold to the moving pictures, six were produced. To have one's first six novels sold and produced may be a record. Seven of these novels were serialized — five in the *Post*, one in *Collier's* and one in *College Humor*. Three were resold to newspaper syndicates. Two movies, "Kid Galahad" and "Touchdown" (from the book *Stadium*), were smash hits. *Kid Galahad* first appeared as a *Post* serial in 1936. It was published as a book in the United States, England and in an armed forces edition and is now translated into Norwegian. The movie, produced by Warner Brothers, starred Bette Davis, Humphrey Bogart, Edward G. Robinson, Wayne Morris and Jane Bryan. There were three radio dramatizations and the book is "still selling well" after fifteen years.

Another of Mr. Wallace's books, *Explosion* (1943), a novel based on a coal mine disaster, received creditable reviews as a serious work and was cited in Pegler's column as "the most understandable authority on these terrifying matters." Mr. Wallace's 13th book, *Dementia Pigskin*, was published in September 1951. His other books are: *Huddle; Stadium; That's My Boy; O'Reilly of Notre Dame; Autumn Madness; Big Game; Razzle Dazzle; Little Hercules; Big League Rookie*. He is now working on *Front Man* for 1952, after which he plans a series of small town novels.

Since 1930 he has done intermittent work in Hollywood studios, at M.G.M., 20th Century-Fox, Paramount and Warner Brothers.

He is a member of the Screen Writers' Guild, Kiwanis, Elks,

Knights of Columbus, Baseball Writers, Football Writers, Belmont Hills Country Club, Fort Henry Club (Wheeling, West Virginia) and the Newman Club, Los Angeles, California.

His hobbies are football, golf (which he plays in the high eighties), swimming, traveling, music and the theatre.

In 1949 he was National President of the Notre Dame Alumni Association; and in 1950 Honorary President of the same group.

M. A. H.

Hugo Wast. See under *Martinez*

Dorothy G. Wayman (Theodate Geoffrey)   1893–

Dorothy Wayman commences her autobiography, *Bite the Bullet*, dramatically. "At the age of twenty-seven, I suddenly found myself alone in the world; guardian and support of three boys, the oldest five years old; with all my personal possessions in four trunks and a handbag; with my cash assets amounting to $1.56, and a 'passport' in the shape of an X-ray film showing tubercular mottlings on one lung."

She had just returned to New England from Japan where she had spent several years with her husband, an export-import agent, and where she had learned to speak Japanese fluently. On her return, a doctor of practical turn of mind, realizing that Dorothy would not be parted from her children, said: "You must look after your children, earn a living, and cure your disease." This triple task Dorothy Wayman achieved, making her living and supporting and educating her children, through her daring and skill as a reporter.

Her friends did not want her to take up writing but she insisted and repaired to a psychologist, Dr. Langfeld. Dr. Langfeld, noting her mental gifts and how "she likes to watch how other people do things," approved her idea of devoting herself to writing. His advice in this respect was excellent but he was incorrect when he jotted down the observation, "she dislikes above all to sell things." Dorothy was in fact, as her success soon showed, a most brilliant saleswoman. Books, stories, plans, ideas of every kind — always she could sell them. Not even Henry Ford (or Charles Lindbergh) could resist her salesmanship.

Above all, however, her art consisted in watching and describing what she saw. Gifted with an eye that saw even more than she knew she saw — that "eidetic imagery" or faculty of reproducing at will and in detail (including details not consciously noted) things her eye had encompassed — she had in addition a facile pen. She watched and wrote. "I write what other people do — and that is the pleasure of a reporter's job. I'm a connoisseur of other people's actions and emotions. . . . I'm never bored with watching people do things and how they do them and what they look like when they are doing them; and that's what I try to write. . . . Part of my job is waiting for things to happen or to start." Dorothy Wayman's task, in her reporting, was not to make deep analyses of people or situations but just to describe. And with her eidetic faculty she took herself in as part of the *mise en scène* and could subsequently tell in *Bite the Bullet*, with no little objectivity, the varied and sometimes amazing things she did, or experiences that she underwent.

When her emotions are aroused by the spectacle of beauty, as for instance when, during her journey to Japan in 1939, she kept "dawn watch" on deck to see "a full moon set as the round red sun rose," she writes with rare beauty. The ship was running southward down the coast of Japan. "To port, rosy streaks in the sky warned of the sun's imminence. To starboard, a huge silver wafer of a moon dropped nearer and nearer to the black, tossing waves. Then, for a breath-taking space, the crimson sun orb shone across the shadows opposite the ghostly moon disk. The chief mate and the barefooted sailors were silently saying their morning prayer." One can understand Dorothy Wayman's boast that "color to me is an emotion with a tangible physical thrill."

That journey to Japan in 1939, as a representative of the Boston *Globe*, marked the climax of fifteen years of brilliantly successful work as reporter and writer. The world was hers. Frankly she says: "I was (at that hour) independent, competent, successful. I could get along under my own steam. I was filled with pride. I ran on pride the way an automobile runs on gasoline. I radiated a broad tolerant philosophy of successful materialism." But, within a few months, by the grace of God, a humble faith in religion, the Catholic faith, came to this Protestant New England writer. It came suddenly, mysteriously, as she knelt before the tabernacle in the Sophia University chapel in Tokyo. "I know I knelt," she writes, "on a dark wooden bench. I saw an altar carved with design of lotus leaves, a tabernacle with the curving lines of an Oriental tiled roof, a statue of Our Lady with slanting eyes, and the rosy flicker of the sanctuary lamp. And like the quiet flooding of a tide sweeping through my mind, I received the gift of faith."

Dorothy G. Wayman (née Godfrey) was born in 1893 in Moreno Valley, San Bernardino County, California, of New England stock. There was Indian blood in her veins, but for the most part her ancestry went back to the English blood of early settlers. "My own home," she says, "was not a religious one. I never remember saying a prayer or hearing my parents speak to me about God." After returning to New Hampshire, Dorothy was sent to a convent school, Mount St. Mary's (Hooksett, New Hampshire), for the excellent training that the nuns offered. The nuns were warned not to interfere with her Protestantism, and for her part, Dorothy was instructed by her mother to beware of popish superstitions. After Mount St. Mary's she was sent to Bryn

Mawr for one year, and then, in 1914, she graduated from Simmons School for Social Workers. After her marriage, she accompanied her husband to Japan, where the social life described in *Immigrant in Japan* was her lot. Following the earthquake in 1923, Dorothy Wayman and her three sons returned to New England and her hard fight for survival began. Then indeed she herself had "to bite the bullet" . . . an expression handed down in her family from Revolutionary days, when wounded soldiers, facing operations without pain-killing drugs, were given a bullet to bite on, to keep them from chewing their tongues to rags.

Having trained for a while in the art of writing and reporting, Dorothy Wayman's first official jobs were Cape Cod correspondent for the Boston *Globe*, and until 1933 managing editor of the Falmouth *Enterprise*. Meantime she wrote her first book, published as a serial in *The Saturday Evening Post* (1925), and later as an independent book, *Immigrant in Japan*. The cover-leaf read: "Japan as seen by an American woman who learned the language and lived as the Japanese live." She had lived in a fishing village among lowly Japanese and had come to know and to love them dearly. Since 1933 she has been on the Boston *Globe* staff in Boston.

As a reporter, Dorothy had to do with crimes of every kind and with underworld characters, in particular, during prohibition, with bootleggers. In conjunction with Eddie Doherty she wrote about them in the novel *Dark o' the Moon*. It was at a time when her sons were ill and hospital and doctors' bills mounted up. "Odd," she says, "how you can have your heart bleeding inwardly, your tears running involuntarily, and still whip yourself to write joyously of love and liquor and adventure on the high seas." In 1938, in collaboration with Major Willis Fitch, she wrote *Wings in the Night*, a biography of an American flier brigaded with the Italian Flying Corps in the First World War. The book was honored by the Italian Government. Two years later she won the *Atlantic Monthly* essay prize, and the Gold Medal awarded by the Institut Litteraire et Artistique, France. Ill health struck again in 1941 in the form of cancer, from which, however, after a long period under surgery and treatment, Dorothy Wayman recovered. Always grateful and hopeful she thus sums up her life: "I've had the best of two worlds. I was born a New England Yankee and whatever is lovely in New England culture or customs or people is part of my memory and being: and then, by God's grace, I stepped through into an irradiated world of Catholic culture and people and the Church."

Apart from her articles and news stories Dorothy Wayman has published the following books: *Immigrant in Japan* (1926); *Powdered Ashes* (1927); *John Holmes at Annapolis* (in conjunction with Comdr. V. H. Godfrey, U.S.N.) (1928); *Suckanesset* (a history of Falmouth, Massachusetts) (1930); *Dark o' the Moon* (co-author with Eddie Doherty) (1933); *Wings in the Night* (in conjunction with Major Willis Fitch) (1938); *Fifty Hours to Breathe* (1939); *Edward Sylvester Morse* (a biography) (1942); *Bite the Bullet* (an autobiography) (1948). The nom de plume, Theodate Geoffrey, was used by Dorothy Wayman in her first seven books. Theodate was chosen to symbolize her soul in quest of God. She is at present writing the first biography of the late United States Senator, David I. Walsh (1872–1947), first Catholic ever elected Governor and Senator in Yankee Massachusetts.

In spite of much illness, much "biting o' the bullet," Dorothy Wayman has lived to see her three sons, veterans of World War II, happily married. Their work took them far from her but her religion gives her solace. "It is strange," she writes, "to my former Protestant mentality — and so beautiful to my present point of view — to look back over my one small life and see how one human affection or attachment after another has been stripped from my life and yet to find how God fills the emptiness with His own fullness and peace." As she began her autobiography with a dramatic cry of near-despair, she concludes it with an equally dramatic prayer of joy and hope, using words from the Psalms: "I was glad when it was said unto me, Let us go into the House of the Lord."   E. B. B.

Oliver John Grindon Welch   1902–

Oliver John Grindon Welch was born at Kidderminster, England, on October 23, 1902. His father, John Grindon Welch, had returned to England from North America, where he had been in business at St. Louis, Missouri, and at St. John, New Brunswick. In 1910 he moved his family to Clifton, Bristol, and it was there that Oliver Welch had his home for the remainder of his boyhood.

He went to a preparatory school in Clifton, and has never ceased to be thankful that it was a school of the old-fashioned sort which really taught boys something. Just before his thirteenth birthday he went as a boarder to Downside School, then rising to the peak of its reputation under Dom Leander Ramsay, O.S.B. His six years at Downside were marked by a total failure to achieve even moderate distinction in the athletic field, combined with a regular, if unspectacular, success in public examinations. He writes: "Considerable credit should be given to the masters who got me over the necessary hurdles in mathematics; those who taught me the humane subjects had an easier task. Among these was Dom Lucius Graham, whose forceful and discursive teaching of history gave to this pupil, as to so many others, his first real taste for that subject."

In 1921 Oliver Welch, having won an open scholarship at Merton College, went to Oxford. Here again he was fortunate in the teaching he received, for he was given as tutor the late Idris Deane-Jones, who had just been elected to a fellowship at Merton. To the latter's brilliant tuition he ascribes much of the credit for his having won first-class honors in modern history in 1924. After taking his B.A. he stayed in Oxford for a postgraduate year and studied the English Reformation.

He competed for the annual prize fellowship at All Souls College, but, on being defeated by that now well-known historian, A. L. Rowse, he abandoned the hope of becoming a don and decided to become what he then regarded, but soon ceased to regard, as the next best thing — a schoolmaster.

He became senior history master at the Oratory School, Cardinal Newman's famous foundation, in 1926, and in the same year he married. He has a son and a daughter. In 1941 he left the Oratory School and, after teaching for two years at Bradfield College, became senior history master at Douai School, thus returning to the English Benedictines by whom he had been educated at Downside.

In 1934 his first book, *The Middle Ages, 1046–1494*, was published by Victor Gollancz, being the first of four volumes forming *A Modern History of Europe*, edited by J. Hampden Jackson. The Middle Ages had been his chief interest at Oxford, but in recent years modern history has increasingly claimed his attention. In 1947 appeared *Great Britain, 1485–1714*, published by Hollis & Carter. Though designed as a school textbook for those aged 15–16, it expresses the author's conviction that the nerve of historical writing should be the pursuit of a vigorous narrative.

If a teacher of history is obliged to attend to a wide field of study, a writer usually finds his private enthusiasm narrowing to a selected plot. With Oliver Welch this is the French Revolution, and his first work on this subject, *Mirabeau, a Study of a Democratic Monarchist*, was published in 1950. He hopes to follow this up with other studies of a period which increasingly fascinates him.   **M. A. H.**

Antonia White   1899–

Antonia White's father was the Senior Classics Master at St. Paul's School, London, where G. K. Chesterton was educated. He was an admirer of Chesterton and became a Catholic several years before him. His own conversion took place when he was thirty-five, after a long period of struggle and study and at a point in his career which meant real renunciation since no Catholic can be headmaster of an English Public School. He refused a professorship of Greek at Dublin University, preferring to remain at St. Paul's for the rest of his life. Antonia White's parents were received into the Church on the same day and Antonia, then aged seven, was conditionally baptized a few months later.

"Being an only child I read voraciously," she says, "from the age of four onwards and began to write almost as soon as I could read. I have to admit that the first thing I remember writing is a review of several imaginary books of my own. The books themselves never got further than their titles and I am afraid that, when I die, the books I meant to write will considerably outnumber the books I actually did. When I was seven, I won a prize for a fairy story in an inter-schools competition. It was neat, competent and perfectly flat, with none of the enchanting simplicity or flashes of real imagination one usually finds in children's work. When I was nine I went as a boarder for six years to a Sacred Heart convent. There I was known as 'good at composition' and wrote stories and poems for pleasure as well as for my classwork. Composition was my downfall for I began a novel and, as a result, was made to leave the school in exactly the same circumstances as the girl in *Frost in May* (her first novel). It was a severe shock and, though it happened long ago and the nuns have since shown me much kindness and understanding, I have never recovered my old pleasure in doing original work and am always burdened by guilt and anxiety about the writing of anything in which I am free to choose my own subject. In my teens, being quick and imitative, I had a certain flair for writing magazine stories; I also got myself a job as an outside copy-writer for an advertising agency. Later I worked for many years on the regular staff of an agency (one of them at the London office of J. Walter Thomson) and did a great deal of journalism of all kinds, ranging from serious critical articles in the reviews to editing the fashion page of a popular daily paper. My 'serious' work has always been done at long intervals, nearly always with a considerable lapse between the inception and the working out; usually, too, with much labour and anxiety. During the years when I was working full time in advertising and journalism I married and had two daughters. It was soon after the birth of the second that *Frost in May* came to be written. Like most writers, I had made several attempts at novels and abandoned them. One day in 1932 I was turning out some old papers and came across the early chapters of one I had begun when I was sixteen and had completely forgotten. I sat on the floor, so absorbed in the atmosphere of my convent schooldays, that my husband made me read aloud what was amusing me so much. His comment was: 'You've got to finish that book,' and he stood over me till I did. I wrote it in six months in the intervals of a full-time job but I have worked on and off on my second novel, *The Lost Traveller*, which was published in England and America (Viking Press) in 1950, for fifteen years. Richard Church in *John O'London's Weekly* (Apr. 14, 1950), writes: 'The two books together are a work of art worthy to stand beside the novels of Maurice Baring.'

"During those fifteen years I have written otherwise a few short stories and poems (only two of my stories have, I think, appeared in the United States, 'The Saint' and 'The Moment of Truth') and a translation of Maupassant's novel *Une Vie*, which won the Denyse Clairouin prize of 1950." Miss White has contributed occasional articles in French, one on Graham Greene, to the French Dominicans' review *La Vie Intellectuelle*. During the war she worked full time, first in the BBC in London (they were bombed out twice in a few months) and later in P.I.D. (the British equivalent of O.W.I.). It was not till 1945 that she decided to give up office work and concentrate on writing. Now, at the age of fifty-three (1952), "I am having all the difficulties most writers have when they are young," she writes, "trying to make both ends meet, by reviewing and so on, while I get on slowly with a new novel.

"For many years I lapsed so completely from Catholic faith and practice that no one was more surprised than myself when I was 'reconverted' in 1940. Returning to the Church has been like making my own choice to become a Catholic instead of being automatically 'brought over' with my parents when I was a child. Those years away have given me considerable insight into the difficulties both of the 'lapsed' and of people who find it hard to accept any form of religion nowadays. In my next two novels I shall attempt to go into the psychology of the lapsed Catholic.

"It is difficult for me to give any account of my private life beyond saying that during my lapse I married another writer, Tom Hopkinson, in circumstances that were not valid for a Catholic and that, before my return, there was a civil divorce. I live in London with my two daughters, the elder of whom has just left Oxford University (1951); the younger has been studying at the Old Vic Theatre School. I have always been interested in the theatre; I was on the stage for a short time and lectured and wrote scenarios for Michel St. Denis, the French producer, who was one of the directors of the Old Vic. Up to now I have only written one play, a light comedy, which has been several times produced in the provinces but not in London. But I hope, before I die, to write at least one serious play."

Mrs. Peter White See. Sheila John Daly

Edmund Taylor Whittaker   1873–

In June, 1930 Edmund Taylor Whittaker, Fellow of the Royal Society and Professor of Mathematics in Edinburgh University, was received into the Catholic Church.

Sir Edmund was born October 24, in 1873, the son of John Whittaker, Birkdale, and was educated at Manchester Grammar School and at Trinity College, Cambridge, where he became Wrangler and First Smiths Prizeman. He was a Fellow and Lecturer of Trinity College, Cambridge from 1896 to 1907; Royal Astronomer of Ireland from 1906 till 1912, when he was appointed Professor of Mathematics in Edinburgh University, a post which he filled till 1946. In 1901 he married Mary Boyd, the daughter of Reverend Thomas Boyd.

His attainments and distinctions make an imposing list. He has been President of the Royal Society of Edinburgh; President of the

London Mathematical Society; President of the Mathematical Association; Rouse Ball Lecturer at Cambridge; Herbert Spencer Lecturer at Oxford; President of Section A of the British Association; and a member of the Pontifical Academy of Sciences, Rome. He is also a foreign member of the R. Accademia dei Lincei and of several other foreign societies. The Universities of St. Andrew and of California have conferred on him an Honorary LL.D., and four universities, Dublin, Manchester, Birmingham and the National University of Ireland, an Honorary Sc.D.

In 1931 he was awarded the Sylvester medal by the Royal Society for his work on both pure and applied mathematics. Four years later the Holy Father awarded him the Cross Pro Ecclesia et Pontifice in recognition of his work for the Catholic Students Union and the Graduates Association. He has been President of the Newman Association. He was knighted in 1945.

He is the author of: *Modern Analysis; Analytical Dynamics; Calculus of Observations; History of the Theories of Aether and Electricity; Theory of Optical Instruments; The Beginning and End of the World; Space and Spirit; The Modern Approach to Descartes' Problem;* and *From Euclid to Eddington.*

Mrs. Canice Whyte. See May Nevin

Reverend Franz Michel Willam
1894–

Franz Michel Willam was born on July 14, 1894, in Schoppernan, situated in a valley of the Alps of Western Austria; there he attended the two primary grades of the village school. At the age of eleven he came to Brixen in the Southern Tyrol where he did his humanistic studies at the gymnasium (i.e., college) of the Boys' Episcopal Seminary. Then he pursued theological courses in Brixen, Vienna and Innsbruck; in the upper classes of the gymnasium he studied Greek with great enthusiasm. About this time — especially during vacation — he also began to occupy himself with the religious customs of his homeland.

After the completion of his studies, Willam worked as a parish priest in various places of his country, which activity (from 1917 onward) gave him a new impetus to continue those folklore studies.

In 1921, and during the following years, he wrote many stories, describing more or less the sorrows and the joys of the people of his homeland, such as: *Vorarlberger Erzählungen* (1921); *Der Sonnensteg* (1922); *Auf dem Tannenhof* (1923); *Der Lügensack* and *Der Streit der*

Friedfertigen (1923); *Knechte der Klugheit* (1924); *Der starkste Bräutigam; Die Sieben Könige* (1926); *Der Mann mit dem Lächeln* (1928). Besides those tales which were published by Herder, Freiburg and Hansen, Saarlouis, Willam — within three years — contributed weekly articles on Faith, Morals, and Grace to the well known Sunday paper *Himmelreich.*

In 1928 Willam (cooperating with Herder, Freiburg) conceived a plan to write a popular *The Life of Jesus* according to the four Gospels. To prepare himself for the task he made, in 1929, a trip to the Holy Land. Now all his folkloristic studies of many years were to stand him in good stead. It was then so easy for him — when wandering or riding through the countryside of Palestine — to keep in view all the places mentioned — often without detailing — in the gospels. While traveling there, he went through good and bad days; bad ones insofar as he fell sick, and had therefore to go — for months — to a hospital in Cairo which was in care of the Borromeo Sisters. But he was fortunate to recover, and this is why he could return to Palestine, seeing it now not in hot summer as formerly, but after the first rainy season, when nature was "dressing in green." After coming home, he sat down to work; it was, however, not easy to compile a really popular book. In our days, it is true, there were several books of the kind published: a *Life of Jesus* by the Frenchmen, Dr. Ferdinand Prat, S.J. and Dr. Jules Lebreton, S.J., also one by an Italian author of the name Dr. Giuseppe Ricciotti. But in those days, when Willam was to compose his book, there was no other *Life of Jesus* to serve him as a textual pattern.

Willam especially wanted to let the text grow out of the general situation; in one word, he wanted to follow the general directions, or guiding principles, as given in an encyclical concerning the Bible (1943): "What the old Orientals meant to say by their words cannot be verified by the rules of grammar, or philology, or the context itself, but the exegete must in spirit go back to those Oriental centuries gone by, and by means of history, archaeology, ethnology, and other disciplines ascertain the literary forms those writers wanted to use, and really used; very often those old Orientals do not express their ideas according to our mind, but have their own ways according to their countries and times. The exegete cannot prove the forms of speech a priori, but only by perusal of the ancient Oriental literature. Biblicists must therefore use all the findings and attainments of archaeology, ancient history, and literature, and whatever might be useful for the understanding of the old writers." In writing his book, Willam wished to answer the aforementioned purpose; this and only this was his intention, and owing to it he gave his book the significant title: *Das Leben Jesu im Land und Volk Israel (The Life of Jesus Christ in the Land of Israel and among Its People).* If he had intended more, it would have filled more than one volume; as it is he had to cut out a third of every chapter.

Das Leben Jesu im Land und Volk Israel was published in 1932, and in the following years translated into English, French, Italian, Spanish, Portuguese, Dutch, Polish, Czech, Slovak, Hungarian, and even Japanese.

In the year 1936 the author issued a supplement to this work. From Holy Scripture he extracted all quotations pertaining to our Blessed Mother and blended them into one picture of her. This supplement was published in 1936 and translated into nearly all the languages as his previous work, *Das Leben Jesu im Land und Volk Israel*, had been translated. Its English title is *Mary, the Mother of Jesus*.

In 1930, on the thousandth anniversary of the death of St. Olaf, Willam — at the invitation of Sigrid Undset and others — he made a trip to Norway. "Of course not in order to enjoy the fjords, but the life of the people in the land of the midnight sun." Two years after that he published the translation of three most important essays by Sigrid Undset under the title: *Begegnungen und Trennungen*. As a result of his interest in religious folklore and intense studies of the history and system of the Rosary devotion, two books, *Die Geschichte und die Gebetsschule des Rosenkranzes* and *Der Rosenkranz und das Menschenleben*, appeared in 1948, and at the same time also a little book about the Rosary. Translations of the former two books are in preparation. In 1946 appeared another book about catechetical problems, *Katechetische Erneuerung*, in which he discusses the necessity of having a good modern catechism. In 1949 still another treatise about catechetical work followed: *Der Lehrstück-Katechismus als ein Träger der Katechetischen Erneuerung*. It deals with the methods of teaching religion in different countries, and is illustrated by examples.

In writing his latest book, *Unser Weg zu Gott, ein Buch zur religiösen Selbstbildung* (1951), Father Willam was assisted by his bishop, Dr. Paul Rusch, and Professor Dr. Joseph Andrew Jungmann. It is a book for religious self-instruction.   **W. B.**

Mother Mary Paula Williamson, R.C.

Her native state is Iowa. She was born in Cedar Rapids, a small city of long avenues lined by tall elm trees and crossed by streets which paralleled the Cedar River. Her education began in one of the public schools, Polk — to be exact. Her home was on an avenue that bordered the campus of Coe College. Instead of going to high school, she entered Coe Academy and was in the last graduating class of that preparatory school. At the end of her freshman year at Coe College, and having decided definitely upon a teaching career, she went to the Iowa State Teachers College at Cedar Falls. Her first position as a teacher was in the Cedar Rapids School and from that time on she moved from one position to another, from Iowa to Oklahoma, to end up as supervisor of the Primary Department and Practical School of the Ada State Teachers College. For several years she taught in various summer schools — University of West Virginia; State College in Raleigh, North Carolina; Johns Hopkins University, Baltimore, Maryland. In 1914 she went to Teachers College, Columbia University, to specialize in School Administration, finishing in 1916 with a B.S. degree from Columbia. She accepted a position as supervisor of the Dorchester County Schools at Cambridge, Maryland. While teaching at the Johns Hopkins University Summer School in 1917, she met the Sisters of the Holy Nativity in Baltimore. In October 1918 she went to New York City to teach in the Lincoln School of Teachers College. In the fall of 1919 she entered the Episcopalian Sisterhood of the Holy Nativity whose mother house is at Fond du Lac, Wisconsin. She followed the usual course of novitiate and vows until 1927. By that time she had recognized the weakness of the claims for Catholicity in the Protestant Episcopal Church and the weak reflection of them in the Anglican religious life. On May 3, 1927, she left the Order and was received into the Catholic Church May 7, 1927. The following November she began her religious life all over again from the bottom, and was solemnly professed July 2, 1935, in the Society of Our Lady of the Retreat in the Cenacle.

While she had written many papers and prepared many addresses for various educational meetings, large and small, she had never thought of writing anything for publication.

Her Society had sent her to England; this was at the beginning of World War II. In 1938 she returned owing to a breakdown in health. After a year in Newport, she was sent to the Boston Cenacle.

"Then I began to try my hand at writing," she says. "My first article, 'Anglicanism Is Not Catholicism,' was published in *The Catholic World*, in February, 1944. Having the urge to write something for children, I wrote *Our Lady Goes A'Maying* in 1945; and in 1947 followed that book by *Little Brother Ben*, St. Anthony Guild, publishers."

In collaboration with Mother Clelia Maranzana she translated, from the Italian, two books by Dr. Igino Giordani: *St. Paul Apostle and Martyr* and *Mary of Nazareth: A True Portrait*, both of which were published by the Macmillan Company. "It is my conviction," she says, "that translations are now an art which practically gives us the original text and are of true literary value." *Faith in God's Love* is a translation from the French by Mary S. Garrity and herself, but which comes from the pen of a Sister of Providence (Sister Jean Baptiste who died April 17, 1950, Montreal, Canada). It was published by P. J. Kenedy and Sons, New York City, in 1950.

"My writing, such as it is," she says, "has become my apostolate of the pen. What I write is fortuitous and what the Holy Spirit of God seems to direct. My essay on the portrait of Mother Thérèse, Foundress of the Society of the Retreat in the Cenacle, was first published in *The Magnificat*, August, 1948, reprinted in brochure form and again in the *Retreat World* to which paper I frequently contribute. 'The Virgin with the Golden Curls,' a short story of South America, appeared in November, 1945, in *The Catholic World*; 'Mother's Beatitudes' in September, 1946; 'My Giuseppina,' 1949, in *The Magnificat*. Three essays: 'A Study of the Conversion of John Henry Newman,' in 1945; 'The Story of

Religious Confession,' in 1947; 'Suzanne Nedoncelle: Catholic Action in France,' 1949, were all published in *The Epistle.*"

That All May Be One is the story of a Trappistine nun, Mother Maria Gabriella, who offered her life for the cause of Church Unity. (P. J. Kenedy & Sons, Publishers.) The book makes a strong and vibrant appeal to souls who desire the healing of Christ's Mystical Body caused by divisions and separations among those who call themselves Christians. The title by happy choice reechoes the appeal of Our Holy Father Pope Pius XII for the Holy Year, that the prayer of Christ at the Last Supper may be answered completely by our separated brethren who, recognizing their indigence and spiritual poverty, will respond to his appeal for the Great Return. This is what the young Trappistine prayed and suffered for.

She is now working on two books: *The Beata of the Spiritual Exercises* and another translation of a biography from the Italian.

Reverend Christopher John Wilmot, S.J. 1868–

Despite his age — he is now in his eighty-fourth year — Father Wilmot is still able to work, to write and give retreats. For years he has been Spiritual Father to the Jesuit students of Philosophy at Heythrop College.

Christopher John Wilmot was born on June 10, 1868, at Port Elizabeth, South Africa, the son of the late Count Alexander and Alice Mary (Slater) Wilmot. At about the age of seven he entered the lowest class (preparatory) of St. Aidan's College, Grahamstown, South Africa, which was built and opened in 1876 by Bishop Rickards and entrusted to the Jesuit Fathers of the English Province of the Society. In the class of preparatory, made up of three students at first and then four boys, Father Wilmot had as his master, Father Augustus Law, one of the pioneers of the Zambezi Mission. When his father returned to London, England, in 1881, Christopher went to Mount St. Mary's College in Chesterfield where he finished his school career, and subsequently, in 1887, joined the English novitiate of the Society of Jesus at Manresa House, Roehampton.

Ordained a priest July 31, 1902, he served as a chaplain in the Boer War, and afterwards in the First World War in 1914. He returned to South Africa in 1916 to be Rector of St. Aidan's College until 1922. From 1922 to 1932, he was first on the Mission of Saint Aloysius, Oxford, and afterwards as superior of the Mission of the Sacred Heart, Bournemouth. At the latter place, he built new elementary schools and enlarged the church and presbytery. Later (1935–1942) he was on the staff of Farm Street Church, London, until a throat ailment necessitated his retirement. While at the Farm Street Church during the war, he was singing the 11 o'clock Mass when the first hostile airplane warning was given. The majority of the congregation as well as the choir left the church to seek shelter in the basement or elsewhere. As there was no choir, the Mass could be continued only as a low Mass. It was discovered later that the warning was a false one.

At Farm Street Church, he instructed many converts. "It was remarkable," he writes, "how many persons sought admission into the Catholic Church when the Second World War broke out."

The writing career of Father Wilmot began when he was a boy of sixteen at school. He sent some verses to *The Catholic Fireside*, a journal that still flourishes. They published them.

During his retirement he has written several books. Among them are: *The Priest's Prayer Book* (1942); *Lift Up Your Hearts* (1949); *The Hymns of the Little Hours*, translations and meditations.

He has also contributed a number of articles to various periodicals, mostly unsigned.   M. A. H.

Right Reverend Boniface Wöhrmüller, O.S.B.   1885–1951

Abbot Boniface Wöhrmüller was born at Altötting, in the very heart of Catholic Bavaria, on December 15, 1885. His father was a brewer.

After completing his humanistic studies in 1904 under the supervision of the Benedictine Fathers at Metten, Bavaria, he applied for admission to St. Boniface's Abbey in Munich. Professed in 1905, he pursued his philosophical and theological studies at the University of Munich under the renowned professors Hertling, Bardenhewer, Knöpfler and others. In 1909, Andrew Frühwirth, the Nuncio of the Holy See, who later became Cardinal, ordained him a priest. He was immediately assigned to do parish work in the large church of the abbey. He labored as a fervent assistant, catechist and preacher until he was appointed prior in 1917. When the abbot died two years later, Father Boniface was elected to succeed him. Despite his frail health, he had shouldered this burden for more than thirty years. He went through turbulent times and difficult conditions. He witnessed two world wars. The existence of the monastery itself was threatened by Nazism. Later both the wonderful basilica and the monastery were destroyed by bombs. The lives of the priests and brothers were saved by seeking refuge in the crypt. To the abbot befell the task of restoring both church and monastery. Much reduced in size, the church was rebuilt and was ready for service in May, 1951, when the monks celebrated the one hundredth anniversary of their foundation — the favorite foundation of their benefactor, King Louis I. The parish has been reduced from twenty-five thousand people to eight thousand. Many of those who survived the bombing had to move to other districts because of the destruction of their homes.

Interested in asceticism and history, Abbot Boniface wrote three books: *Das Königliche Gebot, Kleines Kapitel von der Nächstenliebe* (1911); *Mannhaftes Christentum* (1934); and *Frohe Botschaft* (1919), besides some important historical brochures. His principal work (*Das Königliche Gebot*) had world wide success. This work was honored by the Theological Faculty of the University of Munich by conferring on its author the title S.T.D. It has been translated into five languages. In Germany alone the sales reached over fifty thousand copies. The English edition was printed in London in 1931 under the title *The Royal Law*.

(Abbot Boniface Wöhrmüller died in 1951, and was succeeded by the writer of this sketch, Rev. Dr. Hugo Lang, O.S.B. Editor.)

H. L. (O.S.B.)

Hans Conrad Ernest Zacharias
1874–

Professor Hans Zacharias has traveled long and far in body and mind. From his native Germany he went to England, then to North Borneo and Malaya, then to India, Belgium, France, Switzerland, China, the Philippines, where he was interned by the Japanese (1942–45), next, to the United States, back to China to resume his chair of history in the Catholic University of Peking, where he remained as professor from 1946 to 1949 but had to leave in the fall of the latter year owing to the change of regime in China. Meanwhile his mental and spiritual journeyings were equally fantastic. Born a Lutheran, he became successively Atheist, Agnostic, Deist, Freemason, Occultist, Vedantist, High Church Anglican, and, lastly and finally, Roman Catholic.

The story of his conversion, as told in his booklet, *Dominus Illuminatio Mea*, is a fascinating adventure in which Light Divine leads him step by step to the eternal truth. Apparently haphazard encounters with persons, places and books provoked his mind to fresh enquiry. A retreat at Caldey Abbey, a visit to the Holy Land, Father Michael Maher's *Psychology* (Stonyhurst Series), the New Code of Canon Law, the *Summa* (English translation), and Leo XIII's "Rerum Novarum" were among such contacts. "Slowly, painfully, hesitatingly I followed the light as far as at any time of my long wandering I had seen it. And now," he tells us joyfully, "He who is Light of the whole world . . . came to inflame me with the fulness of His own 'Love Divine, all love exceeding' . . . and to permeate my whole being with gratitude."

Hans Conrad Ernest Zacharias was born in 1874, at Nordhausen in the Hartz Mountains, Germany, of partly Jewish and partly Polish descent. His father, John Paul Zacharias, was a Protestant; his mother,

Maria Josepha de Rabatinska, a Catholic. After studying *Humaniora* at college and natural science at the Universities of Heidelberg, Berlin and Zurich, he obtained the degree of Ph.D. at Giessen University. He was at the time working at the Natural History Museum (London), and at the Marine Biological Station at Jersey (Channel Islands).

After a year's planting experience in British North Borneo (1897–98), he returned to London and became there a pioneer in the motor car industry. (He still is a life member of the Royal Automobile Club of London.)

In 1901 he went to Kuala Lumpur (British Malaya) to engage in business. For seventeen years he held the position of Secretary to the Planters' Association of Malaya. From 1912 to 1914 he was chairman of the Kuala Lumpur Chamber of Commerce. Dissatisfied with the pursuit of making money, he began to spend all his leisure time studying philosophy and theology. It was during this period that he began to try out Christianity, even venturing on a Sunday evening to go to church instead of to a local club, "The Spotted Dog." Being British, it seemed natural to him to be an Anglican. One of Professor Zacharias' most astonishing experiences was his visit (as a High Church Anglican) to the Abbey of Caldey, on the little island off the coast of South Wales. It was six months before the entire community of Anglican monks submitted to Rome. "The Abbot," recounts the Professor, "at our first interview startled me exceedingly, by asking me, why on earth I, who was not English by birth, did not become a Roman Catholic instead of messing about with Anglicanism." In 1919 Zacharias resigned from business and went to India where he spent a year with the schismatic Jacobite Church, teaching philosophy and theology at their seminary. Rebuffed there as "too Catholic," he went to Poona, joined the staff of an Indian weekly, *The Servant of India*, and was put in charge of its foreign affairs section. He lived there entirely as an Indian among Indians.

In the meantime he had been received into the Catholic Church in 1926 and in the year following launched a similar weekly, but in the Catholic sense — *The Week*, which did much to convince the Indian public that an Indian could be both a good Catholic and a patriot.

On medical advice he left India and returned to Europe, where he joined the staff of the *Bulletin des Missions* at the Abbaye de St. André-lez-Bruges, in Belgium. Simultaneously from 1932 to 1935 he lectured at the Catholic University of Lille, France, on Indian history and civilization, and published a book called *Renascent India*. In Lille he became "grandfather" of the famous lay-apostolate "Ad Lucem" and after a year in Switzerland (at Fribourg and Geneva) he was offered and accepted a professorship in history at the Catholic University of Peking (China) where he taught for five years (1936–1941).

At the outbreak of war he fled to the Philippines, where during his internment as a prisoner of the Japanese, he commenced writing his *Protohistory*, an explicative account of the development of human thought from paleolithic times to the Persian monarchy. Liberated in February, 1945, Professor Zacharias went by transport to the United States and worked at the Oriental Institute of the University of Chicago. From Chicago he returned in 1946 to resume his post at the Catholic University of Peking. Since November 1949, he has been residing at St. Mary's Mission Guest House in Techny, Illinois.

Professor Zacharias has contributed to many periodicals, among others: *La Vie Intellectuelle* (Paris); *Blackfriars* (Oxford); *The New Review* (Calcutta); *The Review of Politics* (Notre Dame); *Social Justice* (St. Louis); *Il Pensiero Missionario* (Rome); and the *Chinese Social and Political Review* (Peking). Among his books are: *Dominus Illuminatio Mea* (1926); *Renascent India* (1933); *Protohistory* (1947); *Human Personality: Its Emergence in India, China and Israel* (1950). The Catholic University Press of Peking has published texts of Professor Zacharias' lectures on "The Economic History of Europe," "Politology," and "Prolegomena to a History of the World."

E. B. B.

Jacques Zeiller 1878–

Combining a continued interest in the great practical works of Christian charity with a most erudite perusal of the study of the early Church, Jacques Zeiller has for some years been an outstanding French Catholic savant. Students of primitive Christian origins and archeology have been guided in these later decades of the twentieth century by his researches in these fields.

Jacques Zeiller was born in Paris, March 31, 1878, the son of René Zeiller, member of the Academy of Science and the Inspector General of Mines, and Marie Ollé Laprune, the sister of the philosopher, Léon Ollé Laprune. He received a licentiate in philosophy and law and a fellowship in history and geography and finally in 1918 a doctorate of literature from the University of Paris. He was, from 1902 to 1905, a member of the École Française in Rome. Afterwards, until the outbreak of the First World War, he taught at the University of Fribourg in Switzerland as Professor of Greek and Roman history. During the war, until 1918, he served in a volunteer capacity with the 185th Infantry Brigade as a secretary. Also during the war, he edited, with some other university fellows, the *Bulletin de l'Alliance française*, published in eight languages, to explain to various countries the causes and progress of the war.

He has been a director of studies in the "École pratique des Hautes Études" of the Sorbonne since 1920. He was elected a member of the "Academy des inscriptions et belles-lettres" of the Institut of France on May 8, 1940 and was president of the Academy for the year 1949. He has also been an associate member of the Royal Academy of Belgrade and a correspondent for the Pontifical Academy of Archeology.

His chief publications are: *Les origines chrétiennes dans la province romaine de Dalmatie* (1908); *L'Idée de l'état dans Saint Thomas d'Aquin*

(1910). He has had a fervid interest in early church history of the Danubian lands and Illyria, as evinced by one of his doctoral theses, *Les origines chrétiennes dans les provinces danubiennes de l'Empire romain* (1918). His other thesis was *Paganus, étude de terminologie historique* (1917). He wrote *L'Empire romain et l'Église* for the fifth volume of the world history published under the direction of Cavaignac in Paris in 1928. From his pen appeared a biography of his uncle, *Léon Ollé Laprune*, in the collection of Christian Moralists in 1930. In collaboration with Father Lebreton, he wrote *l'Église primitive* in the collection of the *History of the Church* of Fliche and Martin in 1934 and later in 1935, in the same work, he wrote *De la fin du deuxieme siecle a la paix constantinienne*. A work in preparation deals with the Latin inscriptions found in Algeria.

Doctor Zeiller is married, the father of three living children and of two dead, one of whom, a son, died in 1944 while an aviator in the recent war. Ever since his youth, Jacques Zeiller has been an active member of the Society of St. Vincent de Paul and has served, from 1943 to the present, as its president-general.   K. M.

Gustavo Martínez Zuriria (Hugo Wast). See under Martínez

(Ut in Omnibus Glorificetur Deus)